The Sino-Japanese War of

The Sino-Japanese War of 1894–1895 is a seminal been virtually ignored in the Western literature. This is not the case in the East, where, ever since the war, the focus of Chinese foreign policy has been to undo its results whereas the focus of Japanese foreign policy has been to confirm them. Japan supplanted China as the dominant regional power. Such a seismic reversal in the traditional power balance fractured the previous international harmony within the Confucian world and left an aftershock of enduring territorial and political fault lines that have embroiled China, Japan, Korea, Russia, and Taiwan ever since.

The book examines the war through the eyes of the journalists who filed reports from China, Japan, Russia, Germany, France, Britain, and the United States to show how the war changed outside perceptions of the relative power of China and Japan and to plot the consequences of these changed perceptions, namely, the scramble for concessions in China and Japan's admission to the ranks of the great powers.

S. C. M. Paine is Associate Professor of Strategy and Policy at the U.S. Naval War College and author of *Imperial Rivals: China, Russia, and Their Disputed Frontier,* winner of the 1997 Jelavich Prize for diplomatic history.

The Sino-Japanese War of 1894–1895

Perceptions, Power, and Primacy

S. C. M. Paine

U.S. Naval War College

CAMBRIDGE UNIVERSITY PRESS

CAMBRIDGE UNIVERSITY PRESS
Cambridge, New York, Melbourne, Madrid, Cape Town, Singapore, São Paulo, Delhi

Cambridge University Press
32 Avenue of the Americas, New York, NY 10013-2473, USA

www.cambridge.org
Information on this title: www.cambridge.org/9780521617451

First published 2003
First paperback edition 2005
Reprinted 2006

A catalog record for this publication is available from the British Library

Library of Congress Cataloging in Publication data
Paine, S. C. M., 1957—
When Japan became a world power : the Sino-Japanese War of 1894—1894 / S. C. M. Paine.
p. cm.
Includes bibliographical references and index.
ISBN 0-521-81714-5
1. Japan — Foreign relations — 1868—1912. 2. China — Foreign relations — 1644—1912.
3. Japan — relations — Chinda. 4. China — Foreign relations — Japan. 5. Chinese-
Japanese War, 1894-1895. 6. East Asia — Foreign relations. I. Title.
DS882.6P35 2002
951'.035—dc21 2002071575

ISBN 978-0-521-81714-1 hardback
ISBN 978-0-521-61745-1 paperback

Transferred to digital printing 2009

To BAE

who said, "You should write a book about this,"
when I ran into the negotiating records for the Treaty
of Shimonoseki in the Japanese Foreign Ministry
Archives.

Contents

List of Maps

Acknowledgments

This book is both a by-product of many years of living in and conducting research on China, Japan, and Russia and also a preliminary study for a book about Sino-Russo-Japanese rivalries in northeast Asia during the 1930s and 1940s. The current work has the modest ambition of synthesizing current secondary research on the Sino-Japanese War of 1894–1895 and supplementing this synthesis with an extensive reading of newspapers published around the world during the war. The purpose is to plot the evolution of European and American thinking about the balance of power in the Far East, and in doing so discuss the perceptions that both reflected and created that balance of power. The thesis is that military hardware and economic output alone do not determine international power, perceptions also play an important role. This book is aimed at a general audience of those interested in understanding the origins of such key security issues still bedeviling the Far East as the two-China problem, Korean instability, Sino-Japanese animosity, and Russian Far Eastern ambitions.

It is my great pleasure to acknowledge the help of many persons and also to absolve them of any responsibility for the errors that remain in this book. I would like to start by thanking all of my colleagues in the Strategy and Policy Department at the United States Naval War College who collectively have worked to develop and teach a unique and powerful methodology to analyze wars. The combination of civilians, with doctorates in both political science and history, and officers from the different branches of the military set the Strategy and Policy Department apart from so much of academia where theoreticians too often do not come into regular contact with practitioners.

I would also like to give particular thanks to those who took so much of their time to read a draft of this book and correct my many novel departures from standard English usage and from logical presentation. In alphabetical order, they are my best colleague, Bruce A. Elleman; my supportive brothers, John B. Paine III and Thomas M. Paine; the eminent historian of Russia, Marc Raeff; and, special and most well read of family friends, Alice R. Riley. Cambridge University Press was also kind enough to provide the reports of three anonymous readers. One of them, whom I soon tracked down, proved to be the eminent historian of China, Arthur Waldron, who provided extremely helpful suggestions for restructuring the manuscript. I would like to thank my current seminar co-moderator, Colonel Paul L. Aswell USA, for drawing up the maps; my friend and colleague of many years, Yu Minling, for proofreading the Chinese; Colonel Arakawa Ken-ichi, an expert on Japanese military history, for proofreading the Japanese; Nishikawa Sumi, for so patiently tutoring me in reading hand-written documents in archaic Japanese; and my aunt, Elizabeth N. Nicholson, for reading the manuscript in part. At Cambridge University Press, Mary Child, Cathy Felgar, and Frank Smith worked to produce this book, while Elise Oranges oversaw the proofreading.

A variety of libraries made available their collections and their staff. I am most grateful to them for, without their books, this book could never have been written. In chronological order, they are the Diplomatic Record Office of the Japanese Ministry of Foreign Affairs for allowing me to use the minutes to the negotiations terminating the Sino-Japanese War; International Christian University in Tokyo for making available not only its books but also its photocopying machines; Joyce Martindale at the interlibrary loan department at Texas Christian University for delivering endless reels of microfilm and unusual titles from faraway places; the Mary Evelyn Blagg Huey Library at Texas Woman's University for more microfilm; Princeton University for so generously sharing its collections, curators, and electrical current so I could both research and write; Yasuko Makino, Martin Heijdra, and Chongsook Lee Kim at Princeton University's Gest Library for help finding obscure books and information in Asian languages; Alice K. Juda for finding the unfindable and Robin A. Lima for getting the found sent to me at the Henry E. Eccles Library at the United States Naval War College; the Fairbank Center for providing an *entrée* to Harvard University's massive collections; Kuniko Yamada McVey at the Harvard-Yenching Library for help with obscure references; and Peter Harrington at Brown University's John Jay Library for making available the cover illustration.

In addition to acknowledging the help of all the persons and institutions listed above, I would like to explain the rationale for my decision to use the word "face" throughout this work. My use of this term is in no way intended to offend anyone; rather, the choice comes from Chinese usage. Chinese today still frequently use the term in such idioms as "to lose face," "to give face," "to have face," or "not to have face." The terminology is theirs and not mine. For doubters, I refer them to the references listed in the following footnote.[1]

Finally, a technical note: My computer is unable to produce one diacritical mark necessary for Romanizing Korean, therefore, I have used the French circumflex accent instead. This is an upside down rendition of the correct mark. The Romanization systems used are as follows: *pinyin* for Chinese, *Kenkyusha*'s *Dictionary* for Japanese, and the Library of Congress System for Russian. Chinese and Japanese names have been written surname first, given name second.

---

[1] Research on "face" has been conducted mostly by anthropologists. Historians do not generally avail themselves of these sources. To quote a recent anthropological work on the subject: "Chinese is rich in portraying things that can happen to face. Besides 'wanting face' (*yao mianzi*), 'losing face' (*diou [sic] mianzi*), and 'having face' (*gei mianzi*), one can also 'borrow face' (*jie mianzi*), 'give face' (*gei mianzi*), 'increase face' (*zenglia mianzi*), 'contest face' (*zheng mianzi*), 'save face' (*liou [sic] mianzi*), and compare face as in the expression 'His face is greater than ours' ('Tade mianzi bi bieren da'). The larger one's face, the more prestige and security one possesses and, therefore, the more self-determination one enjoys in social transactions" (Mayfair Mei-hui Yang, *Gifts, Favors & Banquets: The Art of Social Relationships in China* [Ithaca: Cornell University Press, 1994], 196). "Face" also appears in contemporary movies. See director Zhang Yimou's *Shanghai Triad*, when the Triad boss refers to face to explain his reasons for preserving the reputation of his mistress even as he has her murdered for infidelity, or director Wayne Wang's *Eat a Bowl of Tea*, whose entire plot revolves around the theme of losing face. For examples involving the two key diplomats discussed in the current work, see Foreign Minister Mutsu Munemitsu's memoirs, *Kenkenryoku: A Diplomatic Record of the Sino-Japanese War, 1894–95*. Gordon Mark Berger, ed. and trans. (Princeton: Princeton University Press, 1982), page 126; and Li Hongzhang's remarks after the attempt made on his life discussed in Chapter 7 in the present volume. For other standard academic references, see the extensively footnoted section on "face" in Chapter 9, which cites numerous anthropological, historical, and other works.

Part I

The Clash of Two Orders:
The Far East on the Eve of the War

For hundreds of years, Japan and China have enjoyed a history of intercourse and communication as friendly neighbors. We share the same roots in politics, law, literature, the arts, morals, religion, and all other elements of civilization; and in ancient times, Japan was often blessed with the introduction into the country of many splendid aspects of China's civilization. Hence, China assumed the position of an advanced nation while we took something of the role of being a more backward one.[1]

> Mutsu Munemitsu, foreign minister of Japan, 1895

Japan...was organized...So when the West impinged on her, she put what it had to tell her in a sieve and sifted out the parts useful to her – for example, all the sciences and the art of war. She looked at what was left behind...and most of it she threw in the dustbin. But what she sifted out she absorbed into her body political as a lump of sugar is absorbed in a glass of water...[I]n China Western knowledge and Western cults descended on her unguided and uncontrolled. There was no winnowing of it; there was no sifting of what was good for China from what was bad...The simile here is not the lump of sugar....here it is that of blobs of oil floating in the water and tending to go putrid.[2]

> William Ferdinand Tyler, naval adviser to China during the war

---

[1] Mutsu, Munemitsu, *Kenkenryoku: A Diplomatic Record of the Sino-Japanese War, 1894–95,* Gordon Mark Berger, ed. and trans. (Princeton: Princeton University Press, 1982), 27.

[2] William Ferdinand Tyler, *Pulling Strings in China* (London: Constable & Co., 1929) , 96–7.

1

The Reversal in the Far Eastern Balance of Power

Japan has leaped, almost at one bound, to a place among the great nations of the earth. Her recent exploits in the war with China have focused all eyes upon her, and the world now comprehends the startling fact that this small island kingdom, so little taken account of heretofore in the calculations even of students and statesmen, has within a few decades stridden over ground traversed by other nations only within centuries.[1]

The Honorable Hilary A. Herbert, U.S. Secretary of the Navy, 1895

Those who most despair of China are those who know her best.[2]

Western missionary in China, late nineteenth century

The Sino-Japanese War of 1894–5 is a seminal event in world history. Yet it has been virtually ignored in the Western literature. This is not the case in the East. Ever since this war, the focus of Chinese foreign policy has been to undo its results whereas the focus of Japanese foreign policy has been to confirm them. Japan used war to supplant Chinese regional primacy, but China refused to acknowledge the consequences of defeat. The war delivered a *coup de grâce* to the expiring traditional international order in the Far East: It shattered Chinese hegemony and demonstrated to an astonished West that Japan had become a modern great power. Such a seismic reversal in the traditional balance of power fractured the previous international harmony within the Confucian world and left an aftershock of enduring territorial and political fault lines that have embroiled China, Japan, Korea, and Russia ever since. The war has left an ominous territorial legacy in the

---

[1] Hilary A. Herbert, "Military Lessons of the Chino-Japanese War," *The North American Review* 160, no. 463 (June 1895): 685.

[2] Quoted by Sir Henry Norman in the preface to Pierre Leroy-Beaulieu, trans. Richard Davey, *The Awakening of the East: Siberia – Japan – China "* (London: William Heinemann, 1900), xi.

3

form of the disputed status of Taiwan and the Korean Peninsula; an equally ominous political legacy in the form of enduring political instability in China and Korea; and enmity among Japan, China, and Korea. This struggle between China and Japan for primacy in the Far East is still ongoing; the jury is out, but the outcome will have global implications.

The war changed perceptions in both the East and West, and these changed perceptions had a direct impact on the foreign policies of all parties engaged in the Far East. The perception of Chinese weakness led to far more aggressive intrusions by the foreign powers in China, whereas the perception of Japanese strength led to the inclusion of Japan in the ranks of the imperial powers. Japan had transformed itself from the object of imperialism into one of its perpetrators. The war marked the terminal decline of the old inward-looking Confucian order and ascendancy of the Western order of global politics.[3] A new balance of power had emerged. China's millennia-long unquestioned dominance had abruptly ended. Japan was on the rise with momentous consequences in store for the East and West. In today's terminology, Japan had become the first successful developing country. It had demonstrated the potentially global consequences of rapid economic growth coupled with political transformation. In doing so, it had proven that industrialization was not the cultural monopoly of the West.

The Western perception of Japan as a great power was born in September of 1894. In a three-day period, Japan used modern arms so professionally and defeated China on land and sea so decisively that quite suddenly the Western world perceived Japan as a modern power. Japan became the first non-European power in modern times to do so. This is not to say that Western nations believed that Japan could stretch its military might to Europe, but rather that Japan had become a modern nation whose economy was expected to achieve European levels of industrialization in the foreseeable future. As a result of the war, Japan became and has remained an integral part of Western power calculations.

If this first Sino-Japanese War catapulted Japan into the ranks of the powers, it hurtled China on a long downward spiral. Some observers considered the war's Battle of the Yalu to have been the most important naval battle since Admiral Horatio Nelson's obliteration of Napoleon Bonaparte's navy during the 1805 Battle of Trafalgar.[4] Just as Napoleon's hopes to invade England had been

---

[3] William L. Langer, *The Diplomacy of Imperialism 1890–1902*, 2nd ed. (New York: Alfred A. Knopf, 1956), 190.

[4] John Blake, *How Sailors Fight: An Account of the Organisation of the British Fleet in Peace and War* (London: Grant Richards, 1901), 122–3, cited in "Extracts (not literal quotations) from John Blake, 'How Sailors Fight,' *Chino-Japanese War, 1894–95*, in N. W. H. Du Boulay, "Chino-Japanese

dashed, so had China's pretenses of military power been shattered. To the present day, China has yet to recapture its position as a major naval power that it forfeited by defeat in this war.[5]

The war was a turning point for China. The war shattered any basis for China's tenacious sense of unbreachable superiority and forced a Chinese reappraisal of their place in the world. Defeat by Japan, a member of the Confucian world, did this much more decisively than any Western defeat, including those in the Opium Wars, ever did or ever could.[6] This was because defeat at the hands of an alien civilization could be discounted whereas defeat by a member of the Confucian order could not. Equally shattered were any vestiges of political stability in China. Victory by a transformed former member of the Confucian order fatally undermined the legitimacy of that order. For the Chinese, the war kicked the bottom out of their world. A century later, they had yet to find a satisfactory replacement for the stable Confucian order that so long had formed the bedrock of Chinese thought.

The war also marked a turning point for Korea. While problems had been brewing on the Korean Peninsula from the 1860s onward, until the 1880s foreign intervention had been on a modest scale. On the eve of the war – when only a few westerners could locate Korea on the globe – Japan, China, and Russia had become embroiled in a no-holds-barred conflict for control over this very strategic peninsula.[7] Each considered predominance over the area to be vital to its national

War, 1894–95" (London: typescript, ca. 1903), 1; Arthur Diósy also considered the Battle of the Yalu to be "the most important naval action since Trafalgar." (Diósy, *The New Far East* [New York: G. P. Putnam's Sons, 1899], 1.)

Vice-Admiral B. A. Ballard of the British Navy disputed this assessment but still regarded the Japanese naval victory during the first important naval engagement of the war, the Battle of the Yalu, to be "a very honourable victory considering the relative strength of the forces involved" and that it "raised their navy to a point of the highest esteem, retained ever since." He also noted that the battle was the first large-scale naval engagement in a generation, the last having been the Battle of Lissa, when Austria defeated Italy in 1866. (G. A. Ballard, *The Influence of the Sea on the Political History of Japan* [New York: E. P. Dutton, 1921], 151–3). The combined naval battles of the Sino-Japanese War together did have equally significant long-term implications for China as the Battle of Trafalgar did for Napoleon. This issue will be discussed at length in Chapter 8.

[5] Martin van Creveld, "Through a Glass Darkly: Some Reflections on the Future of War," *Naval War College Review* (Autumn 2000): 30.

[6] According to China's preeminent expert on the Sino-Japanese War, Qi Qizhang, compiler of an eleven-volume collection of documents on the war as well as a 600-page history of it, of the five large-scale wars fought between the Qing Dynasty and the imperialist powers – two opium wars, the Sino-French War, the Sino-Japanese War, and the Boxer Rebellion – "the influence caused by defeat in the Sino-Japanese War was the most profound and far reaching." Qi Qizhang 戚其章, 甲午战争 (*Sino-Japanese War*). (Peking: 人民出版社, 1990), 585. See the bibliographic essay for more information about Qi Qizhang.

[7] *Königlich privilegirte Berlinische Zeitung* noted that, prior to the war, Korea was "not known in

security. China had traditionally faced barbarian incursions from the north – its other borders were either mountainous or maritime and therefore comparatively secure until the arrival of European navies in the mid-nineteenth century. Japan viewed the Korean Peninsula as the launch point for any invasion from the Asian mainland, and Russia considered its vast and sparsely populated Siberian frontier to be inherently vulnerable to foreign encroachments.

First Japan ousted China from the Korean Peninsula with the Sino-Japanese War; in 1904–5 it expelled Russia during the Russo-Japanese War; and then in 1910 it formally annexed the Korean Peninsula, keeping it until 1945. Unification of China under the communists in 1949 returned China to the fray. The inconclusive Korean War from 1950 to 1953 left Korea divided into Sino-Soviet and American spheres of influence. For the Koreans, the Sino-Japanese War ushered in an era of war and devastation with no resolution to the underlying geopolitical problem of terrible internal instability due to its precarious location at the grinding point among three acquisitive imperial powers: Russia, China, and Japan. For the world, Korea emerged as a thorny international security concern.

A second territorial legacy of equal import is the two-China problem. The war settlement made Taiwan a Japanese colony, transforming Japan into an imperial power. Previously, Taiwan had been a peripheral part of the Chinese empire; it had not become a province until 1885 and remained one for a mere decade before being ceded to Japan.[8] Thereafter, Taiwanese political and economic development diverged from that of China as Japan implemented a development program there based on its own domestic models. This colonial experience was far less bitter for the Taiwanese than for the Koreans. Korea became not only the battleground for the Sino-Japanese War, but also the staging ground for the subsequent Russo-Japanese War. Moreover, throughout both wars and even after the Japanese annexation in 1910, Korea was the scene of a long and bloody guerrilla war to expel the Japanese. When Japan deposed the Korean emperor in 1910, it ended nearly a millennium of rule by Korean dynasties. Some Koreans would argue that their country had been independent for nearly five millennia.[9] In contrast, Taiwan lacked such a tradition of native rule. The guerrilla war of resistance in Taiwan was

the political geography" of the world (" Korea," *Königlich privilegirte Berlinische Zeitung* [*Royal Berlin Newspaper*], 7 August 1894, p. 1). See also "Das Königreich Korea" (Kingdom of Korea), *Neue Preussische Zeitung* (*New Prussian Newspaper*) (Berlin), 26 July 1894, evening edition, p. 1.

[8] Kwang-ching Liu and Richard J. Smith, "The Military Challenge: The North-West and the Coast," in *The Cambridge History of China*, John K. Fairbank and Kwang-ching Liu, eds., vol. 11 (Cambridge: Cambridge University Press, 1980), 258–61.

[9] Syngman Rhee, *The Spirit of Independence: A Primer of Korean Modernization and Reform*, trans. Han-kyo Kim (Honolulu: University of Hawai'i Press, 2001), 139.

correspondingly short, largely over within a year.[10] As a result, the Taiwanese as a group do not harbor the bitterly anti-Japanese sentiments that are so pervasive in Korea. The Japanese destroyed the illusion of Korean independence whereas the Taiwanese in the nineteenth century never had been formally independent.

For the overwhelming majority of Koreans in both the north and south, the war left deep-seated hostilities. Japanese and Korean relations had long been strained, but the war greatly magnified Korean resentment. Worse still was the effect on Sino-Japanese relations, which, prior to the war, had been very cordial. Educated Japanese had felt a deep admiration for Chinese high culture and had been gracious hosts to visiting Chinese scholars. During the war, Japanese respect rapidly degenerated into contempt while the Chinese learned to loathe the Japanese. Although this Chinese animosity is generally associated with the second Sino-Japanese War of 1937 to 1945, it actually dates to the earlier war when Japan first became China's nemesis.

The war also rattled the European presumption that all important world events emanated from their activities. Previously, the Far East had been the outback of European politics. Certainly, European rivalries had played themselves out in the Far East in a small way, but the real cat-fights had been reserved for more "vital" parts of the globe, such as the Near Eastern shores of the Mediterranean and Black Seas. With the Sino-Japanese War, the cat-fight came to Asia. The Battle of the Yalu had become a testing ground for state-of-the-art European technology: For the first time ironclads and quick-firing guns had been used in naval combat.[11] The Battle of the Yalu, unlike the Battle of Trafalgar, however, was fought not between European powers but between Asian powers. For the first time, Western militaries scrambled to study the lessons to be learned from a purely Asian war.[12]

The Japanese navy was considered state-of-the-art. This caused grave fears, particularly in Great Britain, concerning the maintenance of the empire. Previously, no foreign navy had been strong enough to threaten seriously its far-flung colonies. The Sino-Japanese War signaled that times were changing. Great Britain concluded that its navy, on whose supremacy the empire rested, would have to be rapidly

---

[10] Lieutenant Maxime Joseph Marie Sauvage, *La Guerre Sino-Japonaise 1894–1895* (*The Sino-Japanese War 1894–1895*) (Paris: L. Baudoin, 1897), 273–9.

[11] George Alexander Lensen, *Balance of Intrigue: International Rivalry in Korea & Manchuria, 1884–1899*, vol. 1 (Tallahassee: University Presses of Florida, 1982), 186.

[12] Frank Marble, "The Battle of the Yalu," *Proceedings of the United States Naval Institute* 21, no. 3 (1895): 479–521; Herbert, 685–98; Ballard, 125–84; Du Boulay; H. W. Wilson, *Ironclads in Action: A Sketch of Naval Warfare from 1855 to 1895* (Boston: Little, Brown, 1896); Auguste Huet, *Quelques réflexions sur la Guerre Navale sino-japonaise* (*Some Reflections on the Sino-Japanese Naval War*) (Paris: Bergen-Levrault, 1896); Sauvage.

expanded to meet the offensive capabilities of modern navies so effectively demonstrated by the Japanese. Great Britain responded with a major naval expansion program.[13] By 1902, the reigning superpower would establish an alliance with Japan. This would be Britain's only formal long-term alliance between the settlement of the Napoleonic Wars in 1815 and the outbreak of World War I in 1914.[14] This was the concrete proof that Japan sat at the select table of the great powers.

Russia drew equally dire conclusions from the war. Prior to the Second World War, Russia is not usually considered in connection with the Far East. Yet the Sino-Japanese War marked a key and very fateful turning point in Russian foreign policy. Ever since members of the Russian government acquired accurate maps of Siberia (from mid-nineteenth-century geographic expeditions), they had become concerned about the security of their long and vulnerable Far Eastern frontier. Japan's rapid and total defeat of China and consequent domination over Korea flabbergasted responsible officials in St. Petersburg. Complacency about the sleepy Far East was transformed into frenetic action.

In an unprecedented move, Russia reoriented its foreign policy away from Europe to the Far East. It stepped up the construction of the Trans-Siberian Railway and chose a new route for the last section. Instead of running the line along the Amur River as it does today, the Russian government sent it directly across Manchuria, making a straight shot between Lake Baikal and the port of Vladivostok. Vladivostok's name encapsulated Russia's Far Eastern foreign policy agenda: The Russian, Владивосток, translates as "the ruler of the East." The rerouting of the railway was an attempt to consolidate a Russian sphere of influence in northeastern Asia at Japanese expense. The new railway route would allow the Russian government to concentrate troops rapidly on the border and transform the former *pas de deux* between Japan and China into a *ménage à trois* with the addition of Russia. The new railway line then spurred Japanese officials into action with a massive post-war rearmament program. A Far Eastern arms race was on. This would lead to the militarization of the Siberian border and the emergence of Russia as a Pacific Ocean power. Because of this war, Russia had entered into the thick of things in the Far East and has remained there ever since.

By war's end Russia, Germany, France, and Britain all were bending over backward to reap benefits at the expense of the others. For China, the treaty-port era, when the Western powers had confined their interests to trade and missionary

[13] Peter Burroughs, "Defence and Imperial Disunity," in *The Oxford History of the British Empire: The Nineteenth Century,* Andrew Porter, ed., vol. 3 (Oxford: Oxford University Press, 1999), 338.

[14] S. C. M. Paine, *Imperial Rivals: China, Russia, and Their Disputed Frontier* (Armonk, New York: M. E. Sharpe, 1996), 219–25.

work, had ended. The partition of China had begun. The period immediately following the war has been dubbed "the scramble for concessions," in reference to the European scramble to carve out exclusive zones in China. These comprised not just the major ports as in the past, but entire provinces of China, where one European country's interests would predominate over the others. It marked the end to effective Chinese sovereignty for many a long decade. Dynastic disintegration, warlordism, civil war, foreign occupation, and more civil war all followed in dizzying succession.

Western rivalries now played themselves out in Asia on a grander scale, giving regional issues a new international significance: Domestic instability in China created grave concerns in the West; Korea became an enduring international security conundrum; and deep hostilities fractured the previous international harmony within the Confucian world. These fractures provided foreign countries in the East and West both the incentive and opportunity to intervene more vigorously in China and Korea. The Far East was no longer peripheral to European politics; now it was an integral part. Right after the war, a reporter at the British-owned and Shanghai-based *North-China Herald* mulled over its consequences: "A great war not infrequently affects the interests and relations of neutral onlookers quite as profoundly as those of the belligerents themselves; but seldom has so sudden and dramatic an illustration of the fact been witnessed as in the changes immediately wrought by the war between China and Japan in the relative position of the foreign Powers at Peking...[T]o-day we are compelled to realise more forcibly how fierce the competition has grown."[15]

In this way, the modern international order of the Far East was born. International politics became truly global with the advent of the first non-European great power, Japan. The United States would soon follow in 1898 with its victory in the Spanish-American War. The United States had not been a major participant in the post-war fray to partition China because it had been preoccupied with a revolution against Spanish rule taking place in Cuba. In 1898 this culminated in the Spanish-American War. As in the case of Japan three years earlier, victory brought the United States great powerhood. America acquired colonies in the Philippines, Guam, the Wake Islands, Puerto Rico, and Hawaii.[16] From unencumbered isolationism, the United States emerged from the war with far-flung colonies around the globe. Thus, in the 1890s both Japan and the United States entered the

---

[15] "The Far Eastern Question," *The North-China Herald* (Shanghai), 6 December 1895, p. 952.

[16] George Brown Tindall and David E. Shi, *America: A Narrative History*, vol. 2, 4th ed. (New York: W. W. Norton, 1996), 978–87; Fareed Zakaria, *From Wealth to Power: The Unusual Origins of America's World Role* (Princeton: Princeton University Press, 1998), 160.

arena of international relations and for the first time were considered important international powers. Henceforth, Europe would no longer monopolize key diplomacy since two new non-European players had entered the field. This would transform international relations, bringing into being the phenomenon so visible in our own day – that of global, as opposed to strictly regional, politics.[17]

The reversal in the Far Eastern balance of power at Chinese expense endured beyond the end of the twentieth century. The American occupation after World War II was but a brief hiatus in the general trend of Japanese regional dominance. China would not reestablish itself as a power of consequence until after the communists reunited the country in 1949. Even then the Japanese eclipse of China endured. Within a decade of the end of World War II, Japan was expanding at double-digit economic growth rates.[18] By the 1960s it had reestablished itself as the dominant economy of the Far East.[19] In 1964, almost exactly a century after the Meiji Emperor's ascent to the throne, Japan's admission to the Organization for Economic Cooperation and Development signified its status as one of the world's economic elite.[20] By the mid-1970s its economy was the second largest in the world, surpassed only by that of the United States.[21] By the 1980s it had the largest foreign currency holdings in the world, followed, in second place, by its former colony of Taiwan.[22] At the end of the twentieth century, it alone among non-Western nations sat on the prestigious Group of Seven, which coordinated world economy policy.[23] China remained in the shadows of this virtuoso economic performance that dazzled the West throughout most of the twentieth century. Psychologically, the Chinese never abandoned their claim to preeminence. This made Japanese economic success that much more bitter for the Chinese. Both

---

[17] Walter LaFeber, *The American Age: United States Foreign Policy at Home and Abroad,* 2nd ed. (New York: W. W. Norton, 1994), 193–5, 226–7; Zakaria, 159; Warren I. Cohen, *America's Response to China: A History of Sino-American Relations,* 3rd ed. (New York: Columbia University Press, 1990), 38.

[18] Kazushi Ohkawa and Henry Rosovsky, "Capital Formation in Japan," *The Cambridge Economic History of Europe,* Peter Mathias and M. M. Postan, eds., vol. 7, part 2 (Cambridge: Cambridge University Press, 1978), 156.

[19] Kenneth B. Pyle, *The Making of Modern Japan,* 2nd ed. (Lexington, MA: D.C. Heath, 1996), 244; Gary D. Allison, *Japan's Postwar History* (Ithaca: Cornell University Press, 1997), 88, 122–4.

[20] Akira Iriye, *Japan & the Wider World* (London: Longman, 1997), 148.

[21] Allison, 122.

[22] Ezra F. Vogel. *The Four Little Dragons: The Spread of Industrialization in East Asia* (Cambridge, MA: Harvard University Press, 1991), 2.

[23] After the fall of the Soviet Union, Russia joined the group under special terms and not because of its strong economic performance. The group became the Group of Eight.

Western technological superiority and Japanese military and then economic superiority defied long-standing Chinese assumptions concerning the natural order of the world – meaning a world with China at its apex. The war shattered long-established wisdoms in the East and the West concerning the nature of international relations and the natural hierarchy among nations.

For all of these reasons – the Far Eastern balance of power, enduring regional instability, and the globalization of politics – the first Sino-Japanese War is a seminal event in world history.

* * *

Underlying these changes was a revolution in Western perceptions concerning Chinese and Japanese power and their relative positions in the world. Before the war, the most widespread Western image of Japan was undoubtedly provided by William S. Gilbert and Arthur Sullivan, the famous operetta duo more commonly known as Gilbert and Sullivan. The year 1885 marked the première of what became their most popular operetta, *The Mikado* (帝) or "The Emperor of Japan."[24] While the librettist William S. Gilbert knew little about Japan, the popularity of the work made his ludicrous image stick. The story is about a maiden Yum-yum who jilts her betrothed, Ko-ko (Pickles), the Lord High Executioner, in favor of a wandering minstrel, Nanki-poo. The operetta opens with a chorus of samurai announcing to the Western audience, "If you want to know who we are, / We are gentlemen of Japan: / On many a vase and jar – / On many a screen and fan, / We figure in lively paint: / Our attitudes queer and quaint." The next verse proceeds: "If you think we are worked by strings, / Like a Japanese marionette, / You don't understand these things: / It is simply Court etiquette."[25] This was the European view: A quaint Japan preoccupied with stultifying rules of etiquette instead of the serious pursuits of European powers.

In line with the prevailing European views concerning Oriental despotism, a key character, the Lord High Executioner, emphasizes the arbitrariness of governmental rule with his little ditty explaining that he has "a little list" of "society offenders...who never would be missed." Those available for execution include "the piano-organist," "the lady novelist," and "apologetic statesmen of a compromising kind" as well as "the idiot who praises, with enthusiastic tone, /

---

[24] Philip H. Dilard, *Sir Arthur Sullivan: A Resource Book* (Lanham, MD: The Scarecrow Press, 1996), 49–52, 54, 77–8; Stanley Sadie, ed., *The New Grove Dictionary of Opera*, vol. 4 (London: Macmillan, 1992), 597.

[25] W. S. Gilbert, *The Mikado or the Town of Titipu* (1885, reprint; New York: Macmillan, 1979), 3–4. For similar views about Japan, see Rudyard Kipling, *From Sea to Sea Letters of Travel* (New York: Doubleday, Page & Co., 1909), 291–2, 403, 416.

All centuries but this, and every country but his own."[26] Later, he rhapsodizes about his preferred execution implement, which he fondly refers to as "my snickersnee."[27] In the Western mind, Asians, in general, were associated with a twisted fondness for decapitation and the Japanese, in particular, with a pathological reverence for their execution hardware of choice, the samurai sword.

This libretto has managed to irritate generations of Japanese because of its perceived mockery of Japanese culture.[28] Actually, William S. Gilbert was an equal-opportunity wit. When he wrote the libretto for *The H.M.S. Pinafore* in 1878, the British empire and its vehicle, the royal navy, were at their peak. Yet Gilbert had the cheek to make fun of the navy that at the time was superior to the combined forces of its two strongest rivals.[29] The head of the admiralty attributes his rise from office boy in an attorney's firm to his exalted position in the Royal Navy to his brass-polishing skills – pun intended: "I polished up the handle of the big front door...so carefullee, / That now I am the ruler of the Queen's Navee." He admits that his promotion to "junior partnership... / Was the only ship that I ever had seen." Later he went on to Parliament representing a pocket borough where "I thought so little, they rewarded me, / By making me the ruler of the Queen's Navee." He concludes with a Golden Rule for the upwardly mobile: "Stick close to your desks and never go to sea, / And you all may be rulers of the Queen's Navee."[30] Gilbert was no more derisive of the Japanese than he was of his own countrymen. While Queen Victoria knighted Sir Arthur, she allegedly found Gilbert's lyrics sufficiently irksome to pass him over. Gilbert had to await the next reign for the honor. So the Japanese were not alone in their irritation but were in royal company.

Another Englishman reflected on his time in Japan before the outbreak of Sino-Japanese War: "One used to look upon Japan as a kind of dolls' house, or, at the best, as a sort of Feast of Girls, where they had wooden images in gorgeous, mediæval Oriental dresses, and wonderful miniature sets of every kind of curious furniture and utensils used in an odd country." He added: "The idea that Japan would ever be a factor in the world's politics was too absurd to contemplate –

---

[26] Ibid., 15–17.

[27] Ibid., 72.

[28] Toshio Yokoyama, *Japan in the Victorian Mind: A Study of Stereotyped Images of a Nation 1850–80* (Houndmills, Basingstoke, Hampshire: Macmillan, 1987), xix.

[29] William L. Langer, *The Diplomacy of Imperialism, 1890–1902*, 2nd ed. (New York: Alfred A. Knopf, 1960), 422–4; Burroughs, 338.

[30] W. S. Gilbert, *The H.M.S. Pinafore* (1878, reprint; Milwaukee: G. Schirmer, n.d.), 10–11; Sadie, vol. 4, 597.

their rôle was to be absurd, and supply the suburbs with cheap decorations."[31]

In the pre–Sino-Japanese war period, there is no equivalent to *The Mikado* for expressing Western perceptions of China. Rather, there are a variety of travel books written mainly by missionaries to China. The earliest and most famous of these was not written by a missionary but by the adventurer, Marco Polo, whose *The Description of the World* of 1298 hooked many well-placed Europeans on a lifelong fascination with the East. One of the most notable of these was Christopher Columbus, who made a career of searching for a sea route to China. Systematic Western study of China did not begin until 1583, when the Jesuit Matteo Ricci established the first Catholic mission in China in over two and a half centuries. At his death, Ricci left a body of work that influenced generations of westerners. These works presented China as a well-ordered polity unified by Confucianism. This image of stability stood in stark contrast to a Europe rocked by the division of Christendom during the Reformation, the Catholic Reformation, and the following decades of vicious warfare. Ricci's successors perpetuated this positive image of Chinese stability.[32] In 1736, the French Jesuit Jean Baptiste du Halde, described China as "the most remarkable of all Countries yet known."[33] His influential *General History of China* was based on the work of his Jesuit colleagues in China.[34] After Europe recovered from the religious wars of the seventeenth century and entered into a period of relative prosperity and stability in the eighteenth century, Europeans took a more critical look at China. Enlightenment thinkers such as Montesquieu criticized China for its lack of liberty while Voltaire pointed to an underlying stagnation. Yet many Enlightenment thinkers still considered China an exemplary enlightened monarchy.[35] Voltaire applauded the Chinese examination system for government service, writing, "The human mind certainly

---

[31] Douglas Sladen, *Queer Things about Japan* (London: Anthony Treherne & Co., 1903), xiii. For a similar view, see David Murray, *Japan,* 6th ed. (London: T. Fisher Unwin, 1906), 397–8.

[32] Jonathan D. Spence, *The Chan's Great Continent: China in Western Minds* (New York: W. W. Norton, 1998), 15, 31–6; Nigel Cameron, *Barbarians and Mandarins: Thirteen Centuries of Western Travellers in China* (New York: Walker/Weatherhill, 1970), 149–94; D. E. Mungello, *The Great Encounter of China and the West, 1500–1800* (New York: Rowan & Littlefield, 1999), 7, 59, 75, 89.

[33] Jean Baptiste du Halde, *The General History of China* (London: J. Watts, 1741), Preface. The original French edition was published in 1736: Jean Baptiste du Halde, *Description géofraphique, historique, chronologique, politique, et physique de l'empire de la Chine et de la Tartarie Chinoise* (La Haye: H. Scheurleer, 1736).

[34] "Travel Literature," *New Catholic Encyclopedia,* vol. 14 (New York: McGraw-Hill, 1967), 266–7. This work puts the original publication date of du Halde's work as 1735. Ibid., 267.

[35] Spence, *The Chan's Great Continent,* 83–7, 92–9; Mungello, 87.

cannot imagine a government better than this one."[36] European thinkers still considered China an important country for drawing lessons relevant to Europe.

Although China's defeat by Britain and France in the mid-nineteenth-century Opium Wars caused another Western reappraisal, there still lingered an afterglow of respect for a venerable civilization. In 1870, Reverend Alexander Williamson applauded the Chinese for adopting "every manifest improvement which has presented itself for these many centuries."[37] A decade later, a long-term missionary to China praised its "system of government and code of laws which will bear favorable comparison with those European nations." He predicted that the Chinese would adapt to changing circumstances so that they "will be but little behind the Japanese in the march of progress, and will show themselves superior to them in prudence, sagacity and persistency."[38] In 1891 another long-term missionary in China described how he had found the country "old and decrepit in 1861...But China in 1891 is almost like a newfound land, notwithstanding the fact that the process of renovation is slow, and checked again and again by inroads of the old spirit."[39] That same year, Reverend John Ross praised the "high" intellectual character of the Chinese and suggested that the intelligence of the Chinese peasantry exceeded that of any peasantry elsewhere. He lavished praise on "the greatness of service done her by her excellent education."[40] In 1894, Lord George Nathaniel Curzon – one of Britain's foremost statesmen, well-traveled expert on Asia, and future viceroy of India – described China as a "mysterious anachronism" but populated by an "amazing people."[41]

Other foreign observers were impressed by the recent Chinese efforts at military modernization. In 1894, foreigners attended an inspection of the Chinese land and sea forces being carried out by China's greatest modernizer of the nineteenth century, Viceroy Li Hongzhang (李鴻章). The naval correspondent of the British-owned *Peking and Tientsin Times* reported that Viceroy Li "may be proud indeed

[36] John Merson, *The Genius that was China: East and West in the Making of the Modern World* (Woodstock, NY: Overlook Press, 1990), 121.

[37] Alexander Williamson, *Journeys in North China, Manchuria, and Eastern Mongolia; with Some Account of Corea* (London: Smither, Elder & Co., 1870), 9.

[38] John L. Nevius, *China and the Chinese* (Philadelphia: Presbyterian Board of Publication, 1882), 279, 445.

[39] Arthur E. Moule, *New China and Old: Personal Recollections and Observations of Thirty Years* (London: Seeley and Co., 1891), vi.

[40] John Ross, *The Manchus, or The Reigning Dynasty of China: Their Rise and Progress* (1891; reprint, New York: AMS Press, 1973), xvi, xxviii.

[41] George Nathaniel Curzon, *Problems of the Far East*, 3rd ed. (London: Longman's, Green, and Co., 1894), ix.

of the herculean work created in so short a time by his initiative and supervision, and well pleased he seemed on beholding the fine fleet, the efficient army, the powerful coast defences and the railway; and he is sure to appreciate the merits of his able co-adjustors, both Chinese and foreign."[42] On the eve of the war, *The North-China Herald* still described China as the "only great Asiatic State that really commands the respect of the Great Powers of the World."[43] It was amazing how fast these ideas would change once the war started.

The war precipitated a rash of publications concerning the Far East. Previously, Western works on Japan had almost without exception praised the reforms undertaken to modernize the country in the 1870s and 1880s. Unlike China, which continued to resist the inroads of Western civilization, the Japanese reformers intended to harness many pieces of this alien world to serve their own national interests. In 1887, Major-General James Harrison Wilson praised "the genuine progress made by the Japanese people in all that pertains to modern civilization,"[44] while in 1890, a British observer went so far as to praise Japan as "the only nation in the Orient which has shown itself possessed of the true instinct of civilised progress."[45] In July of 1894, just days before the outbreak of hostilities, a British book reviewer patronizingly praised Japan as "our rapidly developing *protégé.*"[46]

---

[42] Cited in "The Viceroy Li's Inspection," *The North-China Herald and Supreme Court & Consular Gazette* (Shanghai), 8 June 1894, p. 883.

[43] "The Corean Embroglio," *The North-China Herald and Supreme Court & Consular Gazette* (Shanghai), 20 July 1894, p. 107.

[44] James Harrison Wilson, *China: Travels and Investigations in the "Middle Kingdom": A Study of Its Civilization and Possibilities with a Glance at Japan* (New York: D. Appleton and Co., 1887), 1. For other similar favorable pre-war opinions of Japan, see "Political Progress of Japan in 1893," *Japan Weekly Mail* (Yokohama), 9 June 1894, p. 686; William Elliot Griffis, *The Mikado's Empire* (New York: Harper & Brothers, 1876), Preface; John R. Black, *Young Japan. Yokohama and Yedo.* (London: Trubner & Co., 1880), 2; Edward J. Reed, *Japan: Its History, Traditions, and Religions with the Narrative of a Visit in 1879*, vol. 1 (London: John Murray, 1880), 349, 365; Bayard Taylor, *Japan in Our Day* (New York: Charles Scribner's Sons, 1881), Prefatory Note; W. Henry Barneby, *The New Far West and the Old Far East, Being Notes of a Tour in North America, Japan, China, Ceylon, Etc.* (London: Edward Stanford, 1889), 221; Eliza Ruhamah Scidmore, *Jinrikisha Days in Japan* (New York: Harper & Brothers, 1891), 371–2; Edwin Arnold, *Seas and Lands*, rev. ed. (London: Longmans, Green, and Co., 1892), 429–46, 558, 570; William Elliot Griffis, *Japan in History, Folk Lore and Art* (Boston: Houghton, Mifflin and Co., 1892), 227; H. Loomis, "Progress in Japan," *Chinese Recorder and Missionary Journal* 25, no. 5 (May, 1894): 221; Akira Iriye, "Minds Across the Pacific: Japan in American Writing (1853–1883)," *Papers on China* 1 (June, 1961): 22, 33.

[45] Arnold, 446.

[46] Ernest Wilson Clement, *The Dial*, reprinted in "Japanese History and Civilization," *Japan Weekly Mail* (Yokohama), 14 July 1894, p. 55.

After the war, the praise became cacophonous.[47] "In less than twenty years Japan has acquired the knowledge it has taken us centuries to learn...Japan really made her début in the world-history when she declared war on China...Everyone considered them a nation of dolls and pretty toys, and were astonished when they found brains in their heads and courage in their hearts,"[48] extolled one American observer. An American missionary noted: "Seldom, perhaps never, has the civilized world so suddenly and completely reversed an estimate of a nation as it has that with reference to Japan."[49] In 1894, Lord Curzon had described Japan as "still in pupillage,"[50] whereas in the post-war edition of the same book he praised "the confident ambitions and swelling power of Young Japan."[51] The British journalist

[47] Henry Dumolard, *Le Japon politique, économique et social* (*Japan: Politics, Economics and Society*) (Paris: Librairie Armand Colin, 1903), 239, 278-9, 321-9; Arthur Diósy, "The New Japan," in *Japan as Seen and Described by Famous Writers*, Esther Singleton, ed. and trans. (New York: Dodd Mead and Co., 1904), 356-63; Henry Norman, *The Peoples and Politics of the Far East* (London: T. Fisher Unwin, 1901), 375-95; H. Loomis, "The Status of Japan among the Nations, and her Position in regard to Korea," *Chinese Recorder and Missionary Journal* 25, no. 12 (December 1894): 566-70; W. A. P. Martin, *A Cycle of Cathay or China, South and North with Personal Reminiscences*, 3rd ed. (New York: Fleming H. Revell Co., 1900), 403; Robert P. Porter, *Japan the New World Power Being a Detailed Account of the Progress and Rise of the Japanese Empire* (London: Oxford University Press, 1915), *passim;* Robert Porter, *Japan: The Rise of a Modern Power* (Oxford: Clarendon Press, 1918), *passim;* Walter Weston, *Mountaineering and Exploration in the Japanese Alps* (London: John Murray, 1896), vii; John W. Foster, *American Diplomacy in the Orient* (Boston: Houghton, Mifflin, 1903), 342; G. Waldo Browne, *The New American and the Far East*, vol. 2 (Boston: Marshall Jones, 1910), 347-8; Valentine Chirol, *The Far Eastern Question* (London: Macmillan, 1896), 108-9, 138-40; William Eleroy Curtis, *The Yankees of the East: Sketches of Modern Japan*, vol. 1 (New York: Stone & Kimball, 1906), 1-2; Joseph D'Autremer, *The Japanese Empire and Its Economic Conditions* (London: T. Fisher Unwin, 1910), 2; R. H. Graves, *Forty Years in China or China in Transition* (1895; reprint, Wilmington, DE: Scholarly Resources, 1972), 177-80; Lafcadio Hearn, *Japan: An Attempt at Interpretation* (New York: Macmillan Co., 1913), 501; Arthur May Knapp, *Feudal and Modern Japan*, 2nd ed., vol. 1 (Boston: L. C. Page, 1897), ix; George Trumbull Ladd, *Rare Days in Japan* (New York: Dodd, Mead and Co., 1910), 341; Leroy-Beaulieu, vi, viii., 118, 185; H. Loomis, "The Status of Japan": 570; J. Morris, *Advance Japan: A Nation Thoroughly in Earnest* (London: W. H. Allen, 1895), ix; R. B. Peery, *The Gist of Japan: The Islands, Their People and Missions* (1908; reprint, Austin: Book Lab, Inc., 1995), 49; Stafford Ransome, *Japan in Transition: A Comparative Study of the Progress, Policy, and Methods of the Japanese since their War with China* (New York: Harper & Brothers, 1899), 179-80, 189; James A. Scherer, *Japan To-day* (Philadelphia: J. B. Lippincott, 1904), 13-14, 26, 251-4; John L. Stoddard, *Japan* (Chicago: Belford, Middlebrook & Co., 1907), 4; Joseph Walton, *China and the Present Crisis with Notes on a Visit to Japan and Korea* (London: Sampson Low, Marston & Co., 1900), 257-8.

[48] George H. Rittner, *Impressions of Japan* (New York: James Pott & Co., 1904), 142-3.

[49] Sidney L. Gulick, *Evolution of the Japanese: Social and Psychic* (New York: Fleming H. Revell Co., 1903), 23.

[50] Curzon, 3rd ed., ix.

[51] George N. Curzon, *Problems of the Far East*, 4th ed. (New York: Longmans, Green, 1896).

and expert on Asia, Sir Henry Norman, wrote mid-war: "The war with China and the treaty with England [of 1894, according Japan juridical equality] will at last force foreigners to see Japan as she is. The Japanese are a martial and a proud race, with marvellous intelligence, and untiring energy and enthusiasm." He believed that their goal in Asia mirrored England's in Europe, namely, "to hold the balance of power in the Far East."[52]

A new literary image of Japan supplanted that provided by *The Mikado.* Giacomo Puccini's opera, *Madama Butterfly,* premièred in 1906 but was based on a play written by David Belasco in 1900. Belasco, in turn, had based his work on Pierre Loti's best-selling and much-translated novel, *Madame Chrysanthème,* published in 1887.[53] The evolution of the story line from Loti to that of Puccini's librettists parallels the evolution of pre-war and post-war Western perceptions of Japan. Loti's book is about a casual love affair between an American naval officer, Pinkerton, and a Japanese woman. When the officer's term in Japan expires, he hands his mistress silver dollars for the services rendered, she gleefully counts the change, and there are no hard feelings on either side. The book regularly likens the Japanese to monkeys and presents Butterfly as a charming but shallow opportunist devoid of moral scruples or sense of honor.[54]

In the opera the roles reverse. A self-centered Pinkerton, against all advice, lures Butterfly from her family, goes through a mock marriage ceremony, and then abandons her when he sets sail for America. Three years later, a still-faithful Butterfly turns down a wealthy Japanese suitor. She and her son from the affair continue to await the return of Pinkerton, only to learn that he has married an American woman. Pinkerton, lacking the courage to tell Butterfly himself, foists the unpleasant business on his wife, whereupon Butterfly takes the news with dignity and gives the American woman her blessings. But when left alone, Butterfly kills herself with her father's samurai sword. The sword bears the

---

[52] Henry Norman, *Contemporary Review,* republished as "The Question of Korea," *Japan Weekly Mail* (Yokohama), 20 October 1894, p. 462. For biographical background on Norman, see Jean-Pierre Lehmann, *The Image of Japan: From Feudal Isolation to World Power, 1850–1905* (London: George Allen & Unwin, 1978), 184. For other positive post-war views concerning Japan, see H. Loomis, "The Status of Japan among the Nations and Her Position in Regard to Korea," *The Japan Weekly Mail* (Yokohama), 27 October 1894, pp. 488–9.

[53] Sadie, vol. 3, 136–7; Sadie, vol. 1, 380; Setsuko Ono, *A Western Image of Japan: What did the West See through the Eyes of Loti and Hearn?* (Geneva: Imprimerie du Courrier, 1972), 8–9.

[54] Pierre Loti, *Madame Chrysanthème,* Laura Ensor, trans. (Paris: Edouard Guillaume et cie., 1889), 198, 230, 319–24; William Leonard Schwartz, *The Imaginative Interpretation of the Far East in modern French Literature, 1800–1925* (Paris: Librairie Ancienne Honoré Champion, 1927), 131.

inscription: "To die with honour when one can no longer live with honour."[55] All the esteem goes to the Japanese side, none to the American.

Japan had grown greatly in Western estimations, yet a certain ambivalence remained that reflected prevailing racial prejudices. This ambivalence is well illustrated by the views of the American president Theodore Roosevelt. Although he greatly admired the diligence and martial abilities of the Japanese, he also supported strict restrictions to prevent their immigration to the United States.[56] The Western preference was to admire the Japanese from afar.

In contrast to Japan, the post-war Western view of China was anything but flattering. "Corrupt to the core, ill-governed, lacking cohesion and without means of defending herself...China stands to-day as a sort of political Tom Tiddler's ground, on which the representatives of the various Powers disport themselves while making up their minds as to which particular corner they will finally occupy." The author continued, "To believe in the recuperative power of China is mere wasted faith. The people are too ignorant, the rulers too obtuse...There is nothing in common between the situation in China to-day and that which existed in Japan thirty years ago...what has been feasible in Nippon could never come to pass in Chrisé. China as a political entity is doomed."[57] Another author concurred that China "has been dying of old age and senile decay for all of this century."[58] The much-traveled director of the foreign department of the London *Times*, Valentine Chirol, concluded, "This distant thunder of the Japanese guns may have disturbed for a moment the heavy slumber of the worn-out giant, but the nightmare has passed away, and after the vain attempt to stretch his inert limbs, he has sunk off into a deeper sleep than ever."[59] China had assumed the decrepit Ottoman Empire's ignominious title of "Sick Man of Asia." According to the French writer and lecturer, Pierre Leroy-Beaulieu, the war had revealed "the existence in the East of Asia...of another Sick Man, an even greater invalid and infinitely richer than the better known patient at Constantinople."[60]

---

[55] Luigi Illica and Giuseppe Giacosa, *Madam Butterfly*, Rosie Helen Elkin, trans. (New York: G. Ricordi & Co., 19??), 1–2.

[56] Thomas G. Dyer, *Theodore Roosevelt and the Idea of Race* (Baton Rouge: Louisiana State University Press, 1980), 136–40.

[57] Alexis Krausse, *China in Decay: The Story of a Disappearing Empire*, 3rd ed. (London: Chapman & Hill, 1900), 324, 383–4.

[58] Eliza Ruhamah Scidmore, *China: The Long-Lived Empire* (New York: The Century Co., 1900), 1.

[59] Chirol, 19; see also pages 5, 9–18. Lehmann, 182.

[60] Leroy-Beaulieu, 183; Lehmann, 184. The protracted collapse of the Ottoman Empire had earned Turkey the name "the Sick Man of Europe."

For similar post-war views of China, see Baron Charles William De la Poer Beresford, *The*

In the space of one year, the Western image changed from perceiving Japan primarily as an insignificant land populated by horticulturists, rickshaw drivers, trinket makers, and geishas. Suddenly, the Western press started regularly referring to it as a great power and one belonging to that very select club of the so-called "civilized nations." It was the first non-Western nation to do so. The only two other non-Western countries that would follow suit in the twentieth century would be Japan's former colonies of Korea and Taiwan.[61]

At the turn of the twenty-first century, it was taken for granted in the West that Japan ranked among the most industrialized countries; that its citizenry had a high standard of living; and that, because of these achievements, it was a country to be accorded the highest degree of respect. This was not always so. The change in Western perceptions took place as a result of the Sino-Japanese War of 1894–5. The war fixed Japan in the Western mind. It has remained there ever since as the object of enormous attention, curiosity, and of emotional swings ranging from great apprehension to equally great admiration. In contrast, China has yet to recover fully from all the consequences of its defeat. The war undermined the Confucian order and a satisfactory replacement has yet to be found on the mainland. Meanwhile, the Taiwanese hybrid of traditional China, Meiji Japan, and Western thought is as vulnerable as it is promising. Only time will tell what the ultimate consequences of the Sino-Japanese War will be.

What follows is the story of how this fundamental reorientation in Western perceptions occurred and its consequences. This is not a military or diplomatic history, but a hybrid emphasizing the interplay between policy and perceptions. It focuses on the impact of diplomacy, military operations, and public opinion on the international balance of power. If nothing else, this work endeavors to show that perceptions matter.

This book has been divided into three parts. Part I describes the situation on the eve of the war. After an introductory chapter, the next two focus on the key Far Eastern protagonists: first China and Korea and then Russia and Japan. The first pair of countries remained part of the traditional Confucian order while the second pair embarked on industrialization programs aimed at achieving military parity

---

Break-up of China (New York: Harper & Row, 1900), *passim*; Archibald C. Coolidge, "The Position of China in World Politics," in *China and the Far East: Clark University Lectures*, George Hubbard Blakeslee, ed. (New York: Thomas Y. Crowell, 1910), 3; Graves, 187; "China's Extremity," *Blackwood's Edinburg Magazine* 157, no. 954 (April 1895): 501–16.

[61] The term "Little Tigers" has been used to indicate the four Asian success stories: Korea, Taiwan, Singapore, and Hong Kong. The latter two are cities of the former British empire and belong to a separate category. In the 1990s, there were only three non-Western countries that had achieved a high per capita standard of living and industrialized economy: Japan, Korea, and Taiwan.

with the Western powers. The differing national aspirations described in Part I set China, Japan, Korea, and Russia on a collision course.

Part II turns to the war. The account of the hostilities is largely based on wartime newspaper reports published in China, Japan, Europe, and the United States. As much as possible, I have allowed those who lived through the war to speak for themselves. Their views possess a freshness and natural understanding of the connections among contemporary events that the modern historian can rarely improve upon. In addition, newspapers document the day-by-day evolution of such perceptions and the implications drawn by people at the time. This is not to say that these views were necessarily right, but rather that widely held views, regardless of their accuracy, can be extremely influential.

The first chapter of Part II compares the pre-war military balance between China and Japan, and then describes the outbreak of hostilities. The following two chapters each focus on a pair of battles: With the capture of P'yông-yang, the Japanese army expelled the Chinese forces from the Korean Peninsula and, with the Battle of the Yalu, the Japanese navy secured command of the sea. Then, with the capture of Port Arthur, the Japanese army completed its preparations for one pincer aimed at Peking and, with the obliteration of the Chinese navy at Weihaiwei, completed the preparations for the second pincer. This put Peking and the Manchu or Qing Dynasty (1644–1911) at the mercy of the Japanese army.

Part III describes the capitulation of the Qing Dynasty and the consequences of the war. The first chapter discusses the bilateral and then the multilateral settlements of the war, while the second chapter focuses on the long-term consequences of the war, namely, the globalization of international relations. The third chapter examines the underlying cultural factors explaining why China found it so difficult to meet the challenge posed by Japan and, by extension, the West. Finally, the epilogue attempts to draw some more general lessons from the war and the connections among perceptions, power, and primacy. For those interested in the bibliographic fine print, an essay introduces the bibliography.

2

The Decline of the Old Order in China and Korea

Korean rulers, under whatever impulse they act, seem determined to create causes of international friction; petty causes, it is true, but these littles may make a mickle one fine day.[1]

The Japan Weekly Mail, February 17, 1894

Korea seems a very poor place to fight for. Its people are plunged in the most miserable poverty of any in the poverty-stricken East....Japan, in spite of all her mistakes, stands for light and civilization; her institutions are enlightened; her laws, drawn up by European justice, are equal to the best we know, and they are justly administered; her punishments are humane; her scientific and sociological ideals are our own. China stands for darkness and savagery. Her science is ludicrous superstition, her law is barbarous, her punishments are awful, her politics are corruption, her ideals are isolation and stagnation.[2]

Sir Henry Norman, British journalist, 1894

In 1894, the great Pullman Railway Strike paralyzed the economy of the Western half of the United States; the muckraking journalist Henry Demarest Lloyd published his exposé of John D. Rockefeller's Standard Oil Company; and the United States remained in the throes of the Depression of 1893. In France, 1894 marked the beginning of the long, drawn-out Dreyfus affair, when anti-Semitism led to the court-martial and imprisonment on Devil's Island of an innocent Jewish officer. There were headlines concerning the assassinations of President Carnot of France and the Bulgarian nationalist, Stefan Stambulov. Tsar Alexander III of Russia

[1] "Korean Affairs," *The Japan Weekly Mail* (Yokohama), 17 February 1894, p. 199.

[2] Henry Norman, *Contemporary Review*, republished as "The Question of Korea," *The Japan Weekly Mail* (Yokohama), 20 October 1894, pp. 461–4.

unexpectedly died, leaving the throne to his unprepared and panic-stricken twenty-six-year-old son, Nicholas II. Robert Louis Stevenson, the author of *Treasure Island,* also died. An anti-dynastic rebellion broke out in Korea. Ottoman troops massacred Armenian subjects of the Porte while there was a wave of lynchings in the American South. Kitasato Shibasaburo (北里柴三郎) of Japan and Alexandre Yersin of France independently identified the germ causing bubonic plague. The American, Jesse W. Reno, invented the escalator; the Frenchmen, René Panhard and Émile Levassor, invented the gasoline-engined truck while the Italian, Guglielmo Marconi, invented the wireless telegraph.[3] As Britain and Belgium came to an agreement on how to carve up Central Africa and France was poised to take over Madagascar, the Empress Dowager of China redirected naval funds to renovate the Imperial Summer Palace in anticipation of her sixtieth birthday celebrations.

The 1890s were the heyday of Western imperialism. The emergence of centralized industrial states led to a new world view in the West. It took as scientific truth that domestic prosperity and national security depended on the possession of far-flung colonies or spheres of influence.[4] The European powers were rapidly dividing up Africa and the Near East. Before long their colonial appetites would start craving larger portions of the Far East. In 1890, Captain Alfred Thayer Mahan of the United States Navy published his influential and much-translated book, *The Influence of Sea Power upon History, 1660–1783.* His message of the importance of sea power in the age of commercial empires struck chords around the world.[5] To make such overseas adventures more palatable for domestic consumption, governments in the pursuit of empire presented it as a noble civilizing mission.[6] In 1899, Rudyard Kipling, the grand bard of British imperialism, described this task in the most elevated and selfless terms: "Take up the White Man's burden – / Send forth the best ye breed – / Go bind your sons to exile / To serve your captives' need /...Take up the White Man's burden – / And reap his old reward: / The blame of those ye better, / The hate of those ye guard." It was "the white

---

[3] For references to discoveries and inventions, see Claire L. Parkinson, *Breakthroughs: A Chronology of Great Achievement in Science and Mathematics 1200–1930* (Boston: G. K. Hall, 1985), 428; Kevin Desmond, *The Harwin Chronology of Inventions, Innovations, Discoveries from Pre-History to the Present Day* (London: Constable, 1986), 1894. All other references are drawn from a general knowledge of American history and from extensive reading of contemporary newspapers in the United States, Europe, and the Western press in China and Japan. These were the headlines.

[4] Akira Iriye, "Japan's Drive to Great Power Status," in *The Cambridge History of Japan,* Marius B. Jansen, ed., vol. 5 (Cambridge: Cambridge University Press, 1989), 725, 727.

[5] Alfred Thayer Mahan, *The Influence of Sea Power upon History, 1660–1783* (1890, reprint; Boston: Little, Brown, 1935), 1–2, 25–8.

[6] Iriye, "Japan's Drive to Great Power Status," 725, 727.

man's burden" to uplift the teeming throngs populating the benighted and poverty-stricken non-Western world.[7] This is the ideology of imperialism that Karl Marx and, more effectively, his Soviet and Chinese Communist disciples made a generic term for "evil" and "exploitation," with all the virtue going to the colonies and none to the imperialists. In the late twentieth century, in the afterglow of the Soviet Union, the prevailing view among Western scholars attested to the influence of the Marxist interpretation of imperialism: In academic circles the policies of imperialism were generally considered to have been universally pernicious.

Back in the 1890s, scholars had actively sponsored the imperial mission. In 1893, the Englishman Herbert Spencer completed his eight-volume life's work, *The System of Synthetic Philosophy,* which unabashedly described and applauded a philosophy of social Darwinism: Nature dictated a ruthless "survival of the fittest" for societies as well as organisms.[8] It would be a duel to the death between Western and non-Western cultures. In 1881, France took Tunis; in 1882, Britain subjugated Egypt; in 1883, Germany made forays into Southwest Africa; from 1884 to 1885 Britain took Burma while France took Indochina; and in 1889 Germany, Britain, and the United States divided up Samoa.[9] The tempo of Western imperialism had quickened.[10]

Responses to imperialism varied. China and Korea resisted change whereas Russia and Japan embraced elements of it. This chapter will discuss the traditional world still inhabited by China and Korea. The next chapter will turn to an examination of the changes underway in Russia and Japan. On first consideration, Russia may seem an inappropriate inclusion, but along with China and Korea these constitute the countries bordering on Korea, the initial seat of hostilities. Moreover, Japanese policies in Korea often reflected its interpretation of Russian intentions in the Far East. Russia is the all-too-often-ignored essential factor in the Far Eastern equation.

The era of expanding Western commercial interests and Russian territorial interests in Asia coincided with a long period of dynastic decline in China. The Qing Empire had reached its zenith during the reign of the Emperor Qianlong (乾隆皇帝), whose actual rule from 1736 to 1799 was the longest in Chinese history. This was the period when the French philosophe Voltaire had helped popularize

---

[7] Rudyard Kipling, "The White Man's Burden," in *Complete Verse* (1940; reprint, New York: Doubleday, 1989), 321–2. Kipling wrote the poem in 1899 in response to the United States' occupation of the Philippines. Ibid., 321.

[8] Tindall and Shi, vol. 2, 902.

[9] Iriye, "Japan's Drive to Great Power Status," 747.

[10] Langer, 74–166.

the achievements of Chinese civilization in Europe.[11] The Qianlong Emperor had acceded to the throne immediately following two other long reigns, those of the Kangxi (康熙皇帝) and the Yongzheng (雍正皇帝) Emperors. Their combined rule extended from 1661 to 1799. This prolonged period of stability had permitted a very rapid growth of population, which in Qianlong's time began to outstrip the available land supply and technological means for food production. The Qianlong Emperor's crowning achievement was his conquest of much of Central Asia, doubling the size of the empire.[12] Eventually, many of these lands would be formally integrated into the empire as the province of Xinjiang (Sinkiang).[13] The occupation of these vast territories had a very unexpected and long-concealed consequence: They constituted an important drain on government revenues.[14] Therefore, although the Qing Empire reached the peak of its prosperity under the Qianlong Emperor, the harbingers of decline were already appearing.

Botched border campaigns against the Burmese in the 1760s and the Vietnamese in the 1780s indicated problems within the military. Anti-dynastic rebellions confined to single provinces in the 1770s and 1780s indicated scattered but deep-seated grievances. Empty emergency granaries and silting problems in the Grand Canal – the major artery for transporting the rice tax to Peking – indicated failures of fundamental governmental institutions. In later reigns problems would extend to the maintenance of the vital dikes necessary to prevent devastating flooding. The bureaucracy was riddled with factions. Corruption had become so rampant that it had started to impede the flow of accurate information to the emperor and to undermine government efficiency. For the West, this corruption became the hallmark of the Qing Dynasty.[15] According to one British observer, "In China the offices of State are farmed. The greater the emoluments accruing to their holders the heavier the correlated responsibilities."[16] At the time of the

---

[11] Jonathan D. Spence, *The Search for Modern China* (New York: W. W. Norton & Co., 1990), 90; Pamela Kyle Crossley, *The Manchus* (Cambridge: Blackwell Publishers, 1997), 137–40.

[12] Susan Mann Jones and Philip A. Kuhn "Dynastic Decline and the Roots of Rebellion," in *The Cambridge History of China*, John K. Fairbank, ed., vol. 10 (Cambridge: Cambridge University Press, 1978), 108–10; Spence, *Search for Modern China*, 90–7. Although Qianlong officially ruled until 1796, he actually retained control until his death in 1799. In 1796, he abdicated in favor of his son as an act of filial piety so that his own reign would not exceed that of his grandfather, the Kangxi Emperor, who ruled from 1661 to 1722. Ibid., 116.

[13] Paine, 166.

[14] James A. Milward, *Beyond the Pass: Economy, Ethnicity, and Empire in Qing Central Asia, 1759–1864* (Stanford: Stanford University Press, 1998), 58–63.

[15] Spence, *Search for Modern China*, 110–4; Jones and Kuhn, 110–62.

[16] "The Korean Situation," *The Japan Weekly Mail* (Yokohama), 7 July 1894, p. 17.

Sino-Japanese War, a London paper explained to its readers, "The officials in China are very badly paid. The consequence is, they eke out their fortune by extortion and tyranny. Bribery is universal."[17] In the face of such widespread malfeasance, the roots of rebellion rapidly spread. In the final three years of the Qianlong Emperor's reign, the rebellions threatened to become national. The White Lotus Sect rose up to expel the Manchus and restore a native Han Chinese dynasty. The White Lotus Rebellion lasted from 1796 through 1804 and devastated the five central provinces of China.[18] This uprising was the first of the great nineteenth-century rebellions that by the mid-nineteenth century had nearly toppled the Qing Dynasty.

These later rebellions were of two types: secessional and anti-dynastic. The former prevailed in border areas whose local populations presumably resented the influx of Han Chinese trying to escape the population explosion in central China. Secessional rebellions included the Miao people's revolt in the south in Hunan and Guizhou (Kweichow) (1855–73); the Moslem revolt against Chinese rule in the southern province of Yunnan during the Panthay Rebellion (1856–73); and the great Moslem rebellions (1862–78) in Xinjiang and the three western provinces bordering Mongolia. In these rebellions, the goal was secession or at least expulsion of the Han Chinese newcomers.[19]

The anti-dynastic rebellions were far more dangerous because they did not threaten to whittle away the Qing empire at the geographic or cultural periphery, but to deliver a *coup de grâce* in Peking toppling the whole dynasty. Moreover, they were not generically anti-Chinese like the secession movements, but specifically anti-Manchu. These rebellions included the Eight Trigrams, the Triads, the Nian, and the Taiping. In 1813, a secret society called the Eight Trigrams breached the gates of the Forbidden City, the imperial residence in Peking, before succumbing to superior force.[20] By the early nineteenth century, a secret brotherhood known as the Triads had spread from Taiwan across the Taiwan Strait to the provinces of Fujian (Fukien), Guangdong (Kwangtung), and Guangxi (Kwangsi) and from there

---

[17] "Society in China," *The Pall Mall Gazette* (London), 7 August 1894, 4th ed., p. 4.

[18] Hsü, *Rise of Modern China*, 129; Jones and Kuhn, 136–44; "川楚白莲教起义" ("Sichuan–Hubei White Lotus Rebellion") in 中国大百科全书 (*Chinese Encyclopedia*), 中国历史 (*Chinese History*), vol. 1 (Peking: 中国大百科全书出版社, 1992), 113–14.

[19] Jones and Kuhn, 132–6; Frederic Wakeman, Jr., *Strangers at the Gate: Social Disorder in South China 1838–1861* (Berkeley: University of California Press, 1966), 118–9, 136–52; Kwang-ching Liu, 211–43; Paine, 110–25; Bruce A. Elleman, *Modern Chinese Warfare, 1795–1989* (London: Routledge, 2001), x, 57–68.

[20] Susan Naquin, *Millenarian Rebellion in China: The Eight Trigrams Uprising of 1813* (New Haven: Yale University Press, 1976), 1, 176–84, 265.

northward to the Yangtze River provinces. They dreamed of restoring the previous Han Chinese dynasty of the Ming. What began as scattered revolts in 1843 culminated in the Red Turban Revolt (1854–5) when Canton almost fell to the rebels. The Nian Rebellion (1851–68) evolved from isolated acts of banditry into visions of a new dynasty. This rebellion took place against a backdrop of great hardship. The Qing had failed to maintain the dikes on the Yellow River. In 1851, the flooding was on such a scale that the river radically changed its course from the southern to the northern side of the Shandong (Shantung) Peninsula. The ensuing rebellion ravaged the central provinces of Shandong, Jiangsu (Kiangsu), Henan (Honan), and Anhui (Anhwei) and spilled over into four others. Without a doubt, the greatest rebellion in Chinese history was the Taiping (1851–64). It ravaged sixteen provinces; devastated more than 600 cities; founded a competing but short-lived dynasty based at the Yangtze River city of Nanjing (Nanking); reached within twenty miles of Tianjin (Tientsin), the port city to Peking; and almost toppled the Qing Dynasty. Had they coordinated with the Nian and Moslem Rebellions, they would have succeeded.[21] No one knows the precise extent of the casualties. Suffice it to say that they were evidently in the millions.

This list of rebellions is by no means inclusive. There were innumerable smaller ones. Their combined effect was to devastate numerous provinces, empty government coffers, and brutalize a nation. As a last resort, the Qing Dynasty relied increasingly on provincial armies to suppress the unrest. In contravention to rules of the past, provincial leaders raised and funded their own armies, making them independent of central control. After the suppression of the great rebellions, these armies were not disbanded but presented a growing and competing force with the central authority.[22] After the American Civil War, there was a Reconstruction, which, despite its well-known problems, succeeded in reintegrating the South into the American political and economic system. In China a Tongzhi Restoration (同治中興) was attempted during the rebellions, but there was no Reconstruction afterward. The unrest had sapped the strength of the political system. The central government never fully reestablished its control over the provinces. Because the unrest had been so widespread, the Manchus could not conceal their weakness.

---

[21] Spence, *Search for Modern China*, 165–93; Philip A. Kuhn, "The Taiping Rebellion," in *The Cambridge History of China*, John K. Fairbank, ed., vol. 10 (Cambridge: Cambridge University Press, 1978), 264–317; Hsü, 221–56.

[22] Philip A. Kuhn, *Rebellion and Its Enemies in Late Imperial China: Militarization and Social Structure, 1796–1864* (Cambridge: Harvard University Press, 1980), 211–25; Kenneth E. Folsom, *Friends, Guests, and Colleagues: The Mu-fu System in the Late Ch'ing Period* (Berkeley: University of California Press, 1968), 122–4.

Everyone knew that their mandate from heaven was rapidly disappearing. It took the American South over a century to recover fully from the devastation of a five-year civil war. The turmoil in China lasted in one form or another right through the Great Proletarian Cultural Revolution (1966–76). The number of Chinese who died during this century and a quarter of bloodletting make even the extraordinary Russian losses suffered in World War II pale in comparison. Arguably, China has yet to recover.

The Chinese have pejoratively labeled all these many uprisings as "rebellions" and westerners writing about China have taken this cue. The Chinese terminology reflects an imperial view regarding subject peoples and those challenging the established political order. A more accurate term would be "independence movements" for the attempts at secession and "civil wars" for the attempts to overthrow the dynasty. But this perspective threatens the Chinese myth of their country's homogeneity, their history's continuity, and their empire's legitimacy.

Unfortunately for China, the period of great rebellions coincided with the quickening tempo of Western imperialism in the form of expanding commercial demands. These culminated in the First Opium War (1839–42) and the Second Opium War, also known as the Arrow War (1856–60). In settlement of the first war, China abolished its monopolies previously controlling foreign trade; opened five so-called treaty ports, where British consuls and merchants could reside; accorded them extraterritoriality; extended most-favored-nation treatment to Britain; set the export and import tariff rate; ceded Hong Kong as a permanent base to Britain; and paid an indemnity for all the inconvenience.[23] The settlement for the second war permitted foreign representatives to reside in the capital; opened ten additional treaty ports; allowed foreigners and missionaries to travel throughout China; set maximum levels for inland transport duties on imports; and levied additional indemnities for Britain and France.

These treaties were the first of the so-called unequal treaties.[24] Extraterritoriality, externally fixed tariffs, and treaty ports were the essential features of the treaty-port system governing China's trade relations. Westerners might force the Chinese to sign unequal treaties, but the latter had no intention of enforcing them. So there were regular complaints among westerners that the Chinese did not adhere to their treaties.[25] The Chinese loathed the system and their subjugation that it so blatantly

---

[23] Hsü, *Rise of Modern China*, 190.

[24] Hsü, *Rise of Modern China*, 210–11.

[25] Immanuel C. Y. Hsü, *China's Entrance into the Family of Nations: The Diplomatic Phase, 1858–1880* (Cambridge: Harvard University Press, 1968), 46, 89–90, 111–2, 139–40; Spence, *Search for Modern China*, 162, 181; Hosea Ballou Morse, *The International Relations of the Chinese Empire: The Period*

symbolized, yet it endured in full until 1943, that is, soon after the Japanese bombing of Pearl Harbor, when Britain and the United States relinquished their privileges, and endured in part until 1955, when the Soviet Union belatedly gave up its privileges in Manchuria after the Korean War.[26]

To insure the collection of the customs mandated by the new treaties and to guarantee their full payment to the Chinese government, the British took the lead in establishing a small Foreign Inspectorate of Customs in Shanghai in 1854. In 1858 it was expanded to become the Imperial Maritime Customs whose senior personnel were foreigners but officially in the employ of the Chinese government.[27] The system was not without its ironies. Although a creation of Western imperialism and the object of enormous Chinese rancor, its primary function was to insure the equitable collection of tariffs primarily paid by foreigners and then to make sure that all of this money made it into Qing Dynasty coffers. By all accounts, the customs administration was the unique and shining example of bureaucratic efficiency and, by Western standards, of ethical conduct in a governmental system otherwise bogged down in a morass of corruption. It is doubtful that native control of customs collection would have increased revenues for China; rather, the money would have been siphoned off to line deep pockets. Yet, like the treaty ports, the customs inspectorate remains a potent symbol for the Chinese of their years of internal unrest and deeply felt humiliation.

Westerners have tended to emphasize their own role in the decline of the Qing Dynasty. There is a large literature on the Opium Wars and on China's failure to meet the challenge posed by Western civilization. In terms of impact, the Opium Wars cannot be compared to the secession movements and civil wars afflicting China. During the Opium Wars, casualty figures ranged from the hundreds to the thousands, certainly not in the tens of thousands let alone tens of millions for the

of Conflict 1834–1860, vol. 1 (Shanghai: Kelly and Walsh, 1910), 333–4, 530; Hosea Ballou Morse, *The International Relations of the Chinese Empire: The Period of Submission: 1861–1893*, vol. 2 (Shanghai: Kelly and Walsh, 1918), 52, 191; Lloyd E. Eastman, *Throne and Mandarins: China's Search for a Policy during the Sino-French Controversy 1880–1885* (Cambridge: Harvard University Press, 1967), 41; S. M. Meng, *The Tsung-li Yamen: Its Organization and Functions* (Cambridge: Harvard University Press, 1962), 17; "The Envoys of 'Peace,'" *The North-China Herald and Supreme Court & Consular Gazette* (Shanghai), 15 February 1895, p. 223.

[26] Hsü, *Rise of Modern China*, 219, 567; Klaus Mehnert, *Peking and Moscow*, Leila Vennewitz, trans. (New York: G. P. Putnam's Sons, 1963), 249; Bruce A. Elleman, *Diplomacy and Deception: The Secret History of Sino-Soviet Diplomatic Relations, 1917-1927* (Armonk, NY: M. E. Sharpe, 1997), *passim*.

[27] John King Fairbank, *Trade and Diplomacy on the China Coast: The Opening of the Treaty Ports, 1843–1854* (Stanford: Stanford University Press, 1969), 453–61; Hugh B. O'Neill, *Companion to Chinese History* (New York: Facts on File Publications, 1987), 128–9.

civil wars and failed secession movements.[28] Whereas the Opium Wars were largely confined to a few treaty ports and surrounding coastal areas, the rebellions devastated the economies of entire provinces. The Chinese continue to emphasize the evils of the treaty-port system in order to scapegoat foreigners for their tragic century.[29] Mainland China uses a Marxist framework, juxtaposing evil Western imperialists with virtuous Chinese victims and freedom fighters. In reality, almost all of the killing during these years was done by Chinese to Chinese, most of whom were probably civilians.

After the Opium Wars and during the final years of the rebellions, China made an attempt at internal reform in the guise of the Tongzhi Restoration (1862–74), named after the boy emperor Tongzhi (同治), who never actually ruled. De facto power remained in the hands of his mother, the Empress Dowager Cixi (Tz'u-hsi, 慈禧皇太后), and his uncle, Prince Gong (Kung, 恭親王奕訢). The restoration, however, was not of their making. Rather, numerous talented Han provincial leaders took the salvation of China into their own hands and, in their separate ways, independently strove to adapt to the new age by using the new to restore the old. They were concerned about the lethal combination of internal and external threats to traditional Chinese institutions. Some were also aware of the rapid reforms taking place in Japan. Their goal was the restoration of Confucian government in China. Li Hongzhang (李鴻章) was the most famous of these provincial leaders, but there were many others. Most had become prominent for their roles in suppressing the various rebellions. Thereafter, they recognized the urgent need for reform. These reforms included: reinvigorating the Confucian educational system; supplementing the curriculum with the study of a variety of technical subjects imported from the West; reorganizing the military; developing a modern armaments industry; constructing railway and telegraph lines; and westernizing those institutions responsible for the conduct of foreign relations. These measures all focused on protecting the country's national security, not on spurring economic growth – an unknown concept in China at the time. Their intent was overwhelmingly military. Collectively these measures became known under the rubric of "self-strengthening" (自強). Ironically, they were funded by one of the institutional consequences of the very imperialism that the self-strengtheners were trying to combat. Revenues from the Imperial Maritime Customs made the self-strengthening projects possible. These talented Han Chinese provincial leaders breathed life into the expiring Qing

---

[28] Gerald S. Graham, *The China Station: War and Diplomacy 1830–1860* (Oxford: Clarendon Press, 1978), 214, 216, 273–4, 400.

[29] Hu Sheng (胡绳), *Imperialism and Chinese Politics*, translation from Chinese (Beijing: Foreign Languages Press, 1981), *passim*.

Dynasty, extending its allotted span for another half-century.[30]

The treaty-port system was a Western creation. It was based on international law, as this had developed in Western Europe. It entailed the enforcement of treaties, concluded by equal sovereign nations (a Western concept). Its purpose, in the spirit of *The Wealth of Nations*, Adam Smith's seminal work in economics, was to facilitate trade by minimizing regulations. This Western system all but eradicated the traditional way in which China had conducted political and economic relations with the outside.

Traditionally the Qing government had managed these through the tributary system. Those unsinicized peoples (barbarians) who insisted on interacting with the Chinese had to recognize Chinese suzerainty by making periodic tribute missions to Peking along accepted routes and under a Chinese escort. Either they followed Chinese norms for behavior or they could expect to be annihilated. In China, annihilation was the standard remedy for rebels of all kinds and helps to explain the enormity of the casualties suffered during the periods of unrest.

The Confucian framework, with the emperor as harmonizer of the cosmos through the proper performance of ritual, had no place for sovereign nation-states interacting on the basis of equality as demanded by European international law. China occupied the pinnacle of a pyramid of relations; others interacted with China from a mutually accepted position of inferiority. This was symbolized by the tribute ritual and its most graphic part, the mandatory performance of the kowtow to the Chinese emperor by the envoys of his tributary peoples. The kowtow required three obeisances, each entailing three total prostrations with foreheads touching the ground. The rituals of the tribute system served to insulate the Chinese from foreign influence and to provide the imagery of utter superiority to legitimize the dynasty.[31] Westerners considered the kowtow demeaning and would rarely do it. This want of decorum inflamed Chinese sensibilities.

The treaty-port system was no mere infraction of these rules. It rewrote them. The Court of Colonial Affairs (理藩院) and the Bureau of Receptions of the Ministry of Rites (禮部主客司), which had traditionally handled barbarian affairs, were excluded from matters concerning the Europeans and the Americans, who would become the responsibility of a new, westernized institution, the Central Administrative Office for Foreign Affairs, often known as the Zongli Yamen (總理

---

[30] Mary Clabaugh Wright, *The Last Stand of Chinese Conservatism: The T'ung-Chih Restoration, 1862–1874* (1957; reprint, Stanford: Stanford University Press, 1962), 7–8, 193–6; Hsü, *Rise of Modern China*, 261–91; Spence, *Search for Modern China*, 194–221; Chu, "China's Attitudes," 82.

[31] Paine, 50–1.

各國事務衙門).[32] This was the first major institutional innovation in the central government since the creation in 1729 of the Grand Council, the supreme advisory body to the emperor.[33]

Previously, with the exception of certain clerics, no westerners, and especially no diplomatic representatives, had been permitted to reside permanently in Peking. Rather, they could come to Peking only on prearranged tribute missions. Those who did so came, dropped off their tribute, kowtowed to the emperor, picked up their presents, and left. If they were lucky, they got some courtesy days to conduct a little commerce before departing. They certainly did not come to make suggestions, much less demands about altering the system.[34] Enter Great Britain et al.

It is hard to tally the "loss of face" incurred by the Manchus, who, as the ruling dynasty, reaped the blame for abandoning a system whose rules it was their filial duty to enforce. Failure to perform rituals correctly was the mortal sin of the Confucian order. Confucius had exhorted rulers to lead their subjects "by means of virtue and keep order among them by means of ritual."[35] Failure to perform these rituals correctly led to calamity. Many Chinese interpreted the gathering unrest as a sign of heaven's retribution. Just before the Anglo-French occupation of Peking in 1860, the Xianfeng Emperor (咸豐皇帝) fled the city, never to return. He kept putting it off, and, within the year, he was dead anyway. He was only thirty. Had he lived, the new rules of diplomacy would have required him to receive the despised foreign envoys whose continued presence polluted his capital city. Worse yet, these brash barbarians would no longer perform the kowtow.[36] How could he fulfill his imperial obligations to his ancestors to insure the correct performance of rituals? What disasters would follow such breaches? How could the foreigners demand that he "lose face" in a way so total as to threaten his throne? Had he not always treated them in a manner befitting their station? What perversion of propriety was this?

This blatant breach with tradition put a permanent wedge between the Manchus and the many Han Chinese manning all levels of the bureaucracy – the lettered

[32] Paine, 51, 93.

[33] Spence, *Search for Modern China*, 199.

[34] Masataka Banno, *China and the West, 1858–1861: The Origins of the Tsungli Yamen* (Cambridge: Harvard University Press, 1964), 3–4; Mark Mancall, *China at the Center: 300 Years of Foreign Policy* (New York: Free Press, 1984), 22–39.

[35] Confucius, *The Analects*, book 2.3, Raymond Dawson, trans. (Oxford: Oxford University Press, 1993), 6.

[36] Paine, 90.

elite or literati.[37] What better excuse to blame the alien Manchus for all the turmoil besetting China? Politics had been becoming increasingly factionalized since the reign of the Qianlong Emperor, but with the era of unprecedented internal rebellions and foreign challenges these factions grew until they paralyzed the dynasty's ability to respond creatively to the enormous challenges before it. Moreover, they added to the Manchu's problem of insuring the loyalty of the Han officials whose cooperation they required. Questions of loyalty made the Manchus reluctant to grant these Han officials undue military might. The regional armies created to suppress the rebellions were more effective than the traditional Manchu banner forces. To prevent this gap from widening, the Manchu military elite tried to limit the rearmament of the provincial forces.[38] In addition, they resisted centralizing their land or naval forces. The Manchus dared not create an effective centralized military for fear that they would become its first victim. All of this would have devastating consequences during the war with Japan.

China's humiliations were not confined to internal unrest and Opium Wars. Russian officials took advantage of all the turmoil to play a deft game of diplomacy. They manipulated the Manchus into ceding to their country vast territories on the previously undelineated Russo-Chinese frontier. The land acquired by Russia from 1858 to 1864 was not some small piece of tundra real estate but exceeded the size of Japan and included the only arable land in the Russian Far East.[39]

Westerners tend to write about China's foreign relations primarily in terms of China's relations with themselves. The preceding paragraphs are very much in keeping with this tradition. In reality, however, the powers presenting the most direct military threat to China were not Britain, France, or the United States, but Russia and Japan. The Russians and Japanese shared a common interest in territorial expansion that was not a particularly strong motivating force for the Western Europeans, who focused on commerce. The first bone of contention among Russia, Japan, and China would be Korea.

* * *

Just when the Qing Dynasty had largely quelled the unrest within its borders and settled boundary matters with Russia and commercial matters with the West, new problems started brewing in their most important tributary. This was Korea, also known at the time as the "hermit kingdom." Korea had become a tributary of

---

[37] Crossley, 109, 137, 153, 160, 175, 192–4; James M. Polachek, *The Inner Opium War* (Cambridge: Harvard University Press, 1992), 95–9, 234, 274–5.

[38] Polachek, 275.

[39] Paine, 352, 49–97.

China in 1637 and since that time had sent three tribute missions a year to Peking. The Chinese emperor officially conferred authority to each new Korean king while the Chinese government was responsible for Korea's foreign policy and national defense. China did not interfere in Korean domestic affairs. For centuries this relationship had worked to the satisfaction of both parties.[40] The Manchu conquest of China, however, had introduced tensions into the relationship. The instinct of the Korean government was to remain loyal to the defeated Ming Dynasty, but the Manchus invaded in order to make Korea their tributary.[41] The reality of Qing power forced a new accommodation: on the one hand, the policy of *sadae* (事大) or "serving the great," which meant "subordination" to China by assuming the role of a docile tributary, and, on the other hand, the policy of *kyorin* (交鄰) or "befriending the neighboring country," which entailed "appeasing" Japan by permitting limited trade privileges. All other powers had been excluded in its policy of seclusion, a form of extreme isolationism.[42] Accelerating foreign imperialism in the Far East would make this policy untenable.

The Korean Peninsula is one of the most strategic locations in the Far East. It is the meeting place of the three major Far Eastern powers: China, Japan, and Russia, all of which consider Korea vital to their national security. Korea is the promontory that juts out toward Japan. Alternatively, it is the most convenient debarkation point for Japanese troops on the Asian mainland.[43] It is the location of the warm-water ports potentially threatening the Russian Far East, whose harbor at Vladivostok freezes for four months out of the year. It forms the eastern boundary of the Yellow Sea, flanking the maritime approaches to Peking through which passed the large annual rice tribute from southern China and other vital food

[40] James B. Palais, *Politics and Policy in Traditional Korea* (Cambridge: Harvard University Press, 1975), 9; Chu Djang, "Chinese Suzerainty: A Study of Diplomatic Relation between China and Her Vassal States (1870–1895)" (Ph.D. diss., Johns Hopkins University, 1935), 39; Bonnie Bongwan Oh, "The Background of Chinese Policy Formation in the Sino-Japanese War of 1894–1895" (Ph.D. diss., University of Chicago, 1974), 14.

[41] Andrew Changwoo Nahm, "Kim Ok-kyun and the Korean Progressive Movement, 1882–1884," (Ph.D. diss., Stanford University, 1961), 64, 70.

[42] C. I. Eugene Kim and Kan-kyo Kim, *Korea and the Politics of Imperialism 1876–1910* (Berkeley: University of California Press, 1967), 13; Bonnie B. Oh, "Sino-Japanese Rivalry in Korea, 1876–1885," in *The Chinese and the Japanese: Essays in Political and Cultural Interactions*, Akira Iriye, ed. (Princeton: Princeton University Press, 1980), 38; Takemichi Hara, 392, 426–7; In K. Hwang, *The Korean Reform Movement of the 1880s: A Study of Transition in Intra-Asian Relations* (Cambridge, MA: Schenkman Publishing, 1978), 48; Nahm, "Kim Ok-kyun," 153.

[43] Itō Hirobumi explained to the Imperial Diet: "From the close proximity of Korea to our shores, it follows that her tranquility or disorder, her prosperity or decline, have most important bearings upon this country's welfare" ("Imperial Diet," *The Japan Weekly News*, 27 October 1894, p. 484).

supplies.[44] The Korean Peninsula borders on Manchuria, the homeland of the Qing Dynasty and, in later years, the most industrialized part of China. These security concerns were not directed at the Koreans but at the foreign power dominating their country. The Koreans had the terrible misfortune of occupying the lands perennially near the eye of a hurricane created by external forces, whose movements brought it devastation and sorrow.

About the time that the Qing Dynasty had started to decline, so did the Yi (李) or Chosôn (朝鮮) Dynasty (1392–1910) in Korea. (Yi refers to the surname of the imperial family while Chosôn is the historical name for Korea.) In 1800 a ten-year-old boy acceded to the throne under the domination of a strong in-law family. This marked the beginning of what is known in Korean history as "the era of in-law government," which lasted for the next century. All four nineteenth-century kings came to the throne as minors, so that their in-law clans established regencies. This greatly weakened the government. In the absence of legitimate authority, the in-laws struggled to consolidate their power in other ways. Bribe money flowed to secure offices and was obtained by increasing the tax burden on the peasantry.[45] As in China, an increasingly impoverished peasantry would rise up in revolt. In this manner, political instability in the capital fanned out into the countryside. A rebellion broke out in 1862 and continued through 1863.[46]

At that moment, the Yi Dynasty faced a succession crisis. In 1864, King Ch'ôlchong (哲宗) (r. 1849–64) died at age thirty-two without a male heir or designated successor. In such cases, the widow of the deceased king chose the next ruler unless the widow of the previous king was still living. In this case, the senior widow made the choice. At the time, there were three surviving dowagers. The eldest was the widow of King Sunjo (純祖) (r. 1800–34), Queen Dowager Cho, also known as Queen Sinjông (趙大妃, 神貞王后) (1809–1890).

Queen Dowager Cho chose Yi Myông-bok (李命福), the second son of Yi Haûng (李昰應), (1821–98) to reign as King Kojong (高宗) (1852–1919, r. 1863–1907) and elevated his father, Yi Haûng, to the position of Grand Prince Hûngsôn or Hûngsôn Taewôn'gun (興宣大院君). Theirs was the closest house to the main line, but the connection came from adoption, not from blood. Grand Prince Hûngsôn was a fourth son of a direct descendant of a seventeenth-century king. By royal appointment, he had been chosen to represent the long-discontinued

---

[44] Ballard, 125–7.

[45] Carter J. Eckert, et al. *Korea Old and New: A History* (Cambridge, MA: Harvard University Press, 1990), 178–9; Palais, 24–5.

[46] Ching Young Choe, *The Rule of the Taewôn'gun, 1864–1873: Restoration in Yi Korea* (Cambridge: Harvard University Press, 1972), xv.

line of Prince Yi Ûnsin, a half-brother of King Chôngjo (正祖) (r. 1777–1800), the king whose death had started all the dynastic troubles. Grand Prince Hûngsôn's son, Queen Sinjông's choice, was but a boy of eleven and a half. Although she remained regent by right until the boy's majority, from the very beginning she let the Grand Prince rule as de facto regent.[47] The Grand Prince was the fifth generation descended from a prince of the Blood. By court usage in Korea, that was as far removed a kinship as was recognized in the royal house. This meant that, without Queen Sinjông's intercession, the son would not even have been recognized as a prince of the Blood much less as the sovereign.[48]

This very complicated succession meant that the Grand Prince Hûngsôn had a very tenuous claim to power: It was based on the Confucian order's supreme moral principle of filial piety, in this case, the obligation of his son, the king, to honor his opinions.[49] In the absence of legitimate authority, his first order of business was to consolidate his actual power. This included bringing the previous in-law clan under control, which he did through strategic changes in appointments.[50] This was part of a larger campaign to shift the balance of power within the Korean government from the aristocracy to the throne and to transform the government he had inherited – one paralyzed by infighting – into an effective central government. His was an ambitious dynastic restoration program. He almost succeeded.[51]

Government under the Yi Dynasty was extremely centralized but inefficient. The king of Korea was, in principle, an absolute monarch, the owner of the land and the people. He decreed the law but was not subject to it. In reality, the central government had great difficulty in controlling the local administration, while the king had difficulty asserting control over governmental institutions, his wife, or her family. Competing with his power were the great clans making up a small aristocracy or *yangban* (兩班). Originally it had been composed of distant relatives of the royal family, those who had distinguished themselves in government service, scholars of high reputation, and persons honored for their filial piety. From this small minority the government drew its civil and military officials. The

---

[47] Choe, xv, 32; Palais, 1; Young Ick Lew (Yu Yông'ik), "The Kabo Reform Movement: Korean and Japanese Reform Efforts in Korea, 1894" (Ph.D. diss., Harvard University, 1972), 4; Bruce Cumings, *Korea's Place in the Sun: A Modern History* (New York: W. W. Norton, 1997), 92–3; "His Majesty, the King of Korea," *Korean Repository* 3 (Nov. 1896): 424–6.

[48] For information concerning the Korean rules determining princes of the Blood, see "Korean News," *The Japan Weekly Mail* (Yokohama), 11 May 1895, p. 528.

[49] Palais, 29.

[50] Kim and Kim, 14; Choe, 52.

[51] Palais, 5; Oh, "Background," 20–36.

status was hereditary, and by the nineteenth century had become a deeply entrenched interest group opposed to any reforms that threatened its privileged position. The main issue dividing the competing factions within the aristocracy was political power and the wealth that this provided. The arrival of foreigners greatly complicated the power struggle, since any adaptation of domestic institutions to meet the Western challenge affected the precarious balance of factions within Korea. On the eve of the Sino-Japanese War Korean factions included: conservatives, progressives, and independents as well as pro-Japanese, pro-Chinese, pro-Russian, and pro-American groups, and a constant movement among them.[52]

Factional strife and nepotism undermined governmental efficiency while a lack of development in agriculture, industry, and commerce meant a weak economy and a vulnerable peasantry.[53] It was a subsistence economy, in part, because any visible wealth outside the aristocracy was instantly taxed. Only the aristocracy could purchase government offices, so other classes had no hope of influencing government policies.[54] According to Walter Caine Hillier, the British consul-general in Seoul, "Commerce is strangled in Corea by the unscrupulous oligarchy under whose oppressions the patient people groan."[55] The vast majority of Koreans were commoners responsible for paying all the taxes but entitled to no compensatory privileges. The monopolizers of privilege, the aristocracy, financed themselves by skimming its take from this hard-earned tax revenue. Such endemic corruption ultimately had a corrosive effect on the popular acquiescence necessary to maintain the status quo. Most commoners were peasants, although some were engaged in artisanry and commerce. At the bottom of the social pyramid were the lowborn, who were mainly slaves.[56]

Upon assuming the regency, Grand Prince Hûngsôn immediately faced the same three problems confounding the Chinese government: internal rebellion, governmental corruption, and foreign confrontation. In 1862, during the penultimate year of the reign of King Ch'ôlchong, serious uprisings occurred in five of Korea's eight provinces. Peasants as well as members of other social groups rose up in protest against local governmental corruption in the collection of grain taxes.[57]

---

[52] Marius B. Jansen, Samuel C. Chu, Shumpei Okamoto, and Bonnie B. Oh, "The Historiography of the Sino-Japanese War," *International History Review* 1, no. 2 (April 1979): 227.

[53] Kim and Kim, 3–5; Choe, xvi–xvii, 42.

[54] "Mr. Hillier on Corea," *The North-China Herald* (Shanghai), 30 March 1894, p. 468.

[55] "Mr. Hillier on Corea," *The North-China Herald* (Shanghai), 30 March 1894, p. 468; Lensen, *Balance of Intrigue,* vol. 2, 990.

[56] Palais, 6.

[57] Choe, 24

Although the rebellion had been quelled in 1863, the year before Grand Prince Hûngsôn assumed power, the underlying causes – endemic poverty, rapacious local officials, and inequitable taxation – remained. Grand Prince Hûngsôn focused on reducing corruption and on governmental reform.[58]

Unlike the Chinese government, Grand Prince Hûngsôn initially was quite successful at reducing corruption, strengthening the authority of the throne, and restoring governmental finance without resorting to tariffs, but he did so at the cost of rising opposition from the aristocracy. His dynastic restoration program was ambitious. He instituted an anti-corruption campaign and prosecuted offenders; he tried to make the tax system more equitable; he reorganized the government by restoring the Council of State at the expense of the Board of Military Defense; he tried to make governmental appointments open to qualified candidates from all social backgrounds; he curtailed the privileges accorded to the aristocratic educational institutions or *sôwôn* (書院) as a way to rein in the power of the literati in the provinces; he revitalized Confucian education in Seoul; he undertook a massive recompilation of legal and cultural works, which had not been done for centuries; and he also introduced new taxes to fund his defense and public works programs. In short, he shook up the government from top to bottom, unsettling numerous entrenched interest groups in the process.[59]

Yet he did this within a traditional Confucian framework. He did not desire to wipe the aristocracy off the political map or seek a social revolution. Rather, he intended to restore the Yi Dynasty and its governmental institutions to their height and leave the country with a strong monarchy and strong central government. This goal reflected his own educational background. He had received an excellent classical education – stressing Confucianism, the Chinese classics, calligraphy, and painting. Moreover, he was quite accomplished in the latter two subjects.[60] He never had the opportunity, much less the desire, to travel to Europe. From his insulated vantage point, he had no conception of the new world born from the Industrial Revolution. Like his contemporaries in China, the self-strengtheners, he saw his role in terms of perfecting the Confucian order, not in overturning it. The key difference between the two reform movements was that reform in China originated from the literati and military leaders in the provinces, whereas in Korea it came from the one at the top. In neither case was restoration the answer.

Over the years Grand Prince Hûngsôn has received very poor press. Lord

---

[58] Palais, 3; Oh, "Background," 44.

[59] Eckert et al., 192–8; Choe, 32–81; Palais, 275.

[60] Choe, xvi, 178; Palais, 273.

Curzon, a man never in want of a pithy phrase, noted "the corrupt though picturesque imbecility of Korea"[61] in the preface to the revised edition of his book, *Problems of the Far East*, updated in 1896 to reflect the post-war situation. The prevailing orthodoxy was and remains that Grand Prince Hûngsôn was an unscrupulous conservative intriguer who helped bring Korea to its knees.[62] This view does not jibe with the facts of his extensive reforms but with the sad future in store for the Korean Peninsula.

Much of the negative view of Grand Prince Hûngsôn emanates from his foreign policy of seclusion. The Grand Prince adhered to the traditional policy employed by both China and Japan of minimizing contacts with the West. The Opium Wars forced China to change. The Japanese government drew its conclusions from China's fate and peacefully opened to the West in 1854, when the arrival of Commodore Matthew Calbraith Perry of the U.S. Navy and his famous black ships brought matters to a head.[63] Today with the advantage of twenty-twenty hindsight, it is obvious that the Grand Prince's inflexible isolationism went against the march of time and therefore was destined to fail. In mid-nineteenth century Seoul, the future was far less clear.

Unlike in China, Grand Prince Hûngsôn was initially successful in maintaining Korea's traditional policy of seclusion. In 1866, to drive out foreign influences, he authorized the massacre of Korean and French Catholics, leading to thousands of deaths (mainly Koreans). He got away with it. By the end of the year there were no foreigners left in Korea and the French were unsuccessful in their attempted reprisal. No foreign war, no indemnity, no treaty ports. Similarly, in 1871 the Americans were unable to force Korea to open up to foreign trade. These successes seemed to vindicate Grand Prince Hûngsôn's foreign policy.[64] He had commemorative monuments erected throughout the country bearing the inscription: "Not to fight back when invaded by the Western barbarians is to invite further attacks, and selling out the country in peace negotiations [is] the greatest danger to be guarded against."[65] In recognition of the growing foreign threat, between 1866 and 1873, he went on a military spending spree involving the construction and arming of new

---

[61] Curzon, 4th ed., viii.

[62] Kim and Kim, 14; Yur-bok Lee, *West Goes East: Paul George von Möllendorff and Great Power Imperialism in Late Yi Korea* (Honolulu: University of Hawaii Press, 1988), 38. In contrast, Ching Young Choe documents the extensive reform program of Grand Prince Hûngsôn in his book, *The Rule of the Taewôn'gun, 1864–1873*.

[63] W. G. Beasley, *The Modern History of Japan*, 2nd ed. (New York: Praeger, 1974), 57–61.

[64] Choe 48–9, 95, 108; Wright, "Adaptability of Ch'ing Diplomacy": 368–77.

[65] Oh, "Background," 36.

fortresses and garrisons, reorganization of the armed forces, and the manufacture of armaments. He believed that these improvements would be sufficient to keep the West at bay.[66] In fact, Japan, not the West, opened Korea. And when Japan did, Grand Prince Hûngsôn was no longer in power.

In 1873, twenty-one-year-old King Kojong decided formally to take the reins of power. Since the 1860s he had gradually been increasing his involvement in governmental decisions and had actually been ruling since mid-1870. Grand Prince Hûngsôn had no legitimacy as a regent during his son's minority, much less during his son's majority. Once the son had decided to rule, the father had to step down. During Prince Hûngsôn's years as de facto regent, he had failed to train his son in such a way as to insure the continuation of his reform program. Rather, he had delegated the boy's education to tutors who provided twice daily Royal Lectures on Confucian statecraft. After a decade of this, the son possessed a narrow view of limited royal authority, not a broad vision of imperially sponsored reforms. The son concluded that his father had violated Confucian rules against excessive expenditure and excessive taxation of the peasantry. In contrast, King Kojong envisioned himself as a model Confucian monarch. In December 1873, Grand Prince Hûngsôn retired to the countryside.[67]

Upon assuming power, its effective exercise turned out to be more difficult than Prince Kojong had expected. After a brief attempt at tax relief, he gravitated more and more to a policy of inaction.[68] Simultaneously he became increasingly constrained by the growing power struggle between his father and the Min (閔) clan of his wife, Queen Min Myôngsông (閔妃,明成皇后) (1851–1895). In 1866, the year that the regency of Queen Dowager Cho ended, Grand Prince Hûngsôn had chosen as his son's bride his wife's niece. Not only the Grand Prince's own wife but also his mother belonged to the same clan. Up until that point, the Mins had not been particularly powerful and both of the prospective bride's parents were dead, so it seemed unlikely that the Min would threaten the Grand Prince's power. During his years as de facto regent, he took no action to limit their infiltration into the bureaucratic structure. His calculations proved to be incorrect. The Min would be the most power-hungry consort clan in nineteenth-century Korean history.[69]

---

[66] Choe, 48–9, 95, 108; Mary C. Wright, "The Adaptability of Ch'ing Diplomacy: The Case of Korea," *The Journal of Asian Studies* 17, no. 3 (May 1958), 368–77.

[67] Palais, 23–4, 30–1, 33–5, 274, 281–2; "Taewôn'gun," in *Encyclopedia of Asian History*, Ainslie T. Embree, ed., vol. 4 (New York: Charles Scribner's Sons, 1988), 39.

[68] Palais, 284–5.

[69] Roy Hidemachi Akagi (赤木英道), *Japan's Foreign Relations, 1542–1936, A Short History* (Tokyo: Hokuseido Press, 1936), 114; Martina Deuchler, *Confucian Gentlemen and Barbarian Envoys: The*

Grand Prince Hûngsôn was not satisfied to rule until his son, King Kojong, reached adulthood but wanted to remain in power thereafter. There was no rule that set the age of majority and formally terminated the regency. When Queen Dowager Cho chose to abdicate in 1866, Grand Prince Hûngsôn continued with business as usual for seven more years, until 1873.[70] Meanwhile, his niece and daughter-in-law, Queen Min, was equally intent that her husband should rule and that her numerous relatives should hold high offices. When her first child died in 1871, it was alleged that the Grand Prince Hûngsôn had had the infant boy poisoned. He then tried unsuccessfully to have a son of one of the king's concubines made crown prince. This action earned him the eternal enmity of Queen Min.[71] By early 1875, Min relatives and their sympathizers occupied the chief governmental posts and undid most of the Grand Prince's reforms. There was a resurgence of corruption and a rapid deterioration of the economy.[72] In the ensuing power struggle, the Grand Prince murdered the queen's brother, a political rival, with an incendiary package bomb that blew up the brother and burned to death his mother and nephew as well. In 1875, the Grand Prince detonated the queen's bed chamber, reducing the palace to ashes but leaving the queen unscathed.[73] Such family exchanges continued for the next two decades. It would take a specialized monograph to discuss all those who perished in the waves of retaliatory executions that characterized Korean politics in the final years of the Yi Dynasty.

Both Grand Prince Hûngsôn and Queen Min had survived the vicissitudes of their youths by developing strong personalities. In contrast, King Kojong had led a sheltered life from age twelve on. In his youth, Grand Prince Hûngsôn had operated on the periphery of court politics and was at times poor. He often felt slighted by the wealthy in-law rulers controlling the previous king.[74] His regency had given him the very pleasant opportunity to settle some old scores. But once out of power, the tables easily turned. The queen was reputedly very intelligent,

Opening of Korea, 1875–1885 (Seattle: University of Washington Press, 1977), 230; Eckert, et al., 200; Kim and Kim, 14; Palais, 23, 274; Choe, 32, 177, 237; Oh, "Background," 228; Harold F. Cook, *Korea's 1884 Incident: Its Background and Kim Ok-kyun's Elusive Dream*, Royal Asiatic Society, Korea Branch (Seoul: Taewon Publishing, 1972), 16; Nahm, "Kim Ok-kyun ," 21.

[70] Palais, 29.

[71] "Min, Queen," in Embree, vol. 3, 1; "Min, Queen," in *Korea: A Historical and Cultural Dictionary*, Keith Pratt and Richard Rutt, eds. (Surrey: Curzon, 1999), 288–9.

[72] Choe, 175–6; Lew, "Kabo Reform," 4.

[73] Lensen, vol. 1, 18–9; F. A. McKenzie, *The Tragedy of Korea* (1908; reprint, Seoul: Yonsei University Press, 1969), 15; Key-hiuk Kim, *The Last Phase of the East Asian World Order: Korea, Japan, and the Chinese Empire, 1860–1882* (Berkeley: University of California Press, 1980), 249.

[74] Choe, xvi; Palais, 32.

astute at political intrigue, well acquainted with the Chinese classics, and an avid reader of government documents. She also had an eye for fine jewelry, which she imported from China. She and her family became known for their extravagance. Undoubtedly her position as a female orphan in such a patriarchal and clan-oriented society as Korea made her all the more aware of her vulnerability and intent upon cementing her status as queen.[75] There was also a touch of the bizarre in the later part of her reign. Her only surviving son was born with a host of physical ailments, the most notable being mental retardation. In 1894, an American reporter described the prince as "a half-witted, open-mouth youth."[76] Yet Queen Min was determined that one day he would rule. In fact, he did manage to stay on the throne for the three-year interim between his father's forced abdication by Japan and the Japanese annexation of Korea in 1910. Like Tsarina Alexandra Fedorovna, the wife of Nicholas II and also the mother of an invalid heir to a throne, Queen Min found her own version of Rasputin in a variety of sorceresses and Buddhist monks from whom she vainly sought a cure for her incapacitated son.[77] Such sorceresses acted as shamanesses. They were often psychotics and generally from the lowest social class.[78]

The Min clan did not ally itself with the throne but focused instead on its own self-aggrandizement.[79] Therefore, King Kojong found himself alone, caught between his filial duty to honor his father's wishes and the creeping ambitions of his in-law clan. Since he was the font of legitimacy, all ambitions focused on manipulating him. Unlike the father, who had been an active and pragmatic ruler willing to bend particular elements of Confucianism to save the Confucian social order, the son sought no dynastic restoration but rather a preservation of the social and political status quo, which meant, in practice, an oligarchy composed of a dominant but factionalized aristocracy and a weak throne.[80] Effective government meant reining in the aristocracy, but Confucian principles demanded honoring its status. Initially, King Kojong chose to rule according to the tenets of his educators, but his ideas continued to evolve until he developed a great curiosity about the outside world,

---

[75] Choe, 237; Oh, "Background," 230; Seung Kwon Synn, *The Russo-Japanese Rivalry over Korea, 1876–1904* (Seoul: Yuk Phub SA, 1981), 107.

[76] James Creelman, "Corea's King Talks," *The World* (New York), 3 December 1894, p. 2.

[77] Lew, "Kabo Reform," 36; "Kojong, King," in Pratt and Rutt, 227.

[78] "Mudang," in Pratt and Rutt, 295.

[79] Deuchler, 222; Kwang Hai Ro, "Power Politics in Korea and Its Impact on Korean Foreign and Domestic Affairs, 1882–1907" (Ph.D. diss., University of Oklahoma, 1966), 7.

[80] Palais, 285.

which was not shared by his father, Grand Prince Hûngsôn.[81]

Many historians have disparaged King Kojong for being a malleable pawn of his wife and father.[82] Yet to save his wife's life during an 1882 attempted coup, he faced off armed insurgents, and, in 1895, he put himself in full view of and but a sword-point away from Japanese assassins, in the vain hope of gaining enough time to allow his wife to flee.[83] A fairer assessment might be that King Kojong faced terrible dilemmas that few chroniclers of history have ever had to confront in their own lives. A new world had dawned, yet nothing in King Kojong's life had prepared him to understand the nature of the new era. It is easy to forget how dramatically the Industrial Revolution changed the world. In the nineteenth century, the economic, political, and military changes underway in the West truly bewildered those living in pre-industrial societies whose frameworks for understanding the world had no categories suitable for accommodating, let alone understanding, these unprecedented changes.

In 1875, Queen Min made her move to cement her status. The Korean Court formally requested Peking to perform the investiture of her second and only surviving son as heir to the throne. This timing was unusually early, since the child was only a year old and the father was still in his twenties. Moreover, it was already evident that the child was mentally retarded and had other physical problems. For Queen Min, formal investiture would legitimize her status as mother of the heir and eliminate other succession possibilities, such as the illegitimate siblings of her son or aspiring cousins. When the Qing envoys visited Seoul to deliver their emperor's edict granting the investiture, King Kojong took the opportunity to ask for China's advice on a pressing foreign policy matter.[84] It concerned Japan.

For two and a half centuries Korean and Japanese relations had been remarkably stable, regulated by a treaty concluded in 1609. This treaty limited Japanese trade to a location near Pusan and restricted the amount of trade by a quota and passport system.[85] The Japanese government believed that it was time for a change. It was

---

[81] Yur-bok Lee, 38; Deuchler, 221.

[82] McKenzie, 15; Lew, "Kabo Reform," 4. This view is explicit in McKenzie and Lew but only implicit in other works that generally focus on the activities of the Grand Prince and Queen Min.

[83] Lensen, vol. 1, 20; Oh, "Background," 80; Lensen, vol. 2, 538. See also Robert R. Swartout, Jr., *Mandarins, Gunboats, and Power Politics: Owne Nickerson Denny and the International Rivalries in Korea*, Asian Studies at Hawaii, no. 25 (Hawaii: University of Hawaii Press, 1980), 60.

[84] Key-hiuk Kim, 249–52; Eckert et al., 200–1; Lew, "Kabo Reform," 35–6; Nahm, "Kim Ok-kyun," 22.

[85] Palais, 21; Oh, "Background," 48.

intent on opening up the Korean market to Japanese exploitation. Moreover, it looked forward to inaugurating Japan's "civilizing mission" in Korea: The Japanese government planned to do unto Korea what the United States had done unto Japan two decades earlier and recoup some "face" in the process. Japan would open Korea and make a high-profile debut as a modern international power. However, its enormous gain in "face" was being made at Chinese and Korean expense.

The Koreans still deeply resented Japan's invasion, occupation, and desecration of their country from 1592 to 1599 under Toyotomi Hideyoshi (豊臣秀吉). His troops had looted the country, enslaved the people, and desecrated the imperial tombs. Succeeding generations of Koreans kept these memories vivid.[86] The Japanese also unwittingly helped keep the wound open with its Korean ear-tomb in Kyoto, the so-called Monument of Forty Thousand Ears (*Mimi-zuka*, 耳塚), which commemorated the human booty collected during Toyotomi Hideyoshi's invasion.[87] In contrast to the Koreans, the Japanese revered Toyotomi Hideyoshi as the national hero who had quelled their destructive civil wars, making possible the years of stability under the Tokugawa shoguns (1603–1867).[88] On the eve of the war, *The North-China Herald* reported, "The Corean people – the masses – in fact the entire population with the exception of a few officials, hate the Japanese with an undying hatred. The invasion of 1592 is kept fresh by oral tradition in the recollection of all. Relics of it, not flattering to the Japanese, are still sacredly preserved...It is significant that no greater term of contumely is possessed by the Coreans than the name for a Japanese."[89]

In 1875, Japan provoked an incident with Korea. It sent a boat into Korean waters off Kanghwa Island (江華). The island lies opposite the mouth of the Han River, which provides the water route to Seoul. As expected, the Koreans opened fire, whereupon the Japanese expressed great indignation. At the time, King Kojong was as isolationist as his father, but he believed that Korea was militarily

---

[86] J. E. Thomas, *Modern Japan: A Social History since 1868* (London: Longman, 1996), 127–8; Key-hiuk Kim, 176–7; Oh, "Background," 47–8; Iriye, "Japan's Drive to Great Power Status," 746; Akagi, 118.

[87] "The Corean Embroglio," *The North-China Herald* (Shanghai), 20 July 1894, p. 109; "The Hon. J. A. Bingham on the War," *The North-China Herald* (Shanghai), 16 November 1894, p. 804; Scidmore, *Jinrikisha Days*, 234. For a map of Kyoto showing the location of the monument, see Scidmore, 234; T. Philip Terry, *Terry's Japanese Empire Including Korea and Formosa* (Boston: Houghton Mifflin, 1914), 400, 430. For a map showing the location of the *Mimi-zuka* monument in Kyoto, see Terry, 400.

[88] Thomas, 127–8; Key-hiuk Kim, 176–7; Oh, "Background," 47–8; Iriye, "Japan's Drive to Great Power Status," 746; Akagi, 118; Pyle, *Making of Modern Japan*, 11.

[89] "The Corean Embroglio," *The North-China Herald* (Shanghai), 20 July 1894, p. 109.

too weak to fight Japan. He considered it essential to reach some kind of accommodation to prevent the outbreak of war.[90] As a devout Confucian, he sought the advice of his suzerain.

Since 1867, the Chinese had been warning the Koreans of the threat posed by Japan and had been recommending that Korea sign treaties with the Western powers as a counterbalance.[91] This was the standard strategy in Chinese diplomacy of using one barbarian to control another (以夷制夷). King Kojong had resisted doing so because it ran counter to the policy of seclusion favored by himself, his father, and the literati, that is, all the major sources of power in Korea. At the time, there was only a tiny reform constituency supporting relations with the outside world. In 1875, Japan had upped the ante, and this time Korea folded. Two days after seeking the advice of the Qing envoys, the Korean government authorized its negotiators to accept Japanese commercial demands; one week later, on February 22, 1876, Japan and Korea signed the Treaty of Kanghwa; and six months later they concluded a Supplementary Treaty and Trade Regulations.[92]

The main treaty opened three treaty ports to Japan and granted its citizens extraterritoriality and most-favored-nation treatment, but it made no mention of tariffs. The Western "unequal" treaties had set tariffs, which had galled the Japanese and Chinese, but the money had been paid primarily by westerners into Japanese and Chinese governmental coffers. In Japan's first "unequal" treaty with Korea, it did not offer to pay any tariffs at all. Japan, which objected so strongly to its own "unequal" treaties, had no qualms about imposing an even more restrictive regimen on Korea.[93] At the time, British Asian expert extraordinaire Lord Curzon noted that "it is very amusing to contrast the extreme sensitiveness of Japan towards the Treaty Powers in her own territories and her indignant protest against the severity of the Treaties, with the domineering callousness with which she, the first of the Treaty Powers in Korea, treats the latter unfortunate country because of its weakness, and exacts every ounce of flesh permitted by the Treaties between them."[94] Many Japanese goods soon flooded the Korean market, undermining local producers while growing Japanese rice imports from Korea drove up Korean prices and

---

[90] Eckert et al., 200–1; Palais, 284; Key-hiuk Kim, 337.

[91] Wright, 380; Yur-bok Lee, 18.

[92] Key-hiuk Kim, 249–52; Eckert et al., 200–1. For texts of the treaties, see "Treaty of Amity, Friendship, Commerce and Navigation (English), February 26, 1876," in *Korean Treaties*, Henry Chung, ed. (New York: H. S. Nichols, Inc., 1919), 205–8; "Supplementary Treaty relating to Trade Regulations (English)," in Chung, 209–12.

[93] Yur-bok Lee, 20.

[94] Curzon, 3rd ed., 205.

created a food shortage in an already extremely troubled economy.[95]

The most important provision of the new treaty concerned the international status of Korea. It proclaimed Korea to be a sovereign nation. According to the opening line of Article 1: "Chosen [Korea] being an independent state enjoys the same sovereign rights as does Japan."[96] In other words, Korea was no longer a tributary of China. This, in combination with the commercial provisions, was aimed at undermining China's suzerainty over Korea and paving the way for Japanese penetration. Neither the Koreans nor the Chinese chose to recognize the full significance of the treaty but continued tributary relations as usual.[97] To draw attention to the decline in China's fortunes in Korea would have magnified the "loss of face" to the Manchus and confirmed the destruction of the basis for the perpetuation of the status quo in Korea. If Korea were truly independent of China, this could be expected to have a cascade effect throughout the domestic power structure in Korea, opening a free-for-all to oust Chinese supporters in the government. So the Chinese and Koreans tried to ignore the implications of the treaty in the hope that this would eventually make the treaty a dead letter. Success would require Japanese passivity.

The alternative for China was war with Japan.[98] At the time, China was in the midst of quelling the Moslem Rebellion in Xinjiang. This included the further complication of a Russian occupation of strategic parts of the area. Meanwhile, Britain was pressing China with a host of demands, related and unrelated to a pretext: the murder on the Burmese frontier of one Augustus Margary, who went where he was warned not to go.[99] From 1871 to 1881, China remained on the verge of war with Russia over Xinjiang.[100] Then, from 1882 to 1885, China was first covertly and then overtly at war with France over control of China's tributary, Annam (Vietnam).[101] These years would have been extraordinarily bad timing for a war with Japan over Korea. China waited. But the "loss of face" required revenge.

The Chinese government had concluded that, for the time being, it would be wiser to placate than to confront the Japanese. Moreover, concerns over further Russian expansion in the Far East made Japan a potentially useful counterbalance

[95] Oh, "Background," 75, 168–70.

[96] "Treaty of Amity, Friendship, Commerce and Navigation (English), February 26, 1876," in Chung, 205.

[97] Oh, "Background," 54–7.

[98] Wright, 381.

[99] Eckert et al., 200–1; Key-hiuk Kim, 253–4; Hsü, *Rise of Modern China*, 305; Paine, 110–24.

[100] Paine, 110–25.

[101] Hsü, *Rise of Modern China*, 325–30.

against Russia in Korea.[102] The Japanese, however, were unwilling to leave well enough alone. From 1876 to 1881, they negotiated seven additional agreements with Korea, and in 1880 they established the first foreign legation in Seoul.[103] This confirmed Chinese fears that the Japanese government was on the move and undoubtedly had territorial ambitions as well. Another sign of incipient Japanese expansionism was its seizure from China in 1879 of the disputed Ryūkyū Islands (Liuqiu or Liu-ch'iu Islands).[104]

That year, the Qing government authorized the great Chinese statesman, Grand Minister for the Northern Seas, Governor-General of Zhili (Chihli) Province, Commander of the Huai Army, Associate Controller of the Board of the Admiralty, and Grand Secretary Li Hongzhang to handle relations with Korea.[105] This represented a turning point in Sino-Korean relations. Since Li would remain the central figure determining Chinese policies concerning Korea and the Sino-Japanese War, it is worth digressing to describe the man who dominated Chinese foreign policy for a quarter-century.

People who met Viceroy Li generally mentioned his tall stature – he was six feet tall and dwarfed persons such as Count Itō Hirobumi (伊藤博文), his Japanese opposite number, a man known for his unusually short stature. Westerners also usually remarked on Li's fine physique, vigor, piercing eyes, commanding presence, and no-nonsense approach to visitors. He cut quite a figure, dressed in multicolored silk robes and a hat bearing a brilliant diamond and three-eyed peacock feathers.[106] According to Foreign Minister Mutsu Munemitsu (陸奥宗光), "His demeanor brought to mind Tseng Kuo-fan's comment that Li possessed a bearing and manner of speech sufficient to bring men to their knees."[107] Zeng Guofan (Tseng Kuo-fan, 曾國藩) was one of China's greatest statesmen and generals of the

---

[102] Key-hiuk Kim, 254, 294, 297, 300.

[103] M. Frederick Nelson, *Korea and the Old Orders in Eastern Asia* (Baton Rouge: Louisiana State University Press, 1945), 301; Eckert et al., 201.

[104] Key-hiuk Kim, 345.

[105] Key-hiuk Kim, 345; Oh, "Sino-Japanese Rivalry," 45–6; Arthur W. Hummel, *Eminent Chinese of the Ch'ing Period (1644–1912)* (1943; reprint, Taipei: Ch'eng Wen Publishing Co., 1970), 466. An alternate translations of "the Grand Minister for the Northern Seas" include "Imperial Commission for the Northern Ports" and "Superintendent of Northern Trade."

[106] Alicia Bewicke Little, *Li Hung-chang His Life and Times* (London: Cassell, 1903), 1, 196; Norman, 251–2; George F. Seward, "Li Hung-chang," *Chinese Recorder and Missionary Journal* 25, no. 12 (December 1894): 584–5; J. W. Robertson-Scott, *The People of China: Their Country, History, Life, Ideas, and Relations with the Foreigner* (London: Methuen & Co., 1900), 188; Martin, 349; Folsom, 111–2; Foster, *Diplomatic Memoirs*, 125; citing G. N. Curzon, *Problems of the Far East*, 1894, J. A. G. Roberts, *China through Western Eyes: The Nineteenth Century* (Bath: Alan Sutton, 1991), 26.

[107] Mutsu, 167.

nineteenth century, famous for suppressing the Taiping and Nian Rebellions and also as a key proponent of "self-strengthening."[108]

Li was also known for his stinginess, brusqueness, love of reading, courage, shrewdness, personal magnetism, and for the grillings he gave his foreign guests.[109] He was determined to pump them for information but imparted little of his own.[110] As a young man, his Chinese acquaintances noted his arrogance and ambition.[111] His friends emphasized both his warmth and sense of humor as well as his temper and pride.[112] He was loyal to his friends and the throne, regardless of their political fortunes. Indeed, his whole personal power structure was built on the principle of loyalty and a personal connection or *guanxi* (關係) network of stupendous proportions.[113] He was steeped in Confucian traditions.[114] Like his Chinese contemporaries, he had no qualms about the liberal use of capital punishment or torture.[115] Nor, in distinction to his contemporaries, did he shy away from difficult tasks or heavy responsibilities in public affairs. On the contrary, he was known for taking the initiative.[116]

The former minister of the United States to China, George F. Seward, described Li as "a giant among his fellow-Chinese," adding, "the best foreigners who have met him in affairs will not hesitate to accord to him intellectual powers, which would command admiration in any cabinet or council."[117] Count Sergei Iul'evich Witte, Russia's architect for its impressive industrialization program in the last two decades of the nineteenth century, was not a man known to overstate the abilities of others. He described Li as follows: "I have met many notable statesmen in my career and would rate Li Hung-chang high among them. In fact, he was a great statesman; to be sure he was Chinese, without any kind of European education, but a man of sound Chinese education, and what is more, a man with a

---

[108] Hummel, 751–5.

[109] Little, 194, 196; Norman, 253; James Harrison Wilson, *China: Travels and Investigations in the 'Middle Kingdom' – A Study of Its Civilization and Possibilities together with an Account of the Boxer War*, 3rd ed. (New York: D. Appleton and Co., 1901), 103–4; Walton, 43; Martin, 353; John O. P. Bland, *Li Hung-chang* (1917; reprint, Freeport, New York: Books for Libraries Press, 1971), 51, 67; Folsom, 120, 157; Foster, *Diplomatic Memoirs*, 93; Swartout, *Mandarins*, 5; Little, 194.

[110] Douglas, 109.

[111] Folsom, 84.

[112] Folsom, 115–25.

[113] Folsom, 115–25.

[114] Douglas, 114, 250.

[115] Bland, 51; Douglas, 42–3, 126.

[116] Folsom, 111.

[117] Seward, 587.

remarkably sound mind and good common sense."[118] The socialist French newspaper, *Le Siècle,* called him "the yellow Bismarck."[119]

Japanese statesmen were jealous of Li's high reputation in the foreign community. By their own enormous achievements (to be discussed in detail in the next chapter), they must have felt that they deserved the accolades that Li had received throughout much of his career. Foreign Minister Mutsu Munemitsu believed that "Westerners have tended to overestimate him grossly."[120] From this period onward, the Japanese were to feel that China received undeservedly preferential treatment by the West – that the Chinese were permitted to evade the Western rules governing diplomacy and commerce which the Japanese so scrupulously strove to follow.[121]

Li Hongzhang was a Han Chinese, the son of one of his father's inferior wives.[122] He came from a family of moderate wealth but of great academic accomplishments. Six of seven generations had passed the official examinations.[123] At age twenty-four he had passed third-highest out of 4,000 competitors for the highest imperial degree, thereby earning a place in the prestigious Hanlin Academy. His beautiful calligraphy was the object of much admiration.[124] Despite these literary accomplishments, Li rose to power through the military as the protégé of General Zeng Guofan, whom Li had helped to quell the Taiping and Nian Rebellions. By the time they ended, he had built his own army, known as the Huai Army, which rapidly became the strongest and most modern army in China. Li took advantage of the Qing Dynasty's break with precedent in allowing provincial figures to raise and fund their own armies. The self-strengtheners used personal funds to hire corps of employees to do their bidding. This gave them independent power from the court. Li was the most notable of these provincial figures.

Because Li possessed the most powerful army in China, he was appointed the Viceroy of Zhili in 1870. This made him the youngest viceroy at age forty-four. Zhili was the most important province of the empire because within it lay Peking, and with this came the responsibility for defending the capital. That year, he was

---

[118] Sergei Iul'evich Witte, *The Memoirs of Count Witte,* Sidney Harcave, trans. and ed. (Armonk, NY: M. E. Sharpe, 1990), 232.

[119] G. Gareàu, "Chine et Japon" (China and Japan), *Le Siècle* (*The Century*) (Paris), 8 November 1894, p. 1.

[120] Mutsu, 60.

[121] Mutsu, 164. According to Mutsu, "[T]he Western powers had long accepted the fact that China's actions were frequently inconsistent with the rules of international law." (Ibid.)

[122] Martin, 350.

[123] Wilson, 1887 ed., 118.

[124] Bland, 39.

also made the Grand Minister for the Northern Seas. This office oversaw the foreign affairs for North China, again including the capital. There was a corresponding Grand Minister for the Southern Seas based in Canton.[125] This administrative division reflected the underlying north–south division of China that the Manchus had not succeeded in overcoming. Li resided in Tianjin, the port city for the capital. This meant that he met foreigners on their way to and from Peking. In 1873, he was made Grand Secretary. There were only four grand secretaries in the empire: two Han Chinese and two Manchu. He remained at his posts in Zhili for twenty-five years – an exception to Qing rules concerning the rotation of offices – and he dominated Chinese foreign affairs from the 1870s until his death in 1901. Before the war, he established such preeminence in diplomacy that he issued orders directly to China's ministers abroad without going through the Zongli Yamen, the foreign office. Similarly, he received constant reports directly from China's representatives abroad, giving him a monopoly on this information.[126] Many of these diplomats had been his protégés since Viceroy Li had overseen the training of much of China's diplomatic corps. To supplement these sources of information, he had his own sons learn English. His adoptive son, Li Jingfang (李 經方), was sufficiently fluent to conduct the negotiations terminating the Sino-Japanese War in English.[127]

The Empress Dowager Cixi had a special long-standing relationship with Viceroy Li Hongzhang. The latter had become indispensable when his troops had allowed her to install as emperor her nephew, the son of her youngest sister and Prince Chun (醇親王) in 1875. Li Hongzhang had his army suppress the opposition so that the Guangxu Emperor (光緒皇帝) could take the throne.[128] In a great euphemism for all the sordid behind-the-scenes political maneuvering, the reign title translates as "Illustrious Succession."[129] In later years, when the emperor attempted to establish independent rule, Li remained loyal to the Empress Dowager and not to his sovereign.[130]

---

[125] Charles O. Hucker, *A Dictionary of Official Titles in Imperial China*, Taiwan ed. (Taipei: Southern Materials Center, 1988), 342.

[126] Stanley Spector, *Li Hung-chang and the Huai Army: A Study in Nineteenth-Century Chinese Regionalism* (Seattle: University of Washington Press, 1964), xl–xli, 67, 234–5, *passim*; Folsom, 38, 77, 91, 100, 102–3, 161, *passim*; Chow Jen Hwa, *China and Japan: The History of Chinese Diplomatic Missions in Japan 1877–1911* (Singapore: Chopmen Enterprises, 1975), 76–8.

[127] Martin, 353.

[128] "The Birthday of the Empress Dowager," *The North-China Herald* (Shanghai), 9 November 1894, p. 766; Little, 92–3; Bland, 98, 101; Folsom, 168–70.

[129] "Chinese Titles," *The Pall Mall Gazette* (London), 7 August 1894, 4th ed., p. 3.

[130] Demetrius Boulger, *The History of China*, rev. ed., vol. 2 (London: W. Thacker, 1898), 537–8.

Li's preeminence in Chinese foreign affairs was indisputable. He negotiated China's first modern treaty with Japan in 1871; served for many years as China's chief representative in charge of negotiating the fate of the Ryūkyū Kingdom; advised Korea in its negotiations with Japan in 1876 for the Treaty of Kanghwa and in 1882 for the Treaty of Amity and Commerce between the United States and Korea; and concluded the Li-Itō Convention of 1885 regulating Japanese and Chinese activities in Korea.[131] Li also dominated Chinese modernization efforts. He was involved in numerous pioneer undertakings, such as the arsenals at Suzhou, Shanghai, and Nanjing; the China Merchants' Steam Navigation Company; China's first modern mines; the construction of China's first railway and telegraph lines; China's first cotton spinning mill; the Tianjin Military Academy; and the Chinese Educational Mission to send students to the United States.[132]

During these years he was alleged to have become fabulously wealthy but seems to have spent less on personal consumption than on maintaining his political machine.[133] Viceroy Li has been much criticized, however, for the rampant corruption permeating his activities. One of his foreign employees later wrote, "The Viceroy was a diplomat of world-wide fame; but to his countrymen – before the war – he was chiefly reputed as a great military and naval organizer. He was not nor could he be that; for the corruption, peculation and nepotism which infested his organizations had their fountain-head in himself, and to an extent which was exceptional even for a Chinese official. He was himself enmeshed in the national machine of organized inefficiency; to him also it was a normal condition, and any other, had it been indicated, would have been incomprehensible to him."[134]

In China, personal wealth, public funds, and business capital were all drawn from the same well. They were not separate items as in the West. Modern accounting practices were unheard of. Li's commercial and military activities had enormous scope and required commensurate funds. These activities all took place within China's system of *guanxi* networks, which could not function without constant gift-giving. The flow of bribe money was a normal source of political influence. Westerners considered the astute channeling of monetary gifts as bribery, whereas in nineteenth-century China it was just part of politics and *guanxi* as usual. In imperial China where official salaries were insufficient, bribery, kickbacks,

---

[131] Folsom, 101–2; Andrew C. Nahm, *Korea Tradition & Transformation: A History of the Korean People* (Elizabeth, NJ: Holly International, 1988), 154.

[132] Spector, 234–5; Folsom, 77, 102–3.

[133] Folsom, 103–9.

[134] Tyler, 42.

padded accounts, and so on, were the norm.[135] This was how self-strengthening enterprises were funded. Li was a master of this system.

Not only did Li's activities have enormous scope, but they were also very unpopular. In the insular Confucian world of China in the late nineteenth century, the vast majority of the literati vehemently opposed all hints of westernization. The literati were the lettered class who had passed the government examinations enabling them to populate the civil service and govern the country. Given the unpopularity of Li's modernization ideas, his slush fund was essential for his projects and even for his own physical survival.[136] One of the key tactics for political intrigue was accusations made against a rival in a memorial to the court. Even if the charges were subsequently proven to be false, the accused often never recovered from the slander. In such politically hazardous times, money doled out to the appropriate places could silence an accuser or better yet preemptively stifle a would-be accuser.[137] Therefore, money was crucial for political survival.

Viceroy Li did not create this political system. As a Han Chinese with considerable independent power, the Manchus were certainly not about to permit him to reform it. They could not afford to let provincial Han Chinese officials become powerful enough to threaten the dynasty. Rather, Li was a master operator within the political and social system of his day; he surpassed his contemporaries at greasing the wheels of power. Under these circumstances, his only way to help China modernize was to use this system to his advantage.[138] As he wrote, "I can only measure my strength and tread on reality."[139] Unlike others, he had the personal courage to take on the majority view among the literati that China should hermetically seal itself off from Western influence. Unlike the Meiji generation in Japan, which was made up of many daring reformers, Li Hongzhang cut a very lonely figure in China.

It was his personal tragedy to be ahead of his times and yet culturally imprisoned by a political and social framework that impeded his every move. It is to his credit that he was able to initiate so many modernization projects in such an inhospitable environment. Li Hongzhang never traveled to the West until after the war. In the absence of the formative experience of his having seen the West with

---

[135] Chun-ming Chang (張純明), "The Chinese Standards of Good Government: Being a Study of the 'Biographies of Model Officials' in Dynastic Histories," *Nankai Social & Economic Quarterly* 8, no. 2 (July 1935): 226–7.

[136] Bland, 84, 87, 95, 118; Folsom, 108.

[137] Folsom, 27–9.

[138] Folsom, 151–2.

[139] Cited in Folsom, 114.

his own eyes, his ability to understand the world beyond China and to impress its representatives is truly remarkable. Some of his Japanese counterparts possessed a more profound understanding of the outside, but they had spent years abroad. To this day his countrymen have followed the lead of the old Qing literati who savaged him after the war. These Han literati were precisely those who had prevented Li from building a more extensive railway system. The one line he had managed to build was essential for troop deployments during the war. His severest critics were also those who had insisted on waging a war that Li had done his best to avoid. Yet Li reaped the blame for consequences of the ill-conceived policies demanded by his accusers. His own countrymen have blamed him personally for the faults of the country into which he was born and whose faults he, much more than others, strove to overcome.[140] He would die two months to the day after the signing of the 1901 Boxer Protocol. He had been assigned to negotiate this after the court had ignored his warnings to put down the Boxer Uprising before it was too late. His name became associated not with his timely warnings but with the bitter defeat and enormous indemnity incurred from the reckless disregard of his warnings. A century later, he remains despised by many in his native land.[141]

As Grand Minister for the Northern Seas, the unraveling situation in Korea fell under Li Hongzhang's jurisdiction. In 1879 he wrote his Korean counterpart, "There is no human agency capable of putting a stop to the expansionist movement of Japan: has not your Government been compelled to inaugurate a new era by making a Treaty of Commerce with it? As matters stand, therefore, is not our best course to neutralize one poison by another, to set one energy against another? You should seize every opportunity to establish treaty relations with Western nations, which you can use to check Japan."[142] King Kojong eventually took the advice. In 1882, he solicited Viceroy Li to negotiate on his country's behalf a treaty with the United States.[143] This was followed the next year by similar treaties with Great Britain and Germany, and before the end of the decade with Italy, Russia, and France.[144] While the Chinese and Korean intent behind these treaties was to use the West to counterbalance Japan in Korea, the new treaties also worked to

---

[140] For example, see Yuan Tao-feng (袁道豐), "Li Hung-chang and the Sino-Japanese War," *T'ien Hsia Monthly* 3 no. 1: 12.

[141] Thomas J. Christensen, "Posing Problems without Catching up," *International Security* (Spring 2001): 15.

[142] Djang, 149.

[143] Djang, 149. For the treaty text, see "Treaty of Amity and Commerce (English), May 22, 1882" in Chung, 197–204.

[144] Chung, 107–16, 133–42; Eckert, 204; Djang, 160.

undermine Chinese influence in Korea. These treaties collectively shattered Korea's policy of seclusion and constituted a broadside at China's suzerainty over the peninsula. The Korean literati were outraged and regarded Japan's escalating ambitions as proof of the failure of the new policy. Their reaction was very similar to that of the vast majority of the Chinese literati, who were equally intent upon returning to an irretrievable past.

The plans of the outraged Korean literati started to coalesce around the political ambitions of Grand Prince Hûngsôn. In the past, they had considered his domestic reforms to have been unfaithful to Confucianism, but the recent flurry of treaty-making had put his sins into a new perspective. They now more fully appreciated his orthodox foreign policy. In 1881, they tried unsuccessfully to replace King Kojong with the king's elder but illegitimate brother, Yi Chae-sôn (李載先), but the plot was discovered and, with the exception of Grand Prince Hûngsôn, all plotters were executed, including the brother.[145] Family feuding had become fratricidal.

Another opportunity soon presented itself to Grand Prince Hûngsôn. King Kojong and the Min clan had managed to deplete the financial reserves accumulated under the Grand Prince to such an extent that the military payrolls and rations for troops in the capital had not been met for fourteen months. King Kojong had favored new military forces, established the previous year under Japanese tutelage. This preference stirred up xenophobic passions at a time when a severe drought was causing crop failures. The populace blamed the economic turmoil on the opening of the country to foreign trade. Then, when the regular troops finally did receive rations in 1882, the rice was found to be adulterated with chaff. Such tampering with rations was but one example of the many ways in which officials creatively supplemented their incomes. This time it precipitated a rebellion, the Soldiers' Riot of 1882 (*Im'o kunnan,* 壬午軍亂), which Grand Prince Hûngsôn was quick to use.

On July 23, 1882, the rioters went on a rampage, killing all Japanese in their path and unsuccessfully trying to murder their icon for corruption, Queen Min. Although Queen Min escaped piggyback on one of her servants, the rioters did manage to dispatch to the next world the Japanese military adviser to the Korean Army as well as three of his aides. Grand Prince Hûngsôn reportedly exhorted the mob to oust the Min and expel the Japanese. King Kojong saw the writing on the wall, capitulated to their demands, and restored his father to power.[146] The father

---

[145] Eckert et al., 205; Palais, 284; Frederick Foo Chien, *The Opening of Korea: A Study of Chinese Diplomacy, 1876–1885* (Hamden, CT: Shoe String Press, 1967), 96; Lew, "Kabo Reform," 19; Nahm, "Kim Ok-kyun ," 27–8.

[146] Chien, 97–8; Eckert et al., 205–9; Oh, "Sino-Japanese Rivalry," 50; McKenzie, 16–17.

immediately dismissed all senior officials from the Min clan and had his own pro-Min brother, Prime Minister Yi Ch'ae-ûng (李最應), murdered. Queen Min was thought to be dead and Grand Prince Hûngsôn relished the funeral preparations. Imperial family relations had reached a new low.[147]

Among Grand Prince Hûngsôn's first acts of state was a petition to China seeking its sanction for the change in regime. Just before the crisis broke out, Li Hongzhang had left his post on a leave of absence because of the death of his mother. Rules of filial piety demanded that he spend a prescribed period in mourning. This left China's de facto foreign minister out of touch. Japan reacted to the murder of its nationals by dispatching troops to Korea. Li's temporary replacement responded in kind. This was China's first military intervention in Korea since 1636, during the turmoil at the succession between the Ming and Qing Dynasties. It constituted a major departure in China's Korean policy. China had abandoned its distant suzerain–tributary relationship to assume a forward policy in Korea. Li's representative dispatched three warships under General Wu Changqing (吳長慶) and two negotiators – Circuit Intendant Ma Jianzhong (馬建忠), a returned student from France, and Admiral Ding Ruchang (丁汝昌). A decade later, during the ensuing war, Ding would earn the admiration of the world, not for his military prowess but for his suicide upon the destruction of his fleet.

Grand Prince Hûngsôn's *coup d'état* posed three problems for the Chinese government: It had overthrown the pro-Chinese Min clan; it had deposed a lawfully constituted tributary government; and, most important, the attacks on Japanese nationals had precipitated the Japanese military intervention.[148] Once Chinese troops entered Seoul, Wu, Ma, and Ding invited Grand Prince Hûngsôn to call on them. When he did, they read him the riot act. Ma accused him of acting against the Chinese emperor by unseating a duly invested king. "Your sin is unpardonable. Considering the fact that you are the father of the King, we will not press hard on you. Please go to Tientsin [Tianjin] to receive whatever punishment is to be bestowed upon you."[149] This must have been quite a conversation stopper for the Grand Prince. Before he had time to respond, Chinese troops hustled him off into a sedan chair to an awaiting ship bound for Li's stronghold of Baoding (Paoting) outside of Tianjin. There he remained under house arrest until October of 1885.[150]

---

[147] Chien, 98; Kim and Kim, 35.

[148] Chien, 98; Kim and Kim, 35, 37; Djang, 16; Key-hiuk Kim, 349–50.

[149] Djang, 152.

[150] Dong Jae Yim, "The Abduction of the Taewôngun: 1882," *Papers on China* 21 (February 1969): 118–9; Lew, "Kabo Reform," 79–80.

Li Hongzhang was extremely proud of this piece of commando work. He later wrote: "Our country regarded [Korea] as part of the empire and dispatched...troops. We arrested the evil ringleader, the Taewôngun [Grand Prince Hûngsôn], and detained him at Paoting. The [Korean] masses were awed. Now the entire world knows that Korea is our dependency."[151] In addition to power politics, Li was playing an elaborate game of "face" to which westerners were blind, but which the Japanese and Koreans could not possibly miss. Inability to control a tributary constituted a major "loss of face," but hauling off the main instigator of the troubles gave China enormous "face." It gained even by being lenient with him and merely putting him under house arrest in Tianjin. This leniency was in keeping with the Confucian norms for the treatment of seniors, and particularly this one who was father of the king of Korea. The Qing were demonstrating their benevolence, a necessary quality of a legitimate suzerain. More "face" accrued when Chinese troops gallantly escorted Queen Min back to Seoul.[152]

The Qing had gotten so much "face" that they had some to spare for Japan, on whose behalf they intervened to secure Korean cooperation in redressing Japanese grievances. The removal of Grand Prince Hûngsôn led to the appointment of Korean negotiators supporting the opening of the country. Under the resultant Treaty of Chemulp'o (Inch'ôn) of August 30, 1882, Korea agreed to pay Japan an indemnity, to send an envoy to Japan to apologize, and to permit Japanese legation guards in Seoul. Amendments to two prior treaties permitted the Japanese access to the Korean interior and opened an additional treaty port near Seoul.[153] For a brief moment, China recaptured the image of benevolent suzerain and grand puppeteer of barbarian affairs. The Japanese negotiators politely accepted Chinese help but seethed inside. For the Koreans, the kidnapping of their regent was both an insult and a humiliation: China's gains were the result of their loss of "face."[154]

The incarceration of Grand Prince Hûngsôn in China allowed the Min clan to become more firmly entrenched in power than ever.[155] But the riot had been a close call. The Min clan became effusively pro-Chinese. In 1882, Korea signed a commercial treaty granting China exclusive economic privileges that would enable it to dominate Korean trade. Li Hongzhang's policy was to manipulate Korean policies from behind the scenes, so that within a year Korea became a Chinese

---

[151] Yim, 122.

[152] Ro, 10–11.

[153] Palais, 38; Eckert et al., 207.

[154] Nahm, "Kim Ok-kyun ," 78.

[155] Oh, "Sino-Japanese Rivalry," 52.

protectorate in all but name. Integral to this plan was Li's appointment of two governmental advisers – Ma Jianchang (馬建常), the brother of one of the kidnappers of Grand Prince Hûngsôn and former Chinese consul at Kobe, and Paul von Möllendorff, formerly of the German Foreign Office but lately in Li's employ. In addition, Li established a Capital Guard Command under Yuan Shikai (袁世凱), who, after the fall of the Qing Dynasty, would become the first president of China. Ma immediately carried out a governmental reorganization on Chinese lines.[156]

Von Möllendorff was an accomplished linguist, able to read over a dozen languages including Chinese, Manchu, Japanese, and, before long, Korean. He cut quite a striking figure in the round-rimmed glasses and the traditional Korean garb that he chose to wear. The first westerner King Kojong had ever met, he soon earned the king's respect and trust. In 1883, von Möllendorff helped negotiate Korea's treaties with Japan, Britain, Germany, Italy, and Russia. The treaty with Russia granted reciprocal rights for the warships of each to visit any of the ports of the other. Contrary to Li's expectations, von Möllendorff did not promote Chinese interests in Korea, but redirected his loyalties to Korea. In contrast, Yuan soon became known for his arrogance and increasing interference in Korean affairs. On at least one occasion he was alleged to have spat in the face of a high Korean minister.[157] In 1883, Li was so satisfied with his success that he boasted to the American minister in Peking, "I am the king of Corea, whenever I think the interests of China require me to assert the prerogative."[158] Between the kidnapping of Grand Prince Hûngsôn and the prolonged deployment of Chinese troops in Seoul, anti-Chinese sentiments mushroomed in the xenophobic climate of Korea. King Kojong started toying with the idea of seeking an alternate foreign protector to China. Von Möllendorff recommended Russia.[159]

Hemmed in by insatiable in-laws and a Chinese military occupation, King Kojong's options were narrowing by the minute. A small but outspoken group of so-called Progressives developed after the Soldiers' Riot and got the ear of the king, who had suddenly become very receptive to the idea of reform. The Progressives favored a Meiji-style restoration that would have gone beyond Grand Prince

---

[156] Nahm, "Kim Ok-kyun," 187.

[157] Chien, 97–103, 144; Eckert et al., 205–9; Yur-bok Lee, 31–2, 44–8, 55, 62, 64–5; Key-hiuk Kim, 348; Lensen, vol. 1, 74–92; Lew, "Kabo Reform," 38–9; "Korean Affairs," *The Japan Weekly Mail* (Yokohama), 14 July 1894, p. 40; T. F. Tsiang, "Sino-Japanese Diplomatic Relations, 1870–1894," *The Chinese Social and Political Science Review* 17, no. 1 (April 1933): 78; Nahm, "Kim Ok-kyun," 187.

[158] Lensen, vol. 1, 23.

[159] Yur-bok Lee, 31–2, 94–112; Lensen, vol. 1, 32, 52.

Hŭngsŏn's earlier reforms. They planned to revamp the underlying social structure. Needless to say, the aristocracy in general and the Mins in particular did not look favorably upon this. The Min clan made sure to block all appointments of Progressives to important positions. This included their embittered leader, Marquis Kim Ok-kyun (金玉均), whose gruesome death would help precipitate the Sino-Japanese War a decade later. When the Sino-French War broke out in 1884, China withdrew three of its battalions from Seoul. The Progressives thought they could seize this moment to expel the Chinese and their Confucian-bound ideas. The Japanese also saw their opportunity to act. Their minister to Seoul, Takezoe Shin'ichirō (竹添進一郎), started making plans with Kim Ok-kyun.[160]

Kim belonged to the aristocratic Andong Kim clan that had been in power for several decades prior to the rule of King Kojong. The Japanese had taken advantage of its frustrated ambitions to cultivate this clan in opposition to the government.[161] Kim's own family was poor, but adoption at the age of six by a wealthy uncle gave him a classical education, connections in the capital, and rapid advancement up the government career ladder.[162] By 1880, while still in his twenties, Kim had obtained high government office, at one time serving as a councilor in the Foreign Office and becoming acquainted with King Kojong. His clan was extremely powerful, having provided four queens to successive kings since the reign of King Chŏngjo. His family was one of the strong imperial in-law clans that had dominated Korean politics. The negative example of China's inability to fend off the West convinced him that Korea must reform and made him curious about reports of recent Japanese reforms. He visited Japan in December 1881 and was still there during the insurrection in Seoul in 1882. Queen Min was also interested in learning more about Japan. Kim became an official Korean representative sent to Japan in 1882 to apologize for the mayhem during the failed *coup d'état*. He remained in Japan until 1884.[163] While in Japan, he met and was profoundly influenced by Fukuzawa Yukichi (福沢諭吉), the famous writer and promoter of a westernized curriculum and industrial civilization. Kim concluded that Korea must free itself from Chinese domination by overthrowing the Min clan so that it could

---

[160] Chien, 97–103; Eckert et al., 205–9; Yur-bok Lee, 66–7; Djang, 155; Oh, "Sino-Japanese Rivalry," 53.

[161] Synn, 105–6.

[162] Nahm, "Kim Ok-kyun," 82–9.

[163] Kimitada Miwa, "Fukuzawa Yukichi's 'Departure from Asia': A Prelude to the Sino-Japanese War," in *Japan's Modern Century: A Special Issue of "Monumenta Nipponica" Prepared in Celebration of the Centennial of the Meiji Restoration,* Edmund Skrzypczak, ed. (Tokyo: Sophia University, 1968), 8; Oh, "Background," 184; "Kim Ok-kyun," in Embree, vol. 2, 325; Nahm, "Kim Ok-kyun," 93, 105; Hwang, 79–89.

commence a Japanese-style reform program.[164] By this time, Min rule had become notorious. According to one observer, "Korea is a country in which misgovernment and extortion have flourished luxuriantly for centuries, but under the recent MING [Min] administration a serious change for the worse has taken place."[165]

Despite the name "Progressive," the Japanese-inspired reformers fell back on "the old Korean method of political transformation by murder."[166] On December 4, 1884, the Postal Administration hosted an inaugural banquet. The guests included the king, the commanders of the troops garrisoned in Seoul, and senior conservative officials. The plan was simple: Kill the commanders and officials at the banquet and, in the manner of the Meiji reformers, hijack the king to legitimize their reform program. Their program included the repatriation of Grand Prince Hŭngsŏn, the severance of tributary ties with China, the curtailment of aristocratic privileges, and the creation of an efficient modern state. The reality was summary decapitations of six ministers and sundry other murders, the occupation of the royal palace by Japanese troops, and the opening act of a foreign imbroglio.[167] This was the *coup d'état* of 1884 (*Kapsin chŏngbyŏn,* 甲申政變). The father of the murdered postmaster general, who had hosted the unexpected slaughter, was so appalled by the stain on the family honor that he later invited all eighteen of his relatives to dinner and killed them and himself by poisoning.[168]

The result of the attempted coup was not what the planners had envisioned. The Japanese minister, Takezoe, reneged on his promise of continued military aid; Chinese troops in the city outnumbered the Japanese by seven to one; and on December 6, Yuan Shikai retook the palace, routed the Japanese troops, and rescued the king, whom the rebels were trying to take with them. The king immediately telegraphed Li Hongzhang for reinforcements. Yuan had wanted to dethrone the king,[169] whom he considered a "dim-witted monarch,"[170] for complicity in the coup but was overruled by his superiors. Japan compelled Korea to pay it an indemnity for the losses of life and property incurred, make a formal apology,

---

[164] Beasley, *Modern History,* 151–4; Kim and Kim, 42–3; Oh, "Sino-Japanese Rivalry in Korea," 52–3.

[165] "The Cause of the War," *The Japan Weekly Mail* (Yokohama) 4 August, p. 129.

[166] McKenzie, 34.

[167] Eckert et al., 210; Djang, 156; Yur-bok Lee, 67, 73–4; Lensen, vol. 1, 26; Hilary Conroy, *The Japanese Seizure of Korea: 1868–1910: A Study of Realism and Idealism in International Relations* (Philadelphia: University of Pennsylvania Press, 1960), 153–6; Nahm, "Kim Ok-kyun," 272–313.

[168] Lensen, vol. 1, 27.

[169] Eckert et al., 211; Djang, 156; Yur-bok Lee, 74–6; Ro, 16.

[170] Yur-bok Lee, 148.

and promise to punish the guilty. Korea signed the Seoul Protocol of January 9, 1885, in the presence of 600 well-armed Japanese troops and under the threat of war if it did not cooperate.[171] The main negotiations, however, took place without the participation of the allegedly independent Korean government but between representatives of Japan and China. These did not start until the day the Chinese and French agreed to an initial peace protocol settling the Sino-French War.

The Treaty of Tianjin was signed on April 18, 1885, and negotiated by Li Hongzhang and his equally distinguished counterpart, Itō Hirobumi, soon to become Japan's first premier and about whom much more will be said in the next chapter. The convention called for a bilateral troop withdrawal, a proscription against sending military instructors, and prior notification for any future troop deployments to Korea.[172] On the surface, it constituted a diplomatic victory for Japan. China had been unable to have Takezoe punished for his complicity in the attempted subversion of a Chinese dependency. China lost its exclusive claim to armed intervention in Korea since Japan acquired equal rights in this regard. The treaty represented another curtailment of Chinese suzerainty over Korea.[173]

Yet the failure of the coup marked a dramatic decline in Japanese influence over Korea. In contrast to its diplomacy, Japanese political intrigue was a failure.[174] Far from expelling the Chinese, the coup led to a drastic increase of Chinese influence. Because of heavy-handed diplomacy and Minister Takezoe's complicity in the coup, the popularity of Japan plunged to new lows in Korea.[175] Japan got the booby prize: Kim Ok-kyun and his co-conspirators sought and were granted asylum in Japan.[176] Failure transformed Kim from a potential political asset into a political liability, so in 1886 the Japanese government exiled him to various remote locations in Japan.[177] When Kim finally left Japan in 1894, his immediate assassination would cause enormous problems for Japan. Even in death Kim was a political liability. So much for plans of a Meiji-like restoration. In reality, the treaty opened the door to Russia with a provision stipulating that Korea seek military advisers from a third country.[178]

Meanwhile, in June 1885, China signed the final peace protocol with France.

---

[171] Kim and Kim, 38; Djang, 157; Yur-bok Lee, 78; Oh, "Sino-Japanese Rivalry," 54.

[172] Eckert et al., 210–12; Djang, 157–9; Yur-bok Lee, 76, 79, 100–1; Hummel, 246.

[173] Chien, 168; Kim and Kim, 57.

[174] Kim and Kim, 58.

[175] Key-hiuk Kim, 350; Oh, "Sino-Japanese Rivalry," 55; Ro, 13–15.

[176] Eckert et al., 210–11; Djang, 156; Yur-bok Lee, 67, 73–6.

[177] Hwang, 134; Nahm, "Kim Ok-kyun ," 317–19.

[178] Lensen, vol. 1, 30.

For the first time since the Russian invasion of Xinjiang in 1871, China was free from the threat of war from Russia and then France. This gave the Chinese government the opportunity to take a more aggressive stand in Korea. It did so. Upon the advice of Grand Prince Hûngsôn, who was still in Viceroy Li's custody, Li revived the Yuan (Mongol) Dynasty (1279–1368) custom of appointing a supervisor to Korea. Li appointed his protégé, the twenty-six-year-old Yuan Shikai as proconsul with the specific goal of supplanting Japanese influence. Yuan and his troops occupied Seoul, where he operated as if he were above the law. He replaced reform-minded officials with pro-Chinese members of the Min clan. He sought to minimize Korean contacts with the outside by interposing himself as the necessary intermediary. He stopped all attempts at military reform or the development of modern industry. His personal behavior was equally lamentable. He acquired a reputation for kidnapping young Korean women and making them his concubines – nineteenth-century "comfort women." Koreans and foreigners alike loathed him.[179]

From the 1876 Treaty of Kanghwa until war broke out with Japan in 1894, China was remarkably successful at retaining its preeminence in Korea. China and the Min clan had used the two abortive *coups d'état* to wipe out the political opposition. In 1882, they had purged the far-right, represented by Grand Prince Hûngsôn, who desired to return to the pre-treaty status quo. In 1884 they had purged the pro-Japanese radical left represented by Kim Ok-kyun. The coups had been equally important for thoroughly entrenching China's local protégés, the Min clan. By 1890, the Min oligarchy had become known as one of the most corrupt regimes of the Yi Dynasty.[180]

Historians have considered Yuan Shikai's decade-long residency as "a dark age" for Korean development.[181] Yet Li's policy initiatives in Korea seemed thoroughly vindicated. The viceroy stood at the pinnacle of his career. The lesson the Japanese government drew from its debacle in 1884 was not to eschew further entanglements in Korea; on the contrary, next time it would make sure that its troops outnumbered those of the Chinese. King Kojong also drew a lesson. China's new hands-on suzerainty seemed as dangerous as Japan's Western-style imperialism. He still believed that the Yi Dynasty could not survive without a foreign protector, but after the 1884 coup he gravitated toward Russia.[182] It was also a new age of direct foreign interference in Korea's internal affairs. For China

---

[179] Eckert et al., 210–13; Djang, 163; Key-hiuk Kim, 350; Oh, "Sino-Japanese Rivalry," 55; Lew, "Kabo Reform," 42–8, 148; Swartout, *Mandarins,* 87; Hwang, 136.

[180] Palais, 284; Lew, "Kabo Reform," 4–16.

[181] Eckert et al., 213.

[182] Djang, 157–9; Yur-bok Lee, 76, 79, 100–1.

and Japan, this was something new – traditionally they had focused on the foreign rather than the domestic policies of their neighbors. For Russia it was something very old indeed – the manipulation of the domestic politics of weak neighbors was a key instrument of empire.

3

The Rise of a New Order in Russia and Japan

[When Tsesarevich Nicholas] reached his majority...it was decided to send him abroad to round out his political development. At this point Emperor Alexander III had the idea of sending the Tsesarevich to the Far East...In addition to leaving him with a hostile feeling toward the Japanese, the journey produced in him an unreal sense about the East...This journey would put its stamp on Emperor Nicholas II's reign.[1]

Minister of Finance Sergei Iul'evich Witte

The political objective of the Russians has always been focused on taking land that belonged to other people. They would seize an opportunity and employ a stratagem, offer a favor and win over the person who was in power, or use whatever other means necessary to place a piece of land, however small, under their influence. They would then establish permanent control over the land.[2]

Syngman Rhee, future president of South Korea, 1904

The Western challenge proved highly disruptive not only for China and Korea, but also for Russia and Japan. The Industrial Revolution was an epochal change in human history. Prior to it, economies were comparatively static: They did not grow much, if at all. In the first half of the eighteenth century, English industry grew at only 0.7 percent per annum. Per capita standards of living did not change much either. Similarly, technological change was minimal. This meant that people's lives varied little from generation to generation. Once the Industrial

---

[1] Witte, 126–7.

[2] Rhee, 202. Rhee wrote the book while imprisoned in Seoul from 1899 to 1904. It was not published until 1910 (Ibid., xi–xii).

Revolution hit, England started to grow at about 3 percent per year.[3] By late twentieth-century standards, when the most successful developing countries grew at double-digit rates, 3 percent seems to be very modest indeed. Then, it was revolutionary. It meant that a country with a stable population would double its per capita standard of living in one generation.[4] After several generations of compounded growth rates, industrializing countries found that they had left their nonindustrializing counterparts in the dust.

Those in industrializing countries became accustomed to rapid changes in all facets of their lives and tended to forget the mentality of those living in long-static societies. Industrialization also brought a cornucopia of gadgetry ranging from the hardware to exterminate humankind to convenient implements of daily life. This latter category includes such humble items as more effective soap, electricity, cheap cloth, better farm implements, and so on. These collectively created a higher standard of living that most people from most cultures value. The Industrial Revolution did not acquire the label "revolution" by accident, but because it truly was a revolution: a clear divide separating what came before from what came after.

Until the late nineteenth century, all of the countries of Asia were pre-industrial. This meant that contact between them and the industrializing West was inherently destabilizing for them. Whether they liked it or not, their world had changed because of exogenous factors taking place in Europe. The development of steam navigation meant that westerners would arrive in Asia in ever greater numbers; the demand for Asian goods in Europe meant that westerners intended to engage in commerce; the production of more effective weaponry meant that when Asians resisted, westerners had the wherewithal to enforce their will. Given the relatively small numbers of westerners traveling overseas compared to the vast local populations in Asia, it seems surprising that imperialism ever succeeded. American colonists had thrown out the British in the late eighteenth century, when the relative populations of England and America favored England by a margin of three to one. In the mid-nineteenth century, China's population outnumbered England's by a ratio of over forty to one, and still tiny Britain defeated China, a country over four

---

[3] H. N. R. Crafts, *British Economic Growth during the Industrial Revolution* (Oxford: Oxford University Press, 1985), 32, cited in John P. McKay, Bennet D. Hill, and John Buckler, *History of Western Society*, vol. 2 (Boston: Houghton, Mifflin, 1995), 729.

[4] The formula for compounded rates of growth is as follows: $(1.03)^n = 2$. The 1.03 represents a 3 percent growth rate and 2 indicates a doubling, in this case of the economy. The variable n represents the number of years of compounded growth necessary to double the size of the economy. In this case n equals 23.5 years or approximately one generation.

times more distant from its shores than its recalcitrant American colonies.[5]

Before the development of nationalism in Asia and Africa, imperialism was extremely successful. Nationalism is directly related to people's perception of themselves and of their connection to their neighbors. Once Asians saw matters less locally and began to feel common bonds with their countrymen, their world would change because of their changed perceptions of it. Nationalism allowed people to unite in a common cause. Even if they were able only to engage in concerted passive resistance, this eroded the profit margins underlying the imperial enterprise. When local populations united to resist, imperialism became a net money loser for the combined pockets of the public purse and private bank accounts. It is no coincidence that colonial empires crumbled with the upsurge of nationalism after World War II. Imperialism was no longer sustainable and, given the new spirit of resistance, no longer even desirable from the point of view of the perpetrators. When the Western powers realized this, they threw in the towel.

As shown in the previous chapter, China and Korea did not respond to Western military superiority by industrializing themselves. Rather, their approach of self-strengthening was both fragmented in its scope and limited in its application. Here and there it produced a model factory or an arsenal or a shipyard, but not the full complement of infrastructure and related industries necessary for sustained industrialization. More often than not, when the self-strengtheners of China and Korea lost power, their modernization projects disappeared with them. China and Korea were not alone in their troubles. Russia too had extreme difficulty responding to the Industrial Revolution. Because of its military victories over Napoleon in the early nineteenth century and long interaction with Western Europe, Russia is generally pigeonholed along with the Western European powers of the nineteenth century. This is a mistake. Russia differed from them in fundamental ways.

In the late nineteenth century, Russia, China, and Turkey were the last lingering great continental empires. The Russian empire did not belong to the new wave of commercial maritime empires but remained a traditional continental one, whose primary goal was not commercial but territorial aggrandizement. This reflected the traditional way in which Russia continued to deal with its national security concerns. Moreover, the Russian response to the Industrial Revolution differed fundamentally from its Western European counterparts. These differences had enormous consequences.[6]

---

[5] Tindall and Shi, vol. 1, 110; Spence, *Search for Modern China*, 210. The distances refer to the sea routes before the construction of the Suez Canal.

[6] My previous book was devoted to the topic of Russian expansion in the Far East. It has an extensive bibliography of relevant primary and secondary sources. See S. C. M. Paine, *Imperial*

Both Russia and China were greatly impeded in their efforts to modernize by their intoxicating self-images of being a great power, in the case of Russia, and of being a great civilization, in the case of China. In contrast to the false sense of superiority that distorted China's perspective, Russia's great-power syndrome masked a deep and abiding sense of insecurity concerning its place in the international pecking order.[7] Russia faced unique national security problems. Historically, its expansion had been the elusive quest for defensible borders largely absent on the great plains of Russia.[8] But expansion created only very long and remote borders that proved extremely costly to defend. Enormous funds had to be funneled away from the civilian economy in order to defend the empire.[9]

The Industrial Revolution heralded a new age of maritime empires, based on the latest industrial technology: railroads, telegraphs, steamships, repeating rifles, and so on. This new age proved extremely threatening to Russia since it had been a major importer rather than a great center of technological innovation. Before the Industrial Revolution, the gadgetry had been much more limited and therefore not as fundamental to state power; afterward, it became the basis for that power. Worse for Russia, its key rival since the Napoleonic Wars was Britain, the source of the new economic order. Still worse, the British Empire seemed to be swallowing up the globe. As the Industrial Revolution progressed in Britain, the Russians found it ever more difficult to keep up. Despite enormous Russian efforts at

Rivals: China, Russia, and Their Disputed Frontier, 1858–1924.

[7] Dietrich Geyer, *Russian Imperialism: The Interaction of Domestic and Foreign Policy, 1860–1914*, Bruce Little, trans. (New Haven: Yale University Press, 1987), 49, 64, 271–2.

[8] Richard A. Pierce, *Russian Central Asia 1867–1917: A Study in Colonial Rule* (Berkeley: University of California Press, 1960), 17–8; Geyer, 88–98; Morris Rossabi, *China and Inner Asia: From 1360 to the Present* (New York: Praeger Press, 1975), 181; Kenneth Bourne and D. Cameron Watts, eds., *British Documents on Foreign Affairs: Reports and Papers from the Foreign Office Confidential Print, Part I, From the Mid-nineteenth Century to the First World War, Series A: Russia: 1859–1914*, vol. 1 (University Publications of America, 1983), 287–8.

[9] William L. Blackwell, *The Beginnings of Russian Industrialization 1800–1860* (Princeton: Princeton University Press, 1969), 179–82, 409–10; Olga Crisp, *Studies in the Russian Economy before 1914*, School of Slavonic and East European Studies, University of London (London: Macmillan Press, 1967), 7–11, 96–7, 110, 217; Alexander Gerschenkron, *Economic Backwardness in Historical Perspective: A Book of Essays* (Cambridge: Belknap Press, 1962), 17, 131; M. C. Kaser, "Russian Entrepreneurship," in *The Cambridge Economic History of Europe*, Peter Mathias, ed., vol. 7 (Cambridge: Cambridge University Press, 1978), 459; John L. H. Keep, *Soldiers of the Tsar: Army and Society in Russia 1462–1874* (Oxford: Clarendon Press, 1985), 335; William C. Fuller, Jr., *Strategy and Power in Russia 1600–1914* (New York: Free Press, 1992), 175; Paul R. Gregory, *Russian National Income 1885–1913* (Cambridge: Cambridge University Press, 1982), 252; Aleksei Nikolai Kuropatkin, *The Russian Army and the Japanese War*, A. B. Lindsay, trans., W. D. Swinton, ed., vol. 1 (New York: E. P. Dutton, 1909), 3; Geoffrey Parker, *The Geopolitics of Domination* (London: Routledge, 1988), 157, 161.

industrialization, the gap in per capita standard of living kept widening.[10] Moreover, Russia lacked China's convenient backup position: a conviction that its own cultural superiority would some day overcome its embarrassing but temporary technological inferiority. Russian attempts to portray itself as the Third Rome lacked the authenticity of China's claim to cultural dominance in Asia. Russia had never been at the cultural epicenter of Europe as China had been for Asia. Rather, Russia had always been at the cultural periphery of Europe, more often than not, derided for its lack of sophistication.[11] Russian industrialization efforts were sufficiently successful to shift the balance of power in Russia's favor *vis-à-vis* China, which did not engage in large-scale industrialization until after the fall of the Qing Dynasty. This shift was bad news for the Qing Dynasty.

As Britain and the other European powers started checkmating Russia in Eastern Europe and the Middle East, the members of the Russian Foreign Ministry fumed. For centuries Russian elites had considered their country to be a great power. For the Romanov family, the ruling dynasty (1613–1917), the erosion of this status would simultaneously erode its authority to rule because Russian elites and autocrats both considered the preservation of the empire and Russia's international status to be a key responsibility of the dynasty. The Romanov regalia abounded in the symbols of empire: The double-headed eagle clutched the imperial orb in one talon and the scepter of dominion in the other.[12] The orb was a globe surmounted by a Russian Orthodox cross. The Romanovs were the lords of Christendom. After the defeat in the Crimean War (1853–6), Russia remained a great power only in terms of geographic extent and in the size (not effectiveness) of its army, for during that war France and Britain had been able to transport their troops to the Crimea and defeat Russia on its own soil.[13] In the absence of a

---

[10] Crisp, *Studies*, 5, 7, 112; Geyer, 49, 64, 271–2; W. Bruce Lincoln, *The Great Reforms: Autocracy, Bureaucracy, and the Politics of Change in Imperial Russia* (Dekalb: Northern Illinois University Press, 1990), 37–9.

[11] Alfred J. Rieber, "Persistent Factors in Russian Foreign Policy: An Interpretive Essay," in *Imperial Russian Foreign Policy*, Hugh Ragsdale, ed. and trans. (Cambridge: Cambridge University Press, 1993), 322, 344.

[12] "Герб Российской Империи" (Heraldry of the Russian Empire), in *Советская историческая энциклопедия* (*Soviet Historical Encyclopedia*), E. M. Zhukov, ed., vol. 4 (Moscow: Государственное научное издательство «Советская энциклопедия», 1963), 255; Gustave Alef, "The Adoption of the Muscovite Two-Headed Eagle: A Discordant View," *Speculum: A Journal of Mediaeval Studies* 41, no. 1 (Jan. 1966): 1–2.

[13] Milan Hauner, *What Is Asia to Us? Russia's Asian Heartland Yesterday and Today* (Boston: Unwin Hyman, 1990), 69–70; W. Bruce Lincoln, *The Conquest of a Continent: Siberia and the Russians* (New York: Random House, 1994), xix; Henry Kissinger, *Diplomacy* (New York: Simon & Schuster, 1994), 176; Lincoln, *Great Reforms*, 37–9.

world-class standard of living like that of Great Britain or of a preeminent cultural influence like that of China, the maintenance of the empire became the essential legitimizing symbol important for the continuation of autocratic rule.[14]

In the preceding chapters, Russia has been mentioned tangentially with reference to its vast territorial acquisitions in northeastern Asia during the Opium Wars and its invasion of Xinjiang in 1871. But in the late nineteenth century Russia was anything but tangential to the Far East. Although Great Britain has received the limelight in the East and West for its influence and predations in the Far East, in reality Russia constituted the fundamental security threat animating Chinese and Japanese policymakers. Russia, not Britain, took the most territory and eventually acquired by far the largest concessions.[15] In keeping with the axiom of political science that power recognized is power diminished,[16] Russia operated behind the scenes and as often as possible along its border with China. This area was remote from the interests and activities of the other European powers but at the heart of the interests and activities of the other Asian powers. Russia bridged both worlds. From the Chinese point of view, Britain's beloved and all-important Hong Kong was the barren rock that they had ceded in order to keep the British as far away as possible from anything truly important. Manchuria, however, was the birthplace of the dynasty. It and Korea were the focus of Chinese rivalries with Japan.

For over a century prior to the Opium Wars, Russo-Chinese relations had been very stable and relatively harmonious. The 1689 Treaty of Nerchinsk, the 1727 Treaty of Bura, and the 1727 Treaty of Kiakhta had remained in force until the mid-nineteenth century. The Treaty of Kiakhta had established China's first two "treaty ports" with a European power; however, these towns were not ports but trading posts along the long Russo-Chinese frontier.[17] Although Russia did not

---

[14] Geyer, 20–1, 31–9, 49, 64, 86, 95–9, 102, 126, 136, 147; D. C. B. Lieven, *Russia and the Origins of the First World War* (New York: St. Martin's Press, 1983), 153; N. V. Riasanovsky, *A Parting of Ways: Government and the Educated Public in Russia 1801–1855* (Oxford: Clarendon Press, 1976), 255; Robert Wesson, *The Russian Dilemma*, rev. ed. (New York: Praeger Special Studies, 1986), 8–9; Adam B. Ulam, "Nationalism, Panslavism, Communism," in *Russian Foreign Policy: Essays in Historical Perspective*, I. J. Lederer, ed. (New Haven: Yale University Press, 1962), 44; Parker, 88.

[15] R. Quested, *"Matey" Imperialists? The Tsarist Russians in Manchuria 1895–1917* (Hong Kong: University of Hong Kong Press, 1982), 106; C. Hou, *Foreign Investment and Economic Development in China 1840–1937* (Cambridge, MA: Harvard University Press, 1965), 65; Langer, 487–8.

[16] My acquaintance with this axiom came from a freshman course in American government, taught by James Q. Wilson, Samuel Huntington, and H. Douglas Price.

[17] Joseph Fletcher, "Sino-Russian Relations, 1800–62," in *The Cambridge History of China*, John K. Fairbank, ed., vol. 10 (Cambridge: Cambridge University Press, 1978), 318; Mark Mancall, *Russia and China, Their Diplomatic Relations to 1728* (Cambridge, MA: Harvard University Press, 1971), 249–55; 262–5

acquire extraterritoriality, it received the unique privilege of establishing a permanent language school and ecclesiastical mission in Peking. No other foreign country would be permitted to station permanent residents in Peking until 1861, as part of the settlement of the Second Opium War. From the beginning, the mission functioned as the de facto agent of the Russian government. Unlike the other Europeans, whose relations with China were handled by the Bureau of Receptions of the Board of Rites (禮部主客司), Russian relations fell under the jurisdiction of the Court of Colonial Affairs (*Lifan Yuan* or 理藩院). Both the Bureau of Receptions and the Court of Colonial Affairs handled tributary affairs, but originally the former oversaw relations with the sinicized world of Japan, Korea, Annam (Vietnam), the Ryūkyū Kingdom (Liuqiu or Liu-ch'iu), Siam (Thailand), and Burma, while the latter administered relations with China's unsinicized tributaries. These were the Inner Asian lands of Tibet, Mongolia, and Xinjiang. From the beginning China pigeonholed Russia with its unsinicized tributaries, not with the other Europeans. Russia's inclusion under the institution governing Inner Asian relations made geographic sense.[18] This was because contacts with Russia came by land, not by sea, as in the case of the other European powers. Indeed, prior to the Opium Wars, China explicitly excluded Russia from the British treaty-port system and refused to grant Russia the same privileges as the maritime powers.[19]

Like the Japanese government in the Meiji period (1868–1912), the Russian government would not long tolerate being treated by the Chinese as inferior to the Western powers. Inferiority grated. Securing equal treatment became a powerful motivating force for both the Russian and Japanese governments, but for many years their Far Eastern military forces were inferior to those of Britain. Russia, in particular, had no practical way to deploy troops in the Far East prior to the construction of the Trans-Siberian Railway. This was not begun until 1891 and was not completed until 1904, through Chinese territory via Manchuria and, until 1916, through Russian territory along the northern bank of the Amur River.[20]

Until Russia and Japan changed the military balance in the Far East in their favor, diplomacy was the only avenue open to them. Russian diplomacy was masterful. Prior to the Opium Wars, the Chinese did not appreciate the European connection between Russia and the Western powers. Worse still for the Chinese,

---

[18] Eric Widmer, *The Russian Ecclesiastical Mission in Peking during the 18th Century* (Cambridge, MA: Harvard University Press, 1976); John K. Fairbank, "Preliminary Framework," in *The Chinese World Order*, Fairbank, ed., 10; Mark Mancall, "The Ch'ing Tribute System: An Interpretive Essay," in *Chinese World Order*, Fairbank, ed., 72–4.

[19] Paine, 33.

[20] Paine, 185, 274.

they misconstrued the relative balance of power in Europe, believing that Russia had crushed Britain and France in the Crimean War.[21] Nor did the Chinese realize how few and far between Russian forces were scattered in Siberia.[22] This led the Chinese to be less confrontational and more wary of the Russians than of the British. This was a tragic miscalculation for the Chinese. Had they reversed their treatment, they might have kept southern Siberia, whose people were Chinese tributaries, and minimized China's costly indemnities to the West.[23] From the Russian point of view, this was a golden opportunity, which they seized.

Russia took advantage of the Second Opium War fought by Britain and France to walk away with the choicest fruits of victory without ever having participated in or been blamed for the fighting. For several years the governor-general of Eastern Siberia, Nikolai Nikolaevich Murav'ev, later to be named Murav'ev-Amurskii in honor of the Amur River that he secured for Russia, had been pressing the Chinese to enter into boundary negotiations. They finally did. On a cruise down the Amur, he encountered his Chinese opposite number, the cousin of the Xianfeng Emperor (咸豐皇帝) (r. 1851–62) and military governor of Heilongjiang (Amur) Province, Yishan (奕山). After six days of acrimonious negotiations during which the Russians shot off guns and cannons by night and threatened the local Manchu residents with expulsion by day, Yishan capitulated. At the time, the Chinese did not consider treaties to be permanent legal documents. Rather, Yishan considered the Treaty of Aigun he signed on May 28, 1858, to be a temporary expedient to buy a little time from the Russians before dealing with them more firmly. In fact, he had ceded a vast swath of territory.[24]

The Treaty of Aigun set the boundary on the Amur River and opened the entire border to trade, but only between Russia and China.[25] With this treaty 185,000 square miles of territory officially became Russian.[26] This was an area between the size of California and France and comprises the only really livable land in eastern Siberia. Land much north of the Amur was and still largely remains inaccessible,

---

[21] Paine, 52.

[22] Ivan Platonovich Barsukov, *Граф Николай Николаевич Муравьёв-Амурский* (*Count Nikolai Nikolaevich Murav'ev-Amurskii*), vol. 2 (Moscow: Синодальная Типография, 1891), 154–5.

[23] Paine, 57–64.

[24] Paine, 67–70.

[25] For a text of the Treaty of Aigun, see William Frederick Mayers, *Treaties between the Empire of China and Foreign Powers* (1877, reprint, Taipei: Ch'eng-wen Publishing, 1966), 100.

[26] Alan J. Day, ed., *Border and Territorial Disputes* (Detroit: Gale Research, 1982), 259, 261; Alastair Lamb, *Asian Frontiers: Studies in a Continuing Problem* (New York: Frederick A. Praeger, 1968), 193, 207.

unarable, and unpleasant year round. For several years, the Chinese refused to ratify the treaty, but Russia had de facto control of the disputed territory. China was still in the throes of suppressing internal rebellions and also trying to fight off the British and French. By this time, there were no troops to spare for the far north.[27] China's window of opportunity to deter the Russians had closed.

Two weeks later, on June 13, 1858, Russia concluded the Treaty of Tianjin. China concluded three other treaties of Tianjin with the British, French, and the Americans, respectively. This was the initial fruit of the Second Opium War. For the first time, Russia was included in the treaty-port system. The Xianfeng Emperor was no more interested in ratifying this set of treaties than he had been the Treaty of Aigun. Therefore, the British and French pursued the war.[28]

In the midst of the hostilities, St. Petersburg dispatched a new diplomatic agent to Peking, the twenty-six-year-old Nikolai Pavlovich Ignat'ev. He was essentially a one-man operation since St. Petersburg declined to send him forces or funds. What he lacked in materiel he more than compensated with determination and pugnaciousness. For months despite his unrelenting and very creative efforts, his Chinese counterparts refused to budge, leading to angry outbursts on his part and stony faces on theirs. According to Confucius, "The gentleman is calm and peaceful; the small man is always emotional."[29] Those who lost their tempers lost "face." His conduct was absolutely unacceptable under Confucian norms for propriety. Gradually, Ignat'ev became wiser. Since his harangues led nowhere, he took a new tack; he would interpose himself as intermediary between China and the West by convincing the Qing that he was indispensable for the dynasty's survival.

Events worked in Ignat'ev's favor. The Second Opium War and the Taiping Rebellion reached critical stages in March 1860. Anglo-French forces had blockaded the sea routes to Peking and were preventing rice shipments from reaching the capital while a huge force of Taipings was rumored to be headed toward the capital. By September, Anglo-French forces were on the march toward Peking, reaching it on October 13. Like King Kojong (高宗) in Korea at a later date, the options open to the Chinese government were narrowing by the minute. The British and French gave the Chinese a two-day ultimatum. Ignat'ev's offer to mediate suddenly became very attractive. In return he required that they accede to all of Russia's territorial, commercial, and other demands. They did. It was all a bluff, since Ignat'ev's intercession brought the Chinese no additional benefits.

---

[27] Paine, 70, 79–80, 83.

[28] Paine, 65–6, 89.

[29] Confucius, *The Analects*, book 7.37, 27; Rosemary K. I. Quested, *The Expansion of Russia in Asia, 1857–1860* (Kuala Lumpur: University of Malaya Press, 1968), 46, 48, 51–2, 70, 221.

Contrary to Manchu fears, the British and French had never intended to topple the dynasty. It was commerce, not conquest, that motivated them. Russia was the one interested in territory and ultimately in the dynasty's Manchurian homelands.[30]

The British and the French soon concluded their own treaties of Peking, which included recognition of the treaties of Tianjin, permanent diplomatic representation in Peking, and some finishing touches on the new treaty-port system. On November 14, 1860, Russia and China signed their Treaty of Peking. In addition to granting Russia the commercial and diplomatic privileges accorded to the others, this treaty contained boundary provisions. It set the easternmost section of the boundary on the Ussuri River and mandated surveys for the Xinjiang frontier. These were formalized in the Treaty of Tarbagatai (Chuguchak) signed on October 7, 1864.[31] Russia acquired 130,000 square miles of territory under the Treaty of Peking and about 350,000 square miles of territory under the Treaty of Tarbagatai.[32] These territorial changes approximate the sizes of one Italy and three Italies, respectively. It took the Chinese a number of years to figure out what had happened, and, when they did, they were extremely angry. To this day this loss of territory is considered a national humiliation,[33] in contrast to which Hong Kong was small pickings. China finally regained Hong Kong in 1997, but the lands north of Xinjiang and the Amur and east of the Ussuri constitute a permanent and bitter loss.

The Russian government made these enormous territorial gains in the shortest possible time and with the most minimal effort. It succeeded through bluff, bravado, and brilliant diplomacy. Its attention, however, was soon diverted to internal matters. Since the Crimean War, the institution of serfdom had been becoming an increasingly divisive national issue. It was cited as a primary reason for the endemic economic and military problems that had led to Russia's humiliating defeat. Others cited the gross injustice of the enslavement of the many for the benefit of the few. Yet serfdom was the foundation for the way of life of the

---

[30] Paine, 84–97.

[31] Paine, 89–91.

[32] Day, 259, 261; Lamb, 193, 207.

[33] John W. Garver, *Sino-Soviet Relations 1937–1945: The Diplomacy of Chinese Nationalism* (New York: Oxford University Press, 1988), 4–8; William L. Tung, *China and the Foreign Powers: The Impact of and Reaction to Unequal Treaties* (Dobbs Ferry, NY: Oceana Publications, 1970), vii; Luke S. K. Kwong, *A Mosaic of the Hundred Days: Personalities, Politics, and Ideas of 1898* (Cambridge: Harvard University Press, 1984), 17; Ting Tsz Kao, *The Chinese Frontiers* (Aurora, IL: Chinese Scholarly Publishing, 1980), 124; Byron N. Tzou, *China and International Law: The Boundary Disputes* (New York: Praeger, 1990), 13; C. Kwei, *Plain Speaking on Japan: A Collection of Articles on the Sino-Japanese Conflict, Originally Published in the Shanghai Evening Post and Mercury under the Column, "As a Chinese Sees It."* (Shanghai: China Institute of International Relations, 1932), 196–8.

Russian elite. To tamper with it threatened the power base of the Russian autocracy. As in China and Korea, reform in Russia was extremely difficult, and the following century proved to be equally tragic.

In 1861, Tsar Alexander II (r. 1855–81) emancipated the serfs. The reality proved to be more quasi- than actual liberation, for there were all sorts of strings attached to the emancipation. Nevertheless, the change was fundamental. A country of free men required a full complement of related reforms concerning local government, the judiciary, educational institutions, and the military. The 1860s became known in Russian history as the era of "the Great Reforms." Tsar Alexander had tampered with the social hierarchy precisely as the ruling dynasties in China and Korea had eschewed the problem. They had no taste for the consequences facing Russia in the form of escalating reforms. Russia became engulfed in a national debate and political struggle to control the development of a post-emancipation social hierarchy. The struggle would cost Alexander his life in 1881, when he fell to an assassin's bomb thrown by one who considered the reforms insufficient.[34]

In response to the assassination, his son, Alexander III (r. 1881–96), stopped further political reforms and strove to limit those already in place in what became known in Russian history as the period of "counterreforms." Great progress, however, was made in the economic sphere under the vigorous leadership of the Ministry of Finance. The Russian government funded a massive industrialization program. It focused on the creation of a national railway and telegraph system and on the development of heavy industry.[35] The need for this industrialization program was not seen in the civilian terms of raising the general standard of living, but in the traditional military terms of creating a modern military to maintain the empire. Unlike industrialization in the West, which was spontaneous, primarily a response to consumer demand and only secondarily a consequence of government policy, Russian industrialization was state directed and state controlled – the antithesis of the free-market system developing in the West. Russian business activities were highly regulated and frequently possible only through government-chartered monopolies.[36]

---

[34] Nicholas V. Riasanovsky, *A History of Russia,* 5th ed. (New York: Oxford University Press, 1993), 368–90.

[35] Riasanovsky, *History,* 391–6.

[36] Gerschenkron, 60, 62, 186; Olga Crisp, "Labour and Industrialisation in Russia," in *The Cambridge Economic History of Europe,* Peter Mathias, ed., vol. 7, part 2 (Cambridge: Cambridge University Press, 1978), 385; Tibor Szamuely, *The Russian Tradition* (New York: McGraw-Hill, 1974), 409; Peter Gatrell, *Government, Industry and Rearmament in Russia, 1900–1914: The Last Argument of Tsarism* (Cambridge: Cambridge University Press, 1994), 326; Thomas C. Owen, *The Corporation under Russian Law, 1800–1917: A Study in Tsarist Economic Policy* (Cambridge: Cambridge University

Nevertheless, an autonomous Russian merchant class developed, as did a heterogeneous educated group of persons outside of the high aristocracy, but autocracy barred their way to political influence proportionate to their economic standing. From the defeat in the Crimean War onward, a widening chasm developed between the autocracy and the educated public, the very people on whose support autocratic rule depended.[37]

Meanwhile, Russians from a variety of backgrounds, like so many of their European contemporaries, felt the growing call of nationalism. Some Russians recognized that Russia lacked the industrial base to undertake an aggressive foreign policy. They were the intellectual descendants of the Westernizers who favored Russian development along Western lines. In the reigns of Alexander III and Nicholas II (r. 1896–1917), they favored avoiding foreign adventures to focus on domestic reforms. Others ignored or did not perceive Russia's economic inferiority but proclaimed its spiritual superiority. They were the intellectual descendents of the Slavophiles. While the Slavophile–Westernizer debate was primarily a phenomenon of pre-emancipation nineteenth-century Russia, these two divergent responses to the West endured.[38] As Russian nationalism developed and as educated Russians became more politically outspoken, Slavophile beliefs in Russia's civilizing mission abroad combined with the long-standing great-power mentality embraced by many Russians. These expressed themselves in public demands for an active and highly visible foreign policy. This put pressure on the Russian government to intervene in the Balkans to protect co-religionists and fellow Slavs. Successful intervention proved ever more difficult because of the competing interests of the other powers and because of the rising national sentiments fragmenting the Balkans. Instead, Russia turned eastward in search of a proxy proving ground for its imperial prowess. The Far East and Persia were the only remaining large areas where Russia could play the role of a great power.[39]

While Alexander II had dared tamper with the lower end of the social order, he dared not interfere with the upper end. His successors dared not even to do that much. The result, in Russia as in China and Korea, was a fragmenting social

---

Press, 1991), 1–36, 53–6, 79–80, 115, 121, 156, 195–203, 210, 214, 216.

[37] Dominic C. B. Lieven, *Russia's Rulers under the Old Regime* (New Haven: Yale University Press, 1989), 153–4, 296; Dominic C. B. Lieven, *Nicholas II: Emperor of All the Russias* (London: John Murray, 1993), 20, 54; W. E. Mosse, *Alexander II and the Modernization of Russia* (London: I. B. Tauris, 1992), 78–9; Riasanovsky, *Parting of the Ways, passim.*

[38] Riasanovsky, *History of Russia,* 362–4.

[39] Russian activities in Persia paralleled those in China. Firuz Kazemzadeh, *Russia and Britain in Persia 1864–1914: A Study in Imperialism* (New Haven: Yale University Press, 1968), *passim.*

order that inevitably had dire political consequences for the reigning dynasty. Like their Chinese and Korean contemporaries, the Russians zeroed in on the gadgetry of Western Europe and the United States and shunned the underlying cultural bedrock. Russia, China, and Korea all wanted the fruits of modernization: the power that industrial technology provided, but not the garden in which it grew. The issue was and remains a conundrum in the field of economics. Is it possible to have the one without a good deal of the other? Over a century later, many people living in the developing world still believe just as fervently as the late Qing literati that it is possible to have the fruits without the garden. History has yet to bear them out. Yet the deep-seated hostility to Western ideas endures.

The Great Reforms preoccupied Russia during the 1860s. Its attention did not turn eastward again until events in China started spilling over to its side of the border. The fighting during the great Moslem rebellions (1862–78) in Xinjiang and the three western provinces bordering Mongolia was brutal on all sides. Qing provincial officials requested military aid from their Russian counterparts while Moslem refugees fled from the fighting into Russian territory. The rebellion began to spread to coreligionists under Russian jurisdiction, disrupted the main Russian communication route to Peking, and threatened to coalesce into a khanate straddling the border along the Ili Valley. This was important because the Ili Valley is the most strategic part of Xinjiang. The valley provides access to the key passes through the Tianshan Mountains, which divide Xinjiang into its northern and southern halves. In Chinese history, the Ili Valley has been a key barbarian invasion route and its occupation has determined control over the region. The Ili River provides access to the Ili Valley not only in the east but also in the west, in the direction of Russia, and flows into Lake Balkhash, located in Russian territory. By the time of the rebellion, Russian colonization efforts had reached their section of the Ili River right up to the border.

In 1871, the Russian government intervened to quell the rebellion. The governor-general of Turkestan sent troops to occupy the Chinese section of the Ili Valley and seal off the unrest. There they sat to await the outcome of the rebellion. Much to the surprise of the Russian government, the Chinese did manage to restore order in Xinjiang, although it took another seven years, until 1878. Meanwhile, in 1873, Russia had reorganized the disputed territory into the border province of Kuldzha, but China was determined to regain the territory. China's large armies, used to quell the rebellion, remained in Xinjiang to put pressure on the Russians to withdraw. Russia's inability to deploy its own troops along the border became a decisive factor in its eventual withdrawal from the Ili Valley. Another factor was the potential cost of fighting China. Russia had just emerged from a disappointing war with Turkey (1877–8) that had cost the imperial treasury dearly but brought little compensatory influence in the contested Balkans. When China offered Russia an indemnity in lieu of the occupied territory, Russia accepted the much-needed cash. But cash on the barrel head did little to assuage Russian pride or quell its subliminal fears of invasion over its weakly defended far eastern frontiers. Until Russia and China settled their differences in a treaty signed in 1881, they remained on the verge of war. These were the years when China felt hamstrung in Korea by Russian expansion in Xinjiang.

As the Korean situation had continued to degenerate, Russia had watched with great interest. The year 1885 was an important one for Korea: Karl Ivanovich Veber[40] arrived to take up his appointment as Russian consul general and chargé in Seoul; Yuan Shikai (袁世凱) returned in his new capacity as proconsul; and China let Grand Prince Hûngsôn (興宣大院君) return home.[41]

The Sino-Japanese rivalry over Korea disturbed the Russian government. Russian strategy had long been to surround itself with weak neighbors and to destabilize those who threatened to become strong.[42] This was a logical strategy for a large continental empire. Russia would do what it could to prevent a third power from absorbing and revitalizing Korea. It instructed Veber to assure Korea of Russian support in the event of a threat to Korean territorial integrity or independence.[43] Veber carefully cultivated Korean ties and was aided and abetted by King Kojong's adviser and employee of Viceroy Li Hongzhang (李鴻章), Paul von Möllendorff, who disliked the Japanese and favored Russia as Korea's new protector. Von Möllendorff was part of the official Korean delegation sent to Japan to offer an apology for the Japanese deaths during the 1884 coup attempt. It was another example of "face" in action: Korea had to prostrate itself before Japan to restore the "face" lost by Japan during the violence. Von Möllendorff took this opportunity to sound out the Russian legation in Tokyo and negotiate a secret agreement on behalf of the Korean government. Russia was to provide Korea protection and military instructors in return for a Russian leasehold at Yônghûnghang (Port Lazareff, 永興港), located not far from Wônsan[44] on the northeastern coast of Korea. When the British government learned of this, it immediately occupied Kômundo (Port Hamilton, 巨文島), an island situated off the southern tip of the

---

[40] Alternate spellings include Weber and Waeber.

[41] Lensen, vol. 1, 69–70.

[42] John P. LeDonne, *The Russian Empire and the World, 1700–1917: The Geopolitics of Expansion and Containment* (New York: Oxford University Press, 1997), xiii; *passim*.

[43] Yur-bok Lee, 151.

[44] Alternative spellings include Gensan.

Korean Peninsula. Yuan Shikai became irate at King Kojong for seeking Russian protection and immediately set about intimidating the king. Yuan quashed von Möllendorff's plans to secure Russian military advisers for the Korean army. By the time all these plans had leaked out, the diplomatic community was in an uproar. All except Russia agreed that von Möllendorff should go, and Li dismissed him.[45] To check this growing Russian influence, Foreign Minister Inoue Kaoru (井上馨) recommended to Viceroy Li that he send Grand Prince Hûngsôn home. Li complied. Li hoped that the Grand Prince would check the Min (閔) clan, which had played along with von Möllendorff and the Russians. Grand Prince Hûngsôn complied. This time around he allied himself with Yuan Shikai since they shared a common cause in deposing King Kojong.[46]

Yuan's growing interference in Korean affairs boomeranged. It simultaneously made Chinese suzerainty more onerous and made a Russian protectorate more enticing to the Koreans. King Kojong approached Veber again in 1886 with a second request to establish a Russian protectorship. When one of the king's advisers leaked the information to Yuan Shikai, he started making plans to depose King Kojong, before being overruled by Viceroy Li. King Kojong was equally unsuccessful at securing the recall of Yuan.[47] Meanwhile, Britain and Russia continued sparring over their respective occupations of Kômundo and Yônghûnghang. They did not back down until 1887, when they both withdrew.[48]

The deteriorating situation in Korea seemed to offer the Russia government new opportunities in the Far East. Russia had resented being checkmated by the decrepit Qing Dynasty in Xinjiang. As Russian finances improved in the 1880s, the time seemed ripe to solve Russia's Far Eastern security problems once and for all. Russia made two fateful decisions. In 1888, it decided to facilitate Japan's attempts to undermine Chinese influence in Korea in order to weaken Anglo-Chinese relations. This decision rested on a gross underestimation of Japanese power and a corresponding overestimation of Chinese potential.[49] The second decision concerned railway lines. There had long been talk in Russia about building a great eastern railway to link European and Asiatic Russia. But the project was breathtakingly expensive, particularly relative to the negligible size of Siberia's population and economy. The outcome of the Ili crisis favored building the railway. In the 1880s

---

[45] Lensen, vol. 1, 73–4; Yur-bok Lee, 102–3, 129–33; Djang, 161–4.

[46] Yur-bok Lee, 37–8, 134, 144; Lew, "Kabo Reform," 40.

[47] Yur-bok Lee, 157–65.

[48] Lensen, vol. 1, 54–68; Yur-bok Lee, 53, 61.

[49] Harold Perry Ford, "Russian Far Eastern Diplomacy, Count Witte, and the Penetration of China, 1895–1904" (Ph.D. diss., University of Chicago, 1950), 75.

the Russian railway system was extended through the Ural Mountains and preliminary surveys for a trans-Siberian railway were undertaken. Construction began in 1891. Diplomats around the world immediately realized that completion of the Trans-Siberian Railway would alter the balance of power in the Far East.[50] Russia would suddenly be able to deploy troops along the Chinese border, whereas China lacked any railway system on its side. Korea would be defenseless while neither China nor Japan would be in much of a position to intervene. The Koreans had reason for particular concern since Russia remained preoccupied with locating a suitable Asian warm-water port as the final destination for the new railway. The Russian government considered Vladivostok inadequate since, even with modern icebreakers, it remained frozen for nearly two months out of twelve. For years, Russian policymakers had been toying with the idea of a Korean or a Chinese port as a fitting terminus for their glorious East Asian enterprise.[51] No consideration seems to have been taken concerning the likely Japanese response to the construction of such a railway line.

* * *

If neither Russian nor Chinese policymakers were happy about the situation in Korea, Japanese policymakers were distraught.[52] Because of domestic upheaval, the Japanese government was not in a position to take a decisive role in Korea for a long time. At about the time that Grand Prince Hûngsôn was establishing his regency, the 200-year-old Tokugawa shogunate (徳川幕府) (1603-1867) of Japan fell. It took the new government almost three decades to implement enough domestic reforms before key policymakers considered Japan strong enough to attempt to project its influence abroad.

Japan under the Tokugawa shogunate had a decentralized government composed of a military elite. The head of the Tokugawa clan was the *shōgun* (将軍) or generalissimo who ruled over the shogunate or *bakufu* (幕府). *Bakufu* meant "tent government," referring to the field headquarters of a campaigning general, for the Tokugawa military establishment ruled in the name of the Japanese emperor.[53]

---

[50] Andrew Malozemoff, *Russian Far Eastern Policy 1881–1904 with Special Emphasis on the Causes of the Russo-Japanese War* (Berkeley: University of California Press, 1958), 55–6; Langer, 172; Ian Nish, *Japanese Foreign Policy, 1869–1942* (London: Routledge & Kegan Paul, 1977), 45–6; Curzon, 4th ed., 363; Morinosuke Kajima, *The Emergence of Japan as a World Power 1895–1925* (Rutland, VT: Charles E. Tuttle, 1968), 37; "The Siberian Railway," *The North-China Herald* (Shanghai), 29 June 1894, p. 1025.

[51] Nish, *Japanese Foreign Policy*, 22, 24, 267–8; Akagi, 115, 116, 132–4; Djang, 160–1, 165.

[52] Peter Duus, *The Abacus and the Sword: The Japanese Penetration of Korea, 1895–1910* (Berkeley: University of California Press, 1995), 49.

[53] W. G. Beasley, *The Meiji Restoration* (Stanford: Stanford University Press, 1972), 38; Yasuda

The emperor constituted the *tatemae* (建て前) or facade while the real locus of power, the *honne* (本音), rested with the shogunate. While the emperor reigned from Kyoto, the shoguns ruled from Edo, the name used for Tokyo in the Tokugawa period. The Tokugawa shogun ruled over numerous local feudal lords or *daimyo*, meaning "big names" (大名), each controlling separate and often competing domains. Samurai (侍) were the military retainers of the *daimyo*. The word "samurai" means warrior and is derived from the verb "to wait upon" or "to serve."[54] This was a political system based on military not civil authority, where military service was the most honorable of professions.

Since 1639, Tokugawa Japan had maintained a foreign policy of seclusion or "a locked up country" (鎖国). This policy applied to westerners but not to other Asians. That year Japan had expelled the Portuguese, eradicated Christianity, and granted a monopoly on European trade to the Dutch but confined them to Nagasaki. From 1639 through the fall of the shogunate, Japan maintained its Asian contacts.[55]

The Japanese watched in horror as the Europeans forced their way into China during the Opium Wars.[56] Japan's first taste of imperialism came in 1854, when the Americans forced it to sign the Treaty of Kanagawa, which opened two ports to the United States for provisioning its ships and for consular representation, but not for trade. The treaty also granted America most-favored-nation treatment. In 1858, Japan succumbed to continuing Western pressure and signed a set of treaties with the United States, Holland, England, France, and Russia. The American treaty opened more treaty ports, allowed commerce, and set tariff rates.[57] The Americans replicated in Japan the British treaty-port system of China. Like the Qing Dynasty, the Tokugawa shogunate then tried to "expel the barbarians" (攘夷) but failed at an attempt to close the Shimonoseki Straits to foreign ships.

Motohisa, "Shogunate," in *Kodansha Encyclopedia of Japan*, vol. 7 (Tokyo: Kodansha, 1983), 160–1; John M. Maki, "Emperor," in Ibid., vol. 2, 203.

[54] Andrew N. Nelson and John H. Haig, *The New Nelson Japanese-English Character Dictionary*, rev. ed. (Rutland, VT: Charles E. Tuttle, 1997), 86; Kenneth B. Pyle, *The New Generation in Meiji Japan: Problems of Cultural Identity, 1885–1895* (Stanford: Stanford University Press, 1969), 11–12.

[55] Ronald P. Toby, *State and Diplomacy in Early Modern Japan: Asia in the Development of the Tokugawa Bakufu* (Stanford: Stanford University Press, 1991), xiii, 4–7.

[56] Masuda Wataru, *Japan and China: Mutual Representations in the Modern Era*, Joshua A. Fogel, trans. (New York: St. Martin's Press, 2000), 43–7.

[57] Arthur Power Dudden, *The American Pacific: From the Old China Trade to the Present* (New York: Oxford University Press, 1992), 19; Hirakawa Sukehiro, "Japan's Turn to the West," Bob Tadashi Wakabayashi, trans., in *The Cambridge History of Japan*, vol. 5, Marius B. Jansen, ed. (Cambridge: University of Cambridge Press, 1989), 467.

These straits separate the main island of Japan, Honshū, from the more southerly island of Kyūshū. In 1864, the Chōshū batteries, located on the southern extremity of Honshū, succumbed to a joint bombardment by British, French, Dutch, and American ships. As in China, such resistance led to new and more intrusive commercial treaties. This occurred in 1866. The shogunate also tried its version of self-strengthening, but with equally limited success.[58]

Japan's inability to stem such Western encroachments led significant groups of samurai to question the policy of seclusion and the wisdom of continued Tokugawa rule. After the Western bombardment of the Chōshū batteries, samurai in the Chōshū domain rose up to take their *daimyo* hostage and plot the downfall of the shogunate. Before long, samurai in the Satsuma domain reached similar conclusions. Satsuma was located on the southern extremity of Kyūshū. Both domains focused on modernizing and expanding their military forces. On July 20, 1866, the twenty-year-old Shogun Tokugawa Iemochi (德川家茂) died, leaving the office to a twenty-nine-year-old distant cousin, Tokugawa Yoshinobu (德川吉宗). Then, on December 25, 1866, the thirty-six-year-old Emperor Kōmei (孝明) died, leaving the throne to his fifteen-year-old son, the new Emperor Meiji (明治).[59] This turmoil at the top gave the rising samurai in Chōshū and Satsuma an opportunity to threaten Kyoto, the seat of the emperor, with their military forces while the change in reigns gave them the opportunity to proclaim a new era.[60]

A cardinal difference between the Chinese and the Japanese reactions to the West was that the Qing clung to power whereas the last Tokugawa shogun stepped down. When he did so on November 9, 1867, he spared the country a civil war. The Japanese considered the Tokugawa shogunate's capitulation to Western demands to have been a national humiliation of such magnitude that it helped overcome regional and social fragmentation, on which Tokugawa rule had depended, and made possible the overthrow of the shogunate.[61] The shogunate had lost too much "face" for effective rule. Tokugawa Yoshinobu, in stark contrast

---

[58] Beasley, *Meiji Restoration,* 242; Beasley, *Modern History of Japan,* 84–9.

[59] Before becoming shogun, Tokugawa Yoshinobu was known as Hitotsubashi Keiki (一橋慶喜). Conrad Totman, *Early Modern Japan* (Berkeley: University of California Press, 1993), 554; James Murdoch, *A History of Japan,* rev. and ed. by Joseph H. Longford, vol. 3 (1926, reprint, Hertford: Stephen Austin & Sons, 1996), 764; Beasley, *Meiji Restoration,* 438. There is some disagreement on the dates of death for the Emperor Kōmei and Tokugawa Iemochi. I have relied on those in *The Encyclopedia Nipponica 2001* "德川家茂" ("Tokugawa Iemochi") in 「日本大百科全書」 (*Encyclopedia Nipponica 2001*), vol. 16 (Tokyo: 小学館, 1986), 873, 878; 「孝明天皇」 ("Emperor Kōmei"), in ibid., vol. 9, 42.

[60] Beasley, *Modern History,* 89–97.

[61] Beasley, *Meiji Restoration,* 407; Beasley, *Modern Japan,* 96.

to Empress Dowager Cixi, chose the solution that was best for Japan as a whole and quietly bowed out of politics. With the last Tokugawa shogun went the stain of having capitulated to the West. This freed his successors to deal more creatively with the Western challenge. In contrast, Empress Dowager Cixi and Grand Prince Hûngsôn became ever more preoccupied with the mere retention of power, rather than with its creative exercise.

The policy of expelling the barbarians and the political institution of the shogunate succumbed to a new idea. This was the philosophy of "enrich the country, strengthen the army" (富国強兵) that animated the Meiji reformers. The emperor, as usual, remained above the conflict and continued to reign. The men who took the reins of government were mainly middle- and low-level samurai from the Satsuma and Chōshū domains, domains that had been marginalized under the shogunate since they had opposed its original accession to power two centuries earlier.[62] They took over the legitimizing symbol of the royal house and proclaimed a new era under an imperial restoration of the Meiji Emperor (明治天皇). This became known in Japanese history as the Meiji Restoration or "the restoration of enlightened rule" (明治維新).[63] The Meiji reformers went far beyond the isolated modernization projects of their predecessors to revamp the entire political system and reform the underlying social and economic structure of the country as well. They set to work on the bedrock that the Chinese dared not disturb and which the Russians dealt with only partially.

To succeed in their ambitions, they nurtured and then harnessed the force of nationalism. The combination of far-reaching reforms and nationalism allowed the Japanese to regroup and present the West with a united front on issues of foreign relations.[64] Nationalism would be the Japanese remedy for Western encroachments. They discovered for themselves what the American colonists had developed during their protracted war for independence.[65] Japan, like America before it, harnessed patriotism to bring the imperial powers to more equitable terms. Patriotism and its modern incarnation, nationalism, constituted the most effective solvent to dissolve empires. Many lands would make effective use of it only after World War II to create a wave of decolonization. The Americans and the Japanese discovered it early in the game.

The overriding objective of the Meiji leaders was to transform Japan into a great

---

[62] Beasley, *Meiji Restoration*, 78–81, 208, 240, 373–4; Pyle, *New Generation*, 13, 69–70.

[63] Marius B. Jansen, "Introduction," in *The Cambridge History of Japan*, Marius B. Jansen, ed., vol. 5 (Cambridge: University of Cambridge Press, 1989), 23.

[64] Beasley, *Meiji Restoration*, 412–3.

[65] Tindall and Shi, vol. 1, 195–280.

power. In the near term, this meant renegotiating the "unequal" treaties so that the Japanese would no longer suffer foreign discrimination. In the longer term, this meant creating within Japan the institutional sources of military and economic power sufficient to face off the powers. As a first step, Meiji leaders focused on modernizing their legal and political institutions. They believed that this would undermine the Western rationale for the "unequal" treaties. Such reforms would enable the Japanese to renegotiate the "unequal" treaties out of existence and replace them with "equal" treaties, or treaties providing fully reciprocal rights to both signatories.[66] Unlike the Chinese, Japanese statesmen recognized the intimate connection between domestic reforms and national security. While reforming governmental institutions in pursuit of the foreign policy objective of treaty revision, the Japanese government also took stringent measures to insure that on-going foreign affairs did not sabotage domestic reform: It banned attacks on foreigners and, unlike China, took systematic measures to enforce the ban.[67]

This Japanese pragmatism reflected a shrewd understanding of the West. Japanese leaders were far more knowledgeable about the West than were their Chinese counterparts. In part, this reflected Japan's long tradition of learning from others. In the sixth and seventh centuries the Japanese had sent numerous embassies to China and had maintained these links thereafter. These contacts led to the introduction of Chinese characters (*kanji* in Japanese), political institutions, Confucianism, Buddhism, medicine, literature, and art forms.[68] In the mid-seventh century, this was done under the slogan of "Japanese spirit and Chinese learning" (和魂漢才).[69] Until the Sino-Japanese War, educated Japanese continued to revere Chinese scholarship, calligraphy, and art.[70] In the 1860s, the Tokugawa shogunate sent half a dozen missions to the West. In addition, some of the more important domains, such as Satsuma and Chōshū, smuggled students overseas to study.[71] At this time, a new slogan emerged: "Eastern virtue, Western technology" (東洋 道徳、西洋芸術).[72] Before long, the original was updated to "Japanese spirit and

[66] Jansen, "Introduction," 33.

[67] Iriye, "Japan's Drive to Great Power Status," 734–8.

[68] W. G. Beasley, *Japan Encounters the Barbarian: Japanese Travellers in America and Europe* (New Haven: Yale University Press, 1995), 9–16.

[69] Hwang, 23.

[70] Mutsu, 27–8.

[71] Marius B. Jansen, "The Meiji Restoration," in *The Cambridge History of Japan*, Marius B. Jansen, ed., vol. 5 (Cambridge: University of Cambridge Press, 1989), 336; Hirakawa, 459.

[72] Hwang, 23.

Western learning" (和魂洋才) – the word "Western had replaced "Chinese."[73]

In 1871, just four years after the restoration, the new Meiji government sent some of its most important leaders on an eighteen-month tour of Europe and the United States. The mission was led by the vice president of the Council of State, Iwakura Tomomi (岩倉具視), and became known as the Iwakura Mission. Although the mission was an unsuccessful attempt to renegotiate the "unequal" treaties, it became a pivotal educational experience for its members. A year and a half abroad profoundly influenced their understanding of the world and had an enormous impact on subsequent Japanese history. In the United States mission members saw the centrality of public education and in Britain they observed the importance of industrial development. Members of the mission concluded that Japan had to go far beyond importing articles of technology to adopting Western institutions and educating their countrymen in Western subjects.[74] When they returned home, in contrast to the few low-ranking Chinese who had gone abroad in this period, their advice was heeded. Such a formative experience was precisely what Chinese leaders lacked. In 1872, a member of the Iwakura Mission, Itō Hirobumi (伊藤博文), spoke to Californians in Sacramento: "We came to study your strength, that, by adopting widely your better ways, we may hereafter be stronger ourselves...We shall labor to place Japan on an equal basis, in the future, with those countries whose modern civilization is now our guide."[75] Over the next decade and a half, Itō would become one of the most powerful of the *genrō* (元老) or senior statesmen in Japan. His centrality to the course of the Sino-Japanese War and to the negotiations ending the hostilities calls for a digression to describe the man.

Itō was the son of a low-ranking samurai from Chōshū but was adopted, along with his father, into the Itō family. In 1862 he participated in the burning of the British Legation in Shinagawa, located on the southwestern gateway to Edo. The next year, to learn more about the enemy, he went to England, where he quickly realized that forcible expulsion of the foreigners from Japan would not succeed. He returned home in 1864 upon learning that the Chōshū batteries had opened fire on foreign ships in the Shimonoseki Straits. In 1871, he joined the Iwakura Mission. From 1882 to 1883, he returned to Europe to study Western constitutions in preparation for the drafting of one for Japan. In 1885 Itō became first modern prime minister of Japan, formed the country's first modern cabinet, and set about

---

[73] Koh Masuda, ed., *Kenkyusha's New Japanese-English Dictionary,* 4th ed. (Tokyo: Kenkyusha, 1983), 1944.

[74] Jansen, "Introduction," 26; Beasley, *Meiji Restoration,* 370.

[75] Quoted by Hwang, 35.

drafting the country's first constitution, which was promulgated in 1889.[76]

Unlike the towering Li Hongzhang, Itō was short in stature even by contemporary Japanese standards. Chronically insecure, he craved praise to his face and decorations on his chest while easily dismissing others as incompetent.[77] Also unlike Li, he displayed no loyalty to his subordinates but rapidly dispensed with those who were no longer useful.[78] Among his countrymen he was known for his conceit. He flaunted his self-importance, writing such self-adulatory poems as: "With high spirits soaring to the heavens, / Who under the rising sun / Has exalted the emperor's honor? / At work in my fine mansion, draining three cups of wine, / I have as my friends all the Great Heroes of the nation."[79] He also used his poetic skills to entertain geishas by singing them ribald ditties of original composition.[80] His womanizing was extreme enough to draw the ire of the emperor. During the Sino-Japanese War he was often late to meetings of the War Cabinet because of their distance from his preferred geisha houses. This caused the Meiji Emperor to lament, "The only ones taking this war seriously are me and my horse."[81] Had Itō lived in a later era, his diminutive height, expansive ego, and constant womanizing would have led to speculation about a possible short-man's complex.

Like Li Hongzhang, Itō was a voracious reader, his interests focusing on politics, economics, Chinese poetry, British newspapers, and biographies of great men. He was particularly fascinated by another short man and originator of the complex, Napoleon Bonaparte. Itō accurately gauged the opposition to his policies, flexibly adapting them when necessary. Although his ego irritated his colleagues, his undisputed and enormous talent kept him in high office. He showed no particular interest in acquiring great wealth, nor did he have an ostentatious life-style. He was known for his ability to hold his drink, his ever-present cigar, his long hours devoted to work, practical jokes, and repetitious heroic tales of his

---

[76] Kaju Nakamura, *Prince Ito: The Man and Statesman: A Brief History of His Life* (New York: Japanese-American Commercial Weekly, 1910), xii–xiii; Yoshitake Oka, *Five Political Leaders of Modern Japan: Itō Hirobumi, Ōkuma Shigenobu, Hara Takashi, Inukai Tsuyoshi, and Saionji Kimmochi,* Andrew Fraser and Patricia Murray, trans. (Tokyo: University of Tokyo Press, 1979), 3–12; Beasley, *Meiji Restoration,* 367–9; Hirakawa, 433; W. G. Beasley, "Meiji Political Institutions," in *The Cambridge History of Japan,* Jansen, ed., 660; Beasley, *Modern History of Japan,* 87; W. G. Beasley, *The Rise of Modern Japan* (New York: St. Martin's Press, 1990), 85.

[77] Walton, 276; Oka, 19–41.

[78] Nakamura, 76–83, 102–3; Oka, 38.

[79] Oka, 16.

[80] Oka, 37–8; Hamada, 212.

[81] Quoted in Donald Calman, *The Nature and Origins of Japanese Imperialism: A Reinterpretation of the Great Crisis of 1893* (London: Routledge, 1992), 19–20.

youth. Like Li, he prided himself on his poetry and his calligraphy. His hobbies included collecting old swords and playing *go*, a game of strategy and hegemony over the game board. At home he dispensed with pretensions, hosted local fishermen at his villa at Ōiso, and bantered with the village shopkeepers.[82]

Foreign observers remarked on Count Itō's talent, shrewdness, and force of character.[83] Valentine Chirol, the much-traveled editor of the London *Times*, described his acquaintance with the man: "Count Ito not only talked with me in my own language, slowly and somewhat laboriously, yet with correctness and lucidity, but displayed, in the course of a long conversation, a profound acquaintance with the ideas and methods of European civilisation, together with an independent and sometimes critical but always friendly and thoughtful judgement concerning the limits within which their assimilation was desirable or possible from the point of view of his own country's material needs and ethical idiosyncrasies."[84] Because of the postmaster's infamous 1884 banquet that had ended in a bloodbath in Seoul, Li and Itō had met during the following year to conclude the Treaty of Tianjin. At that time, Li had reported to his country's foreign office, the Zongli Yamen, that "The Ambassador had travelled much in Europe and America, and is doing his best to learn what the West has to teach. He really has the capacity for ruling a nation. He emphasizes the development of commerce, the cultivation of friendly relations with foreign nations, the increase of national wealth, and the strengthening of national defenses...In about ten years, the wealth and strength of Japan will be admirable. This is China's future, not present, source of trouble. I pray those controlling China's policies to pay early heed to this."[85]

Upon his return from the Iwakura Mission in 1873, Itō addressed students on the occasion of the founding of a government engineering school: "It is imperative that we seize this opportunity to train and educate ourselves. On this solemn occasion, I urge all ambitious youths to enroll in this school, to study assiduously, to perfect their talents, and to serve in their various posts with dedication." The employment of foreign experts would be temporary. He continued, "We ourselves will fill the realm with railroads and other technological wonders that will form the basis for further developments to continue for a myriad of generations. The

---

[82] Nakamura, 76–83, 102–3; Oka, 19–41; Marius B. Jansen, "Mutsu Munemitsu," in *Personality in Japanese History*, Albert M. Craig and Donald H. Shively, eds. (Berkeley: University of California Press, 1970), 310, 332; Walton, 276.

[83] Walton, 276; William Franklin Sands, *At the Court of Korea: Undiplomatic Memories* (1930; reprint, London: Century, 1987), 29.

[84] Chirol, 116; Lehman, 182.

[85] Cited in Tsiang, 106. There are various translations of this famous quotation. See also Chien, 185.

glory of our Imperial Land will shine forth to radiate upon foreign shores, while at home, high and low will share in the benefits of a great civilization. Therefore, let all ambitious youths throughout the land proceed vigorously with their studies."[86] Another Japanese leader exhorted a delegation being sent abroad: "The most vital task for all of you who are being sent to Europe is to inspect the various European countries and institutions and then adopt their strong points while discarding their weaknesses." He urged the observation of European ways "in a spirit of critical inquiry."[87] How different this response was from that of China.

In 1909 Itō would be murdered in the Harbin railway station, located in what had become the Russian concession in northern Manchuria. As he lay dying and learned that his murderer was a Korean nationalist, he exclaimed, "What a fool!" He had come to reach an understanding with the Russians in a final effort to forestall a Japanese annexation of Korea. The assassin is reputed to have confessed, "I came here with the fixed purpose of assassinating Prince Ito, whose policy ruined my mother country. I am satisfied with the success of my revenge."[88] In an expression of enduring Korean sentiment on the subject, today on the site of Itō's Residency General in Seoul there is a statue of his assassin. Thus, the assassin of Japan's preeminent modern statesman remains a national hero in Korea.[89]

Upon news of the assassination, the Japanese Ministry of Education had all schools deliver moral lectures using Itō's womanizing as the prime negative example.[90] The official sanction for such criticism probably had the purpose of defusing any possible *casus belli*: Itō had been assassinated by a Korean nationalist; the attack had taken place in front of Russian officials; and it had occurred in Manchuria, where Japan had just defeated Russia in a war four years earlier. Some might have expected the Russians to have desired to wreak revenge upon the man who had helped wage that war. To be fair to the Russians, Itō also had powerful rivals in Japan who did not lament his passing. The Koreans also had ample reasons to make him the target of their antipathy toward the Japanese. In 1910, Japan did just as Itō had feared, annexing Korea and keeping it until the end of World War II. And so the Korean problem lived on to haunt future generations.

Unlike the Chinese, the Koreans, or even the Russians, who ultimately allowed their foreign policy to drive and undermine their domestic policy in the years

---

[86] Quoted in Hirakawa, 469–70.

[87] Quoted in Hirakawa, 476–7. These were Etō Shimpei's (江藤新平) instructions to Inoue Kowashi before a trip to France sponsored by the Ministry of Justice.

[88] Nakamura, 92–3; Calman, 153–4.

[89] M. R. Jansen, *The Making of Modern Japan* (Cambridge: Harvard University Press, 2000), 445.

[90] Oka, 37–8; Kengi Hamada, *Prince Ito* (Tokyo: Sanseido, Co., 1936), 212.

leading up to the Russo-Japanese War and then World War I, the Japanese acquired a greater appreciation for the essential economic basis underlying Western power. Like the Chinese, the Japanese coveted the Western military hardware, but, unlike the Chinese, they quickly perceived that Japan would never be able to produce this hardware without first adopting many of the educational, legal, and even philosophical underpinnings of a modern Western industrial society. They realized that mere armament purchases would be useless in a time of war. Even if they were not boycotted, long overseas supply lines would render the purchases futile. Also unique among the governments of the four countries, the Meiji reformers realized that such an economic transformation could not be orchestrated only from above but would require an educated citizenry to push forward modernization from below as well. Unlike educated Russians, who eschewed occupations tainted by commerce,[91] the Meiji reformers set out to train precisely such people. Finally, unlike the Chinese, they understood that, to a great extent, foreign gadgets and foreign culture were a package deal. Their fact-finding missions attempted to isolate those parts of the cultural package that were absolutely necessary for Japan to adopt in order to become a modern industrial state. Modernity, they believed, would liberate Japan from the resented Western domination and allow Japan to become a world power in its own right and capable of protecting vital national interests. This became Japan's overriding aim and enduring ambition. In the nineteenth century, the Japanese saw this primarily in military terms; after their defeat in World War II, they came to see it in economic terms.

Whereas the Russian government focused on the lower end of the social structure to emancipate the serfs, the Meiji leaders turned their attention to the middle and upper end of the scale. They abolished the privileged position, but not the influence, of the samurai class through the removal of its traditional subsidies and tax exemptions.[92] The reform was successfully undertaken by the rising segments of the samurai class at the expense of its tradition-bound segments who did not pull their own weight in the emerging social order. The goal was to restore consistency among wealth, status, and office.[93] This was a problem that the Qing and Romanov dynasties both failed to resolve. As the Industrial Revolution progressed in Russia, wealth and status sharply diverged with an increasingly impecunious nobility at odds with an increasingly wealthy and outspoken but politically excluded educated public. Russia gravitated toward state-directed

---

[91] Gerschenkron, 60, 62, 186; Crisp, "Labour," 385; Szamuely, 409; Gatrell, 326; Owen, 35–6, 53, 115, 197–200, 210, 214.

[92] Beasley, *Meiji Restoration*, 382–90.

[93] Beasley, *Meiji Restoration*, 388–90.

industrialization in part because of its unstated goal of preserving the upper end of the social order come what may. The explicit goal was the preservation of empire, which meant, in effect, the maintenance of a militarized economy instead of the development of the strong civilian economy that fueled growth in the West. In China, as the decay of the Qing Dynasty set in, office and status also diverged with the devolution of central authority to regional strongmen. Both situations had corrosive effects on their respective dynasties.

The reforms of the Meiji period are impressive. In 1869, the feudal domains were returned to the emperor, ending the feudal era; in 1872, elementary education became compulsory, creating a literate citizenry to modernize the country; in 1873, universal military conscription began, thus ending the formerly exclusive military prerogatives of the samurai; in 1878, the Army General Staff was created, totally reorganizing the army; in 1882, the Bank of Japan opened, forming the basis for a modern financial system; in 1885, a cabinet subordinate to the prime minister was instituted, creating a westernized form of government; in 1886, Tokyo Imperial University was founded, providing a center for westernized higher education; in 1887, a modern civil service examination system was implemented, ending the traditional correlation between birth and status; and, the crowning achievement, in 1889 the constitution was promulgated and in 1890 the first Diet was convened.[94] Legal reforms included a new criminal code in 1882 and in 1890 both a reorganized court system and a code of civil procedure.[95]

These changes are difficult to assess because so often what seems to be the case in Japan actually is not so at all. In politics, the facade or *tatemae* of parliamentary government did not conform to the reality or *honne* of behind-the-scenes power. Even on the surface, the Meiji leaders had not chosen the British constitution as their model but that of Prussia. Under the Prussian system the balance of power lay not with the parliament but with the cabinet.[96] The underlying reality was less democratic still. Unlike in the West, where the people constituted the basis for sovereignty, in Japan the figurehead emperor did. Itō explained that, in the absence of the superior authority of Christianity and the constitutional theory that preserved the governmental framework in Western Europe, the emperor fulfilled this role in Japan. The Meiji reformers relied on the Shinto doctrine of divine

---

[94] Beasley, "Meiji Political Institutions," 648–50; David J. Lu, *Japan A Documentary History: The Late Tokugawa Period to the Present* (Armonk, NY: M. E. Sharpe, 1997), Appendix 3, XII–XIII; Beasley, *Meiji Restoration*, 39; Beasley, *Modern History of Japan*, 136.

[95] Ernest Wilson Clement, *A Handbook of Modern Japan*, 7th ed. (Chicago: A. C. McClurg & Co., 1907), 161.

[96] Beasley, "Meiji Political Institutions," 657–8.

imperial descent to justify the position of the emperor as being above the law and as the source of governmental authority and power. Because of his divine origin, the Japanese people owed unquestioning loyalty to his spokesmen and cabinet ministers.[97] Despite the very westernized appearance of the new political institutions, actual power was extraparliamentary, extraconstitutional, and oligarchical: in the hands of the cabinet and of the *genrō* or elder statesmen. These latter were those from Satsuma and Chōshū who had created the Meiji Restoration. As long as they lived, they retained enormous influence. When political parties became too obstreperous, the cabinet dissolved the Diet. At best, the Diet sat in session for no more than ninety days during the year and had limited power even then. The Meiji reformers had created a westernized government but not a liberal democratic or republican one.[98]

There was tremendous frustration in the Diet over its inability to affect policy. The political parties used foreign policy as the vehicle to attack the oligarchs.[99] And the program of westernization introduced by the Meiji leaders was by no means popular. The newspapers joined the political parties in their outspoken criticism of the policies of the cabinet. The British-owned *Japan Weekly Mail* observed that "Journalistic unanimity of opinion in Japan is limited to abusing officialdom."[100] In another edition, it observed: "No political party in Japan to-day, no section in the House of Representatives, openly supports the Government." This was because "not one of the so-called political parties enjoys the sweets of office. In other countries the party in opposition alone is excluded from the administration. Here, all are excluded. Therefore all alike are interested in pulling down the Government."[101] This resulted in government censorship of the newspapers and the expulsion of many opposition leaders from Tokyo.[102] The constitutional framework in Japan left the Diet with little power other than obstreperous obstructionism, the course chosen by its members. The first sessions of the Diet were stormy. At issue was whether or not the cabinet and executive branch of

---

[97] W. G. Beasley, *The Rise of Modern Japan*, 2nd ed. (New York: St. Martin's Press, 1995), 7–80, 127.

[98] Beasley, "Meiji Political Institutions," 666–8, 671–3; J. A. A. Stockwin, "Political System," in *Kodansha Encyclopedia of Japan*, vol. 6 (Tokyo: Kodansha, 1983), 214; "The Coming Session of the Diet," *The Japan Weekly Mail* (Yokohama), 15 December 1894, p. 670.

[99] Pyle, *New Generation*, 169.

[100] "Japanese Men-of-War," *The Japan Weekly Mail* (Yokohama), 28 April 1894, p. 489.

[101] "The Latest Phase of the Parliamentary Struggle," *The Japan Weekly Mail* (Yokohama), 26 May 1894, p. 628.

[102] Akagi, 99–100; Pyle, *New Generation*, 165.

government would be responsible to elected representatives. The Diet was dissolved in 1891, 1893, and a month before the war, in June of 1894. The 1893 Diet had sat for only a month while the 1894 Diet was out after eighteen days.[103] In the last case, Itō chose as the pretext disagreements concerning the delicate on-going treaty-revision negotiations with Britain. The real reason was the unraveling situation in Korea. Treaty revision and Korean instability constituted the two main foreign policy issues in the first quarter-century of the Meiji period.[104]

Japanese nationalism expressed itself most vocally in foreign policy, where public opinion demanded a more active and visible stance. Delineation of boundaries was one of the main issues motivating modern states in the second half of the nineteenth century. Of primary concern to the great powers were their own national boundaries, which they defined more precisely in this period. Where ambiguities remained, such as in Alsace-Lorraine and in the Balkans, armed conflict arose. This concern for formal boundaries extended to the world beyond Europe and North America. The then dominant foreign policy in the West, that of imperialism, entailed, at its most basic level, a division of the world into definable spheres of influence.[105] This policy was very powerful at home and abroad. In the industrializing world, it unified citizens behind their governments in pursuit of aggressive foreign policies while it prostrated those who resisted in the unindustrialized world. The political landscape changed forever for the peoples whose lands were divided up among the imperial powers. The map changed beyond recognition in Africa and, to nearly as great an extent, in the Middle East. Domestically, national sentiment could be easily rallied to support territorial claims and, by extension, to support the ruling government. However, nationalistic fervor turned out to be a two-edged sword since once aroused it was difficult to cool without concrete territorial gains. This tended to push governments into more aggressive policies than perhaps originally intended.

As the Meiji Restoration progressed, Japanese leaders adopted the foreign policy of imperialism. The prevailing Western ideas concerning social Darwinism developed by Charles Darwin and especially Herbert Spencer found great resonance in Japan. This philosophy of survival of the fittest tailor-fit the Japanese imperative to find a way to survive with dignity in the new and hostile industrial world.[106]

---

[103] Beasley, *Modern History of Japan*, 133; Oh, "Background," 294; Conroy, 212.

[104] Hugh Borton, *Japan's Modern Century* (New York: The Ronald Press, 1955), 203; Mutsu, 69.

[105] Iriye, "Japan's Drive to Great Power Status," 739.

[106] Kimitada Miwa, "Fukuzawa Yukichi's 'Departure from Asia': A Prelude to the Sino-Japanese War," in *Japan's Modern Century: A Special Issue of "Monumenta Nipponica" Prepared in Celebration of the Centennial of the Meiji Restoration*, Edmund Skrzypczak, ed. (Tokyo: Sophia

Japanese officials in the Meiji period came to believe that in order to be a modern state a country had to become an imperialist power and that economic modernization could not be successfully undertaken without a military foundation. This was the lens through which Meiji statesmen viewed the world.[107]

Like the imperial powers of its day, Japan set about defining the boundaries of and commercial relations in its sphere of influence in the Far East. In 1871, it concluded its first treaty with China, a commercial treaty notable for its provision for mutual extraterritoriality. When the two countries ratified it in 1873, the Japanese representative mentioned to Li Hongzhang that extraterritoriality was not the norm for Western nations, which subjected each other to municipal jurisdiction. This apparently amazed Li. He had not realized that extraterritoriality was not universal.[108] In 1875 Japan concluded a treaty with Russia ceding Sakhalin Island (Karafuto) in return for Japanese sovereignty over all the Kurile Islands. Japan also resolved the ambiguous status of the Ryūkyū Kingdom – a Chinese tributary since 1372 and concurrent district of the Satsuma domain since 1609. The Ryūkyū Island chain includes Okinawa and is roughly equidistant from Japan, Korea, and Taiwan. In 1871 Ryūkyū fishermen had been shipwrecked and then murdered in Taiwan. After inconclusive talks with the Chinese, the Japanese government had sent a punitive expedition to Taiwan in 1874. The three-year delay in the Taiwan expedition indicated that it was not intended to avenge the deaths of the fishermen but to be a sop for roused domestic opinion in Japan. That year China and Japan signed an agreement whereby China agreed to compensate the families of the dead Ryūkyū fishermen in return for a Japanese withdrawal from Taiwan. The Chinese leaders, including Li, did not realize that the 1874 agreement gave legal standing to Japan's claim that the inhabitants of the Ryūkyū Islands were Japanese subjects. Fruitless negotiations to resolve the status of the islands continued until 1879, when Japan unilaterally annexed them.[109]

Li considered China's loss of the Ryūkyū Islands a bad portent for Korea. He wrote: "As the Liu-ch'iu [Ryūkyū] have been annexed, Korea is in a position of imminent danger. In view of this and of the growing interest of the Occidental nations in Korea, we can no longer refrain from devising ways and means for the

University, 1968), 2–3.

[107] Iriye, "Japan's Drive," 782.

[108] Tsiang, 11–5; Mayers, 178–82.

[109] Iriye, "Japan's Drive to Great Power Status," 739–44; Nish, *Japanese Foreign Policy*, 23; Noriko Kamachi, *Reform in China: Huang Tsun-hsien and the Japanese Model* (Cambridge, MA: Harvard University Press, 1981), 103, 108–9; Oh, "Sino-Japanese Rivalry in Korea," 45–6.

security of Korea."[110] This signaled the beginning of his much more intrusive policies in Korea, described in the last chapter. Japanese leaders took this as a personal challenge, so that Li's new policy resulted in greater not less Japanese involvement in Korean affairs, the very consequence the policy was intended to prevent. From the Japanese point of view, China had simply upped the ante. The new stakes would be a win-or-lose-all contest for control over the Korean Peninsula.

As in the case of the Kurile and the Ryūkyū islands, Meiji leaders also sought to resolve ambiguities in Korea. Geographically, Korea is much closer to Japan than it is to China proper. The Tsushima Islands are only about 30 miles from Pusan,[111] which is 122 miles from Shimonoseki. In contrast, the Yalu River, defining the Chinese border with Korea, is 400 miles from the Great Wall, the demarcation of the northernmost extent of China proper – as opposed to Manchuria, the domain of the Manchus. Similarly, Seoul is 309 miles from the Yalu but only 274 miles from Pusan. The available modes of transportation reinforced these relative distances, since the sea trip between Japan and Korea was relatively simple whereas the land trek from the Great Wall was arduous.[112]

In the 1870s Korea had become important for the Meiji government as the proxy issue on which to focus domestic rivalries. Under the Tokugawa shogunate, the Tsushima fief had been responsible for contacts with Korea.[113] When the new Meiji government absorbed the feudal domains, it also assumed their governmental responsibilities. Korea stirred up a political storm in Japan when it refused to recognize the new Meiji government, despite repeated overtures from 1869 to 1872. By 1873 this had fueled a debate in Japan over the advisability of invading Korea.[114] Members of the Iwakura Mission had an immediate impact on foreign policy. Upon their return in 1873, they scotched the plans for invading Korea drawn up in their absence.[115] This precipitated Japan's first cabinet crisis.[116] The mission members realized that the policy was reckless since Japan was not yet strong enough to subdue Korea. In the intervening two decades before the Sino-Japanese War, the Meiji reformers consistently focused on internal reforms at the expense of foreign adventures. They believed that Japan had to modernize at home

---

[110] Quoted in Oh, "Background of Chinese Policy Formation," 70.

[111] Alternate spellings include Fusan.

[112] Payson J. Treat, "China and Korea, 1885–1894," *Political Science Quarterly* 49, no. 4 (December 1934): 506–7.

[113] Iriye, "Japan's Drive to Great Power Status," 744–7.

[114] Beasley, *Meiji Restoration*, 373–6.

[115] Hirakawa, 465.

[116] Akagi, 115.

before it could be adventurous abroad. In particular, they feared that hostilities would give Russia an opening to extend its influence in the Far East.[117] In contrast, there was no consensus in the upper echelons of the Chinese government concerning the imperative to minimize foreign conflicts; rather, its policies lurched inconsistently in tandem with the demands of the faction of the hour. As a result, Chinese foreign policy remained ineffectual and tragically reckless.

In contrast to the Meiji leaders but like the Han literati, the Japanese public took a highly volatile approach to foreign insults. The Japanese public is an ill-defined group including members of the old samurai class, the rising commercial elite, and the growing group of Japanese who had benefited from the broadening of public education and were vocal on political issues. The enfranchised were men of property about half a million in number.[118] The depth of the moral indignation felt by the Japanese public can be explained by a combination of a traditional sense of "face" and a new sense of nationalism. The unwillingness of the Korean government to respect Japanese overtures to establish relations suggested that the Koreans questioned Japan's international standing. This was perceived as a deliberate attempt to make Japan "lose face." Therefore, it constituted an act of aggression to be answered by the force of arms. The Japanese had so resented being pushed around by the West that their leaders had reinvented themselves with the Meiji Restoration. This fragile new government was struggling to establish itself in a very turbulent domestic and international environment. Domestically, a nascent and rapidly growing sense of nationalism among the general public was leading to increasing demands for foreign adventures while the absence of an established track record for the new government meant that it lacked the legitimacy necessary to resist such domestic demands without difficulties. This made the new government particularly vulnerable to any attacks on its national honor from abroad. Under these circumstances, they were not about to endure slights from what they considered a backward little country like Korea. Meanwhile, many unemployed samurai were itching for an excuse to demonstrate their military prowess. The Taiwan expedition of 1874 had temporarily defused this domestic pressure, but the tinder was laid to be ignited with the next whiff of troubles from Korea.[119]

The 1876 Treaty of Kanghwa, opening Korea, was another foreign adventure with a domestic motivation: The goal this time was not yet empire, but rather a foreign success to consolidate power at home. Several of those who had resigned

---

[117] Beasley, *Modern History of Japan*, 141–2; Marlene J. Mayo, "The Korean Crisis of 1873 and Early Meiji Foreign Policy, *Journal of Asian Studies* 31, no. 4 (August 1972): 819.

[118] Jansen, *Making of Modern Japan*, 379, 383, 403–11, 414–5, 422.

[119] Nish, *Japanese Foreign Policy*, 23.

in protest in 1873 against what they considered a pusillanimous Korea policy took to armed revolt. Discontented samurai began organizing, most notably in the former Satsuma domains. They represented those who resented the loss of traditional samurai privileges and opposed the westernizing reform program. In 1876, three issues made this simmering discontent boil over into rebellion: First, the discontented samurai considered war, not negotiation, as the honorable course of action; thus the Treaty of Kanghwa was an anathema to them. Then a few months later, the samurai lost their right to bear swords, the last visible symbol of their once superior status. Finally, later that same year, they lost their stipends. Sporadic samurai revolts rippled through the prefectures. In January 1877, when the government tried to empty the arsenals in the capital of Satsuma prefecture, a rebellion broke out which lasted six months and took the combined forces of the entire standing army and reserves to quell. The defeat of the Satsuma Rebellion proved that the traditional samurai understanding of the world was obsolete. Sword-bearing samurai proved to be no match for a peasant conscript army with modern communications and Western training. This was the last feudal uprising against the Meiji rule. Thereafter, restive samurai channeled their discontent into political opposition and into support for overseas expansion.[120] Many disaffected samurai became journalists to vent their spleen. For this reason almost every newspaper was critical of, if not outrightly hostile to, the government.[121]

Korea was also becoming economically important to Japan. The Korean ports of Pusan, Wônsan, and Inch'ôn[122] were opened to foreign commerce in 1876, 1880, and 1881, respectively. This led to an influx of Japanese merchants who specialized in the importation to Korea of coarse cotton fabrics from Britain and the exportation of rice, soybeans, other agricultural products, and gold. This disrupted local Korean markets, sending prices upward and causing food shortages in times of poor harvests.[123] According to a report published by the British Foreign Office, "The Japanese are the chief exporters of rice and beans, advancing money on growing crops, and obtaining half the proceeds of the harvest. This is a most lucrative business, for a foreign resident who tried it, found that, with no pressure or supervision on his part, the value of the crop, which was rice, amounted to fifty per cent per annum on his outlay. In good years accordingly the profits of the Japanese are enormous, while in bad years their loss is trivial,

---

[120] Beasley, *Modern History*, 117–9.

[121] G. B. Sansom, *The Western World and Japan: A Study in the Interaction of European and Asiatic Cultures* (New York: Alfred A. Knopf, 1951), 424–5.

[122] Alternate spellings include Chemulpo and Jinsen.

[123] Kamachi, 110.

because their advances are far below the value of the crop mortgaged to them."[124]

In the late 1880s there were successive poor rice harvests in Korea. In 1888, drought in the southern rice bowl and floods in the north led to a nationwide famine.[125] The Korean economy was in turmoil. Many Koreans blamed this on the opening of their country's markets to foreign trade. Hostility to Japanese merchants grew apace.[126] By the 1880s, Japan generally purchased 90 percent of Korean exports, although this trade represented only from 2 to 7 percent of Japanese exports from 1889 to 1893. Yet from the mid-1880s to the early 1890s, Japanese exports to Korea increased by over 90 percent.[127] Japan dominated shipping by transporting 304,244 tons of the 387,507 tons of material sent through Korea's open ports in 1893.[128] More notable than changes in Korean trade were changes in Japanese trade. In 1884, Japan had a total foreign trade of 63.5 million *yen*, whereas in 1893 this almost trebled to 176.4 million *yen*.[129]

In the first two decades of the Meiji period, Japan had focused on internal reforms. It was now on the verge of directing its attention outward. As Japanese thoughts turned to empire, the Korean market was seen in terms of future importance. This was in line with the prevailing ideas in Europe that economic prosperity depended on access to foreign markets. Therefore, from the 1880s forward, the Japanese government made foreign trade an important policy objective.[130]

In response to the Korean *coup d'état* of 1882, the Meiji government funded a major military build-up, particularly of the navy. This was in anticipation of future military action in Korea. At the time Japan was preoccupied with treaty revision: The time was not ripe for war.[131] Korea sent an official mission to convey its apology for the lives lost and paid an indemnity. The mission gave Japan enough "face" to assuage public opinion until the 1884 *coup d'état*, which again electrified Japanese public opinion. This time the discontent was harder to quell. A new rhetoric of Asianism emerged in the public opinion critical of the

---

[124] "Mr. Hillier on Corea," *The North-China Herald* (Shanghai), 30 March 1894, p. 469.

[125] Oh, "Background," 230.

[126] Oh, "Sino-Japanese Rivalry in Korea," 50; Kamachi, 110.

[127] Iriye, "Japan's Drive to Great Power Status," 751, 758; Ernest P. Young, "A Study of Groups and Personalities in Japan Influencing the Events Leading to the Sino-Japanese War (1894–1895)," *Papers on China*, Harvard University 2 (August 1963): 240.

[128] "The Commerce of Korea," *The Pall Mall Gazette* (London), 7 August 1894, 4th ed., p. 5.

[129] "Commerce extérieur du Japon en 1893" (Foreign trade of Japan in 1893), *Le Siècle* (*The Century*) (Paris), 24 January 1895.

[130] Iriye, "Japan's Drive to Great Power Status," 758.

[131] Iriye, "Japan's Drive to Great Power Status," 753–8; Kim and Kim, 43.

government. It was the Japanese version of Kipling's "white man's burden": Japan had a civilizing mission in Asia whereby it must direct China and Korea to their salvation.[132] In June of 1894, according to the *Chūō Shinbun* (中央新聞), "Japan's mission is to extend her sway over the continent of Asia. We are not designed by Heaven to remain cooped up within these narrow islands."[133] Chinese or Russian consolidation of control over Korea would dash Japan's visions of great powerhood via an empire on the Asian mainland.[134]

Sino-Japanese relations continued to worsen after the 1884 *coup d'état*. In 1883, Japan had signed a secret agreement with Korea guaranteeing that all telegrams out of Korea would go via the Pusan–Nagasaki submarine cable line for the next two decades. After the failed coup Korea ignored the agreement with Japan to sign one with China, allowing China to extend the Shanghai–Tianjin telegraph line to Seoul and operate the concession for the next twenty-five years. Later Korea allowed the Chinese to construct and operate a telegraph line from Seoul to Pusan. Japanese protests of these violations of its prior treaty rights were to no avail.[135] Until the outbreak of war, China, not Japan, controlled Korea's communications with the outside world. Japan had no secure transmission route since the Chinese controlled the vital Seoul–Pusan link. This undermined the value of the submarine cable. On the eve of the war, the Seoul–Pusan link was broken so that the Japanese had to route their telegrams to Seoul via Nagasaki, Shanghai, Tianjin, and on to Seoul.[136]

In addition to telegraph lines, there were squabbles over commerce. In 1889, Korea enacted laws limiting rice exports in the event of a domestic food shortage. Japan protested this as a violation of the Treaty of Kanghwa and demanded an indemnity to compensate its merchants for their financial losses from the embargo. In 1890, Korea repealed the laws but refused to pay the indemnity. Only in 1893 did Korea agree to indemnify the Japanese.[137] Then in October 1893, the Korean government exercised its right to give one month's notice for another prohibition of rice exports. This reduced rice exports by 26,000 tons in 1893 from the level set in 1892.[138] The rice trade was not scheduled to be resumed until Chinese New

---

[132] Iriye, "Japan's Drive to Great Power Status," 753–8.

[133] Quoted and translated in "The Spirit of the Vernacular Press during the Week," *The Japan Weekly Mail* (Yokohama), 9 June 1894, p. 682.

[134] Borton, 203.

[135] Akagi, 134.

[136] "The Impending War," *The North-China Herald* (Shanghai), 29 June 1894, p. 1010.

[137] Akagi, 134–5.

[138] "The Commerce of Corea," *The Pall Mall Gazette* (London), 7 August 1894, 4th ed., p. 5.

Year's Day on February 22, 1894. The deadline came and went.[139] The Japanese press was full of articles about the Korean grain embargo and the losses being incurred by Japanese merchants.[140] There were also continual complaints of the preferential treatment accorded to Chinese merchants by the Koreans.[141]

The final and most explosive issue that set off Japanese public opinion was the assassination of Kim Ok-kyun (金玉均). The Min family and King Kojong loathed Kim for his leading role in the assassinations of highly placed Min family members during the coup of 1884. The victims had been summarily beheaded at the postal banquet. Revenge was in order. In the Far East, decapitation was considered a particularly odious form of execution since it mutilated the body so that it would not be intact for the next world. The more mutilated the body, the more punitive the execution. Hence the variations, ranging from mandatory suicide (which leaves the body whole) to decapitation, quartering, and all the way to slicing (which leaves the body in innumerable small pieces). By the nineteenth century in the West the issue was the infliction not the mode of the death penalty. In the East, the issue was how finely the victim had been carved up – in the Western mind, form over content. It also was a reflection of "face"; the nastier the execution, the greater the dishonor to the family of the deceased.

After the failed coup of 1884, Kim had fled to Japan. Meanwhile, the Min clan and King Kojong had tried repeatedly to have him extradited from Japan and, failing in this, had kept trying to assassinate him.[142] Far from acceding to Korean demands, the Japanese government had provided Kim with a monthly allowance while Count Itō and former Foreign Minister Count Inoue Kaoru (井上馨), who

---

[139] "Korean News," *The Japan Weekly Mail* (Yokohama), 27 January 1894, p. 118; "Latest Telegrams," *The Japan Weekly Mail* (Yokohama), 27 January 1894, p. 125; "Korean Affairs," *The Japan Weekly Mail* (Yokohama), 17 February 1894, p. 199; "Latest Telegrams," *The Japan Weekly Mail* (Yokohama), 24 February 1894, p. 252; "朝鮮出米解禁實行彙報" (Bulletin on the implementation of the lifting of the Korean embargo on grain exports), 朝日新聞 (*Rising Sun Newspaper*) (Tokyo), 16 March 1894, p. 2.

[140] "朝鮮出米解禁實予告" (Preliminary announcement of lifting of the Korean embargo on grain exports), 朝日新聞 (*Rising Sun Newspaper*) (Tokyo), 21 January 1894, p. 2; "朝鮮出米解禁の郵報" (Report of lifting of embargo on grain exports), 朝日新聞 (*Rising Sun Newspaper*) (Tokyo), 24 January 1894, p. 1; "朝鮮出米禁止令彙報" (Bulletin of lifting of law forbidding grain exports), 朝日新聞 (*Rising Sun Newspaper*) (Tokyo), 25 January 1894, p. 2; "出米解禁の通牒" (Notification of lifting of embargo of grain exports), 朝日新聞 (*Rising Sun Newspaper*) (Tokyo), 23 February 1894, p. 1.

[141] "朝鮮に於ける日清貿易" (Japanese and Chinese trade in Korea), 朝日新聞 (*Rising Sun Newspaper*) (Tokyo), 1 April 1894, p. 2.

[142] "Corea and Japan," *The North-China Herald* (Shanghai), 20 April 1894, pp. 585–6; Lensen, vol. 1, 110–3; Oh, "Background," 201–3.

would serve as Japanese minister to Korea during the war, allegedly were giving him additional funds.[143] In 1894 a fellow Korean who later admitted to being in the employ of King Kojong befriended Kim, lured him from Japan to Shanghai, and murdered him there on March 28, 1894.[144] The assassin, Hong Chong-u (洪鐘宇),[145] came from a distinguished scholar-aristocratic family.[146] That same day an assassination attempt was made on Kim's friend and fellow exile, Pak Yŏnghyo (朴泳孝), in Tokyo.[147] Although Japanese interest in the Korean reformers had been on the decline, the murder instantly changed this. British authorities in Shanghai arrested the accused assassin and, in accordance with their treaty obligations, surrendered him to Chinese authorities for trial. The Chinese immediately freed him, whereupon he became a celebrity. The Chinese, however, declined to give custody of the corpse to Kim's Japanese friends but on April 12 delivered to Korea both the corpse and the assassin on the same Chinese warship.[148] In the Japanese mind, this implicated the Chinese government in the crime. Instead of trying the accused they had helped him escape.[149] The Japanese public became outraged when the assassin returned home to a hero's welcome while the victim arrived shrouded in a cloth bearing the inscription: "Ok-kiun, arch rebel

---

[143] "Was Kim-Ok-Kiun a Naturalised Japanese?" *The North-China Herald* (Shanghai), 11 May 1894, p. 720.

[144] "The Political Assassination in Shanghai," *The Japan Weekly Mail* (Yokohama), 7 April 1894, p. 401–2; "A Sensational Political Murder in Shanghai," *The North-China Herald* (Shanghai), 30 March 1894, p. 488; Conroy, 223.

[145] Alternate spellings include Hong Tjyong-Ou.

[146] Oh, "Background," 204.

[147] "Corea and Japan" *The North-China Herald* (Shanghai), 20 April 1894, p. 586. Pak was known in Japan by the Japanese pronunciation of his name, Boku Eikō. "朴李等の豫審決定" (Decision of the pretrial hearing for Pak, Yi, etc.), 朝日新聞 (*Rising Sun Newspaper*) (Tokyo), 29 April 1894, p. 1; "李逸植の奸謀" (Wicked plot of Yi Il-chik), 朝日新聞 (*Rising Sun Newspaper*) (Tokyo), 29 April 1894, p. 1

[148] Lensen, vol. 1, 113–7; "金洪の朝鮮著" (Arrival of Kim and Hong in Korea), 朝日新聞 (*Rising Sun Newspaper*) (Tokyo), 15 April 1894, p. 1; "金の死体引取委員談判結果" (Results of the negotiations by the committee for the return of Kim's corpse), 朝日新聞 (*Rising Sun Newspaper*) (Tokyo), 19 April 1894, p. 1; "金の屍体引取委員" (Committee for the return of Kim's corpse), 朝日新聞 (*Rising Sun Newspaper*) (Tokyo), 25 April 1894, p. 1; "金氏の頭首八道梟示の議決" (Decision to display the decapitated head of Mr. Kim in the eight provinces), 朝日新聞 (*Rising Sun Newspaper*) (Tokyo), 29 April 1894, p. 1; Bruce A. Elleman, *Modern Chinese Warfare, 1795–1989* (London: Routledge, 2001), 96.

[149] "又同模樣" (Same pattern again), 朝日新聞 (*Rising Sun Newspaper*) (Tokyo), 5 April 1894, p. 1; "洪の重賞と金の死体" (Hong's great reward and Kim's body), 朝日新聞 (*Rising Sun Newspaper*) (Tokyo), 12 April 1894, p. 1. Details of the assassination filled the papers. See, for instance, the entire first page of the April 6, 1894 issue of 朝日新聞 ; Elleman, *Modern Chinese Warfare*, 96.

and heretic." On April 14, by order of the king, the body was decapitated, so that the head could be displayed in Seoul while the rest of the body was subdivided into eight parts so that one piece could be sent to each of Korea's eight provinces.[150] Even this did not go smoothly, since the head was soon stolen from its display in Seoul.[151] Before long, Kim's father was hanged and his brother, wife, and only daughter were all imprisoned by Korean authorities.[152] Under Korean practice, the family of the guilty was often punished as well. The wife and daughter were made slaves to a government office, the standard punishment for the female household members of rebels.[153] For weeks, Kim's postmortem made headlines in the Japanese press.[154] One of the murdered man's traveling companions, a linguist attached to the Chinese legation in Tokyo, claimed that they had come to Shanghai on the invitation of Lord Li Jingfang (李經方), the former Chinese minister at Tokyo and adopted son of Li Hongzhang.[155] Japanese newspapers interpreted this to implicate Lord Li in the plot. Viceroy Li was alleged to have sent a congratulatory telegram to the Korean government for an assassination well done. Others pointed to King Kojong since the assassin claimed to be under

---

[150] "The Korean Assassination Affair," *The Japan Weekly Mail* (Yokohama), 7 April 1894, p. 400; Young, 233–4; Hosea Ballou Morse, *The International Relations of the Chinese Empire*, vol. 3 (Shanghai: Kelly and Walsh, 1918), 20; "Kim Ok-kyûn's Body and Hong Tjyong-on's Fate," *The Japan Weekly Mail* (Yokohama), 14 April 1894, pp. 439–40; "Korean News," *The Japan Weekly Mail* (Yokohama), 28 April 1894, p. 502; "Korean News," *The Japan Weekly Mail* (Yokohama), 5 May 1894, pp. 530–1; "The Political Murder," *The North-China Herald* (Shanghai), 4 May 1894, p. 696; Vladimir [Zenone Volpicelli], *The China-Japan War Compiled from Japanese, Chinese, and Foreign Sources* (Kansas City, MO: Franklin Hudson Publishing, 1905), 38; "金の訃告と韓廷" (Kim's obituary and the Korean Court), 朝日新聞 (*Rising Sun Newspaper*) (Tokyo), 11 April 1894, p. 1; "金の死骸と洪" (Kim's body and Hong), 朝日新聞 (*Rising Sun Newspaper*) (Tokyo), 12 April 1894, p. 1; "金の屍体到著の模様" (Condition of Kim's corpse upon arrival), 朝日新聞 (*Rising Sun Newspaper*) (Tokyo), 22 April 1894, p. 1; "金の遺骸と洪鍾宇" (Kim's remains and Hong Chong-u), 朝日新聞 (*Rising Sun Newspaper*) (Tokyo), 22 April 1894, p. 2; Elleman, *Modern Chinese Warfare*, 96.

[151] "Political Murder," *The North-China Herald* (Shanghai), 25 May 1894, p. 819.

[152] "The Family of Kim Ok-kyûn," *The Japan Weekly Mail* (Yokohama), 16 June 1894, p. 715; "金の梟首外二件" (Two deaths in addition to the decapitation and hanging of Kim's head from a pole), 朝日新聞 (*Rising Sun Newspaper*) (Tokyo), 15 May 1894, p. 1; Nahm, "Kim Ok-kyun," v, 315.

[153] "Kim-ok-Kiun's Family," *The North-China Herald* (Shanghai), 25 January 1895, p. 112.

[154] Akagi, 135; "The Spirit of the Vernacular Press during the Week," *The Japan Weekly Mail* (Yokohama), 7 April 1894, p. 398; "The Korean Assassination Affair," *The Japan Weekly Mail* (Yokohama), 7 April 1894, p. 400; "The Spirit of the Vernacular Press during the Week," *The Japan Weekly Mail* (Yokohama),14 April 1894, pp. 426–8. See also issues of 朝日新聞 (*People's Newspaper*) (Tokyo) from March 30 through April 12, 1894.

[155] "A Sensational Political Murder in Shanghai," *The North-China Herald* (Shanghai), 30 March 1894, p. 488.

orders from the king.[156] The Chinese mission in Japan was also implicated in the assassination for complicity in luring Kim to China.[157]

Again the issue of "face" came into play. From the Japanese point of view, Kim had been a guest of Japan, yet the Chinese had not protected him. When he was murdered, the Chinese authorities had made no attempt to bring the assassin to justice but had returned him to a hero's welcome in Korea. The Chinese had returned the corpse too, knowing full well that the Koreans would dismember it, as was the custom in cases of treason. They had known that dismemberment would outrage Japanese sensibilities.[158] Actually, the Chinese had recommended that the Koreans not disfigure the corpse or reward the assassin, but the communication arrived too late to prevent the former, and the Korean government went ahead and gave the assassin a hefty reward along with a big house.[159] From the Japanese point of view, the Chinese had gone out of their way to insult the Japanese in every possible manner. From the Chinese point of view, Kim had committed high treason in the postal massacre and deserved his fate.

The Chinese reaction also reflected their deep-seated prejudices concerning the Japanese. Even in official communications, the Chinese routinely referred to them as dwarf pirates (倭寇). During the war a Chinese official expressed these widely held sentiments: "It took them 48,000 years before they made contact with China, while in 3,600 years they still have not accepted our celestial calendar...illegitimately assuming the reign title of Meiji (Enlightened Rule), they in reality abandon themselves all the more to debauchery and indolence. Falsely calling their new administration a 'reformation' they only defile themselves so much the more."[160] Captain William M. Lang, the British officer who had helped train the main Chinese fleet, the Beiyang Squadron, from 1881 until 1890, noted that the Chinese "treated Japan with the utmost contempt, and Japan, for her part,

---

[156] "The Spirit of the Vernacular Press during the Week," *The Japan Weekly Mail* (Yokohama), 7 April 1894, p. 398; "The Japanese Press on the Assassination Affair," *The Japan Weekly Mail* (Yokohama), 7 April 1894, p. 400; "The Spirit of the Vernacular Press during the Week," *The Japan Weekly Mail* (Yokohama), 5 May 1894, p. 523; "He Asserts He Acted under Instructions from the King of Corea," *The North-China Herald* (Shanghai), 30 March 1894, p. 490.

[157] Chow, 181–2.

[158] "The Korean Assassination Affair," *The Japan Weekly Mail* (Yokohama), 7 April 1894, pp. 400–1; Lensen, vol. 1, 115; Oh, "Background," 209.

[159] Lensen, vol. 1, 116.

[160] Cited in Samuel C. Chu, "China's Attitudes toward Japan at the Time of the Sino-Japanese War," in *The Chinese and Japanese: Essays in Political and Cultural Interactions,* Akira Iriye, ed. (Princeton: Princeton University Press, 1980), 74–5.

has the same feeling towards China."[161] A German reported that the Chinese looked upon "Japan as a traitor towards Asia."[162] Before the war, the Chinese considered the Japanese to be another inferior neighboring people below the status of a tributary since Japan no longer shared this intimacy with China. They were not a people to be taken seriously. As the war progressed the Chinese reacted by viewing the Japanese with contempt: subjects of ridicule included communal bathing, the attire of Japanese women, and their imitation of Western ways.[163]

The Japanese intensely resented such contemptuous attitudes. Kim's Japanese acquaintances established the Society of the Friends of Kim, which tried unsuccessfully to secure the return of the body while others supported military retaliation, founding the Society of Heavenly Salvation for the Oppressed.[164] On May 20 many Diet members attended the grand funeral held for him in Tokyo.[165]

While the Japanese public and the press were going wild over Kim's assassination, some very delicate negotiations between Britain and Japan were coming to a head. Japan had long requested that the powers renegotiate their "unequal" treaties with Japan but had made little progress over the years. The situation started to change in the 1890s. The forced resignation of Prince Otto von Bismarck in 1890 marked the end of the long-standing Russo-German alliance. This left Russia in diplomatic isolation to face the British Empire on the one hand and the Triple Alliance of Germany, Austria-Hungary, and Italy on the other. Russia resolved this through the Franco-Russian alliance that started to take shape in 1891 and reached its final form in January 1894. This, in turn, left Britain less secure in its "splendid isolation."[166] After the Russians announced in 1891 their intention to build the Trans-Siberian railway, the British suddenly became more receptive to Japanese demands for treaty revision.[167] Meanwhile, most of the Japanese government's domestic and legal reforms were in place, depriving the powers of any justification for the asymmetrical treaty system.

---

[161] "The Chinese Navy," *The Japan Weekly Mail* (Yokohama), 17 November 1894, p. 572; John King Fairbank, Katherine Frost Bruner, and Elizabeth MacLeod Matheson, eds., *The I. G. in Peking: Letters of Robert Hart Chinese Maritime Customs 1868–1907*, vol. 1 (Cambridge, MA: Harvard University Press, 1975), 797.

[162] Citing *Der Ostasiatische* in "Japan's Armies," *The North-China Herald* (Shanghai), 27 July 1894, p. 151; "The Fighting in Korea," *The Japan Weekly Mail* (Yokohama), 11 August 1894, p. 163.

[163] Chu, "China's Attitudes," 77–80.

[164] Young: 234, 238; "Kim's Friends," *The Japan Weekly Mail* (Yokohama), 28 April 1894, pp. 487, 489; "Obsequies of Kim Ok-kyŭn," *The Japan Weekly Mail* (Yokohama), 26 May 1894, p. 624.

[165] Oh, "Background," 212.

[166] Riasanovky, *History of Russia*, 399–400; Langer, 45–50.

[167] Kajima, *Emergence of Japan*, 37, 39–40.

The Japanese public and political parties long ago had run out of patience on the treaty revision issue. The Diet had protested its political impotence by embarrassing the government with criticisms concerning foreign policy. Political parties in the Diet had fanned the flames of public dissatisfaction. This actually constrained the government in the area of foreign policy, because it resulted in constant goading by the public for the Foreign Ministry to take more forceful measures. The newspapers demanded treaty revision. An editorial in June of 1893 complained that "the most progressive, developed, civilized, intelligent, and powerful nation in the Orient still cannot escape the scorn of white people."[168]

Foreign Minister Mutsu Munemitsu (陸奥宗光) responded to this growing public dissatisfaction with a more aggressive stance toward treaty revision. In April 1894, he told the British minister that the Japanese could not "go on maintaining indefinitely a system of relations with foreign Powers which they considered to be no longer compatible with the progress and changed institutions of the country."[169] Britain finally acquiesced in return for a commercial treaty.[170] On July 16, 1894, Japan and Britain signed a treaty ending extraterritoriality in five years and restoring tariff autonomy in seventeen years.[171] In return, at the end of the five-year period Japan would open the entire country to British trade, travel, and residence. British subjects would be able to lease but not buy land in Japan. Britain and Japan both pledged to protect the privileges, liberties, and immunities of the subjects of the other country in a completely reciprocal manner. Japan also promised to protect foreign patents and trademarks, something that still remained difficult for China over a century later. Similar treaties with the other powers followed in rapid succession.[172] *The Japan Weekly Mail* applauded Japan for assuming "an international position consistent with her modern progress."[173]

---

[168] Cited by Pyle, *New Generation*, 167.

[169] Cited by Pyle, *New Generation*, 171.

[170] Pyle, *New Generation*, 171–2.

[171] For a copy of the treaty see "Treaty of Commerce and Navigation between Japan and Great Britain," *The Japan Weekly Mail* (Yokohama), 1 September 1894, pp. 265–7, or "Treaty of Commerce and Navigation between Japan and Great Britain," *The North-China Herald* (Shanghai), 14 September 1894, Supplement, pp. i–iii. The treaty was signed in London on July 16, and ratifications were exchanged in Tokyo on August 15, 1894, Ibid. For attached notes, see "Diplomatic Notes Accompanying the New Treaty," *The Japan Weekly Mail* (Yokohama), 8 September 1894, p. 291.

[172] Iriye, "Japan's Drive to Great Power Status," 766; Akagi, 111–2; Tatsuji Takeuchi, *War and Diplomacy in the Japanese Empire* (Garden City, NY: Doubleday, Doran & Co., 1935), 105, 107; "The New Treaty between England and Japan," *The Japan Weekly Mail* (Yokohama), 1 September 1894, p. 262.

[173] "The New Treaty between England and Japan," *The Japan Weekly Mail* (Yokohama), 1 September 1894, p. 262.

With this the Japanese government had resolved one of its two outstanding foreign policy issues. The other issue was Korea.

For reasons exogenous to Korea, in the 1890s the Korean situation had become critical for Japanese policymakers. In 1891, Alexander III issued a special imperial rescript announcing his intention to build a trans-Siberian railway. From the Japanese point of view, this amounted to a foreign policy manifesto on the order of the Monroe Doctrine. Just as the American government had attempted to exclude other powers from the Americas, so, it seemed to the Japanese, the Russians intended to keep Japan off the Asian mainland. A year earlier, Premier Count Yamagata Aritomo (山県有朋) had warned that Russian possession of a trans-Siberian railway would pose a direct security threat to Japan via Korea.[174] As the founder of the modern Japanese army, Yamagata was an expert on such matters. The Japanese knew from experience that Russian domination of Korea would be exclusionary in nature. Since the Opium Wars, when the Russians had expanded eastward, they had rapidly transformed their new spheres of influence into an exclusionary zone where merchants from other nations were not welcome.[175] Sir Ernest Satow, the British minister to Tokyo and one of the most knowledgeable Western experts on the Far East, was to venture, "Whatever the ostensible reason for going to war with China may have been, there can be little doubt that the main object was to anticipate the completion of the Siberian Railway and to prevent Russia's gaining free access to the Pacific Ocean."[176] Indeed, in 1887 the Japanese General Staff obtained a secret memorandum by a lieutenant-general in the Russian General Staff recommending a four-stage Russian conquest of China.[177] Japanese concerns about Russian interference in Korean politics were evident from the 1873 debate over invading Korea onward. The threat did not actually materialize until after the failed *coup d'état* of 1884 with the activities of von Möllendorff and the Russian minister, Veber.[178] Japanese policymakers believed that the Trans-

---

[174] Marius B. Jansen, *Japan and China: from War to Peace 1894–1972* (Chicago: Rand McNally College Publishing Co., 1975), 113–4; Miwa, 25; Robert Britton Valliant, "Japan and the Trans-Siberian Railroad, 1885–1905" (Ph.D. diss., University of Hawaii, 1974), 49–50, 56, 61; Duus, 64–5.

[175] Paine, 69, 124, 135, 209.

[176] Cited in Ford, 78; Sidney Giffard, *Japan Among the Powers* (New Haven: Yale University Press, 1994), 17.

[177] Valliant, 61.

[178] Nish, *Japanese Foreign Policy*, 22, 24, 267–8; Akagi, 115, 116, 132–4; Djang, 160–1, 165; Henry Norman, *Contemporary Review*, republished as "The Question of Korea," *The Japan Weekly Mail* (Yokohama), 20 October 1894, p. 463. The Japanese were not the only ones to recognize a potential Russian threat to Korea. From the 1880s on, British and Chinese were also concerned. Chien, 57–60, 68; Giffard, 17.

Siberian Railway would permit Russia to take control of Korea. They believed that this would permanently deprive Japan of any hopes for empire and thereby of the great power status that they coveted. Once the Russian government had announced its intention to build the Trans-Siberian Railway, Japanese leaders knew that they had approximately one decade to resolve matters in Korea before the completion of the railway would irrevocably alter the balance of power in the Far East and preclude Japanese influence in Korea.[179]

In fact, this was a perfectly correct assessment of Russian intentions, as was made clear after the war by the Triple Intervention, when Russia joined with Germany and France to prevent Japanese occupation of the strategic Liaodong (Liao-tung) Peninsula in Manchuria and its ports of Dalian (Dairen) and Port Arthur (Lüshun). Throughout the war the Russian press would run stories stating that Russia would not tolerate a Japanese occupation of Korea or Port Arthur.[180] The Russian press also recognized that the construction of the Trans-Siberian Railway had been a key factor precipitating the hostilities. Afterward a reporter for the Moscow paper, *Moskovskie vedomosti,* wrote that "one of the reasons for this haste by the Japanese was the incomplete construction of the Great Siberian railway. It is absolutely clear that with its construction our interests on the Pacific Ocean will be protected not only by more or less significant land and sea forces, but likewise by the full power of the Russian people."[181] Key members of the Russian government shared this view.[182] The architect of the railway, Minister of Finance Count Sergei Iul'evich Witte, confirmed this interpretation. At a meeting of Russian ministers held on April 11, 1895, he suggested "that the war launched

---

[179] "Progress of the Great Siberian Railway," *The Peking and Tientsin Times,* 22 December 1894, p. 168; "The Siberian Railway," *The Japan Weekly Mail* (Yokohama), 19 January 1895, p. 59; G. V. Glinka, ed., *Азиатская Россия (Asiatic Russia),* vol. 2 (1914; reprint, Cambridge: Oriental Research Partners, 1974), 517. Once the war broke out, the Russians accelerated this schedule, planning to complete the entire line in 1901. Ibid. See also "The Great Siberian Railway," *Peking and Tientsin Times,* 15 September 1894, p. 111; "Men and Things in Russia," *The Pall Mall Gazette* (London), 7 December 1894, 4th ed., p. 2.

[180] "Японско-Китайская война и Россия "(The Sino-Japanese war and Russia), *Московские ведомости* (*Moscow Gazette*), no. 203, 27 July 1894 (8 August 1894), p. 2; "По поводу событий в Корее" (Regarding the events in Korea), *Новое время* (*New Times*), no. 6609, 5 August 1894, p. 2; "Корейский вопрос и Россия" (The Korean question and Russia), *Московские ведомости* (*Moscow Gazette*), no. 209, 2 August 1894 (14 August 1894), p. 3;"Война в Корее"(The war in Korea), *С.-Петербургские ведомости* (*St. Petersburg Gazette*), no. 272, 18 October 1894,p. 1; "Нынешняя политическая минута" (Current politics), *Новое время* (*New Times*), no. 6863, 21 April 1895, p. 1.

[181] "Великая Сибирская дорога" (The great Siberian railway), *Московские ведомости* (*Moscow Gazette*), no. 104, 17 April 1895 (29 April 1895), pp. 1–2.

[182] Malozemoff, 55–6, 64.

by Japan is the consequence of the construction of the Siberian Railway begun by us. All the European powers, and likewise even Japan, apparently, recognize that the partition of China will take place in the not distant future, and [they] see in the Siberian railway a significant improvement of our chances in the event of such a partition. The hostile actions of Japan are directed mainly against us."[183]

In 1891, three months after the imperial Russian rescript, a young Japanese vented these deep fears concerning Russia's Far Eastern ambitions. At the time, Tsarevich Nicholas Aleksandrovich was on a Far Eastern tour that had included a ceremony inaugurating the construction of the railway in the Far East. In Ōtsu (大津), a lakeside town near Kyoto, a Japanese youth slashed Tsarevich Nicholas's forehead in a failed assassination attempt. Japanese newspapers brimmed with stories about possible Russian retaliation.[184] The attack made an indelible impression on the future tsar of Russia; henceforth he referred to the Japanese as monkeys.[185] Meanwhile, by the spring of 1894 matters in Korea were coming to a head and the Japanese press was urging its government to take decisive measures.[186]

In 1894, on the eve of the war, Count Yamagata Aritomo, now minister of the army, told his interviewer: "Countries of the Occident have long been regarding China and Korea with a greedy eye. Thus far they have not attempted to satisfy their appetite for aggrandisement, simply because the present facilities of land and marine transport are insufficient for their purpose." He then referred to the Trans-Siberian Railway and France's expanding influence in Southeast Asia: "With increasing facilities of communication and transportation, dangers to the peace of the East will inevitably increase also. A general complication in this quarter of the globe is only a question of time. It is well said that to forestall others is to control them. Granted that complications are destined to arise in the Orient at no distant date, Japan's wisest plan is to take some decisive action before other Powers become provided with wings of mischief."[187]

---

[183] "Первые шаги русского империализма на Дальнем Востоке (1888–1903 гг.)" (The first steps of Russian imperialism in the Far East [1888–1903]), *Красный архив* (*Red Archive*) 52 (1932): 80.

[184] Pyle, *New Generation*, 163–4; Mutsu, 280*n*.13.

[185] Witte, 126–7.

[186] "The Spirit of the Vernacular Press during the Week," *The Japan Weekly Mail* (Yokohama), 9 June 1894, p. 682; "Korean Insurrection," *The Japan Weekly Mail* (Yokohama), 9 June 1894, p. 685; "The Spirit of the Vernacular Press during the Week," *The Japan Weekly Mail* (Yokohama), 23 June 1894, p. 746; "Korean Affairs," *The Japan Weekly Mail* (Yokohama), 30 June 1894, p. 782; "Counts Yamagata and Okuma on the Korean Question," *The Japan Weekly Mail* (Yokohama), 7 July 1894, p. 9; "Korean Affairs," *The Japan Weekly Mail* (Yokohama), 21 July 1894, p. 70.

[187] "Counts Yamagata and Okuma on the Korean Question," *The Japan Weekly Mail* (Yokohama), 7 July 1894, p. 9.

Yamagata Aritomo was one of the key figures in the Meiji Restoration. He had been the first prominent Japanese to travel abroad after the Restoration with the task of studying the Western military. His traveling companion, Saigō Tsugumichi (西郷従道), was to make a parallel study of their navies. They spent a year in Europe from 1869 to 1870. Immediately thereafter, the government entrusted Yamagata with the task of creating a modern national army based on nationwide conscription. In addition to his military service, he also served on the cabinet as minister of home affairs, during which time he modernized and standardized the country's police force. In 1888 he traveled to Europe again, this time to study local government and military developments. He subsequently served as prime minister.[188] At the time of the war he was the most powerful official in Japan with protégés placed throughout the military and government.[189]

There was some Western sympathy with the sentiments expressed by Yamagata Aritomo. Many British, in particular, were convinced that Korea's on-going domestic mismanagement was providing a tempting opportunity for Russian interference. According to *The Japan Weekly Mail*, "Korea has been an impossibility for the past thirteen years; a perpetual menace to the peace of the Far East. Japan is geographically forbidden to regard the fate of the peninsula with indifference. She cannot allow it to fall into the hands of a great and growing Power." The author added, "Emeute [French for riot] has followed emeute with wearisome iteration. Japan can not tamely endure such anarchy. Twice her Legation in Sŏul [Seoul] has been burned and twice her Representative has been obliged to flee for his life. Time and again the legitimate commerce of her subjects in the peninsula has been deliberately interrupted by official interference, the outcome of bribery and corruption. Diplomatic negotiation is virtually a farce."[190]

From the Chinese point of view, the construction of the Trans-Siberian Railway was even more threatening than it was for Japan: The railway would allow Russia to deploy troops along the Chinese border in areas where it would be very difficult for the Chinese to deploy their own troops because of the absence of a railway system anywhere near the frontier.[191] Worse still for the Chinese, Japanese modernization efforts were permitting Japan to pursue an increasingly aggressive

---

[188] Hackett, Roger F. *Yamagata Aritomo in the Rise of Modern Japan, 1838–1922* (Cambridge, MA: Harvard University Press, 1971), 1–2, 51–3, 58–60, 101–3, 115, 125.

[189] Stewart Lone, *Japan's First Modern War: Army and Society in the Conflict with China, 1894–95* (London: St. Martin's Press, 1994), 31.

[190] "The Korean Situation," *The Japan Weekly Mail* (Yokohama), 7 July 1894, p. 17.

[191] "A Chinese View of the Russian Trans-Siberian Railway," *The North-China Herald* (Shanghai), 12 January 1894, p. 60.

foreign policy, focusing ever more sharply on the Korean Peninsula. Chinese strategists had long considered Korea to be an essential buffer for Chinese defenses. With Russians moving in from the west and Japanese from the east, Viceroy Li may have felt that he had little choice but to take a more aggressive stance in Korea. China's two main security threats, Russia and Japan, were both zeroing in on Korea. How could China not but respond in kind?

Meanwhile, disaffected samurai and the Japanese general public were primed and eager to support the government in an aggressive policy in Korea.[192] The Japanese government had opened Korea and wished to help her modernize, yet the Chinese government had hindered Japan at every turn, condemning the Koreans to a life of poverty and thwarting Japan's growing ambitions. After the 1884 coup attempt, the influential writer and educator, Fukuzawa Yukichi (福沢諭吉), had already despaired of Japan's Asian neighbors independently becoming enlightened. He blamed their close-minded attitudes toward westernization. In 1885, Fukuzawa published his famous essay, "On Saying Good-bye to Asia," (「脱亜論」), in which he recommended to his countrymen: "We do not have time to wait for the enlightenment of our neighbors so that we can work together toward the development of Asia. It is better for us to leave the ranks of Asian nations and cast our lot with civilized nations of the West."[193] China, by its own domestic paralysis, had abdicated its leadership role in the Far East. Japan was ready to take up the torch and show benighted Asia the way to civilization. For years the Japanese had endured Chinese arrogance, insults, and highly visible domestic incompetence.

Many Japanese must have felt that it was high time to teach the Chinese a lesson. It was time for Japan to humble China. The confluence of events – treaty revision, the Trans-Siberian Railway, and military modernization – against a backdrop of hopeless decay in Korea and increasingly vocal public dissatisfaction in Japan were all so much tinder. The Japanese government merely awaited a pretext to light the fuse.

---

[192] "The Spirit of the Vernacular Press during the Week," *The Japan Weekly Mail* (Yokohama), 16 June 1894, p. 714. For similar opinions, see "The Spirit of the Vernacular Press during the Week," *The Japan Weekly Mail* (Yokohama), 30 June 1894, p. 774; "The Spirit of the Vernacular Press during the Week," *The Japan Weekly Mail* (Yokohama), 7 July 1894, p. 2.

[193] David J. Lu, ed., vol. 2, 353; Miwa, 1, 17, 22. Lu provides a complete English translation of the essay (Ibid., 251–3).

Part II

The War:
The Dividing Line Between Two Eras

We have hitherto been favoured with one Eastern question [the crumbling Ottoman Empire], which we have always endeavoured to lull as something too portentous for our imagination, but of late a Far Eastern question has been superadded, which, I confess, to my apprehension is, in the dim vistas of futurity, infinitely graver than even that question of which we have hitherto known.[1]

> Prime Minister Archibald Philip Primrose,
> 5th Earl of Roseberry, 1895

This at least I can tell you for certain, we neither can nor will leave Korea again until our aim has been attained in one way or another. We are fighting in Korea for our own future – I might also say for our independence. Once let Korea fall into the hands of a European power, and our independence will be threatened.[2]

> Japanese diplomat in Europe, July 25, 1894

---

[1] Cited in "England's Position before and after the War," *The Times* (London), 24 September 1895, p. 3. The first "Eastern question" refers to the disintegration of the Ottoman Empire and European competition for its spoils, while the "Far Eastern question" refers to the disintegration of China. In both cases, the respective countries were sometimes referred to as "the Sick Man of Asia."

[2] *Kölnischer Zeitung*, 25 July 1894, from its London correspondent, cited in *The Times* (London), 7 September 1895, cited in Morse, vol. 3, 29.

4

The Beginning of the End: The Outbreak of Hostilities

> The present war will, perhaps, go far to make the public of western countries understand that China and Japan are *not* different parts of the same country.[1]
>
> The Japan Weekly Mail, August 1894

> They [the Japanese] know that the eyes of the civilized world are upon them and do not neglect any means to make their *debût* [sic] – as an Asiatic power fighting on modern principles – as impressive and imposing as possible.[2]
>
> The Peking and Tientsin Times, March 1895

Before the onset of hostilities, the European and American press at home extended negligible coverage to the disintegrating situation in Korea. The notable exception was the Western press located in the Far East. Worthy of particular note were the British-owned weeklies: *The Japan Weekly Mail,* published in Yokohama, the sister city of Tokyo; *The North-China Herald and Supreme Court and Consular Gazette,*[3] published in Shanghai, the great commercial metropolis of China; and *The Peking and Tientsin Times,*[4] published in Tianjin, the official seat of Viceroy Li Hongzhang (李鴻章), who for many years served as China's quasi-foreign

---

[1] "Another Affront to Japan," *The Japan Weekly Mail* (Yokohama), 11 August 1894, p. 152.

[2] "The War. – The Situation," *The Peking and Tientsin Times,* 16 March 1895, p. 215.

[3] *The North-China Herald*, which began publication in 1870, was the weekly version of *The North-China Daily News,* which had begun publication in 1864. The latter seems to have survived only in part. As far as I know, the issues for the war period no longer exist. *The North-China Herald,* however, seems to have survived in its entirety, probably because it was the mail edition. Frank H. H. King and Prescott Clarke, eds., *A Research Guide to China-Coast Newspapers, 1822–1911* (Cambridge, MA: Harvard University Press, 1965), 28–9, 77, 87.

[4] *The Peking and Tientsin Times* only began publication in January of 1894 (King and Clark, 182).

minister. These papers were distinguished by their detailed and passionate coverage of Far Eastern events. There were many other Western papers published in Asia as well, but most have not survived or are difficult to obtain.

For Westerners then and today, the most accessible were *The North-China Herald* and *The Japan Weekly Mail*. The former provided perceptive coverage about China but presented a very limited understanding of Japan, while the latter provided excellent coverage of Japan due, in part, to its section entitled, "Vernacular Press." This abstracted key articles from numerous Japanese newspapers, some of which seem to have survived only in this form.

These British papers belonged to an era when Western journalists covering Asia had no qualms about ruthlessly criticizing Asian countries or about prescribing home remedies for their ills. The era preceded the two world wars of the twentieth century that would cause self-doubt to creep into the Western psyche. In the final decade of the nineteenth century, European confidence in the superiority of Western civilization and belief in their inescapable civilizing mission were at their zenith. A want of tact and overly exuberant self-assurance among European and American journalists do not negate the underlying perspicacity of many of their observations about the China and Japan that they saw with their own eyes and where some of them had lived for many years. The often sharp criticism by the foreign press in Asia did not generally emanate from hostility toward Asia or Asians but rather from a desire to see the peoples of Asia prosper.[5] Many Western missionaries devoted their lives to this cause, particularly in China, by living there for years, primarily engaged in what today would be called social work: spreading knowledge of public health, providing medical care, caring for foundlings, opening Western schools, and so on. Some gave their lives doing so. Friction arose when Eastern and Western recipes for prosperity did not jibe. More fundamentally, it arose from the different ways in which easterners and westerners perceived the world and their rightful places in it.

When the war broke out, the Western press in Europe and the United States scrambled to learn something about the enigmatic East but lacked correspondents in Asia. The British papers based in China and Japan were their logical starting point. The foreign press in the Far East had a high enough reputation that, in the case of *The North-China Herald,* Chinese officials, including Viceroy Li, had it translated for their perusal. There was some doubt among the newspaper staff about the accuracy of these translations, but the fact that the Chinese leaders went to

---

[5] "The Peking and Tientsin Times," *The Peking and Tientsin Times,* 9 March 1895, p. 209.

these lengths suggests the value of the reporting.[6] In general, the British and, to a lesser extent, the American press provided the best coverage because they had many more independent sources of information than other countries, due to their larger missionary and commercial presence in China and Japan. Only the British press and especially the British press in Asia followed domestic Chinese and Japanese events in any detail. Given the British domination of the Chinese Imperial Customs Service, the British had many more official Chinese contacts than did the other Western nationals. The French, German, and Russian press focused almost exclusively on the implications of the war for Europe.[7]

The following account is based on the reporting of the British press in Asia and on the columns of some of the leading papers of Great Britain, the United States, Russia, Germany, France, Japan, and China. The story is one of rapidly changing European and American perceptions of China and Japan. It is the story of a rising power, Japan, using the strategy of war to secure its policy objective of becoming an internationally recognized power. That is, Japan would use victory in war to alter the perceptions of the other powers in order to insert itself into the upper level of the international pecking order. The common view in our own time – that of Japan as an exemplary Eastern power – came into being as a result of this war. This is the story of the reversal of the roles of China and Japan in the Far East. For the first time in history, Japan became the ascendant power in the East, where it has remained to the present day. In contrast, China as the traditionally dominant power in the Far East was a status quo power. The Confucian international order put China at the summit of human achievement, so the Chinese government had no conceivable interest in upsetting this order; rather, it acted only when compelled to respond to Japanese initiatives. This is also a story told, as far as possible, in the words of those who were alive at the time, for it is their story – what they saw and what they thought about it.

* * *

For the Japanese government to succeed in its plans, it needed a pretext to go to war in Korea. This would be provided by the deteriorating internal situation there. It would modify Kipling's idea of the "white man's burden" to create a civilizing mission for itself in Korea. This would become the moral justification to legitimize its actions. A headline from *Kokumin shinbun* encapsulated this idea by describing Japanese–Korean relations as "Teacher–Student Relations."[8] In 1894, the first

---

[6] King, 80.

[7] For more information about the press coverage of the war, see the Bibliographic Essay.

[8] "我邦と朝鮮とは師弟の關係あり" (Our country and Korea have teacher–student relations), 國

mention of Korea in *The Japan Weekly Mail* did not appear until January 27, in an article about the Korean rice embargo on Japan. The paper's Seoul correspondent took the opportunity to expound his views concerning the Korean situation: "If 'nothing succeeds like success,' then Korea has illustrated in the past ten years of intercourse with western nations that nothing is more conducive to failure than failures. They have failed in everything, from the time of the match factory (which made matches, 'mitout heads') was built, down to the present."[9] Western papers paid scant attention to Korea until the assassination of Kim Ok-kyun (金玉均) on March 28, 1894. Although most of the domestic European and American press did not cover this story, the Japanese press pounced on it.[10] Just as the furor over the assassination was dying down in Japan, a new Korean story started receiving media coverage.[11] This was the Tonghak (東學) or "Eastern Learning" Rebellion of 1894, the largest peasant rebellion in Korean history.[12]

The Tonghak movement had begun in 1860 as a new religion, emphasizing salvation and providing its own rituals to achieve this. It juxtaposed itself to Roman Catholicism or Western learning and had many parallels with the Taipings of China. Like the Taipings, it was both greatly influenced by Christianity but also intensely hostile to it. Both movements constituted an anti-foreign reaction to shut out the winds of change blowing from the West. The peasantry of southern Korea found the Tonghak doctrine particularly appealing. Although the government executed the founder in 1866, the movement continued underground. By 1892 and 1893 followers held mass rallies protesting government attempts to suppress the movement. The hue and cry was for the expulsion of the foreigners and the punishment of corrupt officials, but the goals were essentially conservative: the improvement, not the overthrow, of dynastic institutions.[13]

The Tonghak Rebellion followed a series of lesser rebellions against excessive taxation by local government officials. There had been revolts in 1885, 1888,

---

民新聞 (*People's Newspaper*) (Tokyo), 29 June 1894, p. 2. See also "國際法上清國に對する日本の地位." (Japan's status under international law *vis-à-vis* China), 國民新聞 (*People's Newspaper*) (Tokyo), 24 July 1894, p. 4.

[9] "Korean News," *The Japan Weekly Mail* (Yokohama), 27 January 1894, p. 118.

[10] See citations in the previous chapter for the reaction of the Japanese press to the assassination of Kim Ok-kyun.

[11] "Korean Affairs," *The Japan Weekly Mail* (Yokohama), 28 April 1894, p. 495; "Insurrection in Korea," *The Japan Weekly Mail* (Yokohama), 26 May 1894, p. 624; "Insurrection in Korea," *The Japan Weekly Mail* (Yokohama), 2 June 1894, p. 635; "The Korean Disturbance and the Japanese Government," *The Japan Weekly Mail* (Yokohama), 9 June 1894, pp. 688–9.

[12] Eckert et al., 221; Lew, "Kabo Reform," 1.

[13] Kim and Kim, 75–6; Lensen, vol. 1, 122; Lew, "Kabo Reform," 51, 73, 90–3.

1889, 1890, 1891, 1892, and 1893.[14] In February 1894, the unrest bubbled up again and spread rapidly. By late April of 1894, the long-suffering Korean peasantry once more rose up in open rebellion against oppressive taxation and incompetent financial administration. While the British press in Asia immediately recognized the importance of the rebellion, the European and American press at home only mentioned the spreading unrest in occasional single-paragraph stories.

Here is the story not covered in the West: Rumors reached the Tonghaks that China and Japan were on the verge of sending troops. On June 1, 1894, the rebels agreed to a cease-fire in order to remove any grounds for foreign intervention.[15] On June 2, the Japanese cabinet decided to send troops to Korea should China do so and also to muzzle the political opposition by having the emperor dissolve the Lower Chamber of the Diet.[16] On June 3, the Korean king, on the recommendation of the Min (閔) clan and at the insistence of Li Hongzhang's proconsul in Korea, Yuan Shikai (袁世凱), requested that China send troops to help suppress the rebellion. In doing so, he unwittingly handed the Japanese military leaders the pretext they had long desired to intervene massively in the Korean Peninsula. The Mins may have believed that they had little choice. The Tonghaks considered them the source of much government corruption, and the rebels were rumored to be in contact with Grand Prince Hûngsôn (興宣大院君).[17]

Within days, Japan was on a military footing. On June 5, the first Imperial Headquarters (大本営) was established.[18] On June 6, the ministries of the army and the navy issued instructions to the press not to print any information concerning warlike operations. Many papers ignored the order and were promptly suspended for a day.[19] China, after notifying Japan on June 7, according to the stipulations of the Treaty of Tianjin, sent 2,000 troops to Nanyang (南陽), located on the coast

[14] Lew, "Kabo Reform," 17.

[15] Oh, "Background," 366–7, 305, 325; Ro, 25–6; Conroy, 267–83.

[16] Hackett, 160; Mutsu, 287. For an English translation of this memorial, see "The Cabinet's Memorial to the Throne about the Dissolution of the House of Representatives" *The Japan Weekly Mail* (Yokohama), 9 June 1894, p. 691.

[17] "The Troubles in Korea," *The North-China Herald* (Shanghai), 22 June 1894, p. 985; Mutsu Munemitsu, *Kenkenryoku: A Diplomatic Record of the Sino-Japanese War, 1894–95*, Gordon Mark Berger, trans. (Princeton: Princeton University Press, 1982), 287; Vladimir, 44; Oh, "Background," 268–78; Jansen, et al., 222; Ko Seok-kyu, "Activities of the Peasant Army During the Chipkangso Period," *Korea Journal* 34, no. 4 (winter 1994): 40.

[18] Young: 249.

[19] "The Newspapers and the Korean Affair," *The Japan Weekly Mail* (Yokohama), 9 June 1894, pp. 684–5; "Suspensions," *The Japan Weekly Mail* (Yokohama), 9 June 1894, p. 685; "The Vernacular Press and Its Troubles," *The Japan Weekly Mail* (Yokohama), 16 June 1894, p. 717.

between Seoul and Asan (牙山).[20] Within hours of receiving this notice, Japan gave its own notice to China and also sent troops.[21] *Asahi shinbun* also reported that Russia had sent troops and deployed naval warships to Korea, although the Western press never mentioned these reports.[22] Editors at the paper hoped that the Western powers would compare Japanese to Chinese troops and take note of the extent of Japan's modernization programs.[23] Within days over 2,000 Japanese troops had landed and marched on to Seoul despite the Korean request that Japan refrain from sending troops. It was too late; the troops were on the way. The rapidity of the Japanese response indicated that preparations in Japan had been going on for some time. Yet, according to the 1885 Treaty of Tianjin, the end of the rebellion meant that China and Japan no longer had any grounds to send troops and should have withdrawn any fresh deployments.[24] The Japanese government claimed the troops were necessary to protect its embassy, consulates, and nationals.[25]

A month before the hostilities broke out, the Japanese press was full of articles concerning the Japanese and Chinese war preparations.[26] By mid-June the harbor of Inchôn (仁川),[27] the port city for Seoul, looked like the site of an international naval show. At anchor on June 13 were nine Japanese men-of-war and transports, along with four Chinese men-of-war and one war vessel each from Russia, Great Britain, the United States, and France. On June 15, eight more Japanese transports arrived and 6,000 fully equipped troops disembarked.[28] By mid-June, ten Japanese

---

[20] "The Troubles in Korea," *The North-China Herald* (Shanghai), 22 June 1894, p. 985; U.S. Adjutant-General's Office, Military Information Division, *Notes on the War between China and Japan* (Washington: Government Printing Office, 1896), 9; "清國より出兵の知照" (Reports that troops sent from China), 朝日新聞 (*Rising Sun Newspaper*) (Tokyo), 8 June 1894, p. 1.

[21] Mutsu, 14–15, 287; Lensen, vol. 1, 126–7.

[22] "露兵朝鮮に入る" (Russian troops enter Korea), 朝日新聞 (*Rising Sun Newspaper*) (Tokyo), 8 June 1894, p. 1; "露兵のに入韓に就て" (Concerning the Entry of Russian Troops in Korea), 朝日新聞 (*Rising Sun Newspaper*) (Tokyo), 9 June 1894, p. 1; "露國艦隊朝鮮に向て" (Russian Fleet Approaching Korea), 朝日新聞 (*Rising Sun Newspaper*) (Tokyo), 13 June 1894, p. 1.

[23] "日清兩國兵の出兵" (Troop Deployments by Both Japan and China), 朝日新聞 (*Rising Sun Newspaper*) (Tokyo), 10 June 1894, p. 1.

[24] Oh, "Background," 366–7, 305, 325; Ro, 25–6; Conroy, 267–83; Grimm, 91.

[25] "出兵の目的" (Reason for sending troops), 朝日新聞 (*Rising Sun Newspaper*) (Tokyo), 14 June 1894, p. 1.

[26] "Imperial Ordinance," *The Japan Weekly Mail* (Yokohama), 7 July 1894, p. 8.

[27] Other spellings include Jinsen and Inch'ôn. The old name was Chemulp'o (濟物浦).

[28] "The Troubles in Korea," *The North-China Herald* (Shanghai), 22 June 1894, p. 985. Foreign Minister Mutsu Munemitsu wrote that 7,000 troops were encamped between Seoul and Chinchôn (Mutsu, 19).

warships were patrolling the Korean waters[29] and on June 18 the Ministry of the Navy issued new Naval Fleet Regulations.[30] At about this time, Yuan Shikai decided it was time to leave. On June 27, he requested Viceroy Li for permission to return to China, but Li delayed for twenty days before granting it.[31] Finally, on July 19, Yuan Shikai fled Seoul disguised as a Chinese servant of the Russian military attaché who was on his way to Peking.[32] Apparently, Russian diplomats were in the thick of things.

In June, the Korea question dominated Japanese newspapers to such an extent that, according to *The Japan Weekly Mail,* "It is apparent that the restless energies of the people yearn for employment in a foreign war."[33] A week later it reported, "The Tokyo journals unite in urging upon the Government the importance of utilizing the present opportunity for wiping away the stain left on the national honour by the fatal error of 1884."[34] At that time, the failed pro-Japanese coup had obliterated Japanese influence in Korea and left China ascendant. It was now time for Japan to regain the "face" then lost to China. Count Ōkuma Shigenobu (大隈 重信), the leader of the *Rikken Kaishinto* (立憲改新党) or Constitutional Reform Party, also a former cabinet member intimately involved in securing treaty revision for Japan and a key rival of Itō Hirobumi (伊藤博文), argued that "It was Japan that first opened the Hermit Kingdom to the beneficent influence of modern civilization, and Japan also introduced Korea to the world as an independent State." Therefore, it was Japan's "duty to lead the little Kingdom along the path of civilization and help it to grow in prosperity and power. Thus Japan's duty is to suffer no other Power to retard the progress or endanger the independence of Korea."[35] In other words, it was time to oust China. Here, in a nutshell, was

---

[29] "Summary of News," *The Japan Weekly Mail* (Yokohama), 16 June 1894, p. 713. Other boats soon followed. "Korean Affairs," *The Japan Weekly Mail* (Yokohama), 7 July 1894, p. 12.

[30] For an English translation of the regulations, see "Fleet Regulations," *The Japan Weekly Mail* (Yokohama), 23 June 1894, p. 760.

[31] Oh, "Background," 349–50.

[32] Lensen, vol. 1, 140.

[33] "The Spirit of the Vernacular Press during the Week," *The Japan Weekly Mail* (Yokohama), 16 June 1894, p. 714. For similar opinions, see "The Spirit of the Vernacular Press during the Week," *The Japan Weekly Mail* (Yokohama), 30 June 1894, p. 774; "The Spirit of the Vernacular Press during the Week," *The Japan Weekly Mail* (Yokohama), 7 July 1894, p. 2.

[34] "The Spirit of the Vernacular Press during the Week," *The Japan Weekly Mail* (Yokohama), 23 June 1894, p. 746.

[35] Cited and translated in "Count Okuma on the Korean Question," *The Japan Weekly Mail* (Yokohama), 16 June 1894, p. 721. The original article appeared in *Hōchi Shinbun.* (報知新聞). For similar attitudes regarding Japan's civilizing mission in Asia, see "The Spirit of the Vernacular Press during the Week," *The Japan Weekly Mail* (Yokohama), 30 June 1894, p. 774; "The Japanese Government

Japan's growing sense of its special civilizing mission in Asia. Japan would bring its understanding of modernity to the East: westernized political, legal, financial, and educational institutions and a modern industrial and infrastructural base. This sense of mission would form the moral basis for Japan's territorial expansion in the first half of the twentieth century.

War preparations continued apace. In the last week of June, public petitions from Japan's prefectures requested permission to raise troops.[36] In early July, an imperial ordinance established extraordinary powers to regulate the sale of goods with military applications.[37] By the third week of July, the Korean question so engrossed the Japanese press that "scarcely any other subject" was being discussed. Based on the Japanese press, *The Japan Weekly Mail* predicted: "It now looks as though war is inevitable."[38] A week later they noted that the Japanese newspapers "write as though war has already commenced."[39]

Initially China sent 2,000–3,000 troops while Japan sent 5,000–8,000 troops (or over twice as many).[40] Compared to the huge discrepancies in troop and casualty estimates that came later, the ranges for these figures indicate general agreement on the size of the forces initially deployed in Korea. In the beginning, journalists must have staked themselves out at the ports and counted the incoming troop transports. But as soon as the fighting started, forces from both sides began pouring into Korea, making the counting game much more difficult. Once the Japanese took control over Korea, which happened almost immediately, they must have removed journalists from the port areas. In any case, with the outbreak of hostilities, the estimates suddenly varied widely from article to article even within the same newspaper, let alone among newspapers. As the most famous European military strategist of the nineteenth century, Carl von Clausewitz, has written, "Casualty reports on either side are never accurate, seldom truthful, and in most

and the Korean Question," *The Japan Weekly Mail* (Yokohama), 7 July 1894, p. 10; Lone, 42. For biographical information on Ōkuma, see "The Kaishinto," *The North-China Herald* (Shanghai), 31 May 1895, p. 818; "Ōkuma Shigenobu," Embree, vol. 3, 151–2; "Ōkuma Shigenobu," *Kodansha Encyclopedia of Japan,* vol. 6, 95–6.

[36] "Summary of News," *The Japan Weekly Mail* (Yokohama), 30 June 1894, p. 773.

[37] "Imperial Ordinance," *The Japan Weekly Mail* (Yokohama), 7 July 1894, p. 8.

[38] "The Spirit of the Vernacular Press," *The Japan Weekly Mail* (Yokohama), 21 July 1894, p. 62.

[39] "The Spirit of the Vernacular Press," *The Japan Weekly Mail* (Yokohama), 28 July 1894, p. 90.

[40] In the first week of June, Viceroy Li sent 3,000 troops whereas Japan was reported to have sent 5,000 troops. "The Korean Insurrection," *The Japan Weekly Mail* (Yokohama), 9 June 1894, p. 685; "The Cost of the Korean Trouble," *The Japan Weekly Mail* (Yokohama), 16 June 1894, p. 719; "Korean Affairs," *The Japan Weekly Mail* (Yokohama), 16 June 1894, p. 725. Foreign Minister Mutsu stated in his memoirs that Japan sent 7,000 troops. Mutsu, 19. The U.S. military estimated that the Japanese had deployed 8,000 troops (U.S. Adjutant-General's Office, 9).

cases deliberately falsified."[41] A century later there is no way to determine the reliability of the many casualty figures circulating during the war.

It is doubtful that accurate statistics were ever available for Chinese losses. The Chinese government lacked precise information concerning the size of its own forces when still alive, let alone when dead. This was because its armies were provincial, not national, and because Chinese commanders were notorious for padding their rolls to enrich themselves with the extra ration allowances.[42] Since China's was an army in retreat, there would have been little time or desire to compile accurate casualty figures. While the Japanese government probably knew exactly how many troops it had in the field, there is no reason to believe that it would have made the actual figures public or that the Japanese military would publish accurate casualty figures. For reasons of national security and domestic tranquility, neither side was interested in revealing information about its troop strength or losses. Therefore, in the following narrative there has been minimal attention to the number of troops and casualties. Let the uninterrupted sequence of Japanese victories and steady advance of the Japanese army through China suffice to establish which country suffered the brunt of the losses.

After the initial troop deployments, Viceroy Li made no further war preparations nor did he attempt to match Japanese troop deployments in Korea. His strategy remained to avoid hostilities with Japan. He hoped to keep up the pretence of China's guardianship role in Korea by sending some troops but to avoid sending enough to give Japan a *casus belli*. The main thrust of his strategy throughout the war was to secure European intervention to rein in the Japanese. As commander of China's most modern military forces and as stepfather to China's recent ambassador to Japan, he, better than anyone else, must have known that his soldiers were no match for the Imperial Japanese Army. Although he worked feverishly behind the scenes to secure the mediation of the European powers, he overestimated their willingness to intervene and underestimated their disgust with Chinese political institutions.[43] Sir Robert Hart, the British subject who served as the inspector general of the Imperial Maritime Customs from 1863 to 1908 and in so doing became the foreigner with the closest contacts at the Manchu Court, commented in

[41] Carl von Clausewitz, *On War*, Michael Howard and Peter Paret, eds. and trans. (Princeton: Princeton University Press, 1976), 234.

[42] For information concerning the padding of Chinese military payrolls, see "Foreigners and the War," *The North-China Herald* (Shanghai), 24 August 1894, p. 293; Powell, 17.

[43] Oh, "Background," 326–7, 410; Robert K. Douglas, *Li Hungchang* (New York: Frederick Warne, 1895?), 206; Alexander Michie, *The Englishman in China during the Victorian Era*, vol. 2 (Edinburg: William Blackwood and Sons, 1900), 408.

mid-July of 1894 that the "Yamen [the Chinese foreign office] is calculating with too much confidence on foreign intervention."[44] Li also seems to have misread the domestic political situation in Japan. Many of the Chinese officials who were aware of the constant feuding between the Diet and the cabinet seem to have concluded that these political divisions would prevent Japan from launching an effective military campaign.[45] Perhaps these Chinese were reading China's own political problems into the Japanese domestic situation. Whereas the Manchu–Han division did impede Chinese foreign policy, the Japanese shared a national identity and an evolving foreign policy mission, both of which distinguished Japan from China and served to mend Japanese political divisions once the war broke out.

Li first sought the intercession of Russia in June, but this came to naught. Britain then made a more concerted effort prior to the outbreak of war. The Italians also gave mediation an unsuccessful shot. Finally, King Kojong (高宗) requested American help, but the United States had an isolationist foreign policy.[46] None of the powers was willing to go beyond negotiation to put significant pressure on the belligerents. The foreign community had complained for years about official corruption in China. Time and again they had urged China to reform. From their perspective, this well-meant and wise advice had fallen on deaf ears. Many foreigners concluded that the current predicament served China right. Indeed, it seemed as if some derived a certain amount of satisfaction from the unfolding spectacle.[47] According to *The North-China Herald,* "the majority of the foreign residents in China...generally think that it would be a very good thing for everybody if China, at the beginning of the war at any rate, were seriously defeated by her confident little antagonist."[48] Perhaps in war the Japanese would teach the Chinese the salutary lesson that the Europeans had been unable to communicate in peace.

When the foreign press first reported that 6,000 Japanese troops had landed on Korean soil, such a large deployment baffled them. It far exceeded the number needed to insure the safety of Japanese nationals in Korea. To the editors of *The North-China Herald,* it seemed "a very expensive demonstration" given the high price the Japanese government had been willing to pay to secure the necessary transport and coal and given the disruption in trade likely to result from the

---

[44] Hart to Campbell, 15 July 1894, in Fairbank et al., *The I. G. in Peking,* vol. 2, 976. For biographical information on Hart, see O'Neill, 113–4.

[45] Douglas, 238.

[46] Oh, "Background," 444–75, 484–5.

[47] See foreign opinions cited in Chapter 1.

[48] "The Situation," *The North-China Herald* (Shanghai), 13 July 1894, pp. 51–2. For a similar view see Hart to Campbell, 26 August 1894, in Fairbank et al., *The I. G. in Peking,* 984.

government's attempt to block coal exports from Japan.[49] In an interview, Count Ōkuma Shigenobu agreed that the size of the Japanese forces sent to Korea far exceeded the small contingent necessary to protect Japanese residents. He elaborated, "By making judicious use of the present unique opportunity, it will be possible...for the Japanese Government to retrieve all past errors and make the Empire respected and feared not only by Korea but also by the rest of the world."[50] After a quarter-century of domestic reforms to make Japan strong, many Japanese felt that it was time for their country to make its debut on the international stage.

The North-China Herald editorialized: "If Japan is not deliberately provoking a war with China, it is difficult to know what her aggression on Corea means. She is rapidly increasing her military and naval forces there, on the pretext – the only one we have seen put forward – that her residents in Corea require protection, though no one is menacing them." The article concluded, Japan "drives China into a war."[51] Although this newspaper sympathized with the Chinese throughout the war and consistently (and quite correctly) argued that Japan had been the aggressor, it remained highly critical of the Chinese leadership. "[T]here can be little question that it would be much better for the Coreans if their country came under Japanese control. China does nothing to mitigate the intolerable misgovernment and oppression under which, as every traveller and writer tells us, the whole country groans and travails; Japan is willing and eager to introduce reforms."[52]

On June 16 the Japanese government invited the Chinese government jointly to sponsor a reform program for Korea. The goal would be to improve Korean administration, finances, and policing.[53] On June 21, the Chinese government turned down the offer, saying that "the idea may be excellent, but the measures of improvement must be left to Korea herself. Even China herself would not interfere with the internal administration of Korea, and Japan, having from the very first recognized the independence of Korea, cannot have the right to interfere with the same."[54] The Japanese government responded that it did not intend to withdraw

---

[49] "China, Corea, and Japan," *The North-China Herald* (Shanghai), 22 June 1894, pp. 966–7. For similar reports, see "The Troubles in Korea," *The North-China Herald* (Shanghai), 29 June 1894, p. 1030; Mutsu, 19.

[50] "Count Okuma on the Korean Question," *The Japan Weekly Mail* (Yokohama), 16 June 1894, p. 721.

[51] "Japan's Attack on Corea," *The North-China Herald* (Shanghai), 29 June 1894, p. 1008.

[52] "China, Japan, and Corea," *The North-China Herald* (Shanghai), 29 June 1894, p. 1010. For a similar opinion, see "Japan's Intentions," *The North-China Herald* (Shanghai), 6 July 1894, p. 10.

[53] For translations of the correspondence, see Vladimir, 228–31; Mutsu, 22–4.

[54] Vladimir, 229; Mutsu, 24.

from Korea until a reform program had been implemented.[55] Viceroy Li responded, "On the approach of the Chinese forces the insurgents [Tonghaks] dispersed. China now desires to withdraw, but Japan refuses to evacuate simultaneously with China, and proposes a joint occupation, the administration of Korean finances, and the introduction of reforms. These are tasks which China cannot accept."[56] After the war, Foreign Minister Mutsu Munemitsu (陸奥宗光) described Japan's rationale: Endemic instability in Korea had led high officials in the Japanese government to conclude that "Korea lacked some of the elements most necessary for her to fulfill her responsibilities as an independent state...Japan's many interests in Korea were too important and far-reaching to allow us to ignore the deplorable conditions there without standing accused of betraying both our sentiments of good neighborliness and our own security."[57] In other words, Korean independence from China would no longer satisfy Japanese security requirements. For reasons of national security, the Japanese government intended to reform Korean administration whether the natives (or anyone else) liked it or not.

As the Japanese poured troops into Korea, their diplomats put relentless pressure on King Kojong to implement a far-reaching reform program to bring his country more in line with European norms concerning penal codes and governmental administration. The Korean government tried unsuccessfully to convince the Japanese to withdraw their troops before implementing any reforms.[58] The Japanese, however, were not about to abandon their main source of leverage. They were in no mood for another diplomatic dance with the Koreans. According to Mutsu, the cabinet decided to "seize control of the King's person" in order to "oblige the Korean government to comply" with Japanese demands.[59] On July 22, the Japanese government realized that Li Hongzhang had finally overcome domestic opposition in China to sending large reinforcements to Korea. By this time, his original policy of conflict avoidance was being superseded by a conflicting imperative to keep up Chinese pretences of overlordship in Korea in order to help maintain the legitimacy of the Manchu Dynasty in China. As a result of the delay, these reinforcements would not arrive in time for the first two battles.[60] Unlike the Meiji

---

[55] For translations of the correspondence, see Vladimir, 228–31.

[56] "The Situation in Korea," *The Times* (London), 27 June 1894, p. 5; "The Rising in Korea," *The Times* (London), 28 June 1894, p. 5.

[57] Mutsu, 26.

[58] "Japan Defied by Corea," *The New York Times*, 23 July 1894, p. 5; "公使要求の箇條て" (List of demands made by minister), 朝日新聞 (*Rising Sun Newspaper*) (Tokyo), 24 July 1894, p. 1.

[59] Mutsu, 81–3.

[60] Mutsu, 64.

reformers, who had carefully minimized foreign entanglements until after the completion of the domestic reform program, both the Empress Dowager and the self-strengtheners such as Viceroy Li lacked the power either to conduct a national reform program or to contain their country's foreign policy extremists. Instead, the Japanese government easily baited China into hostilities.

Early the next morning, on July 23, Japanese troops stormed the Korean royal palace in Seoul and took the king captive. *The New York Times* reported, "The Japanese have announced that they will hold the King of Corea as a hostage until the internal reforms demanded by Japan shall have been satisfactorily guaranteed."[61] Apparently, the Japanese did not care that such interference with the person of the king would guarantee a bountiful harvest of Korean hostility.[62] It is no coincidence that the Tonghak Rebellion soon flared up again and rapidly gained momentum, transforming itself from a regional into a national uprising.[63] Japanese brutality in suppressing the rebellion only fueled Korean hostility toward them.[64] Moreover, kidnapping the Korean sovereign provided an undeniable *casus belli* for the Chinese. Either China would rise to the challenge or give up its suzerainty over Korea – either way, the Japanese government got what it wanted.

On the afternoon of July 23, the same day they occupied the royal palace, Japanese troops disarmed the Korean garrisons in Seoul. This put Japan in possession of the capital. For lack of a better alternative, the Japanese recalled the bitterly anti-foreign but domestically very popular Grand Prince Hûngsôn for the most unlikely role. He was to oversee a far-reaching Japanese reform program. For lack of a better route back to power, he accepted on the condition that Japan refrain from any territorial annexation in Korea. That day the Grand Prince and the king had an emotional meeting in the royal palace; they had not seen each other for a decade. The father scolded the son for misrule, the son apologized and requested the father again become regent. After the father agreed, he immediately banished members of the Min clan to various remote islands. The new government then renounced its three treaties with China, severing its last tributary ties.[65]

---

[61] "Corean King Is a Captive," *The New York Times*, 28 July 1894, p. 5.

[62] Japan, Imperial General Staff, *History of the War between Japan and China*, vol. 1, Major Jikemura and Arthur Lloyd, trans. (Tokyo: Kinkodo Publishing Co., 1904), 60, 63.

[63] Suh Young-hee, "Tracing the Course of the Peasant War of 1894," *Korea Journal* 34, no. 4 (Winter 1994): 17–30.

[64] Synn, 128; Cho Jae-gon, "The Connection of the Sino-Japanese War and the Peasant War of 1894," *Korea Journal* 34, no. 4 (Winter 1994): 46.

[65] "Korea," *The Japan Weekly Mail* (Yokohama), 11 August 1894, p. 159; Eckert et al., 223; Conroy, 304; Oh, "Background," 384–5.

After the war began, the Japanese immediately imposed a detailed reform program on Korea. This became known as the Kabo Reform (甲午更張) movement, which lasted from July 1894 until February 1896. The goal was to create an efficient and honest government administration. Nepotism, sinecures, and redundant posts were to be eliminated; posts were to have fixed responsibilities and salaries; a national budget was to be established; the tax structure, the military, the judiciary, and the educational system were all to be reformed; and the country's infrastructure was to be modernized.[66] The most significant reform measure was the end of the monopoly on public offices held by the *yangban* (兩班) or aristocracy and the end of the Chinese-style examination system. In one stroke the Japanese undermined the basis of power for the Korean elite.[67] The inspector general of Chinese customs, Sir Robert Hart, commented on how the Japanese were "ramming independence and reforms down the King's throat in a really masterful way." He noted that the Western powers were "*against* Japan's method but with her aims."[68] In addition to accepting these reforms, the Koreans were expected to send a special envoy to Japan to "express Korea's thanks."[69] This was another entracte of "face," whereby the inferior, Korea, "gave face" to the superior, Japan, by sending a mission to kowtow at the court of the superior.

The Koreans bristled and dragged their feet at every opportunity. Whereas Japanese relations with Chinese civilians were generally quite good throughout the war, their relations with Korean civilians, whose interests they had come allegedly to defend, were generally hostile. In contrast to the Chinese territories occupied by Japan later in the war, where the Japanese minimized their interference with local customs, laws, and religious practices, they sought to reform these sensitive areas of Korean life. In addition, the Japanese wartime tax moratorium for the Manchurians must have been popular.[70] The Japanese did not consider themselves to be at war with the Chinese people but with the dynasty; therefore, the term for this war in Japanese was 日清戦争 or the Japanese-Qing War, whereas the name in Chinese was 中日戰爭 or the Sino-Japanese War.[71]

---

[66] For an English translation of the reform proposal, see "Japan's Proposals to Corea," *The North-China Herald* (Shanghai), 3 August 1894, pp. 179–80; or Vladimir, Appendix A, 223–4; or Kajima, *Diplomacy of Japan*, vol. 1, 123–4. See also Eckert et al., 224.

[67] Kim and Kim, 82.

[68] Hart to Campbell, 15 July 1894, in Fairbank et al., *The I. G. in Peking*, vol. 2, 976.

[69] For a summary of the initial set of reforms introduced by the Japanese in Korea, see "Korean Reforms," *The Japan Weekly Mail* (Yokohama), 18 August 1894, p. 195.

[70] Lone, 131, 139, 141.

[71] Lone, 137.

As Japanese–Korean relations declined, the Grand Prince proved less tractable than anticipated. Before the key Battle of P'yôngyang in mid-September of 1894, he tried to link up with the Chinese. He envisioned a pincer movement on Seoul with the Tonghaks approaching from the south and the Chinese from the north. The Japanese learned about this when they found incriminating documents upon the capture of P'yôngyang. When he subsequently tried to stage a coup to install his favorite grandson at the expense of King Kojong and the Min clan, the Japanese had had enough and hauled out the incriminating documents to retire the old gentleman in October 1894.[72] Thereafter, the Japanese issued another decree concerning internal reforms.[73] For lack of any other alternative, the Japanese went back to working with King Kojong. Meanwhile, Min family intrigues continued unabated. In mid-December, the Japanese reshuffled officialdom again in another attempt to weed out Min sympathizers.[74] King Kojong could not have been pleased with the Japanese-orchestrated game of musical thrones. On January 7, 1895, he was reported to have been cured of an eye ailment. Now he could (and would, as far as the Japanese were concerned) take a fourteen-part oath before the tombs of his ancestors promising to cooperate with the reforms and to keep his wife out of politics.[75] Both were easily said but neither was done. Later, the Japanese sent King Kojong back to the royal tombs for a formal proclamation of Korean independence. The number of Japanese troops occupying Korea must have detracted from the ceremony. *The New York Times* pointed out that the "royal party was escorted by a body of soldiers armed and equipped in modern style."[76] The Korean government remained a shambles for the duration of the war and beyond. A month after the Sino-Japanese War ended, Japan gave up on reforming Korea, whereupon King Kojong promptly reversed the major Japanese reforms.[77]

In the countryside, Tonghak resistance continued unabated only to be quelled,

---

[72] Eckert et al., 228; Synn, 121; "La Guerre entre la Chine et le Japon" (War between China and Japan), *Le Journal des débats politiques et littéraires* (*Journal of Political and Literary Debates*) (Paris), 13 March 1895, p. 1; Ko, 41.

[73] "The Representation to the King of Korea," *The Japan Weekly Mail* (Yokohama), 15 December 1894, p. 672; "Korean News," *The Japan Weekly Mail* (Yokohama), 15 December 1894, p. 673.

[74] "Korean News," *The Japan Weekly Mail* (Yokohama), 29 December 1894, p. 725; Lew, "Kabo Reform," 393–401, 428–9; Synn, 123–4.

[75] "The Oath of the King of Korea," *The Japan Weekly Mail* (Yokohama), 5 January 1895, p. 7; "Japan in Korea," *The Japan Weekly Mail* (Yokohama), 12 January 1895, p. 46; "Korean News," *The Japan Weekly Mail* (Yokohama), 26 January 1895, p. 99.

[76] "Independence of Corea," *The New York Times*, 9 January 1895, p. 5.

[77] Kim and Kim, 84.

temporarily, at about the time the war ended.[78] This meant that, throughout the hostilities, the Japanese army had to fight a rear-guard action in Korea. It is interesting that virtually no information appeared in the Western press concerning the suppression of the rebellion or the number of Japanese troops tied down by these operations. Once the Japanese had invaded, the rebellion became specifically anti-Japanese and the Japanese army became an army of occupation.[79]

From Japan's aggressive actions a reporter at *The North-China Herald* concluded, "There is no impartial person who can deny that the war has been forced on China by Japan."[80] The rest of the Western press agreed.[81] Viceroy Li and his patroness, the Empress Dowager Cixi (慈禧太后), went to war only with the greatest reluctance. As Korea's suzerain, the Qing Dynasty had to comply with King Kojong's original request for troops. To do otherwise would have been to abandon once and for all the suzerain–tributary relationship with Korea. Not only would this have removed Korea as a defensive buffer zone on China's perimeter, but it also would have constituted an enormous loss of "face." Given Russia's railway plans, Japanese aggression in Korea could not have come at a worse time for China. Two powerful neighbors were simultaneously becoming more threatening.

From the point of view of the Empress Dowager Cixi, 1894 was a particularly awkward year to fight any war, for it coincided with her sixtieth birthday on November 29. According to *The Japan Weekly Mail,* "[S]hould such an auspicious year be stained with bloodshed, dire misfortunes must ensue to the Middle Kingdom."[82] China was a land in which people took omens very seriously. According to *The North-China Herald,* "Events this year do not appear to be very propitious to the dynasty or the birthday celebrations. The breaking out of war, the scourge of plague and cholera, and the floods all seem to point to heaven's displeasure and to predict the end of the dynasty." The Chinese believed, "Heaven cannot lie and events about to occur on the earth have their previous warnings in the sky. This was clearly indicated and so interpreted at Peking on the 2nd day of

---

[78] "The Ton-haks," *The Japan Weekly News,* 9 March 1895, p. 285.

[79] Eckert et al., 221–2.

[80] "The Declaration of War," *The North-China Herald* (Shanghai), 3 August 1894, p. 165.

[81] "Japan Seems Aggressive," *The New York Times,* 26 July 1894, p. 5.

[82] "The Japanese Government and the Korean Question," *The Japan Weekly Mail* (Yokohama), 7 July 1894, p. 10. *The North-China Herald,* intimated that the Chinese might even "put forward the fact that this, as the sixtieth anniversary of the Empress-Dowager's birthday, is a sacred year, as reason for refusing to fight the Japanese, and they will make it the excuse for tolerating the loss of honour involving accepting the Japanese demands." It went on to predict that such a refusal would make the Manchu Dynasty even more unpopular among the Han Chinese. "A Peace Possibility," *The North-China Herald* (Shanghai), 29 June 1894, p. 1001.

the 2nd moon of this year [March 8, 1894], when a strange double halo was observed round the sun." The article continued, "China is able to cope with one or even two of these visitations, but when three are launched upon her in one year, the struggle seems futile, and defeat is certain."[83] As matters went from bad to worse, the Empress Dowager honored herself with "the presentation of an extra auspicious name,"[84] 崇熙, meaning "exalted and glorious," but to no avail.[85]

Viceroy Li Hongzhang continued to do his utmost to avoid hostilities and still maintain China's presence in Korea. He knew that his army could not take on the Japanese forces. Zhili, Shandong, and Fengtian[86] provinces had 40 battalions with 20,000 men good for first-line action and another 20 battalions good only for garrison duty. All the rest belonged to the Green Standard Army (the name for the regular Han army) and were useless for fighting. To match a 50,000-man Japanese army, China would have to recruit 20 to 30 additional battalions at a cost of two to three million *taels*.[87] According to William Ferdinand Tyler, who served in China's Beiyang or northern squadron and saw action at the battles of the Yalu and Weihaiwei: "the Viceroy's game was merely bluff, not genuine defence; his army and navy were the equivalent of the terrifying masks which Eastern medieval soldiers wore to scare their enemy. He knew that if it came to actual blows he would stand but little chance; but he carried on his bluff so far that withdrawal was impossible, and the Empress Dowager urged him on – probably much against his will. And Japan 'saw him,' as they say in poker."[88] Others described Li's military machine as an "elaborate system of make-believe."[89] This strategy of bluff was in keeping with China's most renowned strategist, the late Zhou Dynasty (1122–255 B.C.) military master, Sunzi (孫子), who considered the optimal war strategy to be

---

[83] "Peking," *The North-China Herald* (Shanghai), 9 November 1894, p. 774. For another view on the importance of superstitions pervading Chinese daily life, see Holcombe, 144.

[84] "Abstract of the Peking Gazette," *The North-China Herald* (Shanghai), 7 December 1894, p. 935.

[85] Little, 213.

[86] Fengtian province was often referred to as Shengking (Shengjing or Shengching). After the Qing conquered China, they renamed the Ming city of Shenyang (瀋陽), calling it Shengjing (盛京). In 1657, the Manchus created Fengtian prefecture with Shengjing as its capital. Thereafter, the two names of Fengtian and Shengjing were often used interchangeably to refer to the prefecture. The other two Manchurian prefectures of Jilin (Kirin) and Heilongjiang (Heilungkiang or Amur) were established in 1653 and 1683, respectively (Robert H. G. Lee, *The Manchurian Frontier in Ch'ing History* [Cambridge, MA: Harvard University Press, 1970], 4–5).

[87] Sung-ping Kuo, "Chinese Reaction to Foreign Encroachment with Special Reference to the First Sino-Japanese War and Its Immediate Aftermath" (Ph.D. diss., Columbia University, 1953), 32.

[88] Tyler, 43. For similar views, see Kuo, 32.

[89] Boulger, vol. 2, 529.

avoidance of hostilities: "To subdue the enemy without fighting is the acme of skill."[90] A reporter at *The North-China Herald* correctly perceived Li's predicament if not China's military readiness: "For years he has had a free hand, and has been allowed to lavish money in the creation of a modern fleet, the construction of fortifications, and the organisation of an army; and he could not now allow that China is unprepared to fight such a comparatively insignificant enemy."[91]

Li worked tirelessly to avert war and, once it had started, to bring it to a rapid conclusion. The outbreak of hostilities in 1894 disrupted his whole strategy, which required years of peace in order to finish the task of modernizing China's armed forces.[92] Rapidly escalating Japanese demands and mounting Chinese accusations of his being too conciliatory forced Li into war.[93] Once the war had started, Li was constantly harried by his political enemies in Peking, who soon coalesced around the Guangxu Emperor (光緒皇帝).[94] The emperor, in contrast to his aunt, the Empress Dowager Cixi, seemed eager for a fight.

Most members of the Chinese literati were far less circumspect than Viceroy Li. They assumed that China would rapidly crush Japan.[95] *The North-China Herald* reported, "The national feeling, as expressed in the newspapers, is that Japan deserves to be chastised and that China is able to chastise her."[96] Just after the war began, a well-educated Manchurian merchant told a foreign correspondent, "But Japan! It's such a small country and of no importance. It's a small affair to crush

[90] Sun Tzu, *The Art of War*, Samuel B. Griffith, trans. (London: Oxford University Press, 1963), 77.
[91] "Japan's Attack on Corea," *The North-China Herald* (Shanghai), 29 June 1894, p. 1008.
[92] Kuo, 51–2; Folsom, 187–9.
[93] Oh, "Background," 290–1.
[94] Tabohashi Kiyoshi (田保橋潔), 日清戦役外交史の研究 (*A Diplomatic History of the Sino-Japanese War [1894–1895]*) (Tokyo: 刀江院刊, 1951), 268–9.
[95] "The Danger of War between China and Japan," *The North-China Herald* (Shanghai), 29 June 1894, p. 1014; Samuel C. Chu, "The Sino-Japanese War of 1894: A Preliminary Assessment from U.S.A.," 近代史 – 行究所集刊 (*Proceedings of the Institute for Modern History*) 14 (June 1985): 354, 365.
[96] "A Chinaman's Brain," *The North-China Herald* (Shanghai), 20 July 1894, p. 90. This article presents what the author considers to be a scientific examination of the brain structure of a Chinese. A century later, the racism underlying the inquiry all but leaps out from the page and assaults the reader. On the basis of one dissected brain, the author launches into a comparison between the brains of the Chinese and great apes. The author concludes that "there is as great a disproportion between their [the Chinese] intellectual triumphs and those of Europe, as there is between the comparative size of the Chinese cerebrum and the European cerebrum" (Ibid., pp. 90–1). For another article of misapplied social Darwinistic pseudo-science, see "Professor Robert Kennaway Douglas on the Chinese Situation," *The Pall Mall Gazette* (London), 5 February 1895, 4th ed., p. 3.

her after all, like one of our robber risings up North."[97] Sir Robert Hart noted that "999 out of every 1000 Chinese are sure big China can thrash little Japan."[98] China's ministers to Japan had not helped disabuse officials in Peking but had themselves generally not been fully cognizant of the significance for China of Japan's internal reforms. While a few Chinese had written perceptive accounts concerning Japan, high officialdom did not seem to read them.[99] Those who wrote about the outside were highly unusual in such an inward-focused nation as China. The profound faith of the literati in their own superiority meant there was no need to study the outside – the few who did were considered eccentrics with bizarre interests. Whereas Japanese representatives abroad focused on gathering intelligence about their host country, Chinese representatives in Japan devoted much time to cultural activities. Japanese intellectuals revered the same belletristic achievements stressed by the Chinese civil service examination system.[100] As scholars upholding an ancient tradition, they did not see the ramifications of industrialization. Their tradition looked backward to past sages for guidance, not forward into the future for the harbingers of the world yet to come. Such harbingers as could be discerned usually came in the form of dark omens read into natural disasters. Industrialization existed entirely outside of their philosophical system and their 5,000-year supply of historical analogies. They were not prepared to grasp the unprecedented because they came from an educational system stressing precedent above all else. What were the classics but the collection of relevant precedents? Anything falling beyond their scope was considered unimportant if perceived at all.

Court politics greatly complicated Chinese strategy. Since the Empress Dowager's claim to authority was tenuous and since – through undisguisable incompetence – the basis for continued Manchu rule in Han China was growing weaker daily, she could not afford to have a unified government. Such a government would have unified first against her and then against the Manchus. To stay in power, she used the opinions of low- and middle-ranking officials to check possible rival sources of power, such as Li Hongzhang. Such lower officials were known as the *Qingliudang* (清流黨) or Party of Purists and their opinions were known as *qingyi* (清議) or "pure views." Their views were notable for their chauvinism. The Party of Purists had risen to prominence during the 1884–5 Sino-French War, when its members had demanded an aggressive policy against France and had criticized Viceroy Li

---

[97] "Manchuria," *The North-China Herald* (Shanghai), 17 August 1894, p. 264.

[98] Hart to Campbell, 27 July 1894, in Fairbank et al., *The I. G. in Peking*, vol. 2, 979.

[99] Chu, "China's Attitudes," 85–8.

[100] Chu, "China's Attitudes," 85.

for being too cautious.[101] In the Sino-Japanese War, they again rose to prominence and, as in the last war, criticized Li for being pro-foreign and not getting on with the fighting.[102] Members of the Party of Purists could not see that they and not Li were the problem. China's lack of military preparations had resulted from factional rivalries within the capital and between the capital and the provinces. Viceroy Li had tried to maintain the Huai Army but favorites of the Empress Dowager controlled the funds for the navy. The favorites had siphoned off naval funds to renovate the Summer Palace, but Viceroy Li could not bring this matter to the attention of the Empress Dowager if he expected to remain in power. Nor could he admit to military unpreparedness lest he appear to be a fool.[103] Meanwhile, the Manchus were leery of permitting any Han Chinese to control overly effective military forces lest the forces be turned against Manchu rule.

In another layer of complexity, the emperor and the Empress Dowager had a convoluted political relationship. When the emperor had assumed his majority in 1887, the Empress Dowager had agreed to step down but only after two additional years of tutelage for her charge.[104] Finally, in 1889, the emperor had assumed the reins of power in principle. In fact, he remained in the shadow of his aunt.[105] Undoubtedly, the war offered him an opportunity to strike out on his own and set himself apart from the aunt who, like the Grand Prince Hûngsôn, had no legitimate right to rule after her charge had come of age.[106] Her authority was even more tenuous than that of the Grand Prince. In 1852 she had been designated as an imperial concubine of the fourth rank. After bearing the sole son to the Xianfeng Emperor (咸豐皇帝), she rose six years later to a concubine of the first rank, but she could never completely escape her humble beginnings.[107] Like the Grand Prince, the Empress Dowager tried to overcome such shortcomings in the area of legal formalities with shrewd calculations in the area of her own political survival.

---

[101] Oh, "Background," 389–92; Immanuel C. Y. Hsü, "Late Ch'ing Foreign Relations, 1866–1905," in *The Cambridge History of China,* vol. 11, John K. Fairbank and Kwang-ching Liu, eds. (Cambridge: Cambridge University Press, 1980), 96–99; Ding Richu, "Dowager Empress Cixi and Toshimichi: A Comparative Study of Modernization in China and Japan," in *China's Quest for Modernization: A Historical Perspective*, Frederic Wakeman Jr. and Wang Xi, eds. (Berkeley: University of California Press, 1997), 180.

[102] Kuo, 33–9.

[103] Oh, "Background," 438.

[104] Oh, "Background," 396.

[105] Kwong, 26–8, 55–8.

[106] Kuo, 58–68, 92–101.

[107] Kwong, 31.

By all accounts she was a very canny woman and a deft political operator.[108] She had fled the imperial city once in her youth during the Second Opium War. That flight had taken place in the face of a much smaller invading army. Her consort, the Xianfeng Emperor, had never returned to Peking but had died in Rehe (Jehol).[109] The current situation must have conjured up some of these old nightmares.

In contrast, the Guangxu Emperor was still a raw youth of twenty-three who had little experience outside the confines of the Forbidden City. He soon fell under the influence of the war party, for which it was an article of faith that Chinese forces would have no trouble bringing the Japanese to their knees. Chinese forces would thrash the insolent dwarfs. Such ideas dominated the thinking of the Han literati throughout the war.[110] The war party played to the youthful vanities of the emperor that China could win and that he could rule effectively where his aunt could not. A small minority took a different view. These tended to be persons with significant dealings with foreigners. Members of the peace party had greater respect for Japan's military forces and sought to avoid and then terminate the hostilities through diplomacy. The unpopular peace party coalesced around the Empress Dowager and Li Hongzhang.[111] The war presented the Empress Dowager with the opportunity to give her unworldly and idealistic charge enough rope to hang himself and then insinuate herself back into power. And hang himself he did. He left a paper trail of edicts documenting his vacuous exhortations to behead unsuccessful generals without offering any realistic policy alternatives. Meanwhile, his armies met an uninterrupted string of defeats in the field.

The press outside of Asia took a long time to realize that China and Japan were on the brink of war. The London *Times* provided the most detailed reporting of any Western paper, but the coverage was minimal until two days before the outbreak of hostilities, when it started devoting multiple-paragraph stories to the unfolding events in Korea.[112] Only two days after the war began did the degenerating

---

[108] Kwong, 28–9.

[109] Hsü, *Rise of Modern China*, 263. Rehe (熱河) is referred to variously as Reho, Jehol, and Chengde (承德).

[110] Kuo, 58–68, 92–101.

[111] Irwin Jay Schulman, "China's Response to Imperialism, 1895–1900" (Ph.D. diss., Columbia University, 1967), 30, 93; Oh, "Background," 391, 397–9.

[112] "Korean Question," *The Times* (London), 23 July 1894, p. 5. Similarly, *Journal des débats politiques et littéraires* did not start covering the Korean situation until two days before the war ("Les Affaires de Corée" [Korean Affairs], *Journal des débats politiques et littéraires* [*Journal of Political and Literary Debates*] [Paris], 23 July 1894, evening edition, p. 1).

Similarly, *The Pall Mall Gazette* and *Königlich privilegirte Berlinische Zeitung* predicted war only two days before the onset ("Critical Situation in Korea," *The Pall Mall Gazette* [London], 23 July

Far Eastern situation finally make it to the front pages in London.[113] In contrast, a month before hostilities broke out it was obvious to foreign observers in the Far East that war was imminent. Unless China conceded Korea to Japan, according to *The North-China Herald*, "the breaking out of war between China and Japan is only a question of days, perhaps of hours." It suggested that the real reason for Japan's desire for war was "that the Japanese government prefers a foreign to a civil war. The discontent of the majority of the House of Representatives was getting serious...A foreign war, however, is expected to reunite the people; it is an outlet for the bad blood which has been accumulating of late years in the body politic."[114] In another article, *The North-China Herald* simultaneously accused the Japanese of launching "a war for glory" and a war to overcome a crumbling domestic situation: It was "a war undertaken by the desperately situated statesmen of the Mikado to preserve to him and his dynasty the empire of his ancestors."[115] A reporter for *Moskovskie vedomosti* agreed, "[I]n Japan they have resorted to the usual remedy of a weak government – they have started a foreign war."[116]

The renowned British poet, journalist, and expert on Asia, Sir Edwin Arnold, dismissed this interpretation. He wrote that "in the present struggle Japan unquestionably stands the champion of progress, justice, and of international development, so that the partisanship shown in certain quarters against her has in it an element of stupidity which cannot, therefore, be easily excused."[117] He correctly saw through the facade of westernized institutions in Japan to their true

1894, 4th ed., p. 7; "Die Wirren in Korea" [Turmoil in Korea], *Königlich privilegirte Berlinische Zeitung* [Berlin], 23 July 1894, p. 1). A day later, on July 24, *The Pall Mall Gazette* then jumped the gun by a day to report that the hostilities had already started ("Heavy Fighting in Korea," *The Pall Mall Gazette* [London], 24 July 1894, 4th ed., p. 7).

[113] "Fides Japonica," *The Pall Mall Gazette* (London), 30 July 1894, 4th ed., p. 1.

[114] "The Impending War," *The North-China Herald* (Shanghai), 29 June 1894, p. 1009. See also "Japan," *The North-China Herald* (Shanghai), 20 July 1894, p. 94; "The Corean Embroglio," *The North-China Herald* (Shanghai), 20 July 1894, p. 106; "The War Cloud in Corea," *The Peking and Tientsin Times*, 28 July 1894, p. 82; Hart to Campbell, 8 July 1894, in Fairbank et al., *The I. G. in Peking*, 975.

[115] "The Corean Embroglio," *The North-China Herald* (Shanghai), 20 July 1894, p. 108. See also "War and Peace," *The North-China Herald* (Shanghai), 14 December 1894, p. 966.

[116] Louise McReynolds, *The News under Russia's Old Regime: The Development of a Mass-Circulation Press* (Princeton: Princeton University Press, 1991), 21; "Японско-Китайская война и Россия" (The Sino-Japanese War and Russia), *Московские ведомости* (*Moscow Gazette*), no. 203, 27 July 1894 (8 August 1894), p. 2. For a similar opinion see G. Gareau, "Autour de la Corée" (Around Korea), *Le Siècle* (*Century*) (Paris), 8 August 1894. G. Gareau authored most front-page stories about the war in this newspaper.

[117] Sir Edwin Arnold, *New Review*, quoted in "Sir Edwin Arnold's Defence of Japan," *The North-China Herald* (Shanghai), 12 October 1894, pp. 596–7.

oligarchic and nondemocratic nature. No significant power had ever rested in the parliament – it was but democratic window dressing – therefore, the war was not primarily a response to the revolt in the Diet.[118] Although the opposition parties were very vocal, they were weak.

Rather, the issue of governmental legitimacy ran much deeper to the new institutions themselves, not merely to the people occupying public office. On the eve of the war, the Japanese Minister to the United States, Tateno Gōzō (建野郷三), told the secretary of state, Walter Q. Gresham, "Our situation at home is critical, and war with China would improve it by arousing the patriotic sentiment of our people and more strongly attaching them to the Government."[119] The issue was not the balance of power between the political parties and the government but public support for the new westernized governmental institutions. Thus the war was connected to the larger problem of nation-building. Meiji institutions were new and unpopular among many. A *modus vivendi* between the oligarchs and the political parties had not been reached. If the oligarchs could demonstrate that their modernization efforts of the last quarter-century had propelled Japan into the ranks of the powers, this would greatly enhance the legitimacy of the government and help pacify Japan's turbulent domestic politics. Treaty revision meant Japan had achieved juridical equality under international law, but the powers still ignored its security concerns. A successful war could change this. With the domestic agenda largely completed, the attention of Japanese statesmen turned abroad.

While the Japanese were doing their best to stir up hostilities, Viceroy Li continued to do his utmost to avoid them. He had been very careful to keep Chinese troops out of Seoul to minimize the possibility of clashing with Japanese troops. They had encamped about eighty miles to the south of the capital at Asan and near the Tonghak rebel area. Yet he had to be prepared in the event of hostilities. On July 20, nearly two weeks before the formal declarations of war, the Chinese had started massing troops in Korea in preparation for a possible pincer

---

[118] Sir Edwin Arnold, *New Review*, quoted in "Sir Edwin Arnold's Defence of Japan," *The North-China Herald* (Shanghai), 12 October 1894, pp. 596–7. Gordon Mark Berger, the editor and translator of Foreign Minister Mutsu Munemitsu's memoirs, agrees with this interpretation. He notes quite rightly that Mutsu repeatedly writes of the need to secure public support for government policies. My reading of the memoirs is that when Mutsu refers to "the public" quite often he actually seems to mean the Japanese military and its supporters but is hesitant to be too specific. See especially his concluding chapter, where he emphasizes how Japanese diplomats had difficulty harmonizing international realities with popular demands to occupy the Liaodong Peninsula (Mutsu, 252–4, 263n.8). It was actually the demand of the Japanese army to occupy the peninsula. Perhaps Mutsu was hesitant to refer directly to the army.

[119] Cited in Jeffery M. Dorwart, *The Pigtail War: American Involvement in the Sino-Japanese War of 1894–1895* (Amherst: University of Massachusetts Press, 1975), 23.

movement on the capital: They deployed troops to the south at Asan and to the north at P'yŏngyang. The Japanese military realized that these troops would be easier to dispose of at sea before they dug in on land. The most vulnerable and threatening were those being deployed nearest to Seoul. Therefore the Japanese navy went after the reinforcements being sent to Asan. As tensions continued to escalate, General Ye Zhichao (葉志超) had requested Li to send reinforcements since his position at Asan was isolated.[120] On July 22 eight transports set off from Dagu,[121] the fortified city at the mouth of the Hai River, which provided access to Tianjin and Peking. Two were directed to go to Asan, where they arrived safely on the 24th.[122] That day news reached Asan that the Japanese had occupied the royal palace in Seoul. In response, Chinese warships were ordered back to China.[123]

* * *

The Japanese would begin the war with a surprise attack at sea without a prior declaration of war. They would follow this pattern in both of their major twentieth-century wars: the Russo-Japanese War and World War II.[124] On July 25, on the return voyage from Asan, two of the Chinese warships ordered back to China ran into three Japanese cruisers near Feng Island (豐島),[125] located on the sea approaches to Inch'ŏn and Asan.[126] The Japanese ships disabled one Chinese vessel and damaged the other. While pursuing the damaged vessel, the Japanese sighted another transport, the Chinese-leased but British-owned steamship, the *Kowshing* (高陞).[127] According to the captain, Thomas Ryder Galsworthy, the steamer had

---

[120] Japan, Imperial General Staff, 48; Oh, "Background," 306; Sun Kefu and Guan Jie, 122.

[121] Alternative spelling: Taku.

[122] U.S. Adjutant-General's Office, 12.

[123] Other spellings include Yasan, Gazan, and Yashan. Japan, Imperial General Staff, 47.

[124] David C. Evans and Mark R. Peattie, *Kaigun: Strategy, Tactics, and Technology in the Imperial Japanese Navy, 1887–1941* (Annapolis, MD: Naval Institute Press, 1997), 41.

[125] Other spellings include Phung-do, P'ung Island, Poung Do, Fengdao, and Baker Island. For information concerning the hostilities at Feng Island, see U.S. Adjutant-General's Office, 12–13.

[126] Japan, Imperial General Staff, 47.

[127] The correct Romanization is the *Gaosheng* (or *Kao-sheng* under the Wade Giles system), but the spelling used in the text was the one used at the time.
  For information concerning the sinking of the *Kowshing* see "Korean Affairs," *The Japan Weekly Mail* (Yokohama), 4 August 1894, pp. 127–8; "The Recent Naval Fight," *The Japan Weekly Mail* (Yokohama), 4 August 1894, p. 131; "The 'Kowshing'," *The Japan Weekly Mail* (Yokohama), 4 August 1894, p. 132; "The 'Tsao-kiang' and the 'Kowshing'," *The Japan Weekly Mail* (Yokohama), 11 August 1894, pp. 158–9; "The Sinking of the 'Kowshing'," *The Japan Weekly Mail* (Yokohama), 11 August 1894, p. 160; "The 'Kowshing' Affair," *The Japan Weekly Mail* (Yokohama), 11 August 1894, pp. 162–3; "The White Flag," *The Japan Weekly Mail* (Yokohama), 18 August 1894, p. 195; "Mr. von Hanneken," *The Japan Weekly Mail* (Yokohama), 18 August 1894, p. 196; "The 'Kowshing'

picked up 1,100 Chinese troops and officers at Dagu. On July 23 it had left for Asan but was intercepted by three Japanese men-of-war. The Chinese generals on board refused to heed the Japanese order to follow them to port, whereupon the crew mutinied and demanded to be returned to Dagu. During the several hours of fruitless negotiations, during which the Chinese refused either to heed the advice of their European crew members to follow Japanese orders or to allow the Europeans to leave, the Japanese commander, Tōgō Heihachirō (東郷平八郎), carefully examined the relevant provisions of international law. Upon finding the law to be on his side, he sank the *Kowshing*. A decade later, he would command the Japanese fleet in the Russo-Japanese War and have the pleasure of annihilating the Imperial Russian Navy.[128] Unlike most of the Chinese, many of the Europeans knew how to swim and so jumped ship as the *Kowshing* started to go down. The Chinese responded by opening fire on them.[129] Many observers considered the Chinese troops lost on the *Kowshing* to have been the best in the land.[130]

Affair: Captain Galsworthy's Report," *The Japan Weekly Mail* (Yokohama), 18 August 1894, p. 199; "Versions," *The Japan Weekly Mail* (Yokohama), 18 August 1894, pp. 200–1; "Korean News," *The Japan Weekly Mail* (Yokohama), 18 August 1894, p. 203; "The 'Kowshing' Affair," *The Japan Weekly Mail* (Yokohama), 18 August 1894, pp. 203–4; "The China-Japan War," *The Japan Weekly Mail* (Yokohama), 15 September 1894, pp. 320–2; "The Korean War," *The Japan Weekly Mail* (Yokohama), 15 September 1894, pp. 322–3; "The Sinking of the Kowshing," *The North-China Herald* (Shanghai), 3 August 1894, extra edition; "The Sinking of the Kowshing," *The North-China Herald* (Shanghai), 3 August 1894, pp. 171–4; "The Sinking of the Kowshing," *The North-China Herald* (Shanghai), 10 August 1894, pp. 209–10; "Captain Galsworthy's Report," *The North-China Herald* (Shanghai), 10 August 1894, p. 211; "The Sinking of the Kowshing: The Japanese Communiqué," *The North-China Herald* (Shanghai), 10 August 1894, pp. 215–7; "Oh, East is East and West is West," *The Pall Mall Gazette* (London), 6 August 1894, 4th ed., p. 1.

See in particular the official report presented to the Japanese government by the president of the Imperial Board of Legislation, Kencho Suematsu (末松謙澄), "The Report relating to the 'Kowshing' Affair," *The Japan Weekly Mail* (Yokohama), 18 August 1894, pp. 205–8; and reports by those on board: "The War: Mr. von Hanneken's Report," *The North-China Herald* (Shanghai), 10 August 1894, pp. 216–7; "The Sinking of the Kowshing," *The North-China Herald* (Shanghai), 10 August 1894, pp. 236–9; "Capt. Galsworthy's Report," *The North-China Herald* (Shanghai), 17 August 1894, pp. 275–6; Statement by Mr. Tamplin, doc. 471, *British Documents on Foreign Affairs: Reports and papers from the Foreign Office Confidential Print*, part 1, series E, vol. 5, Ian Nish, ed. (University Publications of America, 1989), 251–4; Report relating to the "Kow-Shing" Affairs, 10 August 1894, no. 487, *British Documents*, Nish, ed., 267–70; The Destruction of the "Kow-Shing," Statement of the Survivors, 2 August 1894, doc. 529, *British Documents*, Nish, ed. 293–5; Messrs. Jardine, Matheson, and Co. to Mr. O'Conor, 1 August 1894, doc. 530, *British Documents*, Nish, ed., 295–6; Vladimir, Appendix C, 232–44.

[128] "The 'Kowshing' Affair: Captain Galsworthy's Report," *The Japan Weekly Mail* (Yokohama), 18 August 1894, p. 199; Ballard, 142; Evans and Peattie, 82–3.

[129] "The 'Kowshing' Affair: Captain Galsworthy's Report," *The Japan Weekly Mail* (Yokohama), 18 August 1894, p. 199.

[130] Allen Fung, "Testing Self-Strengthening: The Chinese Army in the Sino-Japanese War of

A foreign commentator observed, "It was truly a pitiable sight that such a number of officers [on the *Kowshing*], amongst whom were two generals, should not have sufficient military experience to understand the absurdity of attempting resistance in a merchant vessel against a powerful man-of-war."[131] The Japanese made an effort to pick up the Europeans stranded in the water but made little attempt to help the many drowning Chinese. On the contrary, there were reports that some Japanese had opened fire on them. Westerners subsequently criticized them for this neglect of the Chinese.[132] With one major exception at the end of the war, the Japanese did not repeat this kind of public relations blunder.[133] The Japanese then damaged a cruiser, captured one gunboat and sank another, while two other war vessels escaped.[134] A reporter at *The Japan Weekly Mail* concluded that "the Chinese ships made a miserable fight." He also noted the problem of bad ammunition. Apparently, in the one hit that the Chinese had scored, the shell had failed to explode and thus did no significant damage. The article suspected "bad equipment or careless inspection."[135]

The owners of the sunken *Kowshing,* the British firm of Jardine, Matheson and Co., known for its commerce in opium, aggressively sought compensation from the Japanese government. For a time it had the support of the British press. But the British government eventually exonerated the Japanese of any wrongdoing. Since both China and Japan had been on a war footing as of the hostilities at Feng Island, since the *Kowshing* was carrying troops, and since it refused to follow reasonable Japanese orders, the British government considered the Japanese to have been justified in sinking a hostile ship.[136] With this explanation the issue disappeared from the press.

The hostilities at Feng Island and the sinking of the *Kowshing* precipitated

---

1894–1895," *Modern Asian Studies* 40, no. 4 (1966): 1015.

[131] Vladimir, 72.

[132] "The 'Kowshing' Affair," *The Japan Weekly Mail* (Yokohama), 11 August 1894, p. 163; Elleman, *Modern Chinese Warfare*, 98.

[133] "The 'Kowshing' Affair: Captain Galsworthy's Report," *The Japan Weekly Mail* (Yokohama), 18 August 1894, p. 199.

[134] "Japanese victory in Korea," *The Japan Weekly Mail* (Yokohama), 4 August 1894, p. 124; "Korean Affairs," *The Japan Weekly Mail* (Yokohama), 4 August 1894, pp. 125–6; Kencho Suyematsu, "The Report relating to the 'Kowshing' Affair," *The Japan Weekly Mail* (Yokohama), 18 August 1894, pp. 205–8; Evans and Peattie, 41.

[135] "The Fight on the 25th Ultimo," *The Japan Weekly Mail* (Yokohama), 11 August 1894, p. 154.

[136] Earl of Kimberley to O'Conor, 26 February 1895, doc. 137, *British Documents*, Nish, ed., 93–4; "The Kowshing Inquiry," *The North-China Herald* (Shanghai), 31 August 1894, p. 344; Ballard, 142; Holland, 128.

formal declarations of war. On August 1, 1894, Japan declared war on China. According to the imperial rescript, "Korea is an independent State. She was first introduced into the family of nations by the advice and under the guidance of Japan. It has, however, been China's habit to designate Korea as her dependency, and both openly and secretly to interfere with her domestic affairs." It accused China of turning down Japan's offer to sponsor reforms jointly, which would "procure for Korea freedom from the calamity of perpetual disturbance." It justified the Japanese declaration of war on the grounds that China had made "warlike preparations," sent "large reinforcements," and had opened fire on Japanese ships.[137] It neglected to note that the Chinese warlike preparations were simply a response to Japan's far greater warlike preparations. It also misrepresented the opening of hostilities since Japanese, not Chinese forces, had kidnapped the Korean king and had taken aggressive actions against Chinese troop transports. The Japanese for their part considered the Chinese and Koreans to be totally obstructionist and unwilling to take the actions necessary to create regional stability in the Far East.

According to *The Japan Weekly Mail,* the declaration of war was greeted in Japan "with universal joy and enthusiasm"[138] and "a mania for war."[139] The political parties immediately fell into line to support the government and, in distinct contrast to the pre-war period, remained faithful throughout the war.[140] "The Japanese people are stirred to their depths by the present complication with China. The affair absolutely engrosses the attention of the people, high and low. So soon as matters assumed a serious complexion, petitions began literally to pour into the Central Staff Office from country localities asking permission to serve in the army."[141] On July 28, 1894, the London *Spectator* took the seen-one-Asian-seen-them-all view. It lumped the Chinese and Japanese together and denied that "national feeling" existed in Asia. The editor of *The Japan Weekly Mail* ridiculed this ignorance of Japanese patriotism.[142] Throughout the war Japanese popular

---

[137] "Imperial Rescript," *The Japan Weekly Mail* (Yokohama), 4 August 1894, pp. 133–4. The original declaration of war is also reprinted in Vladimir, 245–6.

[138] "The Spirit of the Vernacular Press during the Week," *The Japan Weekly Mail* (Yokohama), 4 August 1894, p. 118.

[139] "Japanese Jingoism," *The Japan Weekly Mail* (Yokohama), 4 August 1894, p. 123.

[140] "The Spirit of the Vernacular Press during the Week," *The Japan Weekly Mail* (Yokohama), 8 September 1894, p. 278; "The Spirit of the Vernacular Press during the Week," *The Japan Weekly Mail* (Yokohama), 6 October 1894, p. 38; "The War in the East," *The Times* (London), 22 October 1894, p. 5; "The Spirit of the Vernacular Press during the Week," *The Japan Weekly Mail* (Yokohama), 27 October 1894, p. 470; Conroy, 255–6.

[141] "Japanese Jingoism," *The Japan Weekly Mail* (Yokohama), 4 August 1894, p. 123.

[142] "An Asiatic War," *The Spectator,* 28 July 1894, quoted in "Yamato-Damashi a Chimera," *The*

support for the military never wavered. "The complete harmony that prevails among Japanese of all sorts and conditions, irrespective of party or faction, with regard to the prosecution of the present war is very striking."[143] Unlike the Chinese, whose regional loyalties and Han–Manchu divisions prevailed over national sentiments, the Japanese of the 1890s shared a deep sense of national unity, national pride, and national mission abroad.[144]

In contrast, foreign commentators despaired at the total absence of patriotism in China.[145] An American adviser to the Beiyang Squadron wrote afterward, "In a sense it was Li Hung-chang and not China that was fighting, and it may well have been that the majority of the Chinese people knew nothing of the war."[146] He added that people in China "never really serve a cause – only their master's interests or their own."[147] The Qing Dynasty had very successfully perpetuated the myth that it ruled over a homogeneous and unified country populated by Han Chinese who spoke dialects of a common language and lived harmoniously in the eighteen provinces of China proper, plus or minus a few former tributaries. Westerners generally did not question this Chinese myth of their homogeneity. In fact, China had always been a heterogeneous empire of mutually antagonistic parts. Long before segregation was ever dreamed up in the United States, the Manchus had segregated China among the many ethnic groups, but most rigidly between the Manchu and non-Manchu. The Qing Dynasty had conjured up a false image of a monolith precisely in order to counteract the centrifugal pull of ethnic and regional affiliations. The evidence, however, did not support the myth: The history of China under the Qing is one of continuous internal rebellions; during the Sino-Japanese War Chinese troops, many of whom were not from the areas under attack, repeatedly refused to fight; and China lacked some of the most basic elements of a unified country: namely a national army and a national navy.

The same day that the Japanese government declared war, the Chinese did

---

Japan Weekly Mail (Yokohama), 15 September 1894, p. 316. *Yamato damashi* (大和魂) refers to "the spirit of Japan."

[143] "The Spirit of the Vernacular Press during the Week," *The Japan Weekly Mail* (Yokohama), 1 September 1894, p. 246.

[144] "The China-Japanese War," *The Pall Mall Gazette* (London), 4 September 1894, 4th ed., p. 7.

[145] "The War in the East," *The Times* (London), 26 December 1894, p. 4; "China and Japan," *The North-China Herald* (Shanghai), 14 December 1894, p. 964; "War and Peace," *The North-China Herald* (Shanghai), 14 December 1894, p. 966; "La Chine et le Japon" (China and Japan), *Le Temps* (*The Times*) (Paris), 2–3 January 1895; MacGowan, 601; Boulger, vol. 2, 528; Leroy-Beaulieu, 213.

[146] Tyler, 61.

[147] Tyler, 95.

likewise.[148] According to *Le Temps*, Prince Qing (慶親王奕劻),[149] chief member of the Zongli Yamen, China's foreign office, had been one of the few high officials to oppose declaring war and even he bowed to the overwhelming majority in the Yamen. "All the other ministers were indignant at the audacious perfidy of Japan and it was decided to advise the emperor to declare war immediately in order not to expose China to the ridicule of the world."[150] Again "face" was at issue. So China justified its intervention in Korea on the grounds of its suzerain–tributary relationship. The declaration of war accurately accused the Japanese of forcing "the Korean King to change his system of government," of being "bellicose," and of violating international law by "sending large armies to bully a country in this way, and compel it to change its system of government."

The Guangxu Emperor also unwittingly revealed one of the primary irritants fueling the Japanese determination to expel China from Korea. The declaration repeatedly referred to the Japanese as *woren* (倭人) or "dwarfs," an ancient and highly derogative term for the Japanese.[151] To make sure that no one missed the point, the Chinese, who had the document translated into English, provided an explanatory note saying that the word was used in an "opprobrious sense."[152] In a part of the world so dominated by "face," such a public and so oft-repeated insult – the word appeared six times in the declaration of war – would have been the equivalent, in the West, to spitting the Japanese sovereign six times in the face. The Japanese had striven for years to modernize their country while, in their mind, the Chinese had remained in indolent decay. Still the Chinese had the affront to treat them with contempt. Such a declaration could only have made the Japanese even more determined to ram victory down China's throat. Whereas China was the land of proud pretensions and philosopher kings known for sermonizing recalcitrant inferiors, Japan was the country of understatement and indirect speech until the growing internal rage burst forth to burn all bridges of propriety.

---

[148] For a translation of the Chinese declaration of war, see Vladimir, 246–7.

[149] Also spelled as Ch'ing.

[150] "Les Affairs de Corée" (Korean Affairs), *Le Temps* (*The Times*) (Paris), 15 August 1894, p. 1; Hummel, 964–5.

[151] "China's Declaration of War," *The Japan Weekly Mail* (Yokohama), 11 August 1894, p. 178; "Declaration of War by the Emperor of China," *The North-China Herald* (Shanghai), 3 August 1894, p. 191; "Abstract of Peking Gazette," *The North-China Herald* (Shanghai), 9 November 1894, p. 776. A ten-year resident of China gives the translation for *woren* as "lickspittle." "'Wo-jen,'" *The Japan Weekly Mail* (Yokohama), 1 September 1894, p. 268; "The Emperor's Proclamation and the Circular Note," *The Peking and Tientsin Times*, 11 August 1894, p. 90; "The 'Wo Jen,'" *The Peking and Tientsin Times*, 1 September 1894, p. 102.

[152] "'Wo-jen,'" *The Japan Weekly Mail* (Yokohama), 1 September 1894, p. 260.

The Japanese press was quick to respond in kind. Prior to the insult, the press in Japan had referred to the Chinese as *shinjin* (清人), meaning "Manchu," or *shinajin* (支那人), meaning "Chinese." Afterward, it employed a host of epithets: *chanchanbōzu* (ちゃんちゃん坊主), or "Buddhist priests in baby clothes"; or *tonpi* (豚尾), literally "pig-tail," referring both to the hind end of a swine and the long queues worn by Chinese men; *tonbikan* (豚尾奸), or "pig-tailed vagabonds"; and *tenkan* (天奸) or "Celestial vagabonds." It referred to China as *meisokoku* (迷想国), or "the country of mistaken ideas."[153] Various derogatory terms also made the rounds through the Western press. These included "Japs," "Chinamen," "les jaunes" (the yellows), and "Celestials" (in reference to the English translation of 天下 as Celestial Empire).[154]

At the beginning of the war, the European and American press outside of Asia tended to believe that sheer numbers dictated a Chinese victory over Japan.[155] On July 24, *The Times* of London predicted that, due to the size of China and its population, time would be on its side.[156] *The Pall Mall Gazette* interviewed Sir Edward J. Reed, former Chief Constructor of the British navy, Knight of the Rising Sun of Japan, and designer of Japanese warships. He believed that a lack of armored ships would fatally weaken the Japanese navy.[157] The Russian Foreign

---

[153] "'Wo-jen,'" *The Japan Weekly Mail* (Yokohama), 8 September 1894, p. 282; "Events in Japan," *The North-China Herald* (Shanghai), 10 August 1894, p. 239.

[154] "The Japanese in Corea," *The North-China Herald* (Shanghai), 10 August 1894, pp. 239–40; "Corea," *The North-China Herald* (Shanghai), 17 August 1894, p. 263; "Corea," *The North-China Herald* (Shanghai), 17 August 1894, p. 263; "Corea," *The North-China Herald* (Shanghai), 24 August 1894, p. 305; "Les Affairs de Corée" (Korean Affairs), *Le Temps* (*The Times*) (Paris), 15 August 1894, p. 1; "La Chine and le Japon" (China and Japan), *Le Temps* (*The Times*) (Paris), 30 December 1894, p. 1.

After the Japanese victories at Port Arthur and the Yalu, calling the Japanese "Japs" virtually ceased. "Corea," *The North-China Herald* (Shanghai), 17 August 1894, p. 263; "Japs and Chinamen Start," *The New York Times*, 20 August 1894, p. 5; "Chinese or Jap," *The North-China Herald* (Shanghai), 1 March 1895, p. 305; "The Future of China," *The North-China Herald* (Shanghai), 14 June 1895, p. 897.

[155] "Corean King Is a Captive," *The New York Times*, 28 July 1894, p. 5; "Japan Has Declared War," *The New York Times*, 2 August 1894, p. 5; "'China's Defeat Impossible'," *The New York Times*, 13 August 1894, p. 5; "Японско-Китайская война и Россия" (The Sino-Japanese War and Russia), *Московские ведомости* (*Moscow Gazette*), no. 203, 27 July 1894 (8 August 1894), p. 2; "Китай и Япония. Война с Китаем" (China and Japan. War between Japan and China), *Московские ведомости* (*Moscow Gazette*), no. 203, 27 July 1894 (8 August 1894), p. 4.

[156] "English, American, and Russian Opinions on the War," *The Japan Weekly Mail* (Yokohama), 8 September 1894, p. 288.

[157] "The Navies of Japan and China. A Talk with Sir Edward J. Reed, K.C.B., M.P.," *The Pall Mall Gazette* (London), 1 August 1894, 4th ed., pp. 1–2.

Ministry's *Journal de St-Pétersbourg* extolled: "Firmness and persistence are special qualities of the Chinese race and justify its superior role in the history of humanity."[158] Although Chinese political weakness was recognized, the same editorialist ventured: "We believe in how important its military and economic resources will soon be: agriculture, industry, commerce, armies, naval forces."[159]

A solitary voice aired in *The Pall Mall Gazette* on July 28 countered: "I observe that most people who are supposed to be in a position to give an opinion...assert that China in time will be certain to crush Japan." The author then mentioned his travels in China, Japan, and Korea, continuing, "I cannot help coming to the conclusion that unless the 'Japs' at the very outset commit some terribly stupid strategical blunder they will carry everything before them, capture or destroy the Chinese fleet and transports, and possibly the same fate awaits the Chinese army."[160] The next week a reporter for *The New York Times* also seemed more inclined to believe that Japan would triumph because of its modernization programs.[161] In Asia, the Western residents of China generally took a very dim view of the country's military potential, whereas those in Japan usually extolled Japan's rapid economic progress.[162]

The Russian press lacked the special correspondents available to the British and American press. Instead, it devoted considerable attention to interpreting the significance of Western reports. Unlike the other powers, Russia bordered on the war theater. Therefore the hostilities had a direct impact on Russian national security. One of the best-known conservative newspapers, the St. Petersburg daily, *Novoe vremia*, was among the first to devote serious articles to Japan.[163] In one written just after the Battle of Asan, it shared the prevailing assumption in Russia

---

[158] "Chine et Japon" (China and Japan), *Journal de St-Pétersbourg* (*St. Petersburg Journal*), no. 198, 8 August 1894, p. 2.

[159] "Chine et Japon" (China and Japan), *Journal de St-Pétersbourg* (*St. Petersburg Journal*), no. 198, 8 August 1894, p. 2. For another generally positive article about Chinese military potential, see "По поводу событий в Корее" (Regarding Events in Korea), *Новое время* (*New Times*), no. 6606, 2 August 1894, p. 1.

[160] *The Pall Mall Gazette*, 28 July 1894, reprinted in "Summary of News," *The North-China Herald* (Shanghai), 12 October 1894, p. 595. I was unable to find the original article in the fourth edition of *The Pall Mall Gazette*. Perhaps *The North-China Herald* is citing a different edition of the paper. I did find one article, an interview, which was very similar in tenor and could have been the same person quoted by *The North-China Herald*. See "Comparison of the Belligerents' Chances," *The Pall Mall Gazette* (London), 28 July 1894, 4th ed., p. 7.

[161] "Japan Has Declared War," *The New York Times*, 2 August 1894, p. 5.

[162] "The Situation," *The North-China Herald* (Shanghai), 13 July 1894, pp. 51–2; Spenser Wilkinson, "China and Japan," *The Pall Mall Gazette* (London), 11 August 1894, 4th ed., p. 1.

[163] For this and other characterizations of the Russian press, see McReynolds, 25.

and the West that Japan was just another backward Asian country: It italicized the sentence: *"The Japanese cannot regenerate themselves, although sometimes they strive for this."* The same article was even more negative about the Chinese: *"The Chinese never will regenerate themselves and they do not want this."*[164] Despite such prejudices, in an article published on August 6, 1984, less than two weeks after the start of the war, *Novoe vremia* provided a detailed comparison of the Chinese and Japanese navies. It concluded that the Japanese navy was superior.[165]

Less than a month after the onset of hostilities, the Russian Foreign Ministry's *Journal de St-Pétersbourg* reported that Japan had become the master of the seas due to the "inertia of the Chinese navy."[166] By the end of August, it would no longer be devoting long or positive feature stories to China but to Japan.[167] "The Japanese naval administration can bear perfectly the comparison with a European navy, equally well in what concerns the vessels as in the officers and in the equipment...the army of the Mikado is the only military force in the Far East set up according to European methods."[168] By the first of September, the *Journal de St-Pétersbourg* was waxing: "All the world knows about the efforts made by Japan to assimilate the progress of our European societies; but what is less well known is that our civilization has been grafted onto a very remarkable indigenous civilization, having numerous traits in common with ours, all of it being much more ancient. Only this can explain the rapidity with which the Japanese have put themselves on a par with Western civilization and the astonishing progress without

---

[164] "По поводу событий в Корее" (Regarding Events in Korea), *Новое время* (*New Times*), no. 6609, 5 August 1894, p. 2. Italics from the original.

[165] "Военные флоты Китая и Японии" (The Naval Fleets of China and Japan), *Новое время* (*New Times*), no. 6610, 6 August 1894, p. 1.

[166] "Chine et Japon" (China and Japan), *Journal de St-Pétersbourg* (*St. Petersburg Journal*), no. 207, 17 August 1894, p. 2.

[167] "Chine et Japon" (China and Japan), *Journal de St-Pétersbourg* (*St. Petersburg Journal*), no. 210, 21 August 1894, p. 3; "Chine et Japon" (China and Japan), *Journal de St-Pétersbourg* (*St. Petersburg Journal*), no. 212, 23 August 1894, p. 2; "Chine et Japon" (China and Japan), *Journal de St-Pétersbourg* (*St. Petersburg Journal*), no. 220, 1 September 1894, p. 2; "Chine et Japon" (China and Japan), *Journal de St-Pétersbourg* (*St. Petersburg Journal*), no. 292, 13 November 1894, p. 2; "Chine et Japon" (China and Japan), *Journal de St-Pétersbourg* (*St. Petersburg Journal*), no. 340, 1 January 1895, p. 2. For positive coverage of Japan in other newspapers, see A. Molchanov, "Корея и Япония" (Korea and Japan), *Новое время* (*New Times*), no. 6653, Sep. 18, 1894, p. 1.

[168] "Chine et Japon" (China and Japan), *Journal de St-Pétersbourg* (*St. Petersburg Journal*), no. 212, 23 August 1894, p. 2. For other articles praising Japanese military achievements, see "Японско-китайская война" (The Sino-Japanese War), *Русские ведомости* (*Russian Gazette*) (Moscow), no. 271, 1 October 1894 (13 October 1894), p. 3.

historical precedent, which have characterized this transformation."[169]

At this juncture, it would be useful to compare the Chinese and Japanese military forces. Unlike Japan, China lacked a national military force. The Chinese army was composed of a hodgepodge of regional forces. A journalist at *Le Journal des débats politiques et littéraires* put his finger on the key Chinese military weakness: "There are Chinese troops: there is no Chinese army, or rather there are as many armies as there are regions."[170] These consisted of (1) the eight banners, segregated into Manchu, Mongol, Moslem, and Han Chinese banners;[171] (2) the Green Standard forces or Chinese army; (3) braves or hired mercenaries; and (4) the foreign-drilled army. The practice of the Manchus had been to segregate themselves from the other ethnic groups in order to maintain the purity of their bloodlines and culture.[172] Manchus traditionally served in their own banner forces. The Han Chinese served in some segregated banners (as did Mongolians and Moslems), but they mainly manned the regular Chinese army, or Green Standard Army, as well as served in the various provincial armies throughout the empire. The banner forces had been an innovation of the Manchus. In the seventeenth century, these banner forces had conquered China. Their status was hereditary and over the intervening years their fighting capacity had atrophied. Banner membership conferred unique privileges: The pay was much better than that in the Green Standard Army. Bannermen were usually immune from civil law, subject to lesser punishments than Han Chinese, put before a separate examination system, granted faster promotion, and accorded those privileges particular to the Manchus in general. For instance, certain key positions were reserved exclusively for Manchus. These included membership in the imperial house, elevation to prince or duke, and participation in the elite guards.[173] In the late Qing, banner troops were mainly stationed around the capital and had increased to twenty-four banners, eight for each ethnic group.[174]

---

[169] "Chine et Japon" (China and Japan), *Journal de St-Pétersbourg* (*St. Petersburg Journal*), no. 220, 1 September 1894, p. 2.

[170] Charles Malo, "Revue militaire: Les armés de la Chine et du Japon" (Military Review: The Armies of China and Japan), *Journal des débats politiques et littéraires* (*Journal of Political and Literary Debates*) (Paris), 30 July 1894, evening edition, p. 1.

[171] Robert H. G. Lee, 62.

[172] Joseph Fletcher, "Ch'ing Inner Asia c. 1800," in *Cambridge History of China*, Fairbank, ed., 39.

[173] Mark Christopher Elliott, "Resident Aliens: The Manchu Experience in China, 1644–1760" (Ph.D. diss., University of California, Berkeley, 1993), 391–3, 472.

[174] "Extracts from An Epitome of the Chino-Japanese War," in Du Boulay, 1–3. This work is generally referred to as being written by Du Boulay. Actually, he was simply the author of the greater part, the book being a typewritten collected work concerning the Sino-Japanese War. Only some of the parts have their own internal pagination; therefore, I have given the titles of the parts as

The Green Standard Army was the descendant of the Ming Army. It was entirely composed of Han Chinese and was garrisoned throughout the empire. By the late Qing period it was broken down into relatively independent small units used for constabulary, not combat, duty. Contrary to the name of Green Standard Army, it was not actually trained for war. The braves or hired mercenaries were organized by province to serve as a national guard to be sent to any hot spots in the empire. They were descendants of the Ever-Victorious Army, which had been trained by foreigners to help put down the Taiping Rebellion, but the foreign advisers had long since departed. The trained army simply consisted of those braves who had received some European-style military training. It formed a microscopic percentage of the total Chinese armed forces. Of the Chinese armed forces, the Green Standard troops were the most numerous, followed by bannermen. Braves and trained recruits together represented perhaps 10 percent of the total. But this is just a guess, since the Chinese government did not maintain accurate statistics. The Chinese army lacked an organized engineer corps, a commissariat, transport services, and a medical division. A German article singled out the cavalry for particular criticism and also noted that the lack of a commissariat meant that troops in the field had to find their own provisions.[175] Therefore local inhabitants, far from supporting Chinese troops, lived in dread of their arrival since they acquired their provisions at gunpoint from civilians. In 1891, a physician who had long served in China had accurately predicted the consequences: "[I]n time of war the peasantry would be at the mercy of the soldiery, who would be compelled to take provisions where they could be found."[176]

During the war, *The New York Times* described the consequences: "The Chinese Army of the North is reported to be in a terrible plight, suffering from starvation and exposure to the extremely cold weather."[177] Another article noted, "In great contrast to this are the Japanese troops. The discipline under which they are kept is remarkable, while in the entire conduct of their enterprise Corea has not been laid under contribution for anything. The Chinese troops have no commissariat, are living off the country through which they pass. One of the most prominent features of the Japanese is their commissariat. All supplies which have been

well as any page number, if available.

[175] Citing *Der Ostasiatische* in "China's Armies," *The North-China Herald* (Shanghai), 27 July 1894, p. 150.

[176] Robert Coltman, Jr., *The Chinese, Their Present and Future: Medical, Political, and Social* (Philadelphia: F. A. Davis, Publisher, 1891), 209–10.

[177] "Japan's Victorious Warfare," *The New York Times*, 10 November 1894, p. 5.

purchased from the Coreans have been paid for at 100 per cent advance."[178]

Li Hongzhang had created his personal army, the Huai Army, to fight the Taiping Rebellion in 1862 and had never subsequently disbanded it. Rather, it had become a key element of his personal power base. The Huai Army was composed of braves and trained troops. As Li had aged, he had been less able to oversee its operations. In addition, the court was reluctant to fund it for fear of allowing any army under Han control to become too powerful lest the Han commander put it to such domestic uses as unseating the dynasty.[179] As a result, its forces had deteriorated. At the time of the war, Li also controlled the provincial troops of Zhili under the command of General Ye Zhichao. Such militia armies as the Huai Army were not imperial troops but the private armies of their creators who provided for their needs independently of the central government. These regionally financed armies constituted a threat to central control. Therefore, the government consciously tried to curtail their power. For example, Viceroy Li, as Commissioner for the Northern Seas, was in command of all the troops engaged during the war except for the Manchu forces from Manchuria, or about three-fifths of the total. Similarly, as governor-general of Zhili, the metropolitan province, he controlled all military forces except the Imperial Guards in Peking, the bannermen under Manchu control who were responsible for guarding the capital.[180]

China's army and navy were fractured by command, organization, province, race, and training. Nothing about them was unified. In 1900, Alexander Michie, who had served as a Chinese envoy to help mediate the end of the Sino-Japanese War, described its forces: "Every military corps raised is essentially territorial; and if ever it is moved from one province to another, it looks to a territorial chief, and no stranger can command it."[181] The Chinese navy also lacked a unified command and was severely weakened as a result. It was divided into four autonomous squadrons: the Beiyang (northern), Nanyang (southern), Fujian, and Guangdong Squadrons. Only the Beiyang possessed a modern fleet. It was based at Weihaiwei and was under the control of Viceroy Li.[182] Similarly, China's arsenals and naval academies were the property of their province of origin and could not be counted

---

[178] "Corean Light on the Far East," *The New York Times*, 27 October 1894, p. 12.

[179] Allen Fung, 1027–8.

[180] Vladimir, 48–52; Japan, Imperial General Staff, 26–32, 40–2; Intelligence Division to Foreign Office, 16 July 1894, *British Documents*, Nish, ed., 54–6; Ralph L. Powell, *The Rise of Chinese Military Power 1895–1912* (Princeton: Princeton University Press, 1955), 11–45; "Extracts from An Epitome of the Chino-Japanese War," Du Boulay, 1–3.

[181] Michie, vol. 2, 399–400.

[182] Japan, Imperial General Staff, 32.

on to supply other provinces in the event of hostilities. During the Sino-French War of 1884–5, Viceroy Li had declined to heed the call from the south for aid. His fleet, the Beiyang Squadron, had remained in North China. Ten years later, the southern fleet would pay him back during the Sino-Japanese War by ignoring his calls for help.[183] Even within the Beiyang Squadron guns and ammunition were not standardized. The gunpowder was local and not of the appropriate grade for the imported guns. This greatly complicated supplying the correct ammunition in adequate quantities. The supply system was ad hoc and flawed so that the Beiyang Squadron was grossly undersupplied with ordnance. Foreign employees had complained about these problems for at least a year prior to the war.[184]

In other words, Chinese naval forces and particularly the Chinese land forces had negligible logistical competence and a highly flawed organization. Nearly two generations earlier, the Crimean War (1853–6) had demonstrated the critical importance of railways for efficient troop deployments, yet this lesson failed to make an impression on the majority of the Chinese leadership.[185] Then, a generation later, Prussia, under the guidance of Otto von Bismarck, had again demonstrated to his European rivals the power of superior logistics and organization. The Japanese military had studied the lessons of the wars of German unification and particularly of the Franco-Prussian War of 1870–1 while the Chinese government had ignored them but for compelling internal reasons, namely, fears that an efficient Han military force might overthrow the Manchu Dynasty.[186]

The Manchus had deliberately prevented the creation of a unified national army. This was an integral part of their strategy to maintain their minority rule over a vast land teeming with Han Chinese. Preserving the separation of the banner forces and Manchu privileges were prerequisites to keeping Manchu status distinct.[187] Fracturing the command of the far more numerous Han Chinese forces was necessary to prevent the Han from unifying to depose the Qing Dynasty. The system worked well enough for maintaining the peace on the central Asian frontier, the traditional origin of foreign encroachments. It was disastrous when it was used against the technologically superior peoples of the Industrial Revolution.

---

[183] John L. Rawlinson, *China's Struggle for Naval Development 1839–1895* (Cambridge, MA: Harvard University Press, 1967), 81–2, 94, 120–1.

[184] Rawlinson, 148–50.

[185] Geoffrey Wawro, *The Austro-Prussian War: Austria's War with Prussia and Italy in 1866* (Cambridge: Cambridge University Press, 1996), 10.

[186] Bismarck was instrumental in unifying the German states under Prussian hegemony in a series of wars fought against Denmark in 1864, Austria in 1866, and France from 1870 to 1871.

[187] Elliott, "Resident Aliens," 489.

On the eve of the war, an article in the German press focused on this fundamental weakness of Chinese land forces: the lack of a unified command. Each of the provincial armies was the personal creation of that province's governor. "It is naturally in the interest of each [provincial] Viceroy to retain the fruit of his exertions for himself; in no case is he inclined to come to the assistance of a neighbour who is worse provided, and incur the danger of denuding his own province, for whose safety he is responsible with his head." The same system of individual responsibility applied down through the military ranks. It squelched initiative and promoted defensive rather than preemptive action. "By this system, common action is virtually excluded."[188]

This article came closest to pinpointing the predicament of Chinese officers in the field. The Qing legal code, 大清律例便覽, devoted much attention to regulating the army. The code required that officers depart for expeditions on the scheduled date and only engage in authorized troop movements. The punishments for failure to do so were severe, ranging from military exile on a remote frontier to enough cudgel blows to kill an ordinary man.[189] Those who failed to hold their positions against enemy attack could be decapitated.[190] Destruction of arms issued by the government would also incur a potentially lethal number of cudgel blows.[191] In an era of very slow communications, such limitations made it difficult for commanders in the field to adjust tactics to reflect changing circumstances. Moreover, the regulations precluded an orderly retreat since commanders could not destroy weapons to prevent their falling into enemy hands, nor could they abandon a position without fear of decapitation.

Such a fractured command and rigid rules of engagement presupposed a technologically inferior enemy – one whom China could defeat if given enough time. This was indeed the case for most of Chinese history. Such rules also assumed that the enemy's strategy was predictable and would not require significant modifications in the field. So the rules focused on forcing Chinese officers to go into battle as scheduled and stay there until victory. In the face of a technologically equal or superior enemy, these rules hamstrung Chinese officers, making them more vulnerable to a far more dangerous enemy than that contemplated in the regulations. Commanders dared not change plans made far away that no longer

---

[188] Citing *Der Ostasiatische* in "China's Armies," *The North-China Herald* (Shanghai), 27 July 1894, p. 150.

[189] Guy Boulais, *Manuel du Code Chinois* (大清律例便覽) (*Chinese Legal Code Manual*) (Chang-hai: Imprimerie de la Mission Catholique, 1924), 415, 418.

[190] Boulais, 420.

[191] Boulais, 418.

reflected current circumstances. Similarly, they dared not destroy equipment to keep it out of enemy hands. All of this would spell military disaster for China in the Sino-Japanese War.

In contrast, a sister article on Japan in the same German newspaper opened: "When three decades ago, Japan awoke out of the sleep of her isolation and attached herself to the civilisation of the West, her first care was the re-organisation of her army. The result may truly be called astonishing." It concluded: "The Japanese army is in reality a European force and any one of their army divisions, with the exception of the cavalry, which is small and would look badly mounted, might march through the streets of any town on the Continent, without, at first sight, being recognised as Oriental troops." The article lavished praise on the infantry in drill and on the skill of the artillery. Nevertheless, the author implied that in a long war, China's numbers would overcome Japan's crack forces.[192]

The Times of London provided a similarly positive description of the Japanese army. The author of the article considered their domestically manufactured Murata magazine rifle to be equal to the best in Europe and commended the artillery. Particularly praised was the discipline of the troops. The article concluded, "They are brave, temperate, patient, and energetic, and though the Chinese might be made, under European officers, as fine soldiers as they are, at this moment they are about 200 years behind them; and, although the victory is not always to the strong, as found out in the Boer campaign, from every *data* that a soldier can judge by the Japanese should beat the Chinese in Korea with the greatest ease."[193] (Prior to the Boer War [1899–1902], the British colonial government of southern Africa had had difficulty controlling the Dutch settlers under its jurisdiction.)

Chinese financial institutions to fund the war were no more well organized than the land or naval forces. While Japan had a unified system of public finance to raise funds for fighting a war, China did not. Before the war, Li Hongzhang had borrowed from the customs revenues of Ningbo (寧波)[194] and Shanghai to buy armaments.[195] Later, the Chinese government created a war fund by authorizing a voluntary deduction of thirty percent from the salaries of civil officials of all ranks

---

[192] Citing *Der Ostasiatische* in "Japan's Armies," *The North-China Herald* (Shanghai), 27 July 1894, pp. 151–2. For other positive views of the Japanese army, see "The Situation in Korea," *The Pall Mall Gazette* (London), 11 July 1894, 4th ed., pp. 1–2; "Comparing the Chinese and Japanese Forces," *The Pall Mall Gazette* (London), 26 July 1894, 4th ed., p. 7.

[193] Cited in "The Japanese Army in Korea," *The Japan Weekly Mail* (Yokohama), 8 September 1894, p. 295.

[194] Also spelled Ningpo.

[195] "At Weihaiwei," *The North-China Herald* (Shanghai), 8 February 1895, p. 188.

and military officers not in active service.[196] How voluntary the contributions or how widespread the collection are unknown. In addition, the emperor ordered four Chinese banks to cough up 10 million *taels* for the war.[197] A loan of 10 million *taels* or approximately one and a half million pounds sterling at 7 percent was raised at the Hong Kong and Shanghai Bank in London. It was the first loan in Chinese history to be negotiated directly by the Peking government instead of through a provincial authority. Therefore, the money would go directly to governmental and not to provincial coffers.[198] But China's continued ability to raise foreign loans depended on its success in the battlefield.[199] When this proved elusive, the Chinese government tried to raise money domestically and among overseas Chinese.[200] In December 1894, the Chinese government tried to exact money from Cantonese pawnbrokers.[201] That same month, the Shanghai Customs Bank issued a loan of 5 million *kuping taels*, using customs revenues as the security.[202] Various war loans were raised regionally.[203] In contrast, Japan financed the war in the way of wealthy Western nations. It did not resort to foreign borrowing but issued domestic loans to create a national war fund.[204]

In addition to these numerous organizational deficiencies there remained the problem of the Chinese soldier. He was the despair of the Western observer in China. A German article pointed out the low prestige of military service: "The military calling enjoys in China less consideration than any other occupation soever."[205] Thus the Chinese proverb, "Good iron is not beaten into nails; good men are not made into soldiers" (好鐵不打釘,好男不當兵).[206] Foreigners believed

---

[196] "The War," *The North-China Herald* (Shanghai), 31 August 1894, p. 360.

[197] "Japanese Moving North," *The New York Times*, 20 September 1894, p. 5.

[198] "Peking," *The North-China Herald* (Shanghai), 9 November 1894, p. 774; "The Silver Loan," *The Peking and Tientsin Times*, 10 November 1894, p. 142.

[199] "Chinese Loans," *The North-China Herald* (Shanghai), 14 December 1894, p. 959.

[200] "The War Loan in the Coast Districts" and "The Chinese War Loan," *The North-China Herald* (Shanghai), 21 December 1894, p. 1023; "The Chinese War Loan," *The North-China Herald* (Shanghai), 21 December 1894, pp. 1024–5.

[201] "The War Loan at Canton," *The North-China Herald* (Shanghai), 28 December 1894, pp. 1055–6.

[202] "The Kiangsu Imperial Loan," *The North-China Herald* (Shanghai), 11 January 1895, p. 55.

[203] "The War Loan in Kuangtung," *The North-China Herald* (Shanghai), 18 January 1895, p. 89.

[204] Vladimir, 220. For more information about Japanese war loans, see Eastlake and Yamada, 446–64.

[205] Citing *Der Ostasiatische* in "China's Armies," *The North-China Herald* (Shanghai), 27 July 1894, p. 150. For a similar view see Alfred Cunningham, *The Chinese Soldier and Other Sketches* (London: Sampson, Low, Marston, 1899?), 29.

[206] Cited in Powell, 16.

that this attitude had a significant impact on the caliber of the persons serving in arms and particularly on the officers.[207]

In 1892, the New York *World* interviewed the inspector general of the Imperial Maritime Customs, Sir Robert Hart. The interviewer remarked on what he considered an astonishing parade of Chinese soldiers that he had just seen. He noted that the soldiers were "actually armed with bows and arrows and firearms of the most antique pattern." "Most people are surprised," Hart replied, "for incredible as it may appear, while possessing as she does some of the finest types of modern warships, the Chinese army is still in many respects absolutely what it was three hundred years ago – merely an armed undisciplined horde. There seems as yet no signs of her waking up from this lethargy."[208]

Two years later, at the outbreak of hostilities, the situation remained the same. A foreign observer described the Chinese troops being sent to Korea: "In front marched their leader with fixed bayonet and a very conscious sense of his own importance. Next came a heavily laden Pekingese small cart, going faster than I ever succeeded in getting a carter to drive me; on the back of this there were slung, without any protection whatever, perhaps three dozen mud-bespattered and rusty old-fashioned rifles. This cart was followed by an open farmer's wagon laden with cases and kegs of gunpowder, atop of which perched a new-enlisted rustic complacently nursing his water-pipe. These are fair specimens of the 'brave' procession."[209]

In 1894 Lord Curzon wrote, "Of discipline in the highest sense the Chinese have none; and no arms in the world...placed in untrained hands, can make them follow leaders who are nincompoops, or resist an enemy whose tactics...they do not understand. They have no idea of marching or skirmishing, or of bayonet or musketry practice. The only recruiting test is the lifting to the full stretch of the arms above the head of an iron bar, from the ends of which are hung two stones, weighing 9 1/2 stone the pair. Their drill is a sort of gymnastic performance, and their ordinary weapons are tufted lances, spears, battle-axes, tridents, and bows and arrows, with an ample accompaniment of banners and gongs. Rifles of obsolete pattern, bought second-hand or third-hand in Europe, are dealt out to those who are on active service. These and their ammunition are mostly worthless from age.

---

[207] "An Epitome of the Chino-Japanese War," Du Boulay, 3; Intelligence Division to Foreign Office, 16 July 1894, *British Documents*. Nish, ed., 56; Herbert, 689; Powell, 16, 35; Curzon, 3rd ed., 353.

[208] Julius M. Price, *World*, quoted in "A Talk with Sir Robert Hart at Peking," *The North-China Herald* (Shanghai), 21 September 1894, p. 500.

[209] "Brave" is a pun on the word's use, in its conventional sense as an adjective, and, in its Chinese military sense, as a noun. Troops of the Manchu banner forces were referred to as "braves." "Manchuria," *The North-China Herald* (Shanghai), 17 August 1894, p. 264.

The weapon of the majority is, however, an ancient matchlock, of which the most familiar pattern is the *jingal,* which requires two men to fire it. All these drawbacks or delinquencies, however, shrink into nothingness when compared with the crowning handicap of the native officer." [210]

Unbeknownst to these foreign observers, the prevalence of bows and arrows had a cultural dimension. As foreign occupiers of an alien land, the Manchus strove hard to preserve their ethnic and cultural identity against the strong pull of the Han Chinese civilization. The Qing Dynasty focused on preserving the "Manchu Way," which found its expression in the dexterity with both horse and arrow, fluency in the Manchu language, and adherence to a simple traditional life-style. [211] Those armed with bows and arrows were undoubtedly in large part Manchu banner forces. Bows and arrows were part of their standard military issue and visible proof of their pride in their cultural heritage.

During the war a reporter for *The New York Times* described the sad pageant: "The Chinese troops have proved to be a heavy burden on Corea already. Rapine and violence have marked their course. It is notorious that no good Chinaman enters the army, and, with the exception of a few thousand foreign-drilled troops, her multitudes of braves are hordes of freebooters. They neither give nor take quarter." [212] According to the Intelligence Division of the British Government, despite the importation of huge quantities of firearms, "the majority of the Chinese army is to this day armed with the now almost prehistoric matchlock." [213] The Japanese general staff estimated that only three-fifths of the Chinese army was armed with some kind of rifle. The rest had only a pike, spear, or sword. [214]

Le Journal des débats politiques et littéraires noted that, in contrast to the "spirit of banditry" of the Chinese soldiers, Japanese troops were "well-disciplined." [215] The Intelligence Division of the British Government observed that the Japanese army was "well equipped and organized and ready for work." It predicted a Japanese victory. [216] Indeed, the Japanese army was national, organized

---

[210] Curzon, 3rd ed., 351–2. For similar opinions, see "Les Affaires de Corée: La Situation militaire" (Korean Affairs: The Military Situation), *Journal des débats politiques et littéraires* (*Journal of Political and Literary Debates*) (Paris), 26 July 1894, morning edition, p. 1.

[211] Elliott, "Resident Aliens," 406.

[212] "Corean Light on the Far East," *The New York Times,* 27 October 1894, p. 12.

[213] Intelligence Division to Foreign Office, July 1894, doc. 91, *British Documents,* Nish, ed., 54–6.

[214] Powell, 39.

[215] "La Guerre entre la Chine et le Japon" (War between China and Japan), *Journal des débats politiques et littéraires* (*Journal of Political and Literary Debates*) (Paris), 28 July 1894, morning edition, p. 1.

[216] Intelligence Division to Foreign Office, July 1894, doc. 91, *British Documents,* Nish, ed., 54–6.

on the Prussian model, and based on universal conscription with a standard term for service. Likewise, the organization of the Japanese navy conformed to the most modern navies of its day. Less needs to be said about either than about their Chinese counterparts because in structure the Japanese army and navy were very similar to those of Europe. Universal conscription had been instituted in 1872. Men served for three years in the regular army, followed by four years in the reserves. They were uniformly armed with the Japanese-made single-shot Murata breech-loader rifle. Similarly, the artillery and soldiers' kit were all standardized. The army was composed of six divisions. During the war, commanders were given precise objectives but with the freedom to decide how to reach them.[217] In 1892, the Japanese army had engaged in comprehensive war games. A French observer had come away with "the best impression" of the Japanese army.[218] On July 30, 1894, *Le Journal des débats politiques et littéraires* ran a long article comparing the Chinese and Japanese armies. The author concluded that "one can only note an appreciable difference and all to the advantage of the latter. In twenty-five years they have been able to create a really homogeneous army and with an incontestable solidity due to a remarkable spirit for results and an absolute unity of direction and instruction." He had praised their modernization methods: "The Japanese moreover do not conceal at all their intention to free themselves little by little from foreign instructors as well as foreign industry." But the author did not dare predict whether or not the Japanese would ultimately succeed; he took the attitude that only time would tell.[219] For the navy, Japan had three bases – at Yokosuka, Kure, and Sasebo – each with its own squadron. In addition to these three locations, there were also excellent dockyards at Nagasaki. During the war these forces were subdivided into groups composed of four vessels.[220] The Meiji government had modeled its fleet on the British navy and its doctrine on the teachings of Captain Mahan. More of Mahan's writings were translated into Japanese than into any other language.[221] Captain John Ingles, who had taught for six years at the Naval Staff College in Japan, said in an interview, "Japanese naval

---

[217] Vladimir, 56–62; Japan, Imperial General Staff, 33–7; "An Epitome of the Chino-Japanese War," Du Boulay, 4–6.

[218] "L'Armé japonaise aux grandes manœuvres de 1892" (Japanese army at the major maneuvers of 1892), *Le Journal des débats politiques et littéraires* (*Journal of Political and Literary Debates*) (Paris), 8 August 1894, morning edition, pp. 1–2.

[219] Charles Malo, "Revue militaire: Les armés de la Chine et du Japon" (Military Review: The Armies of China and Japan), *Journal des débats politiques et littéraires* (*Journal of Political and Literary Debates*) (Paris), 30 July 1894, evening edition, p. 1.

[220] Vladimir, 63; "An Epitome of the Chino-Japanese War," Du Boulay, 4.

[221] Evans and Peattie, 11, 24.

officers are much impressed with the advantage in a land war of superiority at sea. They have been, I know, faithful students of the American naval historian, Captain Mahan." He presciently noted that "the modern and well-equipped Japanese army is entirely a new factor in a war among Eastern nations."[222]

When Japan initially mobilized well over 100,000 troops,[223] even the editors at *The North-China Herald* were impressed. "No one can help admiring the ability and thoroughness with which the Japanese carried out their mobilisation, and the completeness of their preparations, a strong contrast to those of China."[224] The Japanese military strategy was first to seize control of the sea so that the navy could transport soldiers at will to the mainland. Then the Japanese army would invade Korea to expel China. After the occupation of Korea, Japan would take the Chinese naval base at Weihaiwei on the southern shores of the Bohai (渤海), providing naval access to Peking. This would be followed by an invasion of the metropolitan province of Zhili. If the grand plan proved unfeasible, Japan would simply expel China from Korea. However, if disaster struck and China, not Japan, took command of the sea, then Japan would focus on its own coastal defenses to prevent a Chinese invasion. Within the first week of the war, the Japanese army decided on the military strategy.[225] It divided its forces into two armies: the First Army under Yamagata Aritomo (山県有朋) would invade Korea and enter Manchuria from the north, while the Second Army under the minister of war, Marshal Ōyama Iwao (大山巌), would invade Manchuria from the south to take the naval base on the Liaodong Peninsula and, once the two armies met, leave for Shandong Province to take the naval base at Weihaiwei.[226] Under this strategy, after the first phase of the war, the Japanese navy would play a secondary role to the army.[227] Once the navy had secured command of the sea it would be reduced to a transport service to ferry soldiers to the Asian mainland. This would mean that when victory came much of the glory would go to the Japanese army as its troops converged on

---

[222] "The Chino-Japanese War," *The Pall Mall Gazette* (London), 18 August 1894, 4th ed., p. 7; Evans and Peattie, 36.

[223] "Telegraphs in Korea," *The Japan Weekly Mail* (Yokohama), 4 August 1894, p. 122.

[224] "Foreigners in Japanese Service," *The North-China Herald* (Shanghai), 20 July 1894, p. 89. For other positive reports on the Japanese troop mobilization, see "Japanese Eager to Enlist," *The New York Times*, 29 July 1894, p. 5.

[225] Lone, 33; 高橋秀直 (Takahashi Hidenao), 日清戦争の道 (*Road to the Sino-Japanese War*) (Tokyo: 東京創元社, 1995), 484–5.

[226] "Movements of the Headquarters of the Japanese Armies" and "A Summary of the Port Arthur Campaign," Du Boulay, n.p.; Chang Chi-yun (張其昀), 中國歷史地圖 (*Historical Atlas of China*), vol. 2 (Taipei: 中國文化大學出版部印行, 1984), 117.

[227] Takahashi, 484.

Peking and compelled the Chinese government to capitulate. As a freshly minted service, only organized as a fleet in 1887, and as a service whose leaders began their own careers in the land forces, the navy at this time was only in the process of developing a separate service identity.[228] While the navy was amenable to playing second fiddle to the army in this war, it would become increasingly restive in Japan's subsequent wars against Russia and the United States.

In the first phase of the war, however, naval force played the key role. The only efficient way for either Japan or China to deploy troops in Korea was by sea. There could be no war if Japan could not ferry its troops to Korea. China, though connected to Korea by land, was actually in a similar position. It possessed only one short railway line between Tianjin, the seat of Viceroy Li, to the coast and then north to Shanhaiguan, where the Great Wall meets the sea.[229] The line was good as far as it went, but it ended a long way from the Korean border. China had no railway lines beyond the Great Wall, and the road system in Manchuria and Korea was woefully inadequate.[230] The Japanese government had long recognized the importance of the ability to conduct rapid and massive troop deployments. It had subsidized the country's large steamship companies so that their vessels would be available in times of war. The Japan Mail Steamship Company (日本郵船株式会社) supplied almost ninety steamships for transport service during the war.[231] In contrast, the Chinese merchant marine was only about one-third that of Japan.[232] A front-page article in the Berlin *Neue Preussische Zeitung* painted a more extreme picture with only 40 troop transports belonging to China versus 450 to Japan.[233] Even so, Japan required the services of foreign merchant ships to help supply her troops on the Asian mainland.[234] Whereas the Japanese cobbled together adequate transport capacity or what we call today adequate "lift," China could

---

[228] Evans and Peattie, xxi–xxii.

[229] Japan, Imperial General Staff, 21.

[230] At the time, the Tianjin-Mukden (Shenyang) railroad was still under construction. It reached from Tianjin to six miles beyond the Great Wall. Although the earth work for the line was nearly complete for 150 miles beyond the Great Wall, the track had yet to be laid. "Japanese Next Station," *The New York Times*, 20 February 1895, p. 5.

[231] "Compilers' note, Mil. Inf. Div., War Dept. on 'Notes on the Japan-China War' General Inf. Series, No. XIV, Off. of Naval Intelligence." Du Boulay, 1; Eastlake and Yamada, 434–45.

[232] Herbert, 690–1.

[233] "Der chinesisch-japanische Konflikt" (Sino-Japanese Conflict), *Neue Preussische Zeitung* (*New Prussian Newspaper*) (Berlin), 25 July 1894, p. 1.

[234] John Robert Russell, "The Development of a 'Modern' Army in Nineteenth Century Japan" (Master's thesis, Columbia University, 1957), 86–7.

not.[235] Transport capacity had not been the focus of the influential American naval strategist, Captain Alfred Thayer Mahan, who was so popular in Japan. Yet this logistical capability would prove critical to the outcome of the Sino-Japanese War.

However, the lessons that the West did derive from the war supported Mahan's emphasis on the command of the sea. From the point of view of the Japanese navy, once it had secured command of the sea through victory in a showdown between major battleships, the army would simply be engaged in a mopping up operation in China. When *The Pall Mall Gazette* interviewed a long-time resident of Japan, the resident predicted that the war would be a naval war: "Which ever side holds the chief commercial ports of Korea...with the capital, completely controls the country. If Japan succeeds at the outset in sweeping the Chinese from those waters...she wins the key to the whole situation. It would be impossible for China to send up troops" since the land route entailed "an enormous distance" where provisioning and feeding a large army would be unmanageable even for "a well-organized European nation."[236] The British press reiterated that the war would be won or lost at sea.[237] *Neue Preussische Zeitung* predicted that these naval battles would offer lessons for all sea powers concerning the effectiveness of such naval innovations as the latest armored ships and quick-firing guns.[238]

Given the relative states of the Japanese and Chinese armies and of the domestic political situations in both countries, rapid command of the sea would indeed prove decisive for the outcome of the Sino-Japanese War. If Japan could not secure command of the sea, it could not safely transport its troops to the mainland. If China could not command the sea or at least deny access to the Korean and Manchuria littoral to Japan, it would have to depend on its antiquated and fragmented land forces to defend Peking. The Chinese government believed that in this unhappy scenario the bitter Manchuria winter in combination with its land forces would still prove adequate to wear out the Japanese. Most Chinese believed time to be on their side so that, even under the worst-case scenario, an attrition

---

[235] "The Japanese Navy," *The Pall Mall Gazette* (London), 26 July 1894, 4th ed., p. 3.

[236] "Comparison of the Belligerents' Chances," *The Pall Mall Gazette* (London), 28 July 1894, 4th ed., p. 7.

[237] Spenser Wilkinson, "China and Japan," *The Pall Mall Gazette* (London), 11 August 1894, 4th ed., p. 1.

[238] Count v. Dürkheim, "Der Seestreitkräfte Chinas und Japans und die aus dem entbannten Kriege für uns zu schöpfenden Lehren I" (The Chinese and Japanese Naval Forces and the Lesson for Us to Learn from the Unfolding War I), *Neue Preussische Zeitung* (*New Prussian Newspaper*) (Berlin), 4 August 1894, morning edition, p. 1; Count v. Dürkheim, "Der Seestreitkräfte Chinas und Japans und die aus dem entbannten Kriege für uns zu schöpfenden Lehren II" (The Chinese and Japanese Naval Forces and the Lesson for Us to Learn from the Unfolding War II), *Neue Preussische Zeitung*

strategy would prove sufficient to send the Japanese packing.

Unlike Chinese land forces, the Beiyang Squadron was supposed to be one of the top ten navies of its day.[239] As hostilities began to seem imminent, European papers began running articles comparing the Chinese and Japanese navies.[240] Since both the Beiyang Squadron and the Japanese navy had state-of-the-art equipment, there was no consensus on which was superior, but before the first major engagement in mid-September the coverage of China from abroad was very favorable.[241] In May of 1894, Viceroy Li made a three-week triennial inspection of the northern coastal defenses. At Weihaiwei, he hosted foreign observers. Li impressed Westerners personally with his unflagging energy despite his seventy-two years and militarily with the precise maneuvers of his fleet.[242] According to the naval correspondent of *The Peking and Tientsin Times,* "The officers in command of the navy...have strikingly shown to the world at large that they have the ability to manage their

---

(*New Prussian Newspaper*) (Berlin), 4 August 1894, evening edition, p. 1.

[239] Benjamin Franklin Cooling, *Gray Steel and Blue Water Navy: The Formative Years of America's Military-Industrial Complex 1881–1917* (Hamden, CT: Archon Books, 1979), 136. Cooling provides a list of the top European navies in 1896. By capacity, China and Japan would have been in the top ten in 1895.

[240] "The Peiyang Squadron," *The North-China Herald* (Shanghai), 29 June 1894, p. 1009; "The Japanese Navy," *The Pall Mall Gazette* (London), 26 July 1894, 4th ed., p. 3; "La Guerre entre la Chine et le Japon" (War between China and Japan), *Journal des débats politiques et littéraires* (*Journal of Political and Literary Debates*) (Paris), 28 July 1894, morning edition, p. 1; "Summary of News," *The Japan Weekly Mail* (Yokohama), 23 June 1894, p. 745; "Les Affaires de Corée: La Situation militaire" (Korean Affairs: The Military Situation), *Journal des débats politiques et littéraires* (*Journal of Political and Literary Debates*) (Paris), 26 July 1894, morning edition, p. 1; Charles Malo, "Revue militaire: Les armés de la Chine et du Japon" (Military Review: The Armies of China and Japan), *Journal des débats politiques et littéraires* (*Journal of Political and Literary Debates*) (Paris), 30 July 1894, evening edition, p. 1.

"The Chinese Navy," *The Japan Weekly Mail* (Yokohama), 8 September 1894, pp. 294–5; "Korean Affairs," *The Japan Weekly Mail* (Yokohama), 7 July 1894, pp. 13–4; "The Peiyang Squadron," *The North-China Herald* (Shanghai), 29 June 1894, p. 1009. The reports in the two newspapers are identical. For other reports on the relative strengths of the Chinese and Japanese navies, see "China's Navy" and "Japan's Navy," *The Peking and Tientsin Times,* 8 September 1894, p. 108.

[241] For a view more critical of the Chinese navy see Count v. Dürkheim, "Die Seestreitkräfte Chinas und Japans und die aus dem entbannten Kriege für uns zu schöpfenden Lehren I" (The Chinese and Japanese Naval Forces and the Lesson for Us to Learn from the Unfolding War I), *Neue Preussische Zeitung* (*New Prussian Newspaper*) (Berlin), 4 August 1894, morning edition, p. 1; Count v. Dürkheim, "Die Seestreitkräfte Chinas und Japans und die aus dem entbannten Kriege für uns zu schöpfenden Lehren II" (The Chinese and Japanese Naval Forces and the Lesson for Us to Learn from the Unfolding War II), *Neue Preussische Zeitung* (*New Prussian Newspaper*) (Berlin), 4 August 1894, evening edition, p. 1.

[242] "The Viceroy Li's Inspection," *The North-China Herald* (Shanghai), 8 June 1894, p. 883; "Li Hung-chang's Tour of Inspection," *The North-China Herald* (Shanghai), 15 June 1894, p. 925.

own naval affairs without assistance from outside...The discipline of the crews seems to be of the first order and the cleanliness and smartness of the ships, material and men, leaves nothing to be desired." The maneuvers "were carried out with astonishing precision," while the heavy artillery and quick-firing guns displayed "deadly effect" and the "torpedo practice under steam of the ships...proved another feat of the highest order." The correspondent also admired the "powerful forts, dock yards, work shops, armouries, piers, store-rooms, colleges, hospitals, etc., etc.," at Port Arthur, Dalian, and Weihaiwei. He concluded that this proved Viceroy Li, "with his unique knowledge of men and things, has put the right men in the right place."[243] Foreign observers made little of it at the time, but the outbreak of the Tonghak Rebellion forced Li to cut short his tour and return to Tianjin. It turned out that the viceroy was a better judge than they on the severity of the unraveling situation in Korea.[244]

Despite the well-orchestrated naval maneuvers of May, other commentators took a less sanguine view. In 1890, the long-time British naval adviser, Captain William M. Lang, along with the other commissioned officers of the British navy at the Beiyang Squadron had resigned in protest because, during the leave of absence of Admiral Ding Ruchang (丁汝昌), their authority had been ignored. Afterward, peculation had become rampant and efficiency had declined.[245] There were reports of serious financial irregularities. In 1893, the Board of War had complained that Viceroy Li's accounts for the expenses of the squadron for 1887 to 1890 were inaccurate, incomplete, and inflated.[246] One newspaper report pointed to the "gross nepotism" and the tendency of the Chinese to rest on their laurels instead of pressing forward with reforms.[247] Another mentioned pervasive gambling (suggesting a lack of discipline) and "systematic peculation," but then noted with undue optimism that these problems had been endemic in Chinese society for millennia and yet China had survived.[248]

Before the war, a Chinese officer had shown off one of the Beiyang Squadron's two great iron-clad battleships to Sir Henry Norman, the noted writer on Asia.

---

[243] Citing *The Peking and Tientsin Times*, 2 June 1894, in "The Chinese Naval Manœuvres," *The North-China Herald* (Shanghai), 8 June 1894, p. 904.

[244] "The Viceroy Li's Inspection," *The North-China Herald* (Shanghai), 8 June 1894, p. 883.

[245] Ballard, 136; Michie, vol. 2, 412; Lee McGiffin, *Yankee of the Yalu: Philo Norton McGiffin, American Captain in the Chinese Navy (1885–1895)* (New York: E. P. Dutton, 1968), 107–11.

[246] "Finding Fault," *The North-China Herald* (Shanghai), 4 May 1894, p. 685.

[247] "Li Hung-chang's Tour of Inspection," *The North-China Herald* (Shanghai), 15 June 1894, pp. 925–6.

[248] "The Chinese Navy," *The Japan Weekly Mail* (Yokohama), 8 September 1894, pp. 294–5.

When Norman had requested to be shown one of the quick-firing guns, an officer had ordered the protective canvas to be removed from the gun only to expose a barrel "filled with chop-sticks and littered with rice and pickles." Norman then described a feud between two mandarins over an arms shipment. In the end they had split a shipment between their two arsenals located hundreds of miles apart, so that neither possessed a working gun. He also reported that a well-known European manufacturer had delivered cocoa powder to Port Arthur in lieu of gunpowder, with both Europeans and Chinese pocketing the difference in value.[249]

The North China Daily News also provided ominous reports: "As to their ships, they could only fight one battle, for no reserves of coal have been provided, or of gunpowder, or other stores. The officers and men are good enough, and they are quite ready to fight, but in their unprovided condition it would be grossly unfair to pit them against such a thoroughly organised, and well-provided navy as that of Japan."[250] According to *The North-China Herald,* "Enormous sums have been spent on ships and forts and naval stations; and the naval stations have no coal, the ships and forts have no ammunition, the regiments have not half the number of men for whom pay is drawn, and the warships are commanded by men whose last thought is fighting, and who try to get below the water line when they see an enemy's ship. The only officers who have shown themselves of any use so far are the young men who have been educated abroad, or under foreign supervision in the naval academies and training ships."[251] This was the minority opinion provided by long-term European residents in China. In Europe, numbers were still believed to be decisive: China was big, therefore it would win.

Prior to the major naval engagements of the war, Reuter's Agency interviewed Captain William M. Lang, formerly an admiral of the Chinese fleet. "As compared with the Japanese, the Chinese Navy is about equal. Probably, the Japanese have more dash and go, and there is among them more *esprit de corps*. Otherwise the two naval forces are about the same."[252] He described Admiral Ding Ruchang of the Beiyang Squadron in the most flattering terms and predicted, "In the end there is no doubt that Japan must be utterly crushed."[253] Ōkuma's official organ, *Hōchi*

---

[249] Norman, 265–6. For other similar stories, see Michie, vol. 2, 412–3.

[250] Quoted in "Shanghai News," *The Japan Weekly Mail* (Yokohama), 14 July 1894, p. 42.

[251] "Foreigners and the War," *The North-China Herald* (Shanghai), 24 August 1894, p. 293.

[252] "The Chinese Navy," *The North-China Herald* (Shanghai), 21 September 1894, p. 501; "China and Japan," *The Peking and Tientsin Times,* 3 November 1894, p. 139.
  For other early comparisons of the Chinese and Japanese naval and land forces, see "Forces of China and Japan," *The New York Times,* 23 July 1894, p. 5.

[253] "The Chinese Navy," *The North-China Herald* (Shanghai), 21 September 1894, p. 501; "China

Shinbun (報知新聞), agreed that the navies and officers were roughly equivalent, but the Chinese sailors were described as a bunch of indolent opium addicts unfamiliar with firearms.[254] Officers of the Japanese navy, however, were less optimistic, fearing the enemy possessed both quantitative and qualitative superiority. The Chinese navy possessed twice as many warships, the best two of which were superior in armaments and armor to anything possessed by Japan, and its naval bases were nearer the war theater. In reality, most of China's vessels were out of date, while Japan had faster ships overall and an advantage in quick-firing guns.[255]

After the declarations of war, the Japanese poured troops into Korea. As long as the Beiyang Squadron remained intact, the Japanese military had to be very cautious about transporting these troops. The Japanese government was also aware that its troops were the most vulnerable to attack when en route to Korea in transport ships. Disposing of Japan's troops at sea would have been China's most effective means to undermine Japan's military strategy. Therefore the initial Japanese landings took place in Wônsan (元山), on the central part of the eastern coast, as far away as possible from the Chinese naval bases at Weihaiwei and Port Arthur. Other landings occurred at Pusan, on the southern tip of the Korean Peninsula, nearest to Japan. These deployments entailed arduous marches to Seoul. In late August, the Japanese army concluded that considerations of disease, fatigue, and time made landing at Inch'ôn worth the risk.[256]

Viceroy Li missed a key opportunity by not targeting the Japanese troop transports. He made a crucial strategic error by ordering his fleet not to sortie east of the Yalu River–Weihaiwei line, that is, anywhere off the Korean Peninsula. He wanted to minimize the risk of engaging the Japanese fleet in order to save his two ironclad battleships to deter attack on the coast and to use his fleet for convoy duty to protect Chinese troop deployments.[257] Li focused on a prevent-defeat strategy, that is, on a strategy to preserve his modern navy intact to fight Japan another day. This decision ceded the initiative to the Japanese. The Japanese would choose the

and Japan," *The Peking and Tientsin Times*, 3 November 1894, p. 139. This article was translated in 朝日新聞. "清國北洋艦隊の勢力及組織" (Strength and Organization of the Chinese Beiyang Squadron), 朝日新聞 (*Rising Sun Newspaper*) (Tokyo), 17 June 1894, p. 6.

[254] "Fighting Strength of the Japanese and Chinese Navies," *The Japan Weekly Mail* (Yokohama), 23 June 1894, p. 748. The story was reprinted in "The Fighting Strength of the Japanese and Chinese Navies," *The North-China Herald* (Shanghai), 29 June 1894, p. 1014.

[255] Evans and Peattie, 38–9; Vladimir, 63; "An Epitome of the Chino-Japanese War," Du Boulay, 4.

[256] Chang Chi-yun, vol. 2, 117; Lone, 35; Sun Kefu and Guan Jie, 孙克复 (Sun Kefu) and 关捷 (Guan Jie), eds., 甲午中日陆战史 (*History of the Land Engagements of the Sino-Japanese War*) (Harbin: 黑龙江人民出版社, 1984), 119.

[257] Samuel C. Chu, "Sino-Japanese War," 366; Ballard, 144–6.

timing and location of hostilities. This meant that China would be fighting on Japan's, not China's, terms. Viceroy Li must have believed time to be on his side so that an attrition strategy by Chinese land forces would yield victory. There was a strong tradition in Chinese military thought favoring the defense over the offense unless possessed of greatly superior numbers. The idea was to prolong hostilities in order to undermine the logistical lines of the attacking enemy. Driving up the costs of war would simultaneously drive the Japanese to the negotiating table.[258] If hostilities dragged on into the winter months, the viceroy may have believed that the bitter Korean winter would take its toll on the Japanese troops and their long logistical lines. The British press in China predicted that the Japanese army would "never stand a winter campaign in Corea."[259] Viceroy Li did not appreciate the imperative for China to destroy Japan's land forces at sea, where they were most concentrated and vulnerable.

The next significant battle after Feng Island and the sinking of the *Kowshing* took place four days later, on the night of July 28, 1894, at Sônghwan (歡成),[260] about ten miles northeast of Asan. As mentioned earlier, the Chinese had deliberately encamped their troops outside of Seoul in order to minimize the chances of hostilities, but Japanese forces under the command of Major General Ōshima Yoshimasa (大島義昌) marched to them from Seoul. The Chinese seemed aware of the impending arrival of the Japanese for they had erected forts, dug trenches, constructed new earthworks, and flooded the surrounding rice paddies. The Japanese divided their forces to make a night attack: A small diversionary force engaged the Chinese from the front while the main force marched to the rear of the Chinese flank.[261] Fighting concentrated on opposite banks of the Ansông River (安城). To cross it, the Japanese army surprised the Chinese forces with their successful flanking maneuver. The Chinese fought hard but were unable to hold the town. The Japanese army captured many armaments and pursued the fleeing enemy to Asan for the next battle.[262] The ill-fated *Kowshing* had been bringing reinforcements

---

[258] Allen Fung, 1019–20.

[259] "The Japanese in Corea," *The North-China Herald* (Shanghai), 10 August 1894, p. 240. For similar views that the Japanese would not bear up in a winter campaign, see "Peking," *The North-China Herald* (Shanghai), 9 November 1894, p. 774.

[260] Other spellings include Sông-hwan and Chenghuan.

[261] Eastlake and Yamada, 16–21.

[262] "Japanese Victory in Korea," *The Japan Weekly Mail* (Yokohama), 4 August 1894, p. 124; "Korean Affairs," *The Japan Weekly Mail* (Yokohama), 4 August 1894, p. 127; "Korean Affairs," *The Japan Weekly Mail* (Yokohama), 11 August 1894, pp. 156–8; "The First Land Battle," Du Boulay, 1; Elleman, 98; Russell, 90; Sun Kefu and Guan Jie, 102–13.

to Asan, but Japanese interference had prevented most of them from arriving.[263] Although the Chinese had spent three weeks prior to the battle fortifying the area so that it should have been difficult for the Japanese to take, the defeat at Sŏnghwan seemed to have broken the Chinese morale. Most troops at Asan seemed to have fled in advance of the arrival of Japanese troops, so that the Japanese took the city with ease on the next day. This broke the Chinese encirclement of Seoul. The Chinese had been preparing for a pincer movement against the capital by massing troops at P'yŏngyang in the north and Asan in the south.[264]

The apparent ease of the Japanese victory confounded columnists, who could only conclude that "the Chinese forces fight badly and are ill equipped."[265] A reporter for the Yokohama-based *Japan Weekly Mail* derisively commented: "The Chinese are indeed skilled in the art of running away. As they fled they generally cast off their uniforms and donning the clothes of Koreans made the best of their way to what they considered safe places. The directions toward which they fled are unmistakably indicated by the cast-off uniforms. Even the Vice-commander of the Chinese troops appears to have been tempted to avail himself of this method, for his uniform was left behind in camp."[266] Throughout the war, fleeing Chinese soldiers tried to disguise themselves as civilians. This caused Japanese troops to question whether Chinese men out of uniform near battlefields were actually civilians. Undoubtedly Chinese troops felt that they had no choice, since, according to Chinese military practice, no quarter was given to enemy troops. The Chinese generally summarily executed captives, noncivilian and civilian sympathizers alike.[267]

In contrast, a commentator from the Shanghai-based *North-China Herald* reported that heroic Chinese forces had succumbed to overwhelmingly superior numbers: "The Chinese have retired from the Yashan [Asan] district after several day's heavy fighting, 10,000 Japanese against 3,500 Chinese. In the first days, the Japanese met with a sharp reverse and severe losses, the Chinese loss being unimportant. On July 29th the Chinese withdrew, leaving the camp in charge of a

---

[263] Japan, Imperial General Staff, 47.

[264] Russell, 90; Eastlake and Yamada, 21.

[265] "Korean Affairs," *The Japan Weekly Mail* (Yokohama), 4 August 1894, p. 127; "Korean Affairs," *The Japan Weekly Mail* (Yokohama), 11 August 1894, p. 156; "The Fighting in Korea," *The Japan Weekly Mail* (Yokohama), 11 August 1894, pp. 163–4.

[266] "Korean Affairs," *The Japan Weekly Mail* (Yokohama), 11 August 1894, p. 158.

[267] Chinese unwillingness to take prisoners of war caused friction during the Taiping Rebellion, when the British mercenary Charles G. "Chinese" Gordon, commander of the "Ever-Victorious Army," secured a surrender of Taiping leaders at Suzhou (Soochow) under the protection of a white flag. Viceroy Li overrode Gordon's promise of leniency and summarily executed them all. Kwang-ching Liu, "The Ch'ing Restoration," in *The Cambridge History of China,* Fairbank, ed., 432.

guard of 300 men, who were attacked and captured by an overwhelming force of Japanese before dawn. The guard was killed. The Japanese lost 500 men, found only heavy baggage in the camp, and took no prisoners, many Chinese noncombatants in the vicinity being slain."[268] This report was nonsense.

The Japanese had not engaged a small guard left behind at Asan but the main body of Chinese troops. It had handily defeated them, bagging lots of armaments in the process.[269] The Chinese Court, however, had no way of knowing this. Rather, it issued an imperial decree on August 3 congratulating General Ye Zhichao (葉志超), the commander of the Chinese forces in Korea, for killing over 2,000 "dwarfs" and remunerating him and his troops.[270] Later, when the court found out the real story, General Ye escaped decapitation only through the astute use of "money and influence" – *guanxi* or personal connections in action.[271]

In early August, a reporter for *The Pall Mall Gazette* began wondering about the conflicting reports from correspondents in Japan and China. "From the East comes a perfect Babel of rumours...First we hear of the Japanese victory at sea, and then of a repulse of the Japanese forces by land, culminating in a loss of 2,000 men; and now we are assured, officially, that the Chinese have been routed at Asan, and, unofficially, that three of their war vessels have been captured...If you cannot win a battle on land or sea, you can win it on paper, and let the West know about it...All that we can definitively believe is that fighting has taken place near Asan, and that people have been killed."[272] A month later, *The North-China Herald* was still repeating concocted Chinese stories of victories in the field.

A little article appeared that was a harbinger of things to come: "I read somewhere during the Franco-Chinese war [of 1884–5] the native papers of Shanghai reported the death of Admiral Courbet thirty-seven times, while the number of the killed among the French, according to these reliable (?) sheets reached 1,600,000. The amount of falsehood which these papers have poured forth since the commencement of the 'War of Pygmies and Pigtails' is simply astounding. O, that the word 'liar' had the same force in Chinese as in English for no other

[268] "The War," *The North-China Herald* (Shanghai), 24 August 1894, p. 299.

[269] "Korean Affairs," *The Japan Weekly Mail* (Yokohama), 4 August 1894, p. 27.

[270] "Abstract of Peking Gazette," *The North-China Herald* (Shanghai), 9 November 1894, p. 776. See also "Abstract of Peking Gazette," *The North-China Herald* (Shanghai), 23 November 1894, pp. 857–8; "The War," *The North-China Herald* (Shanghai), 31 August 1894, p. 360; "Abstract of Peking Gazette," *The North-China Herald* (Shanghai), 9 November 1894, p. 776; "The War. Imperial Decrees," *The Peking and Tientsin Times*, 8 September 1894, p. 107.

[271] "The New Chihli Commander-in-Chief," *The North-China Herald* (Shanghai), 30 November 1894, p. 903; Oh, "Background," 348.

[272] "Oh, East is East and West is West," *The Pall Mall Gazette* (London), 6 August 1894, 4th ed., p. 1.

purpose than to enable one to tell a celestial, 'You are a liar!'"[273]

From the onset of the war, the Chinese government had a policy of publicizing false war bulletins. Belligerents often try to arouse public sympathies by selectively releasing and distorting information. The Chinese variation was highly unusual – at least in European and American eyes – because the Chinese officials in Beijing and commanders in the field falsified information that could not be concealed. During the war, the Chinese government reported each battle as a Chinese triumph.

There are a variety of reasons for such blatant lying. Undoubtedly, in the beginning there was the hope that the defeats would prove only temporary and would soon be buried by an accumulation of victories. Had this happened, the initial falsifications would have been soon forgotten in a blaze of victories. There was another reason for the false reports from the front. In China, a lost battle often translated into a lost head for the responsible commander. The Board of Punishments had no qualms about executing loyal, but unsuccessful, officers. There was a well-known sequence of events: The emperor would recall the luckless commander to Peking, have him put before the Board of Punishments, and, with breathtaking rapidity in a land not known for its dispatch, the man would be beheaded in a market square, ending his life in a public spectacle. This created a powerful incentive to conceal the actual military situation from the court. As a result, the court did not have the faintest idea what was going on at the front. Eventually, the movement of the hostilities to locations ever closer to Peking and the reports from foreign witnesses thoroughly undermined the credibility of the Chinese battle reports. The embattled Manchus needed to blame Han commanders for military defeats in order to protect the flagging legitimacy of the dynasty. Therefore, as defeats escalated so did the pressures on the court to execute more Han commanders. Hence the litany of Wonderland-like calls of "Off with his head!"

Once the Chinese Court realized that the victory reports were false, it did not stop the spectacle but continued to issue ludicrously inaccurate reports itself (although it no longer passed out any rewards to its commanders in the field).[274] The policy of lying had its domestic dynastic purposes. Most of the Han literati never understood the extent of China's defeat. This accounted for the ludicrous

---

[273] "Pygmies" refers to the derisive Chinese term for Japanese (dwarfs or 倭人). "Pigtails" refers to the Chinese who wore their hair in a queue. "A celestial" also refers to the Chinese, since another name for China was the Celestial Empire. N. Arraisso, "An Asiatic's Ruminations," *The North-China Herald* (Shanghai), 7 September 1894, p. 408.

[274] For other examples of the false information being circulated in China, see "論日本舉動之可笑" (Concerning the Laughableness of Japanese Conduct), 申報 (*Shanghai Report*) (Shanghai), 13 September 1894, p. 1; "平倭芻議" (Humble Opinion on Quelling the Dwarfs), 申報 (*Shanghai Report*) (Shanghai), 29 September 1894, p. 1.

policy suggestions found in memorials to the throne even very late in the war. The increasingly discredited Manchu Dynasty teetered on the brink of being toppled by the Han Chinese. To stay in power, it had to manipulate domestic sentiment so that the Han Chinese response to the foreign threat would be to remain loyal to the dynasty rather than to join with the Japanese to expel the Manchus. So it continued trying to manipulate domestic sentiment by heaping the blame on its Han Chinese commanders.

After the defeat at Asan, there were rumors that the emperor had degraded Li by stripping him of the Order of the Yellow Riding Jacket. *The Pall Mall Gazette* attributed this to intrigue in Peking, not to false reports of victories in Korea.[275] Former U.S. Secretary of State John W. Foster, who had considerable experience in the Far East and who would later play a key role in the peace negotiations, had a more perceptive observation. "It must have been a very grave neglect that would bring about such a severe measure...It is...an indication of loss of the confidence of the Government in the administrative head of affairs."[276] Some speculated that Li had been demoted because his diplomatic efforts failed to avert war and, consequently, was blamed for his dilatoriness in prosecuting the war.[277] Since Li could no longer wear the yellow riding jacket, it was immediately clear to everyone he met that he had been officially degraded.[278] This enormous loss of "face" cast a shadow over his official dealings. As *The New York Times* described him reviewing troops shortly afterward, "The absence of the yellow jacket was the subject of much remark."[279] "Nevertheless Li Hung Chang retains office, and, inasmuch as he has been given entire charge of the naval and military forces, enjoys all the privileges of Viceroy."[280] Li would be a useful scapegoat for the dynasty.

In contrast, the Japanese government had little cause to lie to the press on most issues since it was winning. Early on, *The North-China Herald* accused the Japanese of an adroit use of war propaganda.[281] There is much truth in this

---

[275] "The Chino-Japanese War," *The Pall Mall Gazette* (London), 4 August 1894, 4th ed., p. 7; "May Aid Japan's Chances," *The New York Times*, 4 August 1894, p. 5; "Imperial Decrees," *The North-China Herald* (Shanghai), 7 December 1895, p. 935.

[276] "The Loss of the Yellow Coat," *The New York Times*, 6 August 1894, p. 5.

[277] "Li Hung Chang Was for Peace," *The New York Times*, 10 August 1894, p. 5; "Marching Against Seoul," *The New York Times*, 11 August 1894, p. 5.

[278] *The Pall Mall Gazette* notes that Viceroy Li was seen without the yellow riding jacket but does not comment on its import. "The Chino-Japanese War," *The Pall Mall Gazette* (London), 6 August 1894, 4th ed., p. 1.

[279] "Li Hung Chang in Command," *The New York Times*, 7 August 1894, p. 5.

[280] "Li Still Acting as Viceroy," *The New York Times*, 13 August 1894, p. 5.

[281] "The Future of China," *The North-China Herald* (Shanghai), 14 June 1895, p. 897.

accusation. The Japanese regularly issued bulletins with the latest battle information. While the Japanese casualty figures were ludicrously low, the rest of the information was far more plausible than what was available from the Chinese side. Since the information was accessible, foreign correspondents used it. There are allegations that the Japanese attempted to bribe the Western press.[282] With the sinking of the *Kowshing,* they started a propaganda campaign in the American and European press.[283] According to a contemporary report, the Japanese sought to "capture the European press" by demonstrating that they were "engaged in a crusade against darkness and barbarism, and were spreading light with which they had themselves been illumined by Christendom."[284] The overarching policy objective of Japan was to demonstrate to the industrialized world that it had become a modern power. Therefore, the battle for world public opinion became a key theater for the Japanese. In international affairs, blatant Chinese lying served Japanese purposes since it sharpened the unfavorable comparison between China and Japan.

Internationally, all the lying backfired. The distortions were too obvious and thus served no useful purpose *vis-à-vis* the foreign community. Instead, they destroyed any vestiges of credibility of the Chinese government.[285] Chinese commanders in the field were still reporting mythical victories to the court in December 1894, when Chinese defeat was considered only a matter of time by reputable military experts.[286] As the war progressed such distortions seemed ever more brazen to the foreign community.[287] In their eyes, China was worse than unrepentant: It was hell bent. The effect on the foreign community would entail serious consequences after the war. Foreign disgust combined with Chinese military defeat would open the floodgates to foreign imperialism.

---

[282] Mutsu, 271n.18; James Creelman, "Bloodthirsty Japan," *The World* (New York), 7 January 1895, p. 2; "Japan Tried Bribery," *The World* (New York), 13 January 1895, p. 1; "The Japanese Embroglio," *Blackwood's Edinburgh Magazine* 158 (Sept. 1895): 313–15.

[283] Dorwart, 32, 96–8.

[284] "Japanese Embroglio," 313.

[285] "Chine et Japon" (China and Japan), *Journal de St-Pétersbourg (St. Petersburg Journal)*, no. 218, 30 August 1894, p. 3; "Китайско-японская война " (The Sino-Japanese War), *Московские ведомости (Moscow Gazette)*, no. 265, 27 September 1894 (9 October 1894), p. 2. For other examples of Chinese attempts to downplay the magnitude of their military predicament, see "Японско-Китайская война" (The Sino-Japanese War), *Русские ведомости (Russian Gazette)*, no. 283, 13 October 1894 (25 October 1894), p. 3.

[286] "Imperial Decree," *The North-China Herald* (Shanghai), 18 January 1895, p. 82.

[287] "Conflicting Stories," *The Japan Weekly Mail* (Yokohama), 16 February 1895, p. 197.

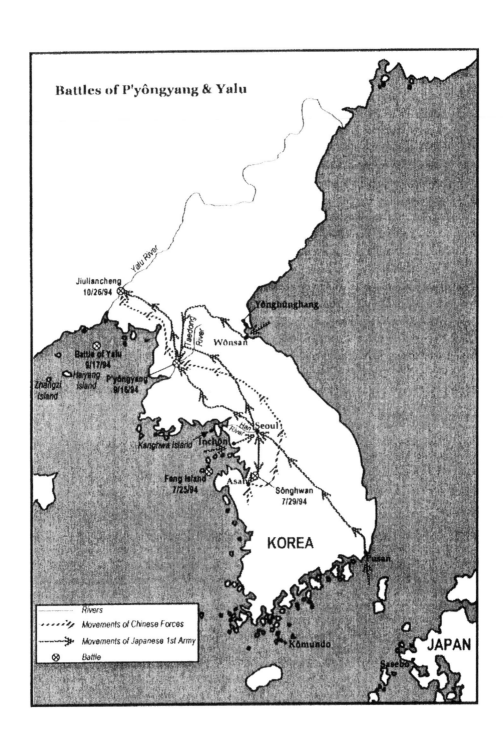

Battles of P'yôngyang & Yalu

Yalu River

Jiuliancheng
10/26/94

Yônghûnhang

Taedong River

Wônsan

Battle of Yalu
9/17/94

Haryang
Island

P'yôngyang
9/16/94

Zhangzi
Island

Han
River

Seoul

Kanghwa Island

Inchôn

Feng Island
7/25/94

Asan

Sônghwan
7/29/94

KOREA

Pusan

Rivers
Movements of Chinese Forces
Movements of Japanese 1st Army
Battle

Kômundo

JAPAN

Sasebo

5

Japan Triumphant:
The Battles of P'yôngyang and the Yalu

The Chinese have sent an army to Korea...But it would be as reasonable to match brave men armed with pitchforks against brave men armed with rifles, as to pit, man for man, the Chinese in their present condition against the Japanese.[1]

The Times of London, September 1894

The Japanese by their victories have drawn the attention of Europe and it is now acknowledged that they have become a great Power. An insular Empire on the Pacific, she has in a generation made herself a strong nation with an army and navy which have won victories over a proud enemy.[2]

The Japan Weekly Mail, September 1894

Between the outbreak of the war in late July and the early fall of 1894, there was no heavy fighting, only some preliminary skirmishes. Two of the four major battles of the war would be fought in a three-day period in mid-September. The final two would be fought in late November of 1894 and early February of 1895. The first of these important battles took place at P'yôngyang (平壤),[3] the former capital of Korea and the future capital of North Korea. The outcome of this battle would determine which country would control the Korean Peninsula. If the Chinese forces could not hold P'yôngyang, they would probably be expelled from the country since the next defensible position was on their bank of the Yalu River, which forms the border with Manchuria. If this happened and the Japanese army

---

[1] Cited in "The Japanese Army in Korea," *The Japan Weekly Mail* (Yokohama), 8 September 1894, p. 295.

[2] "Another Great Power," *The North-China Herald* (Shanghai), 7 December 1894, p. 923.

[3] Other spellings include Pyŏng-yang, Phyŏng-yang, Pingyang, Heijō, and Pingrang.

165

crossed the Yalu River, the rest of the war would be on Chinese territory.

P'yôngyang was surrounded by a wide river to the east and the south, cliffs along the river bank, mountains to the north, and massive city walls that had been fortified to withstand a prolonged siege. Before the battle, all the advantages seemed to belong to the Chinese. They had been massing troops and supplies and constructing fortifications at P'yôngyang for almost two months. At the time of the battle, the Chinese had approximately 13,000 troops dispersed in 27 forts surrounded by trenches and moats. The city lies on the right bank of the Taedong River (大同江), which was large enough to provide a shipping route to the Bohai. Eight thousand of the Chinese troops deployed at P'yôngyang arrived by boat, so that only 5,000 had to make the arduous overland journey from Manchuria. In contrast, because all the Japanese troops had initially been deployed in central or south Korea, they had to make the journey over Korea's miserable roadways through mountainous terrain and across the Taedong River to reach the city. Since the Chinese had made P'yôngyang their base of operations in Korea, it was supplied not just for the defense of the city but for the recapture of the rest of the country.[4] The Chinese sent their most modern equipment there.[5]

The reality of the Chinese situation may have been less favorable. Before the battle, *The Pall Mall Gazette* reported that dispatches "from more than one source agree that the Chinese army in Northern Korea is in a deplorable condition. The generals are said to be grossly incompetent, the minor officers discontented and disheartened, and the rank and file exhausted and dispirited. What roads there were a month ago have been washed away by floods. Transport through Manchuria to Korea is impossible; guns, ammunition, and food stores are blocked, and spoiling all along the long route southward. Food is becoming scarcer every day at the front."[6] The four Chinese commanders in P'yôngyang each commanded his own army and none adequately coordinated with the others. They did parcel out static defensive sectors, but after the Japanese attacked such static demarcations became more of a hindrance than a help. They had only the most general plans: If their lines failed to hold at P'yôngyang, surely their lines would hold at the Yalu River.[7] Weak logistics and organization would plague the Chinese forces throughout the war. Moreover, the Chinese had not planned for a worst-case scenario.

For the Japanese the city had tremendous symbolic importance as the northernmost

---

[4] "The Battle of Phyongyang," Du Boulay, 8; Lone, 35; Eastlake and Yamada, 27–8, 31–2; Sun Fuke and Guan Jie, 122, 128; Russell, 97.

[5] Allen Fung, 1016–17.

[6] "The Chino-Japanese War," *The Pall Mall Gazette* (London), 11 September 1894, 4th ed., p. 7.

[7] Chu, "Sino-Japanese War," 362–5.

point of advance by Toyotomi Hideyoshi's invading army in the sixteenth century.[8] Japanese troops advanced from Wônsan and Seoul to attack the Chinese troops entrenched at P'yôngyang. The main force followed the west coast of Korea to approach the city, while two smaller forces took different inland routes and a final detachment marched from Wônsan. All converged on P'yôngyang to storm the city from four directions. The geography of P'yôngyang made the city difficult to approach from the south or the east but easier from the north, provided that the attacking army was already on the right bank of the Taedong River. Focusing the attack on the north was a high-risk, high-reward strategy. Had the Chinese been prepared, which they were not, the strategy risked the annihilation of the army at the difficult river crossing, but it also promised to deliver the city if successful.[9]

From September 15 to 16, approximately 16,000 Japanese troops made a three-pronged attack on P'yôngyang. The Japanese began the attack from the east at 4:30 A.M. on September 15 with an artillery barrage on the forts on the west bank of the Taedong to divert the Chinese from the main attack, which came from the north and the northwest.[10] The Japanese also feigned an attack from the south while forces under Lieutenant-General Viscount Nozu Michitsura (野津道貫) and Major-General Ōshima Yoshimasa (大島義昌) made a flanking maneuver to deliver the massive blow from the north.[11] The main Japanese force, originally assigned to attack from the southwest, did not end up participating in the main attack that broke through the principal Chinese fortifications, but focused on annihilating Chinese forces as they retreated. Fighting was fierce, with the Chinese launching

---

[8] Vladimir, 103.

[9] Eastlake and Yamada, 28–40; "The Battle of Phyongyang," Du Boulay, 1; Allen Fung, 1020.

[10] Eastlake and Yamada, 28–40; "The Battle of Phyongyang," Du Boulay, 1; Allen Fung, 1020.

[11] "Korean Affairs," *The Japan Weekly Mail* (Yokohama), 22 September 1894, p. 336; "The Battle of Phyông-yang," *The Japan Weekly Mail* (Yokohama), 22 September 1894, p. 337; "The Pyông-yang Prisoners," *The Japan Weekly Mail* (Yokohama), 22 September 1894, pp. 335–6; "The Japanese and Chinese Forces at Phyông-yang," *The Japan Weekly Mail* (Yokohama), 22 September 1894, pp. 344–5; "War Items," *The Japan Weekly Mail* (Yokohama), 29 September 1894, pp. 363–6; "The Fall of Pyông-yang," *The Japan Weekly Mail* (Yokohama), 29 September 1894, p. 369; "War Items," *The Japan Weekly Mail* (Yokohama), 6 October 1894, pp. 388–93; "The War," *The North-China Herald* (Shanghai), 12 October 1894, pp. 617–8; "The Fall of Pingyang," *The North-China Herald* (Shanghai), 12 October 1894, pp. 619–20; "The Contrast between the Japanese and Chinese at Pyông-yang," *The Japan Weekly Mail* (Yokohama), 13 October 1894, p. 413; A. B. De Guerville, "The Battle of Phyông-yang," *The Japan Weekly Mail* (Yokohama), 20 October 1894, pp. 452–4; "平壤占領" (P'yôngyang Occupied), 朝日新聞 (*Rising Sun Newspaper*) (Tokyo), 16 September 1894, p. 1; "平壤の激戰" (Fierce combat at P'yôngyang), 朝日新聞 (*Rising Sun Newspaper*) (Tokyo), 29 September 1894, supplement, pp. 1–2; "平壤の大戰鬥" (Great Battle at P'yôngyang), 朝日新聞 (*Rising Sun Newspaper*) (Tokyo), 30 September 1894, p. 2; "平壤の落す" (Fall of P'yôngyang), 國民新聞 (*People's Newspaper*) (Tokyo), 18 September 1894, p. 2.

repeated cavalry charges, igniting prearranged blazes, and subjecting the Japanese forces to continuous fires. The Chinese put up one of their stiffest resistances of the war, but they committed a gross strategic error when they did not take advantage of the natural barrier created by the river. They made no attempt to attack the Japanese columns while the latter were crossing the river and were at their most vulnerable; rather, they waited behind their fortifications, which proved insufficient. For their part, the Japanese had remarkably poor logistics. Although their strategy required crossing the Taedong River, they had made no advance provisions for doing so. Since they had no pontoon bridges, they had to scrounge up enough Korean river boats to ferry their troops across in secret. In addition, their commissariat was grossly understaffed and their Korean carriers deserted whenever possible. Nevertheless, the Japanese successfully deceived the Chinese as to the main direction of their attack, carried the day, and ripped the Chinese army to shreds. The Japanese victory seems to have had a devastating impact on Chinese morale, for they did not attempt to make another stand until the Yalu River, over 100 miles to the north.[12]

Many believed that "the flower of the Chinese Army was all but annihilated" at P'yŏngyang. If true, this meant the end of the foreign-drilled regiments of the Huai Army and thereby of Li Hongzhang's essential power base.[13] Another view was that Viceroy Li had held back his best troops for this very reason.[14] Even if he had held back his best troops, he still lost a significant portion of his best weapons when his troops left behind the stockpiles of war materiel.[15] A reporter at *The Japan Weekly Mail* doubted that the Chinese had fought very hard: "What resistance was made could not have been very great. This is the more surprising, as the Chinese took possession of the city on the 4th of August and had ample time to thoroughly entrench themselves."[16] Colonel J. F. Maurice, commander of the British Royal Artillery at Colchester, provided his evaluation of the battle: "Field-Marshal Yamagata has conducted the campaign in the most brilliant manner, and

[12] Russell, 96–8; "The Battle of Phyongyang," Du Boulay, 1; Allen Fung, 1020.

[13] "Extracts from 'Advance Japan' by J. Morris, 1895," Du Boulay, 1; John Morris, *Advance Japan: A Nation thoroughly in Earnest*, 2nd ed. (London: W. H. Allen, 1896), 343. For a similar view, see William Elliot Griffis, *The Mikado: Institution and Person* (Princeton: Princeton University Press, 1915), 11; U.S. Adjutant-General's Office, 12n. Kuo concludes that the best Chinese troops were lost in Korea, but he puts their loss at the earlier battle of Asan (54, 72); Allen Fung, 1028.

[14] J. W. Robertson-Scott, *The People of China: Their Country, History, Life, Ideas, and Relations with the Foreigner* (London: Methuen & Co., 1900), 188.

[15] Allen Fung, 1018.

[16] "The Fall of Pyŏng-yang," *The Japan Weekly Mail* (Yokohama), 29 September 1894, p. 369.

his tactics would not have disgraced a Western general."[17] A column in *The Japan Weekly Mail* predicted, "The path to the frontier now lies open to the Japanese."[18]

An article in *The North-China Herald* noted ethnic loyalties that did not bode well for the Manchu dynasty: Troops under the Moslem general Zuo Baogui (左寶貴) had fought very well until he had perished in combat. In contrast, "the Manchu troops have hitherto proved themselves utterly untrustworthy. The Kirin [Jilin] Manchus are far more intent on hunting for something to fill their opium pipes, than on doing anything to uphold the dynasty which has pampered them for so long a time that they seem to have concluded that the dynasty exists for their special benefit."[19] The forces of the Jilin division remained under the separate command of a Manchu general.[20] *The North-China Herald* continued that the Manchu forces at P'yôngyang "retreated almost intact" rather than fight.[21] This was a devastating commentary on the Qing Dynasty. If their own people would not fight for them, why should the Han Chinese? Foreign commentators often noted in passing various examples of tensions between the Han and the Manchus, but they failed to put these tensions in a broader context of explaining the very notable and much-commented-on fact that the Han Chinese troops generally fought miserably throughout the war. Perhaps the Han troops did not consider the fight to be for China but rather for an alien dynasty as detestable as the Japanese. Certainly, the Manchus had failed to supply them with armaments comparable to the routine issue for the Japanese army. It could not have taken the Han conscripts long to figure this out. Later in the war, there were reports of enmity between the Han and Manchu troops. According to *The New York Times*, "The Chinese and Manchou soldiers frequently attack one another, and many bloody fights have taken place."[22]

Prior to the battle, the perception abroad had been that the Chinese were fighting on their own terms at P'yôngyang – the Japanese had needed to do most of the marching to get there and upon arrival had been required to storm well-fortified positions. These perceptions increased the impact of the Japanese victory on the European press. With such a prominent victory, the Russian press took another look at the Chinese military. It ran a stream of articles concerning the endemic

[17] "War News," *The Japan Weekly Mail* (Yokohama), 3 November 1894, p. 509.

[18] "The Chinese Loss at Phyŏng-yang," *The Japan Weekly Mail* (Yokohama), 22 September 1894, p. 343.

[19] "The Fall of Pingyang," *The North-China Herald* (Shanghai), 12 October 1894, p. 620.

[20] "The War in the East," *The Times* (London), 3 October 1894, p. 3.

[21] "The Fall of Pingyang," *The North-China Herald* (Shanghai), 12 October 1894, p. 620.

[22] "Moukden in Anarchy," *The New York Times*, 4 January 1895, p. 5.

problems in the Chinese army and navy.[23] These problems included a lack of training and discipline; cowardice pervading all ranks; and rampant insubordination, desertion, and corruption. Time and again, Chinese officers and troops fled their posts. Time and time again Chinese forces allowed quantities of valuable military supplies to fall into Japanese hands instead of destroying them before retreating.[24] At P'yôngyang, they reportedly left behind 35 good field guns, hundreds of magazine rifles, hundreds of breechloaders, 2,000 tents, and 1,700 horses. The magazine rifles were superior to the Japanese Murata rifles.[25] Some of the hallmarks of the Chinese campaign became evident at P'yôngyang: the abandonment of quantities of ammunition and armaments in the field,[26] the looting and abuse of the local civilian population,[27] the torture and mutilation of prisoners of war,[28] and

[23] "Корея" (Korea), Московские ведомости (Moscow Gazette), no. 258, 20 September 1894 (2 October 1894), p. 3; "Безпорядки в китайской армии" (Disorder in the Chinese Army), Московские ведомости (Moscow Gazette), no. 263, 25 September 1894 (7 October 1894), p. 3; "Оборонительные средства Китая" (The Defenses of China), Новое время (New Times), no. 6690, 25 October 1894, pp. 1–2.

[24] "Китай. Война с Японией" (China. The War with Japan), Московские ведомости (Moscow Gazette), no. 303, 4 November 1894 (16 November 1894), p. 3; "Китай. Война с Японией" (China. The War with Japan), Московские ведомости (Moscow Gazette), no. 304, 5 November 1894 (17 November 1894), p. 4; "Китай. Война с Японией" (China. The War with Japan), Московские ведомости (Moscow Gazette), no. 305, 6 November 1894 (18 November 1894), p. 5; "Chine et Japon" (China and Japan), Journal de St-Pétersbourg (St. Petersburg Journal), no. 289, 10 November 1894, p. 3.

[25] Allen Fung, 1016–17; "平壤分捕の大砲" (Artillery Seized at P'yôngyang), 朝日新聞 (Rising Sun Newspaper) (Tokyo), 27 September 1894, p. 1; "平壤の分捕品" (Articles seized at P'yôngyang), 朝日新聞 (Rising Sun Newspaper) (Tokyo), 28 September 1894, p. 1. The estimates of the exact amounts of equipment vary slightly.

[26] For other examples, see "Korean Affairs," The Japan Weekly Mail (Yokohama), 4 August 1894, p. 127; "Japan. Fall of Phyongyang," The North-China Herald (Shanghai), 28 September 1894, p. 525; "The War in the East," The Times (London), 3 October 1894, p. 3; A. B. De Guerville, "The Battle of Phyöng-yang," The Japan Weekly Mail (Yokohama), 20 October 1894, pp. 452–4; "War News," The Japan Weekly Mail (Yokohama), 3 November 1894, pp. 508–9; "The Progress of the War," The North-China Herald (Shanghai), 2 November 1894, p. 758; "Japan," The North-China Herald (Shanghai), 9 November 1894, p. 771; "War News," The Japan Weekly Mail (Yokohama), 10 November 1894, p. 533; "War News," The Japan Weekly Mail (Yokohama), 24 November 1894, p. 583; "War News," The Japan Weekly Mail (Yokohama), 24 November 1894, pp. 587–8; "War News," The Japan Weekly Mail (Yokohama), 5 January 1895, pp. 10–1; "Panic in China's Capital," The New York Times, 23 January 1895, p. 5; "Latest Telegrams," The Japan Weekly Mail (Yokohama), 2 March 1895, p. 270; "War News," The Japan Weekly Mail (Yokohama), 9 March 1895, p. 281; "Letter from Hushan," The Japan Weekly Mail (Yokohama), 16 March 1895, p. 312; "Stores and Ammunition Captured," The North-China Herald (Shanghai), 15 March 1895, p. 384.

[27] For other examples, see "The Situation in Korea," The Japan Weekly Mail (Yokohama), 1 September 1894, p. 250; "The War in the East," The Times (London), 3 October 1894, p. 3; A. B. De Guerville, "The Battle of Phyöng-yang," The Japan Weekly Mail (Yokohama), 20 October 1894, pp. 452–4; "War News," The Japan Weekly Mail (Yokohama), 24 November 1894, p. 58; "Moukden,"

the use of civilian attire by combatants as a disguise when fleeing the field.[29] From the Japanese point of view, the abandoned war materiel greatly simplified their logistical problems. Throughout the war, as the Chinese fled, the Japanese picked up the abandoned supplies.

The New York Times described the track of the fleeing Chinese as "only too apparent. Rifles, swords, and ammunition, which they had thrown away in their haste to escape, were constantly being found. The fugitives had acted the part of bandits. Villages had been pillaged and afterwards set on fire. Farms had been destroyed and all the stored produce burned. The Korean natives who had resisted the robbers had been ruthlessly slaughtered. Many bodies were found hacked with spear thrusts. The whole line of retreat was one scene of desolation."[30] Korean farmers were extremely poor and had little food to share; therefore, they had no choice but to resist Chinese attempts at requisitioning or starve to death themselves. Either way they died. According to a reporter at *Moskovskie vedomosti*, "The people fear Chinese soldiers much more than the invasion by the Japanese."[31]

Chinese soldiers had little choice but to plunder or starve because they had no commissariat and they were notoriously poorly paid. China remained in the traditional mode of wars of booty fought by mercenaries. Plunder was about the only perk to soften the miserable lot of the ordinary soldier. Unlike Japan, China

---

The North-China Herald (Shanghai), 12 October 1894, p. 605; "Tientsin," *The North-China Herald* (Shanghai), 23 November 1894, p. 854; "Japan-China," *The North-China Herald* (Shanghai), 7 December 1894, p. 924; "Imperial Decrees of the 17th of December," *The North-China Herald* (Shanghai), 21 December 1894, p. 1021; "The Fall of Port Arthur," *The North-China Herald* (Shanghai), 21 December 1894, p. 1021; "Sacked by the Chinese Soldiery," *The North-China Herald* (Shanghai), 4 January 1895, p. 9; "Imperial Edicts," *The North-China Herald* (Shanghai), 4 January 1895, p. 13; "Moukden in Anarchy," *The New York Times,* 4 January 1895, p. 5; "Imperial Decrees," *The North-China Herald* (Shanghai), 11 January 1895, p. 47; "Another 'General Wei' in Trouble," *The North-China Herald* (Shanghai), 25 January 1895, p. 123; "Planning to Save Pekin," *The New York Times,* 11 February 1895, p. 2; "La Guerre en Chine" (The War in China), *Le Temps* (*The Times*) (Paris), 24 March 1895.

[28] For other examples, see "Interview with the Correspondent of the 'New York Herald,'" *The Japan Weekly Mail* (Yokohama), 20 October 1894, p. 441; A. B. De Guerville, "The Battle of Phyŏng-yang," *The Japan Weekly Mail* (Yokohama), 20 October 1894, pp. 452–4; "The Taking of Port Arthur," *The Japan Weekly Mail* (Yokohama), 8 December 1894, p. 644; "The Fall of Port Arthur," *The Peking and Tientsin Times,* 15 December 1894, p. 163; "The Fall of Port Arthur," *The North-China Herald* (Shanghai), 21 December 1894, p. 1021.

[29] A. B. De Guerville, "The Battle of Phyŏng-yang," *The Japan Weekly Mail* (Yokohama), 20 October 1894, pp. 452–4; "Moukden," *The North-China Herald* (Shanghai), 12 October 1894, p. 605.

[30] "The War in the East," *The Times* (London), 3 October 1894, p. 3.

[31] "Китай. Война с Японией" (China. The War with Japan), *Московские ведомости* (*Moscow Gazette*), no. 303, 4 November 1894 (16 November 1894), p. 3.

had not entered the new era of national armies fighting wars of ideology.[32] Later, when the Chinese army retreated across Manchuria, Reverend John Ross noted how "the country traversed by the Chinese army has been stripped of its vegetation and resembles nothing so much as fields over which locusts have passed."[33] Undoubtedly this was the way the Chinese had always waged war during their many campaigns to suppress ethnic minorities and internal rebellions. This time, however, there were Western observers from wealthy lands who could afford to maintain well-supplied armies. They observed China's traditional methods of warfare and were appalled. As Japan had modernized and become wealthy relative to China, it could afford to fight in the modern way. The Japanese brought their supplies with them. What they lacked, they reputedly bought locally at the going rate.[34] Western observers were struck by the contrast.

Westerners were also disgusted by the Chinese treatment of prisoners of war. Many of their countries were signatories of the August 22, 1864, Geneva Convention mandating protections for prisoners of war. Perhaps this legal system already in place in the West contributed to the opprobrious tone of many of the Western articles concerning Chinese behavior. Two decades later, in World War I, westerners would have a chance to reflect further on barbarity and warfare. During the Sino-Japanese War, the Chinese seemed to revel in torturing the captured and in decapitating the fallen. Part of the Chinese propensity to decapitate the enemy simply reflected the official reward system of payment per head.[35] Undoubtedly it also reflected the inability of the Chinese to care for prisoners of war – they had trouble feeding their own soldiers and provided their own no formal medical care. The easy solution was to execute all prisoners. This does not explain the other mutilations: disembowelment, removal of facial features, extraction of livers, and so on. One can only speculate on the reasons for the widespread mutilation of captives and corpses. According to the Qing penal code, the direst crime was that of insurrection. It was the worst of the ten "abominations."[36] The Chinese probably considered Japanese actions to be a rebellion against the Confucian order meriting

---

[32] Lone, 58.

[33] "The War in the East," *The Times* (London), 23 November 1894, p. 5.

[34] "Corean Light on the Far East," *The New York Times*, 27 October 1894, p. 12; "The War," *The North-China Herald* (Shanghai), 7 December 1894, p. 944; Kuo, 82–3.

[35] See for instance, "Proclamation by the Kiangnan Arsenal Authorities, Near Shanghai," *The North-China Herald* (Shanghai), 7 September 1894, p. 411; "The Port Arthur Atrocities," *The Japan Weekly Mail* (Yokohama), 22 December 1894, p. 702; "Japan on Its Behavior," *The New York Times*, 18 December 1894, p. 5.

[36] Boulais, 28.

the most severe punishment. It could be argued that the entire Qing penal system was a codified system of torture, where physical abuse was a routine part of interrogations. Punishments short of execution included the cangue, handcuffs, and shackles on the low end and caning, ankle-crushers, finger-crushers, the Chinese rack, and, the simple but excruciating, prolonged kneeling on chains on the high end.[37] Notions of *habeas corpus* and presumption of innocence were strictly Western concepts. They were totally alien to the Chinese tradition of coercing confessions from the incarcerated. The cruel treatment of Japanese captives may also have reflected traditional Chinese views concerning their own cultural supremacy and disgust for barbarians. The mutilations turned stomachs in the West and made the Japanese livid.

A particularly well-documented case of torture occurred when the American secretary of state ordered his consul in Shanghai to hand over to Chinese authorities two Japanese accused of spying.[38] Although Chinese officials in Shanghai had promised not to torture them, this was precisely what happened. The tortures included kneeling on chains while their captors stood on their legs, the removal of fingernails, the crushing of tongues, the pouring of boiling water on their handcuffed wrists until the metal reached the bone, the smashing of their groins, and decapitation just before they expired from all the other abuses. This did not make good press for the Chinese. Americans were outraged. *The New York Times* ran a front-page article with all the details.[39] Given what people knew about China at the time, whether or not the gruesome details were accurate, the account was considered quite plausible. There was no doubt that the men had been decapitated and that the Chinese government had broken its promise to the United States not to mistreat or execute them. China was fast becoming an international symbol of barbarity. It would not take westerners long to conclude that the country deserved its miserable fate.

The Chinese government's on-going stream of lies concerning the actual (and obvious) military situation only heightened these negative perceptions. According to the battle report ostensibly written by General Zuo Baogui, commander-in-chief of the Fengtian divisions, "on the 17th instant the Chinese army attacked the Japanese at Pingyang [P'yôngyang] and drove them southwards with considerable slaughter to Chungho [Zhonghe], a prefectural city about eleven miles south-west of Pingyang. The Japanese made another stand at Chungho, but were again driven

---

[37] For a list of the mandated punishments, see Boulais, 2–7.

[38] For documents related to this incident, see Vladimir, Appendix E, 248–50.

[39] "Our Naval Force in Asia," *The New York Times*, 28 November 1894, pp. 1, 5; "The Shanghai Incident," *The New York Times*, 29 November 1894, p. 1.

from that city in a southwestward direction the next day, with great slaughter. Chungho is now in the hands of Chinese troops."[40] The evidence of a continued Chinese retreat westward into Manchuria did not conform to General Zuo's report. Nor did the personal history of the general. It became known only several weeks later that he had died in the fighting and therefore would not have been in a position to make the report.[41]

In early October, *The North-China Herald* still did not know what to make of P'yôngyang. It took time for accurate reports to sift out about the land campaign. Telegraph lines were scarce and easily cut while the battlegrounds were distant from the ports. "A special messenger from Pingyang [P'yôngyang] now reports that the Japanese never entered the city at all, and this report is confirmed by two other independent messengers, notwithstanding Oshima's telegrams to the contrary...Oshima seems to follow the methods of Napoleon, who told Prince Metternich that his reports were for the Parisians and as long as the people of Paris believed them it mattered little whether they were true or not." *The North-China Herald* continued, "There was a triumphal entry into Seoul after the Yashan affair [the Battle of Asan], which everyone acknowledges to have been a complete failure from a military point of view. There was an illumination after the Pingyang affair [the Battle of P'yôngyang], which, to say the least, seems to be a very doubtful victory."[42] Major-general Ōshima Yoshimasa (大島義昌) had commanded Japan's original mixed brigade sent to Korea in June of 1894. Thereafter, his troops participated in the campaign to expel Chinese troops from Korea.[43]

In the second week of October, about a month after the battle, more accurate reports started filtering out. The correspondent for *The North-China Herald* reported that the Japanese had taken advantage of the Chinese festivities for the Mid-Autumn Festival (中秋節) to position themselves around P'yôngyang and launch a surprise attack. "The Japanese simply lay on the ground, concealed by the cover, and mowed down the advancing masses. This accounts for the terrible slaughter of the Chinese with very small loss to the Japanese. The Chinese then fled."[44] This

---

[40] "The War, Chinese Victory at Pingyang," *The North-China Herald* (Shanghai), 24 August 1894, p. 300. Zhonghe (中和) was a prefectural city in Pingan (平安) province. Ibid. See also "The War," *The North-China Herald* (Shanghai), 28 September 1894, pp. 534–5.

[41] "Moukden," *The North-China Herald* (Shanghai), 12 October 1894, p. 604.

[42] "Corea," *The North-China Herald* (Shanghai), 5 October 1894, p. 563. Prince Metternich was the foreign minister for the Austro-Hungarian Empire. He was intimately involved in the settlement of the Napoleonic wars and in power for decades thereafter. The allusion is to false reports by Napoleon made to the Parisians. Presumably Napoleon exaggerated his victories and minimized his defeats.

[43] Lensen, vol. 1, 129, 177–8.

[44] "Moukden," *The North-China Herald* (Shanghai), 12 October 1894, p. 605.

account seems plausible. The Japanese were far better armed than the Chinese. Once entrenched, they could easily have mowed down the Chinese in droves. By mid-October, *The North-China Herald* had downgraded Asan, P'yôngyang, and the Yalu from Chinese victories to Japanese "successes," which the Japanese had "failed to follow up" for "want of ability."[45]

The few papers that relied on Japanese, instead of Chinese, sources accurately reported the victor within a day of the battle. The day after the hostilities, *The Pall Mall Gazette* reported that the "Chinese have been utterly routed."[46] As the war continued, more and more papers would abandon their Chinese sources for the Japanese official war bulletins. In the process Japan would acquire a reputation for accuracy and efficiency whereas, from a Western point of view, the Chinese only sank deeper into the mire of their own deceit.

The Japanese government used the Battle of P'yôngyang to score a public relations coup with the West. It had been stung by criticisms of its failure to rescue the drowning during the sinking of the *Kowshing*. This time the Japanese government would use Chinese prisoners of war to showcase modern Japanese medical care and its exemplary treatment of captives. The Japanese military transported approximately 600 prisoners of war to Tokyo. The 111 who were sick or wounded received excellent medical care.[47] This was meant to be a rebuke to the Chinese government, which provided no medical care for its own soldiers let alone for the enemy. The correspondent from *The Japan Weekly Mail* dismissed the details from the battlefield. "What has proved a thousand times more interesting to me is the way the Chinese prisoners and wounded have been treated, and for this I hardly know how to express my admiration...I had some conversation with a captured commander. He said he could not understand the meaning of the Japanese kindness...I went from there to the hospital for wounded Chinese. They were treated exactly as if they were Japanese...I do not see how Japan can be refused the place she rightly claims among the civilized nations of the world."[48]

Although there was extensive reporting on the Chinese prisoners of war captured at P'yôngyang, there were no similar reports for the battles that followed. It is unclear whether other prisoners of war ever received similar treatment. The newspaper record is also silent about prisoner of war camps. Perhaps such camps were simply

---

[45] "The Situation," *The North-China Herald* (Shanghai), 12 October 1894, p. 589.

[46] "The Chino-Japanese War," *The Pall Mall Gazette* (London), 17 September 1894, 4th ed., p. 7.

[47] "Letters from Hiroshima," *The Japan Weekly Mail* (Yokohama), 20 October 1894, p. 451. For more information about these prisoners of war, see "The Chinese Prisoners," *The Japan Weekly Mail* (Yokohama), 10 November 1894, pp. 541–2.

[48] "Letter from Phyŏng-yang," *The Japan Weekly Mail* (Yokohama), 20 October 1894, p. 451–2.

off limits to the press. Or perhaps there were remarkably few prisoners of war. In the general newspaper coverage of the battles, there are numerous accounts of the enemy's being mowed down. This probably was the more usual fate. According to a military analyst, "the Chinese were most frequently found shot or wounded in the back, as a rule without weapons, often only half clothed, as if they had torn their uniforms off in order to be mistaken for non-combatant Chinese."[49] Diaries of Japanese soldiers suggest that Japanese forces were not interested in taking prisoners of war since they would have further burdened Japan's already attenuated supply lines as they later marched deeper and deeper into Manchuria.[50] Other findings later in the war corroborate the information in the diaries.

On March 9, 1895, foreign correspondents arrived on the battlefield an hour after the Battle of Tianzhuangtai (天莊台).[51] It was relatively easy for them to get there since it was located on the Manchurian coast not far from Yingkou (營口), the port for the treaty-port city of Niuzhuang (Newchwang, 牛莊).[52] To the surprise of one correspondent, he found no wounded among the 200 to 300 fallen Chinese but 20 to 30 with cut throats or bayonet stabs in addition to bullet wounds. The gashes suggested that the Japanese had finished them off instead of getting them to medical treatment according to the stipulations of the 1864 Geneva Convention concerning the treatment of soldiers wounded in the field.[53] According to the Geneva Convention, to which Japan but not China was a signatory, the wounded were supposed to be turned over to their respective countries for medical treatment. They were not supposed to be finished off on the ground.[54] A reporter for *The Japan Weekly Mail* excused the apparent murders as a rational response to the Chinese, who tended to empty their final rounds into the nearest Japanese, medical personnel not excepted. Apparently the Chinese could not believe that the Japanese

---

[49] "Port Arthur," Du Boulay, 10.

[50] Lone, 158–9.

[51] Alternate spellings include Tienchwangtai and Tienchuangtai.

[52] The original treaty port had been located at Niuzhuang, up river from the port city of Yingkou. Over time, the foreign settlement swapped from the inland city to the port. The port was referred to as Yingkou and as New Newchwang (Lensen, vol. 1, 191; Chang Chi-yun, vol. 2, 116).

[53] "Tienchwangtai," *The Japan Weekly Mail* (Yokohama), 27 April 1895, p. 483; "A Grave Charge," *The North-China Herald* (Shanghai), 5 April 1895, p. 515; "The Japanese at Newchwang," *The North-China Herald* (Shanghai), 11 April 1895, p. 542.

[54] "War Items," *The Japan Weekly Mail* (Yokohama), 29 September 1894, p. 361; Sakuyé Takahashi, *Cases on International Law during the Sino-Japanese War* (Cambridge: Cambridge University Press, 1899), 1. See article 6 of the Geneva Convention (Switzerland, Politisches Departement, *Documents relatifs à la révision de la Convention de Genève du 22 Août 1864* [Berne: Imprimerie Stæmpfli, 1906], 3).

could possibly intend to help the wounded.[55] Given the negligible Chinese medical care, the Japanese may have regarded any post-battle attempted swap of wounded prisoners to be a dangerous exercise in futility. There was no guarantee that the Chinese would respect the neutrality of the Japanese medical personnel. In addition to suspicious deaths on the battlefield, there were also occasional stories of Japanese massacres of civilians.[56] In any case, after P'yôngyang there were no more stories of Chinese prisoners of war being shipped to Japan for medical care.

Throughout the war there were reports concerning the high professional standards of the Japanese Red Cross. Unlike China, which had no Red Cross until very late in the war, the Japanese had founded their own branch in 1877.[57] The captain of an American warship deployed in Asia described the hospital facilities and staff in the field hospital near Nagasaki: "They had the best modern instruments and systems, the newest antiseptics – everything a hospital on modern lines should have. And all this is the work of a generation. Truly the Japanese is a wonderful man."[58] On September 15, *The Peking and Tientsin Times* contrasted Japan and China, "We know that Japan's ambulances, well provided by the Red Cross Society and by the government are in an effective condition...We await with anxiety to see something of this kind done for the Chinese troops. Many foreigners would gladly contribute towards any rational scheme to benefit the wounded."[59] Only at war's end were foreigners able to organize the bare beginnings of a Red Cross in China. But fears that fleeing Chinese troops would do violence to the medical staff greatly impeded its work.[60] The circuit intendant of Tianjin reportedly shooed away one

[55] "Tienchwangtai," *The Japan Weekly Mail* (Yokohama), 27 April 1895, p. 483; "A Grave Charge," *The North-China Herald* (Shanghai), 5 April 1895, p. 515; "The Japanese at Newchwang," *The North-China Herald* (Shanghai), 11 April 1895, p. 542.

[56] The most notable one was the massacre at Port Arthur, discussed in detail in Chapter 6. In addition, there was a massacre reported at a village on the march to Weihaiwei. A villager took a pot shot at the passing Japanese troops, who responded by massacring the entire village. "Shantung Notes," *The Peking and Tientsin Times*, 6 April 1895, p. 227.

[57] "The Chino-Japanese War," *The Pall Mall Gazette* (London), 5 September 1894, 4th ed., p. 7; "Tokyo in War Time," *The Pall Mall Gazette* (London), 9 February 1895, 4th ed., p. 3; "The Japanese Red Cross Society," *The Times* (London), 8 January 1895, p. 3; "La Chine et le Japon" (China and Japan), *Le Temps* (*The Times*) (Paris), 10 January 1895; Eastlake and Yamada, 418–25, 464–77; "日清戰爭に於ける赤十字社" (Red Cross Society in the Sino-Japanese War), 國民新聞 (*People's Newspaper*) (Tokyo), 10 October 1894, p. 1.

[58] "Battles in the Far East," *The New York Times*, 21 November 1894, p. 5. For more information on Japanese medical services, see S. Suzuki, *The Surgical and Medical History of the Naval War between Japan & China, 1894–95*, Y. Saneyoshi, trans. (Tokyo: Z. P. Maruya, 1901).

[59] "Chinese Administration and Conduct," *The Peking and Tientsin Times*, 15 September 1894, p. 110.

[60] "A Red Cross Society," *The North-China Herald* (Shanghai), 30 November 1894, p. 891; "Tientsin,"

group of foreigners interested in opening a chapter of the Red Cross, saying, "We don't want to save any wounded Chinese."[61] Eventually foreigners set up Red Cross hospitals in the treaty ports of Niuzhuang, Tianjin, and Yantai (Chefoo, 煙 臺), while foreigners in Shanghai raised money to help fund relief work in Shandong Province.[62] Today, the Chinese are still wont to criticize the activities of the Western imperialists in China. In doing so they ignore a wide variety of humanitarian initiatives that foreigners provided because they were appalled that the Chinese would not do so for themselves.

The apparent callousness of Chinese officials and officers toward their own people became another source of Western disgust. A reporter for *The North-China Herald* described the plight of wounded Chinese soldiers: "[T]he terrible sufferings which the poor wretches have undergone cannot but excite the keenest disgust with a Government which treats its employés with such callous neglect. It is well for them that European charity happens to be so well organised here that it is able to do much of the work which any Government with any pretence to being civilised should do itself; but one cannot contemplate without contemptuous disgust the shameless manner in which the officials of a proud and supercilious people resort in their extremity to foreign charity, with hardly an effort to help themselves."[63]

In the beginning of November, a reporter for *The Peking and Tientsin Times* described Chinese forces as "bands of ill fed and undisciplined mobs to be slaughtered or put to flight by the Japanese." The author wondered why the Chinese government had done so little to rectify this problem over the preceding

The North-China Herald (Shanghai), 7 December 1894, pp. 930–1; "Newchwang," *The North-China Herald* (Shanghai), 23 November 1894, p. 852; "Tientsin," *The North-China Herald* (Shanghai), 23 November 1894, p. 854; "The Red Cross Expedition," *The North-China Herald* (Shanghai), 14 December 1894, p. 97; "The War in the East," *The Times* (London), 23 November 1894, p. 5; "The Red Cross Hospital," *The North-China Herald* (Shanghai), 4 January 1895, p. 9; "Newchwang," *The North-China Herald* (Shanghai), 15 March 1895, p. 387; "Battles in the Far East," *The New York Times*, 21 November 1894, p. 5.

[61] "Battles in the Far East," *The New York Times*, 21 November 1894, p. 5. See also Cunningham, 21.

[62] "The Red Cross Hospital," *The North-China Herald* (Shanghai), 8 February 1895, p. 183; "Red Cross Hospitals" and "Can Be Grateful," *The North-China Herald* (Shanghai), 8 February 1895, pp. 184–5; "The Tientsin Red Cross Society," *The Peking and Tientsin Times*, 15 December 1894, p. 162; "China's Stubborn Fight," *The New York Times*, 13 February 1895, p. 5; "Red Cross Hospital Fund," *The North-China Herald* (Shanghai), 15 February 1895, p. 241; "Red Cross Hospital Fund," *The North-China Herald* (Shanghai), 22 February 1895, p. 281; "Planning to Save Pekin," *The New York Times*, 3 March 1895, p. 5; "Pursuing China's Armies," *The New York Times*, 12 February 1895, p. 5; "Oyama Victorious Again," *The New York Times*, 2 March 1895, p. 5; "China's Stubborn Fight," *The New York Times*, 13 February 1895, p. 5.

[63] "The Wounded," *The North-China Herald* (Shanghai), 15 March 1895, p. 384.

three months: "A commissariat and medical department might have been organised, so that the soldiers might at least have been assured that they would be fed and paid while in the field, and would not be left to die of their wounds if they fell in the fight." He lamented that commanders had not been given "any technical training" and speculated that the "Chinese have thought they would prevail by mere force of numbers." He predicted that "the slaughter cannot go on forever."[64]

* * *

The day after P'yôngyang, the second major battle of the war took place. The Japanese fleet had been trying to engage a very reluctant Chinese fleet that had been ordered not to cross the Yalu–Weihaiwei line. So the Japanese crossed it for them, finding the Chinese fleet at anchor at the mouth of the Yalu River. Viceroy Li had decreed a defensive strategy.[65] The Beiyang Squadron had been convoying troop transports to Korea and was on the return voyage to Port Arthur when the Japanese fleet caught up with them in the vicinity of Haiyang (海洋島)[66] and Zhangzi (獐子島)[67] Islands. The islands are located off the coast of Liaodong Peninsula, midway between the mouth of the Yalu River and Port Arthur. There on September 17, one of the two great naval battles of the war erupted. It has become known variously as the Battle of the Yellow Sea (黃海海戰), of Haiyang Island (海洋島海戰), of Dadonggou (大東溝), of Taigozanoki (大孤山沖海戰), or of the Yalu (鴨綠江), the term used in this work.[68] The differing names have to do with the variety of geographic landmarks in the vicinity of the engagement.

Although there is no agreement even among contemporary sources about the

[64] "The Situation," *The Peking and Tientsin Times*, 3 November 1894, p. 138.

[65] Kuo, 67; Ballard, 144–6.

[66] Alternate spellings include Hai-yun.

[67] Alternate spellings include Chang-tzu tao and Blonde Island.

[68] Morse, vol. 3, map; Chang Chi-hun, 117; Tan Qixiang (譚其驤) ed., 中国历史地图集 (*Historical Atlas of China*), vol. 8 (Shanghai: 地图出版社, 1980), 10–11; "The Naval Fight on the 17th," *The Japan Weekly Mail* (Yokohama), 22 September 1894, p. 336; "The Naval Engagement," *The Japan Weekly Mail* (Yokohama), 22 September 1894, p. 338; "War Items," *The Japan Weekly Mail* (Yokohama), 29 September 1894, pp. 361–6; "Japan," *The North-China Herald* (Shanghai), 5 October 1894, pp. 564–5; "The War," *The North-China Herald* (Shanghai), 12 October 1894, pp. 618–9; "The Naval Fight," *The Japan Weekly Mail* (Yokohama), 13 October 1894, pp. 420–1; "War Items," *The Japan Weekly Mail* (Yokohama), 20 October 1894, p. 449; "The Naval Battle," *The Japan Weekly Mail* (Yokohama), 27 October 1894, pp. 481–2; "Some Naval Lessons from the Yalu," *The New York Times*, 15 October 1894, p. 8.; Jukichi Inouye, *The Japan-China War: The Naval Battle of Haiyang* (Yokohama: Kelly & Walsh, 1895); "Letters from Hiroshima," *The Japan Weekly Mail* (Yokohama), 6 October 1894, p. 394; "海軍大勝利" (Great Naval Victory), 朝日新聞 (*Rising Sun Newspaper*) (Tokyo), 21 September 1894, p. 1; "海戰の詳報" (Detailed Report of the Naval Battle), 朝日新聞 (*Rising Sun Newspaper*) (Tokyo), 22 September 1894, p. 1.

exact number of ships engaged, there is agreement that the two fleets seem to have been fairly evenly matched. The Chinese had an advantage in armor and heavy guns, whereas the Japanese had an advantage in speed and quick-firing guns. In addition, most of the Chinese fleet had been built before 1887, while most Japanese ships had been built since 1890.[69] About ten significant ships from each side took part in the battle: The Chinese employed two armored turreted battleships (each with about one-third more displacement than the largest Japanese vessel), three coastal defense ships, and five or six cruisers, while the Japanese deployed three coastal defense ships, five or six cruisers, and a gunboat.[70] The Chinese fleet tried to form a line abreast with the weakest boats on the ends. Because of mixed signals and different speeds, the formation soon degenerated into an asymmetrical wedge shape. The Japanese fleet assumed a column formation with the flying squadron out front. The flying squadron had instructions to attack the right flank of the Chinese to annihilate the weak boats on the end of the formation. Upon seeing this, Admiral Ding Ruchang (丁汝昌) ordered his ships to change course in such a way that would have exposed his ship, the flagship, but put the rest of the squadron in a good position to fire on the Japanese fleet. Ding's subordinate on the flagship ignored the order allegedly out of cowardice. In a nineteenth-century example of fragging, before the Japanese fleet was in range, the subordinate fired the main guns, thereby demolishing the temporary flying bridge on which Admiral Ding was standing. This was a well-known consequence to be expected from firing straight ahead. Ding's leg was crushed so that he could not stand, let alone walk, during the hostilities. This made it impossible for him to repeat his order in time. The wounds would also make it difficult for him to follow the battle.[71]

[69] According to a modern source, each fleet had twelve ships (Rawlinson, 174), while Tyler, who served on the Chinese flag ship, and McGiffen, who served on the other great battleship, said that ten Chinese vessels faced twelve Japanese (Tyler, 50; McGiffin, 118, 122). *The Japan Weekly Mail* reported that eleven Japanese vessels opposed twenty Chinese ("The Naval Engagement," 22 September 1894, p. 338). Other sources agreed that the Chinese had 20 vessels but thought that there were sixteen Japanese ("Extracts from 'Advance Japan' by J. Morris, 1895," Du Boulay, 3; Morris, 344). For a list of the two fleets, see U.S. Adjutant-General's Office, 11. For a detailed comparison of the two fleets, see Marble: 480–5. See also the charts comparing the two fleets in 桑田悦 (Kuwada Etsu), 近代日本戦争史 (*History of Modern Japanese Wars*), vol. 1, 日清。日露戦争 (*Sino-Japanese and Russo-Japanese Wars*) (Tokyo: 同台経済懇話会, 1995), 181–2; "大孤山沖海戦の一大詳報" (Very Important Detailed Report on the Battle of the Yalu), 朝日新聞 (*Rising Sun Newspaper*) (Tokyo), 30 September 1894, special edition, pp. 1–2; "海軍の大勝!!!" (Great Naval Victory!!!), 國民新聞 (*People's Newspaper*) (Tokyo), 21 September 1894, p. 2.

[70] Marble, 482–3; Kuwada, 181–2. These categorizations of the ships are only approximate since technology has changed and heterogeneous boats were grouped within each category.

[71] Evans and Peattie, 42–4; Rawlinson, 178–85; Tyler, 39–41, 48–62; Kuo, 75.

According to Vice-Admiral G. A. Ballard of the British navy, China's battle formation was flawed from the beginning since a line abreast strategy required that the strongest, not the weakest, boats be on the wings in order to prevent the weakest boats from being picked off in detail. The Chinese then had failed to change course to prevent the Japanese from going around their wing with each vessel delivering a full broadside at close range on the wing ships. This destroyed China's right wing while two boats on the left wing took the opportunity to flee from the battle altogether.[72] The Japanese managed to obliterate the flagship's foremast, which ended communications among the Chinese fleet – the vital signals could not be hung from the missing foremast. This gave the Japanese an enormous advantage since they maneuvered and fought by signal throughout the battle.[73] The fighting was brutal, particularly since the wooden decks of the ships caught fire too easily. According to the *Proceedings of the United States Naval Institute*, "the severest damage to both fleets was done by fire."[74]

According to the Yantai correspondent of the Shanghai-based newspaper, *The China Gazette*, "There is no doubt the Chinese fought bravely, but they were no match for the Japanese whose tactics were admirable throughout the fight...The unfortunate Chinese gunners lost their heads and fired wildly, their officers left their ships at the mercy of the enemy by their clumsy seamanship while, on the other hand, almost every shot of the Japanese told."[75] According to a reporter for *The Japan Weekly Mail*, "The Japanese men-of-war preserved their battle array intact from first to last, but the Chinese were soon compelled to fight without any tactical order."[76] *The New York Times* ran the headlines, "China's Waterloo in Corea"[77] and "Japan's Great Naval Victory."[78]

In addition to defective tactics, the Chinese also had defective ordnance. The Japanese discovered, to their relief, that some of the Chinese shells were filled with cement instead of explosives. Other reports described some of the ammunition as being filled with porcelain and others as being of the wrong caliber, making it impossible to fire. These observations were made after the heat of battle. At the time, the Japanese grossly underestimated the degree of Chinese incompetence.

---

[72] Ballard, 147–51.

[73] Wilson, vol. 2, 101.

[74] Marble, 493.

[75] "Another Account of the Naval Battle on the 17th," *The Japan Weekly Mail* (Yokohama), 6 October 1894, p. 396.

[76] "Letters from Hiroshima," *The Japan Weekly Mail* (Yokohama), 6 October 1894, p. 394.

[77] "China's Waterloo in Corea," *The New York Times*, 19 September 1894, p. 5.

[78] "Japan's Great Naval Victory," *The New York Times*, 20 September 1894, p. 5.

Admiral Itō Yūkō (伊東祐亨) did not pursue the fleeing Chinese because he knew that his fleet lacked weapons capable of sinking their two large armored battleships. Unbeknownst to him, the Chinese fleet was nearly out of ammunition and could not have fired many additional rounds from the big guns of the two large battleships.[79] According to Sir Robert Hart, inspector general of Chinese Maritime Customs, on the eve of the battle the Chinese had no shells for their Krupp artillery and no powder for their Armstrong guns – these were some of the main offensive weapons of their fleet.[80] Although the Japanese were subsequently criticized for not pursuing the remnants of the Beiyang Squadron, their decision was based on the knowledge that they had nothing in their navy to match China's two strongest battleships. A European diplomat observed that Japan's naval "victories were due to the skill and daring of her sailors, and not to the ships which they manned."[81] The victory shattered the morale of the Chinese naval forces.[82]

The Chinese defeat at P'yŏngyang followed a day later by its naval defeat at the Yalu dazzled the foreign press. Previously the continental European press had not provided much coverage of the war. With these Japanese victories, the war received front-page coverage in *Le Temps*.[83] No one had suspected such a rapid turn of events. *S.-Peterburgskie vedomosti* credited Japan with "a brilliant victory."[84] The London *Times* wrote that the Japanese displayed "a rare aptitude for the assimilation of the best that has been thought and done by the civilized world, and, what is equally rare, the power of putting into practice the ideas thus assimilated."[85] Within the month, the Japanese would expel the Chinese from Korea (October 9, 1894) and start taking the strategic land and naval approaches to Peking. In early October, a reporter for the Moscow newspaper, *Russkie vedomosti*, observed: "The war which has flared up between China and Japan, indisputably is important not only for the Asiatic East, but also for Europe, and in particular for Russia, whose Asiatic possessions border on Korea and China and are located not far from the possessions of Japan."[86] After the Battle of the Yalu, it was recognized that Japan

[79] Evans and Peattie, 42–4; Rawlinson, 178–85; Tyler, 39–41, 48–62; Kuo, 75.

[80] Hart to Campbell, 2 September 1894, in Fairbank et al., *The I. G. in Peking*, 985.

[81] Vladimir, 62.

[82] McGiffin, 144.

[83] *Le Temps* (*The Times*) (Paris), July–November 1894, *passim*.

[84] "Война в Корее" (The War in Korea), С.-Петербургские ведомости (*St. Petersburg Gazette*), no. 244, 20 September 1894, p. 1.

[85] "The War in the East," *The Times* (London), 22 September 1894, p. 5.

[86] D. A., "Японско-китайская война. Корея и русские интересы на Дальнем Востоке" (The Sino-Japanese War, Korea, and Russian Interests in the Far East), Русские ведомости (*Russian*

controlled the sea.[87] Thereafter *Moskovskie vedomosti* treated an ultimate Japanese victory as a foregone conclusion: "Our readers who were familiar with the condition of the Chinese and Japanese military forces before the war, undoubtedly are not surprised by the victories of the sons of 'the Empire of the Rising Sun,' and should have expected them...there is no doubt that a new strong military power has appeared in the East."[88] China's miserable performance had shattered the pre-war illusion of its military power.

Meanwhile, the official battle report received by the Chinese government claimed that the Chinese fleet had defeated "a numerically superior fleet of the Wojên [dwarfs]...sinking three of the enemy's ships and severely injuring the rest, but losing four of our own in the battle."[89] Japanese findings corroborate the deliberate falsification of battle reports to Peking. Later in the war, the Japanese seized various state papers found in Port Arthur. An undated dispatch to Viceroy Li concerning the Battle of the Yalu described a battle "more terrible than any to be found in the Naval records even of Western countries. The ships of both sides were considerably damaged, especially those of the enemy. The enemy retired first, so that victory may more or less be said to have rested with us. Had not our rear become disordered, the entire victory would have been ours." The dispatch went on to recommend rewards for those who fought bravely.[90]

Viceroy Li wrote a report to the Zongli Yamen, the Chinese foreign office, based on Admiral Ding's report to him, requesting promotions and honors for those who had participated in the battle. According to Ding's account, after hours of fierce fighting and "vowing to die in opposing them we were enabled in our weakness to overcome their strength and to turn defeat into merit. We succeeded at this time in sinking the Admiral's ship with one other war-vessel and one transport, three in all; while the number afterwards sank through inquiries [*sic* injuries?] received was still greater." His ships, he claimed, had succeeded in

Gazette), no. 264, 24 September 1894 (6 October 1894), p. 3. This was the first article in a nine-article series explaining the historical background of the Sino-Japanese War. The series was later reprinted with a three-month lag in Владивосток (*Vladivostok*). See no. 49, 4 December 1894 (16 December 1894), p. 11, for the first article in the series.

[87] "Япония и Китая. Японско-китайская война" (Japan and China. The Sino-Japanese War), *Московские ведомости* (*Moscow Gazette*), no. 257, 19 September 1894 (1 October 1894), p. 3.

[88] "Китайско-японская война" (The Sino-Japanese War), *Московские ведомости* (*Moscow Gazette*), no. 265, 27 September 1894 (10 October 1894), p. 2.

[89] "Abstract of Peking Gazette," *The North-China Herald* (Shanghai), 21 December 1894, p. 1017. The report is alluded to in the imperial decree cited above and dated October 7, 1894. Ibid.

[90] "Documents Seized at Port Arthur," *The Japan Weekly Mail* (Yokohama), 5 January 1895, p. 15; "Imperial Decrees," *The North-China Herald* (Shanghai), 11 January 1895, p. 46.

preventing the Japanese from landing more troops in Korea.[91] By all accounts, Admiral Ding, in stark contrast to so many of his contemporaries in the upper echelons of the Chinese military, was a man of great integrity and humility. Perhaps the errors in his report can be explained by the severe injuries he had received at the onset of the hostilities. It is unclear whether he ever totally regained consciousness during the rest of the battle. Therefore, his report must have been based to large extent on the testimony of his associates.

The editors of *The North-China Herald* dismissed the Japanese reports as untrue because they did not admit to any sunk ships. As it turned out, none of their ships was sunk. The paper concluded that it was "evident" that the battle was a draw.[92] It is unclear how many Chinese boats went down in the battle. Official Chinese reports admitted to a loss of three or four ships; others claimed that the Chinese had lost five ships and that three others had been severely damaged. Estimates of significantly damaged Japanese boats ranged from three to five to all of the Japanese ships involved.[93]

According to the U.S. Secretary of the Navy, Hilary V. Herbert, the Battle of the Yalu "was nearly a drawn battle." Although China lost four boats with an aggregate displacement of 7,580 tons while Japan lost none, "[m]ost of the Japanese fleet had suffered severely." Had Chinese vessels been supplied with the proper ammunition – more common exploding shells instead of armor piercing shell – the Japanese might have lost.[94] In other words, after the Battle of the Yalu, the Chinese navy still could have taken on the Japanese navy to interfere with its on-going troop buildup on the Asian mainland. As Vice-Admiral G. A. Ballard of the British navy later pointed out, China's two main battleships, for which Japan

---

[91] "The Peking Gazette and the Naval Engagement," *The Peking and Tientsin Times*, 10 November 1894, pp. 142–3.

[92] "The War," *The North-China Herald* (Shanghai), 21 September 1894, p. 469; "The Land and Sea Fights," *The Peking and Tientsin Times*, 29 September 1894, p. 118; "Admiral Ito and the Late Naval Battle," *The Peking and Tientsin Times*, 20 October 1894, p. 130.

[93] "Extracts from 'Advance Japan' by J. Morris, 1895," in Du Boulay, 5; Ballard, 147–51; Evans and Peattie, 42–4; Rawlinson, 178–85; Tyler, 39–41, 48–62; Kuo, 75; "The Naval Fight on the 17th," *The Japan Weekly Mail* (Yokohama), 22 September 1894, p. 336; "The Naval Engagement," *The Japan Weekly Mail* (Yokohama), 22 September 1894, p. 338; "War Items," *The Japan Weekly Mail* (Yokohama), 29 September 1894, pp. 361–6; "Japan," *The North-China Herald* (Shanghai), 5 October 1894, pp. 564–5; "The Naval Fight," *The Japan Weekly Mail* (Yokohama), 13 October 1894, pp. 420–1; "War Items," *The Japan Weekly Mail* (Yokohama), 20 October 1894, p. 449; "The Naval Battle," *The Japan Weekly Mail* (Yokohama), 27 October 1894, pp. 481–2; "Some Naval Lessons from the Yalu," *The New York Times*, 15 October 1894, p. 8; Jukichi Inouye, *The Japan-China War: The Naval Battle of Haiyang* (Yokohama: Kelly & Walsh, 1895).

[94] Herbert, 693–4.

had no counterparts, "should have been more than a match for the six best ships of the Japanese Navy."[95] But this presupposed that they were supplied with adequate ammunition, which they were not, even though China had had a month and a half after the onset of hostilities to rectify this problem.

The British press in China failed to catch the significance of a Chinese imperial decree issued on the day of the battle. The decree accused Viceroy Li Hongzhang of not acting "with speed and promptness in his military preparations...We therefore command that his decoration of the three-eyed peacock feather be plucked off from (his hat), and that he be stripped of his Yellow Riding Jacket as a slight punishment."[96] After the Battle of Asan there had been rumors that Li had lost his riding coat, but the imperial decree on September 17 made it official. More importantly, he also lost his feather. Just months before, he had been at the zenith of his power. He had been the second Han Chinese in the history of the dynasty to receive the three-eyed peacock feather, generally reserved exclusively for Manchu Princes. He had received his in anticipation of the Empress Dowager's sixtieth birthday.[97] In 1863, he had been awarded the Yellow Riding Jacket, China's highest military award, for his efforts to suppress the Taiping Rebellion.[98] From a Western point of view, what feather adorns a hat or what color jacket one is permitted to wear may seem to be trivial issues. In a "face" society, such public symbols of status were the currency of political power. Li had been demoted because, in the space of three days, the Japanese had virtually destroyed his army at P'yŏngyang and his fleet at the Yalu.

If Li had been an ordinary high official, he would have been executed for these losses. However inept, his naval and land forces were China's best. The Empress Dowager needed them to prevent a Japanese march on Peking. Therefore, she could not afford to dispense with him altogether. Since the dynasty was implicated in the debacle, she needed her most loyal Han defenders, such as Li Hongzhang, in order to remain in power. Within a week of the defeats, in a ploy to win favor, the Empress Dowager deducted from her birthday fund a substantial contribution of 3

[95] Ballard, 134.

[96] "Li Hung-chang *Versus* the Court Party," *The North-China Herald* (Shanghai), 21 September 1894, p. 495; "The Land and Sea Fights," *The Peking and Tientsin Times,* 29 September 1894, p. 118. See also, "The Northern View of Current Events," *The North-China Herald* (Shanghai), 28 September 1894, p. 519; "Abstract of the Peking Gazette," *The North-China Herald* (Shanghai), 7 December 1894, p. 935.

[97] "Imperial Birthday Honours," *The North-China Herald* (Shanghai), 16 February 1894, p. 145; "Abstract of the Peking Gazette," *The North-China Herald* (Shanghai), 1 June 1894, p. 849.

[98] Folsom, 100–1.

million *taels* for the Board of War to help prosecute the war against Japan.[99]

Li's many enemies, who had long resented his modernization projects of the preceding two decades, seized the opportunity to start undoing his connection network by picking off his subordinates.[100] They called for the execution of his generals. Brigadier-General Wei Rugui (衛汝貴)[101] of the Ningxia Circuit in Gansu and commander of the Sheng division; General Ye Zhichao (葉志超), the commander of Zhili; and General Nie Shicheng (聶士成) were "degraded and disgraced."[102] Wei was subsequently given another chance to prove himself at Port Arthur, where he again fled from his post.[103] After the Battle of Port Arthur, General Wei must have exhausted his connections or *guanxi* network, for this time he paid with his head.[104] In the case of General Ye, who had already once been spared decapitation for defeat at Asan, his *guanxi* network seems to have held out.

In late September, *The North-China Herald* began to suspect that something was afoot. It noted the conspicuous demotions of three relatives of Viceroy Li Hongzhang and interpreted this to indicate that "the anti-Li party is in the saddle."[105] One of those cashiered was his sister's son, who had been director of the Beiyang Board of Ordnance. "The outbreak of hostilities found the Peiyang [Beiyang] squadron almost literally without a shot in the locker," wrote a reporter for *The North-China Herald*.[106] But reporters at the paper still did not associate

---

[99] "The War," *The North-China Herald* (Shanghai), 28 September 1894, p. 534; "China's Missing Transports," *The New York Times*, 24 September 1894, p. 5.

[100] Kuo, 75.

[101] Alternate spellings include Wei Ju-kuei.

[102] "Tientsin," *The North-China Herald* (Shanghai), 23 November 1894, p. 853; "To Await Decapitation," *The North-China Herald* (Shanghai), 14 December 1894, p. 983; "Wei Ju-kuei," *The North-China Herald* (Shanghai), 14 December 1894, p. 984; "Imperial Decrees of the 17th of December," *The North-China Herald* (Shanghai), 21 December 1894, p. 1021; "Imperial Decrees," *The North-China Herald* (Shanghai), 11 January 1895, p. 47; Oh, "Background," 286–7.

[103] "The Fall of Port Arthur," *The North-China Herald* (Shanghai), 25 January 1895, p. 119.

[104] "Another 'General Wei' in Trouble," *The North-China Herald* (Shanghai), 25 January 1895, p. 123; "General Wei," *The North-China Herald* (Shanghai), 15 February 1895, p. 232; "Imperial Decrees," *The North-China Herald* (Shanghai), 22 March 1895, p. 438.

[105] "The Viceroy Li and His Satellites," *The North-China Herald* (Shanghai), 28 September 1894, pp. 515–6.

[106] "The Viceroy Li and His Satellites," *The North-China Herald* (Shanghai), 28 September 1894, p. 515; "The War," *The North-China Herald* (Shanghai), 7 December 1894, p. 944.

After the defeat at Port Arthur at the end of November, Zhang was ordered to report to the Board of Punishments for his transgressions, but he was conveniently away on a trip when officials arrived to escort him to Peking. Eventually officials searched him out and arrested him. He was subsequently exonerated of charges of harboring Japanese spies in his establishment, only to be rearrested on charges brought by the widow of a decapitated general, Wei Rugui (衛汝貴). Wei had been executed

Viceroy Li's troubles with a major military debacle. Another article reported, "In spite of the reiterated denials of the Japanese authorities that any of their vessels were badly injured in the recent naval fight, information which we have been able to gather from quarters entitled to all credence, corroborates in a very circumstantial manner the statement that the Japanese lost four vessels in the actual fight, and more probably later on, as the Chinese heavy guns treated them very severely." The column continued: "The Chinese engaged fought with wonderful bravery; there were no skulkers."[107]

The game was up for the Chinese government on September 20, when the country's foreign military advisers who had participated in the fighting arrived in Tianjin.[108] They would soon tell their story. The Western press could not write off their personal accounts of the hostilities as Japanese propaganda. These foreign survivors corroborated the Japanese reports that four Chinese naval vessels had been sunk but "to a man regard the statement that the Japanese lost no ships as a barefaced lie." They could not believe that the Chinese naval forces had failed to sink any Japanese ships. The foreign military advisers reported that the "aim of the Japanese was to keep the distance long, making the most of their superior speed and their quick-firing guns, in which their armament vastly excelled the Chinese. Our object was to get to close quarters with our slow-firing guns of great calibre." The Japanese naval vessels repeatedly circled the Chinese ships, spraying them with fire. These foreigners also corroborated the reports that the Chinese ships had lacked sufficient shells and that two ships had fled the scene. In punishment, the captain of one was subsequently beheaded (after he had already poisoned himself to death).[109]

These reports must have caused severe misgivings in Peking concerning the accuracy of the accounts being received from the field. In late October, the Guangxu Emperor (光緒皇帝) took the unprecedented measure of summoning for an imperial audience Inspector-General Constantin von Hanneken, a cashiered Prussian officer

for military incompetence at the Battle of P'yôngyang and the fall of Port Arthur, but his widow blamed Zhang for providing "antiquated weapons of sheet iron." It is unclear what happened to him after his second arrest. Perhaps no news was good news and he survived courtesy of the Li family *guanxi* or connection network. "The War," *The North-China Herald* (Shanghai), 7 December 1894, p. 944; "Li Hung-chang's Nephew," *The North-China Herald* (Shanghai), 14 December 1894, p. 985; "Summary of News," *The North-China Herald* (Shanghai), 3 May 1895, p. 649.

[107] "The War," *The North-China Herald* (Shanghai), 28 September 1894, p. 533.

[108] "The Naval Action at the Yaloo," *The North-China Herald* (Shanghai), 28 September 1894, p. 535. The "Yaloo" refers to the Yalu River, forming the border between Korea and China.

[109] "The Naval Fight off the Yaloo," *The North-China Herald* (Shanghai), 5 October 1894, pp. 556–8; "The War," *The North-China Herald* (Shanghai), 5 October 1894, p. 579.

but the chief foreign military adviser to the Beiyang Squadron. Von Hanneken was the Prussian fortifications engineer who had built the defenses at Port Arthur and Weihaiwei. He had been present at the Battle of the Yalu. The Guangxu Emperor wanted to learn directly from him what had actually transpired.[110] It seems tragic that the emperor could not rely on his own subjects but had to call in a foreigner to learn the facts. If the court was misinformed about the war, whose events were difficult to conceal, one wonders about the accuracy of information being supplied to the court on other matters as well. If the Manchus did not know the true state of affairs in their empire, it was small wonder that they found it so difficult to choose appropriate remedies for China's ills.

The press in Europe and the United States were never as taken in by the Chinese war propaganda as were the British papers in China. It did require a number of months for the foreign press at home to plumb the depths of the distortions, but within a week of a battle they generally had pegged which side had won. Conversely, for months there was concern that the Japanese reports on the extent of their victories must have been exaggerated – it defied common logic that China could be so badly beaten. But after several months of fighting, this too became clear. Although members of the British press in China had a good grasp of Chinese domestic problems, they were not especially well informed about the recent Meiji reforms in Japan. Despite China's endemic problems, they long remained loyal to their place of residence. Perhaps in their minds the Chinese reports were more plausible than the Japanese. At war's end, they had a lot of backpedaling to do.

Another reason to doubt the credibility of the Japanese reports was connected with their well-enforced censorship policies: Why would the Japanese have the policy unless they were making good use of it? *The North-China Herald* complained that "the very few correspondents who have received permission to go to the front have to submit everything they send away to immediate censorship."[111] An Imperial Ordinance published on August 2, 1894, had required all newspapers and other publications to submit any information concerning diplomatic or military affairs to government authorities prior to publication.[112] The London *Times* complained in late August that "The Japanese appear to have taken extraordinary precautions to

[110] Tyler, 39, 55, 58; "Herr von Hanneken Summoned to Peking," *The North-China Herald* (Shanghai), 2 November 1894, p. 720; Lensen, vol. 1, 184.

[111] "The Situation," *The North-China Herald* (Shanghai), 12 October 1894, p. 589.

[112] " Supervision of Newspapers," *The Japan Weekly Mail* (Yokohama), 4 August 1894, p. 125. For further information on the development of press censorship, see "The Press Censorship and its Different Methods," *The Japan Weekly Mail* (Yokohama), 22 September 1894, p. 339.

prevent the despatch of information independently obtained." It correctly predicted that "it is possible that the Japanese may come to regret the absence of credible independent witnesses to impending events."[113] In mid-October, according to *The Pall Mall Gazette,* "The reason why the war news is so woefully inaccurate is to be found in the fact that not a solitary European correspondent is permitted to the front by either of the belligerents."[114] *The New York Times* concurred, adding that "The Japanese papers have been prohibited, since the outbreak of hostilities, from publishing anything about Japan, China, or Corea that has not received official sanction."[115] An earlier issue of *The New York Times* had complained that reports available to the press were "either Japanese official tales or wild and garbled native yarns" from China.[116]

After the false Chinese reports of victories in P'yôngyang and near the Yalu, *The Pall Mall Gazette* ran a story entitled, "The Art of Lying as Practiced in the East." At this time, the author considered the lying to be practiced in equal measure by the Chinese and Japanese. "Those who may have been in doubt as to whether the art of lying is in a state of decay should have had that doubt removed by reading the various accounts of the fight at the Yalu, at any rate, as far as the East is concerned. There is a finished effrontery about the telegrams which shows that both sides are splendid liars." The article went on to provide a long inventory of contradictory statements.[117]

After the two great victories, the Japanese government decided to undermine the Chinese war propaganda by allowing foreign correspondents to accompany the Japanese army.[118] Before long the War Department decided to let foreign military attachés tag along as well.[119] From the contemporary Western point of view, this meant that there would be white men on the scene whose observations the Western press would trust.[120] Foreigners were never able to accompany Chinese

---

[113] "The War in the East," *The Times* (London), 30 August 1894, p. 4.

[114] "Why the War News is Inaccurate," *The Pall Mall Gazette* (London), 10 October 1894, 4th ed., p. 7.

[115] "China Will Eventually Win," *The New York Times,* 28 October 1894, p. 28.

[116] "Around Alexander's Pillow," *The New York Times,* 14 October 1894, p. 1.

[117] "The Art of Lying as Practised in the East," *The Pall Mall Gazette* (London), 29 September 1894, 4th ed., p. 7.

[118] "Foreign War Correspondents," *The Japan Weekly Mail* (Yokohama), 15 September 1894, p. 303; "War Correspondents," *The Japan Weekly Mail* (Yokohama), 17 November 1894, p. 556.

[119] "Summary of News," *The Japan Weekly Mail* (Yokohama), 29 September 1894, p. 353.

[120] For example, in an analysis of the Battle of the Yalu, *The North-China Herald* accepts as reliable the reports of the foreigners serving on the Chinese ships. "There were unfortunately no foreigners as far as we know on any of the Japanese ships, and we therefore do not know and probably never

forces. As a reporter for *The Peking and Tientsin Times* pointed out, "no one could guarantee the safety of a foreigner accompanying the Chinese troops."[121] This assessment seemed to be borne out by the facts when a reporter and his two interpreters accompanying the Second Japanese Army were captured and killed by the Chinese.[122]

After China's unanticipated defeat in the Battle of the Yalu, the Empress Dowager Cixi finally abandoned her plans for a gala sixtieth birthday celebration and settled on a more modest affair.[123] On September 25, the Guangxu Emperor issued an edict: "H.I.M. the Empress-Dowager, in view of the continuation of the war with Japan, cannot bear to be celebrating her birthday anniversary with great rejoicing while her subjects and soldiers are all suffering from the hardships of war, hence she has commanded that the triumphal progress from Eho [the Summer Palace or *Yiheyuan*, 頤和園] to the Forbidden City and the celebrations at the former place be given up, and only the ordinary celebrations settled upon in the Palace be observed on the auspicious day. We did our best to try to pray her Majesty to reconsider the above decision, but the grace and virtue of her Majesty has resisted our prayers."[124]

Le Temps had estimated that the Empress Dowager Cixi had already spent more than 80 million francs in preparation for the celebration that was not to be.[125] Reportedly, 30 million *taels* were saved by canceling the celebrations.[126] Since 1889, the Empress Dowager had been siphoning off naval funds to refurbish palaces and lay out gardens in anticipation of her jubilee. She had allegedly devoted 100 million *taels* to this purpose, so that there had been no significant additions to the Chinese navy after 1889. This figure seems rather high. Another estimate put the cost of just the Summer Palace renovations at 12 to 14 million silver *taels*, of which 11 million had come from naval funds. This would have been enough to buy six to seven additional warships. One ironic touch to the Summer Palace face-lift was the refurbishment of a marble pavilion in the shape of a boat originally built by the Qianlong Emperor (乾隆皇帝) and grounded in a lake in the palace gardens. The addition of a marble superstructure to the boat was

shall know what the Japanese losses were." "The Late Naval Battle," *The North-China Herald* (Shanghai), 26 October 1894, p. 673.

[121] "The Lesson of the War," *The Peking and Tientsin Times,* 12 January 1895, p. 178.

[122] "The Chino-Japanese War," *The Pall Mall Gazette* (London), 23 November 1894, 4th ed., p. 7.

[123] "Shanghai War News," *The Japan Weekly Mail* (Yokohama), 13 October 1894, p. 423.

[124] "Abstract of Peking Gazette," *The North-China Herald* (Shanghai), 21 December 1894, p. 1015.

[125] "Les Affairs de Corée" (Korean Affairs), *Le Temps (The Times)* (Paris), 15 August 1894, p. 1.

[126] Treat, vol. 2, 491.

the Empress Dowager's sole contribution to the Chinese fleet between 1889 and 1894. The marble pleasure boat still graces the waters of the Summer Palace and is large enough to hold a modest party. Meanwhile, since 1893 the Japanese government had reallocated one-tenth of civil and military officials' salaries as well as 300,000 *yen* per annum out of court expenses in order to fund warship building and arms purchases.[127]

When the Empress Dowager Cixi's long-anticipated birthday arrived, there "were no public rejoicings or fêtes of any kind."[128] Instead of being the grand event originally envisioned by the Empress Dowager, the day was subordinated to another purpose altogether. The foreign diplomatic community used its leverage in China's time of weakness to pressure the Guangxu Emperor into hosting an imperial audience within the Forbidden City. The ostensible purpose was for the diplomatic community to express birthday salutations to the Empress Dowager Cixi. The choreography of imperial audiences had long been a diplomatic sore point. Because of immutable tradition reinforced by considerations of "face," the Chinese government had bristled at Western demands that China treat foreign envoys in the dignified manner expected in the West but inappropriate in China, where the emperor's own ministers remained his slaves. "Chinese officials are exceedingly tenacious of their dignity. They have a minute and exact line of ceremony of intercourse among their own officials of varying ranks, and they strongly object, and perhaps naturally, to the payment of higher honors to a foreign official than would be conceded to a native of the same or corresponding rank.[129] Over the years the westerners had gradually insinuated their diplomatic norms into the hallowed precincts of the imperial palace. From the birthday forward, foreign audiences would no longer be held in peripheral buildings of the Forbidden City but in the Hall of Blooming Literature (文華殿). On November 12, the Guangxu Emperor held the long-awaited audience.[130] It must have been particularly galling for the Empress Dowager to have been forced to abandon her gala birthday preparations and, instead, have her birthday become the occasion for her despised nephew, the Guangxu Emperor, to hold a precedent-breaking audience

---

[127] Rawlinson, 140–3; Ding, 180. These figures are simply estimates. Needless to say, the Empress Dowager did not make her accounts public. See also Tyler, 113; Powell, 43.

[128] "Peking," *The North-China Herald* (Shanghai), 16 November 1894, p. 844.

[129] Holcombe, 264.

[130] "Peking," *The North-China Herald* (Shanghai), 16 November 1894, p. 815; "Peking," *The North-China Herald* (Shanghai), 30 November 1894, p. 891; "The Audience of the Foreign Ambassadors in Peking at the Celebration of the Sixtieth Birthday of the Empress Ex-regent," *The North-China Herald* (Shanghai), 30 November 1894, p. 903.

in the Forbidden City to the even more detested foreigners. Times had changed.

Columnists from Russian newspapers were quick to realize that the war signified the beginning of a new era in the Far East. Within two weeks of the outbreak of hostilities, *Novoe vremia* was among the first newspapers to point out that the war would undoubtedly change the status quo in the Far East.[131] Two weeks later it expanded on this theme by summarizing the press accounts of the other interested European powers.[132] Implicitly, this report recognized that the Sino-Japanese War had international implications.[133]

Japan's uninterrupted string of victories on the land, crowned by its signal victory over the highly considered Beiyang Squadron, turned heads in Europe. With the battles of P'yŏngyang and the Yalu, many people recognized that the war represented a dividing line between two eras in the Far East. *The Pall Mall Gazette* reported that "it is more than likely that we are on the eve of great changes in the condition and status of China. The sudden and unexpected collapse of Chinese resistance to the Japanese invasion revealed a weakness as grave as that which the march of the Ten Thousand did in the case of the Persian Empire. And the parallel may not improbably be continued, and the success of Japan may be the prelude to the disruption of the Chinese Empire."[134] From 401 to 400 B.C., a Greek revolt that had culminated in a long march to freedom from Persian rule had demonstrated the decrepitude of the Persian Empire.[135] In the estimation of a reporter at *Le Journal des débats politiques et litérraires*, "The Japanese victory over the Chinese at the Yalu has a significance much greater than a simple battle won under unusual circumstances. It is not only a brilliant feat of arms, as are produced in all wars, where there is necessarily a victor and a vanquished. The Battle of the Yalu is an important date in history." He continued, "Who would have believed, in only a quarter of a century, that a power in the Far East, and a

[131] "Внешние известия. Новейший гордиев узел," (Foreign News. The Newest Gordian Knot), *Новое время* (*New Times*), no. 6610, 6 August 1894, p. 1.

[132] "Война в Корее" (War in Korea), *Новое время* (*New Times*), no. 6627, 23 August 1894, p. 1. See also A. Molchanov, "Корея и Япония" (Korea and Japan), *Новое время* (*New Times*), no. 6653, 18 September 1894, p. 1.

[133] See also "The China-Japanese War," *The Pall Mall Gazette* (London), 4 September 1894, 4th ed., p. 7.

[134] "'When You Hear the East A-Callin'," *The Pall Mall Gazette* (London), 19 November 1894, 4th ed., p. 1.

[135] R. Ernest Dupuy and Trevor N. Dupuy, *The Harpers Encyclopedia of Military History from 3500 B.C. to the Present*, 4th ed. (New York: Harper Collins, 1993), 37. The Spartan victory was only temporary, however, for a Persian-financed Greek coalition soon defeated Sparta, forcing her to abandon her hopes to liberate the Greeks of Asia (Strassler, 550).

relatively small power, would so quickly assimilate the techniques of large-scale warfare and put them into practice?...Europe first had to take America into consideration: soon without a doubt she will have to take Asia into account." The author concluded, "If Gœthe had participated in the Battle of the Yalu, it is probable that he would have said as he did to his compatriots at Valmy, 'Here and today begins a new historical era and you can say that you have witnessed it.'"[136] Goethe was referring to the international significance of the French Revolution. This reporter for *Le Journal des débats* was among the first to realize that politics was fast becoming global.

Neue Preussische Zeitung concluded: "Today Japan is now the actual master in Korea and her navy rules the Yellow Sea."[137] *National Zeitung* announced: "Sooner than we could have expected, our claim is being fulfilled that the war in Korea will mark the beginning of a new era for East Asia...For the Europeans and Americans, the Japanese have with one stroke established their spiritual supremacy in Asia."[138] The article concluded by predicting that a defeated China would be devoured by predators. *Moskovskie vedomosti* recognized that "Japan has acquired that status of an important eastern power for which she had been striving. Russia will have to change her attitude of quiet waiting to another one not lacking in anxiety."[139] The Russian newspaper went on to speculate on the possible fall of the Qing Dynasty.[140] *The New York Times* editorialized that the "notion is exploded" that China is the strongest power in Asia. Rather, "Japan has become a first-class power."[141]

The pro-Japanese *Japan Weekly Mail* exulted that the Japanese "have long

---

[136] "La Bataille de Ya-lu" (Battle of Yalu), *Le Journal des débats politiques et littéraires* (*Journal of Political and Literary Debates*) (Paris), 29 September 1894, morning edition, p. 1. Johann Wolfgang von Goethe, the German writer, accompanied the Duke of Weimar on a disastrous campaign into France that included the Battle of Valmy of September 20, 1792. Valmy occurred in the first war of the French Revolution and therefore made a great impression abroad. Goethe later wrote two books about his war experiences.

[137] "Die Bedeutung de Kämpfe bei Pjöng-jang und am Yalu-Fluss" (Importance of the Battles at P'yŏngyang and at the Yalu River), *Neue Preussische Zeitung* (*New Prussian Newspaper*) (Berlin), evening ed., 27 September 1894, p. 1. *National Zeitung* drew a detailed and unfavorable comparison of the governments and militaries of China and Japan (morning ed., 28 September 1894, p. 1).

[138] "China in Vergangenheit und Gegenwart" (China Past and Future), *National Zeitung* (*National Newspaper*) (Berlin), morning ed., 7 October 1894, p. 1.

[139] "Япония и Китай. Поражение китайцев" (Japan and China. Defeat of the Chinese), *Московские ведомости* (*Moscow Gazette*), no. 248, 10 September 1894 (22 September 1894), p. 4.

[140] "Япония и Китай. Поражение китайцев" (Japan and China. Defeat of the Chinese), *Московские ведомости* (*Moscow Gazette*), no. 248, 10 September 1894 (22 September 1894), p. 4.

[141] "Japan and Europe," *The New York Times*. 7 October 1894, p. 4.

chafed under the consciousness that the mood of Europe towards them was one of good natured superciliousness, and that very many people in the west did not even take the trouble to differentiate them from the Chinese. But they have sprung suddenly into respect and consideration...War is an expensive and painful method of compelling the world's attention, but we doubt whether anything less drastic would have served in Japan's case."[142] A reporter for the London *Spectator* reached a similar conclusions: "Japan must be reckoned with as if the people were white men. Japan cannot be coerced, or even bullied any more, for no Power could attack her without all the labour and expense and risk which would attend a European campaign."[143] After the Battle of the Yalu, the Reuter's Agency interviewed Captain John Ingles of the British navy, who had just returned from a six-year stint as naval adviser to the Japanese government. "The Japanese Navy is distinctly comparable with a European Navy, both as regards ships, officers, and men, and in discipline it is quite European...On board ship the Japanese are not the least like ordinary Easterns. Smart, and constantly on the alert – whether in sweeping a deck or in firing big guns – they are just like Europeans."[144] Captain Ingles continued, "In the army of the Mikado we have an entirely new factor in the Far East, for it is the only one in those countries which has been drilled after the most modern method."[145] In an era when racism was taken for granted and generally not considered a point of flawed principles but of self-evident fact, such reports constituted quite a compliment.

What the Western press did not know was that Japanese cryptographers had broken the Chinese code by June of 1894, that is, before the opening of hostilities, and were busily deciphering Li Hongzhang's many communications both to his superiors and to his many subordinates.[146] There is little information concerning the precise details and consequences of this intelligence coup, but one can surmise that the advantage must have been significant, particularly later on during the diplomatic end game terminating the war. During the hostilities foreknowledge must also have considerably simplified Japanese military deployments since they

---

[142] "Great Britain and Japan," *The Japan Weekly Mail* (Yokohama), 29 September 1894, p. 371. See also, "The Chinese and Japanese Navies," *The North-China Herald* (Shanghai), 19 October 1894, p. 660.

[143] Quoted in "English Opinion on the War," *The Japan Weekly Mail* (Yokohama), 24 November 1894, p. 579.

[144] "The Chino-Japanese War," *The Japan Weekly Mail* (Yokohama), 6 October 1894, p. 403.

[145] "The Chino-Japanese War," *The Japan Weekly Mail* (Yokohama), 6 October 1894, p. 403–4.

[146] Chow, 106; Mutsu, 266n.2, 58, 109, 172, 191. Satō Aimaro (佐藤愛麿), the chief of the Telegraphic Section of the Foreign Ministry, had been instrumental in breaking the code (Ibid., 266n.2). For other examples of Japanese decoding of Chinese telegrams, see Japan, Imperial General Staff, 46.

probably understood the general outlines of Chinese plans in advance. Better strategy, better equipment, better supplies, better transportation, better training, better morale, better preparation, better propaganda, plus the enemy's code book – it is a small wonder that the Japanese campaigned so well.

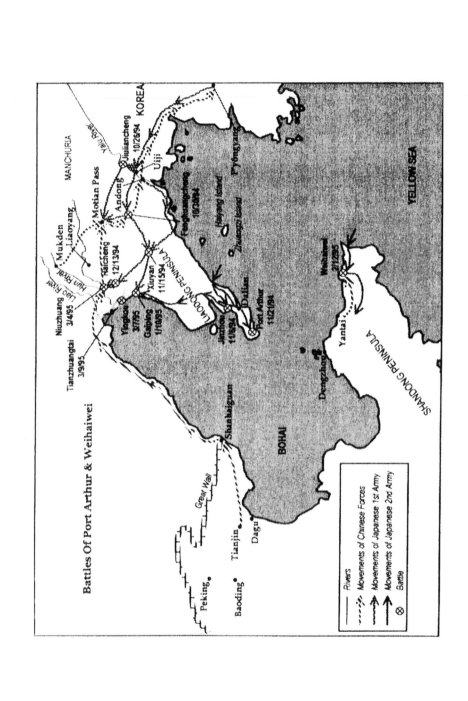

Battles Of Port Arthur & Weihaiwei

KOREA

MANCHURIA

Yalu River

Jiuliancheng 10/26/94

Andong

Uiji

Motian Pass

Mukden

Liaoyang

Haicheng 12/13/94

Niuzhuang 3/4/95

Tianzhuangtai 3/9/95

Yingkou 3/7/95

Gaiping 1/10/95

Xiuyan 11/1/94

Liao River

Hun River

LIAODONG PENINSULA

Fenghuangcheng 10/30/94

Pyongyang

Pyang Island

Zhuangzi Island

Dalian

Port Arthur 11/21/94

Jinzhou 11/6/94

Weihaiwei 2/1/95

Yantai

Dengzhou

SHANDONG PENINSULA

YELLOW SEA

Shanhaiguan

BOHAI

Great Wall

Tianjin

Dagu

Peking

Baoding

Rivers

Movements of Chinese Forces

Movements of Japanese 1st Army

Movements of Japanese 2nd Army

Battle

6

China in Disgrace: The Battles of Port Arthur and Weihaiwei

Everyone knew that a chastising would be highly satisfactory for China, but no one aspired to the privilege of giving it. Japan has. We are now witnessing the soundest thrashing being administered to China which that self-satisfied, ignorant and unprincipled Empire has ever received, and by an irony of fate the thrashing is being administered by the youngster who but a decade or two ago was her own pupil, albeit a conceited one, and by a hand which she thoroughly hates and despises.[1]

The North-China Herald, January 1895

[T]he most pessimistic prophet could hardly have predicted the utter ineptitude of the Chinese military movements.[2]

The Times of London, December 1894

The first two key battles of the war had focused on expelling the Chinese from the Korean Peninsula. The final two major battles focused on the land and sea approaches to Peking. After the Battle of the Yalu, the war theater shifted to Manchuria. The Japanese military wanted to clear the way from the Korean border to the Liaodong Peninsula in preparation for taking the vital fortress and naval refitting station of China's main naval base at Port Arthur (旅順 or Lüshun), located on the northern shore of the Bohai (渤海). The fortifications had taken sixteen years to build, and the naval station was considered superior to that of

---

[1] "Japan's Work," *The North-China Herald* (Shanghai), 18 January 1895, p. 72.

[2] "The War in the East," *The Times* (London), 26 December 1894, p. 4.

Hong Kong.[3] If lost, the Chinese would be unable to repair their men-of-war damaged in battle and could expect to succumb to a Japanese naval attrition strategy if not to outright defeat in a major naval showdown. Guarding the southern shores of the Bohai was China's second most important naval base at Weihaiwei (威海衛) in Shandong Province. These two fortresses controlled the entrance to the Bohai and thereby the sea approaches to Peking. These would be the sites of the two remaining key battles of the war. If Japan could take Port Arthur and Weihaiwei, the rest of the war would become a mopping-up operation.

The Japanese planned to execute a pincer movement on Peking. Their forces would advance in three columns: Part of the First Army would move south through Manchuria toward the Liaodong Peninsula; the Second Army would come by sea to land on the Liaodong Peninsula and move south down the peninsula to take Port Arthur; and the rest of the First Army would head from Korea toward the Qing ancestral home at Mukden (Shenyang, 瀋陽), as a down-payment on their plans to decapitate the dynasty. After taking Port Arthur, the First Army would continue the land campaign in Manchuria to clear the way to Peking, while the Second Army would simultaneously attack the home base of the Beiyang Squadron at Weihaiwei. If successful, the Japanese forces would obliterate the Chinese navy and have Peking at their mercy. To deliver the *coup de grâce* for the Qing Dynasty, the Japanese were organizing a Third Army at Hiroshima in anticipation of an amphibious landing at Dagu on the river approach to Peking.[4] These were the plans of the Imperial Japanese Army. Diplomats in the Japanese Foreign Ministry, however, had grave doubts about the wisdom of undertaking the unlimited war aim of overthrowing the Chinese government. They foresaw great power intervention and argued for much more limited war aims. Their turn would come during the peace negotiations. The Chinese counterstrategy was minimal; it rested on the assumption that the Japanese could not possibly cross the Yalu River.[5]

In early September of 1894, the London *Times* ran an article summarizing the basic strategic situation: "The mouth of the gulf of Pechili [Gulf of Bohai], at the head of which lie Taku [Dagu], Tientsin [Tianjin], and the short route to Pekin, narrows to about 110 miles between Port Arthur and Wei-hai-wei. These ports seem thus marked by nature as the strategic outposts of the north-eastern coast line of China. A hostile force entering the Gulf of Pechili must leave them on its flanks and rear." It cautioned that "the value of Port Arthur and Wei-hai-wei depends

---

[3] Boulger, vol. 2, 528; Kuo, 81.

[4] Ballard, 158; Russell, 95–6.

[5] Chu, "Sino-Japanese War," 365.

entirely on the fighting capacity of the Chinese navy." The article pointed to lessons from history showing that the "proximity of a fortified place of refuge...has frequently supplied counsels of inactivity." After describing Port Arthur's modern defenses (mostly oriented toward the sea), it presciently pointed out: "As usual, the back-door [landward defence] appears to be relatively weak, although, in accordance with all the teaching of history, this would necessarily be the way of approach selected by an enemy." The article concluded that only if Chinese forces prevented the landing of Japanese troops could they secure this back door. "It is almost inconceivable that no attempt would be made to interfere with the delicate operation of landing a large number of men to the east of Port Arthur"[6] – not inconceivable, just "almost inconceivable."

After the defeat at P'yôngyang, the Chinese made their next stand 125 miles to the north at the Yalu River. The river constituted the boundary between Korea and China. It was deep and wide and so presented a formidable obstacle for the advancing Japanese army. Two fortified outposts faced each other from opposite banks of the river, Jiuliancheng (九連城)[7] on the Chinese side and Ûiji (義州)[8] on the Korean side. These became the headquarters for the opposing armies.[9] General Song Qing (宋慶)[10] fortified the northern bank of the river for seven miles to the south as far as Andong (安東)[11] and for ten miles to the north to Hushan (虎山) and beyond. The seventy-four-year-old General Song had made a name for himself thirty years earlier by helping suppress the Taiping Rebellion and had been one of Viceroy Li's subordinates during his campaign against the Nian Rebellion. Since 1880 he had served as an assistant to Li to oversee the defense of Manchuria, and in 1882 he and his troops had been stationed in Port Arthur, where, apparently, he had done little to modernize the Manchurian armed forces. After the Battle of P'yôngyang, he had been made assistant to Li to direct the war and given command of a reorganized army.[12] The appointment was not a success. By the end of the year, "[m]en who were formerly with General Sung [Song] speak of him as a coward, but extol the bravery of the Japanese, their excellent discipline and

[6] "The War in the East," *The Times* (London), 3 September 1894, p. 4.

[7] Jiuliancheng is also spelled as Chiu-lien-ch'eng, Kiulien-ching, and Shiulien.

[8] Other spellings include Yichow and Wiju.

[9] Vladimir, 129; Kuo, 73; Eastlake and Yamada, 110.

[10] Also spelled as Sung Ch'ing.

[11] Andong is also spelled as Antung.

[12] Hummel, 686–8; "The New Chinese Generalissimo," *The North-China Herald* (Shanghai), 5 October 1894, p. 550; Eastlake and Yamada, 111.

firing, and the courage and efficiency of their officers in contrast to their own."[13] He was not a coward; rather, his formative military experiences belonged to an earlier era and had not been sufficiently updated since.[14]

Meanwhile, Japan's First Army, under Field-Marshal Count Yamagata Aritomo (山県有朋), had left P'yŏngyang to reach the Yalu on October 23. The fifty-six-year-old Yamagata was the father of the modern Japanese army and leading Meiji-period statesman. Not only had he overseen the introduction of national conscription in 1873, the reorganization of the army along Prussian lines in 1878, and the adoption of an independent General Staff system, but in the 1880s he had also reorganized the national police force and system of local government. As prime minister from 1889 to 1891, he had helped introduce the imperial rescript on education, westernizing Japanese educational institutions.[15] After the war he described his command appointment in the war as the "happiest moment in my life."[16]

His plan followed Napoleon's successful tactic of making a feint to the front while delivering the main blow on the flank at Hushan. He planned to use a small force to attack the left wing of the enemy in hopes of turning its flank and also as a feint to disguise the movements of the main body of troops. These he planned to concentrate on the center of the Chinese position. To do this, the troops first had to cross the Yalu. The Japanese had learned their lesson at P'yŏngyang and this time had made careful preparations to ford the river. On the night of October 24, they erected a pontoon bridge at Ŭiji to get the main body of their troops across the Yalu. On the next day, the main attack began with a simultaneous diversionary attack on the Chinese flank. This meant that the Chinese were caught between two lines of fire. After defeating the Chinese forces at Hushan on the 25th, the Japanese planned to attack Jiuliancheng in the early hours of the 26th.[17] According to a military analyst, "The Chinese garrison [at Jiuliancheng] which might have inflicted great damage on the hostile army from behind battlements of solid masonry, silently decamped during the night, keeping up a desultory fire in the

[13] "Tientsin," *The North-China Herald* (Shanghai), 18 January 1895, p. 78.

[14] Allen Fung, 1021; Chu, "Sino-Japanese War," 360–1.

[15] "Yamagata Aritomo," *Kodansha Encyclopedia of Japan,* vol. 8 (Tokyo: Kodansha, 1983), pp. 290–2.

[16] Hacket, 161.

[17] "Invasion of Manchuria," Du Boulay, 1–6; "War News," *The Japan Weekly Mail* (Yokohama), 24 November 1894, pp. 584–5; "The Operations in Manchuria," *The Japan Weekly Mail* (Yokohama), 22 December 1894, p. 704; "Newchwang," *The North-China Herald* (Shanghai), 9 November 1894, p. 773; "The War," *The North-China Herald* (Shanghai), 23 November 1894, p. 862; "The New Chihli Commander-in-Chief," *The North-China Herald* (Shanghai), 30 November 1894, p. 903; Eastlake and Yamada, 112–15.

meantime, in order to encourage the belief that they intended to retain possession of the stronghold."[18] When the Japanese scaled the city walls, they found it deserted. The same was true for Andong. As usual, the Chinese left behind enormous quantities of weapons and rice and, in doing so, once again provided commissariat and logistical services for the invading Japanese army.[19] The commanding Chinese generals Yiketang'a (依克唐阿), Ye Zhicheng (葉志超), and Nie Shicheng (聶士成)[20] all retreated to Fenghuangcheng (鳳凰城).[21] Yiketang'a was a Manchu in command of banner forces from Heilongjiang Province and not subject to the command of Viceroy Li Hongzhang.[22] Upon being pursued by the Japanese, they let the city fall on October 30. This time the Chinese forces managed to torch the city before departing.[23] On November 15, the Japanese took Xiuyan (岫巖),[24] the fortified town located west of Fenghuangcheng, south of Mukden and east of Gaiping (蓋平).[25] Thereafter, the Manchurian campaign slowed for the winter months.[26]

Chinese sources no longer claimed victories, but presented their defeats as brave encounters against overwhelmingly superior numbers. "When the Japanese army of forty odd thousand attacked Chiulinch'eng [Jiuliancheng] on the 24th of October there were only a little over 5,000 Chinese troops to oppose the enemy. But it took the latter two whole days to take the city. When the city was abandoned all the modern Krupp and Hotchkiss guns, over twenty in number, were carried along with the army, the ones left to the enemy being some thirty odd old muzzle-loading pieces, a hundred years old, which had been placed there many

---

[18] "Invasion of Manchuria," Du Boulay, 5.

[19] Eastlake and Yamada, 115–17.

[20] Alternate spellings include Nie Sze-chên.

[21] Alternate spellings include Feng-whang-Cheng, Fenghwan and Fênghuangch'eng.

[22] Chu, "Sino-Japanese War," 362; "依克唐阿" (Yiketang'a), in 中国历史大辞典 (*Big Chinese History Dictionary*), 中国历史大辞典编纂委员会 (Compilation Committee for the Big Chinese History Dictionary), comp., vol. 2 (Shanghai: 上海辞书出版社, 2000), 1866.

[23] Eastlake and Yamada, 116.

[24] Alternate spellings include Sui-yen and Hsiu-yen.

[25] Alternate spellings for Gaiping include Kai-p'ing.

[26] "Invasion of Manchuria," Du Boulay, 6; Lone, 39; "Summary of News," *The North-China Herald* (Shanghai), 2 November 1894, p. 758; Eastlake and Yamada, 200. For information about the hostilities, see "War News," *The Japan Weekly Mail* (Yokohama), 24 November 1894, pp. 584–5; "The Operations in Manchuria," *The Japan Weekly Mail* (Yokohama), 22 December 1894, p. 704; "Newchwang," *The North-China Herald* (Shanghai), 9 November 1894, p. 773; "The War," *The North-China Herald* (Shanghai), 23 November 1894, p. 862; "The New Chihli Commander-in-Chief," *The North-China Herald* (Shanghai), 30 November 1894, p. 903.

years ago as a defence against possible native or Corean marauders."[27] Later reports indicated much higher numbers of Chinese soldiers present but still provided ludicrously low casualty figures for both sides. In reference to the latter, *The North-China Herald* remarked, "These Far Eastern combatants must possess a secret unknown to European armies. Happy would be the European general able to contemplate the manœuvring of 20,000 men in the field in the face of a hostile force of equal strength at a maximum loss of say two hundred killed and wounded."[28]

In the absence of many telegraph lines or good roads, communications were difficult and battle details for the Manchurian campaign were slow to emerge. Therefore, the initial coverage tended to be based more on rumor than on fact. Often it took more than a month for more comprehensive accounts to become known. In November 1894, *The North-China Herald* reported: "The native authorities are keeping whatever news reaches them very secret. However, refugees from Chiulienchêng, Fênghuangch'eng, and Liaoyang, are pouring into this port [Yingkou], bringing news of disaster and flight."[29]

General Song's forces retreated in the direction of Liaoyang (遼陽) to protect the provincial capital of Mukden. As the ancestral home of the Qing Dynasty, Mukden had tremendous symbolic importance for the Manchus. It was a city that they could not afford to lose if they hoped to retain any vestiges of legitimacy in China. Since the territory between Fenghuangcheng and Liaoyang "is hilly, and the roads difficult, being very steep in many places, and surrounded by hills," in the estimation of a reporter from *The North-China Herald*, "[i]t will be almost impossible for the Japanese to pass through this country, if the Chinese will only fight."[30] Perhaps the author was thinking of the Opium Wars, when the Chinese had not fought either. The Chinese had not done well in their encounters with foreigners from overseas.

While the Manchu Dynasty considered it essential to retain Mukden for dynastic reasons, the Japanese considered it essential to take Port Arthur to secure their command of the sea. The Manchus were following a traditional strategy focusing on the land war and dynastic continuity while overlooking the need to deny Japanese access to the coast to continue landing troops. Such an outlook made sense before the arrival of the Europeans when the invaders had been mounted nomads from the Asian hinterland, but it would be disastrous against a modern

---

[27] "The War from Native Sources," *The North-China Herald* (Shanghai), 2 November 1894, p. 742.

[28] "Japan," *The North-China Herald* (Shanghai), 9 November 1894, p. 773.

[29] "Newchwang," *The North-China Herald* (Shanghai), 9 November 1894, p. 773.

[30] "Newchwang," *The North-China Herald* (Shanghai), 9 November 1894, p. 773.

army invading from the sea. They assumed that China's vast territory and population would prove too much for the Japanese, so that time was on their side and an attrition strategy would deliver victory. A strong government could have abandoned the capital and continued to fight. The Manchus, however, could not assume that they would survive a prolonged absence from the capital. If they left, the Han Chinese might take the opportunity to cut their losses with the Japanese, strike a deal, and restore Han Chinese rule to China. Therefore, it was imperative for the Manchus to prevent the Japanese navy from delivering reinforcements. This would have entailed a sea denial strategy: They needed to deny Japanese access to the key ports for disembarking their troops on the Asian mainland. To do this required a navy, and to maintain a navy required the facilities at Port Arthur. The Manchus needed to concentrate their forces to protect Port Arthur, not to disperse them in Manchuria. Instead, they tried to keep the Japanese forces divided by successfully engaging them on the south Manchurian plain.[31] The Manchus were not successful. It turns out that the Japanese had actually managed to keep the Chinese forces divided with their feint toward Mukden.

The Japanese strategy was to take Jinzhou (金州)[32] and Dalian (大連) on either coast of the neck of the Liaodong Peninsula to launch a land attack on Port Arthur, whose primary defenses anticipated a sea attack.[33] Troops of the Second Army under Major General Nogi Maresuke (乃木希典) started arriving on the Liaodong Peninsula on October 24.[34] Their first objective was Jinzhou, the most important fortified town in southern Fengtian Province.[35] It commanded the neck of the Liaodong Peninsula and was located at a major transportation intersection. Jinzhou was located at the fork in the road from China proper to the Liaodong Peninsula and to Korea. One route followed the western coast of the peninsula to the treaty port at Niuzhuang and from there to the sea terminus of the Great Wall at Shanhaiguan. The other route went along the eastern coast of the peninsula northward to the Yalu River. Just south of Jinzhou, the Liaodong Peninsula narrowed to a width of 2.5 miles. If the Japanese could take the city, they would be in a position to attack Port Arthur from its vulnerable landward side.

On November 6, the Japanese took Jinzhou with little resistance. It was a very

---

[31] Chu, "Sino-Japanese War," 365.

[32] Alternate spellings include Chin-chow, Kinchow, and Chinchou.

[33] "Is This the End, Is This the End?" *The Pall Mall Gazette* (London), 26 November 1894, 4th ed., p. 1.

[34] "Intelligence of the Second Army," *The Japan Weekly Mail* (Yokohama),10 November 1894, p. 539.

[35] Alternate spellings include Shenking, Shengching, and Shengjing (盛京).

difficult position to defend because it was surrounded by hills, putting the city within artillery range of any attackers. The next day, General Nogi's forces took Dalian, the best anchorage on the peninsula, without firing a shot.[36] The night before, the Chinese forces had abandoned their positions and fled to Port Arthur.[37] The Beiyang Squadron had arrived at Port Arthur in early November but received orders from Tianjin to return to Weihaiwei. So it did not participate in the defense of the Liaodong Peninsula. Worse yet, on the return to Weihaiwei, the *Zhenyuan* (*Chen Yuen*, 鎮遠), one of China's two large battleships for which Japan had no counterpart, had been accidentally damaged while navigating the entrance to Weihaiwei harbor. In the absence of docking facilities – those at Port Arthur were under imminent attack – the ship had to be beached, rendering it useless for the remainder of the war. Commodore Lin Taizeng (林泰曾), the grandson of the famous Commissioner Lin Zexu (林則徐), whose destruction of crated opium had started off the Opium Wars half a century earlier, took a lethal overdose of the opium his grandfather had tried to ban and committed suicide. At his funeral, onlookers spat at his coffin. In the estimation of *The New York Times*, "With the loss of the Chen-Yuen [*Zhenyuan*], her greatest battleship, China becomes practically powerless on the sea."[38]

Western observers could not understand why the Chinese had bought modern battleships if they never intended to use them. With the best of the Chinese army destroyed in Korea, the navy offered an essential means to defend Peking.[39] Half a century later, during World War II, the American general Joseph Warren Stilwell would be equally dumbfounded by Jiang Jieshi's (Chiang Kai-shek or 蔣介石) unwillingness to engage his modern American-supplied weapons to fight the

---

[36] "The War," *The North-China Herald* (Shanghai), 9 November 1894, p. 766; "War News," *The Japan Weekly Mail* (Yokohama), 17 November 1894, p. 559; "A Summary of the Port Arthur Campaign," Du Boulay, 2–4; "Kinchow," Du Boulay, 1; "Extracts from 'Advance Japan' by J. Morris, 1895," Du Boulay, 10; Eastlake and Yamada, 126; Ballard, 159; "金州及大連灣占領報告" (Report that Jinzhou and Dalian Occupied), 朝日新聞 (*Rising Sun Newspaper*) (Tokyo), 13 November 1894, p. 1; "大連灣の大襲擊" (Surprise Attack on Dalian), 朝日新聞 (*Rising Sun Newspaper*) (Tokyo), 21 November 1894, p. 2.

[37] Sun Kefu and Guan Jie, 216.

[38] "China's Best Ship Lost," *The New York Times*, 23 November 1894, p. 1; "Accident to the 'Chenyuen,'" *The North-China Herald* (Shanghai), 23 November 1984, p. 862; "Will China Learn?" *The North-China Herald* (Shanghai), 14 December 1894, p. 972; "From Native Sources," *The North-China Herald* (Shanghai), 4 January 1895, p. 14; U.S. Adjutant-General's Office, Military Information Division, *Notes on the War between China and Japan* (Washington: Government Printing Office, 1896), 11.

[39] Kuo, 54.

Japanese.[40] In both cases, it was as if the military hardware represented poker chips in the scales of *guanxi* (關係) or connections and was more valuable held than spent. In the grand game of bluff played in China, to use it up meant to deplete the stores of *guanxi* whose primary value came from its possession, not from its use. Traditionally, the Chinese had preferred to take on much weaker foes, such as seceding ethnic minorities, whom they have slaughtered without mercy. Their age-old strategy was to divide and rule by playing off one barbarian against another (以夷制夷) and destroying them in detail. Before Stilwell's time, the game was considerably more complicated with the unmentionable but vital tensions between the Manchu rulers and their far more numerous and resentful Han Chinese subjects.

The court hamstrung its officers out of fear that they might turn on their Manchu overlords. It had attempted to impeach Admiral Ding Ruchang (丁汝昌) for his failure to prevent two minor simultaneous Japanese raids on Weihaiwei and Port Arthur on August 10. For Admiral Ding, it must have become clear that if he intended to keep his head, his priority would have to be convoy duty rather than any offensive actions against the Japanese navy or troop transports. In this he was following common sense and orders. After the Battle of the Yalu, both he and his superior, Viceroy Li, made avoiding the loss of ships their top priority.[41] Ding's instructions throughout the war remained to defend the coast of the Bohai from Weihaiwei to the Yalu River – in other words, to protect Peking and the Manchu government ensconced there. This strategy wasted the Beiyang Fleet on convoy duty instead of interrupting the transport of Japanese troops to the war theater.[42] From the Manchu point of view, priority number one had to be the protection of the dynasty. Since they could not assume the loyalty of their subjects, they had to deploy troops defensively. Their most dangerous enemy was not necessarily the Japanese. Rather, the most menacing danger to the dynasty lay in any budding Han Chinese nationalism.

The Western press missed this dimension of the Chinese predicament: "The failure of the Pei-yang [Beiyang] Squadron in failing to make any resistance to the landing of a Japanese army on the Liau-tong [Liaodong] Peninsula, naturally evokes much comment...What is more, not even was warning conveyed to ships engaged in the transport service, the result being that 16 junks laden with material for constructing forts fell into the hands of the Japanese."[43]

---

[40] Barbara W. Tuchman, *Stilwell and the American Experience in China, 1911–1945* (New York: Macmillan, 1970), 388–90.

[41] Rawlinson, 171–3, 187–8.

[42] Evans and Peattie, 40.

[43] "War News," *The Japan Weekly Mail* (Yokohama), 3 November 1894, p. 509.

Before the Battle of Port Arthur, Colonel J. F. Maurice, commander of the British Royal Artillery at Colchester, informed the *London and China Express* that "a comparatively small Chinese naval force" could make it very difficult for the Japanese to transport large quantities of troops to the Asian mainland.[44] Yet Admiral Ding did nothing to impede the Japanese troop buildup in preparation for the assault on Port Arthur. The editors of *The Japan Weekly Mail* were dumbfounded: "When we begin to think what the loss of Port Arthur would signify for the Chinese Fleet, and what the abandonment of the place to its fate would imply under the circumstances, we can not but marvel at China's apparent inaction. Port Arthur is the only dock in north China. Did it come into Japanese possession, the Chinese war-ships would have no place to go for repairs and consequently dare not risk an engagement. Moreover, Port Arthur alone is not invested. The Japanese are holding the entrance to Pechili [Bohai] Gulf...Yet despite its easy accessibility for purposes of relief, and despite the crippling consequences involved in its capture, the Chinese seem resolved to leave it to its fate."[45]

It was incomprehensible to foreigners how China could possess a modern fleet and then not use it to prevent Japan from supplying its forces. The sea lanes were the lifeline for the Japanese military, yet "ordinary unarmed merchantmen, have been regularly plying to and fro without any escort, and they could have been waylaid and sent to the bottom time after time had China but risen to the occasion," wrote a reporter for *The North-China Herald.*[46] "The movements of the Chinese fleet have throughout the war been...utterly and incomprehensibly imbecile...[T]he Chinese fleet has not attempted to meet the Japanese fleet in the open sea, or weighed a single anchor to hinder and debar the unprotected transports of Japan passing to and fro with their freight of eager invaders."[47]

Right after the war, the United States' secretary of the navy, Hilary A. Herbert, provided his analysis. Given the well-known and endemic weaknesses of the Chinese army, "China had in this war a chance, and only one chance to win, and that lay in her fleet."[48] To seize this chance required aggressive and daring use of that navy. Instead, China had "entered upon a losing game of transporting troops to Korea, the battle ground Japan had chosen, in competition with an enemy, whose lines by sea were shorter and whose transports were as three to one. The

---

[44] "War News," *The Japan Weekly Mail* (Yokohama), 3 November 1894, p. 509.

[45] "War News," *The Japan Weekly Mail* (Yokohama), 24 November 1894, p. 584.

[46] "China's Apathy," *The North-China Herald* (Shanghai), 25 January 1895, p. 110.

[47] "The Contending Fleets," *The North-China Herald* (Shanghai), 15 February 1895, p. 214.

[48] Herbert, 689.

result of this game was shortly seen in the numbers that met each other at the battle of Ping Yang [P'yôngyang]." Herbert continued, "Japan, having beaten China in transporting troops to Korea, was then allowed to choose her own time and place for a sea fight in the battle off the Yalu. The first of the untoward results of the unfortunate policy of scattering her war ships upon which China had embarked, was that she was worsted off Asan [at Feng Island], where three of Japan's ships attacked two of the Chinese vessels."[49]

To defeat Japan, China had to be daring. Yet the whole incentive system in China under the Qing Dynasty penalized those who left the beaten path. To break with the norm and to defy hallowed traditions and conventional wisdom meant to create many enemies even in the event of success; and in the event of failure, these enemies would descend in a wolf pack. There was no up side to daring, as illustrated by Li Hongzhang's own fate. A century later, China's great nineteenth-century innovator remains a pariah to many in his native land.

The fall of Dalian left Port Arthur completely surrounded. The Chinese, in their haste to depart, had left behind the plans for the minefields in Dalian harbor as well as the plans for the defenses of Port Arthur. This blunder greatly simplified the task of making the harbor available to Japanese vessels. In no time, Dalian became a convenient base for launching the attack on Port Arthur.[50]

If Dalian had been a rout, the situation was little better at Port Arthur. Rumors of an "absence of discipline" within the fortress at Port Arthur circulated even before the attack.[51] After the fall of Dalian, the harbor master of Port Arthur, Captain Calder, observed "with the growing unruliness of the so-called defenders, that the fabric was tottering." He set off for Tianjin to warn Viceroy Li. "[A]fter infinite difficulty through the hindrances of the viceregal underlings" he "succeeded in having an interview with Li Hung-chang. Li began by enquiring whether it was a fact that one or two forts at Talienwan [Dalian] had been taken. When told that they were all lost he visibly faltered and remarked that it was incredible...his agitation became very marked." Calder told Li how "the Generals did little else but quarrel amongst themselves and act in opposition." For Viceroy Li, the fall of

[49] Herbert, 691.

[50] "The War," *The North-China Herald* (Shanghai), 9 November 1894, p. 766; "War News," *The Japan Weekly Mail* (Yokohama), 17 November 1894, p. 559; "A Summary of the Port Arthur Campaign," Du Boulay, 2–4; "Kinchow," Du Boulay, 1; "Extracts from 'Advance Japan' by J. Morris, 1895," Du Boulay, 10; F. Warrington Eastlake and Yamada Yoshi-aki, *Heroic Japan: A History of the War between China & Japan* (1897; reprint, Washington: University Publications of America, 1979), 126; Ballard, 159; U.S. Adjutant-General's Office, 18.

[51] "Tientsin," *The North-China Herald* (Shanghai), 23 November 1894, p. 854.

Port Arthur would mean the destruction of his life's work of modernizing China's military. It would also threaten him with personal destruction because the dynasty and the Han literati would require a scapegoat to blame for the debacle. Rather than addressing China's long-standing institutional problems at the root of the impasse, it was less mentally taxing to blame one individual for the whole situation. Quick and simple.[52]

When Captain Calder returned to Port Arthur, "Soldiers were wandering about in mobs, taking pot-shots at electric-light lamps and destroying everything in the most wanton way. In some of the smaller forts the soldiers were finding amusement in discharging the smaller guns at everything and anything – a small fishing boat for instance."[53] Chinese troops started looting Port Arthur before the attack. Allegedly, the "commander of the submarine mines and torpedo corps, in his fright, cut the connecting electric wires and carrying away the firing apparatus immediately fled, his example being well imitated by those under him, so that of the 600 odd torpedoes laid in the harbour not a single one was fired against the enemy."[54] On November 17, the Tianjin correspondent for *The North-China Herald* reported that "news of the fall of Port Arthur has been expected every day...Foreigners from Newchwang [Niuzhuang] and Port Arthur give a most deplorable account of the state of things among the common people. All who can are fleeing with such of their possessions as they can take away."[55]

Fighting began on November 20, but the main body of Japanese troops did not arrive until that evening. Although the navy was present, its involvement in the attack was only peripheral. On November 21, the main attack began.[56] The Japanese lacked the proper grade and range of ammunition for their siege guns, so that the Chinese should have been at a real advantage. Yet the Japanese were able to storm the forts. "Chinese gunnery was hopelessly ineffective...What fighting

[52] "The War," *The North-China Herald* (Shanghai), 7 December 1894, p. 943; "Tientsin," *The North-China Herald* (Shanghai), 23 November 1894, p. 853; "Imperial Decrees of the 17th of December," *The North-China Herald* (Shanghai), 21 December 1894, p. 1021.

[53] "The War," *The North-China Herald* (Shanghai), 7 December 1894, p. 943; "Tientsin," *The North-China Herald* (Shanghai), 23 November 1894, p. 853; "Imperial Decrees of the 17th of December," *The North-China Herald* (Shanghai), 21 December 1894, p. 1021.

[54] "The Fall of Port Arthur," *The North-China Herald* (Shanghai), 21 December 1894, p. 1021.

[55] "Tientsin," *The North-China Herald* (Shanghai), 23 November 1894, p. 854.

[56] "War News," *The Japan Weekly Mail* (Yokohama), 1 December 1894, p. 614; "The War," *The North-China Herald* (Shanghai), 7 December 1894, pp. 941–2; "The Taking of Port Arthur," *The Japan Weekly Mail* (Yokohama), 8 December 1894, pp. 644–5; Jukichi Inouye, *The Japan-China War: On the Regent's Sword: Kinchow, Port Arthur, and Talienwan* (Yokohama: Kelly & Walsh, 1895).

followed was mere carnage...The Chinese officers abandoning their men to their fate, got on board two small steamers that remained in the harbour and put out to sea."[57] It proved unnecessary for the Japanese to besiege the fortress since the Chinese gave up so quickly. Defense by land required coordination among the forts on the semicircle of hills surrounding the fortress. In the absence of this coordination, the Japanese picked off the forts one by one and turned the forts' artillery on the arsenal and dockyard.[58] On November 21, the same day the main attack had begun, Port Arthur fell to the Japanese with all the forts and dockyard abandoned and in good condition. The coal supplies left behind would be used to fuel the naval attack on Weihaiwei.[59]

On November 20, when a foreign correspondent had asked Lieutenant-General Yamaji Motoharu (山地元春), the commander of the first division of the Second Army, "When do you expect to take Port Arthur?" he had replied, "Oh, tomorrow." The correspondent gave the general "a dubious smile." The following evening, after the city had fallen, they met again. "Well, you see I was right; here we are," said Yamaji.[60] The fall of Port Arthur was the Japanese birthday present to the Empress Dowager, whose sixtieth birthday came eight days later.

The Japanese victory at Port Arthur was marred in one very important respect. Ever since the sinking of the *Kowshing,* the Japanese had striven to acquire a reputation for impeccable behavior on the battlefield. In addition to demonstrating their military prowess, they had also sought to demonstrate their country's high degree of civilization through the humane treatment of civilians and prisoners of war. For public relations, the policy was brilliant. Even the anti-Japanese *North-China Herald* felt its effects. "Official corruption has certainly sapped China's strength and brought about defeat and loss, and Japan's humane treatment has certainly been the chief cause of her victories."[61] On September 22, 1894, the

[57] "The Taking of Port Arthur," *The Japan Weekly Mail* (Yokohama), 8 December 1894, p. 645.

[58] "Is This the End, Is This the End?" *The Pall Mall Gazette* (London), 26 November 1894, 4th ed., p. 1; "The Taking of Port Arthur," *The Japan Weekly Mail* (Yokohama), 8 December 1894, pp. 644–5.

[59] U.S. Adjutant-General's Office, 19, 21; "旅順口占領" (Port Arthur Occupied), 朝日新聞 (*Rising Sun Newspaper*) (Tokyo), 25 November 1894, pp. 1–2; "旅順口占領の詳報" (Detailed Report of Occupation of Port Arthur), 朝日新聞 (*Rising Sun Newspaper*) (Tokyo), 30 November 1894, p. 1; "旅順口攻擊に關する公報" (Announcement Concerning Attack on Port Arthur), 國民新聞 (*People's Newspaper*) (Tokyo), 22 November 1894, p. 1; "旅順口占領の詳報" (Detailed Report Concerning Occupation of Port Arthur), 國民新聞 (*People's Newspaper*) (Tokyo), 25 November 1894, supplement, p. 1.

[60] "Port Arthur Items," *The Japan Weekly Mail* (Yokohama), 15 December 1894, p. 663; U.S. Adjutant-General's Office, 12.

[61] "China and Japan," *The North-China Herald* (Shanghai), 14 December 1894, p. 973.

Minister of War Marshal Ōyama Iwao (大山巌) had alerted the army that Japan had responsibilities as a signatory since 1886 of the 1864 Geneva Convention. Japanese soldiers "must never forget that however cruel and vindictive the foe may allow himself, he must nevertheless be treated in accordance with the acknowledged rules of civilization; his disabled must be succored and his captured kindly and considerately protected." Soldiers were admonished not to bear animosity toward civilians.[62] Marshal Ōyama later issued a general order to his troops: "Our Army fights for the right and in accordance with the principles of civilization. Our enemies are the military forces of the country with which we are at war, not the individuals of the country. Against the force of our foe we must fight with all resolution, but as soon as any of his soldiers surrender, are taken prisoners, or receive wounds, they cease to be enemies, and it becomes our duty to treat them with all kindness."[63]

By the time that Japanese troops reached Port Arthur, this reputation for restraint had preceded them: "With wonderful unanimity they [the natives] say they had no fear of the Japanese, who had earned the reputation of paying for everything they wanted."[64] This made what transpired doubly tragic. Articles published in mid-January would point out with particular regret that Marshal Ōyama's publicized promises of safety for the civilian population had convinced some to remain in Port Arthur.[65]

Thomas Cowan of the London *Times* and James Creelman of the New York *World* witnessed the fall of Port Arthur together. In December, Creelman's sensational reports would make headlines in the United States and send ripples through the European press. The handsome Creelman was known to be willing to do just about anything for a scoop. At various times he had interviewed European revolutionaries, Indian chiefs, Mexican dictators, and Russian novelists and then sensationalized the results for more interesting reading. In the war zone, he impressed people with his immaculate dress and grooming.[66] Creelman and Cowan rode with the Japanese advance patrol on November 18, when they came upon mutilated Japanese bodies. According to Cowan, "The sight was most revolting and was sufficient to excite revengeful feelings in the hearts of the best disciplined men."[67] Creelman also described other Chinese atrocities in Port Arthur, where

---

[62] "War Items," *The Japan Weekly Mail* (Yokohama), 29 September 1894, pp. 361–2.

[63] "War News," *The Japan Weekly Mail* (Yokohama), 3 November 1894, p. 509.

[64] "The War," *The North-China Herald* (Shanghai), 7 December 1894, p. 944.

[65] "The Slaughter at Port Arthur," *The Peking and Tientsin Times*, 19 January 1895, p. 183.

[66] Dorwart, 106–10.

[67] "The Atrocities after the Fall of Port Arthur," *The Times* (London), 8 January 1895, p. 6. See also

entering Japanese troops found "the heads of their slain comrades hanging by cords, with the noses and ears gone" and "a rude arch in the main street decorated with bloody Japanese heads."[68] Apparently, many Japanese soldiers also saw the heads.[69] Throughout the war, the Japanese had discovered many equally mutilated bodies of their fallen comrades, but until Port Arthur they had not taken revenge in front of westerners.

Another witness, James Allan, wrote a book about it after the war: "Strongly as the massacre by the Japanese troops in Port Arthur is to be condemned, there is not the slightest doubt in the world that the Chinese brought it on themselves by their own vindictive savagery towards their enemies...[O]ne of the first things I saw on the morning of the 19th was a pair of [Japanese] corpses suspended by the feet from the branches of a huge camphor tree...They had been disemboweled; the eyes were gouged out, the throat cut, the right hand severed. They were perfectly naked, and groups of children were pelting them with mud and stones."[70] Allan was allowed to walk about freely and observe the massacre in progress. "Nobody was spared, man, woman, or child, that I could see. The Chinese appeared to offer no resistance. Many of them prostrated themselves on the ground before the butchers with abject submission, and were shot or stabbed in that posture."[71] "The dead were mostly the townspeople; their valiant defenders seemed to have been able to make themselves scarce."[72] He described the events as "the diabolical orgy of murder and mutilation, rape, lust, and rapine."[73]

While Cowan excused the Japanese summary executions during the first day as part of the capture of the city, he said, "I was greatly surprised next day to find them still killing the Chinese. They practically routed out the whole of the town: every house was entered and searched; the Chinese were driven out and killed; some were even killed in the houses." Cowan dismissed the Japanese press reports that the massacres were carried out primarily by "coolies" or porters working for the Japanese. The murders "were all done by soldiers in uniform; not the work of

---

"The Port Arthur Atrocities," *The Times* (London), 1 February 1895, p. 4.

[68] J. Creelman, "The Massacre at Port Arthur," *The World* (New York), 20 December 1894, p. 1.

[69] "The Taking of Port Arthur," *The Japan Weekly Mail* (Yokohama), 8 December 1894, pp. 644–5.

[70] James Allan, *Under the Dragon Flag: My Experiences in the Chino-Japanese War* (London: William Heinemann, 1898), 66–7. For Allan's description of the massacre, see Ibid., 76–93.

[71] Allan, 80.

[72] Allan, 84.

[73] Allan, 89. Similarly, Creelman and Cowan witnessed no evidence of Chinese resistance to the massacre (James Creelman, "The Massacre at Port Arthur," *The World* [New York], 20 December 1894, p. 1).

coolies, so far as I could see." In support of the Japanese claims that it was difficult to distinguish combatants from civilians, Cowan said that "the hillsides around Port Arthur were strewn with their uniforms." This, however, did not explain the killing of women and children.[74] "I saw scores of Chinese hunted out of cover, shot down and hacked to pieces, and never a man made any attempt to fight...I watched intently for the slightest sign of cause, confident that there must be some, but I saw none whatever." He speculated that perhaps the Japanese "also are barbarous at heart, like the Chinese." If not, he admonished them "to prove it, for the fact remains that a dozen white men saw these Japanese commit these savageries for four clear days after the day of the fight."[75] When Cowan left on November 26, five days after the fall of Port Arthur, the massacre was still going on.[76] Diaries of Japanese soldiers engaged in the massacre corroborate the general story recounted in Western press reports.[77]

In Port Arthur Creelman ran into the Japanese legal adviser to the Second Army: "On the night of the second day [of the massacre] the legal adviser of the army told me that Field Marshal Oyama regarded the continued slaughter as quite justifiable. 'Prisoners are a burden.'"[78] The legal adviser, Ariga, appears to be one and the same as Ariga Nagao, who, a year after the war had ended, published in French a book entitled, *The Sino-Japanese War from the Point of View of International Law.* By that time Ariga had become a professor of international law at the War College in Tokyo. In the book, Ariga justified the massacre on the grounds of provocation and reciprocity. In a nutshell, since the Chinese did not adhere to the terms of the Geneva Convention, they got what they deserved.[79] At Port Arthur, Ariga implied to the foreign correspondents that Japan had the option "to kill our prisoners." He continued, "We took a few hundred prisoners at Pingyang [P'yôngyang], and we found it very expensive and troublesome to feed and guard them. We are taking practically no prisoners here."[80] The correspondents

[74] "The Port Arthur Atrocities," *The Japan Weekly Mail* (Yokohama), 22 December 1894, p. 702; "Japan on Its Behavior," *The New York Times*, 18 December 1894, p. 5.

[75] "The Atrocities after the Fall of Port Arthur," *The Times* (London), 8 January 1895, p. 6. See also "The Port Arthur Atrocities," *The Times* (London), 1 February 1895, p. 4.

[76] "The Port Arthur Atrocities," *The Japan Weekly Mail* (Yokohama), 22 December 1894, p. 702; "Japan on Its Behavior," *The New York Times*, 18 December 1894, p. 5.

[77] Lone, 155.

[78] James Creelman, "Bloodthirsty Japan," *The World* (New York), 7 January 1895, p. 2.

[79] James Creelman, "The Massacre at Port Arthur," *The World* (New York), 20 December 1894, p. 1. Nagao Ariga, *La Guerre Sino-Japonaise au Point de Vue du Droit International* (*The Sino-Japanese War from the Perspective of International Law*) (Paris: A. Pedone, 1896), 6, 85–6

[80] J. Creelman, "The Massacre at Port Arthur," *The World* (New York), 20 December 1894, p. 1.

were not particularly argumentative since they were in a war zone in the midst of an on-going indiscriminate massacre.

Since the story of the massacre would not have cleared the Japanese censors, the Western witnesses had to leave the Japanese zone of occupation before filing their news reports. The London *Times* was among the first papers to allude to the massacre. On November 26 it published a one-sentence paragraph stating, "Great slaughter is reported to have taken place."[81] In early December *The Pall Mall Gazette* and *Le Journal des débats politiques et littéraires* mentioned a massacre, but the foreign press at home gave the matter little or no coverage.[82] American newspapers gave much more press to the Armenian atrocities being perpetrated by the Ottoman Empire.[83]

Foreign eyes focused on the behavior of the Japanese army only with the publication of James Creelman's first article on the massacre in *The World* on December 12, 1894. According to the front-page news short, "The Japanese troops entered Port Arthur on Nov. 21 and massacred practically the entire population in cold blood." Creelman continued, "The defenseless and unarmed inhabitants were butchered in their houses and their bodies were unspeakably mutilated. There was an unrestrained reign of murder which continued for three days. The whole town was plundered with appalling atrocities." He concluded, "It was the first stain upon Japanese civilization. The Japanese in this instance relapsed into barbarism."[84]

---

[81] "The War in the East," *The Times* (London), 26 November 1894, p. 5. See also "The War in the East," *The Times* (London), 1 December 1894, p. 5.

[82] *The Pall Mall Gazette* ran only a few short articles buried in the back pages. "The Chino-Japanese War," *The Pall Mall Gazette* (London), 3 December 1894, 4th ed., p. 7; "The Chino-Japanese War," *The Pall Mall Gazette* (London), 20 December 1894, 4th ed., p. 7. The first significant account to appear in *The New York Times* was on December 18 ("Japan on Its Behavior," p. 5). Meanwhile, the London *Times* tended to sympathize with the Japanese faced with an enemy who mutilated captives and disguised himself in civilian dress. "The War in the East," *The Times* (London), 15 December 1894, p. 5; "The War in the East," *The Times* (London), 17 December 1894, p. 5. *Le Temps* mentioned the massacre in passing, simply to say that it was "confirmed" that "atrocities" had been committed. "La Guerre en Chine" (The War in China), *Le Temps* (*The Times*) (Paris), 30 November 1894; "La Guerre entre la Chine et le Japon" (War between China and Japan), *Le Journal des débats politiques et littéraires* (*Journal of Political and Literary Debates*) (Paris), 1 December 1894, evening ed., p. 1; "La Guerre entre la Chine et le Japon: Les Massacres de Port-Arthur" (War between China and Japan: The Massacres at Port Arthur), *Le Journal des débats politiques et littéraires* (*Journal of Political and Literary Debates*) (Paris), 9 January 1895, morning ed., p. 2; "La Guerre entre la Chine et le Japon: La Version officielle japonaise sur les massacres de Port-Arthur" (War between China and Japan: The Official Japanese Version of the Massacres at Port Arthur), *Le Journal des débats politiques et littéraires* (*Journal of Political and Literary Debates*) (Paris), 31 January 1895, morning edition, p. 2.

[83] See for example, "About Armenian Atrocities," *The New York Times*, 22 December 1894, p. 5.

[84] James Creelman, "A Japanese Massacre," *The World* (New York), 12 December 1894, p. 1.

Once Creelman's article came out, the London *Times* and *Le Temps* provided detailed coverage.[85] The massacre threatened to undo Japan's meticulously crafted public image as the only civilized nation in the Far East. In America, it threatened to upset the pending ratification of the American–Japanese treaty providing Japan juridical equality.[86]

The Japanese Foreign Ministry handled the matter deftly. Cowan had gone to Hiroshima on his way home and had met with Foreign Minister Mutsu Munemitsu (陸奥宗光) to relay the story personally. Mutsu "announced that an investigation would be made. He showed no disposition to interfere with the correspondents' duty and the reports were telegraphed on Dec. 1."[87] On December 16, the Japanese Foreign Ministry issued a formal statement to the foreign press: "The Japanese Government desires no concealment of the events at Port Arthur. On the contrary, it is investigating rigidly for the purpose of fixing the exact responsibility and is taking measures essential to the reputation of the empire." It admitted that "Japanese troops transported with rage at the mutilation of their comrades by the enemy, broke through all restraints" and that "exasperated by the wholesale attempts [by Chinese soldiers] at escape disguised at citizens, they inflicted vengeance without discrimination." While the Japanese government "deplores" the excessive violence, it protested "exaggerations" in the press reports and insisted that "the victims, almost without exception, were soldiers wearing the stolen clothes of citizens."[88] Three days later, a *Times* correspondent reported that most foreign reporters "agree that the excesses were committed, but say that they were excusable, and that they have had their parallels in the best European armies."[89] The Japanese military soon promised to launch an inquiry that, after much ado, never wound up punishing anyone.[90] By then Western attention had focused on the peace terms and was no longer concerned with the events at Port Arthur.

In a strange reversal in roles, *The North-China Herald* was far less critical of the Japanese military than *The Japan Weekly Mail*: "There was a foe too impotent and cowardly to stand and fight, who nevertheless did not hesitate to exhibit the most malicious hatred and vindictiveness by torturing and mutilating in the most

---

[85] "La Chine et le Japon" (China and Japan), *Le Temps (The Times)* (Paris), 17 January 1895.

[86] "America is Aghast," *The World* (New York), 13 December 1894, p. 1.

[87] "Japan is Heartsick," *The World* (New York), 11 January 1895, p. 1.

[88] "Japan Confesses," *The World* (New York), 17 December 1894, p. 1.

[89] "The War in the East," *The Times* (London), 19 December 1894, p. 5. "The Port Arthur Atrocities," *The Times* (London), 1 February 1895, p. 4.

[90] "The War in the East," *The Times* (London), 19 December 1894, p. 5. "The Port Arthur Atrocities," *The Times* (London), 1 February 1895, p. 4.

horrible manner a few isolated Japanese who had the misfortune to fall into their power...The circumstances were such as might have taxed the control of any invading force." It then sermonized that "it must be remembered that warfare is warfare and not a drawing-room game."[91] The editors of *The Japan Weekly Mail* excoriated the Japanese military for its barbarous conduct and did not let the matter drop in subsequent issues.[92]

In contrast, the native Japanese press also tended to dismiss reports of the massacre, attributing the allegations to "an invidious desire to detract from the glory of the Japanese Army."[93] Even though most Western papers provided minimal coverage of the massacre, the Japanese press was stung by the criticism. Perhaps its members got a false impression of the attention being given to the story from the pages of *The Japan Weekly Mail*. A reporter for *Shin Chōya* (新朝野) responded: "It is a regular habit with civilized Christians of the West to see no wrong in anything they do themselves to Oriental and other non-Christian races, and to be blind to every element of right or justice in the conduct of the men they call heretics...Civilized Occidentals have often slaughtered Orientals and other heretics or savages, as though they were no better than fattened animals destined to die under the butcher's knife. During the past century, the history of savage nations that have come in contact with Christian Occidentals is all but written in blood." The reporter concluded that, while certain members of the Second Army had

---

[91] "The Japanese at Port Arthur," *The North-China Herald* (Shanghai), 4 January 1895, p. 5. For other articles on the Port Arthur massacre in the same paper, see "The Excesses at Port Arthur," *The North-China Herald* (Shanghai), 4 January 1895, p. 8; "The Port Arthur Atrocities," *The North-China Herald* (Shanghai), 11 January 1895, p. 26.

Similarly, *The Peking and Tientsin Times* did not focus attention on the massacre. "Another Peace Mission," *The Peking and Tientsin Times*, 29 December 1894, p. 170; "The Taking of Port Arthur," *The Peking and Tientsin Times*, 5 January 1895, p. 175; "The Slaughter at Port Arthur," *The Peking and Tientsin Times*, 19 January 1895, p. 183.

[92] "The Taking of Port Arthur," *The Japan Weekly Mail* (Yokohama), 8 December 1894, p. 645; "The Conduct of the Japanese Troops and Coolies at Port Arthur," *The Japan Weekly Mail* (Yokohama), 8 December 1894, pp. 651–2; "Port Arthur," *The North-China Herald* (Shanghai), 7 December 1894, p. 929; "Comparisons – and False Inferences," *The Japan Weekly Mail* (Yokohama), 15 December 1894, p. 679; "Comparisons," *The Japan Weekly Mail* (Yokohama), 15 December 1894, pp. 680–1. For information on other massacres perpetrated by British troops, see "The Massacre of Chinese at Port Arthur," *The Japan Weekly Mail* (Yokohama), 15 December 1894, p. 680.

[93] *Jiyū* (自由) quoted in "The Spirit of the Vernacular Press during the Week," *The Japan Weekly Mail* (Yokohama), 15 December 1894, p. 662. See also "War News," *The Japan Weekly Mail* (Yokohama), 15 December 1894, p. 667; "Advancing on Chin-Chow," *The New York Times*, 13 January 1895, p. 5. Recent Japanese accounts of the war, however, do not dismiss the massacre. See for example Iguchi Kazuki (井口和起), "日清。日露戦争論" (Discussion of the Sino-Japanese and Russo-Japanese wars) , 日本歴史 (*Japanese History*) 8, no. 2 (June 1985): 93; Inoue Haruki (井上春樹), 旅順虐殺事件 (*Lüshun Massacre*) (Tokyo: 筑摩書房, 1995).

committed excesses, the Western stories were laced with gross exaggerations.[94] The Japanese press responded with bitterness that the Japanese army had extended all courtesies to foreign correspondents, only to be subject to such "calumnious criticism"[95] by them.

Meanwhile the Chinese government, far from devoting coverage to the massacre, was trying to deny that Chinese forces had been defeated, let alone massacred, at Port Arthur. According to the Shanghai-based *China Gazette:* "The most strenuous efforts have been made by the Chinese officials to conceal the fact that the great stronghold has passed out of their hands, and is now a *de facto* Japanese naval yard. Telegraphic notices have been sent...all over the empire by the officials saying that a wicked report has been set on foot by the enemy that they have captured Port Arthur, but it was utterly untrue, the place being garrisoned by 30,000 brave Chinese soldiers who would never give it up to the Japanese." The story continued, "Official telegrams to this effect were published to-day in all the native papers, and thousands of Chinese will thereby be kept in blissful ignorance of the terrible position in which China stands to-day. Ostrich-like, most of the Chinese prefer not to believe the unpleasant truth and rather listen to the barefaced mendacity of their wretched rulers. But the stupidity of the latter gentry, who have brought the country to its present desperate plight, is only emphasized by this false manœuvre."[96] A month after the defeat, "By many it is not yet known or admitted that Port Arthur has been taken and is held by the Japanese – even of the 'well-informed' officials. The same is said to be true in Peking."[97]

The court had good reason to desire concealment of their defeat. With Japanese troops pouring into the Manchu homeland of Manchuria, the dynasty's mandate of heaven, already seriously weakened by the long period of internal rebellions, must have seemed to have been hanging from a thread. After the defeats of P'yôngyang and the Yalu, the emperor reportedly had demanded to take personal control over the prosecution of the war in Korea. He wanted to leave the throne under the regency of the Empress Dowager so that he could concentrate on the front, but his advisers eventually dissuaded him.[98] The Manchus had proven derelict in their

---

[94] "The Spirit of the Vernacular Press during the Week," *The Japan Weekly Mail* (Yokohama), 22 December 1894, p. 694.

[95] "The 'Nippon' and the 'Niroku' on Foreign War Correspondents," *The Japan Weekly Mail* (Yokohama), 29 December 1894, p. 726. *Nippon* (日本) and *Niroku* (二六) were Japanese newspapers.

[96] Quoted in "Chinese News," *The Japan Weekly Mail* (Yokohama), 8 December 1894, p. 646.

[97] "Tientsin," *The North-China Herald* (Shanghai), 18 January 1895, p. 78.

[98] "Japan's Great Naval Victory," *The New York Times*, 20 September 1894, p. 5; "Chinese Ammunition Landed," *The New York Times*, 25 September 1894, p. 5.

primary responsibility to maintain the national security of China. Luckily for them, the lack of national sentiments in China coupled with a self-destructive xenophobia allowed them to heap the blame for their defeat on Viceroy Li Hongzhang and his generals.

Personnel changes suggested that something was afoot in Peking. In October 1894, even before the defeat at Port Arthur, Prince Gong (恭親王奕訢) had been reinstated. He had been demoted a decade earlier ostensibly as a result of the Sino-French War but actually because Empress Dowager Cixi considered him a dangerous rival. He was appointed High Commissioner of the Peking Field Forces and co-president, with Prince Qing (Ch'ing) (慶親王奕劻), of the Admiralty, the Zongli Yamen, and of War Operations.[99] For this latter appointment, the government created a quasi-general headquarters.[100] Prince Gong was the sixth and only surviving son of the Daoguang Emperor (道光皇帝); the uncle-in-law of the Empress Dowager; and, with Viceroy Li, one of China's two preeminent experts on foreign affairs. He was well respected in the foreign community but in poor health. In December 1894, he was also made a member and president of the Grand Council, the supreme advisory body to the emperor.[101] Prince Qing had been the head of the Zongli Yamen since 1887.[102] These changes put two Manchu princes, Gong and Qing, in control of the defense of the capital. Although Gong now shared command of the Chinese military with Li Hongzhang, Gong remained in Peking, indicating that his responsibilities were specifically for the defense of the capital, whereas Li retained the general responsibility for prosecuting the war against Japan.[103] The foreign press failed to see that this was an attempt by the Manchus to reassert control over the war effort in general and specifically over the protection of the capital from any attempt – Japanese or Han – to topple the dynasty.

After the fall of Port Arthur, Viceroy Li Hongzhang "had applied to the throne for adequate punishment and within twenty-four hours was deprived of all his titles, honours, and offices." No sooner said than done, yet he remained at his

---

[99] "Prince Kung Reinstated," *The North-China Herald* (Shanghai), 5 October 1894, p. 550; "The War in the East," *The Times* (London), 6 November 1894, p. 5; "The War," *The North-China Herald* (Shanghai), 7 December 1894, p. 944; "Imperial Decrees," *The North-China Herald* (Shanghai), 11 January 1895, p. 47.

[100] Japan, Imperial General Staff, 26.

[101] "Prince Kung Reinstated," *The North-China Herald* (Shanghai), 5 October 1894, p. 550; "The War," *The North-China Herald* (Shanghai), 7 December 1894, p. 944; "The War in the East," *The Times* (London), 14 December 1894, p. 5. "Abstract of Peking Gazette," *The North-China Herald* (Shanghai), 21 December 1894, p. 1015; Ding Richu, 179.

[102] Kuo, 33.

[103] "The War in the East," *The Times* (London), 8 October 1894, p. 5.

post.[104] *The New York Times* ran the headline, "Viceroy Li Hung Chang Has Lost the Rest of His Wardrobe."[105] To the foreign press, the Chinese Court's practice of continually degrading and punishing its officials instead of implementing serious policies had become a subject for derision. Yet Li Hongzhang remained at his post and in power. "Of whatever honorific titles he may have been deprived, it is becoming more apparent that the functions of H. H. Li as Viceroy, have not been disturbed. With all his faults, he is one of the best – if not the very best – of the Emperor's servants."[106]

Li Hongzhang then turned the tables on his opponents. In a memorial defending his actions, he blamed them, quite accurately, for resisting for years his railroad construction plans. A lack of railways made it impossible for China to deploy troops effectively during the war.[107] A month later, a memorial by Viceroy Li's son-in-law, Zhang Peilun (張佩綸), was mysteriously made public. One wonders whether the viceroy himself leaked the document. It had been written in 1882 and had warned that China must prepare for a future contest with Japan. At that time, the document had been forwarded to Li Hongzhang for comment. In his extensive addendum, Li had agreed that the Chinese government must prepare to take on Japan, but only after modernizing its own navy. He had then complained that the promised naval funds were not forthcoming. The release of the document was an indirect I-told-you-so from Li.[108]

In 1874, Li had argued that China's limited resources should be channeled into the navy instead of into central Asian border defenses. At the time Russia was threatening Xinjiang and the money went to fend off Russia, not to create a navy. Central Asian defense had been a conventional strategic concern throughout Chinese history, whereas the idea of naval defenses was a novelty of the late nineteenth century.[109] In 1884 Li had advocated to no avail the creation of a national navy under a unified command. In April of 1894, he had warned the court that the military needed to buy more warships, improve its land defenses, and create better

---

[104] "What Next?" *The North-China Herald* (Shanghai), 14 December 1894, p. 975.

[105] "On the March to Pekin: Viceroy Li Hung Chang Has Lost the Rest of His Wardrobe," *The New York Times*, 28 November 1894, p. 5.

[106] "Battle of Kangwangtsai," *The North-China Herald* (Shanghai), 25 January 1895, p. 117.

[107] "The Chino-Japanese War," *The Pall Mall Gazette* (London), 13 December 1894, 4th ed., p. 7.

[108] "Some Chinese Official Documents," *The Times* (London), 19 January 1895, p. 4.

[109] Key-hiuk Kim, 339–40; Immanuel C. Y. Hsü, "The Great Policy Debated in China, 1874: Maritime Defense vs. Frontier Defense," *Readings in Modern Chinese History* (New York: Oxford University Press, 1971), 258–69.

military schools.[110] After the Battle of the Yalu, when the court had attempted to cashier Admiral Ding, Li had noted that he had not been allowed to purchase any new ships since 1888, whereas nine of Japan's twenty-one fast ships had been purchased since 1889. Because of the technological improvements over the intervening years, the Chinese fleet could not match the Japanese fleet for speed.[111] During the war, Li had complained bitterly about the reluctance of the Guangxu Emperor to meet his repeated requests for money and munitions: "We are merely using the local troops of North China to fight the whole national force of Japan."[112]

According to Colonel J. F. Maurice, commander of the British Royal Artillery at Colchester, "Li Hung-chang is being treated as a scapegoat. He is the only man in China who has advocated European methods, and he is now being punished on account of the failure of the old Conservatives who refused to follow his advice."[113] "The ablest known man in the empire asking to be punished for doing his best, and asking whom? Practically a set of sterilised drones [a reference to the Court eunuchs in service to their queen bee, the Empress Dowager] who for years have been doing their worst to thwart his policy and oppose his measures...Both in insight as to his country's needs and in foresight in his attempts to provide them, he excels all his rivals."[114] Had national sentiments been more fully developed or had the blame for the debacle been focused, not on a few Han Chinese, but on those at the helm in Peking, the Manchus might have been sent packing. However, the foreign powers would prevent Japan from administering the *coup de grâce,* thereby assuring a lingering death for the Qing Dynasty.

Internationally, the rapid defeat at Port Arthur constituted a mortal blow to Chinese military prestige. The modern fortifications should have been very difficult to dislodge since they were well situated, up-to-date, and amply supplied with modern equipment. Yet Chinese officials fled, Chinese troops fought poorly, and once again the Chinese did not manage to destroy the fortifications or munitions before they fell.[115] China's reputation for military incompetence was cemented.

---

[110] Ting-i Li, *A History of Modern China* (Hong Kong: Oriental Society, 1970), 221.

[111] Rawlinson, 66, 144.

[112] Cited by Yuan Tao-feng: 15.

[113] "War News," *The Japan Weekly Mail* (Yokohama), 3 November 1894, p. 509. For similar views, see Treat, vol. 2, 526.

[114] "Responsibility," *The North-China Herald* (Shanghai), 28 December 1894, p. 1043.

[115] "Китай. Война с Японией" (China. The War with Japan), *Московские ведомости* (*Moscow Gazette*), no. 304, 5 November 1894 (17 November 1894), p. 4; "Китай. Война с Японией" (China. The War with Japan), *Московские ведомости* (*Moscow Gazette*), no. 305, 6 November 1894 (18 November 1894), p. 5; "Китай. Взятие Порт-Артура" (China. The Capture of Port Arthur), *Московские ведомости* (*Moscow Gazette*), no. 320, 21 November 1894 (3 December 1894), p. 4.

With the fall of Port Arthur, China's Western friends threw in the towel. On November 26, a reporter for *The North-China Herald* lamented in disbelief: "The news of the fall of Port Arthur reached here on Saturday [November 24], but was scarcely credited at first. So much had been said of its impregnability that it seemed impossible that the Japanese could take it without a sanguinary conflict. But the report was confirmed later on, and that it was captured after only nineteen hours' fighting."[116] An article in *The New York Times* concluded, "It is hard to see how the war in the East can now be prolonged." It recommended that China sue for peace post haste.[117] A commentator for *The North-China Herald* grudgingly admitted: "It is the unexpected which always happens. Japan has done far more than was ever anticipated by her most enthusiastic admirers, and has consequently reaped encomiums which might not otherwise have fallen to her share." He continued, "[S]he has proved herself to be a Power which must be reckoned with in all the future plans and undertakings of the Western Powers." He considered Japan to be "a great Power." "What Japan has accomplished in less than half a century – we might almost say within a quarter of a century – it has taken other countries many whole centuries to perform."[118] A second article in the same issue was entitled, "Another Great Power."[119]

From the war's onset, reporters at *The North-China Herald* had argued that Japan's cause was morally bankrupt since Japan had forced war on China. This was a valid argument, and it was equally applicable to the acquisition of empires by all of the other powers of the day as they expanded their colonies throughout the globe at gunpoint. Contrary to the editor's vision of international affairs, Japan's goal was not primarily one of moral probity, but rather the acquisition of the raw military power believed necessary to secure its independent existence against the predations of the other great powers. Any moral pretexts the Japanese government used to justify the hostilities were simply meant to further this overriding strategic goal.

The Japanese government was determined to become a great power and be treated as such. In an interview, Count Ōkuma Shigenobu (大隈重信), one of the most important political leaders of the Meiji era, pointed out: "Those in power may think it a great achievement to have secured the independence of Korea and to

---

[116] "Tientsin," *The North-China Herald* (Shanghai), 7 December 1894, p. 930.

[117] "The Fall of Port Arthur," *The New York Times*, 25 November 1894, p. 4.

[118] "The Other Side of the Question," *The North-China Herald* (Shanghai), 7 December 1894, p. 917. For similar views that the Japanese were mere imitators, see "The Anglo-Japanese Treaty," *The Peking and Tientsin Times*, 22 September 1894, p. 114.

[119] "Another Great Power," *The North-China Herald* (Shanghai), 7 December 1894, p. 923.

have concluded new treaties with the European Powers. But the nation...has the grander aim of laying a foundation for the dissemination of its influence throughout the world...[T]he European Powers are in a decline, and...in the course of the coming century a complete prostration will overtake them. Who are to take their place?" He concluded that their place "will be taken by our own descendants...To sum up...with treaties revised, and China completely humbled...Japan will have become a Power whose intentions and attitudes must be carefully studied by all other countries of the world."[120]

A consistent goal of the Meiji generation had been to change Western perceptions of Japan. The victory at Port Arthur, even with the massacre, went a long way toward doing this. In Moscow *Russkie vedomosti* captured the new prevailing stereotypes in Russia concerning the belligerents: Korea was described as being weak, little-cultured and peaceful; China was credited with being enormous but poorly united, largely immobile, and conservative; Japan was enterprising and energetic, with a rapidly developing culture, proud pretensions, and great forces on the land and sea.[121] This represented a complete reversal in the perceptions about the relative strength of China and Japan prevailing at the start of the war. An article in the London *Times* described the victory as "an achievement of the first importance" and a decisive turning point. It stressed the rapid progress over rugged terrain by the Japanese forces from the beginning of the war onward. "In looking back upon the course of the war up to the present time, it is impossible not to be struck by the vigour with which it has been prosecuted by the Japanese and the rapid succession of events." The author concluded that the "war in the East will furnish invaluable teaching to the British nation."[122]

In France, an article in *Le Journal des débats politiques et littéraires* described the excellent fortifications in great detail and expressed an equally great disbelief that the Chinese could have lost them so quickly. With the possession of the facilities at Port Arthur, the Japanese "are the uncontestable masters of the sea route which leads to Peking."[123] For the first time, *Le Temps* hired a special correspondent and sent him to Japan, where he reported his agreement with the

---

[120] "Count Okuma on the Situation," *The Japan Weekly Mail* (Yokohama), 1 September 1894, p. 256.

[121] D. A., "Японско-китайская война, Корея и русские интересы на Дальнем Востоке" (The Sino-Japanese War, Korea and Russian Interests in the Far East), *Русские ведомости* (*Russian Gazette*) (Moscow), no. 264, 24 September 1894 (6 October 1894), p. 3.

[122] "The War in the East," *The Times* (London), 26 November 1894, p. 7.

[123] Émile Weyl, "La guerre entre la Chine et le Japon" (War between China and Japan), *Le Journal des débats politiques et littéraires* (*Journal of Political and Literary Debates*) (Paris), 25 November 1894, evening edition, p. 2.

estimate of Jules Ferry, France's premier during its greatest period of territorial expansion from 1881 to 1885, that "China is a negligible quantity." In the opinion of the author of the article, the Chinese aristocracy embodied a "hypocritical venality," giving China "the most worm-eaten and the most corrupt government to exist in the world."[124] In another article the special correspondent expressed the shock felt in France concerning the war. "Since the beginning of this war, China has provided a lamentable spectacle. No one suspected such weakness, [or] an equally total want of foresight. For an army, the hordes do not differ appreciably from the ones Genghis Khan commanded. As naval forces, some superb vessels but not any navy to guide or utilize them. Everywhere an extraordinary disorder, the most shameless peculation," extending to the relatives of Li Hongzhang and a "total indifference" among the general population.[125]

With the rapid Japanese victory at Port Arthur, they had become the talk of Europe while the Chinese government was on the verge of being declared *non compos mentis* by the European press. In an age of enormous racial prejudice, so clearly illustrated in the columns of *The North-China Herald*, Japan's achievement was even more remarkable. Just as Japan was determined to force the Chinese to revise their views about "dwarfs," so it was compelling the Europeans and Americans to change their ideas about "the Japs."[126]

On December 9, there was an enormous victory celebration in Tokyo for the capture of Port Arthur. It was only the second of its kind during the Meiji period. The first such occasion had celebrated the promulgation of the Meiji Constitution, which had marked a new era in domestic politics.[127] The second celebration in honor of Port Arthur anticipated a new era in international politics as well.

* * *

The Japanese did not rest on their laurels but continued their sweep through Manchuria toward Peking. They also began to prepare for another major campaign, their southeastern pincer toward Peking. The next important military objective for

---

[124] "La Chine et le Japon" (China and Japan), *Le Temps (The Times)* (Paris), 30 December 1894, p. 1; Thomas Power, Jr., *Jules Ferry and the Renaissance of French Imperialism* (1944, reprint, New York: Octagon Books, 1977), ix.

[125] "La Chine et le Japon" (China and Japan), *Le Temps (The Times)* (Paris), pp. 2–3 January 1895.

[126] "Corea," *The North-China Herald* (Shanghai), 17 August 1894, p. 263; "Corea," *The North-China Herald* (Shanghai), 24 August 1894, p. 305. After the Japanese victories at Port Arthur, calling the Japanese "Japs" virtually ceased.

[127] "Fete in Honour of the Recent Victories," *The Japan Weekly Mail* (Yokohama), 15 December 1894, pp. 664–5; "Some Details of the Great Fete," *The Japan Weekly Mail* (Yokohama), 15 December 1894, p. 665; "Tokyo en Fête," *The Japan Weekly Mail* (Yokohama), 15 December 1894, pp. 670–1; "Tokio in Holiday Dress," *The New York Times*, 14 January 1895, p. 5.

the Japanese was the naval base at Weihaiwei. It has been suggested that Japan simultaneously pursued the very difficult winter campaign in Manchuria as a diversion. Japan could capitalize on the area's great symbolic importance to the ruling dynasty as their homeland and use this to draw as many Chinese troops as possible far away from the projected campaign on the other shore of the Bohai in Shandong Province.[128] There was also tremendous popular and military pressure in Japan to take Peking. The Manchurian campaign did not disappoint these hopes. The Japanese troops managed to brave the bitter winter weather. They were greatly aided by the Chinese' inability to destroy supplies and weapons before they abandoned a position. While this followed the Qing legal code requirement not to destroy equipment, it undermined the Chinese attrition strategy of drawing the enemy deep into Chinese territory to stretch Japanese logistical lines and allow the bitter Manchuria winter to deliver the *coup de grâce* to the Japanese forces. Instead, the Chinese supplies left behind helped compensate for logistical difficulties experienced by the Japanese army.[129]

The Chinese divided their forces in Manchuria into three armies forming a line between the coastline at Gaiping all the way to Liaoyang: The northernmost army was headquartered at Liaoyang so that it could defend the road to Mukden from the east via the Motian Pass (摩天嶺) and from the south via Haicheng. The Motian Pass formed a bottleneck between Fenghuangcheng and Liaoyang; it was the strongest position in the highlands separating Korea from the Liao River Valley. In mid-December, however, this army was decimated during a failed attempt to push back the Japanese army by recapturing Fenghuangcheng, a town located in a deep mountain gorge. Another army used the treaty port of Niuzhuang and the walled castle-town of Haicheng (海城)[130] as its base for operation. Niuzhuang was the only Manchurian treaty port while Haicheng was situated west of Fenghuangcheng at a key crossroad. Located on the road from Niuzhuang to Mukden via Liaoyang, it was also on the main highway to Peking and on the road to the Liaodong Peninsula and Port Arthur. Mukden, Liaoyang, and Niuzhuang were all located in the valley formed by the Hun (渾河) and Liao Rivers (遼河), which ran roughly parallel and shared a connection near Niuzhuang. A third army was headquartered to the south on the coast at Gaiping and commanded by General Song.[131]

---

[128] "After the Capture of Port Arthur..." Du Boulay, 1.

[129] Ballard, 173.

[130] Alternate spellings include Haiching and Hai-ch'eng.

[131] "Extracts from 'Advance Japan' by J. Morris, 1895," Du Boulay, 5; "The Operations in Manchuria," *The Japan Weekly Mail* (Yokohama), 22 December 1894, p. 704; "The Operations in Manchuria," *The Japan Weekly Mail* (Yokohama), 26 January 1895, p. 106; "The War," *The Japan Weekly Mail*

The next Japanese objective was Haicheng. If they could take Haicheng, they would be able to link land communications between their First Army in eastern Manchuria and their Second Army, which was moving northward up the Liaodong Peninsula. This would cut off the Chinese in three directions, leaving them only the west for retreat.[132] On December 13, Haicheng fell to the Japanese, the day after Chinese forces failed to retake Fenghuangcheng. This both severed the Chinese line of defense and inserted the Japanese army between the northernmost Chinese forces and their natural line of retreat southward. It also separated General Song from his troops. "That has been the strategy of the Japanese Generals throughout the war. They have always succeeded in taking a position such that, while having direct access to the enemy's front, they also threatened his line of retreat."[133]

On December 19, 1894, Japan attacked the retreating Chinese forces under the command of General Song and took Ganwangzhai (感王寨),[134] a town just to the southwest of Haicheng. The Chinese put up a stubborn resistance but were defeated.[135] This victory prevented Song's army from reaching the road to Liaoyang and connecting with the other Chinese army to the north. It also protected the strategic city of Haicheng from any attack from the west.[136] Because this effectively broke the Chinese line from Gaiping to Liaoyang, they tried four times to retake it in January and February.[137] This constituted the only major Chinese offensive of the war. The only other had been the failed attempt to retake Fenghuangcheng.[138]

Then, on January 10, 1895, the Second Army launched a three-pronged attack on the walled city of Gaiping. The Chinese forces had prepared for the attack by causing the water in the stream next to the city to freeze on an incline to make it

---

(Yokohama), 19 January 1895, p. 73; Eastlake and Yamada, 238–9.

[132] Eastlake and Yamada, 230.

[133] "The Operations in Manchuria," *The Japan Weekly Mail* (Yokohama), 26 January 1895, p. 106.

[134] Alternate spellings include Kangwangtsai and Kangwasai. Du Boulay, "Memoranda."

[135] "War News," *The Japan Weekly Mail* (Yokohama), 5 January 1895, p. 9; "Battle of Kangwangtsai," *The North-China Herald* (Shanghai), 25 January 1895, p. 116; "After the Capture of Port Arthur..." Du Boulay, 5.

[136] "The War," *The Japan Weekly Mail* (Yokohama), 19 January 1895, p. 73; "After the Capture of Port Arthur..." Du Boulay, 5–6.

[137] "The Operations in Manchuria," *The Japan Weekly Mail* (Yokohama), 26 January 1895, p. 106; "The Chinese Attack on Haicheng on February 21st," *The Japan Weekly Mail* (Yokohama), 16 March 1895, p. 318; "War News," *The Japan Weekly Mail* (Yokohama), 26 January 1895, p. 97; "The Chinese Attack on Haicheng," *The Japan Weekly Mail* (Yokohama), 16 March 1895, p. 316; "The Chinese Attack on Haicheng on February 21st," *The Japan Weekly Mail* (Yokohama), 16 March 1895, p. 318; Du Boulay, "Memoranda"; U.S. Adjutant-General's Office, 21; Sun Kefu and Guan Jie, 256–61; Eastlake and Yamada, 277–94.

[138] Chu, "Sino-Japanese War," 368.

difficult for the Japanese troops to cross. While this tactic might have been effective in an earlier age, long-range artillery undercut its impact, although it did increase Japanese casualties.[139] The fall of Gaiping made a continuous line of Japanese troops stretching from Gaiping on the western coast of the Liaodong Peninsula northeast to Haicheng. From there the line continued eastward back to the Korean border at Jiuliancheng.[140]

In early March, the three Chinese armies massed to the north of Niuzhuang. Facing them were two Japanese armies: the First near Haicheng and the Second near Gaiping. The Japanese planned to launch simultaneous attacks on the southern and northern segments of the Chinese line. The First Army was to engage the northernmost Chinese army and then to sweep southward to make a pincer movement on Niuzhuang.[141] The fighting was reported to be some of the stiffest of the war and the number of troops engaged was large. The Chinese succumbed only when the Japanese used mountain guns to hit a power magazine, creating an enormous explosion in the city. The foreign settlement at Niuzhuang fell to the Japanese on March 4 and its port city of Yingkou fell on March 7.[142] When the defeated Chinese forces retreated across the Liao River, the fighting in Manchuria ended.[143] The Japanese now threatened to move south of the Great Wall.

Meanwhile, the political reshuffling in Peking continued apace. Viceroy Liu Kunyi (劉坤一) of Liangjiang (Jiangsu, Anhui, and Jiangxi Provinces) had replaced Li Hongzhang as viceroy of the vital metropolitan province of Zhili, where Li had reigned for a quarter-century. Viceroy Liu had also been placed in command of the Xiang Army (湘軍),[144] composed of large numbers of troops from Hunan and

---

[139] "The War," *The Japan Weekly Mail* (Yokohama), 19 January 1895, p. 73; "After the Capture of Port Arthur...." Du Boulay, 5–6; Eastlake and Yamada, 258–63.

[140] "War News," *The Japan Weekly Mail* (Yokohama), 5 January 1895, p. 8; "The War," *The Japan Weekly Mail* (Yokohama), 19 January 1895, p. 73; "Fancies and Facts," *The Japan Weekly Mail* (Yokohama), 16 March 1895, p. 317; "蓋平占領詳報" (Detailed Report on the Occupation of Gaiping), 朝日新聞 (*Rising Sun Newspaper*) (Tokyo), 12 January 1895, supplement, p. 1; "蓋平占領詳報" (Detailed Report on the Occupation of Gaiping), 朝日新聞 (*Rising Sun Newspaper*) (Tokyo), 13 January 1895, p. 1.

[141] "The Campaign in Manchuria," *The Japan Weekly Mail* (Yokohama), 16 March 1895, p. 315.

[142] "Newchwang," *The North-China Herald* (Shanghai), 5 April 1895, pp. 514–5; Sun Kefu and Guan Jie, 413; "牛莊占領" (Niuzhuang Occupied), 朝日新聞 (*Rising Sun Newspaper*) (Tokyo), 8 March 1895, p. 1; "營口占領" (Yingkou Occupied), 朝日新聞 (*Rising Sun Newspaper*) (Tokyo), 10 March 1895, p. 2; "牛莊占領詳報" (Detailed Report of Occupation of Niuzhuang), 朝日新聞 (*Rising Sun Newspaper*) (Tokyo), 10 March 1895, supplement, p. 1; Eastlake and Yamada, 356, 367.

[143] Powell, 48.

[144] Alternate spellings include Hsiang and Siang Army. The Xiang Army was originally General Zeng Guofan's (曾國藩) army used to suppress the Taiping Rebellion (Folsom, 62, 89).

Hubei Provinces.[145] On December 28 he had been made commander-in-chief of the imperial armies within and without the Great Wall, including the war zone of Zhili, Manchuria, and Shandong Province. This meant he was replacing Li Hongzhang. After the fall of Port Arthur, Li had lost his honors; after the loss of Weihaiwei, he lost his positions as well. The next day Liu had unsuccessfully tried to decline the appointment, then he had become ill for a time. He remained in Peking through the end of January 1895 while he continued trying to weasel out of the post. Rumors also circulated of a very serious addiction to opium.[146] He was not alone in this affliction. Generals Wei Rugui (衛汝貴) and Ye Zhichao (葉志超) reputedly were also both opium addicts.[147]

The Japanese did not wait for Liu's indisposition. Their primary objective after the fall of Port Arthur was the great naval base at Weihaiwei. In January 1895, as the march through Manchuria toward Peking slowly progressed, the Japanese divided the Second Army. In the third week of January the entire Second Division and most of the Sixth Division, both under the command of Marshal Ōyama, would be redeployed across the Yellow Sea to Shandong Province in preparation for the attack on the great naval station at Weihaiwei.[148] Whereas at Port Arthur the goal had been the capture and retention of the naval facilities for their present and future Japanese use, at Weihaiwei the goal would be "the destruction of the fleet inside." This would leave China hobbled after the war so that the Japanese navy could dominate the Far East.[149] The Japanese military successes had demonstrated the critical importance of sea power. Without command of the sea, Japan could not have deployed its troops at will. A critical war objective became the long-term neutralization of Chinese sea power.

The move on Weihaiwei began with a diversionary bombardment of the town of Dengzhou (登州)[150] on January 18–19, 1895. Dengzhou was located to the west of Yantai (煙臺 or Chefoo), which in turn was located to the west of Weihaiwei. The goal was to turn Chinese attention westward while the actual landing point

---

[145] "The War," *The North-China Herald* (Shanghai), 9 November 1894, p. 783.

[146] "Liu Kun Yi's Diffidence," *The New York Times*, 5 January 1895, p. 5; "Imperial Decrees," *The North-China Herald* (Shanghai), 8 February 1895, pp. 187–8; "A Prayer to be Excused," *The North-China Herald* (Shanghai), 1 March 1895, p. 308; "The Proposed Spring Campaign," *The North-China Herald* (Shanghai), 25 January 1895, p. 123; "Liu Kun-yi," *The North-China Herald* (Shanghai), 8 March 1895, p. 351.

[147] "Disgraced Warriors," *The North-China Herald* (Shanghai), 29 March 1895, p. 472.

[148] Chang Ch'i-yun, vol. 2, 117; Eastlake and Yamada, 298–9.

[149] Ballard, 161.

[150] Other spellings include Tungchow and Tungchou.

for Japanese troops was thirty miles to the east of Weihaiwei, at the easternmost tip of the Shandong Peninsula at Rongcheng (榮城).[151] Japanese troops left Dalian between January 19 and 22, landing between January 20 and 23. The army divided into two parts and headed westward toward Weihaiwei, one by the coastal road and the other by a parallel road about four miles inland. They began their advance on January 26. The Japanese ushered in the Chinese New Year with an attack on Weihaiwei. With the Meiji Restoration, the Japanese had discarded the old lunar calendar that was still in use in China, while the lunar new year remained the most important holiday in China. The traditional annual celebrations and sacrifices were meant to insure good luck for the coming year. Perhaps the Japanese chose the day not only in hopes of surprising the Chinese but also as one more attempt to drive home to the Chinese the message that the old days were finished: Wake up and modernize or suffer dire consequences.[152]

Weihaiwei had three categories of defenses: those on the two harbor islands, those on the mainland overlooking the northwestern entrance to the harbor, and those on the mainland overlooking the southeastern entrance to the harbor. The fortifications were equipped with the best artillery available and should have been extremely difficult to take. The Chinese had closed the harbor with booms to prevent any unwelcome visitors while the Japanese had laid contact torpedoes and maintained a naval patrol outside to prevent any exits.[153] This left the Beiyang Squadron bottled up in the harbor.[154] The weather was bitterly cold and snow covered the ground.[155] The Japanese launched a three-pronged attack on January 30, 1895, and soon took the main forts to the south and east of Weihaiwei. The next day they attacked the forts in the immediate vicinity of the city.[156] This seems to have shattered the morale of the Chinese troops, for when the Japanese entered the town of Weihaiwei on February 2, they found the garrisons abandoned.[157]

---

[151] "The Tungchow Affair," *The Japan Weekly Mail* (Yokohama), 16 February 1895, p. 196.

[152] "The Attack on Weihaiwei," *The North-China Herald* (Shanghai), 1 February 1895, p. 156; "The Capture of Weihaiwei," *The North-China Herald* (Shanghai), 1 March 1895, p. 321; "The Wei-hai-wei Campaign," Du Boulay, 2–4.

[153] "The Wei-hai-wei Campaign," Du Boulay, 2–4; Eastlake and Yamada, 306.

[154] "The Progress of the War," *The North-China Herald* (Shanghai), 25 January 1895, p. 107.

[155] "War News," *The Japan Weekly Mail* (Yokohama), 9 February 1895, p. 157; "The Weihaiwei Campaign," *The Japan Weekly Mail* (Yokohama), 23 February 1895, pp. 228–31; "The Lost Navy," *The North-China Herald* (Shanghai), 15 February 1895, p. 242; "The Capture of Weihaiwei," *The North-China Herald* (Shanghai), 1 March 1895, p. 321; Tyler, 71; Jukichi Inouye, *The Fall of Weihaiwei* (Yokohama: Kelly & Walsh, 1895).

[156] Eastlake and Yamada, 305–10.

[157] Eastlake and Yamada, 310.

When the siege had begun, the Chinese hospital staff had fled, leaving a few remaining foreigners to take over the medical service.[158]

Admiral Ding Ruchang had succeeded in having only a few of the forts surrounding the harbor destroyed before the Japanese took them on February 2. The conquerors soon trained the repairable guns on the remaining Chinese positions and on the fleet stuck in the harbor.[159] On the night of February 3, the Japanese tried unsuccessfully to remove the booms blocking the entrances to the harbor. The following night, they were successful. Two squadrons of torpedo-boats entered to face heavy Chinese fire. Two boats opened fire as a diversion so that others could disable the flagship. The next night, a squadron of Japanese torpedo-boats repeated their attack on the Chinese men-of-war anchored in the harbor, disabling two other warships and a transport.[160] On February 7, the army and navy launched a combined attack on Weihaiwei.[161] In response, the seaworthy Chinese torpedo-boats mutinied and unsuccessfully tried to run the blockade.[162] The fall of Port Arthur had been the Empress Dowager's birthday present from Japan. Li Hongzhang's turn came at Weihaiwei. On February 12, three days short of his seventy-second birthday, Weihaiwei fell to the Japanese.[163] In the West such anniversaries did not generally affect military planning, but this was not so in the East. The Japanese armed forces went out of their way to make the two key sources of power in China understand that China's loss of "face" was also their personal loss. This was Japan's indirect way of communicating with the Chinese government and people without the notice of the West.

At the surrender, Admiral Itō Yūkō (伊東祐亨) wrote a letter urging his old friend, Admiral Ding, to come with him to Japan. "It is not the fault of one man that has brought China into the position she now occupies. The blame rests with

---

[158] Tyler, 78, 80.

[159] "The Capture of Weihaiwei," *The North-China Herald* (Shanghai), 1 March 1895, p. 321; "The Surrender at Weihaiwei," *The Japan Weekly Mail* (Yokohama), 16 February 1895, p. 198.

[160] "Letter from Hushan," *The Japan Weekly Mail* (Yokohama), 2 March 1895, p. 253; "War News," *The Japan Weekly Mail* (Yokohama), 23 March 1895, pp. 335–6; Rawlinson, 189.

[161] "The Capture of Weihaiwei," *The North-China Herald* (Shanghai), 1 March 1895, p. 321.

[162] Rawlinson, 189.

[163] "Weihaiwei Surrenders," *The North-China Herald* (Shanghai), 15 February 1895, p. 215; "威海衛占領" (Weihaiwei Occupied), 朝日新聞 (*Rising Sun Newspaper*) (Tokyo), 2 February 1895, p. 1; "威海衛砲臺の全領敵艦の現状" (Weihaiwei Gun Emplacements All Taken, Current Situation of Enemy Fleet), 朝日新聞 (*Rising Sun Newspaper*) (Tokyo), 6 February 1895, supplement, p. 1; "北洋艦隊の盡滅" (Complete Destruction of Beiyang Squadron), 朝日新聞 (*Rising Sun Newspaper*) (Tokyo), 10 February 1895, p. 1; "威海衛攻撃に關して" (Concerning the Attack on Weihaiwei), 國民新聞 (*People's Newspaper*) (Tokyo), 2 March 1895, p. 2.

the errors of the Government that has long administered her affairs. She selects her servants by competitive examination, and literary attainments are the test." In the modern age, Itō argued that this system needed to be changed. Japan "owes her preservation and her integrity to-day wholly to the fact that she then [thirty years ago] broke away from the old and attached herself to the new."[164] For years Japanese diplomats had offered this advice to Chinese diplomats and for years the Japanese would continue to repeat the same, only to have the advice fall on deaf ears. From the Chinese point of view, they would be damned before they would take advice from "dwarfs." And damned they were.

Unbeknownst to Itō, Ding had decided to commit suicide. Admiral Ding was a man known for his personal bravery, but he was also a man out of his element. He was a cavalry officer by experience and training and knew little about naval affairs. Nor was he popular with the sailors.[165] This was in large measure because he was from Anhui Province, whereas most of his officers hailed from the southern province of Fujian. In China regional loyalties remained paramount and military service did not overcome such divisions.[166] He had resisted capitulation until the end and had done his best to be killed in action by repeatedly standing exposed during bombardments. According to a foreign adviser, "Ting [Ding] declared at first that capitulation was impossible; but later he said he could arrange it by committing suicide, and so save the lives of many."[167] When mutinous sailors threatened him with knives, he went to his cabin and took a lethal dose of opium.[168] It is unclear whose opium it was, but there seems to have been enough on board to supply any officers contemplating suicide. Two captains followed suit. A third, Captain Yang Yonglin (楊用霖), had served as the second in command onboard the flagship. He shot himself as the Japanese boarded the vessel.[169]

Admiral Ding Ruchang had no choice but to commit suicide. The Guangxu Emperor had already degraded him over the summer for not preventing the Japanese navy from entering the Bohai.[170] After the fall of Port Arthur, the emperor had

---

[164] "War News," *The Japan Weekly Mail* (Yokohama), 23 February 1895, p. 225. The correspondence between Itō and Ding is reprinted in Appendix F of Vladimir, 251–4.

[165] Rawlinson, 174–5; Tyler, 47, 89.

[166] Chu, "Sino-Japanese War," 359; "丁汝昌" (Ding Ruchang), in 中国历史大辞典编纂委员会 (Compilation Committee for the Big Chinese History Dictionary), vol. 1, 29.

[167] Tyler, 79.

[168] Rawlinson, 190; Tyler, 78.

[169] "The Surrender at Weihaiwei," *The Japan Weekly Mail* (Yokohama), 16 March 1895, pp. 313–4; "The Chino-Japanese War," *The Pall Mall Gazette* (London), 19 February 1895, p. 7.

[170] "Admiral Ding Degraded," *The New York Times*, 10 September 1894, p. 5.

degraded him again and attempted to hand him over to the Board of Punishment. This could have meant decapitation had not Viceroy Li intervened to keep Ding at his post.[171] With the destruction of the Beiyang Squadron, China's sole credible military force against the Japanese, certain execution awaited him in Peking. His family would also have suffered. By committing suicide, he chose a noble death and in doing so wiped away the stain of defeat and became a tragic war hero in Japan as well as in China.[172]

The Japanese admired his final act since it fit within their own military code of *bushidō* (武士道) or *The Code of the Samurai*. According to these norms for military conduct, there was no honorable way out for those defeated in battle other than death. If the enemy did not do it, then the honorable warrior must acknowledge his disgrace by taking his own life.[173] Ding's suicide followed this Japanese military creed, whose operative principles were "loyalty, duty, and valor."[174] Admiral Ding and three of his captains had died like samurai and the Japanese honored them for this.[175] The Japanese accorded them full military honors and granted their men extraordinary leniency. It was the honorable response in a profession that in Japan was regarded as the embodiment of honor.

An American professor – a Southerner who had taught English in Japan – described how differently the Chinese and the Japanese, on the one hand, and the Americans on the other hand reacted to defeat. "What would have been the feelings of the North for Robert E. Lee if, at Appomattox [when the South capitulated to the North at the end of the American Civil War], rather than share the fate of the gallant men he had surrendered, he had committed suicide from a

[171] "Yamagi's Army Advancing," *The New York Times*, 24 November 1894, p. 5; "Allies against Europe," *The New York Times*, 25 November 1894, p. 5.

[172] "Count Katsu on Admiral Ting," *The Japan Weekly Mail* (Yokohama), 9 March 1895, p. 285; Lensen, vol. 1, 393n.49; Morse, vol. 3, 40; Donald Keene, "The Sino-Japanese War of 1894–95 and Its Cultural Effects in Japan," *Tradition and Modernization in Japanese Culture*, Donald H. Shively, ed. (Princeton: Princeton University Press, 1971), 140; Kamachi, 193; Jansen, *Japan and China*, 10; "A Tribute to the Late Admiral Ting," *The Japan Weekly Mail* (Yokohama), 9 November 1895, p. 490.

[173] Yamamoto Tsunetomo, *Hagakure: The Book of the Samurai*, William Scott Wilson, trans. (Tokyo: Kodansha International, 1979), 17.

[174] Taira Shigesuke, *The Code of the Samurai*, Thomas Cleary, trans. (Boston: Tuttle Publishing, 1999), 22. See also Yamamoto Tsunetomo, *Hagakure: The Book of the Samurai*, William Scott Wilson, trans. (Tokyo: Kodansha International, 1979), 18–23, 72–3.

[175] "北洋艦隊降服の顛末丁, 劉, 張の殉國" (Complete Story of the Surrender of the Beiyang Squadron, Ding, Liu, and Zhang Die for Their Country), 朝日新聞 (*Rising Sun Newspaper*) (Tokyo), 19 February 1895, p. 2; "丁提督の遺骸" (Remains of Admiral Ding), 朝日新聞 (*Rising Sun Newspaper*) (Tokyo), 20 February 1895, p. 1.

sense of devoted patriotism? Instead of admiring him for the unsullied hero and knightly character that he was, North and South alike would have despised him. And yet nine out of ten of my Japanese schoolboys wrote of the suicide of Admiral Ting [Ding] as the noblest thing of which they had ever heard."[176]

The letter of capitulation delivered to the Japanese and written in the name of the deceased admiral was actually drafted by a foreign adviser and translated into Chinese. This meant that the Japanese received a diplomatically correct letter of capitulation with no references to dwarfs.[177] Upon completion of the negotiation for surrender on March 13, Chinese troops and officers signed promises not to take further part in the war. They were disarmed and set free. This was the Japanese response to Admiral Ding's suicide: leniency for his men. After Port Arthur, another massacre before the foreign community that inhabited coastal China was not in the cards. The Japanese knew that the war was over for the Chinese and so allowed the prisoners to return home.[178] Officers were provided passage on the gunboat *Kangji* (康濟), which would take the bodies of General Ding and the three captains who had committed suicide. The Japanese went out of their way to treat the bodies of the dead with respect. Their ships flew their flags at half-mast and the flagship minute guns gave a long salute as the boat bearing Admiral Ding's body left port. According to *The Pall Mall Gazette*, "Several junks have arrived here, bringing soldiers from Wai-Hei-Wai [*sic*]. The men all express astonishment at the consideration which the Japanese have shown for them, and the tribute which their enemies paid to Admiral Ting's corpse has created a great impression among them."[179] *The Pall Mall Gazette* hailed the victory in a headline: "Brilliant Achievement by the Japanese."[180]

Back in Peking, the Guangxu Emperor, in a fit of pique after the defeat at Weihaiwei, reportedly took the "unusual course of authorizing the Governor of Shantung province [the location of Weihaiwei] to behead all fugitives without previously reporting to the throne."[181] Editors for *The New York Times* expressed their disgust in a headline: "Emulating Alice's Wonderland Queen, China's Emperor Says of Wei-Hai-Wei Defenders, 'Off with Their Heads.'"[182] An article in

---

[176] Scherer, 46.

[177] Tyler, 85.

[178] "The Capture of Weihaiwei," *The North-China Herald* (Shanghai), 1 March 1895, p. 321.

[179] "The Surrender at Weihaiwei," *The Japan Weekly Mail* (Yokohama), 16 March 1895, pp. 313–4; "The Chino-Japanese War," *The Pall Mall Gazette* (London), 19 February 1895, p. 7.

[180] "The Chino-Japanese War," *The Pall Mall Gazette* (London), 2 February 1895, 4th ed., p. 7.

[181] "The Chino-Japanese War," *The Pall Mall Gazette* (London), 18 February 1895, p. 7.

[182] "Intervening in the East," *The New York Times*, 17 February 1895, p. 5.

The North-China Herald had earlier lambasted the Board of Punishments for meting out rewards and punishments on the basis of doctored reports. The board "by indiscriminating executions puts a premium on falsehood and a system of rewards which showers buttons [awards for good service] upon lies." This lead article continued, "Has not the Tsungli Yamen [Zongli Yamen] been in the deepest and most humiliating ignorance of its own defensive operations throughout; in ignorance of the actual events transpiring; in ignorance as to whether victory or defeat attended each new move upon the board; and hemmed in on all sides by the two-edged sword of incipient rebellion?"[183]

After Weihaiwei, some of the Han literati memorialized the throne, recommending that China either hire foreign mercenaries or engage Chinese fishermen to launch an attack on the Japanese homeland.[184] A theme of jingoistic bellicosity ran through these communications.[185] For these men the modern era still had not yet dawned. They inhabited a psychological world that reality no longer supported. The world had changed but they had not. With the advantage of twenty-twenty hindsight, it seems obvious over a century after the war that, with the fall of Port Arthur, China was already finished and should have gotten on with peace negotiations. Yet many members of the upper echelons of the Chinese government did not believe such a turn of events to be possible. "Dwarfs" could not bring China to her knees. It was a logical and physical impossibility. It violated such fundamental beliefs about the natural order that these persons, who were by no means few in number, continued to be convinced that China would crush the Japanese in the end. Over a century later, such thinking seems delusional. But these people believed that they had 5,000 years of uninterrupted Chinese history in support of their views. Surely this world was immutable. How could it be overturned in the space of a few months? The 5,000 years of uninterrupted history was but another myth that the Chinese had fashioned to enhance their prestige, to overawe their enemies, and also to mask the glaring reality of a history fraught with terrible instability and devastating civil wars. Japan's successful reform program presented a change that violated key assumptions underlying how the Chinese perceived the world: The Japanese were inferiors from a minor place across the seas. China was

---

[183] "China Unmasked," *The North-China Herald* (Shanghai), 28 December 1894, p. 1038. A European diplomat criticized "the hasty death-sentence pronounced by literary mandarins ignorant of warfare." Vladimir, 6. There had been a particularly notorious case of a well-respected naval officer, Captain Fang Boqian (方柏謙 or Fong), being beheaded on false accusations of dereliction of duty during the hostilities at Feng Island. Diósy, *New Far East*, 157–8. For the Chinese view, see Kuo, 74–5.

[184] Kuo, 109–11.

[185] Chu, "China's Attitudes," 88–9.

the cultural well from which the Japanese drank, never the reverse. In the cosmos there was a one-way flow of knowledge: always from China outward.

On the eve of the attack on Weihaiwei, Wu Dacheng (吳大澂), assistant imperial commissioner of defense, president of the Board of War, vice president of the Court of Censors, governor of Hunan, and officer of the premier button, had made an official proclamation to the Japanese. He had grandly offered them a chance to surrender. Wu noted that he was "of a charitable state of mind" and so could not bear to see Japanese troops "going to destruction before my fresh battalions in this severe cold."[186] Wu Dacheng was an outstanding Chinese scholar who was famous among the literati for his views that the Chinese could bring the Japanese to their knees.[187] One can only speculate that such a proclamation must have confirmed Japanese intentions to humble the Chinese once and for all. At about the same time, Reuter's Agency reported that the Japanese "Diet unanimously passed a resolution that they consider the objects of the war yet unattained, and are prepared to grant whatever amounts are necessary for military expenses to establish the country's prestige, and adopted this resolution with the express intention of making the country's sentiments generally known."[188] Wu Dacheng was given enough rope to hang himself when, after Weihaiwei, he was put in command of the Hunan and Hubei Armies, which were promptly trounced in their first engagement under his brief command.[189]

Although the Li faction remained in power if not always in official capacity, its position was being steadily eroded by the relentless assault of those still living in the past. "The ignorance and fatal optimism of the great officials is [*sic*] working steadily against the Li party. The utter collapse of the military force of the Empire against a power so despised as Japan, is to them perfectly inexplicable on any other grounds except '*Nous sommes trahis*' [We are betrayed]." They pointed to Li as the betrayer. "Peking official opinion is, on the whole, becoming foolishly optimistic again. By some curious means the vapourings of the European press which treat China's boundless resources, etc., are being taken as gospel, and the officials think if they can prolong the war for one year, they will not only roll back the tide of invasion but punish the Japanese in turn. Utterly ignorant of the nature of modern war, they think that science and discipline may be overcome by numbers. They are even certain in many quarters that the new-fangled foreign arms

---

[186] "A Remarkable Proclamation by Wu Ta-ch'eng," *The North-China Herald* (Shanghai), 1 February 1895, p. 157; "The Chino-Japanese War," *The Pall Mall Gazette* (London), 11 March 1895, p. 7.

[187] Kuo, 115.

[188] "The Diet Militant," *The North-China Herald* (Shanghai), 8 February 1895, p. 171.

[189] Kuo, 115.

of precision are the primary source of the Chinese reverses, and several prominent officials have not hesitated to commend that the repeating rifles should be discarded in favour of the ancient Brown Bess, or gingal requiring two men and four minutes to fire one round." Any attempts by Li's party to dispute these conclusions "are at once quoted against them as proofs of their want of patriotism and their incompetence to conduct affairs."[190]

These officials in Peking concluded that China's military defeats had proven the weakness of European weaponry. Because of the mismatch between inferior Chinese gunpowder and modern breech-loading rifles, there was a movement afoot in "Peking for a return to the use of muzzle-loading rifles and long jingals [*sic*] for arming the Chinese armies." According to the native correspondent in Peking for *The North-China Herald*, the gunpowder stored in the Chinese arsenals before the war was "unfit even for firecrackers" and had been provided "by unprincipled ordnance officials." This inferior gunpowder supplied "to the Chinese armies in Manchuria and elsewhere since the war began, had undoubtedly been one of the chief causes which has made our soldiery appear ridiculous in the eyes of the world." He continued, "The powder in the cartridges has been found either not to carry far enough in nine cases out of ten or not even to explode! This sad state of affairs has been the principal cause of the hitherto astonishing panics of the Chinese soldiery whenever they were confronted by the Japanese." The cartridge casings made it impossible to see the gunpowder within, so that soldiers wanted to return to the old-fashioned weapons whose powder they could easily inspect. More to the point, the older weapons were effective with inferior grades of gunpowder while the modern weapons were not.[191] The Chinese solution to the problem – disposing of the modern guns instead of the defective powder – was yet another example of what many in the West considered to be unfathomable Chinese logic.

Westerners also could not understand the Chinese naval strategy. They wondered why Admiral Ding had refused to vacate the harbor at Weihaiwei before the Japanese had cut off his retreat. If the Chinese had been unable to flee the harbor, the boats should have been sunk "rather than allowed to fall bodily into the enemy's hands."[192] This is what happened. China's loss became a direct contribution

---

[190] "The Situation in Peking," *The North-China Herald* (Shanghai), 25 January 1895, p. 107.

[191] "The Army of the Chinese Troops," *The North-China Herald* (Shanghai), 8 February 1895, pp. 202–3. The Manchus originally introduced gingals when they conquered the Ming Dynasty in the seventeenth century. They required two men to operate because they were very long. One man had to bear the weight of the weapon on his shoulder while a second man took aim and fired. It could be fired with "a handful" of gunpowder and from one to four 2.5-ounce bullets. Ibid., 203.

[192] "China's Apathy," *The North-China Herald* (Shanghai), 25 January 1895, p. 110.

to Japanese naval expansion. Actually, the Japanese netted four warships and six gunboats at Weihaiwei.[193] Unknown to the outside world, Admiral Ding had tried to scuttle his boats at the very end, but by that time his crew had mutinied and refused to carry out the order.[194] He had also ordered that the mainland forts be dismantled but was overruled by a Chinese general, who "declined the responsibility, declaring it might cost him his head."[195] The general's decision simply reflected the reward system that prevented officers from altering plans to meet changed circumstances and a punishment system that sought individual scapegoats to blame for systemic problems. The Qing legal code mandated decapitation for the destruction of twenty firearms or more.[196] One can only speculate on the punishment for scuttling a multi-thousand-dollar imported battleship or for dynamiting a gun emplacement with an imported artillery piece. Ding did succeed in having the engine room of his remaining great battleship dynamited, so that the best remaining ship in his fleet did not fall into Japanese hands in a repairable condition.[197]

Le Temps later provided an accounting for the Chinese navy: During the war, twenty-two of its war vessels had been destroyed and twelve had been surrendered to the Japanese to become additions to the Imperial Japanese Navy. In contrast, the Japanese had lost two vessels. For Japan this became a net gain of ten ships.[198] After the Battle of Weihaiwei, Prince Gong ordered the closing of the Admiralty Board since China no longer possessed a navy. Five million *taels* were discovered missing from the account. Allegedly these too were part of the funds diverted to the Empress Dowager. Her redecorations suffered another setback with the cancellation of the expensive electrification plans for the Summer Palace.[199]

Captain William M. Lang, an Englishman formerly charged with training Chinese naval forces, had stated in the fall of 1894, "In my opinion Weihaiwei is impregnable, and no Japanese fleet dare approach it."[200] Four days after its capture, the Japanese allowed Vice-Admiral Sir Edmund R. Fremantle and about 100 British officers to tour the fallen citadel. "After their examination of the fortress

---

[193] Rawlinson, 190. A contemporary article provides different figures ("The Chino-Japanese War," *The Pall Mall Gazette* [London], 19 February 1895, p. 7).

[194] Rawlinson, 189–90.

[195] Ballard, 168; "The Chino-Japanese War," *The Pall Mall Gazette* (London), 27 February 1895, p. 7.

[196] Boulais, 428.

[197] U.S. Adjutant-General's Office, 22.

[198] "La guerre en Chine" (The War in China), *Le Temps* (*The Times*) (Paris), 5 March 1895.

[199] "Peking," *The North-China Herald* (Shanghai), 10 May 1895, p. 683.

[200] "The Chinese Navy," *The North-China Herald* (Shanghai), 21 September 1894, p. 501.

they pronounced it to be impregnable if any real attempt had been made to defend it by the Chinese."[201] "When the Japanese came to examine the forts, they were found to be practically undamaged. The splendid construction of the forts excited general admiration, and it was pretty evident that but for incipient mutiny and scarcity of provisions they could have held out indefinitely."[202] During the subsequent occupation, the Japanese made sure to destroy these forts in which the Chinese government had invested so much money.[203] This was the end of a world-class Chinese navy for the next century. At the opening of the Sino-Japanese War, the Chinese navy ranked in the top eight in the world.[204]

With the fall of Weihaiwei there was general recognition in Europe that the Far Eastern balance of power had changed. China was no longer the dominant regional power; rather, Japan was and Japanese military achievements were receiving recognition throughout the European press. The Japanese army had been given credit for mastering the Chinese despite the difficult terrain in Korea and Manchuria.[205] During the siege at Weihaiwei, the editors of *Le Siècle*, who throughout the war had been very sparing in their judgments concerning the belligerents, ran a front-page article: "Like Port Arthur, Weihaiwei was well defended by European-style fortifications, and if the Japanese, instead of being the besiegers, had been the besieged, they could not have been subdued except by famine. But the Chinese soldier is so badly commanded, its leaders so slovenly and so incapable, that even behind the most solid walls its resistance cannot last more than a few hours." The final sentence of the article read: "The facility and fullness with which the Empire of the Rising Sun has assimilated the military institutions and the diplomatic customs of our ancient Europe are truly marvellous."[206]

According to the official newspaper of the Russian Foreign Ministry, *Journal de St-Pétersbourg*, "Since the beginning of this war, the Chinese have provided a lamentable spectacle. No one suspected such weakness." The article marvelled, "Japan vanquisher of China!" and continued, "It is remarkable – and this alone is

[201] "The Chino-Japanese War," *The Pall Mall Gazette* (London), 1 December 1894, 4th ed., p. 7.

[202] "The Capture of Weihaiwei," *The North-China Herald* (Shanghai), 1 March 1895, p. 321.

[203] "Stores and Ammunition Captured," *The North-China Herald* (Shanghai), 15 March 1895, p. 384.

[204] Cooling, 136. Cooling provides a table showing the strength of the seven principal navies in 1896. He overlooks the Japanese navy, which was stronger than that of Spain, the seventh on his list.

[205] Quoting an article that first appeared in *Le Temps*, "Chine et Japon" (China and Japan), *Journal de St-Pétersbourg* (*St. Petersburg Journal*), no. 345, 6 January 1895, p. 2.

[206] G. Gareau, "Les Japonais à Weï-Haï-Weï" (The Japanese at Weihaiwei), *Le Siècle* (*Century*) (Paris), 3 February 1895, p. 1. Mon. Gareau was actually jumping the gun because Weihaiwei would not fall for another week and a half.

sufficient to prove the complete absence of any Chinese resistance – that this war, which has been going on for four months, has only caused the Japanese armies insignificant losses, scarcely one thousand men killed, as many in Korea as at sea and during the advance on Port Arthur!" It concluded, "China has no military organization whatsoever...The Japanese, in contrast, have resolutely begun a war European style."[207]

A front-page story in *The New York Times* noted, "You know how it has been the fashion to speak of China with bated breath as a sleeping leviathan, which it was dangerous to stir; how she has been given way to for fear she might close some source of wealth and profit to the traders; how the overweening self-conceit of the people has been fostered and sustained by the cringing attitude of all the powers except Russia and Japan." The article announced: "The time has come now when it should be realized that the continued existence of China, under present methods, is a standing menace to the peace of the world. China is an anachronism, and a filthy one on the face of the earth." The author believed that the world owed Japan "a debt of gratitude" for puncturing the overly positive international image of China.[208] In the United States some went so far as to call the Japanese the "Yankees of the Orient."[209]

After the fall of Port Arthur, a commentator for the London *Times* took stock of the situation, declaring Japan deserving of "little but praise" and China, the opposite; "the only palliation of their failure is that they were wholly unprepared for an unprovoked aggression." The author believed that the war had "brought out in strong relief...the essential differences between the two belligerents. A stronger contrast is scarcely imaginable." He continued, "With passionate effort the Japanese have ransacked the Western world for its treasures of knowledge, and have vigorously applied what they have learned. The Chinese, on the other hand, have set their face against the science of other nations, and, with an unhappy mixture of apathy and contempt, have rejected the teaching which has been pressed upon them." He went on, "Another essential difference between the people is in their exhibition of patriotism. The Japanese are saturated with it, while the Chinese have none." He noted "the incredible difference between the peoples in their treatment of soldiers and sailors. In the one country they are made heroes of...In the other the men are treated worse than dogs, robbed of their small pay, deserted, discarded, or grossly neglected by their leaders whenever they can be dispensed with, and their monthly

---

[207] "Chine et Japon" (China and Japan), *Journal de St-Pétersbourg* (*St. Petersburg Journal*), no. 345, 6 January 1895, p. 2.

[208] "Planning to Save Pekin," *The New York Times*, 11 February 1895, p. 1.

[209] Dorwart, 119.

pay saved...[T]he most pessimistic prophet could hardly have predicted the utter ineptitude of the Chinese military movements."[210]

Just after the war the writer on Asian topics, Demetrius Charles Boulger, criticized, in his *History of China*, "the antiquated views of warfare held by Chinese military men, whose text-books went back for 2000 years...There is no doubt that the Chinese Government gave a deplorable exhibition of itself, and after what occurred it would be impossible to put faith in any military or naval changes carried out under the auspices of the Government then and still existing in Pekin."[211] *The Times* of London expressed a similar view: "The actuality of ineptitude stultifies the imagination...China may henceforth be considered incapable of war either by sea or land, and incapable even of learning it...The single word rabble describes the Chinese army, untrained, unarmed, unpaid, unfed, and uncared for – so grossly ill-used, indeed, that the docility of the poor wretches who are sent in droves to the slaughter would be admirable if it carried any intelligence with it." It described the pathetic sight of "wounded men begging their way some hundreds of miles towards their home."[212] Such beliefs would have consequences. After the war European countries would reorient their own foreign policies to take into account the reversal in the Far Eastern balance of power. For China, the cost of the war went beyond Japan, ultimately to include all of the other powers.

* * *

Despite the harsh criticism often meted out to China in the columns of such papers as *The North-China Herald* and *The Peking and Tientsin Times*, the criticism emanated not from ill-will but from a deep pathos. These critics had been rooting for the Chinese, but at every turn, Chinese actions seemed self-destructive. Generations of missionaries had gone to China to spread the Gospel and scientific knowledge and had been largely unsuccessful on both fronts. They had opened churches, schools, hospitals, libraries, universities, and orphanages. Yet nothing seemed to mitigate the unspeakable tragedies of daily life in China. A reporter for *The Peking and Tientsin Times* lamented, "Two centuries or more of effort have in fact produced next to nothing." He observed, "The native cities or towns adjoining the foreign settlements remain exactly as they were before those settlements were formed. Their streets or lanes contain the same accumulations of filth which breed the same periodical pestilences; they continue to perish by the thousands and to suffer daily discomfort and deprivation from the foul sources of their water supply;

---

[210] "The War in the East," *The Times* (London), 26 December 1894, p. 4. For a similar opinion concerning the lack of patriotism in China, see Boulger, vol. 2, 528.

[211] Boulger, vol. 2, 528.

[212] "The War in the East," *The Times* (London), 2 January 1895, p. 7.

they have no better means of locomotion than they had two thousand years ago; they will adopt no means of saving labour, and no scientific means of saving time." There was a deep sympathy for the plight of the common man in China. "The people are sound at heart, honest, industrious and well meaning."[213] For these foreigners, the sufferings of China were a highly avoidable tragedy. If only the Chinese would listen. Like the Japanese, they never could understand why the Chinese would not.

Westerners did not hate the Chinese, although they often expressed their exasperation in ridicule. It was not that most westerners considered the Chinese people to be inherently incompetent; on the contrary, time and again Western commentators paid tribute to the great industriousness and talent of the general Chinese population. At the beginning of the war, *The North-China Herald* ran a lead article: "There are very few foreign residents in China who have any quarrel with the Chinese people; and those who are brought in contact with Chinese officials rarely condemn them as individuals. On the other hand, there is hardly a foreigner in China, or a Chinaman who has had any relations with the outside world, who does not utterly condemn the Chinese Government, and hope that this war will result in some reform in it. The Chinese Government is rotten through and through."[214] In a later article another reporter lamented "the utter hopelessness of her cause." He continued, "The breadth and wealth of the country; the natural intelligence of its people; the numerical vastness of its population – all these are the corner stones of national resource and are possessed by China above and beyond all nations...We see each and all of these resources rendered a mockery and worse than useless by want of unity and by corruption."[215] *The New York Times* made the most pithy summary of Western views on China in a headline, "System, Not Materials, at Fault."[216]

During the final two decades of the dynasty, as matters went from bad to worse, foreign bewilderment at China's predicament gradually transformed into contempt. To many it seemed incredible that the Chinese had demonstrated so little interest in protecting their homeland. Contempt would later provide a self-justification to carve up China into spheres of influence in the years following the war. An article in *The Pall Mall Gazette* described such views: "The Chinaman at the present moment stands about as low in the estimation of the average Englishman as it is

---

[213] "After the War," *The Peking and Tientsin Times*, 22 December 1894, p. 166.

[214] "Foreigners and the War," *The North-China Herald* (Shanghai), 24 August 1894, p. 293.

[215] "China's Apathy," *The North-China Herald* (Shanghai), 25 January 1895, p. 109.

[216] "China's Settled Method," *The New York Times*, 13 February 1895, p. 5.

possible to be, and to read of his countless defeats, retreats, and incontinent fleeings, this is not to be wondered at." Yet in the next paragraph, the author, a recent resident of China, continued, "Go where you please in China you will find an order-loving people, well built, lithe, robust, and hardy, accustomed to frugal fare, capable of cheerfully sustaining great fatigue, and by no means cowardly." He questioned, "How [can one] reconcile all these essentially manly qualities, which the Chinese undoubtedly possess, with the present piteous fiasco?" He went on to attribute this apparent paradox to the very conservative upbringing of Chinese children and their static view of the world.[217] These Western observers could not crack the riddle of such an accomplished people and civilization and yet such a nonperforming military and political system.

What Western observers failed to see were the national implications of provincial loyalties, Han–Manchu hostilities, and the poor treatment of common soldiers. China was an empire whose parts did not necessarily feel great loyalty to the center; hence the strength of provincial loyalties. Moreover, the ruling dynasty was not even Han Chinese, and for the last half-century had presided over one domestic policy fiasco after another. From the Han soldier's point of view, Manchu indifference to his fate was proven daily by his lack of pay, provisions, and competent superiors. These three factors had further eroded any loyalties of the provinces to the center and of the soldier to his government. While the newspapers often referred to the tensions between the Han and Manchus, they did not draw the logical but unutterable conclusion and the Han Chinese could not openly voice it; that is, they had no intention of risking their lives to preserve a decaying alien dynasty. But the soldiers voted with their feet. They deserted in droves. Foreigners did not want to see the logical consequence of this Han–Manchu division. Given that the vast majority of China's population was Han and that their Manchu rulers were proving themselves ever more incompetent, the logic of the situation suggested a Han overthrow of the Manchu minority rule. Because all of the treaties so laboriously negotiated by the foreigners had been ratified by the Manchus, there were fears that all of their years of negotiations would become null and void should the dynasty fall.

Right after the war, an enterprising reporter of *The New York Times* ventured down Manhattan to Chinatown. The Chinese he interviewed explained Chinese attitudes toward the war: "Chinese don't care. Not like Americans. American all one heart. Each part of China want to go its own way. Emperor not a Chinese, but a Manchu. Chinese rather have a Japanese King than Tartar King, so they not fight

---

[217] "Those Despicable Chinese," *The Pall Mall Gazette* (London), 13 February 1895, 4th ed., pp. 1–2.

hard, but run away. When you run away first you not get killed." The man being interviewed continued, "Four hunder, five hunder, year ago wise Chinese said in what you call almanac, 'Chinese have one King so long, then other King so long.' Chinese have now Manchu King for two hunder fifty year – his time 'bout done. War came same as almanac or 'bout year or two different. So Chinese not care to help him, anyhow...Manchu King never save man's life, no trial, no jury; don't care about his people; people don't care 'bout him."[218] In other words, the Manchus had lost their mandate of heaven; their time was up and their fate sealed. No sensible Han Chinese would support them. Those interviewed repeatedly talked of the lack of Han Chinese support for the Manchu dynasty. In New York City, it was safe to voice such sentiments. Another Chinese residing in New York explained, "Chinese officials squeeze people all they can. Squeeze them more where no English or American see them. Emperor much hated by pure Chinese. Officials nearly all Tartars or Manchus. Common people from China not care how the war goes; think nothing about it; hope the Manchus get beaten."[219]

The Chinese people were not unprincipled cowards; rather, they loathed their government for reasons that were obvious to all and were described at length in the contemporary press, whose articles read like an inventory of governmental malfeasance. From the point of view of the general population in China, the Japanese were at least competent aliens, unlike their own ruling dynasty. But for a Han Chinese to voice such sentiments in China would have entailed instantaneous decapitation and dire consequences for his entire clan. It was not the sort of thing to put in one's diary. But it does explain why Chinese soldiers so often fled the battlefield, a fact that baffled foreign observers who unwittingly bought into the myths concerning Chinese homogeneity, the sinification of the Manchus, and Han loyalty to the Manchus.

These divisions in the Chinese government had plagued and ultimately undermined the war effort from the very beginning. Commanders dared not take the initiative in the field lest they suffer censure for the innovations afterward. Since the anti-Li party was firmly entrenched around the Guangxu Emperor, the military could not count on support within the capital. The Guangxu Emperor and the Empress Dowager had divergent views on the war; the former wanted to pursue hostilities, while the latter wanted to end them. No one was certain which view would prevail, but survival depended on choosing the winning side of the dispute. The imperative to choose correctly also applied to the officials in Peking, who

---

[218] "Says Chinese Don't Care," *The New York Times*, 16 May 1895, p. 1.
[219] "Says Chinese Don't Care," *The New York Times*, 16 May 1895, p. 1.

focused on personal rather than on national survival. Too many devoted themselves to undermining Viceroy Li rather than on uniting the collective energies to defeat the common foreign foe. *The Peking and Tientsin Times* devoted an article to the corrosive effects of these "divided counsels."[220] The political cleavage between the Manchus and Han Chinese and the centrifugal pull of provincial loyalties undermined national unity in China. As President Abraham Lincoln had so eloquently paraphrased the Gospel according to St. Mark during the American Civil War, "A house divided against itself cannot stand."[221]

If Chinese military failings brought a harvest of bewilderment in the West, it sowed a crop of utter contempt in Japan. The pre-war Japanese respect for Chinese high culture had vanished without a trace. Foreign Minister Mutsu Munemitsu wrote after the war: "Japanese students of China and Confucianism were once wont to regard China with great reverence. They called her the 'Celestial Kingdom' or the 'Great Empire,' worshipping her without caring how much they insulted their own nation. But now, we look down upon China as a bigoted and ignorant colossus of conservatism. She, in turn, mocks us as a tiny island of barbarians who have recklessly and impudently rushed forward in a mad effort to imitate the external trappings of Western civilization."[222] By the end of the war intimacy had brought contempt, and the Japanese considered the Chinese and Koreans to be their absolute inferiors.[223]

An article in *The Japan Weekly Mail* summed up the strategic situation after the fall of Weihaiwei: "In the present war between the two Eastern Powers, China has been defeated in every battle. Her frontier line has been pushed back, her cities have been captured, and her armies annihilated. The great forts of Port Arthur and Weihaiwei, that guarded the entrance to the gulf of Pechili [Bohai], have fallen, and with them China has lost defences on which she had exhausted the contents of her treasury for more than twenty years. They failed her at the critical moment. The Peiyang Squadron, too, formed at great cost, fared no better when put to the test. It remained concealed in harbour, and if any of its warships attempted to fight they were burnt or sunk: finally the remnant of the once famous squadron surrendered to the enemy. By the fall of Port Arthur and Weihaiwei, the gateway to the capital of China has been thrown open, and no power in China can stay Japanese entry

---

[220] "Divided Counsels," *The Peking and Tientsin Times*, 16 February 1895, p. 198.

[221] John Bartlett, *Famous Quotations*, 14th ed. (Boston: Little, Brown, 1968), 635.

[222] Mutsu, 27–8.

[223] Lone, 59–69.

into Pekin."[224] At this juncture, the Manchus had no choice but to negotiate. Utter military incapacity meant that a continued Japanese drive to Peking would result in their overthrow either by the Japanese if not sooner by some enterprising Han Chinese. The Manchus correctly concluded that their only hope for survival rested with negotiations.

---

[224] "China," *The Japan Weekly Mail* (Yokohama), 23 March 1895, p. 344. See also "Die Lage in Ostasien" (Situation in East Asia), *National Zeitung* (*National Newspaper*) (Berlin), morning edition, 10 February 1895, p. 1.

Part III

The Settlement:
The Modern Era in Far Eastern Diplomacy

Last July when Japan declared war on China, Europe could not help feeling quite a keen sense of astonishment. It did not fail to find presumptuous this little country which set about playing the role of the aggressor against a much more vast empire, whose population exceeded its own by several hundreds of millions and whose resources are considered inexhaustible.[1]

Le Journal des débats politiques et littéraires, February 1895

In a few months, "frivolous, superficial, grotesquely imitative, little Japan" had become "the predominant factor in the Far East" – "a nation to be reckoned with in all future international combinations affecting Eastern Asia" – "a rising naval power"...Governments that had, in the past, treated Japan with scant courtesy, now seriously considered the question of an alliance with her. Other great Powers paid her the almost equally great compliment of looking upon her as a dangerous rival...Friends and foes alike had begun to grasp the changed situation. The New Far East was born. [2]

Arthur Diósy, London-born writer, founder of the Japan Society, knight commander of Japan's Order of the Rising Sun

---

[1] "La Guerre entre la Chine et le Japon" (War between China and Japan), *Le Journal des débats politiques et littéraires* (*Journal of Political and Literary Debates*) (Paris), 6 February 1895, p. 1.

[2] Arthur Diósy, 363; Lehmann, 183.

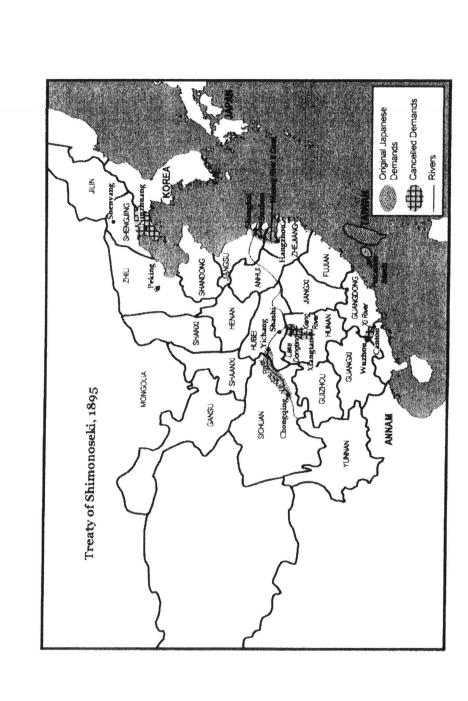

Treaty of Shimonoseki, 1895

Legend:
- Original Japanese Demands
- Cancelled Demands
- Rivers

7

The Treaty of Shimonoseki and the Triple Intervention

The present war is an object lesson in many ways. The positions of the two greatest Eastern Powers of the present day have, within a few short months, been completely reversed. China, regarded as the Bluebeard of the East, is disclosed as a sheep parading in wolf's clothing; while Japan, who has never been seriously thought of at all, has with one bound suddenly entered the comity of nations and become one of us, whether we will it or no...If the Western world has been blind to the fact that Japan was steadily and surely working herself up to a position which should command for her recognition and respect, it has been equally blind to the extent to which official corruption was undermining China. The same period which has loaded Japan with laurels of admiration and applause, has sufficed to cover China with confusion and contempt...[N]othing short of a complete upheaval and breaking down of old systems seems practicable.[1]

The North-China Herald, 28 December 1894

Without losing a single ship or a single battle, Japan broke down the power of China, enlarged her own territory, and changed the whole political face of the Far East.[2]

Lafcadio Hearn, Greek-born U.S. writer resident in Japan, 1896

After the fall of Port Arthur it had become evident to some officials in China that their country had to sue for peace or the Japanese army would march on Peking. In all, China would send three peace missions to Japan, two before the destruction of the Beiyang Squadron at Weihaiwei and the final one afterward. In the end, the

---

[1] "China Unmasked," *The North-China Herald* (Shanghai), 28 December 1894, p. 1037.

[2] Lafcadio Hearn, *Atlantic Monthly,* cited in "The Genius of Japanese Civilization," *The Japan Weekly Mail* (Yokohama), 7 March 1896, p. 282; Timothy Hoye, *Japanese Politics: Fixed and Floating Worlds* (Upper Saddle River, NJ: Prentice Hall, 1999), 164.

Qing Dynasty had to choose between settling the war or risking a *coup d'état*, if not by the Japanese then by their own disgusted Han subjects. The Manchus found the former preferable, particularly since they hoped to enlist foreign intervention in order to mitigate the peace terms. For the Japanese, the problem became how to make their war gains permanent by compelling China to sign a peace treaty without demanding terms that would trigger a foreign intervention. While Japan could defeat China, it could not simultaneously take on the navies of the great powers, let alone in combination with Russian troops in Manchuria. War termination turned out to be a very delicate task, not only internationally but also domestically. The Japanese public and military were demanding peace terms commensurate with their victories in the field. Japanese diplomats, however, were much more aware of the international diplomatic consequences of overly ambitious peace terms. Although the war had made Japan a great power, it was one of the weakest great powers and so could not yet take on the likes of Great Britain or Russia.

Unity between the Japanese diplomats and military leaders began to erode with the taking of Port Arthur. Eight days later, on November 29, 1894, Premier Itō Hirobumi (伊藤博文) arranged to have the emperor relieve Field-Marshal Yamagata Aritomo (山県有朋) of his command, allegedly for medical reasons. In reality, Yamagata favored a march on Peking and there was fear among the diplomats that if Yamagata remained in the field, he might march on Peking regardless of their orders.[3] Itō believed that Yamagata's strategy would backfire because it would cause the collapse of the Qing Dynasty and the consequent disorders would lead rapidly to Western intervention. "'Should that happen,' Itō warned, 'Japan would be negotiating peace not with China but with the Western powers.'"[4] There were also personal reasons. Yamagata was Itō's most powerful rival.[5] On December 20, Yamagata was sidelined as Inspector-General of the Army.[6]

Itō then arranged a complete change in strategy. Peking would no longer be the objective. Instead, the Second Army would take China's second most important naval base, Weihaiwei. This would not threaten Peking directly, but it would allow Japan to destroy China's fleet. This would have important implications for China's post-war relative military power. Then Japan would strike further south to

---

[3] Edward I-te Chen, "Japan's Decision to Annex Taiwan: A Study of Itō-Mutsu Diplomacy, 1894–95," *Journal of Asian Studies* 37, no. 1 (November 1977): 65–6; J. Charles Schencking, "The Imperial Japanese Navy and the Constructed Consciousness of a South Seas Destiny, 1872–1921," *Modern Asian Studies* 33, no. 4 (October 1999): 778.

[4] Cited by Edward I-te Chen, 68.

[5] Oka, 14.

[6] "Field-Marshal Yamagata," *The Japan Weekly Mail* (Yokohama), 22 December 1894, p. 697.

take Taiwan in the belief that the European powers would tolerate Japanese absorption of that island. Like the governments of the other imperial powers, most members of the Japanese government believed that an empire was an essential characteristic of a great power. For Japan, this empire would have to be in the Far East. If the other powers would not yet tolerate such an empire on the Asian mainland, then Japan would start with Taiwan, an island the size of Massachusetts and Connecticut combined. This strategy was highly unpopular with the public and with the army, both of which were intent upon establishing a foothold on the Asian mainland and taking Peking for the final act in the spectacle of "face." In preparation for this spectacle, Field-Marshal Prince Komatsu Akihito (小松彰仁) of the Imperial family had taken command over the march on Peking. A representative of the Japanese royal family would personally seek the capitulation of his Chinese royal counterpart.[7] Most Japanese outside the Foreign Ministry were intent upon bringing China to her knees. They did not understand that the powers would not permit this because the stability of treaty relations hinged on the survival the ruling dynasty. By the end of the war, the army was determined to retain the Liaodong Peninsula. This Japanese diplomats knew to be impossible, since it was too close to the capital for the powers to tolerate. Luckily for the diplomats, the Japanese navy was more interested in taking Taiwan. Meanwhile, Japanese financial experts hoped for a large indemnity. In the end, the diplomats tried to satisfy everyone by including everything in the peace demands: Taiwan, the Liaodong Peninsula, and a large indemnity.[8]

Meanwhile, in October, after the disasters at P'yôngyang and the Yalu, the British government had made an attempt at joint mediation with the Russians, but Tsar Alexander III had fallen ill, the illness had become terminal, and he had died on November 1, so this attempt at intervention had gone nowhere.[9] Before long Port Arthur fell, and when it did the Chinese government suddenly became desperate. In January 1895, the London *Times* editorialized: "China's repeated attempts to procure the intervention of the Western Powers between herself and Japan are provoking surprise and contempt among the Japanese...[China, a] Power that habitually holds Occidental countries at arm's length, that despises their civilization and repels their intercourse, should have more sense of self-respect than

---

[7] "La Guerre entre la Chine et le Japon" (War between China and Japan), *Le Journal des débats politiques et littéraires* (*Journal of Political and Literary Debates*) (Paris), 18 March 1895, p. 1; "支那分割論" (Discussion Concerning the Partition of China), 日本人 (*The Japanese*) (Tokyo), 25 December 1894, p. 5.

[8] Lone, 41–3, 172–3; Edward I-te Chen, 62, 64–6.

[9] Kajima, *Diplomacy of Japan*, vol. 1, 135–51.

to run to them for succor in the first moment of sharp distress. To save her face at home by bowing her head in the dust abroad is a kind of statesmanship, which, though not inconsistent with China's display of miserable incompetence throughout this war, cannot fail to provoke the ridicule and disgust of a proud, high-spirited people like the Japanese."[10] The editors of *The Times* did not realize that those who despised Western civilization and those who sought Western mediation represented two different groups within the Chinese government.

Within a week of the fall of Port Arthur, the Chinese government sent its first peace mission to Japan. On November 26, Gustav Detring, the commissioner of customs at Tianjin, and the journalist Alexander Michie arrived in Hiroshima bearing a letter from Li Hongzhang (李鴻章) to Premier Itō. Detring was a German known for his close connections to Li and for his personal vanity, while Michie was a special correspondent for the London *Times* and the former editor of an English newspaper published in Tianjin. Detring was to deliver the letter and sound out the Japanese on possible peace terms. Itō, however, refused to receive Detring because he was not properly accredited by the Chinese government. Two days after his arrival, the Japanese sent him packing.[11]

The foreign press had no sympathy for the Chinese representatives. It considered the flawed credentials to be proof of the Chinese government's lack of seriousness.[12] A reporter for *The Peking and Tientsin Times* considered China's choice of "two foreigners, one not of the first official position in the service of China and one not in its services at all" to be ludicrous and in keeping with China's past record of dilatory and insincere negotiations.[13] A reporter for *The Pall Mall Gazette* labeled the Chinese peace mission "a diplomatic impertinence." He continued: "China is beaten, and if she will not see it she will be beaten some more."[14] According to *The Peking and Tientsin Times,* "It has been the practice of China in all negociations with foreign powers with which she has hitherto been at war to attempt to open those negociations through inferior emissaries, furnished with incomplete credentials,

---

[10] "China and Japan," *The Times* (London), 9 January 1895, p. 4.

[11] "The Fall of Port Arthur," *The North-China Herald* (Shanghai), 30 November 1894, p. 884; "The Detring Mission" *The North-China Herald* (Shanghai), 28 December 1894, p. 1042; Tyler, 43; "The Abortive Peace Mission" *The Peking and Tientsin Times,* 15 December 1894, p. 163; Mutsu, 127–30; Lensen, vol. 1, 229–30.

[12] "Li," *The Pall Mall Gazette* (London), 21 December 1894, 4th ed., p. 1.

[13] "Rejected Addresses" *The Peking and Tientsin Times,* 15 December 1894, p. 162. The paper cited the example of the tortured negotiations of Lord Elgin, settling the Second Opium War. Ibid.

[14] "Li," *The Pall Mall Gazette* (London), 21 December 1894, 4th ed., p. 1.

which might be disavowed or confirmed as might be most convenient for her."[15]

The Peking and Tientsin Times spotted China's game of "face." It noted, "If the Chinese government imagined that Japan was in the humour to be treated slightingly, how grossly must the Chinese government deceive itself! And what greater slight could be put upon the government of the Micado [the Emperor of Japan] than to accredit to his court on a business of vital importance to the Chinese empire, two gentlemen, estimable in every way no doubt in their respective positions, but absolutely without the slightest qualifications or standing to enable them to treat with authority the important and delicate questions necessary to be discussed in negotiating a treaty of peace." To add insult to injury, the envoys bore letters of credence, not from their emperor but from Li Hongzhang, who had so recently been stripped of his office and honors. The reporter also understood a primary goal of Japan, namely, "to be treated by China with the respect which is due by one empire to the other." He saw no reason why Japan would tolerate this diplomatic snub.[16] *The Pall Mall Gazette* reported, "On Japan's side, we are told authoritatively the war is more one of sentiment than advantage. If she can beat down the arrogance of her hereditary rival she will count the war brilliantly successful."[17]

With the fall of the southern Manchurian city of Gaiping (蓋平) on January 10, 1895, the Chinese government requested a cease-fire, which the Japanese immediately turned down. The Japanese refused to halt the hostilities during any peace talks.[18] They would keep up the military pressure on China in order to secure an optimal settlement. So the war continued.

Meanwhile, within a month of the first failed mission to Japan, China began organizing a second one. This was delayed three weeks while the Chinese government awaited the arrival of John Watson Foster, former United States Secretary of State, whom it had hired as a special adviser.[19] It appointed two commissioners. The first, Zhang Yinhuan (張蔭桓), who ranked as president of a board, was a former minister to the United States, Spain, and Peru; a current senior vice president of the Board of Revenue; and minister of China's foreign office, the Zongli Yamen.

---

[15] "Rejected Addresses," *The Peking and Tientsin Times*, 15 December 1894, p. 162.

[16] "Rejected Addresses," *The Peking and Tientsin Times*, 15 December 1894, p. 162.

[17] "Is This the End, Is This the End?" *The Pall Mall Gazette* (London), 26 November 1894, 4th ed., p. 1.

[18] "媾和中休戰拒絕" (Refusal to Cease Hostilities during Peace Negotiations), 朝日新聞 (*Rising Sun Newspaper*) (Tokyo), 17 January 1895, p. 1.

[19] Lensen, vol. 1, 231; John Watson Foster, *Diplomatic Memoirs*, vol. 2 (Boston: Houghton Mifflin Co., 1909), 102; Vladimir, 201. Documents related to this peace mission have been reprinted in Vladimir, Appendix I, 257–63.

The second commissioner, Shao Youlian (邵友濂), was the former *chargé d'affaires* at St. Petersburg, a past governor of Taiwan, and current officer of the button of the first rank and the acting governor of Hunan. Zhang was the only Chinese member of the embassy able to speak English since he had lived in the United States for several years. At that time he had negotiated with the Americans concerning their restrictions on Chinese immigration. His life would end tragically. During the Boxer Uprising in 1900, the Empress Dowager had him executed for his allegedly pro-foreign sympathies.[20]

The presence of Foster on the Chinese peace embassy gave it some credibility in the eyes of the Japanese press. According to *Tōkyō Jiyū Shinbun* (東京自由新聞), "Were the Chinese peace mission, now alleged to be *en route* for the Court of Japan, entirely of Chinese nationality, one might not unreasonably connect it with some sinister design on the part of the Pekin Government. But the fact that so exalted and learned a personage as Mr. Foster accompanies it, suffices to satisfy any enlightened and impartial observer as to the sincerity of China's desire to sue for peace."[21] Later Foster summarized the problem with China's choice of emissaries: Zhang was qualified but "not of the highest rank." However, "Mr. Shao's selection was most unfortunate, as he was almost an unknown man, his most distinguishing act being the issuance of a proclamation at the opening of the war offering a reward for the head of every Japanese presented to him."[22] In August 1894, the London *Times* had mentioned that the governor of Taiwan had implemented a reward policy of 200 *taels* per head for every Japanese officer and 100 *taels* per soldier. It is unclear how he had distinguished between the two.[23] Such an appointment was but the latest move in China's game of "face." It would continue as long as possible to act as if Japan had lost the war and remained China's inferior. The Japanese understood the game perfectly and would have none of it.

On December 29, 1894, *The Peking and Tientsin Times* reported that Shao Youlian had been governor of Taiwan at the beginning of the war and in that capacity had offered a bounty for Japanese heads. The Japanese had already indicated their displeasure at the practice. *The Times* predicted that the Japanese would not

[20] "The Envoys of Peace," *The North-China Herald* (Shanghai), 28 December 1894, p. 1039; "Chinese News," *The Japan Weekly Mail* (Yokohama), 5 January 1895, p. 13; "The Peace Mission at Kobe," *The Japan Weekly Mail* (Yokohama), 2 February 1895, p. 145; "Imperial Diet," *The Japan Weekly Mail* (Yokohama), 9 February 1895, p. 156; Hummel, 60–3; Foster, *Diplomatic Memoirs*, vol. 2, 160.

[21] "The Spirit of the Vernacular Press during the Week," *The Japan Weekly Mail* (Yokohama), 26 January 1895, p. 86.

[22] Foster, *Diplomatic Memoirs*, vol. 2, 113.

[23] "China and Japan," *The Times* (London), 17 August 1894, p. 3.

accept "as an ambassador of peace, a semi-barbarous official who has recently been capable of offering rewards for the heads of the slain in battle."[24] A reporter for *The North-China Herald* fumed that "it is very difficult to understand how the Chinese Government can have appointed a man of such antecedents for so delicate a negotiation." It also reported that in 1879, Shao had served during the Russo-Chinese negotiations for the Treaty of Livadia.[25] The Chinese side had so bungled these negotiations that the government had actually denounced the treaty and very nearly had gone to war with Russia as a result.[26]

These reporters found China's choice of negotiators perplexing because they were thinking in European terms. The Chinese government, however, was playing an intricate game of "face." It deliberately chose not to send top-ranking diplomats. To do so would have been to accord Japan equal status and thereby give Japan the "face" that China had always withheld not only from Japan but from the Europeans as well. This was but the latest chapter in the endless squabble over the choreography of Chinese imperial audiences for foreign diplomats. At the time of the Opium Wars, the issue had been the mandatory kowtow to the Chinese emperor – the Europeans refused while the Chinese insisted. After many years, the Europeans finally got their way. Then the issue shifted to the venue and frequency of these audiences. If the Chinese were willing to tolerate a certain amount of nonsense from ignorant westerners, they were not about to tolerate such insolence from a country well versed in Confucian traditions. The Chinese did not simply stick to their refusal to treat the "dwarfs" as equals, but it went out if its way to choose someone whose presence would constitute a gross insult in Japanese eyes. It was the Chinese government's way of expressing its utter scorn for the Japanese.

From the Chinese point of view, their choice seemed extremely clever because the westerners would never figure out the game of "face" and would criticize the Japanese should they be less than perfectly courteous. The Japanese fully understood this; indeed, a key war aim had been the public humiliation of China to inflict an enormous "loss of face." In his memoirs, Foreign Minister Mutsu Munemitsu (陸 奥宗光) called it "the war of chastisement against China."[27] Well versed in the traditions of the East and West, the Japanese outfoxed the Chinese. They used diplomatic fine print from the canons of European international law to rid themselves of the unwanted delegation without breaching any rules of courtesy and, in doing

---

[24] "Another Peace Mission," *The Peking and Tientsin Times,* 29 December 1894, p. 170.

[25] "Shao Yu-lien," *The North-China Herald* (Shanghai), 18 January 1895, p. 79.

[26] For a discussion of the Treaty of Livadia, see Paine, 132–50.

[27] Mutsu, 77.

so, made the Chinese look ridiculous. Instead of Japan losing "face," China did.

On January 25, 1895, there was a hint of the problems to come: *The North-China Herald* reported that the two envoys, "who should be proceeding" were still "idling in Shanghai" because they were "unfurnished with proper credentials."[28] This suggests that even before the envoys left China, the Chinese government must have understood that correct credentials would be an issue in the negotiations. The American minister in Peking had been requested to draw up a proper set, which he did, but they were substituted at the last minute with a very vaguely worded document. The Japanese proclaimed this unacceptable. After the war, a foreign commentator observed that with this little ruse, China "exposed herself to the derision of the whole world, thousands of lives and millions of money were wasted, and the whole Pei-yang [Beiyang] Squadron was destroyed or captured."[29] These negotiations preceded the Battle of Weihaiwei, so that China still possessed half of the Beiyang Squadron. Had the Chinese government settled the war at this time, it might have retained the squadron. For this reason, negotiations at this time would have been highly disadvantageous for Japan. It would be better to negotiate after the total destruction of the Chinese navy in order to leave the country bereft of naval defenses.[30]

A few days after the envoys departed for Hiroshima, *The Peking Gazette* (京報), the official organ of the Chinese government for the publication of memorials and edicts, referred to the Japanese, not with the conventional epithet of *woren* or "dwarfs" (倭人), but with the still more derogatory term of *wokou* or "dwarf bandits" (倭寇). *The Peking and Tientsin Times* accused the Chinese government of "colossal conceit" and predicted that such insulting language would only serve "to make the Ministers of the Mikado more than ever determined to humiliate [the Chinese] to the dust."[31] Correct. In a *guanxi* system, in other words a system based on particularistic personal connections rather than universal legal principles, when interpersonal relations have broken down to the point of no return and there are no prospects for future positive interaction, then "face" becomes a way of inflicting the maximum insult on one's adversary. The Guangxu Emperor and the war party still did not comprehend the direness of their negotiating position whereas the Japanese government and the Western nations did.

The Chinese plenipotentiaries arrived in Hiroshima on January 31, 1895. Both

[28] "The Progress of the War," *The North-China Herald* (Shanghai), 25 January 1895, p. 107.

[29] Vladimir, 202.

[30] Lensen, vol. 1, 237.

[31] "Peking Pride," *The Peking and Tientsin Times*, 9 February 1895, p. 194.

were described as very "portly."³² Some of their personal habits set their hosts on edge, particularly their spitting on the floors of their lodgings. A century later, spitting and nose-blowing finesse would remain points of cultural difference between China and the West. Not surprisingly, the Japanese, so famous for their elaborate baths, found Chinese ablutions wanting.³³ In the first meeting held on February 1, Zhang kept up a friendly banter with Premier Itō and Foreign Minister Mutsu. In a total misjudgment of the situation, Zhang repeatedly asked when the Meiji Emperor would be hosting him to an imperial audience. The Japanese politely but repeatedly demurred.³⁴ It was probably just as well for Zhang that he did not seem to have penetrated the facade, presented by his hosts, of perfectly correct manners. The hosts, far from satisfying Chinese pride by giving two low-level representatives an imperial audience, were about to throw Zhang et al. out of the country.

This happened upon the comparison of the plenipotentiary powers provided for the envoys of each country. According to the powers furnished to the Japanese envoys, they had "Full Powers to meet and treat, whether separately or conjointly, with the Plenipotentiaries of China, and to conclude and sign Preliminaries of Peace," whereas the powers vested in the Chinese representatives only empowered them "to meet and negotiate the matter with the Plenipotentiaries appointed by Japan" and await final instructions by telegraph from Peking.³⁵ In other words, they lacked the authority to make any decisions. According to *The North-China Herald*, such credentials "were so much waste paper." Its editors understood that the selection of such envoys was an expression of China's "contempt for Japan," but it did not piece together the on-going shadow play of "face."³⁶

Count Itō responded to these incomplete plenipotentiary powers with a speech addressed to Zhang and Shao: "China has hitherto held herself almost entirely aloof from other Powers, and while she has in some instances enjoyed the advantages accruing to her as a member of the family of nations, she has perhaps more frequently denied the responsibilities of that relation. She has pursued a policy of isolation and distrust and consequently her external relations have not been

³² "Arrival of the Chinese Embassy," *The Japan Weekly Mail* (Yokohama), 9 February 1895, p. 161.
³³ "The Chinese Envoys and Their Suite," *The Japan Weekly Mail* (Yokohama), 23 February 1895, p. 216.
³⁴ Japanese Foreign Ministry, 外務省外交資料館 (Ministry of Foreign Affairs, Diplomatic Record Office), 2.2.1-1-6, 会見条約 (Negotiations and Treaty), "The Proceeding of the Peace Conferences Held at Hiroshima and Shimonoseki in 1895," 6.
³⁵ "Imperial Diet," *The Japan Weekly Mail* (Yokohama), 9 February 1895, p. 156.
³⁶ "The Failure of the Peace Negotiations," *The North-China Herald* (Shanghai), 8 February 1895, p. 176.

characterized by that frankness and good faith which are essential to good neighbourhood." He continued, "Instances are not wanting in which Chinese Commissioners, after having formally agreed to international compacts, have refused to affix their seals, and cases might be cited in which treaties solemnly concluded have been unceremoniously and without apparent reason, repudiated." He continued, "Consequently, the Imperial Government made it a condition precedent to any peace negotiations, that the Chinese Plenipotentiaries should be furnished with full powers to conclude peace, and it was only upon receiving positive assurance from the Chinese Government that that condition precedent had been complied with and that the Chinese Plenipotentiaries were on their way to Japan, that His Majesty the Emperor of Japan conferred upon my colleague and myself full powers to conclude and sign Preliminaries of Peace with the Plenipotentiaries of China."[37] On February 2, 1895, Itō called off the negotiations.[38]

Zhang tried to cut-and-paste a set of credentials over the wires. Itō would have none of it. He told off his guests: "You must surely be aware of our repeated warnings to your Government, made through the United States representatives, that the peace commissioners should be provided with proper and correct documents. And now we find that your Government has not complied with these conditions. We can not be treated lightly in this matter."[39] Two days after their arrival, the envoys were on their way home again.[40] The Chinese government had tried to continue treating the Japanese as inferiors. The Japanese had just fought a war over this issue and had won. But the lesson had yet to percolate into the deeply embedded ideas of the Chinese psyche. One of the most deeply embedded of these was that the "dwarfs" were inferiors, China's students, but under no circumstances, were they her teachers.

In response to the rumored appointment of Prince Gong (恭親王奕訢), *Kokumin shinbun* (国民新聞) reported, "China has at last shown herself serious in her desire for peace. She plays a mere farce...when she sends such men as Chang [Zhang], essentially a second-rate or third-rate statesman, on so important a mission."[41] The Japanese press responded to the repeated Chinese diplomatic

---

[37] "Imperial Diet," *The Japan Weekly Mail* (Yokohama), 9 February 1895, p. 156. Reprinted in Kajima, *Diplomacy of Japan*, vol. 1, 189–91.

[38] "Imperial Diet," *The Japan Weekly Mail* (Yokohama), 9 February 1895, p. 157; "The Peace Mission to Japan," *The North-China Herald* (Shanghai), 22 February 1895, p. 283.

[39] Japanese Foreign Ministry, 16.

[40] Mutsu, 160.

[41] "The Spirit of the Vernacular Press during the Week," *The Japan Weekly Mail* (Yokohama), 26 January 1895, p. 86.

snubs with demands that Japan occupy part of China as a security during any future negotiations. There were also accusations that China's behavior constituted a breach of diplomatic etiquette.[42]

Chinese practices had long been the subject of Western criticism, but the Chinese government had never paid much heed. Military extremity finally seemed to have indicated the validity of some of this criticism. Prince Gong and the other members of the powerful, but reclusive, Grand Council granted an unprecedented interview to the foreign press. At the time, even the diplomatic community residing in Peking was uncertain of the names of all the members, most of whom no foreigner had ever seen.[43] Prince Gong made admissions that must have cut him to the quick. After blaming Japan for starting the war, he "added that he must acknowledge that China had faults. The war, too, had been managed unwisely, and some even of the most exalted and trusted officers have proved incompetent. For those faults China must without doubt suffer."[44] Such admissions would have discomfited the most stalwart of diplomats let alone one from a "face" society. Public admissions of incompetence constituted an enormous and generally irretrievable loss of "face." Whereas in the West, at some level, there is respect for those who have the courage to admit their mistakes, in the East public admission of failure translates into permanent humiliation. There is no recovery from a major admission. The stain remains a permanent blot on the person's record and an eternal dishonor to the achievements of his ancestors.

It took over a month and a half before the departure of the third mission.[45] In the interim the Japanese took Weihaiwei, obliterated or confiscated China's modern warships, and opened the way to Peking by land and sea. This lent some urgency to appointing an envoy whom the Japanese would accept. The Japanese insisted that China send a distinguished diplomat. They had long made it known that they would accept either Grand Secretary Li or Prince Gong, China's two premier foreign policy experts. This would provide the Japanese the opportunity to humiliate the commander of the Chinese naval and land forces in the case of Li or a very distinguished member of the royal clan in the case of Gong. For over four months, the Chinese government resisted giving Japan this satisfaction.[46] There could have

---

[42] "The Spirit of the Vernacular Press during the Week," *The Japan Weekly Mail* (Yokohama), 9 February 1895, p. 150.

[43] Foster, *Diplomatic Memoirs*, vol. 2, 149.

[44] "The Chino-Japanese War," *The Pall Mall Gazette* (London), 28 February 1895, p. 7.

[45] Documents related to this peace mission have been reprinted in Appendices J and K, Vladimir, 264–84.

[46] "Why Was Li Sent?" *The North-China Herald* (Shanghai), 29 March 1895, p. 472.

been no doubt at the Chinese Court that the peace terms would be both onerous and highly unpopular in China.

Naturally, when the choice came, it fell on the Han Chinese. This served as a means to deflect blame from the Manchu Dynasty and onto a simple and highly visible scapegoat. It took no subtlety of thinking to blame all of China's ills on one individual rather than on the complex web of institutional relations and prevailing views that had impeded needed reforms since the time of the late Qianlong reign. It also suited Chinese prejudices to blame the Chinese most associated in the popular mind with foreign ideas, Li Hongzhang. So China's great modernizer and conduit for Western ways became the scapegoat for the calamity he had worked his entire adult life to avoid. China's premier foreign affairs expert and introducer of foreign technology would personally bear China's humiliation. He would negotiate the peace with Japan from a position of abject weakness. It was a way for Li's enemies to finish off the old man's career until the next humiliation arrived with the Boxer Uprising in 1900, when Li was reinstated for another highly distasteful diplomatic assignment and further humiliation.[47]

To ready Li for his new responsibility, the emperor restored the honors so recently stripped. These included the three-eyed peacock feather and the yellow jacket. Li would arrive in Japan in full regalia.[48] To recoup a little "face," the Chinese tried to have the negotiations held in China at Port Arthur or Tianjin. This would create the appearance of Japan as the supplicant coming to petition China.[49] The Japanese refused. The Chinese were able to get permission from the Japanese to communicate with China by coded telegrams.[50] This was only a small inconvenience to the Japanese since they had long ago broken the Chinese code and had already been reading Li's telegrams to Korea and Peking as the situation had degenerated into war in the spring of 1894.[51]

Just before his departure for Japan, Li arrived in Peking on February 21, for several imperial audiences but apparently none with the Empress Dowager. It was rumored that Li had to pay an enormous bribe before he was allowed to enter the city gate. The Guangxu Emperor allegedly told Li that China needed extensive reforms throughout the empire. This was a harbinger of what would become known as the Hundred Days' Reform of 1898, when the emperor would attempt to

---

[47] Paine, 219, 250.

[48] "The Peace Mission," *The North-China Herald* (Shanghai), 8 March 1895, p. 350.

[49] "The Chino-Japanese War," *The Pall Mall Gazette* (London), 19 February 1895, p. 7.

[50] "Documentary History of the Peace Negotiations between China and Japan," *The Peking and Tientsin Times*, 18 May 1895, supplement, p. 1.

[51] Mutsu, 266n.2, 58, 109, 172, 191; Chow, 106.

strike out on his own and implement a far-reaching reform program only to be put under house arrest on the hundredth day and kept there by his aunt until his death in 1908. *The North-China Herald* reported: "Reform is in this air." For five days Li also made the rounds at the various foreign legations.[52] He had not changed his strategy of securing foreign intervention to rein in Japanese ambitions.

The Grand Council ordered all provincial authorities of the top three ranks to make recommendations concerning the wisdom of prolonging or ending the war.[53] The hope was to implicate as many others as possible in the peace settlement so that the Manchus could shift the responsibility for an onerous peace from themselves onto high officials throughout the empire.[54] The responses, however, did not allow for much negotiating flexibility. More than two-thirds of the respondents advocated peace so long as the Japanese government demanded only an indemnity however large, but they demanded a fight to the finish should the Japanese require permanent cession of territory however small. They argued that the emperor's prerogative did not extend to ceding any Chinese territory because these lands had been acquired at the cost of much bloodshed by his ancestors.[55]

Many of the Han literati remained as disconnected from reality as ever. Their hermetically sealed philosophical world continued to flourish within the confines of their minds. Many still did not realize that the world that they understood and the China that they loved no longer existed. The old order survived only in their very vivid memories of it. They were not the first group of people who responded to unacceptable revolutionary changes by retiring into their own mental worlds. Their contemporaries in Russia and particularly the Romanov family also withdrew from reality as that reality diverged ever more sharply from their ideals. The United States is a country famous for groups that bow out of the mainstream to set up independent and, in the minds of their members, ideal communities – the Shakers, the Amish, the Owenites, and the hippies all come to mind. The reaction of the Chinese literati to vast changes from the outside was a very human, if ultimately futile and uncreative response to the winds of change. The Chinese response to the West was characterized by intransigence and withdrawal. In contrast, the Japanese had taken the bull by the horns. Either way was wrenching.

---

[52] "Chinese News," *The Japan Weekly Mail* (Yokohama), 6 April 1895, pp. 401–2; "Peking," *The North-China Herald* (Shanghai), 29 March 1895, pp. 470–2; Little, 233–4.

[53] "The Chino-Japanese War," *The Pall Mall Gazette* (London), 27 February 1895, p. 7. The article erroneously reported that the memorials unanimously recommended suing for peace. The reverse was actually closer to the case. Ibid.

[54] Vladimir, 214.

[55] Little, 234.

On March 19, Li Hongzhang and a suite of over 100 persons divided between two steamers arrived in the port of Shimonoseki (下関) located on the southernmost tip of the main Japanese island of Honshū (本州) and directly across the Korea Strait from Pusan. Premier Itō Hirobumi would serve as the chief negotiator for Japan. Later Itō would describe these negotiations as the most difficult of his life.[56] They were conducted in English, Viceroy Li speaking through an interpreter and Premier Itō in his own words. Somehow in his busy life, Itō had devoted time and energy learning to speak English quite fluently. That day, credentials were exchanged and all were found to be in order, although, as Premier Itō noted, the Chinese documents bore the Guangxu Emperor's seal and not his signature. Viceroy Li explained that this was the Chinese custom, whereupon Premier Itō inquired, "I would not press the matter now; but why does not China observe the rules of all other nations?" Li responded, "We have no such precedent and it would not become me to attempt to press the change."[57] Here in a nutshell was one of China's fatal problems: Even her highest ministers dared not tamper with hallowed traditions to effect reforms. This helps explain the late Qing sclerosis.

Viceroy Li stressed that Japan and China as two Asian countries had much in common, in particular, the common security problem of thwarting European imperialism in Asia. According to Li, "the yellow race" must work together to hamper the designs of the "white race." Itō responded, "When I was at Tientsin [Tianjin ten years ago settling the Korea problem] I gave you my friendly advice that many reforms were most important for your country but I regret very much that no change whatever has taken place." Li expressed regret that "the trammels of antiquated manners and customs in my country are most difficult to shake off and one cannot follow one's own inclination in effecting reform." According to the Japanese version of the minutes, Li urged Japan to form an alliance with China to oppose the West. The Japanese did not take Li up on his offer. That day, Li also

---

[56] Nakamura, 97; Princeton University, Firestone Library, Rare books, John Watson Foster collection, "Diary written by John W. Foster, Shimonoseki, 1895," p. 8.

[57] Japanese Foreign Ministry, 2.2.1-1-6, p. 4; "Letters from Shimonoseki," *The Japan Weekly Mail* (Yokohama), 30 March 1895, p. 366; "War News," *The Japan Weekly Mail* (Yokohama), 30 March 1895, p. 362.

In the dialogues quoted below, I have used the Japanese version of the minutes for Itō and the Chinese version for Li. I will provide only one citation for each day of the negotiations. For March 20, 1895, see Japanese Foreign Ministry, 2.2.1-1-6, pp. 1–12; "Report of the Verbal Discussions During Peace Negotiations," *The Peking and Tientsin Times*, 8 June 1895, p. 263; Foster, *Diplomatic Memoirs*, vol. 2, 127.

For a complete discussion of the various versions of the minutes for the negotiations terminating the war, see the Bibliographic Essay.

presented a proposal for an immediate armistice.[58] The Japanese declined again.[59]

It was not in Japan's interest to conclude an armistice, since its army was making steady progress toward Peking and had yet to occupy Taiwan, which at that time was envisioned by the Japanese navy as an essential territorial cession. According to Foreign Minister Mutsu, the Japanese government deliberately made its terms for an armistice unacceptable to the Chinese.[60] These terms included Japanese occupation and disarmament of Dagu (the military fortress guarding the immediate sea approaches to Peking), Tianjin (the seat of Viceroy Li), and Shanhaiguan (the location of enormous symbolic importance to the Manchus where the Great Wall meets the sea); Japanese control over China's sole railway, which ran between Tianjin and Shanhaiguan; and a monetary contribution from China to finance the occupation. It is important to point out that the Japanese army was in possession of none of these places while all of them fell under Li's jurisdiction as viceroy of Zhili.[61] This was the Japanese way of turning down China flat. According to Mutsu, "As Li read this memorandum to himself, his face changed color and he appeared stunned. Over and over, he muttered that the terms were too severe."[62] Upon communicating with the members of the Zongli Yamen, who had consulted with the foreign representatives in Peking, their unanimous advice to Li was to reject the armistice.[63] He did just that.

On March 24, Li warned Itō: "If the terms [for peace] involve the interests of any other country it would be well to proceed cautiously." This was Li's way of warning Itō that the European powers would intervene if Japan's demands were excessive enough to prejudice European interests. He also grimly pointed out Japan's real reason for turning down the armistice: "Your Excellency said that Japan will attack Formosa [Taiwan]. This explains your objection to the Armistice."[64] When the meeting broke up, Japan had agreed to deliver its peace terms to China at a meeting to be held the following morning.

On Li's way back to his lodgings, however, a Japanese youth, Koyama

---

[58] "Report of the Verbal Discussions During Peace Negotiations," *The Peking and Tientsin Times,* 8 June 1895, p. 263; Kajima, *Diplomacy of Japan,* vol. 1, 201.

[59] Japanese Foreign Ministry, 2.2.1-1-6, pp. 13–26; "Report of the Verbal Discussions During Peace Negotiations," *The Peking and Tientsin Times,* 15 June 1895, pp. 267–8.

[60] Mutsu, 170.

[61] Kajima, *Diplomacy of Japan,* vol. 1, 204.

[62] Mutsu, 169.

[63] Lensen, vol. 1, 241.

[64] Japanese Foreign Ministry, 2.2.1-1-6, pp. 27–38; "Report of the Verbal Discussions During Peace Negotiations," *The Peking and Tientsin Times,* 22 June 1895, pp. 271–2.

Toyotarō (小山豊太郎), approached Li's palanquin and fired a single shot before the police could intervene. The bullet lodged in Li's left cheek, an inch below his eye.[65] During the assassination attempt and while various sets of physicians probed the wound, Viceroy Li impressed people with his fortitude.[66] The Japanese physicians did not dare anesthetize Viceroy Li for fear of killing someone of his advanced years.[67] Since an operation would have entailed a longer recovery period, Li decided not to have the bullet removed. He preferred to get on with the negotiations.[68] The bullet remained lodged deep under his nose, a souvenir from his first trip abroad and a continuing source of discomfort.

Foster described Li's preoccupation with the loss of "face" as a result of the assassination attempt. "He did not seem concerned about his life or worried over the pain he was suffering; what weighed upon his mind was that he, the greatest man in the greatest empire of the world, had been shot down on the public streets of a foreign city by a miserable wretch, a common assassin, a man of no rank or standing. 'I am forever disgraced,' he said; 'I am neither protected nor respected in this land; I ought to have remained at home; I have lost face with my people.'" Foster wryly noted that "His was the most effective shedding of blood on the Chinese side during the entire war, as it brought to him the sympathy of the world, and made the Japanese plenipotentiaries more considerate of him, if not less exacting in the terms of peace."[69] Another foreigner wrote, "All the enemies of the aged Viceroy, all the snarling censors were ready to denounce him as a traitor to his country if he concluded a disadvantageous peace, but the edge was taken off their arguments when the old statesman returned with a bullet lodged in his skull."[70] As for Japan, "For the first time she felt humbled before her adversary. Government and people vied in their efforts to atone for the disgraceful act."[71]

The Emperor Meiji dispatched his personal physician while the empress

---

[65] "War News," *The Japan Weekly Mail* (Yokohama), 30 March 1895, p. 363; "Latest Telegrams," *The Japan Weekly Mail* (Yokohama), 30 March 1895, p. 386; "兇漢小山の裁判宣告書" (Judicial Verdict for the Assassin, Koyama), 朝日新聞 (*Rising Sun Newspaper*) (Tokyo), 2 April 1895, p. 2.

[66] Foster, *Diplomatic Memoirs*, vol. 2, 131–2.

[67] "War News," *The Japan Weekly Mail* (Yokohama), 30 March 1895, p. 363.

[68] "Attempt to Assassinate Chinese Plenipotentiary: Details from Members of Embassy," *The Peking and Tientsin Times*, 18 May 1895, supplement, p. 1.

[69] Foster, *Diplomatic Memoirs*, vol. 2, 134.

[70] Vladimir, 216.

[71] Vladimir, 215. According to Lensen, the United States Library of Congress identifies Vladimir as the pseudonym for Zenone Volpicelli. Other sources provide other guesses at the true identity. All agree that the author was a foreign official with expertise in the Far East. Lensen, *Balance of Intrigue*, vol. 1, 392–3.

personally rolled bandages and sent along a pair of nurses.[72] Emperor Meiji immediately issued a public apology to the Chinese government: "It was of course incumbent on Us, in observance of international usage and on account of the credit of Our country to treat the Chinese Ambassador with proper courtesy and consideration...Most unfortunately, however, a fanatic has come forward and inflicted injury on the Chinese Ambassador. We are profoundly pained by the incident. The fanatic will of course be punished by Our officials in conformity with law."[73] The Diet made a special request to prolong its session long enough so that it could pass a resolution expressing its profound regret and offering its condolences.[74] In the week following the assassination attempt, Li reportedly received from the Japanese general public 10,000 letters of condolence.[75] Upon hearing the news of the assassination attempt, Field-Marshal Yamagata is alleged to have jumped up from his chair to cry out in indignation: "The scoundrel has undone the great achievements of the nation."[76]

The Japanese press expressed its regret *en masse*. The editors of *Nichinichi shinbun* (日日新聞) stated that they "can not but feel keenly pained by the reflection that now, for the first time since the war began, Japan is compelled, by the mad deed of a miscreant, to assume an apologetic attitude toward China. Her honour, hitherto unsullied and even greatly enhanced by the war, has been stained."[77] According to *Yorozu-Chōhō* (万朝報), one of the most popular journals: "From the august Emperor down to the humble cottager, there is not one who does not feel mortified at this incident, which casts the greatest stain on Japan. The whole country is overcome with the sense of shame, horror, and remorse. The enormity of the would-be assassin's crime is so great and no palliation whatever is possible."[78]

---

[72] "Summary of News," *The Japan Weekly Mail* (Yokohama), 30 March 1895, p. 357; "War News," *The Japan Weekly Mail* (Yokohama), 30 March 1895, p. 364.

[73] "War News," *The Japan Weekly Mail* (Yokohama), 30 March 1895, p. 363. A different English translation of the imperial rescript was also reprinted in "Imperial Rescript from Emperor of Japan, Communicated to Chinese Plenipotentiary," *The Peking and Tientsin Times*, 18 May 1895, supplement, p. 2. The basic content of the two versions is the same.

[74] "War News," *The Japan Weekly Mail* (Yokohama), 30 March 1895, p. 363.

[75] "Summary of News," *The Japan Weekly Mail* (Yokohama), 6 April 1895, p. 389; "李鴻章狂漢の為めに狙撃せらる" (Li Hongzhang Attacked Because of Rabid Anger at China), 國民新聞 (*People's Newspaper*) (Tokyo), 26 March 1895, p. 1.

[76] "The Shimonoseki Incident," *The Japan Weekly Mail* (Yokohama), 13 April 1895, p. 429. This was also reprinted in "Some Numerous Expressions of Sympathy in Japan," *The Peking and Tientsin Times*, 18 May 1895, supplement, p. 2.

[77] "The Vernacular Press on the Shimonoseki Incident," *The Japan Weekly Mail* (Yokohama), 30 March 1895, pp. 366–7.

[78] "A Japanese Paper on the Wounding of the Viceroy Li," *The Japan Weekly Mail* (Yokohama), 6

It was an issue of "face." Japan had fought the war to gain "face" in the East and equal treatment in the West. With one shot, the assassin had made a very public breach of the most elementary principle of diplomatic conduct: One does not murder one's diplomatic opposite number. The Japanese government feared that Li might use the assassination attempt as a pretext to break off negotiations and secure the intervention of the European powers.[79] With breathtaking rapidity, the courts brought the assassin to justice. Within the week he had confessed to the crime and was sentenced to life imprisonment.[80]

There was only one way to restore the loss of "face." This would be through magnanimity. The Meiji Emperor made a previously unthinkable offer. He granted a three-week armistice to China. The Japanese public fully understood the rules of "face" and considered the emperor's actions entirely appropriate.[81] Previously the hue and cry had been for a march to Peking; the assassination attempt muted this. The fine print to the agreement indicated that the armistice would be partial and not general: Fighting would continue in Taiwan and the Pescadores (Penghu liedao, 澎湖列島).[82] A reporter for *The North-China Herald* astutely noted, "this voluntary sacrifice on Japan's part, is, as a matter of fact, no sacrifice and no armistice at all...[T]he march to Peking will not be continued...[but she] will go on with the subjugation of Formosa [Taiwan]."[83] On March 25, Japanese troops had landed on Taiwan and the eight-month struggle to subdue the island began.[84] Both sides signed the armistice agreement on March 30, six days after the assassination attempt.

On April 1, Li Jingfang (李經方) or Lord Li, the adopted son and nephew of Li Hongzhang, met in his stepfather's stead with Foreign Minister Mutsu. Given the embarrassing circumstances, Mutsu accepted the plenipotentiary powers telegraphed to him by the Chinese court.[85] Lord Li had passed the first two exams of the

April 1895, p. 391.

[79] Mutsu, 176.

[80] "The Sentence upon Koyama Toyotaro," *The Japan Weekly Mail* (Yokohama), 6 April 1895, p. 404.

[81] "The Vernacular Press on the Armistice," *The Japan Weekly Mail* (Yokohama), 6 April 1895, p. 404.

[82] For a text of the armistice agreement, see Kajima, *Diplomacy of Japan*, vol. 1, 213–5; "Conclusion of an Armistice," *The Japan Weekly Mail* (Yokohama), 6 April 1895, p. 405; "Convention of Armistice," *The Peking and Tientsin Times*, 18 May 1895, supplement, p. 2.

[83] "The Armistice," *The North-China Herald* (Shanghai), 5 April 1895, p. 506.

[84] Schencking: 778; Sauvage, 273–9.

[85] Japanese Foreign Ministry, 2.2.1-1-6, pp. 44–54, 60. *The Peking and Tientsin Times* published no corresponding minutes for the Lord Li–Viscount Mutsu meeting.

three-tiered Chinese examination system and had also learned English. In 1886 he had been sent to Europe for a three-year tour as the secretary to the legations in England and France. Upon his return in 1889, he had served as the Chinese minister to Japan until his mother's death in 1891, when he returned home for the obligatory mourning period.[86] He was his stepfather's right-hand man.

That afternoon, the Japanese provided the Chinese delegation with an eleven-article treaty draft. The draft reflected the interests of key groups within the government: The Japanese navy wanted Taiwan whereas the army demanded the Liaodong Peninsula and the Ministry of Finance wanted a large indemnity.[87] All were satisfied. Premier Itō was a great admirer of Otto von Bismarck. He hoped to emulate Germany's victory over France in the Franco-Prussian War of 1870–1. That war had served both to unify Germany internally and to raise its prestige internationally. Just as Itō had modeled the Meiji Constitution on that of Prussia, so he wanted the Treaty of Shimonoseki to mirror the key features of the 1871 Treaty of Frankfurt: territorial annexation, a large indemnity, occupation of an enemy city to insure payment of the indemnity, and so on. Alas for Itō, just as the possession of Alsace-Lorraine became the occasion for enduring hostilities and another war, World War I, so too would possession of the Liaodong Peninsula lead to future hostilities in the Russo-Japanese War.[88] Foreign Minister Mutsu later indicated to Foster that the army had demanded the Liaodong Peninsula over the objections of Mutsu and Itō, the diplomats.[89] Just as rising civil–military tensions would poison German politics with momentous consequences in the two world wars of the twentieth century, rising civil–military tensions would have a similar impact in Japan in its long war to subdue China (1931–45) and expel the United States from Asia (1941–45). Sad parallels of two rising powers that were only fully integrated into the international system at the tremendous price of world war and prolonged occupation.

The salient features of the draft treaty were (1) the "complete independence and autonomy of Korea"; (2) Chinese cession of (a) the entire coastal region of Manchuria from the Korean border south, including the Liaodong Peninsula and the treaty port of Niuzhuang, (b) Taiwan, and (c) the Pescadore Islands; (3) an indemnity of 300 million Kuping (庫平) *taels*[90] to be paid over four and a half years with a 5

---

[86] Chow, 176–7.

[87] Mutsu, 144.

[88] Edward I-te Chen, 71; Tabohashi, 415, 435; "支那分剖論" (Discussion Concerning the Partition of China), 日本人 (*The Japanese*) (Tokyo), 25 December 1894, p. 3.

[89] Foster, *Diplomatic Memoirs*, vol. 2, 153.

[90] China did not have a unified currency until after the communists took over in 1949. Before then a

percent interest rate on the unpaid portion; (4) mandatory Japanese citizenship for residents of the ceded territories; (5) renegotiation of the Sino-Japanese commercial treaties to bring them into conformity with China's commercial treaties with the Western powers; (6) the opening of seven cities to international commerce, residence, and industry: Peking; Shashi (沙市), Hubei; Xiangtan (湘潭), Hunan; Chongqing (重慶), Sichuan; Wuzhou (梧州), Guangxi; Suzhou (蘇州), Jiangsu; and Hangzhou (杭州), Zhejiang; (7) the opening to international steam navigation of the upper Yangtze River (長江) from Yichang (宜昌) to Chongqing, the Xiang River (湘江) and Lake Dongting (洞庭湖) from the Yangtze River to Xiangtan, the West River (西江) from Canton (廣東) to Wuzhou, and the Wusong River (吳淞江) and canal (運河) from Shanghai (上海) to Suzhou and Hangzhou; (8) exemption for Japanese exports and imports from the *likin* tax (*lijin* or 釐金)[91] and a reduction in transit dues for Japanese imported goods; (9) Japanese occupation of both Weihaiwei and Fengtianfu (奉天府), until the payment of the indemnity; and (10) an end to all offensive military operations upon the ratification of the treaty.[92]

These provisions spelled the end to Chinese influence not only on the Korean Peninsula but also on the Manchurian coastline. In addition, the provisions curtailed Chinese influence in the South China Sea by ceding to Japan Taiwan and the Pescadores, a strategic island chain between Taiwan and the mainland. These territorial changes would transform Japan into an empire. In addition to these territorial losses, the Japanese also expected the Chinese to pay an enormous

whole array of currencies was in circulation even within the same locality. Monetary amounts set in treaties tended to be denominated in Haiguan (海關) or Kuping (庫平) *taels*. The former was a purely theoretical unit of the Chinese customs office (Haiguan). One Haiguan *tael* was 583.3 grains troy 1,000 fine or chemically pure silver. Various formulas were used to convert local currencies into Haiguan *taels*. The Kuping *tael* was that set by the Chinese treasury. One Kuping *tael* was 575.82 grains 1,000 fine and used primarily in Peking. Throughout the nineteenth century, the nominal relationship between the *tael* to the dollar was 72:100 (Frank H. H. King, *Money and Monetary Policy in China 1845–1895* [Cambridge: Harvard University Press, 1965], 80, 82, 189–90, 193). In 1897, the gold standard law fixed the value of the *yen* at 11.574074 grains of pure gold with a par exchange rate of 1 *yen* equal to 24.58217 pence or 49.845 cents (Harold Glenn Moulton and Junichi Ko, *Japan an Economic and Financial Appraisal* [Washington: Brookings Institution, 1931], 148). In 1894, 100 *yen* were worth $50.79 whereas in 1897 they were worth $49.31 (R. L. Sims, *A Political History of Modern Japan 1868–1952* [New Delhi: Vikas Publishing House, 1991], 328).

[91] This internal customs tax was introduced during the Taiping Rebellion. It was levied on goods as they moved from one locality to another, giving imported goods a competitive advantage over locally produced but internally shipped goods ("Likin" in O'Neill, 169).

[92] Japan, Ministry of Foreign Affairs, Diplomatic Record Office, 2.2.1-1-6, 会見条約 (Negotiations and treaty), "The Proceeding of the Peace Conferences Held at Hiroshima and Shimonoseki in 1895," Appendix AA, 1-11. A copy of the Japanese draft treaty was reprinted in *The Peking and Tientsin Times*, 18 May 1895, supplement, pp. 2–3.

indemnity. To put its size in perspective: China's first government budget of 1911 was only 376 million *taels*.[93] Thus, the indemnity constituted three-quarters of an annual budget. This was not all. The treaty also entailed extending foreign influence deeper into the Chinese interior. The seven new treaty ports were not located on the coast, but inland. Similarly, the navigation provisions extended foreign transport deeper into the interior. This expansion focused on three geographic areas: the upper Yangtze Basin, the key cities near Shanghai, and inland from Canton. This was the commercial heartland of China. The renegotiation of Japan's commercial treaties with China would transform Japan into a full member of the treaty-port system and select club of imperial powers. China would also provide Japan with lucrative tax breaks. Finally, the treaty hamstrung China militarily by demanding a cessation of offensive operations combined with a permanent Japanese occupation of the key naval base at Port Arthur and the temporary occupation of Weihaiwei. This would put Japan in control of the sea approaches to Peking. There would also be a temporary occupation of the symbolically crucial ancestral home of the Qing Dynasty, Mukden, located in the district of Fengtianfu. In effect, Weihaiwei and Fengtianfu became hostages to ensure Chinese compliance with the treaty terms. Upon reading these terms, Chinese jaws dropped.

A key Japanese war goal had been to humiliate China. According to Foster, "The Japanese are greatly elated over their [military] successes and feel very keenly the contemptuous treatment which China has extended to them in the past, and are inclined to humiliate her as much as possible."[94] Fengtianfu, a strategically nonessential location, became part of the primary territorial demands. This was because it was the district containing Mukden, the ancestral capital of the Qing Dynasty and the location of the early Qing imperial tombs. In a society whose religious beliefs and ideas of propriety focused on ancestor worship, this would have been the equivalent of ordering the Christians out of Jerusalem and allowing infidels to occupy the holy places. That sort of thing had led to the Crusades.

While Foster was recommending that the Chinese leak to the foreign powers Japanese territorial and monetary demands, the Japanese decided to leak only the commercial demands. The Japanese knew that these would be greatly desired by the other powers since any benefits Japan negotiated on commercial matters

---

[93] Chuzo Ichiko, "Political and Institutional Reform, 1901–1911," in *The Cambridge History of China*, vol. 11, John King Fairbank and Kwang-ching Liu, eds. (Cambridge: Cambridge University Press, 1980), 407.

[94] Foster, *Diplomatic Memoirs*, vol. 2, 112; "支那人の根性" (The Disposition of Chinese People), 日本人 (*The Japanese*) (Tokyo), 25 December 1894, p. 7.

accrued to them all through their most-favored-nation treaty clauses.[95] On April 5 Foster drafted a four-part reply to the Japanese treaty draft. Viceroy Li used it for his official reply after making a few modifications.[96] The points related to the future status of Korea, territorial adjustments, the size of the indemnity, and commerce in China.

(1) China agreed to "the full and complete independence" of Korea but also hoped for a guarantee of its "complete neutrality" with reciprocal promises made by China and Japan. (2) Viceroy Li argued that Japan's territorial claims were excessive. He provided what turned out to be a very prophetic warning: "[I]t is part of wise statesmanship, to negotiate such a peace as will make true friends and allies of these two great nations of the Orient, who are and must remain neighbours, and who have in common so many things in their history, literature, art and commerce...Nothing will so arouse the indignation of the people of China and create in them a spirit of undying hostility and hatred, as to wrest from their country important portions of their territory." He complained in particular about the demands for coastal Manchuria: "In this clause China hears Japan saying, 'I am going to be your ever-threatening and undying enemy, with my army and navy ready to pounce down upon your capital when it suits me; and I propose to humiliate your Emperor by taking from him a valuable portion of his ancestors' home.'"[97] With this Li had addressed both the geopolitical and symbolic consequences of the territorial cessions. War termination is a reciprocal process, and a settlement is unlikely to endure unless both parties can ultimately live with the terms. Otherwise, onerous terms become the pretext for future wars to redress the balance.[98] On this occasion, it was the Japanese who ignored a timely piece of advice from the Chinese.

Japan and China were locked in a battle for "face"; the Japanese were trying to maximize China's loss in retribution for generations of insults, while the Chinese were trying to salvage enough "face" for the ruling dynasty to remain in power. Viceroy Li was quite accurate in interpreting Japanese demands to mean that a lack

---

[95] Lensen, vol. 1, 248–9. After the signing of the Treaty of Shimonoseki, someone in Li Hongzhang's entourage leaked the negotiating minutes and related documents to *The Peking and Tientsin Times* ("The 'Japan Mail' and the Shimonoseki Conference," *The Peking and Tientsin Times*, 3 August 1895, p. 295).

[96] Foster, *Diplomatic Memoirs*, vol. 2, 137–8.

[97] Japan, Ministry of Foreign Affairs, Diplomatic Record Office, 2.2.1-1-6, 会見条約 (Negotiations and Treaty), "The Proceeding of the Peace Conferences Held at Hiroshima and Shimonoseki in 1895," Appendix BB, 2-3. A copy of the Chinese reply is reprinted in Kajima, *Diplomacy of Japan*, vol. 1, 223–31.

[98] Handel, 198.

of Chinese cooperation would transform Japan into an "undying enemy." A blood feud would be the consequence of making one's adversary totally lose "face." If avoiding this had been desired, then the victor would have had to take pains to give "face" to the defeated on some symbolic but highly visible issue. Initially, Japan did not do this. And this neglect was significant. Those in the West fully understood the geopolitical consequences of the cessions, but they did not adequately appreciate their symbolic importance. In 1895, Kang Youwei (康有為), China's famous reformer during the 1898 Hundred Days' Reform, described the war as China's "greatest humiliation in more than two hundred years since the advent of the Qing Dynasty."[99]

(3) China objected to paying "an indemnity for the expenses of a war in which she does not regard herself as the aggressor" – true, but, alas, China was the loser. Viceroy Li realized that this line of argument would not go far in Japan so he set about trying to negotiate a reduction in the amount of the indemnity. He noted that the average annual revenue from the Chinese Imperial Maritime Customs was 22.5 million Haiguan (海關) *taels* for the four years preceding the war. Sixty percent of this had gone to provincial authorities, with additional sums earmarked to pay off war loans. Therefore, China lacked the resources to pay the 300-million-Kuping-*tael* indemnity demanded. Then Viceroy Li took another tack. Based upon Japan's own war loans, he estimated the war to have cost Japan less than 150 million *yen*, from which should be deducted the value of Japan's many valuable spoils of war: naval vessels, military supplies, warships, and so on. During the war, the Japanese government had raised loans totaling 80 million *yen* domestically. This was used to help create a war fund totaling 250 million *yen*, implying that the cost of the war approximated the size of the fund.[100] According to *Keizai Zasshi* (経済雑誌), an authoritative source on financial matters, the cost of keeping more than 60,000 troops in the field during the Satsuma Rebellion had

---

[99] Cited in Hu Sheng, 126.

[100] For information on the finances of the war see "War Fund," *The Japan Weekly Mail* (Yokohama), 25 August 1894, p. 220; "The War Loan," *The Japan Weekly Mail* (Yokohama), 25 August 1894, p. 224; "The War Loan," *The Japan Weekly Mail* (Yokohama), 22 September 1894, p. 339; "The War Loan," *The Japan Weekly Mail* (Yokohama), 24 November 1894, p. 594; "Subscriptions to the Second War Loan," *The Japan Weekly Mail* (Yokohama), 15 December 1894, p. 673; "The Second War Loan," *The Japan Weekly Mail* (Yokohama), 22 December 1894, p. 697; "The New War Loan," *The Japan Weekly Mail* (Yokohama), 2 March 1895, p. 244; "A Japanese War Loan," *The North-China Herald* (Shanghai), 22 February 1895, p. 255; "At Weihaiwei," *The North-China Herald* (Shanghai), 8 February 1895, p. 188; "The War in the East," *The Times* (London), 21 February 1895, p. 5; Vladimir, 220; Eastlake and Yamada, 446–64; "The Indemnity," *The Japan Weekly Mail* (Yokohama), 18 May 1895, p. 554.

been 41 million *yen*.[101] In the 1920s, a representative of the Japanese Ministry of Finance claimed that the war had cost Japan over 200 million *yen*.[102] Yet the indemnity was eventually set at 200 million Kuping *taels* or 311,072,865 *yen*.[103] This represented over a 50 percent profit for the Japanese.

(4) Predictably, Li objected to the reduction in taxes since these were needed to pay the indemnity. He pointed to the hypocrisy of these demands in view of Japan's on-going negotiations with the powers to increase its own tariffs on foreign goods. Viceroy Li also hoped, in vain, to retain most-favored-nation treatment for China in Japan. Finally, he objected to the many provisions expanding commercial rights for the Japanese in China.

The Japanese were not interested in such logic. Their troop deployments put them in a position to use force if logic did not suit. In the official reply of April 6, the Japanese dismissed China's financial concerns, pointing out "that the domestic difficulties of China do not properly fall within the sphere of the present discussion and that demands arising as a consequence of war cannot be regarded as matters for negotiation in the ordinary acceptation of that term."[104] On April 8, at Count Itō's request, he and Lord Li had an informal meeting. Count Itō warned Lord Li that time was running short. The armistice period was already half over. "'We are the conquerors and you the conquered,' said the Count, 'you solicited for peace and we agreed to the negotiations. Should our negotiation fail, the advancement of our troops into the Province of Chi-li [Zhili] cannot now be avoided. Our next move must be to Peking itself.'"[105] He even went so far to suggest that, under such circumstances, Japan would not be able to guarantee the safe return of the Chinese delegation.[106] A would-be assassin had already shot the principal Chinese plenipotentiary in the face and now Premier Itō was threatening the physical safety of the rest of the Chinese delegation. Nevertheless, the Chinese kept stalling on presenting a treaty counterdraft. Foreign Minister Mutsu interpreted Li's reluctance to do so as a reflection of court politics in China: Li "desperately wished to avoid

---

[101] Quoted in "War Expenditure," *The Japan Weekly Mail* (Yokohama), 14 July 1894, p. 47.

[102] Giichi Ono, *Expenditures of the Sino-Japanese War* (New York: Oxford University Press, 1922), 36. Giichi provides a table that categorizes the expenses for each year, claiming amounts through 1903. I have only totaled the amounts for 1894 and 1895.

[103] Giichi Ono, 119.

[104] Kajima, *Diplomacy of Japan*, vol. 1, 231–2.

[105] Japanese Foreign Ministry, 2.2.1-1-6, p. 62. Kajima, *Diplomacy of Japan*, vol. 1, does not cite this exchange.

[106] Japanese Foreign Ministry, 2.2.1-1-6, p. 62. Kajima, *Diplomacy of Japan*, vol. 1, does not cite this exchange; however, Mutsu does (Mutsu, 190).

bearing the responsibility for making the response himself. Indeed, he had pleaded for instructions from the Peking government in an exchange of telegrams several days earlier, hoping to be spared the onus of the decision regarding the Chinese reply to Japan's proposal. The instructions from Peking, however, had as usual been vague and irrelevant, and Li found himself caught between his own government and us."[107] These problems also reflected the lack of a unified government in China: Different factions, instead of working with each other against the common Japanese foe, were still focusing on their domestic hostilities, thereby making the Japanese subjection of China that much easier.

On April 9 the Chinese delegation caved in to Japanese demands to provide a treaty counterdraft. The salient changes were as follows: (1) Both Japan and China would recognize Korean neutrality. (2) Territorial cessions would be limited to the Pescadores and to the part of Manchuria right on the border with Korea. The ceded territory in Manchuria would be limited to the prefectures of Andong (安東縣) and Kuandian (寬甸縣), Fenghuangcheng (鳳凰城), and Xiuyanzhou (秀巖州). These were the territories farthest from Peking and did not include the Liaodong Peninsula, the treaty port of Niuzhuang, or the island of Taiwan. (3) The indemnity would be reduced to one-third of the original demand. (4) The Japanese would extend to nonresident Chinese in the ceded territories the same property rights accorded to Japanese subjects. (5) New Sino-Japanese treaties would be fully reciprocal and not "unequal" as were the treaties between China and the European powers. There would be no opening of additional cities or rivers to international commerce, nor would there be a reduction in taxation. (6) Only Weihaiwei and not Mukden would serve as bail until China paid up the indemnity. (7) Any future disagreements would be submitted to international arbitration. (8) All offensive military operations would cease upon the signing, not the ratification, of the treaty.[108]

On April 10, for the first time since the assassination attempt, Viceroy Li met with Count Itō for negotiations. The talks began with an exchange of small talk and personal flattery, which Viceroy Li ended with a sad commentary: "What you have done for Japan I wanted to imitate for China. Had you been in my place you would know the unspeakable difficulties met with in China."[109] At this point, Count Itō presented Viceroy Li with a revised Japanese treaty draft.[110] (1) Japan

[107] Mutsu, 191.

[108] "Counter-Proposal by Chinese Plenipotentiary," *The Peking and Tientsin Times*, 18 May 1895, supplement, p. 4.

[109] Japanese Foreign Ministry, 2.2.1-1-6, pp. 70–83; "Report of the Verbal Discussions During Peace Negotiations," *The Peking and Tientsin Times*, 29 June 1895, pp. 275–6.

[110] Japanese Foreign Ministry, 2.2.1-1-6, Appendix DD, pp. 66–70.

refused to recognize the neutrality of Korea but demanded that China but not Japan recognize the independence of Korea. (2) Japan agreed to reduce the ceded territory in Manchuria to a narrower band along the coast, excluding Mukden but including the Liaodong Peninsula and Niuzhuang. Taiwan and the Pescadores remained on the wish list. (3) They split the difference on the indemnity to demand 200 million Kuping *taels* but with the repayment period stretched out over seven and a half years. (4) They refused to guarantee Chinese property rights in the ceded territories. (5) Japan would not guarantee China equal treatment in its future treaties. Instead, it would use China's European treaties as a "basis" for the new treaties. The underlying message was that Japan, in emulation of the European powers, intended to have "unequal" treaties of its own with China. (6) Japan did reduce the list of cities to be opened to international commerce from seven to four. Demands to open Peking, Xiangtan, and Wuzhou were eliminated. The new river routes were reduced from four to two. Since Wuzhou and Xiangtan were not to be opened, the relevant river routes were also canceled, but the Japanese still demanded the right to conduct business in the Chinese interior. (7) The Japanese also agreed not to hold Mukden as collateral. They still wanted Weihaiwei to serve that function, but only during part of the payment period. Thereafter, Chinese customs revenues would serve as the security. (8) Japan refused to accept international arbitration to resolve future disputes. (9) Japan also refused to cease offensive military action until China ratified the treaty. This put pressure on the Guangxu Emperor to ratify the document or be deposed. Given the extreme Han opposition to the treaty, this was a way to make the Guangxu Emperor interpret his own best interests in a way compatible with Japanese desires. It also gave Japan another week or two to subdue Taiwan and the Pescadores.

In the end the Japanese did give the Chinese some "face" with the elimination of Peking and the reduction in the number of cities and rivers open to foreign trade, and especially with the end of the demand to occupy Mukden. The Japanese had also reduced the indemnity, their territorial demands in Manchuria, and proposed tax relief. Viceroy Li tried to haggle over these terms, citing European precedents and indicating that the Japanese demands remained excessive. Viceroy Li argued that "Great Britain and France also occupied Chinese territory but never asked for an inch of it." He added, "No Western nation has ever demanded whatever territory it was able to occupy," to which Count Itō shot back, "Moreover to cite a case was not...Eastern Siberia ceded to Russia without occupation?" All Viceroy Li could reply was "The cession was not in consequence of war." The territory lost by China to Russia in Eastern Siberia in the mid-nineteenth century was equal to the area of California plus a quarter of the state of Oregon. China had ceded all of it out of ignorance of European politics and of its own geography.[111]

Tired of Li's arguments, Count Itō turned to the military realities. He pointed out that more than sixty Japanese transports were lying at anchor in Hiroshima's harbor awaiting the expiration of the truce before descending on China. The next day, April 11, Premier Itō sent Viceroy Li an ultimatum. Japan would provide no further amelioration of the conditions. He warned "that war is progressive in its consequences as well as its operations and that it is not to be expected that conditions of peace which Japan is now happily able to accept will be possible later on."[112]

The plenipotentiaries met again on April 15. After much haggling, Count Itō agreed to waive interest payments on the indemnity if China paid off its entirety within three years; to limit Japanese subjects to establishing businesses in the treaty ports; and to make adjustments on other secondary matters.[113] Li kept trying to argue in terms of his personal relationship or *guanxi* with Count Itō: If Count Itō would just back down on a particular issue, this would ease Viceroy Li's position in China and reap his enduring gratitude, with future personal benefits to Itō implied. Count Itō was not interested in *guanxi* but made his arguments strictly on the basis of *realpolitik:* Japan had won, Japan was strong, Japan would take what it wanted. Before the next meeting, the Japanese agreed to extend the armistice and broaden it to include Taiwan and the Pescadores, for they were now under Japanese military occupation, but the other essential terms remained unchanged. Finally, on April 17, the plenipotentiaries signed the peace treaty to be known as the Treaty of Shimonoseki for the locale where it was negotiated.[114]

---

[111] In 1858, by the Treaty of Aigun, China ceded approximately 185,000 square miles of territory to Russia. Paine, 57–69, 352.

[112] Kajima, *Diplomacy of Japan*, vol. 1, 240–1; "Japan's Ultimatum," *The Peking and Tientsin Times*, 18 May 1895, supplement, p. 5.

[113] Japanese Foreign Ministry, 2.2.1-1-6, pp. 84–107; "Report of the Verbal Discussions During Peace Negotiations," *The Peking and Tientsin Times*, 6 July 1895, pp. 279–80; Ibid., 13 July 1895, p. 283.

[114] Japanese Foreign Ministry, 2.2.1-1-6, pp. 108–12. *The Peking and Tientsin Times* did not publish the minutes to the signing of the treaty. For the complete treaty, protocol and armistice agreement, see "Treaty of Peace between China and Japan," *The Peking and Tientsin Times*, 11 May 1895, p. 247; "媾和條件" (Articles of Peace), 朝日新聞 (*Rising Sun Newspaper*) (Tokyo), 18 April 1895, p. 1; "媾和談判成なり！" (Peace Negotiations Completed!), 國民新聞 (*People's Newspaper*) (Tokyo), 18 April 1895, p. 2; "媾和條約の條項" (Articles of Peace Treaty), 國民新聞 (*People's Newspaper*) (Tokyo), 20 April 1895, p. 1.

In addition to the Treaty of Shimonoseki, the negotiators simultaneously signed a protocol dealing with the temporary occupation of Weihaiwei and a convention of armistice prolonging the armistice twenty-one more days.

The Chinese reaction to the treaty was cacophonous. The Manchu Court tried to keep the peace terms secret. It never asked for the advice of the upper echelons of the officials, such as those of ministerial rank on the six boards, the governors-general, or the governors. Between what the Chinese and Japanese had leaked, however, everyone got a pretty good idea of the terms.[115] Moreover, by June of 1895, the Presbyterians would publish in Shanghai the leaked minutes in their Chinese-language monthly journal.[116] Officials throughout the empire deluged the court with memorials demanding that the emperor reject the treaty and continue with the war. Over 2,500 officials presented the court with 130 memorials.[117] The general argument was as follows: Since the indemnity was exorbitant, it would consume ten years' worth of customs revenues and fund a massive Japanese armament program. The cession of territory on the Chinese mainland would set a precedent for the other powers that would be sure to follow suit. Port Arthur was too strategic to let go, while Taiwan had not even been involved in the war until Japan had suddenly launched a peripheral operation there. The commercial demands were also excessive. Most officials believed the Japanese military presented less of a threat than had the Taiping and Nian rebels. Therefore, the Chinese forces should continue fighting.[118]

In particular, the vast majority of Chinese officials did not see the need to cede territory. According to *The North-China Herald*, "For the past fortnight the Emperor has been deluged with memorials from the provinces, not a single Viceroy, Governor, Tartar [Manchu] General or Provincial Commander-in-Chief having abstained from his privilege of memorialising the Throne and advising the rejection of the clauses of the Li-Ito treaty where the cession of territory has been agreed. The vote for a continuance of the war providing Japan insists upon the observance of the whole treaty also seems to have been unanimous on the part of these officials, who furthermore guarantee funds for the prosecution of the war but not for the payment of the indemnity." Liu Kunyi (劉坤一), who had assumed Li's civil duties as viceroy of Zhili but had tenaciously tried to avoid the military duties after the fall of Port Arthur, was among the most vociferous opponents.[119]

A memorial by the governor of Shandong Province, Li Bingheng (李秉衡),

---

[115] Kuo, 121.

[116] "問答節略" (Summary of the Minutes), 萬國公報 (*International Gazette*) (Shanghai) 7, no. 77 (June 1895): 23a–26. For the continuation, see Ibid., no. 78 (July 1895): 3b–10b; no. 79 (August 1895): 7a–13b; no. 84 (January 1896): 25b–28b.

[117] Marcella Bounds, "The Sino-Russian Treaty of 1896," *Papers on China* 43 (July 1970): 110.

[118] Kuo, 121–6; Schulman, 38–59.

[119] "The Effects of the Treaty," *The North-China Herald* (Shanghai), 10 May 1895, p. 683.

encapsulated the sentiments of these provincial officials: "Although your servant is old and exhausted, I am quite willing to lead an army to avenge the accumulated defeats. I would have no regrets even if I should perish. When the enemy is exhausted and we bring them under control, then we can negotiate peace at our own pace. Not only would we not hurt our prestige and incur insults [i.e., lose "face"], but thereby we would dampen the avaricious designs of other nations."[120] This was positive thinking carried to absurdity. Yet to these many officials, the facts so violated the vital assumptions underpinning their mental world that the truth eluded them. China was not superior. Traditional Chinese learning did not comprise all valuable knowledge. In the future, China would not be able to sinicize either East or West. The Japanese did possess superior might. Industrial technology more than compensated for inferior numbers and resources. China could be vivisected by outsiders who would not become sinicized in the process but would leave behind indelible cultural imprints of their own.

Neither the Guangxu Emperor nor the Empress Dowager wanted to settle the matter. He ordered officials to memorialize to her. She dumped the matter back in his lap: "Today we have a sudden influenza; petition the Emperor for an edict to settle the matter."[121] She had never favored the war, while her brash ward had. In the intervening months she had reeled out to him plenty of rope to hang himself, and hang himself he had. He had jumped headlong into the wave of Han literati demands to thrash the "dwarfs." Perhaps Empress Dowager Cixi felt unable to stem this tide and therefore her best solution was to let the reckless youth ride it if he could. The consequences had been bad for China, but they had served to undermine the prestige of the Guangxu Emperor and keep Empress Dowager Cixi within the grasp of power.

The emperor responded by singling out two high officials who had talked a good piece during the war about whipping the "dwarfs." The time had come for them to make good on all the bravado. On April 26, in an ostensibly secret edict, he ordered Liu Kunyi and Wang Wenshao (王文韶), the high-ranking self-strengthener, to recommend whether or not he should sign the peace treaty. The emperor noted in his edict to them, "For successive days we have received innumerable memorials from the Ministers and officers of our Court all of whom denounce the Treaty and declare that it would never do to ratify such a document." He criticized their responses because "they never thought of touching upon *the most important point which induced us to be favourable to a ratification. That was

---

[120] Cited in Chu, "China's Attitudes," 90–1.
[121] Schulman, 59.

our great anxiety for the safety of Moukden and Peking." In other words, the Guangxu Emperor's primary concern was not the welfare of his country, a modern way of looking at the world, but the fate of the two cities symbolically important to his dynasty, a traditional concern. The Qing imperial tombs were located outside of these two cities. The emperor went on to implicate Liu and Wang by quoting back their words: "In Liu K'un-yi's last memorial telegraphed to us he states that 'even if we should be defeated, there are plenty of means to prolong resistance,' while Wang Wên-Shao declared in his memorial that 'the troops commanded by General Nieh Sze-ch'eng [Nie Shicheng (聶士成)] are perfectly organised and prepared to fight the enemy." The Guangxu Emperor wanted to hang some of the responsibility for the treaty around their necks.

In the edict, the emperor continued to refer to the Japanese as "dwarfs."[122] Even as Viceroy Li was preparing to leave for the peace negotiations, the Chinese officials, including Li himself, still used the term "dwarf pirates" (倭寇) in official documents. The Peking correspondent of *The North-China Herald* reported: "The officials outside the Foreign Office, are as haughty and conceited and detest the foreigners as much as ever. They still believe China cannot be conquered by the 'dwarfs.'"[123] Chinese attitudes remained frozen in time and officialdom had yet to digest the enormous implications of their country's defeat.

Upon Li's return, the opposition to ratification was so great that he sent Foster in his stead to Peking to meet with three members of the Grand Council and urge its members to ratify the treaty. This was an unprecedented meeting since most members of the Grand Council had never been seen by a foreign envoy, much less been lectured to by one. According to Foster, "The point which I strongly urged was that it was no longer Li Hung Chang's treaty, but the Emperor's treaty, as every word of it had been telegraphed to Peking before signing it and, with the advice of the Cabinet [the Grand Council], the Emperor had authorized its signature. If he refused to ratify it, he would stand disgraced before the civilized world, and the Cabinet would be responsible for their Emperor's ignominy."[124] Foster was amazed by the hermetically sealed intellectual world encasing the highest echelons of the Chinese government. At the meeting, a key critic of Li Hongzhang, Weng

---

[122] "Peace or War?" *The North-China Herald* (Shanghai), 7 June 1895, p. 876. Another translation of the edict was published several weeks later. Although the two documents are not identical, they are very similar in content. "The Responsibility of Advisers," *The North-China Herald* (Shanghai), 28 June 1895, p. 1002; Kwong, 178–9.

[123] Quoted in "Chinese News," *The Japan Weekly Mail* (Yokohama), 6 April 1895, p. 402.

[124] Foster, *Diplomatic Memoirs*, vol. 2, 147–50; Princeton University, Firestone Library, Rare books, John Watson Foster collection, "Diary Written by John W. Foster, Shimonoseki, 1895," p. 15.

Tonghe (翁同龢), the tutor of the emperor and president of the Board of Revenue, asked Foster whether or not territory had ever changed hands in European wars. At the time, Weng was the most influential government official in China. Foster realized that such a question showed that Weng knew virtually nothing about the world beyond China. Foster must have been diplomatic in his response, for members of the Grand Council paid him a rare compliment when each one called at the American Legation on his departure to leave his farewell card.[125] They went out of their way to give him "face." They also must have heeded his warning, for the Guangxu Emperor soon ratified the treaty.

The Chinese and Japanese exchanged treaties on schedule at Yantai (煙臺 or Chefoo) on May 8.[126] Anchored in the harbor that day were nine Russian men-of-war, the flagship, two torpedo-gunboats, and one torpedo-boat all repainted in battle color in readiness for action. In addition, there were two warships each from Germany and Great Britain and one apiece from France, the United States, and Italy.[127] This international naval attendance was just one more indication of the emerging world of global politics.

With the treaty signed, the enemies of Li Hongzhang turned their attention to him. They arranged to have his adopted son, Lord Li Jingfang, take on the invidious responsibility of handing over Taiwan to Japan. The father had signed the hated Treaty of Shimonoseki. Now the son would sign the documents ceding Taiwan to Japan. As a reporter for *The Peking and Tientsin Times* noted, "[T]he appointment of Lord Li has not been made on public grounds. It is a spiteful move in the endless complication of Chinese domestic intrigue, the object of which is to fix the entire odium of the humiliating conditions of peace upon Li Hung-chang and his family." He lambasted "Peking Mandarindom. Incompetent to carry on the war, incompetent to make peace, they will at least stamp with indelible shame and bring to irretrievable ruin the one man who was capable of seeing the necessity of the situation and strong enough to grapple with it. Whatever view we may hold of the concessions China has been forced to make, no one [outside of China] doubts they were necessary."[128] It was rumored that when

---

[125] Foster, *Diplomatic Memoirs*, vol. 2, 150; Schulman, 87; Allen Fung, 1011.

[126] "The Exchange of Ratifications at Chefoo," *The Japan Weekly Mail* (Yokohama), 25 May 1895, p. 580.

[127] Eastlake and Yamada, 525; Foster, *Diplomatic Memoirs*, vol. 2, 151.

[128] "Changing Hands," *The Peking and Tientsin Times*, 25 May 1895, p. 254. According to Foster, "Viceroy [Li] greatly displeased and alarmed at this [appointment of Li Jingfang], showing interest at Peking to fasten on him and family all odium of treaty." Princeton University, Firestone Library, Rare books, John Watson Foster collection, "Diary 30 January to 8 June 1895," 18 May 1895.

Viceroy Li was recalled to Peking after the signing of the treaty, he had to distribute the enormous sum of eight million *taels* or about eight and one-half million dollars to ward off his political enemies.[129]

The court had Li negotiate the new trade treaty demanded by Japan. In the end, it was signed on July 21, 1896, by Zhang Yinhuan, who had accompanied the Japanese head-hunter Shao Youlian on the ill-fated second diplomatic mission to Japan.[130] The Sino-Japanese Treaty of Commerce and Navigation formally ended the era of reciprocal relations between China and Japan. The treaty accorded Japan most-favored-nation treatment in China but not the reverse. Similarly, Japanese consuls in China had consular jurisdiction but not the other way around.[131] Japan had transformed itself from the object of imperialism into one of the perpetrators.[132] Meanwhile, on August 7, *The Peking Gazette* reported the appointment to the Zongli Yamen of two of Li's harshest critics and members of the war party: Weng Tonghe, whose ignorance of foreign affairs Foster had noted, and Li Hongzao (李鴻藻), the seventy-five-year-old former tutor to the Tongzhi Emperor (同治皇帝), the deceased son of the Empress Dowager, and court official closely associated with the Tongzhi Restoration. According to *The Peking and Tientsin Times*, "These two appointments to the Chinese Foreign Office at Peking are quite in harmony with the wave of anti-foreign feeling now sweeping over south China."[133] They forced into retirement Li's two closest allies on the Grand Council and the Zongli Yamen, Sun Yüwen (孫毓汶) and Xu Yongyi (徐用儀).[134]

A reporter for *The Peking and Tientsin Times* observed, "The Peace Mission, though successful is not anything of which China or Her great statesman can feel proud. Apart from material considerations altogether, though these have been hard to comply with, and we think excessive, she suffers, still more keenly in the humbled pride and lost prestige which the signing of this Treaty involve. It sets the seal of acknowledged weakness upon Her defeat. The pity felt for Her by

---

[129] Folsom, 108.

[130] Henri Cordier, *Histoire des relations de la China avec les puissances occidentales 1860–1902* (*History of the Relations of China and the Occidental Powers 1860–1902*), vol. 3 (Paris: Ancienne Librarie Germer Baillère, 1902), 325; Hummel, 62. For the text of the agreement, see John V. A. MacMurray, *Treaties and Agreements with and Concerning China 1894–1919*, vol. 1 (New York: Oxford University Press, 1921), 68–74.

[131] Chow, 88–9.

[132] Marius B. Jansen, *Japan and China from War to Peace, 1894–1972* (Chicago: Rand McNally College Publishing Co., 1975), 25.

[133] "New Blood in the Tsung-li Yamen," *The Peking and Tientsin Times*, 17 August 1895, p. 303; Schulman, 87–8.

[134] Schulman, 81, 90.

outsiders is too closely akin to contempt to be other than bitter in Her mouth. Her greatest lovers and admirers must now apologize where they were wont to boast...She has been defeated under such circumstances as once and for all preclude the exercise of faith in Her power of regeneration."[135] Even in the West, where a watered-down version of "face" exists in ideas about national dignity, China's failure was so complete as to draw enormous attention. Westerners clearly saw that China's prostration meant a free-for-all for the foreign powers in China. Internationally, the scramble for concessions was the logical consequence of the publicity given to China's weakness so clearly demonstrated by its rapid and utter defeat in war. Internally, a much more thorough soul-searching and more widespread call for reforms would lead to a reevaluation of many traditional Chinese assumptions concerning the natural order of the world and their place in it.

Japan had mastered China. The next question was whether Japan could master the European powers as well.

* * *

The Japanese Foreign Ministry made every effort to forestall foreign intervention. Days before the outbreak of war, the Japanese government took care to notify the British government that Shanghai would be outside the sphere of hostilities.[136] This was a costly decision, since the main Chinese arsenal was located there and Chinese ships freely transported munitions from the port for the duration of the war.[137] But Shanghai was also a key center of British commerce, which the Japanese did not want to disrupt. On July 25, 1894, the day the war began, the Japanese government issued instructions to the governors of Japan to prevent Japanese youths from harassing Chinese residents living under their jurisdictions. On July 27, the number of constables stationed in the foreign settlement in Yokohama was increased.[138] On August 4, an imperial ordinance guaranteed Chinese residents in Japan the same protections concerning life and property as Japanese subjects. This ended Chinese extraterritoriality in Japan.[139] The 1871 Sino-Japanese

---

[135] "The Viceroy's Return," *The Peking and Tientsin Times*, 27 April 1895, p. 238.

[136] "Shanghai to Be Respected," *The North-China Herald* (Shanghai), 27 July 1894, p. 131.

[137] Morse, vol. 3, 31.

[138] "Summary of the News," *The Japan Weekly Mail* (Yokohama), 4 August 1894, p. 117; "Yokohama News," *The Japan Weekly Mail* (Yokohama), 4 August 1894, p. 121; "Mutual Protection," *The Japan Weekly Mail* (Yokohama), 4 August 1894, p. 122.

[139] "The Imperial Ordinance of the 4th," *The Japan Weekly Mail* (Yokohama), 11 August 1894, pp. 161–2. For an English translation of the ordinance, see "Imperial Ordinance," *The Japan Weekly Mail* (Yokohama), 11 August 1894, p. 170. Apparently the Japanese suspended extraterritoriality in retaliation for a Chinese suspension of extraterritoriality to Japanese subjects. "The War in the East," *The Times* (London), 5 September 1894, p. 3.

treaty had provided fully reciprocal rights including mutual extraterritoriality.[140]

The Japanese government also sought to insure that its citizens in the West provoked no incidents. For instance, in early August of 1894, the Japanese consul in Portland, Oregon, issued a circular to Japanese nationals on the west coast of the United States ordering them not to engage in any military activities "or act in any way contrary to the laws which are binding on neutral countries" and "to be very careful" in their "daily intercourse with Chinese residents of this country" to prevent any outbreak of disorders.[141] During the war a lawyer with expertise in international law was assigned to each Japanese army corps and fleet to prevent any international incidents.[142] As Foreign Minister Mutsu wrote afterward, "As both we and the Chinese were seeking the sympathy of the Western powers for our respective positions, we deemed it prudent to avoid any Japanese action which might alienate foreigners and cause them to align themselves against us."[143] These precautions extended to sending authorities to the public schools in Hiroshima on the eve of the second peace mission led by Zhang and Shao in order to impress upon students not to "hoot and jeer at foreigners" who would soon be arriving for the peace talks.[144]

Ever since the Battle of the Yalu, the Japanese press had been speculating about a possible foreign intervention terminating the war in a manner prejudicial to Japanese interests.[145] After the Battle of Gaiping, Count Ōkuma Shigenobu (大隈 重信), a key political rival of Itō Hirobumi, gave another interview to the press in which he warned of the possibility of foreign intervention.[146] From the first major battles of the war onward, French and Russian papers repeatedly brought attention to the likelihood of foreign intervention to prevent Japan from taking more compensation than was in the interests of the European powers. After the Battle of Weihaiwei, a reporter for *Le Siècle* predicted that Japan would get Taiwan but

---

[140] Miwa, 3.

[141] "Japanese in This Country," *The New York Times*, 9 August 1894, p. 5.

[142] William Elliot Griffis, *Corea: The Hermit Nation* (New York: Charles Scribner's Sons, 1911), 477.

[143] Mutsu, 66.

[144] Foster, *Diplomatic Memoirs*, vol. 2, 119–20.

[145] "The Spirit of the Vernacular Press during the Week," *The Japan Weekly Mail* (Yokohama),17 November 1894, p. 554; "支那分剖論" (Discussion Concerning the Partition of China), 日本人 (*The Japanese*) (Tokyo), 25 December 1894, p. 5; "今日誰か戰爭を欲し誰か平和を欲するや" (Now Who Wants War and Who Wants Peace?), 日本人 (*The Japanese*) (Tokyo), 3 February 1895, p. 7; "露國の干渉來らん" (Russian Intervention Coming), 國民新聞 (*People's Newspaper*) (Tokyo), 18 April 1895, p. 2.

[146] Citing *Kokumin* (国民新聞), "Count Okuma Interviews," *The Japan Weekly Mail* (Yokohama), 26 January 1895, p. 88.

noted "luckily for China certain European powers are there to warn the Mikado of the dangers of indigestion."[147] The diplomatic community was also aware that Russia would not sit idly by and let Japan carve out a concession on the Asian mainland. Russian diplomats also made this abundantly clear to their Japanese counterparts on every possible occasion.[148]

In early August of 1894, two weeks after the opening of hostilities, a reporter for the *S.-Peterburgskie vedomosti* suggested that Korea had provided Japan with the pretext to demonstrate to the world the success of its recent domestic reforms, to show off its modern military, and to seek hegemony in the Far East.[149] This was one of the first indications that the initial Russian admiration for Japanese military prowess would rapidly be overtaken by Russian fears for its borders. As the Russians began to appreciate Japan's strength, they soon feared that Japan might pose a security threat to their long and sparsely populated Siberian frontier. Specifically, they feared that Japan would seek to establish its hegemony in the Far East.[150] This turned out to be a perfectly accurate but premature assessment of the future direction of Japanese foreign policy. Japan would attempt to do this only in the 1930s. So Russian praise rapidly degenerated into anti-Japanese diatribes.[151] Growing anti-Japanese sentiments would be one of the consequences of the Sino-Japanese War. In the ensuing years, these would develop into fears of a "yellow peril," which became widespread a decade later during the Russo-Japanese War.[152]

Moskovskie vedomosti was among the first newspapers to advance this more sinister interpretation of Japanese motives. It attributed the rapidity of their military successes to Japanese plans made three years earlier in 1891 to take Korea: "Such speed was only possible because everything had been prepared beforehand."[153] Within the week it revised this time frame of "three years earlier" to "from time immemorial the Japanese have harbored pretensions to Korea...Their goal consists

---

[147] G. Gareau, "Les Japonais à Weï-Haï-Weï" (The Japanese at Weihaiwei), *Le Siècle* (*The Century*) (Paris), 3 February 1895, p. 1.

[148] Treat, vol. 2, 532–3, 539; Mutsu, 225–7.

[149] "Англия в корейской войне" (England in the Korean War), *С-Петербургские ведомости* (*St. Petersburg Gazette*), no. 201, 8 August 1894, p. 1.

[150] "Отпор Азии" (Rebuff of Asia), *С-Петербургские ведомости* (*St. Petersburg Gazette*), no. 95, 23 April 1895, p. 1; "Высадка Японцев близ нашей границы" (Landing of Japanese Near Our Border), *Новое время* (*New Times*), no. 6688, 23 October 1894, p. 2.

[151] "Китай и Япония" (China and Japan), *Московские ведомости* (*Moscow Gazette*), no. 66, 8 March 1895 (20 March 1895), p. 4.

[152] Paine, 234, 246.

[153] "Корея. Японско-китайская война" (Korea. Sino-Japanese War), *Московские ведомости* (*St. Petersburg Gazette*), no. 228, 21 August 1894 (2 September 1894), pp. 3–4.

in the seizure of power in Korea." It went on to highlight the hypocrisy of Japanese actions by juxtaposing Japan's forcible interference in Korean affairs to Japan's jealous protection of its own internal affairs against European interference.[154]

An article in *Novoe vremia*, entitled "The Yellow War and Its Consequences," warned: "[W]e look, with true alarm, at the emergence of a new world power thirty hours by sea from Vladivostok." The author continued: "[O]f course the strengthening of Japan at the expense of China scares us and makes us carefully consider our own military forces in the Amur region – the way it was before the emergence there of a new world power in the form of a Japan, triumphant on land and sea. Military glory and success in battle are too capable of intoxicating even old states, and because of this ability to intoxicate to the point of losing all prudence, one should fear a young state which has only just stepped out in the role of an enlightener, and partly perhaps, of a liberator for the numerous kindred yellow tribes of the East." The author expressed concerns of an incipient pan-mongolism. He concluded: "[T]he yellows are fighting; the whites must keep a sharp look out!"[155]

Russkie vedomosti published one of the clearest descriptions of the brewing conflict between Russian and Japanese aspirations in the Far East: "Korea, Manchuria and part of China – all of this must be the historical sphere of influence of the Japanese, who, by their geographic location and ethnographic make-up have a greater right to these areas than any other people, and even more so than a newly arrived people alien to East Asia, such as all the European peoples." The author continued, "Of these peoples – the Russians appear, from the point of view of the Japanese chauvinists, to have the fewest rights of all to the domination of East Asia; meanwhile the possessions of Russia have approached Korea itself; a Russian port has sprung up on the shores of the Sea of Japan; and the Siberian Railway, which is under construction, demonstrates the aspirations of Russia to link this great region more firmly to the central state and to strengthen Russian influence and trade in the Sino-Japanese region. However such aspirations run counter to the ideas and plans of the Japanese, and therefore – dream Japanese politicians – the Empire of the Rising Sun must take measures, while it is not too late, in order to guarantee its predominance in the closest parts of the east Asiatic continent and to strengthen its position *vis-à-vis* Russia." He concluded, "As soon as this is successful, it will not be – so they think – particularly difficult to appear more

---

[154] "Япония и Китай. Китайско-японская война" (Japan and China. The Sino-Japanese War), *Московские ведомости* (*Moscow Gazette*), no. 233, 26 August 1894 (7 September 1894), p. 3.

[155] "Жёлтая война и её последствия" (The Yellow War and Its Consequences), *Новое время* (*New Times*), no. 6672, 7 October 1894, p. 2.

decisive even against the aggressive aspirations of Russia, even take from her the Ussuri region and throw her out of eastern Siberia. Asia should belong to the peoples of Asia and the natural eastern border of Russia is the Ural Mountains."[156] Should the Japanese establish themselves in either Korea or Manchuria, the Russians feared that the next objective would be to expel the Russians from eastern Siberia. In fact, during the 1920s and 1930s, this idea did cross Japanese minds on more than one occasion, first during the Russian Civil War (1918–22), when Japanese troops occupied eastern Siberia and were reluctant to withdraw, and then again in 1939, during the Battle of Nomonhan on the Mongolian border, when the Soviet troops defeated Japanese forces.

By early 1895, security concerns had become widespread in the Russian press. Articles began appearing which demanded that Japan be prevented from securing territory on the Asian mainland.[157] Others went further. These included Prince Esper Esperevich Ukhtomskii, a publisher and strong advocate of Russian eastward expansion.[158] His ideas about the East had been shaped several years before the Sino-Japanese War, when he had accompanied then-tsarevich Nicholas on an Asian tour. The trip had included the assassination attempt on Nicholas in Japan.[159] Ukhtomskii devoted a long article in *Moskovskie vedomosti* to the impending Japanese (and continuing British) threat to Russian Asian interests.[160]

To resolve these new security concerns, there were renewed calls for the Russian acquisition of an ice-free port in the Far East. A reporter for *Russkie vedomosti* boldly stated: "It is not necessary even to mention the necessity of such a port, it is obvious in and of itself."[161] The article went on to recommend that such an

---

[156] D. A., "Японско-китайская война. Корея и русские интересы на Дальнем Востоке" (The Sino-Japanese War, Korea and Russian Interests in the Far East), *Русские ведомости* (*Russian Gazette*), no. 264, 24 September 1894 (6 October 1894), p. 3. Other articles also recognized the growing conflict between Russian and Japanese aspirations in the Far East. See "Японско-китайская война" (The Sino-Japanese War), *Русские ведомости* (*Russian Gazette*), no. 275, 5 October 1894 (17 October 1894), p. 3. The Ussuri River forms the easternmost section of the Russo-Chinese boundary. The Ural Mountains conventionally have been considered to be the boundary of European Russia.

[157] "Китай. Сообщение о намерениях держав" (China. Report about the Intentions of the Powers), *Московские ведомости* (*Moscow Gazette*), no. 31, 31 January 1895 (12 February 1895), p. 3; "Мировой прогресс и японцы" (Peace Settlement Progress and the Japanese), *Московские ведомости* (*Moscow Gazette*), no. 114, 27 April 1895 (9 May 1895), p. 2; "Война в Корее" (The War in Korea), *С-Петербургские ведомости* (*St. Petersburg Gazette*), no. 272, 18 October 1894.

[158] Paine, 202*n*.62.

[159] Paine, 202*n*.62.

[160] "Англо-японские виды на Китай" (The Anglo-Japanese Prospects for China), *Московские ведомости* (*Moscow Gazette*), no. 349, 20 December 1894 (1 January 1895), p. 2.

[161] "Незамерзающий порт на Дальнем Востоке" (An Ice-Free Port in the Far East), *Новое время*

ice-free port become the terminus for the Trans-Siberian Railway. The solution to Russia's security concerns would be territorial expansion. This did not take place in the manner envisioned in this article, but, as the Japanese had foreseen, the Trans-Siberian Railway did indeed have security ramifications aimed directly at them. An article written in the same newspaper less than a week later, in early April of 1895, was closer to the mark when it recommended that the Trans-Siberian Railway be run directly across Manchuria. This was exactly what happened.[162]

By the closing months of the war, the Russian press had reached the conclusion that Japan now posed a serious security threat to Russia and that expansion of Russia's Far Eastern railway system would be an appropriate countermeasure. Once the terms of the Treaty of Shimonoseki became known, such security concerns received front-page coverage with special emphasis given to the Japanese occupation of the strategic Liaodong Peninsula.

In late April and early May, *Moskovskie vedomosti* featured a series of long articles entitled, "Complications in the Far East," by an anonymous author who went by the description, "not a diplomat." These articles detailed the strategic implications of Japan's victory and provided summaries of contemporary British, French, German, and American press accounts.[163] One of these French newspapers pointed out that the war had changed the balance of power in the Far East.[164] "The truth is that Japan will demand as the prize for its victories some economic advantages which will give it a certain monopoly."[165] The Foreign Ministry's *Journal de St-Pétersbourg* quoted one formerly pro-Japanese French columnist: "Evidently, from the European point of view, this development of Japan, a people which was considered a negligible quantity and which shows itself invading, cannot but give rise to some anxieties or at least some reflections. If Europe wants to protect its position in the world, it would be desirable that she act with a

(*New Times*), no. 6847, 3 April 1895, p. 2. For other articles pointing to the need for an ice-free port in the Far East, see "Японско-китайская война" (The Sino-Japanese War), *Русские ведомости* (*Russian Gazette*), no. 275, 5 October 1894 (17 October 1894), p. 3.

[162] "Ещё о незамерзающем порте Дальнего Востока" (More on a Far Eastern Ice-Free Port), *Новое время* (*New Times*), no. 6852, 8 April 1895, p. 1.

[163] Не дипломат (Not a Diplomat), "Осложнения на Дальнем Востоке" (Complications in the Far East), *Московские ведомости* (*Moscow Gazette*), nos. 100–13, 13–26 April 1895 (25 April–8 May 1895), p. 2 or 3.

[164] Не дипломат (Not a Diplomat), "Осложнения на Дальнем Востоке" (Complications in the Far East), *Московские ведомости* (*Moscow Gazette*), no. 103, 16 April 1895 (28 April 1895), p. 2.

[165] Quoting a letter from Berlin originally printed in *Le Journal de Genève* (*Geneva Journal*), "Chine et Japon" (China and Japan), *Journal de St-Pétersbourg* (*St. Petersburg Journal*), no. 93, 20 April 1895, p. 2.

certain unity *vis-à-vis* peoples reputed to be barbarian and that she form a kind of syndicate."[166] The general conclusion of such articles was that Russia must redouble efforts to colonize the Russian Far Eastern territories and speed up the completion of the Trans-Siberian Railway.[167] Simultaneously, it would need to shore up its Far Eastern defenses.

As the war progressed and as the Japanese military forces surprised even themselves with the rapidity and completeness of their victories, their war aims grew accordingly. Within three months of the start of the war, Japan had achieved its initial objective to preempt others in Korea. By that time, the Japanese military was just hitting its stride and was not in the mood to quit. A subsidiary goal of the Japanese government had been to cement domestic support for the war in Korea and by extension to the ruling oligarchy in Japan. Its success in this so far exceeded expectations that the government could no longer easily limit its military objectives. Rather, the goals set by the Japanese military and demanded by the Japanese public grew in tandem with Japanese military successes. In the press interview of Count Ōkuma after the Battle of Gaiping, he noted "how the present war has suddenly raised Japan's status in the eyes of European Powers. Both by the prestige and the credit enjoyed by it, Japan has truly come to be regarded as the greatest Power in the Orient, and it has become necessary for her to enlarge her scope of action proportionately."[168] For Japan, its appetite for territory would grow with the eating. The diplomats rode a powerful wave of military and public support for an aggressive foreign policy. Under these circumstances, the diplomats concluded that a "bold policy" was in order. It would be designed to mobilize domestic public support for the Japanese government, not to reassure the powers to head off their possible intervention.[169] They did so despite obvious Russian displeasure. This strategy had culminated in the Treaty of Shimonoseki.

[166] M. Paul Leroy-Beaulieu, originally published in *l'Economiste français* (French Economist), "Chine et Japon" (China and Japan), *Journal de St-Pétersbourg* (*St. Petersburg Journal*), no. 110, 8 May 1895, p. 2.

[167] "Как ускорить постройку Сибирской дороги" (How to Speed up the Construction of the Siberian Railway), Московские ведомости (*Moscow Gazette*), no. 104, 17 April 1895 (29 April 1895), p. 2; Не дипломат (Not a Diplomat), "Осложнения на Дальнем Востоке" (Complications in the Far East), Московские ведомости (*Moscow Gazette*), no. 110, 23 April 1895 (5 May 1895), p. 3; "Колонизация нашего Востока" (Colonization of Our East), С-Петербургские ведомости (*St. Petersburg Gazette*), no. 277, 23 October 1894, p. 1; "В виду сибирской колонизации" (Concerning Siberian Colonization), С-Петербургские ведомости (*St. Petersburg Gazette*), no. 108, 6 May 1895, p. 1.

[168] Citing *Kokumin*, "Count Okuma Interviews," *The Japan Weekly Mail* (Yokohama), 26 January 1895, p. 88.

[169] Mutsu, 205.

Japanese policymakers may have believed that they had a chance of avoiding Russian intervention because key and destabilizing changes in the Russian leadership might make the Russia government more reluctant to take chances abroad. Alexander III died on November 1, 1894, at age forty-nine after a two-month illness. His son, Nicholas II, came to power at least two decades earlier than expected and was thoroughly unprepared educationally and emotionally to rule. Foreign Minister Nikolai Karlovich Girs had been seriously ill since 1892 but was persuaded to stay on by order of the tsar. He finally died on January 26, 1895, after a thirteen-year stint as foreign minister. He was replaced by a foreign minister *ad interim.*[170] A permanent replacement was not found until March 13, 1895, when the seventy-five-year-old Prince Aleksandr Borisovich Lobanov-Rostovskii took office.[171] According to Roman Romanovich Rozen, the future Russian minister to Japan (1897–9), the new foreign minister, "belonged to a generation whose ideas of China and Japan were mostly connected with pictures of pig-tailed mandarins on boxes of tea, or red lacquer cups and saucers brought home by bold travellers."[172] These personnel changes did put Russian foreign policy out of action for a time. Perhaps the Japanese diplomats believed that they could take advantage of the Russian situation.

Yet there was evidence that such a strategy might prove problematic. Since the end of 1894, the Russian government had been concentrating its naval forces in the Far East and deploying some of its land forces in Vladivostok.[173] In March of 1895, the Russian navy dispatched its Mediterranean squadron to the Far East.[174] In April the Russian army began to mobilize its land forces in the Russian Far East in preparation for an invasion of Manchuria.[175] At the time of the treaty ratification, Russia had thirty warships in Pacific waters.[176] It had consistently tried to discourage Japan from annexing any part of the Asian mainland. Instead, it hoped to deflect Japan's acquisitive impulses southward to Taiwan.[177]

---

[170] "The Whisper of the Throne," *The Pall Mall Gazette* (London), 28 January 1895, 4th ed., p. 1; "Death of M. de Giers," *The Pall Mall Gazette* (London), 28 January 1895, 4th ed., p. 7; Paine, 249; Malozemoff, 58–9. Alternate spellings for Girs include Giers and de Giers.

[171] Ford, 96–7.

[172] Roman Romanovich Rosen (Rozen), *Forty Years of Diplomacy,* vol. 1 (London: George Allen & Unwin, 1922), 134; Lensen, vol. 1, 492.

[173] For a list of Russian warships in Far Eastern waters, see "The Japanese and Russian Men-of-War," *The North-China Herald* (Shanghai), 24 May 1895, p. 795; Mutsu, 205, 222.

[174] Morse, vol. 3, 47.

[175] Lensen, vol. 1, 323.

[176] Lensen, vol. 1, 321.

[177] Mutsu, 225–7.

On April 23, six days after the signing of the Treaty of Shimonoseki, the ministers of Russia, Germany, and France called on the Japanese Foreign Ministry to offer some "friendly advice": They recommended that Japan return the Liaodong Peninsula to China on the grounds that Japanese possession of it "would be a constant menace to the capital of China, would at the same time render illusory the independence of Korea, and would henceforth be a perpetual obstacle to the peace in the Far East."[178] There is disagreement over whether the intervention was instigated by Germany or Russia. Given the disarray of the Russian foreign policy establishment at the time of the intervention, Germany seems the more likely mastermind.[179] From the outbreak of hostilities onward, the German press had consistently viewed the war in terms of its probable impact on Russia and Britain, Germany's two key rivals. Also from the beginning, the German press had assumed that the resolution of the conflict would entail European participation.[180] The ambitious thirty-six-year-old Kaiser Wilhelm II was determined to guarantee Germany a major helping during the anticipated post-war feast on a carved-up China. This was the same Kaiser Wilhelm who, in 1890, had fired Germany's greatest diplomat of the nineteenth century, the seventy-five-year-old Otto von Bismarck, the unifier of Germany and father of a stable European alliance system that took shape in the 1860s and did not disintegrate until Wilhelm landed Germany in World War I.

During the Sino-Japanese War, Kaiser Wilhelm II had sent his cousin, Tsar Nicholas II, an enormous allegorical painting depicting persons representing all of the European powers. The figures appeared against a backdrop of ominous storm clouds surmounted with a fiery image of Buddha. The painting was entitled, "The Yellow Peril."[181] However tacky the artwork, the message was clear: Russia must save Europe from the teeming peoples of the East just as it had done during the

---

[178] The oral memorandum presented by the Russian minister and cited in Mutsu, 203; Frank W. Iklé, "The Triple Intervention: Japan's Lesson in the Diplomacy of Imperialism," *Monumenta Nipponica* 22, no. 1–2 (1967): 125.

[179] Iklé, 122–30; Minge C. Bee (皮名舉), "Origins of German Far Eastern Policy," *The Chinese Social and Political Science Review* 21 (1937–38): 76; Ford, 110–18.

[180] See *Neue Preusische Zeitung* (*New Prussian Newspaper*) (Berlin), *passim; Königlich privilegirte Berlinische Zeitung* (*Royal Berlin Newspaper*), *passim; National Zeitung* (*National Newspaper*) (Berlin), *passim.* See especially, "Englische und russische Absichten in China" (English and Russian Intentions in China), *National Zeitung* (*National Newspaper*) (Berlin), 8 October 1894, p. 1. This article is the beginning of a series analyzing the geopolitical consequences of the war. See front-page articles in the morning issues for October 10, October 11, and November 24, 1894.

[181] Ian Littlewood, *The Idea of Japan: Western Images, Western Myths* (London: Secker & Warburg, 1996), 27–8, 209.

Mongol invasions in the thirteenth and fourteenth centuries. The underlying strategy was simple: Kaiser Wilhelm hoped to embroil Russia in the Far East to keep it out of Germany's way in Europe. France was pulled into the intervention by its prior alliance with Russia.[182] French weakness relative to Germany and French revanchism concerning Alsace-Lorraine, the territory lost to Germany during the Franco-Prussian War of 1870–1, had made the Russo-French alliance the cornerstone of French security. France felt compelled to follow Russia's lead in the Far East or jeopardize the alliance.

It was clear to Japanese diplomats that the three powers intended to intervene militarily if Japan did not go along. It did not take them long to conclude that the Japanese navy would be no match for the combined navies of the three. Should the powers become involved militarily, the Treaty of Shimonoseki would become a dead letter. Japan would lose not only the Liaodong Peninsula but also all of the other concessions contained in the treaty. For these reasons, Japanese diplomats rapidly concluded that they had no choice but to accede.

In an effort to keep "face," the Japanese tried to make the retrocession appear to be a "magnanimous gesture."[183] On May 10 the Meiji Emperor issued an imperial rescript: "By concluding the Treaty of peace, China has already shown her sincerity of regret for the violation of her engagements and thereby the justice of Our cause has been proclaimed to the world." He continued, "Under these circumstances, we can find nothing to impair the honour and dignity of Our empire if We now yield to the dictates of magnanimity and, taking into consideration the general situation, accept the advice of the friendly Powers."[184] The glaring fact – and the object of great discussion in the Japanese press – was that Japanese acquiescence did indeed directly "impair the honor and dignity" of Japan.[185] The palliative of an additional 30-million-Kuping-*tael* indemnity did little to mollify the Japanese public.

After Viceroy Li Hongzhang returned home, despite being stripped again of all of his offices save the honorary title of grand secretary, he was called in to negotiate the treaty retroceding the Liaodong Peninsula to China and it was finally

---

[182] Iklé: 122–30; Minge C. Bee (皮名舉), "Origins of German Far Eastern Policy," *The Chinese Social and Political Science Review* 21 (1937–8): 76.

[183] Mutsu, 203–20.

[184] For a text of the Imperial Rescript, see "Imperial Rescript," *The Japan Weekly Mail* (Yokohama), 18 May 1895, p. 565.

[185] "所謂三國同照今如何" (Current Status of the So-Called Triplice), 日本人 (*The Japanese*) (Tokyo), 24 July 1894, pp. 1–3.

signed in Peking on November 7, 1895.[186] No member of the Zongli Yamen would defile himself by negotiating with the Japanese.[187] For the return of the territory, China agreed to pay Japan an additional 30-million-Kuping-*tael* indemnity. Meanwhile, the Russian government wanted to make sure that Japan did not receive what it considered to be an "excessive indemnity," undoubtedly realizing that the Japanese would spend every bit of it on a military expansion program aimed at Russia. The Russians pressured China into demanding the expurgation of a clause in the draft retrocession agreement whereby China pledged not to cede the Liaodong Peninsula to any other power. The Russians correctly interpreted this clause to be aimed at them. The Japanese conceded this point, much to their later regret. Chinese and Japanese representatives signed the agreement on November 8, 1895, and the Japanese completed their evacuation on December 25, 1895. It was their Christmas present to the Christian nations that had intervened.[188] When the Japanese evacuated, they took with them the dockyard equipment and promptly installed it at the Japanese naval base at Sasebo.[189]

Back in May the Tokyo police had made the rounds at the various local newspaper offices to inform them that the *Official Gazette* was about to publish the text of the peace treaty and warned the reporters and editorialists not to vent any criticisms.[190] At the time, the Japanese public did not yet know the details of the settlement but seemed "to be aware that there is some hitch in the proceedings."[191] According to a report in the *Yorozu Chōhō* (万朝報), "the Government prohibited the newspapers publishing anything in connection with the reported modifications. Suspension often means ruination to some papers....Up to the present, forty-five papers of various kinds have been interdicted for publishing some meagre news about the matter...[T]he Government is trying everything in its power to extinguish the fire of popular indignation, while yet smouldering...The demands formulated by Russia are too preposterous. We might say that her actions are nothing short of piracy and such injustice as she desires to inflict upon us we must oppose. We are

---

[186] For a text of the agreement, see MacMurray, vol. 1, 50–3, 119–22, or "Convention between China and Japan for the Retrocession of Liao-tung," *The Peking and Tientsin Times*, 23 November 1895, p. 358.

[187] "The Japanese Commercial Treaty," *The Peking and Tientsin Times*, 12 October 1895, p. 334.

[188] Lensen, vol. 1, 330, 354. For the text of the retrocession agreement, see Kajima, *Diplomacy of Japan*, vol. 1, 382, or "Convention between China and Japan for the Retrocession of Liaotung," *The North-China Herald* (Shanghai), 29 November 1895, p. 912.

[189] "Extracts from 'Japan in Transition' by Stafford Ransome, 1899," Du Boulay, 11–2; Ransome, 280–1.

[190] "Muzzling the Press," *The North-China Herald* (Shanghai), 31 May 1895, p. 818.

[191] "Popular Feeling," *The North-China Herald* (Shanghai), 31 May 1895, p. 818.

determined to shed our blood to the last drop for this purpose."[192]

From the Japanese point of view, the Triple Intervention was outrageous. They believed the hostilities to have been a just war to protect Japan's vital interests on the Asian mainland. The war had demonstrated Japan's independence in international affairs after the dark years of the "unequal" treaties and had propelled Japan to equality with the other powers, which were no less acquisitive than Japan. The war had also anticipated a new role for Japan as the bearer of civilization and progress to its neighbors. The intervention proved these dreams to be premature, for Japan still lacked the military strength to ignore the powers even on vital national security issues. The Japanese concluded that the powers cared not a whit that Japan's cause was just.[193]

The Triple Intervention became public in Japan in the first week of May. After the initial shock, the reaction became one of *ganbaru* (頑張る) or of "grim determination to try harder the next time." *Jiji Shinpō* (時事新報) ran the headline, "Wait for another time." The editors advised their readers that "They must not forget that justice and sentiment find no place in modern diplomacy, but that all questions are in practice solved by mere brute force...[E]ven though there be grounds for complaint and dissatisfaction, let such sentiments be carefully concealed, so that no sign whatever of emotion may be visible to outsiders. Then while stout and persevering endeavours are made honestly and indefatigably to promote the practical interests of the country, its foundations will by degrees, and with the lapse of years, be so strengthened that the desire of the nation may be achieved, and the longed-for opportunity can be taken advantage of when it presents itself, as it will do sooner or later."[194] According to *Kokumin Shinbun* (国民新聞), "To lie on a bed of thorns and to taste gall, as the Chinese proverb goes, forever keeping one's great object in view, and biding one's time, that must be the course adopted by the Japanese people at the present juncture."[195] A reporter for *Nichinichi*

[192] "The Coalition between France, Germany and Russia," *The North-China Herald* (Shanghai), 31 May 1895, p. 841.

[193] John D. Pierson, *Tokutomi Sohō 1863–1947: A Journalist for Modern Japan* (Princeton: Princeton University Press, 1980), 238. Although Pierson is writing about Tokutomi, his comments on this matter apply more generally.

[194] Quoted in "The Spirit of the Vernacular Press during the Week," *The Japan Weekly Mail* (Yokohama), 11 May 1895, p. 522.

[195] Quoted in "The Spirit of the Vernacular Press during the Week," *The Japan Weekly Mail* (Yokohama), 11 May 1895, p. 522. For similar views, see "The Vernacular Press on the Treaty of Peace," *The Japan Weekly Mail* (Yokohama), 18 May 1895, p. 555. See also "如何にして平和條約の實效を見んとする乎" (How to Make the Peace Treaty Work Effectively), 國民新聞 (*People's Newspaper*) (Tokyo), 28 May 1895, p. 3.

Shinbun (日日新聞) concluded "that for diplomatic success the prime necessity is a sufficiency of military strength."[196] Similarly, a reporter for *Mainichi Shinbun* (毎日新聞) believed that "it was absolutely necessary for Japan to augment her navy, so that she may enjoy the supremacy of the sea in the East."[197] It was reported that forty Japanese committed *seppuku* or ritual disembowelment upon hearing the news of the retrocession of the Liaodong Peninsula.[198]

This hostility toward the government led to a wave of retaliatory press suspensions under the terms of the Press Law.[199] A reporter for *The Japan Weekly Mail* commented, "At no time since it began to exist has the Japanese press been subject to more stringent censorship than at present. Of the dozen leading dailies in the capital, as many as seven are under the ban of suspension...The impression left after careful perusal of the metropolitan journals is one of respect for the firm and united determination of the whole nation. The indignation of all classes and parties at the conduct of Russia and her allies is keen and intense...What is more noteworthy about the situation is that, instead of having recourse to excited agitation, the nation seems determined to proceed in a practical manner by increasing the strength of the Navy. All parties are agreed in thinking that the greater portion of the indemnity obtained from China should be employed for this purpose."[200]

Hostility toward the retrocession of the Liaodong Peninsula initially focused on the three intervening foreign powers, but it soon turned against the Japanese government. A reporter for *The Japan Weekly Mail* observed that "A few days ago the general tone of the Press was one of hostility to the triple coalition that obliged Japan to renounce the possession of the Liaotung Peninsula; now, however, the foreign policy of the Government is the principal object of attack." In disgust with their own diplomats, some papers praised the Chinese for their adroit diplomacy. Years later, this view still found resonance in Japan. According to the future Vice-Minister of Foreign Affairs, Count Hayashi Tadasu (林董), Viceroy Li had been an astute negotiator who "surrendered nothing which he was not prepared and glad to get rid of, except the indemnity. He always considered Formosa

---

[196] Quoted in "The Spirit of the Vernacular Press during the Week," *The Japan Weekly Mail* (Yokohama), 11 May 1895, p. 522.

[197] Quoted in "The Spirit of the Vernacular Press during the Week," *The Japan Weekly Mail* (Yokohama), 11 May 1895, p. 522.

[198] Calman, 20.

[199] "The Spirit of the Vernacular Press during the Week," *The Japan Weekly Mail* (Yokohama), 18 May 1895, p. 550. For similar views, see "The Vernacular Press on the Treaty of Peace," *The Japan Weekly Mail* (Yokohama), 18 May 1895, p. 555.

[200] "The Vernacular Press on the Treaty of Peace," *The Japan Weekly Mail* (Yokohama), 25 May 1895, p. 574.

[Taiwan] a curse to China, and was exceedingly pleased to hand it over to Japan, and he shrewdly guessed that Japan would find it a great deal more trouble than it was worth. In this he proved himself a true prophet, for even to-day (1915) the Japanese have not succeeded in pacifying Formosa, and insurrections are frequent, in spite of the drastic methods of the Japanese *gendarmerie*." Similarly, the Pescadores were also "useless to China." [201] Hayashi also believed that had not the Japanese negotiated the commercial privileges, the other powers soon would have – so in his mind, even this success was an illusion. Foster's diary does not bear out this interpretation of Li's views on Taiwan. After the intervention of the powers, Li had wanted to reopen the Taiwan issue but was dissuaded by Foster.[202]

Hayashi also believed that Li had ceded the Liaodong Peninsula to Japan realizing that the powers would not tolerate it. Li "was only too delighted to let Japan have the sensation of owning the place as a preliminary to the chagrin of losing it."[203] In this, Hayashi was probably right on the mark. Viceroy Li understood that the Russians would not permit the Japanese to annex the Liaodong Peninsula – the Russians had repeated this position on numerous occasions to Japanese diplomats. The latter, however, were unsuccessful in making their compatriots in the military see the futility of trying to retain the peninsula. So the Japanese military overplayed their hand and in doing so were far more effective at precipitating foreign intervention than Li had been on his own. With the retrocession of the Liaodong Peninsula, Li finally did succeed in making Japan lose face, but it was the most pyrrhic of victories. In the end there was humiliation for both parties.

The West did not understand the depth of Chinese and Japanese resentment over the war because they did not appreciate the full depth of the humiliation entailed from the loss of "face" for both: China's from its defeat and Japan's from its retrocession. What the general public did perceive was the astonishing success of Japan. As an indication of the popularity with which Japan was viewed in the West, at the time of the peace conference terminating the war, Field-Marshal Yamagata was receiving an average of seventy foreign letters per day congratulating him on the success of the war. Most of the mail came from Great Britain and the United States, but a significant percentage also came from Germany and France. To keep up with it, Field-Marshal Yamagata had hired nearly half a dozen

---

[201] Hayashi Tadasu, *The Secret Memoirs of Count Tadasu Hayashi*, A. M. Pooley, ed. (New York: G. P. Putnam's Sons, 1915), 57.

[202] Princeton University, Firestone Library, Rare Books, John Watson Foster collection, "Diary 30 January to 8 June 1895," 13 May 1895.

[203] Hayashi, 57.

translators.[204] Although the terminology did not exist at the time, Japan had become the first less-developed country to modernize successfully. Japan did so despite its own lack of natural resources, and its success became both the model and the rebuke for all other developing nations that were unable to emulate its rapid economic development. Before the war, there had been grave doubts in Western minds that it was possible for a non-Christian nation to modernize. Afterward, there was no doubt. Westerners recognized the enormity of the achievement and congratulated the Japanese. Sadly, it had taken a war for outsiders to appreciate the transformation underway in Japan.

Japan's miracle became China's great tragedy. Its triumph was China's humiliation. In a reversal of the millennia-old Far Eastern balance of power, Japan replaced China as the dominant power of Asia. China's many friends in Europe and America despaired of ever pulling it away from what they considered to be the path to self-destruction. The war broke the dikes and depleted the reservoir of foreign respect for China. What followed was a crass competition to vivisect the unresponsive patient into a welter of foreign spheres of influence. There followed decades of uninterrupted tragedy for China.

The Japanese drew important lessons from the war, namely, the powers could not care less about moral issues of right and wrong, the traditional concerns of Confucian ethics, and only through military prowess could Japan protect its national interests. Foreign Minister Mutsu concluded that "diplomacy shorn of military support will not succeed, however legitimate its aims might be."[205] For civil and military Japan, the overwhelming lesson of the Sino-Japanese War was that Japan must focus on enhancing its military power to insure its independence. The fruits of the Japanese victory a decade later in the Russo-Japanese War would be taken as further proof positive concerning the accuracy of this assessment.

Those in the West drew a different lesson from the war: Henceforth Japan would be a power to be reckoned with.

---

[204] "Field Marshal Yamagata," *The Japan Weekly Mail* (Yokohama), 27 April 1895, p. 471.
[205] Mutsu, 250.

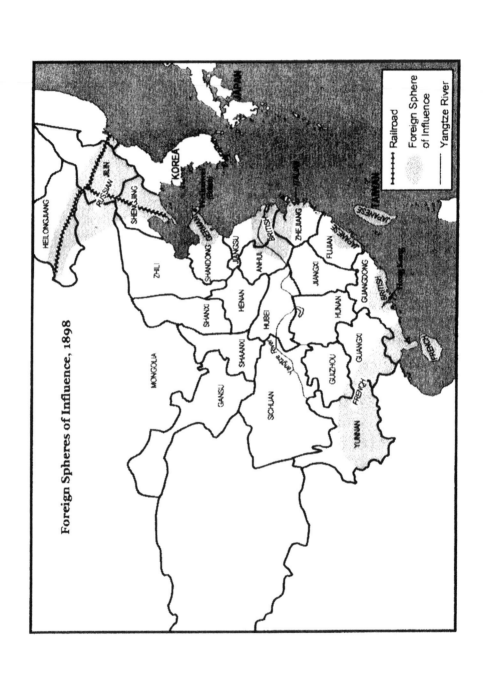

Foreign Spheres of Influence, 1898

8

The Era of Global Politics

A version of the old fable in which a wolf and a jackal quarrel over the prostrate form of a lamb, while an eagle hovers overhead prepared to pounce down so soon as the combatants have reduced themselves to a state of helplessness, is just now being reproduced in North-Eastern Asia. China and Japan are contending for supremacy in Korea, while...the Russians on the northern frontier are prepared to take part in the fray.[1]

The Japan Weekly Mail, September 1894

The present situation in the Far East is not the result of a gradual chain of events, but of the absolute surprise created by the unexpected results of the Chino-Japanese War. No doubt the collapse of China in 1894 was only the last act in a long drama of decadence, but it revealed to astonished Europe the utter incapacity of China either to reform or to defend herself, a fact for which we were quite unprepared...China had systematically fooled both Governments and public alike, who shared the same illusion as to her power...By dissipating these illusions and exhibiting to the world the truth concerning China's decrepitude, the Japanese victories produced almost the effect of an earthquake.[2]

Pierre Leroy-Beaulieu, writer, lecturer, world-traveler, 1900

With the Sino-Japanese War, Japan had achieved the key international goal that had precipitated three decades of Meiji reforms: It had acquired the status of an international power. Gone was the era of unequal treaties for Japan – but not for China. Westerners were falling over themselves to applaud Japan's successes. At the beginning of the war, there had been various predictions concerning the likely outcome, but no one had imagined the extent of Chinese weakness. Surely its vast

---

[1] "Suzerainty in Korea," *The Japan Weekly Mail* (Yokohama), 1 September 1894, p. 270.

[2] Leroy-Beaulieu, 242–3. For biographical details, see Lehmann, 184.

population and size would provide some compensation for the well-known weaknesses of its armed forces. Japan had gained its new-found prestige directly at the expense of the Chinese. This reversal in the traditional Far Eastern balance of power was the most far-reaching result of the war. The effects would be felt throughout the following century and beyond. Premier Itō Hirobumi (伊藤博文) exulted, "I think that the Sino-Japanese War is the greatest event since the beginning of our history." The journalist, Tokutomi Sohō (德富蘇峰), concurred: "Now that we have tested our strength we know ourselves and we are known by the world. Moreover, we know we are known by the world."[3]

Yet the war had not materially changed Chinese political institutions or its legal system. Most of the country had not been touched by the hostilities – life had gone on as usual in twenty out of twenty-four provinces and territories. The Japanese had obliterated China's modern military forces, but westerners had never considered these to be aimed at them. On the contrary, they had actively supported the westernization of the Chinese army and navy through the export of equipment and the furlough of officers to train Chinese forces. The key change resulting from the war took place not so much in the material circumstances of the Far East but in the Western perceptions of China and Japan and their perceptions of themselves. China's miserable showing had finally convinced westerners of the hopelessness of its domestic situation. In their minds, the evidence was now in. The matter was no longer debatable. The Chinese situation was terminal. Since the Chinese government was incapable of reform, each Western power would take independent action to protect its own interests and to preempt the others.

In reality, China's situation had been at least as hopeless before the war, when Chinese reformers such as the self-strengtheners had been voices in the wilderness. The war broke through the pre-war logjam that had prevented far-reaching reforms. In the past, educated Chinese could write off Caucasians and Slavs as depraved barbarians who would ultimately be brought to heel through sinicization in the manner of all obstreperous barbarians. Japan, however, presented a different case. For over 1,000 years, it had shared China's Confucian heritage and its Asian world. It was unprecedented for a former member of the Chinese world to abandon civilization in order to become like the West. Yet the "dwarfs" had broken the rules of filial piety to make war on their older brother, China. Worse still, the Japanese had relied on these foreign ways and had inexplicably defeated civilization

---

[3] Both Itō and Tokutomi are cited in Jansen et al., 190; Mark R. Peattie, "The Japanese Colonial Empire, 1895–1945," in *The Cambridge History of Japan,* John W. Hall, Marius B. Jansen, Madoka Kanai, and Denis Twitchett, eds., vol. 6 (Cambridge: Cambridge University Press, 1988), 221.

as the Chinese understood it.[4] In the Confucian order, this was an impossibility whose reality refuted bedrock assumptions underpinning China's way of perceiving the world. Civilization had failed.

The Chinese came to recognize that civilization was not singular but plural. Theirs was just one among a constellation of civilizations. This realization made them see the world in a very different light: The world was not a simple dichotomy between their civilization and the barbarity beyond. All ambitious peoples would not necessarily ever become sinicized. Sinicization was not an irreversible process. Peoples who disregarded the correct performance of ritual could win the day. Chinese civilization was not the font of all that was worthy in the world. Theirs was not the only way to interpret natural laws. On the contrary, Western technology was based on a completely different understanding of the natural world, an understanding that the Japanese had consciously acquired and used to great effect against China. Japan's victory had powerfully demonstrated the existence of a competing civilization to the Confucian order, a civilization that had an "ization" of its own: "westernization."

Defeat by Japan rattled Chinese confidence in their philosophical system in a way that no barbarian-imposed defeat ever could have done. For this reason defeat in the Sino-Japanese War, in contrast to the defeats in the Opium Wars, made such a profound impression on educated Chinese.[5] Military defeat vindicated the warnings of the Chinese reformers. During the war broad sectors of the literati concluded that China must change and must change radically.[6] Japan's total victory had irrefutably demonstrated the superiority of Western technology and military institutions. It is no coincidence that widespread talk of reform among the Chinese did not take place until after the war. Within two years, the emperor himself was in the thick of the reform movement of 1898. Thus, there was as radical a change in perceptions in China as in the West.

Western perceptions of Japan also made an about-face. Because of the war, the Western powers suddenly considered Japan to be one of them. Japan would participate in the post-war partition of China. Japanese political, military, and legal institutions had not actually changed materially during the hostilities. Certainly

---

[4] D. R. Howland, *Borders of Chinese Civilization: Geography and History at Empire's End* (Durham: Duke University Press, 1996), 233, 238–41; Benjamin Schwartz, *In Search of Wealth and Power: Yen Fu and the West* (Cambridge: Harvard University Press, 1964), 42–3, 49–50, 55; Jerome Ch'en, *China and the West: Society and Culture 1815–1937* (Taipei: Southern Materials Center, 1985), 270.

[5] Lone, 63; Y. C. Wang, *Chinese Intellectuals and the West 1872–1949* (Chapel Hill: University of North Carolina Press, 1966), 41, 43, 225–6, 233–49; Chu, "China's Attitudes," 81.

[6] Hu Sheng, 138.

the Japanese had suffered casualties and losses of equipment, but westerners never considered these forces antagonistic to them. In fact, Japan had possessed modern armed forces since the 1870s, when it had demonstrated its effectiveness during the suppression of the Satsuma Rebellion in 1877, the last gasp of the old samurai order. Those in the West, however, had not paid much attention to internal events in Japan until the Sino-Japanese War. As in the case of China, the revolution was not so much one in the material circumstances within the Far East as in Western perceptions of the Far East.

Finally, the revolution in perceptions extended to the Japanese. The Meiji reforms had entailed the rapid creation of modern institutions and then a gradual process of legitimizing them in the eyes of the Japanese population. The Diet–cabinet feuding before the war had indicated the incompleteness of the legitimization process. The cabinet did not respect the Diet or the political parties while the latter two had rarely cooperated with the cabinet. The war changed this. The Japanese people, although outraged by the Triple Intervention, were jubilant from their victory over China. They derived a strong sense of national unity from their foreign successes. The war had legitimized the Meiji reforms because the Meiji government had delivered in two crucial areas – treaty revision and military victory – and together these had made Japan an internationally recognized power. Domestically, this success vindicated the government's extensive westernization program and its quarter-century-long foreign policy of caution. Despite the enormous public pressure to do otherwise, the government had long eschewed foreign conflicts so that Japan could proceed with necessary domestic reforms. Success in war gave value to the years of patient nation-building. The war had unified the Japanese behind a common purpose and a shared chauvinism while victory had given their political institutions a legitimacy in their baptism by fire.[7] Although the war did not completely overcome divisions within the government, the national unity created by shared foreign policy goals during the hostilities had helped to ease the split. After the war, cabinet ministers were more inclined to create meaningful alliances with political parties, while the latter muted some of their criticism of the cabinet and supported arms appropriations.[8] The goals of the ruling oligarchy had not changed; rather, more members of the Diet embraced the methods chosen by the oligarchy to achieve these goals.

The war changed not only Japanese perceptions about themselves but also their perceptions of others. It permanently undermined a millennium of harmonious

[7] Jansen, *Japan and China,* 71.

[8] Lone, 178.

Sino-Japanese relations. Prior to the Meiji Restoration, the Chinese and Japanese had had a common written language of characters or *tongwen* (同文) and a shared high culture of gentlemen-scholars. The westernization of the Japanese school curricula had gradually eroded these common cultural bonds. Nevertheless, the positive image of Chinese civilization lingered.[9] One Japanese journalist recalled, "The China we children envisioned before the Sino-Japanese War...was noble, romantic, and heroic. China was never disparaged, never regarded spitefully, in any of the things we saw or the stories we heard."[10] Before the war, the Japanese had revered Chinese literati for their *belles-lettres* and Chinese high culture in general. These positive feelings were a casualty of the war. The Chinese wartime combination of breathtaking incompetence and pointless brutality had shattered the formerly positive Japanese image of them.[11] The past achievements of Chinese culture had not changed; rather, the Japanese were no longer interested in them. The Japanese had long been preoccupied with China and before the war had set their course in China's shadow.[12] The war marked the end of that era.

After the war, China would set its course in Japan's shadow. For China this was the most humiliating aspect of the war. Japan became a bone stuck in China's throat, where it has remained lodged, with varying degrees of inflammation and gagging, ever since. If the ascendancy of Japan in Asia made headlines in the West, it sent great seismic waves reverberating throughout China. Japan's victory shattered the lens through which China had been so long accustomed to viewing the world.

* * *

This revolution in the nebulous world of perceptions had very concrete consequences, not only for China and Japan but also for Korea and Russia and, by extension, for the world. International politics had become truly global in the sense that activities not directly involving the European powers could have a global impact, and events in one corner of the world no longer necessarily had strictly regional consequences. The reversal in the traditional balance of power between China and Japan had an immediate global impact through its consequences

---

[9] Howland, 231–3, 238–41; Keene, 122–5.

[10] Quoted in James L. Huffman, *Creating a Public: People and Press in Meiji Japan* (Honolulu: University of Hawai'i Press, 1997), 200.

[11] Keene, 126, 138–43; Shumpei Okamoto, "A Phase of Meiji Japan's Attitude toward China: The Case of Komura Juntarō," *Modern Asian Studies* 13, no. 4 (October 1979): 447; Henry Norman, *Contemporary Review*, republished as "The Question of Korea," *The Japan Weekly Mail* (Yokohama), 20 October 1894, pp. 462–3; Allan, 49; Morris, 400.

[12] David Pollack, *The Fracture of Meaning: Japan's Synthesis of China from the Eighth through the Eighteenth Centuries* (Princeton, NJ: Princeton University Press, 1986), 3.

for the reigning superpower of the pre–World War I period, Great Britain, and for the way it pursued empire.

Prior to the sinking of the *Kowshing*, the British outside Asia had not paid much attention to the brewing conflict in the Far East.[13] The influential *Pall Mall Gazette* had run various serial articles in June of 1894 on topics like "The Ideal Post Office" and "The Alps from End to End." With the opening of hostilities, however, it featured an alarmist series entitled, "Man the Fleet," which deplored the "dangerously weak" state of the British navy.[14] The British instantaneously recognized the implications of Japanese naval supremacy in the Far East. The day after the Battle of the Yalu, *The Pall Mall Gazette* provided the first installment of a front-page serial article entitled, "The Command of the Sea."[15] Other related front-page serials followed.[16] The paper noted: "The *Spectator* said not long ago that 'At no time in living memory has so much space been given by newspapers to the discussion of sea-power and sea-tactics and strategy.' Originally and above all, we have to thank the American Captain Mahan for helping us to the discovery that there is no question of the day so pressing or so momentous for England as her power at sea, actual and relative."[17] Surely the term "relative" referred to Japan.

---

[13] There were occasional articles, such as "The Kingdom of Korea," *The Pall Mall Gazette* (London), 8 June 1894, 4th ed., pp. 1–2; "The Situation in Korea," *The Pall Mall Gazette* (London), 30 June 1894, 4th ed., p. 8; "The March of Events in Korea," *The Pall Mall Gazette* (London), 3 July 1894, 4th ed., p. 7; "The Situation in Korea," *The Pall Mall Gazette* (London), 11 July 1894, 4th ed., pp. 1–2; "The Situation in Korea," *The Pall Mall Gazette* (London), 16 July 1894, 4th ed., p. 7; "The Situation in Korea," *The Pall Mall Gazette* (London), 4th ed., 19 July 1894, p. 7.

[14] "Man the Fleet–II," *The Pall Mall Gazette* (London), 8 September 1894, 4th ed., p. 1. This is just the second installment of a long series of articles.

[15] Spenser Wilkinson, "The Command of the Sea. – 1," *The Pall Mall Gazette* (London), 18 September 1894, 4th ed., p. 1. The seventh and last article in this series was published on October 11, 1894.

[16] See the serial entitled, "The Northern French Dockyards," *The Pall Mall Gazette* (London), 4 October 1894, 4th ed., p. 1. The concluding article appeared on November 19, 1894. See also, "Our New Battleships," *The Pall Mall Gazette* (London), 23 October 1894, 4th ed., p. 1; "The Command of the Sea," *The Pall Mall Gazette* (London), 21 November 1894, 4th ed., pp. 1–2; "The Command of the Sea," *The Pall Mall Gazette* (London), 22 November 1894, 4th ed., p. 1.

With the death of Tsar Alexander III on November 1, 1894, there was a hiatus on coverage of naval matters. Instead, *The Pall Mall Gazette* switched to various serials concerning Russia. Serials on the navy returned at the end of December with "Towards an Ideal Fleet," *The Pall Mall Gazette* (London), 20 December 1894, 4th ed., p. 1; "National Defence," *The Pall Mall Gazette* (London), 4 January 1895, 4th ed., p. 1; "Our Commerce in War," *The Pall Mall Gazette* (London), 3 January 1895, 4th ed., p. 1. The serial entitled, "Towards an Ideal Fleet," was still going strong with the ninth installment, published six months after the first. "Towards an Ideal Fleet," *The Pall Mall Gazette* (London), 18 June 1895, 4th ed., p. 1.

[17] *Spectator* cited by Frederick Greewood, "A Short Way to Set up the Navy," *The Pall Mall Gazette* (London), 26 October 1894, 4th ed., p. 3.

The development of a strong Japanese navy threatened that "command of the sea" which the British considered fundamental for their "national safety and prosperity."[18] After the great Japanese naval victory at the Yalu, the paper ran series after series on the deficiencies of the British navy. The editors clearly considered the existence of a modern and effective navy outside of Europe to constitute a direct threat to the British Empire, whose defense rested primarily on the navy.

After the Battle of Weihaiwei, the British took stock of the situation. *The Pall Mall Gazette* immediately published a long front-page article entitled, "The Lessons of the Naval War in the East." After making an urgent case for military modernization in Britain, the author concluded, "We have now to reckon with a new Power in the East, and a power which success may be expected to render aggressive. The addition of four or five Chinese warships to the Japanese fleet makes it formidable...We are manifestly the Power most affected, as we have colonies and commerce in every quarter of the earth."[19] In September 1895, a reporter for the London *Times* reflected: "Until little more than a twelvemonth ago Great Britain had enjoyed for upwards of 50 years...almost undisputed ascendancy in the Far East...Within the following 12 months the situation was completely changed."[20] Immediately after the war that had made Japan a power came the Triple Intervention, composed of Britain's major European rivals. Britain's nonparticipation in the Triple Intervention signaled the end of its policy of cultivating ties with the Chinese government pursued since the 1860s. This combination of war and intervention made the British government see the Far East in a whole new light. For the quarter-century after the war it would set its sights on Japan.[21] The article went on to stress "the community of interests which exist between the island empires of the West and the East."[22]

Before the Treaty of Shimonoseki had been ratified, there was already serious discussion in Britain of entering into an alliance with Japan.[23] This was a highly unusual proposition. The British had long cherished a foreign policy of "splendid

---

[18] *Spectator* cited by Frederick Greewood, "A Short Way to Set up the Navy," *The Pall Mall Gazette* (London), 26 October 1894, 4th ed., p. 3. See also "Is This the End, Is This the End?" *The Pall Mall Gazette* (London), 26 November 1894, 4th ed., p. 1; "How's That for Wai-Hei-Wai?" *The Pall Mall Gazette* (London), 2 February 1895, 4th ed., p. 1.

[19] "The Lessons of the Naval War in the East," *The Pall Mall Gazette* (London), 2 February 1895, pp. 1–2.

[20] "England's Position before and after the War," *The Times* (London), 24 September 1895, p. 3.

[21] Paul Baker Remmey, "British Diplomacy in the Far East, 1892–1898" (Ph.D. diss., Harvard University, 1964), 86.

[22] "England's Position before and after the War," *The Times* (London), 24 September 1895, p. 3.

[23] "An Anglo-Japanese Alliance," *The North-China Herald* (Shanghai), 3 May 1895, p. 645.

isolation" unencumbered by any foreign alliances. Between 1815 and 1914, Britain had only one formal alliance:[24] Britain, the reigning superpower of the nineteenth century, signed this treaty of alliance with Japan in 1902 and related treaties in 1905 and 1911.[25] More than anything, this alliance concretely demonstrated that Japan had indeed become a world power.[26] The debut of the Japanese navy would help spur an international naval competition and frenzy of naval expansion.[27]

* * *

The revolution in perceptions caused by the war had a devastating impact on the traditional political order in China and Korea. The post-war situation in China was grim. The powers had not permitted Japan to finish off the Qing Dynasty with a march to Peking, since their treaty rights all hinged on the perpetuation of the dynastic status quo. Instead, the dynasty had a lingering death over the following decade and a half. The war left the economies of several provinces devastated, the country indebted, the Manchus discredited, and national defenses utterly compromised.

In the spring of 1895, a French missionary reported that famine in Manchuria seemed imminent: In June of 1894, there had been severe flooding in the great Manchurian plain between Yingkou and Mukden. The high waters had only partly destroyed the wheat and barley crops, but they had devastated the main crops of millet, peas, and sorghum. Once the war had started, the Japanese had then used up the rest of the crop to feed their pack animals and cavalry horses. This suggests that the story of the Japanese army's always having paid as it went was not uniformly the case. Between the Chinese and Japanese armies, the peasantry had lost their seed and their work animals. Worse still, they had little means of getting through the five months until harvest time.[28] In April 1895, there were reports from Tianjin of starvation.[29]

Before the war, China had relatively little foreign debt. During the hostilities, its indebtedness had risen to £7 million. Afterward, the payment of the indemnity to Japan and the costs for rebuilding the country made its debts rise to £48

[24] Paine, 219–25.

[25] A. Gérard, *Ma Mission en Chine (1893–1897)* (Paris: Librarie Plon, 1918), 52; Chung-fu Chang, *The Anglo-Japanese Alliance* (Baltimore: Johns Hopkins Press, 1931), 269–81. For the text of the 1902, 1905, and 1911 agreements, see Chang, 282–91; MacMurray, vol. 1, 324–5, 516–18, 900–1.

[26] Clement, 153–6.

[27] For a table showing naval expansion for 1896, see Cooling, 136.

[28] "The Famine in South Manchuria," *The Japan Weekly Mail* (Yokohama), 25 May 1895, p. 583.

[29] "Tientsin," *The North-China Herald* (Shanghai), 26 April 1895, p. 623.

million.[30] The Empress Dowager Cixi (慈禧太后) allegedly coughed up nearly 13 million *taels* as her personal contribution to the indemnity. The British inspector-general of the Imperial Maritime Customs oversaw the financing of the indemnity, so that the Chinese lost financial autonomy as well.[31]

The Sino-Japanese War was the beginning of the end for imperial China. The rapid defeat discredited the Qing Dynasty both at home and abroad. The Manchus had demonstrated gross incompetence in governance. For many Chinese, the dynasty had lost its mandate to rule and its demise was considered to be a matter of time. To many in the West, the results of the war made clear that the next phase would be the partition of China, and they no longer had many qualms about doing so. In February 1895, Charles Denby, the American minister to China, had pinpointed the fatal flaw of Li Hongzhang's (李鴻章) strategy of courting foreign intervention: "To my view there is no good for China in foreign intervention. It is more likely to produce dismemberment than any action that may be taken by Japan. Unless Russia, and England, and France are more disinterested than history shows them to be they will each demand heavy compensation for any services rendered to China."[32] Events bore him out.

Previously, Spain, Portugal, the Netherlands, Russia, Great Britain, and France had all carved out empires in Asia. After the war, Japan and Germany also took seats at the banquet table. In summarizing the significance of the war for China, a report in *The North-China Herald* described China as an imperial anachronism "doomed to disappearance." The author concluded that "[China] has lost her prestige which was nothing but the shadow of a great name; that she lies exposed as a carcass in the neighbourhood of which a cloud of eagles is hovering; that her independence is gone for the moment, and that on pain of permanent extinction as an autonomous Power she must submit to a prolonged tutelage."[33] He correctly anticipated the scramble for concessions, the inability of the dynasty to reform itself, the demise of the dynasty, and a continuing Chinese unwillingness to follow much Western advice. "Whatever be the terms upon which she may obtain peace, she will, we feel assured from our previous experience, speedily set out evading her obligations."[34] In April 1895 a reporter working for *Le Journal des débats politiques et littéraires* predicted, rather ominously from a Chinese point of

---

[30] Leroy-Beaulieu, 253–4.

[31] "An Imperial Edict," *The North-China Herald* (Shanghai), 10 May 1895, p. 683.

[32] Cited in Treat, vol. 2, 525.

[33] "The Problem of China's Fall," *The North-China Herald* (Shanghai), 5 April 1895, p. 504.

[34] "The Problem of China's Fall," *The North-China Herald* (Shanghai), 5 April 1895, p. 504.

view, "We are at a turning point in economic history."[35] This would certainly be true for China.

A later report in *The North-China Herald* predicted that reform was no longer possible for China. Enough power had devolved onto the provinces to preclude a centrally orchestrated reform program. As for a bottom-up reform from the provinces, "The provincial officials have not felt the direct stress of the war, and they do not understand one very important thing. Foreign Powers before last year accepted very inadequate reparation for outrages [the murder of missionaries, etc.] because they had a belief in the latent strength of China and were unwilling to push their demands to the bitter end. They know better now, and they, it is to be hoped, will make no demands of which they will not exact the fulfillment to the letter. This must end before very long in the disruption of China."[36] Henceforth foreigners would drive a much harder bargain.

Post-war views concerning the power of China and the likelihood for reforms led the powers to conclude that there was nothing to stop them from descending on the country *en masse*. They also could see no alternative to doing so. If the Chinese could not run their own affairs, then the powers would subdivide the country and each administer those areas within its own sphere of influence. The general post-war contempt for China had removed any prior qualms about carving up the country. Actually, the powers felt their decisions were morally justified in the face of rotting Chinese political institutions.

France, the least enthusiastic participant in the Triple Intervention, was the first to cash in.[37] On June 20, 1895, it secured an agreement adjusting the Chinese-Tongking (東京, northern Vietnam)[38] boundary in its favor, opening three new treaty ports, reducing tariffs for the Tongking trade, and acquiring the right of first refusal to develop mines in the three Chinese provinces bordering on Tongking: Yunnan, Guangxi, and Guangdong. In March 1896, a French company acquired a thirty-six-year railway concession for a line to run from Langson,[39] a city in

---

[35] "Les conséquances économiques de la guerre sino-japonaise" (Economic Consequences of the Sino-Japanese War), *Le Journal des débats politiques et littéraires* (*Journal of Political and Literary Debates*) (Paris), 10 April 1895, p. 1.

[36] "The Future of China," *The North-China Herald* (Shanghai), 14 June 1895, p. 898.

[37] For texts of these and all of the other concession agreements, see MacMurray, vol. 1. The table of contents provides a very convenient chronological list of the agreements.

[38] Alternate spellings include Tonkin. Tongking refers to northeastern Vietnam, while Annam refers to the eastern coast of Vietnam south of Tongking. John K. Fairbank, Edwin O. Reischauer, and Albert M. Craig, *Far East: Tradition and Transformation*, rev. ed. (Cambridge, MA: Harvard University Press, 1989), 605.

[39] An alternate spelling is Liang-shan.

northern Vietnam, across the frontier to Longzhou (龍州), Guangxi. The next year, France secured a nonalienation agreement for Hainan, the enormous island located off the shores of Guangdong Province. In 1898, it acquired a lease for Guangzhou Bay (廣州灣), Guangdong on the Gulf of Tongking; a railway concession from Tongking to Kunming (昆明),[40] Yunnan; the right to extend the Tongking railway to Nanningfu (南寧府) in the border province of Guangxi; and a Chinese guarantee not to alienate Guangdong, Guangxi, or Yunnan to another power. In other words, France acquired a sphere of influence in three out of the eighteen provinces of intramural China. These were the provinces abutting its colony in Indo-China, which France had acquired piecemeal from 1859 to 1885 and where France would remain until the Vietnamese were finally able to expel them in 1954, only to endure the Americans in the southern half of Vietnam until 1975.[41]

In October 1895, Germany started to cash in. It acquired two small concessions, one in Hankou (漢口) on the Yangtze River and the other on the coast at Tianjin. Two years later, Germany went whole hog. It carved out a sphere of influence composed of Shandong Province and including the excellent harbor at Jiaozhou Bay (膠州灣) with its port city of Qingdao (青島).[42] On November 14, 1897, Germany acquired a ninety-nine-year lease for the port and port city and in March of 1898 other railway and mining concessions in Shandong. These Germany retained until losing the World War I, when Japan oversaw their return to China.[43]

Russia was the last member of the Triple Intervention to collect on services rendered. In March of 1895, before the peace terms were known or the Triple Intervention contemplated, there was already talk in Russia of running the final link of the Trans-Siberian Railway directly through Manchuria for a straight shot from Lake Baikal to Vladivostok.[44] At the time of the Triple Intervention, members of the British press speculated that the Russians might run the railway through the northern Manchurian province of Heilongjiang.[45] *The Peking and Tientsin Times* had accurately predicted that the price for Russian aid in securing the return of the

---

[40] Kunming was located in the district of Yünnanfu (雲南府).

[41] Fairbank et al., *East Asia*, 603–6.

[42] Alternate spellings for Jiaozhou include Chiao-chou and Kiaochow. Alternate spellings for Qingdao include Ch'ing-tao and Tsingtao.

[43] Bruce A. Elleman, *Wilson and China: A Revised History of the Shandong Question* (Armonk, NY: M. E. Sharpe, 2002). The book is to be published in the summer of 2002. It describes President Woodrow Wilson's role in the return of the German concessions to China after World War I.

[44] "The War in the East," *The Times* (London), 16 March 1895, p. 7; "Corea and Russia," *The North-China Herald* (Shanghai), 6 December 1895, p. 933.

[45] "How Are the Mighty Fallen!" *The North-China Herald* (Shanghai), 10 May 1895, p. 691.

Liaodong Peninsula would be payment "in privileges to Russia – Siberian railway concession – Port Arthur Fleet Anchorage – and, probably, in the long run, the whole prize gulped down by the Bear."[46] There were even rumors that the Russians had already seized Port Arthur.[47] Over the summer of 1895, the Chinese government got wind of the scheme.[48] Russia held off for three more years.

In 1896, both the Grand Secretary Li Hongzhang and Marshal Yamagata Aritomo (山県有朋) attended the coronation ceremonies for Nicholas II in Moscow. Russian treatment of their guests demonstrated that they had mastered the rules of "face" to a much greater extent than had the other Europeans. They assigned Grand Secretary Li the place of honor in the congratulating procession for the coronation while they virtually ignored Marshal Yamagata. In addition, the Japanese learned that the Russians had extended to Li the honor, in principle accorded only to foreign princes, of covering all of his traveling expenses. The matter became a sufficient irritant for the Japanese to question Foreign Minister Aleksandr Borisovich Lobanov-Rostovskii directly.[49] The Russians felt no compunction about adding insult to injury in the form of diplomatic snubs following close upon the Triple Intervention. The Japanese heard the implicit message loud and clear: Russia would deal with China but not Japan. In the West, such ceremonial details were considered to be of secondary importance; in Asia, they were the vernacular of foreign relations. Russia understood this. In the particular case of Nicholas II, he had survived a Japanese assassination attempt just five years earlier and thereafter had referred to the Japanese as monkeys.[50] Only after the Russo-Japanese War did he learn that contempt based on a miscalculation of power had its price.

During the coronation festivities, the diplomatic treatment mirrored the negotiations underway. Both Grand Secretary Li Hongzhang and Marshal Yamagata Aritomo took advantage of the occasion to negotiate secret agreements with Russia. It seems that the negotiations with Japan were instigated by Japan while those with China were instigated by Russia. In the previous month, on May 14, 1896, representatives from Japan and Russia had signed the Komura-Veber Agreement,

---

[46] "The Liao-tung Treaty," *The Peking and Tientsin Times,* 26 October 1895, p. 342; "The Liao-tung Treaty," *The Peking and Tientsin Times,* 16 November 1895, p. 354.

At the time of the Triple Intervention, *The Peking and Tientsin Times* had predicted that the three intervening powers would seek a payback. "Russia, as we have repeatedly pointed out, is setting some advantages for her railway on the Amoor [Amur River]." ("The War – The Situation," *The Peking and Tientsin Times,* 25 May 1895, p. 255).

[47] "More Rumours," *The North-China Herald* (Shanghai), 31 May 1895, p. 820.

[48] Kuo, 185–92.

[49] Lensen, vol. 2, 502, 628, 630–7. For the text of this agreement, see McKenzie, 301.

[50] Ford, 11.

to create an uneasy *modus vivendi* in Korea. Both countries acquired equal rights to advise the king of Korea, while Russia secured the right to deploy equal numbers of troops in Seoul.[51] At the coronation festivities, representatives from the two countries concluded the Lobanov-Yamagata Protocol on June 9, 1896. This was another attempt to establish a *modus vivendi* in Korea, but it also satisfied neither party. The treaty empowered both powers to encourage the Korean government to reform while a secret clause set conditions in the event that either party desired to deploy troops in Korea. Russia was given the right to guard the king, a right that came in very handy before too many months had passed.[52]

Meanwhile, Grand Secretary Li was negotiating a portentous alliance with Russia. Lord Curzon had quite correctly predicted that war could "drive China into the arms of Russia who would have much to gain by such an arrangement" and "confront Japan with an alliance that she would then regret to have provoked."[53] On June 3, 1896, after numerous Russian threats and ultimatums, China signed a secret treaty of alliance whereby Russia agreed to protect China from Japan in return for a huge railway concession in Manchuria to complete the Trans-Siberian Railway. This was just as some newspapers had anticipated. Moreover, the railway would be built with the wide-gauge track in use in Russia, not the narrow-gauge track used in China.[54] This meant that the new railroad would be integrated with the Russian and not the Chinese railway system. The concession would cut a 300- to 400-mile-deep swath across Manchuria along the hypotenuse of the triangle created by the big northward arc of the Amur River and would comprise over 1,000 miles of track. The future Russian minister to Japan expressed satisfaction at the arrangement: "Adequate compensation for our successful intervention...was found in the grant by China of the right of way through Northern Manchuria to our Trans-Siberian Railway."[55]

Thereafter Nicholas II sent an emissary to Peking bearing gifts to the Emperor

---

[51] Malozemoff, 85–7; Eckert et al., 224; Lensen, vol. 2, 589, 625–6. For the text of the agreement, see McKenzie, 299–300; Kajima, *Emergence of Japan,* 68, or E. D. Grimm, Сборник договоров и других документов по истории международных отношений на Дальнем Востоке *(1842–1925)* (*Collection of Treaties and Other Documents on the History of International Relations in the Far East [1843–1925]*) (Moscow: Издание Института Востоковедения Москва им. Н. Н. Нариманова, 1927), 106. The Japanese signatory was Komura Jūtarō (小村寿太郎), the Japanese minister to Korea.

[52] Lensen, vol. 2, 502, 628, 630–7. For the text of the agreement, see Ibid., 634–5.

[53] "The Chino-Japanese War," *The Pall Mall Gazette* (London), 2 August 1894, 4th ed., p. 7.

[54] Lensen, vol. 2, 503–5. For a copy of the agreement, see Grimm, 105–6; MacMurray, vol. 1, 81–2, 74–7.

[55] Rosen, 139.

and Empress Dowager. These surpassed anything ever given to China by a European monarch. The forty-eight crates included large lapis lazuli vases, golden cloisonné goblets, a diamond diadem, a silver dressing table, and one large diamond to adorn the hats of each member of the Zongli Yamen.[56] What more visible gift could have been chosen for the yamen members? The Russians understood Eastern gift-giving etiquette.[57] They had given "face" to all of the relevant parties. The Russians also lavished bribes on the Chinese officials overseeing the railway negotiations, including and especially Li Hongzhang.[58] Then, on March 27, 1898, during the same month when Germany was rounding out its sphere of influence in Shandong, Russia acquired a twenty-five-year lease for the Liaodong Peninsula, the very lease that China had secured this alliance to protect. Russia also added a railway concession to connect the Liaodong Peninsula's warm-water ports of Dalian and Port Arthur to the Manchurian railway system at Harbin. The southern line very inauspiciously traversed the hallowed grounds of Mukden in the vicinity of the Qing imperial tombs and added another 709 miles of track. The 1896 Russo-Chinese agreement did not turn out to be much of an alliance. Within two years, the Russian occupation of the Liaodong Peninsula had undermined the rationale for its creation. Russia would only return the last of these concessions to China in 1955.

The Manchurian railway concessions made Russia by far the largest concession holder in China. A distant second was France, with the 289-mile-long Yunnan Railway.[59] Contrary to the general impression that Great Britain was the most voracious imperialist in China, in terms of territory, without question, the honor belonged to Russia. Great Britain was simply China's largest trading partner. Great Britain belatedly joined the scramble for concessions. In 1897, it secured adjustments to conventions related to Burma and Tibet.[60] In February 1898, China agreed not to alienate territory on the Yangtze River. After Russia took Port Arthur on the northern shores of the Bohai, England responded on October 5, 1898, by taking Weihaiwei on the southern shores. Its lease was specifically made coterminous with that of Russia for the Liaodong Peninsula. This made Russia and Great Britain the sentinels on the sea approaches to Peking. On May 13, 1898, Britain acquired the Shanghai-Nanjing railway concession. On June 9,

[56] Lensen, vol. 2, 507–8.

[57] Mayfair Mei-hui Yang, 3, 6, 67–8, 70, 130–2, 142–4.

[58] Lensen, vol. 2, 510–2.

[59] Paine, 186–94.

[60] Kuo, 181–5.

1898, it negotiated a ninety-nine-year lease of the New Territories to the north of Hong Kong beyond Kowloon. On April 28, 1899, Britain and Russia exchanged notes whereby Russia agreed not to seek railway concessions in the Yangtze River Basin while Britain pledged not to seek any north of the Great Wall.[61] The Russian sphere of influence potentially included not only Manchuria but Mongolia and Xinjiang as well, while the British sphere included the Yangtze River Basin, concessions in the many treaty ports dotting China's coast, and the former Chinese tributaries of Burma and Tibet. Britain also secured mining agreements for Shanxi (Shansi), Henan, and Sichuan Provinces. Finally, Belgium acquired the Peking-Hankou railway concession in June 1897 while the United States secured a concession for the Canton-Hankou Railway in 1898. The final British and American concessions were not relinquished to China until 1943, when the vicissitudes of war made Chinese cooperation more valuable to the West.

Japan, whose military victory had made this post-war feeding frenzy possible, was the last to demand a slice of China proper. In 1898 it acquired a nonalienation agreement for Fujian, the mainland province opposite Taiwan, and a concession in Shashi (沙市),[62] Hubei on the Yangtze River.[63] This had been one of the cities that Japan had included in its original demands during the negotiations at Shimonoseki but had subsequently deleted.

It would take decades for the foreign powers to develop these numerous concessions. An 1899 estimate indicated that although just 317 miles of track had been laid in China, 2,270 miles were under construction.[64] Over the following century, the Chinese would complain bitterly about these foreign concessions. Yet they gained thousands of miles of infrastructure. When the foreigners left, the railways and the treaty-port facilities remained.

This period quite aptly became known as "the scramble for concessions."[65] The term had actually been coined earlier in reference to the partition of Africa.[66] The scramble for concessions proves that perceptions matter. The Sino-Japanese War had fundamentally altered European perceptions of the power of China and Japan. These changed perceptions produced concrete results: They led to Japan's 1902 alliance with Britain and to China's vivisection by the powers.

In 1898, Demetrius Charles Boulger, an expert on China, predicted: "The

---

[61] Lensen, vol. 2, 833.

[62] Alternate spellings include Shasi.

[63] Kuo, 206.

[64] Robertson-Scott, 46–60.

[65] For information concerning the scramble, see Kuo, 181–92, 206; Robertson-Scott, 46–60.

[66] "The Scramble for Africa," *The Times* (London), 29 December 1894, p. 5.

division of the Chinese Empire into what practically amounts to spheres of influence implies that it is moribund, and that the Manchu dynasty which has been in existence for 250 years approaches the term of its power."[67] In 1900, the author, Alexander Michie, who had accompanied Gustav Detring on the first Chinese peace mission to Japan in late 1894, described the post-war treatment of China as more of a "process of unsettlement than resettlement" and quite accurately predicted that "no man now living is likely to see the end of the dislocation effected by the transactions of 1895." He considered the Triple Intervention to be "a remedy which was worse than the disease" because the powers "began whetting their knives to carve the moribund carcass...[and because] China ceased to be a free agent; she became a vassal, and not to one Power only."[68] The war marked an end to Chinese sovereignty and the beginning of far more intrusive foreign intervention.

The war seemed to bring out the worst characteristics of the Chinese political order. During the negotiations at Shimonoseki, Premier Itō Hirobumi had questioned one of the Chinese translators, Luo Fenglu (羅豐祿), a brilliant man who had been educated in the West and had a broad knowledge of Western literature. Premier Itō wondered why China had not learned more from the West, to which Luo responded, "You see, in our younger days we knew each other as fellow-students, and now you are Prime Minister in your country and I am an interpreter in mine."[69] In Japan, those with foreign expertise rose to the top while in China such persons were relegated to inferior positions. People like Luo fully understood the tragedy of their situation. It took the Treaty of Shimonoseki and the scramble for concessions to make many high government officials and Han literati understand the dire implications of the war. During the hostilities, internal factions had used the war to further their own personal political ambitions. For instance, many of the numerous officials, long opposed to self-strengthening and westernization, had used the war to undermine Li Hongzhang's power base rather than to respond creatively to the Japanese threat. The split in the royal household between the Emperor and Empress Dowager factions had only exacerbated the problem.

The war finally destroyed the old consensus among the literati of adamant opposition to self-strengthening as a form of spiritual pollution.[70] Ironically, the modernization measures that Li Hongzhang had so long promoted and over so much opposition became widely accepted as a result of the war that had destroyed

---

[67] Boulger, vol. 2, 546.

[68] Michie, vol. 2, 417–8.

[69] Quoted in Lensen, vol. 1, 239.

[70] Hsü, *China's Entrance*, 168–71; J. D. Frodsham, *The First Chinese Embassy to the West: The Journals of Kuo Sung-t'ao, Liu Hsi-hung and Chang Te-yi* (Oxford: Clarendon Press, 1974).

his career. While the man suffered a political eclipse, many of his ideas lived on. Not only did many officials become interested in the military gadgetry of the West, but some turned their attention to the philosophical and economic underpinnings.[71] The war represented a vital turning point for the Chinese; it marked the terminal phase of the Confucian order and the gathering momentum of various reform schemes.[72]

There was a growing realization that China required a modern infrastructure and functionaries with westernized training. At the time of the war, Japan had laid over 2,000 miles of railway lines to China's 100 miles.[73] By the end of the war, the necessity of railway construction had finally become apparent to the Chinese government, which had so long resisted its development. After the defeat at Weihaiwei, the Guangxu Emperor (光緒皇帝) acceded to a memorial requesting to build a line between Peking and the Yangtze river provinces. Reuter's Agency reported, "The reason given for the memorial was a comparison between the ease with which the Tientsin [Tianjin] railway had transported troops during the war to Shanhaikuan and the difficulties and tardiness of the overland march from the south, in the absence of railways."[74] Also as a result of the war, the language school in Peking, the *Tongwenguan* (同文館), belatedly added Japanese to the curriculum. Previously it had offered English, Russian, and German as well as a variety of Western technical subjects. Other educational reforms followed. The Imperial University of Peking was founded in 1898 to become the leading educational institution in China.[75] The war also led to the development of a modern press in China, so that more information about domestic and foreign politics became available to the literate public. The post-war proliferation of newspapers also provided a wider forum for public debate.[76]

The tragedy for China was that the change in outlook came too little and too late. Long before the war, the reforms necessary for China seemed painfully obvious to westerners. A few more railways would not be sufficient. In their minds, China required a thorough overhaul of its political, legal, educational,

---

[71] Wang, 51; Kamachi, 191; Daniel H. Bays, *China Enters the Twentieth Century: Chang Chih-tung and the Issues of a New Age, 1895–1909* (Ann Arbor: University of Michigan Press, 1978), 19–24.

[72] Douglas R. Reynolds, *China, 1898–1912: The Xinzheng Revolution and Japan* (Cambridge, MA: Harvard University Press, 1993), 1.

[73] "Summary of News," *The North-China Herald* (Shanghai), 12 October 1894, p. 595.

[74] "Fall of Weihaiwei" *The North-China Herald* (Shanghai), 8 February 1895, p. 171.

[75] Chow, 62–3.

[76] Joan Judge, *Print and Politics: 'Shibao' and the Culture of Reform in Late Qing China* (Stanford: Stanford University Press, 1996), 19–24.

social, military, and economic institutions – a daunting task under the best of circumstances, let alone the worst. Valentine Chirol, the globe-trotting director of the Foreign Department of the London *Times* and author of numerous books, traveled to China right after the war. He sadly concluded, "Nowhere in Peking could the faintest indication be detected of a desire to apply, or even of a capacity to understand, the lessons of the recent war." He found it difficult to imagine a "more hopeless spectacle of fatuous imbecility, made up in equal parts of arrogance and helplessness, than the central Government of the Chinese Empire presented after the actual pressure of war had been removed...In and above all things the central Government had to 'save its face' – *i.e.,* to maintain those immutable forms and appearances which, in the private as well as in the public life of the Chinese, having nothing to do with realities, but entirely overshadow them."[77] Westerners forgot that their own Industrial Revolution had taken place over the course of a century. They demanded that China telescope these wrenching changes into a few decades. Because Japan had done so, their expectation now seemed perfectly reasonable. Henceforth, Japan became the yardstick by which China always fell short.

The Chinese were not about to share with westerners their soul-searching after the war. Chirol and others did not appreciate the change in attitudes caused by the hostilities. While the scramble was at full tilt, the Guangxu Emperor decided once again to take matters into his own hands. Empress Dowager Cixi seems to have continued her strategy of acting as his enabler: She reeled out more rope for him to hang himself. He outlined a far-reaching reform program, the so-called Hundred Days' Reform of 1898. The proposed changes in the educational system, governmental administration, and finance stirred up a hornet's nest of vested interests. In the absence of provincial support, the program succumbed to intrigues in Peking. This time, the Empress Dowager was able to put the emperor under house arrest for the duration of his reign and to reinstate herself until her death in 1908. Interestingly, the Guangxu Emperor died the day after her demise. One can only speculate on the connection.

The house arrest of the Guangxu Emperor did not seal the fate of reform in China. On the contrary, many of the more moderate reforms were allowed to stand.[78] After her *coup d'état* of 1898, the Empress Dowager Cixi proved no more able to control events than the Emperor had been. She tried to stem the tide only to be carried along with it. When the populace rebelled in the Boxer Uprising of

---

[77] Chirol, 9, 11; Lehman, 182.

[78] Reynolds, 35.

1900, initially against foreigner and Manchu alike, the Empress Dowager skillfully deflected the blood lust away from the Manchus and onto the foreigners. As in the Sino-Japanese War, the Empress Dowager survived but the state was further weakened in the process. The Boxers did not have faith in modern firearms, believing that proper training would permit the initiated to deflect bullets and even enable them to fly. Needless to say, they were rudely awakened when the Europeans, Japanese, and Americans sent troops to relieve the besieged legations in Peking and mowed down the Boxers in droves.[79]

The powers, which now included Japan, initially kept Peking under military occupation. At the negotiating table in 1901, they saddled China with a large indemnity for the outrages endured.[80] Western disillusionment with China had set in with the Opium Wars. It became far worse with the Sino-Japanese War. The Boxer Uprising left only a handful of optimists remaining on the lunatic fringe of Western opinion. With all the foreign powers irate over the uprising, and with the Guangxu Emperor safely under wraps, the Empress Dowager Cixi felt compelled to introduce a much more far-reaching reform program than that of the Hundred Days'. Just as defeat in the Sino-Japanese War had led to a general recognition in China of the need for self-strengthening, so foreign defeat of the Boxer Uprising led to a general recognition of the desperate need for far-reaching reforms extending well beyond the construction of infrastructure and factories, the focus of the self-strengtheners of the previous generation.

Between 1903 and 1906, these reforms included the beginnings of a constitutional government, the abolition of the Confucian examination system for entry into the civil service, the westernization of the educational system, and the repeal of the ban on the intermarriage between the Han Chinese and the Manchus.[81] These changes effectively undermined the traditional power structure underlying the Qing Dynasty. Nevertheless, the reform program did not equal the scope or the magnitude of the Meiji reforms. This final attempt at reforms from above by the Empress Dowager at long last addressed the difficult problem of creating a unified military. It turned out that the long-standing Manchu resistance to this measure had been justified. Within a decade of the creation of these new and primarily Han Chinese military forces, they turned on the Manchus, overthrew the dynasty in 1911, and the Manchus virtually vanished from the ethnic landscape of China.[82] Unlike

---

[79] Paine, 211–9.

[80] Paine, 211–9.

[81] Y. C. Wang, 50–1.

[82] Spence, *Search for Modern China*, 253–6, 263–8; Elleman, 138–45.

Japan's *genrō* (元老) or elder statesmen, the Manchus were hemmed in by their ethnicity. They became the scapegoat for China's incapacity during the late imperial period.[83]

For China, the Sino-Japanese War had set in motion a most detrimental cascade of actions precipitating reactions until the long chain finally culminated in the far more deadly second Sino-Japanese War of 1937 to 1945: The first Sino-Japanese War, the ensuing scramble for concessions, and China's attempt to respond to the growing crisis with a broadening reform program resulted in the collapse of the dynasty. This fed directly into the era of warlordism that continued through the 1940s. Debilitating warlordism, really a series of multilateral and localized civil wars, lasted until the end of the great Chinese Civil War in 1949. At that time, Mao Zedong (毛泽东) finally defeated Jiang Jieshi (蔣介石), whose name is more familiar in its Cantonese transliteration of Chiang Kai-shek. Jiang and his followers retired to Taiwan, which the Japanese had been forced to evacuate upon their defeat in 1945. The two-China problem, which had originated in the first Sino-Japanese War, lived on.

* * *

Another legacy and enduring international security concern left by the war was the problem of political instability on the Korean Peninsula. Years after the war, a member of the Japanese government aptly described Korea's unique position in Asia: "What the Balkan peninsula has so long been to Europe, the peninsula of Korea has for centuries been to the Far East – a 'haunted place' wherein lurked the unceasing source of danger to the peace of the Orient."[84] Even during the war, when the Japanese had possessed an occupying army at their disposal, they had had great difficulty quelling the Tonghak Rebellion. In late 1894, the Tonghaks had launched a major offensive upon learning that the Grand Prince Hûngsôn (興宣大院君) had again been ousted from power. In the ensuing fighting the Tonghaks had suffered thousands of casualties and the capture of key leaders. At the time of the ratification of the Treaty of Shimonoseki these leaders had been executed. The movement got a new lease on life when the Triple Intervention undermined Japanese influence on the Korean Peninsula. In 1906, the movement assumed the new name of Ch'ôngdogyo or "Religion of the Heavenly Way" (天道教). The movement's members continued to work to oppose Japan and its emerging plan to annex Korea.[85] The Koreans never reconciled themselves to Japanese domination,

---

[83] Ch'en, 275.

[84] Giichi Ono, 3. Unrest in the Balkans had precipitated World War I.

[85] Eckert et al., 221–3, 247; Synn, 182.

nor would they admit to any benefits from the Japanese reform efforts.

The war had caused even those Koreans most receptive to Japanese reform measures to defect from the Japanese camp. On May 29, 1895, just after the furor over the Triple Intervention hit the Japanese press, the Korean prime minister, Kim Hong-jip (金弘集), resigned, causing the fall of the pro-Japanese cabinet. The Koreans realized that the Triple Intervention signaled the end of undisputed Japanese ascendancy in their country and their political allegiances shifted accordingly. Queen Min (閔妃, 明成皇后) once more emerged ascendant. Even the Minister of Home Affairs, Pak Yônghyo (朴泳孝), turned against Japan. He seemed to be taking a chapter out of Grand Secretary Li's tactics to appeal for foreign intervention against Japan.[86] Specifically, he was rumored to be courting the Russians.[87] After his participation in the failed coup of 1884, Pak had lived in exile in Japan for about a decade. The attempt on his life in Tokyo just after the assassination of Kim Ok-kyun (金玉均) had been one of the factors leading to the outbreak of war. Pak had been appointed minister of home affairs when the Japanese had been firmly in control in December of 1894.[88]

Pak's defection from the Japanese camp reflected the deep-seated Korean resentment against the massive Japanese interference in their domestic affairs during the war.[89] The war that Japan had fought ostensibly to save Koreans from outsiders had resulted in the rekindling of their historical hatred of the Japanese. Apparently, Pak also had plans to help Queen Min retire from politics.[90] Having concluded that she intended to eliminate him, he had planned his own preemptive assassination of her. He was found out. While minister to Korea, Inoue Kaoru (井上馨)[91] was absent and before the Cabinet could replace the old Korean royal guards with Japanese troops, the Min faction engineered the downfall of Pak. He fled to Japan in early July, when King Kojong (高宗) ordered his arrest on the charge of high

---

[86] Synn, 133–5; "The Spirit of the Vernacular Press during the Week," *The Japan Weekly Mail* (Yokohama), 25 May 1895, p. 574; Young I. Lew, "The Reform Efforts and Ideas of Pak Yông-hyo, 1894–1895," *Korean Studies* 1 (1977): 29.
  In Japan Pak Yônghyo was known by the Japanese pronunciation of his name: Boku Eikō.

[87] "The Chino-Japanese Settlement," *The Pall Mall Gazette* (London), 24 May 1895, 4th ed., p. 7; Synn, 135.

[88] "韓廷大臣の任命" (Appointment of High Officials to the Korean Court), 朝日新聞 (*Rising Sun Newspaper*) (Tokyo), 16 December 1894, p. 1.

[89] "The Spirit of the Vernacular Press during the Week," *The Japan Weekly Mail* (Yokohama), 25 May 1895, p. 574; Lew, "Reform Efforts," 22.

[90] Eckert et al., 229.

[91] An alternative spelling is Inouye.

treason. The Min clan promptly reclaimed power.[92] Queen Min rapidly eliminated Japanese sympathizers from the government and, just as Pak had been doing, sought Russian intercession.[93]

From the point of view of a very frustrated Japanese military, the country's senior diplomats were not delivering the goods in Korea. Exclusion of Russia from the Korean Peninsula had been a fundamental war goal. According to *Chōya Shinbun* (朝野新聞), "Japan came to the rescue of Korea originally at her request, but we are entitled by the right of self-preservation to take into our hands the task of maintaining the integrity of the peninsular kingdom...We have given up Liaodong; but Korea we can never leave to her own fate."[94] On May 25, 1895, the Japanese government recalled Count Inoue and replaced him with Lieutenant-General Miura Gorō (三浦梧楼) as minister to Korea. Before Inoue left Seoul on June 7, however, he set in motion plans to engineer a *coup d'état* using Japanese troops. General Miura then expanded on these. Miura concluded that Queen Min had to go. Japanese officers had her hacked to death in her palace on October 8, 1895. A Russian eyewitness made it impossible for the Japanese military convincingly to deny its complicity.[95] Apparently, Miura and members of the military believed that they could succeed in Korea where the diplomats had failed. The powers responded by deploying small detachments of marines in Seoul. Two weeks to the day after the murder, foreign outrage compelled Japan to recall Miura for trial, where, after much ado, he was acquitted. The Koreans never forgave the Japanese for the murder of their queen.[96] According to the European practice of inverse responsibility, the Europeans regularly butchered each other's citizenry in wartime but generally refrained from injuring the responsible monarchs. Regicide was a crime for natives, not for foreigners. With the dispatch of Queen Min, Japan had broken with this practice. International pressure and Korean resentment caused the collapse of the Japanese conspiracy.[97]

Again, Grand Prince Hûngsôn made an attempt to fill the political vacuum and

---

[92] Kim and Kim, 84–6; Lensen, vol. 2, 534–40; Synn, 137, 140–1, 233; "The Crisis in Korea," *The North-China Herald* (Shanghai), 19 July 1895, pp. 111–2; Lew, "Reform Efforts," 36–7.

[93] Eckert et al., 229.

[94] "The Spirit of the Vernacular Press during the Week," *The Japan Weekly Mail* (Yokohama), 25 May 1895, p. 574.

[95] Kim and Kim, 84–6; Lensen, vol. 2, 534–40; Synn, 137, 140–1, 233.

[96] Eckert et al., 229; Conroy, 314–22; "The Coup d'Etat at Seoul," *The North-China Herald* (Shanghai), 25 October 1895, p. 678; "The Palace Tragedy," *The North-China Herald* (Shanghai), 1 November 1895, p. 722. For the text of the findings of the Japanese Court that tried Miura, see McKenzie, 263–8.

[97] Lensen, vol. 2, 572, 576–7; Yur-bok Lee, 142.

seemed on the verge of launching another bloodletting. The Tonghak Rebellion continued to bubble up in the provinces. King Kojong reacted to the murder of his wife by fleeing to the Russian Legation on February 11, 1896, upon the arrival of Russian marines in Seoul. A year later he finally dared return to his palace. Within days of his flight, the pro-Japanese ministers were massacred and the Kabo Reform movement came to an end.[98]

The Russians wanted to redress the balance between Japan and Russia in Korea. In 1896, there were 120 Japanese firms operating in Korea but only one Russian one.[99] Despite Japanese protests, Russia sent twenty military advisers who replaced the Japanese military instructors expelled by the pro-Russian cabinet.[100] In September 1896, the Russian Foreign Ministry replaced Veber, who had served for ten years as Russian consul general and *chargé d'affaires* in Seoul, with a very ambitious man with little knowledge of Korea, Alexei Nikolaevich Shpeier (de Speyer), whom the foreign diplomatic community in Seoul considered to be arrogant and tactless.[101] Shpeier intended to take control of the Korean army and government; to acquire timber, mineral, and railway concessions; and to secure a Russian naval base at Deer Island in Pusan harbor, where the Japanese had secured an important coaling station in 1887.[102] Russia also acquired several concessions in Korea: a mining concession near the Tumen River on the Sino-Korean frontier; a railway right-of-way from the border to Seoul; and forestry rights along the Sino-Korean and Russo-Korean frontier in the Yalu and Tumen river regions. Eight years later, these would be the very concessions that would help precipitate the Russo-Japanese War.[103] In September 1897, Kir Alekseevich Alekseev arrived in Seoul to act as the financial adviser to the Korean government. In October, Shpeier demanded that King Kojong replace the British Custom's Administrator, J. McLeavy Brown, with Alekseev even though Brown's contract had several more years to run. When the Korean government dismissed Brown in November, Britain responded by dispatching ten warships to Inch'ôn to restore Brown, who had never actually stepped down. Then, in December five ships of the Russian Asiatic Squadron put in an appearance at Inch'ôn in order to secure the Deer Island naval base.

Such Russian aggressiveness had the same effect as Japanese aggressiveness:

---

[98] Malozemoff, 85–7; Eckert et al., 224; Lensen, vol. 2, 589, 625–6.

[99] Synn, 233.

[100] Ro, 67–8.

[101] Lensen, vol. 2, 572, 576–7, 897*n*.95; Yur-bok Lee, 142, Synn, 248.

[102] "Les Événements de Corée" (Events in Korea), *Journal des débats politiques et littéraires* (*Journal of Political and Literary Debates*) (Paris), 2 August 1894, morning edition, p. 1.

[103] Ro, 67, 80; Paine, 238–9, 244.

Russia's Korean allies melted away until King Kojong dismissed the Russian advisers outright.[104] On February 24, 1897, Japan had published the Komura-Veber Agreement and the Lobanov-Yamagata Protocol in order to smear the Russians in Korean eyes.[105] These agreements showed the Russians operating behind the backs of the Koreans to conclude agreements with their mortal enemies, the Japanese. Shpeier had overplayed his hand. The Korean government turned down the request for a Deer Island naval base and asked the Russian financial and military advisers to depart. Also, the Russian minister in Tokyo warned that Japan would resort to force if Russia attempted to exclude Japan from Korea. By this time, Russia was on the verge of taking over Port Arthur. Once this happened, Russian interests shifted from Korea to Manchuria and Russia complied with the king's request to withdraw the advisers.[106]

Japan and Russia continued to thresh out an agreement over their relative statuses on the Korean Peninsula right up to the outbreak of the Russo-Japanese War (1904–5). The settlement of this war would deprive Korea of its de facto independence while Japanese annexation in 1910 would make the loss *de jure*. The Japanese did their best to force their will upon the Koreans through the end of World War II. Then the Koreans had but a five-year breathing space before the Korean War (1950–3) tore apart the peninsula again and left it divided into North and South Korea. For the Koreans, the Sino-Japanese War was just the beginning of their twentieth-century nightmare. In their history, the war marks an indelible divide between the traditional Confucian order and the modern era of global politics in which their country first became an appetizer for the Russo-Japanese rivalry and then the main course for the first hot war of the Cold War.

* * *

The revolution in perceptions caused by the first Sino-Japanese War also had fateful consequences for Russia. It caused a rapid acceleration of Russian colonization and development plans for Manchuria. The Russian government concluded that Japan constituted a major threat to its weakly defended Siberian frontier. Rectifying the problem would require an extensive sphere of influence in Manchuria and possibly in Korea. In the final months of the war, the Russian government took the unprecedented step of redirecting its foreign policy priorities toward the Far East.[107] Administrative changes reflected this reorientation. In June 1895, the

---

[104] Ro, 80–5, 92; Synn, 244.

[105] Synn, 238–9. The Japanese did not publish the secret articles of the Lobanov-Yamagata Protocol (Ibid.).

[106] Lensen, vol. 2, 641, 674, 687, 698–700, 706, 849–50.

[107] Fuller, 367–77; LeDonne, 200–2.

Asiatic Department of the Ministry of Foreign Affairs was abolished in order to integrate Asian affairs into the primary concerns of the ministry.[108] After the war, Japan replaced Britain as Russia's main rival in the Far East.[109]

There was an important domestic motivation for this foreign policy shift. As the Industrial Revolution had progressed in the West, Russian growth rates had not kept up. This meant that the Russian standard of living relative to that enjoyed in the West fell from the advent of the Industrial Revolution onward.[110] Over the years, this had created a growing discontent in Russia. The Russian people had the mentality of a great power, yet the economic basis for that status was steadily slipping. Attacking the economic origins of this problem would have been extremely complicated and unsettling for many powerful interest groups. It is unclear whether many Russians even grasped what would have been required. A far simpler measure of great-powerhood was to be found in foreign policy. The ruling circles concluded that Russia must have the trappings of a great power abroad as a sop for the growing discontent at home. The Western European powers had cut off this avenue for self-aggrandizement in Europe, most of the Near East, and before long in Persia. The only remaining stage on which Russia could play out its imperial ambitions was East Asia.

The Triple Intervention had been a way for Russia to assuage its anger over the 1878 Congress of Berlin, which had nullified the results of the Treaty of San Stefano settling the Russo-Turkish War of 1877 to 1878. In Berlin, Britain, Austria, and Germany had ganged up to force Russia to disgorge key territorial gains.[111] Russian actions fifteen years later created precisely the same spirit of revanchism in Japan as had been created in Russia by the earlier intervention in the Congress of Berlin.

Russian interests gradually began shifting away from Korea to Manchuria. Once the Russian government had decided to pluck the forbidden fruit of the Liaodong Peninsula, it chose to mollify the Japanese by backing off from Korea without actually formally relinquishing any potential claims. On March 16, 1898, Russia withdrew its advisers from Korea[112] while on March 27, Russia and China signed the lease agreement for the Liaodong Peninsula.[113] A month later, on April 25,

---

[108] Malozemoff, 68.

[109] Ford, 92.

[110] Paine, 251.

[111] Mutsu, 252–3; Hugh Seton-Watson, *The Russian Empire 1801–1917* (Oxford: Oxford University Press, 1967), 457–8.

[112] Ro, 88.

[113] Ro, 101.

Japan and Russia signed the Nishi-Rozen Convention, recognizing Korean independence, promising to send military or financial advisers only by mutual consent, and guaranteeing Japanese economic relations with Korea.[114] Only after Russia had consolidated its leasehold over the Liaodong Peninsula and built the connecting railroad line to Harbin, would it turn its attention back to Korea. Not coincidentally, this would precipitate the Russo-Japanese War.[115]

The two Manchurian railway concessions secured in 1896 and 1898 entailed an enormous financial commitment from the Russian government. From 1897 to 1902, the average annual deficit of the Russian government in the Far East was approximately 171 million rubles. In contrast, the entire government budget for 1903 was only 1.3 billion rubles, of which 22 percent was allocated for interest and loan repayments, 36 percent for the military, and only 42 percent, or 520 million rubles, for everything else. Expenditures in the Far East took about one-third of these discretionary funds. In a chronically capital-short country, such a financial commitment to the remotest part of the empire and beyond into Chinese territory could only have taken capital from the development of European Russia. Yet the railway so lavishly funded at public expense never generated a profit under Russian administration.[116]

The magnitude of this investment made the 1900 Boxer Uprising particularly threatening to the Russians. The Boxers targeted the Manchurian railway system for destruction, which precipitated a massive Russian invasion and prolonged occupation of Manchuria. Russia deployed over 100,000 troops. In 1902, Japan and Great Britain responded by forming their alliance. For Great Britain, this would relieve its navy of the burden of protecting its Far Eastern possessions. For Japan, the alliance would insure that Britain would not side with Russia in the brewing Russo-Japanese rivalry for spheres of influence in northeastern Asia. Once the Chinese government restored order in Manchuria, the Russians still refused to leave. When they would not adhere to any timetable for withdrawal, the Japanese decided to force the issue.

The Japanese could only interpret Russia's enormous financial and military commitment in Manchuria to mean one thing: Russia intended to minimize Japanese infiltration of the Asian mainland. On May 8, 1895, the Japanese minister to Russia, Nishi Tokujirō (西徳二郎), had already pegged Russian objectives:

---

[114] Robert P. Porter, *Japan; The Rise of a Modern Power* (Oxford: Clarendon Press, 1918), 144; Ro, 102–3. Nishi Tokujirō (西徳二郎)) was the Japanese foreign minister, while Roman Romanovich Rozen (Rosen) was the Russian minister to Japan (Lensen, vol. 2, 998, 1000).

[115] Ro, 106.

[116] Paine, 256.

"[W]e can surmise from the [Triple] intervention that Russia does hope ultimately to bring the entire area from northeastern Manchuria down to Manchuria's southern coast under her influence."[117] This was the last thing that the Japanese government wanted; it was not a negotiable element of Japan's foreign policy strategy. Dominance on the Korean and Manchurian littoral *was* its strategy. Fomenting war in Korea to keep out Russia had backfired. The Sino-Japanese War, far from moderating Russian interest in the Far East, had created a Russian obsession. It would take another war to accomplish the objective of expelling Russia from Korea. Defeat in the Russo-Japanese War forced Russia to retrocede not only the contested Liaodong Peninsula but also its railroad empire south of Harbin. Much to the chagrin of the Russian government, within a short time the Japanese had transformed the railway into a profit-making enterprise.[118]

Although the Sino-Japanese War has conventionally been seen as a conflict between Japan and China over Korea, the reality was more complicated. The real struggle, as top Japanese policymakers knew full well, did not concern China but was between Russia and Japan.[119] As Yamagata Aritomo, the father of Japan's modern army, had written in 1893, "Neither China nor Korea is our enemy: it is Britain, France, Russia"[120] – in other words, the three great powers of the time. Japan wanted all of them out of Asia. Once the Japanese government had revised its unequal treaties with the former two, the most odious aspects of their presence in the Far East were removed. Russia, however, remained a special problem because of its unique territorial proximity. The construction of the Trans-Siberian Railway brought special urgency to this problem. The shadow war with China disguised the real opponent, Russia. The same would be true in the Pacific War during the 1930s.[121] Control over Korea and China was not Japan's original objective; minimizing Russian influence in Asia was. By the 1930s, Russia was communist and thus even more threatening from the Japanese point of view. Russia and Japan would slog it out for control over Manchuria, Mongolia, and Xinjiang through the defeat of Japan in World War II. The Sino-Japanese War was the opening act in a drama of Wagnerian proportions that would absorb the Far East for much of the twentieth century.

The Japanese originated the policy of containment generally associated with the

---

[117] Cited in Mutsu, 236.

[118] Paine, 196, 213–25, 238–42; Chung-fu Chang, 282–91.

[119] Lone, 1; Hackett, 158.

[120] Lone, 25.

[121] This is the subject of my next book project, which will be an examination of the Russo-Japanese rivalry for spheres of influence in China during the Pacific War period.

United States and its Cold War policies toward the Soviet Union. The Japanese had been trying to contain the Russians from the late nineteenth century through the end of the Second World War. From the time Russia began work on the Trans-Siberian Railway through the end of the Cold War, first Japan and then the United States sought to minimize Russian influence on the Asian mainland while Russia did its best to expand that influence. Until the communists unified China in 1949, China was a victim, not an orchestrator, of this conflict.

* * *

The change in international perceptions concerning Chinese weakness had unanticipated and dangerous consequences for Japan. Previously, the powers had focused on extracting commercial privileges from China; after the war, they focused on dominating territory.[122] This put foreign spheres of influence at Japan's back door. In addition, Japan had not solved the regional geopolitical problem that had precipitated the war: Korea remained highly unstable and, from an outside perspective, tragically self-destructive. After the war, it became even more vulnerable to outside intervention. The end of the old way of doing things under the tributary system led to a free-for-all to establish an undetermined new equilibrium. Japan had expelled China but had awakened Russia in the process. Russia, long habituated to focusing on its European and Near Eastern frontiers, suddenly riveted its attention on the Far East with a massive redirection of state funds. Thus, the war, far from reducing the threats to Japanese national security, had exacerbated them and embittered the Japanese in the process.

The Triple Intervention left a powerful strain of revanchism in Japan. With it, the Russians had humiliated the Japanese. From the Japanese point of view, Russian government could not have chosen a way to insult them more completely than to seize for itself the very place it had so publicly denied to Japan. However westernized Japan had become, it was still a culture that set great store by public appearances and "face." The Russians had made the Japanese lose "face" twice: first by denying them the Liaodong Peninsula and then by seizing the concession for themselves. There was only one way to restore the honor of Japan: The Japanese would have to teach the Russians an equally public lesson in international relations. In 1895, various Japanese newspapers were already recommending that the war indemnity be used to fund a major expansion of both the army and the navy.[123] One Japanese paper recommended that the Japanese respond to the Triple

---

[122] Schulman, 103; Langer, 190–1.
[123] "The Indemnity," *The Japan Weekly Mail* (Yokohama), 18 May 1895, p. 554.

Intervention with an intent "to repay their kindness on some future day."[124]

Foreign Minister Mutsu Munemitsu (陸奥宗光) provided a clear expression of an underlying Japanese bitterness over what they considered extremely shabby treatment, not just by Russia but by the West in general: "Although the Western powers had over the years watched Japan adopt European modes of military organization and discipline they had remained doubtful whether our extensive emulation of civilized military systems would actually be reflected in warfare." Similarly, "When we reformed our legal codes and established a new judicial system, they ridiculed our laws as impractical, questioned the ability of our judges, and remained apprehensive about permitting their citizens to be subjected to our legal jurisdiction." He continued, "Later, they looked on skeptically and made a number of most offensive criticisms when Japan established a constitutional system, for they doubted whether constitutionalism could actually survive in a non-European society. In short, they presumed that the products of European civilization were a monopoly of the European race and that their value could not be truly appreciated by non-European peoples. Our victories now at last freed them for the first time from the delusion that European-style civilization could survive only in Christian lands."[125] In 1898, the Japanese looked on as the powers allowed the United States to retain as fruits of the Spanish-American War colonies in Puerto Rico, Guam, Wake Island, and the Philippines.[126] In contrast, they had been forced to give up the Liaodong Peninsula.

Their irritation with this unequal treatment grew over the years until the 1930s, when they concluded that white people respected only the conquests of other white people. At that time, former-Foreign Minister Viscount Ishii Kikujirō (石井菊次郎) wrote: "Opportunities to repay the three powers for their kind 'advice' concerning the Shimonoseki Treaty were not long in coming. After biding their time for ten years, the Japanese swept the Russians out of the Liaotung peninsula and South Manchuria [in the Russo-Japanese War]. A decade later, they drove the Germans out of Shantung [during World War I]. In the case of France, however, as her interference had been the result of circumstances [that is, due to the Franco-Russian alliance] rather than choice, friendly relations were restored…Japan's policy of patient waiting to settle old scores was thus amply rewarded."[127]

[124] "The Vernacular Press on the Treaty of Peace," *The Japan Weekly Mail* (Yokohama), 18 May 1895, p. 555.

[125] Mutsu, 108. For similar views, see Pyle, *New Generation*, 177.

[126] Fareed Zakaria, *From Wealth to Power: The Unusual Origins of America's World Role* (Princeton: Princeton University Press, 1998), 159–61.

[127] Kikujiro Ishii, *Diplomatic Commentaries*, William R. Langdon, trans. and ed. (Baltimore: Johns

The war had made Japan a recognized power but it had not solved the problem of regional instability. Japan was a rising power with an unfulfilled agenda. From the point of view of the other powers, a rising power with an agenda constituted a potential security threat since both "rising power" and "agenda" implied changes in the status quo. As a result, a new image of Japan as a potential threat emerged.[128] Visions of a "yellow peril" would surface particularly in the Russian press. At the end of the war, an anonymous author who described himself as "not a diplomat" wrote a series entitled, "Complications in the Far East" for *Moskovskie vedomosti*. He predicted that Japan would eventually try to invade Europe. "If [we] do not stop Japan now, then this invasion must be expected not in 1895 but in 1945."[129] Even if he did not peg the location of the invasion (Japan would take over most of Asia not Europe), he was not so far off on the timing. As the peace envoys were preparing to go to Shimonoseki, *The North-China Herald* had run articles conjuring up images of a hostile Japan that would threaten British supremacy in the East. "It is time that we ceased the easy-going, half amused, half contemptuous allusions to the 'little Jap,' time that we forgot Japan as the delightful home of the *musume* [geisha], the impressionist painter, the carver and ideal hostess...Japan is not Japan pure and simply; the land of courtesy and curios; but an Eastern Power re-awakening from its slumber of centuries; re-awakening to do battle of the fiercest kind with the West and all that therein is."[130] Despite the hostility of the rhetoric, the message was clear: Henceforth Japan had to be taken seriously.

Japan's agenda was its civilizing mission in Asia. The war gave the Japanese a great pride in their own achievements and an equally great ambition to foster the development of similar societies elsewhere in Asia.[131] They invented a new civilizing mission for themselves abroad: They would bring their hybrid civilization to their immediate neighbors; Chinese incapacity had proved that Japan must supplant China as the epicenter of the Far East. Japan would be the conduit for westernization to its neighbors.[132] The Japanese had followed Fukuzawa Yukichi's (福沢諭吉)

Hopkins Press, 1936), 21. For comments in a similar vein, see Rosen, 138.

[128] Lone, 8–9.

[129] He дипломат (Not a Diplomat), "Осложнения на Дальнем Востоке" (Complications in the Far East), *Московские ведомости* (*Moscow Gazette*), no. 100, 13 April 1895 (25 April 1895), p. 3.

[130] "The Revival of Oriental Power," *The North-China Herald* (Shanghai), 22 March 1895, pp. 427, 417–9, 427–9.

[131] For typical examples of Japanese pride in their achievements, see "日本上世に於ける開化中心地の移轉" (Transfer in the Center of Development in Ancient Japan), 國民新聞 (*People's Newspaper*) (Tokyo), 10 May 1895, p. 1; "戰勝の大本を原闡明すべし" (The Key Reasons for Victory in War Should Be Made Clear), 日本人 (*The Japanese*) (Tokyo), 25 December 1894, pp. 17–20.

[132] Miwa, 25.

advice and had psychologically "left Asia." They were determined to become a power on a par with the best of them. Like the other powers of their day, the Japanese shared the belief that colonies were an essential attribute of a great power. Historically, Japan had been vulnerable to attack from the Korean peninsula, so it became the focus of these ambitions and the battlefield for the Sino-Japanese War. By war's end, there was general agreement in Japan that it should seek colonies on the Chinese mainland, in the thicket of European rivalries in the Far East. This set various European powers on edge, for they had not expected competition from this new quarter. At war's end, Japan was poised to give its new status a road test by absorbing Korea and Manchuria, tasks that occupied it through World War II. The idea of a civilizing mission, which had become fully developed during the first Sino-Japanese War, would animate Japanese policy throughout the twentieth century and express itself variously in military, political, and economic terms.

In 1895, the journalist Tokutomi Sohō proclaimed that Japan had an obligation "to extend the blessings of political organization throughout the rest of East Asia and the South Pacific, just as the Romans had once done for Europe and the Mediterranean."[133] Through the 1920s, they would attempt to do this in solidarity with the West. An article in *Hōchi Shinbun* (報知新聞) recommended a policy that Japan would attempt in the 1930s: "After reducing the Chinese Government to submission, if it should prove incapable of inaugurating a new epoch of progress and improvement, or when there is danger of internal commotion or foreign intervention, Japan should take upon herself the responsibility of undertaking the reform of China, just as she is now doing in Korea."[134] In the interim a general consensus concerning Japan's civilizing mission in Asia helped maintain a base level of unity between the people and government in Japan. Many Europeans and Americans considered such ambitions to be extremely dangerous.

From the Japanese point of view, the idea of a "yellow peril" was ridiculous. In Asia, the second half of the nineteenth century had been an uninterrupted string of events providing incontrovertible evidence of a "white peril."[135] They saw their policies as a creative response to a foreign menace that had come from half a world away to threaten Asian shores. They had gone out of their way to frame their response within the accepted Western norms for governance, norms that were quite alien to Japanese political traditions. Nevertheless, these perceptions of threat

---

[133] Cited in Peattie, "Japanese Colonial Empire," 221.

[134] Quoted in "The Spirit of the Vernacular Press during the Week," *The Japan Weekly Mail* (Yokohama), 4 August 1894, p. 118. *Kokkai Shinbun* (国会新聞) wrote in a similar vein. Ibid.

[135] Richard Storry, *Japan and the Decline of the West in Asia 1894–1943* (New York: St. Martin's Press, 1979), 14–33.

expressed themselves in military budgets in Japan and abroad and were one further indication of the globalization of politics.

The war had been so successful at making Japan an internationally recognized power that it was believed by main in the government and public alike that success abroad came through the force of arms. With the victory of Port Arthur and long before the Triple Intervention, signs of a post-war arms race had already appeared. *Mainichi Shinbun* (毎日新聞) quoted a Japanese admiral as recommending that the navy be quadrupled so that it could take on the Far Eastern fleets of England, Russia, and France.[136] *Hōchi Shinbun* (報知新聞) and *Kokumin Shinbun* (国民新聞) ran articles expressing similar views.[137] Before the Treaty of Shimonoseki was ratified, there was talk in the Japanese press of the need for a massive post-war rearmament program.[138] The navy had already publicly broached the subject.[139] According to *Chūo Shinbun* (中央新聞), the organ of the National Unionists (国民協会) under Viscount Shinagawa Yajirō (品川弥二郎), Japan required colonies on the Asian mainland so that "she will be enabled in the future to successfully contend for the supremacy of the Orient with England and Russia."[140] The Japanese reaction to the Triple Intervention was not to be cowed but to redouble its efforts. They would follow the proverb, literally "to lie on kindling and lick gall" (臥薪嘗胆), or "to struggle against difficulties for the sake of vengeance."[141]

The first step toward this rearmament program for Japan had been the addition to the Imperial Japanese Navy of the twelve Chinese warships that had been captured during the hostilities. These warships increased the tonnage of the Imperial Japanese Navy by about one-quarter. In addition, the Japanese navy had captured seven smaller torpedo-boats.[142] The real change came with the indemnity. The anonymous author, "Not a diplomat," of the series published in *Moskovskie vedomosti* under the title, "Complications in the Far East," concluded again quite prophetically: "[O]ne must be concerned that the Japanese will strengthen their armaments by that billion francs which they will receive in the form of war

[136] "The Extension of the Japanese Navy," *The Japan Weekly Mail* (Yokohama), 5 January 1895, p. 11.

[137] "Japan's Needs," *The Japan Weekly Mail* (Yokohama), 5 January 1895, p. 11.

[138] "Naval and Military Expenditure," *The Japan Weekly Mail* (Yokohama), 20 April 1895, pp. 449–50.

[139] "The Japanese Navy," *The Japan Weekly Mail* (Yokohama), 27 April 1895, pp. 485–6.

[140] "The Spirit of the Vernacular Press during the Week," *The Japan Weekly Mail* (Yokohama), 11 May 1895, p. 522.

[141] Evans and Peattie, p. 53; Koh Masuda, 318.

[142] Japan, Imperial General Staff, 37–8, Tables 19–20.

indemnity, in order to take vengeance on us in the future for our interference in the Sino-Japanese quarrel."[143]

That was exactly what happened. Japan used the war indemnity to bankroll a massive rearmament program. Japan spent 47 million *yen* for expansion of the army and 169 million *yen* for expansion of the navy, for a total of approximately 216 million *yen*.[144] In November 1895, the cabinet submitted a budget request to the Diet for an enormous military expansion program that would raise the army's budget from 10 to over 53 million *yen* and increase its share of the national budget from 10.5 to over 30 percent. The Diet approved the measure, in marked contrast to its pre-war obstructionist attitude toward military appropriations. The Japanese government planned to double the strength of the army from six to twelve divisions (not including the Imperial Guard) by 1903. This meant that its peacetime army would increase from 70,000 to 150,000 men, while its wartime army would rise from 275,000 to 550,000 men. Similarly, the fleet would be quadrupled. Before the expansion, the navy had 43 vessels, totaling 78,000 tons displacement and comprising 26 torpedo-boats but no cruisers. The navy was slotted to expand to 67 men-of-war (including, for the first time, top-rated battleships to be seven in number), 11 torpedo-boat destroyers and 115 torpedo-boats, for a new total displacement of 258,000 tons. The naval expansion program was projected to cost 213 million *yen* and be completed in 1906. This would make Japan's navy equal to that of Italy or Germany and superior to any other navy in the Far East. The goal was to create a fleet capable of taking on a combination of France with either Britain or Russia. Given the global commitments of the British navy, it would be hard-pressed to match the Japanese navy in the Far East. Without a doubt, Japan had absorbed Captain Mahan's lesson concerning the necessity of the command of the sea. Japan also expanded its arsenals, railways, telegraphs, ports, and subventions to the merchant marine; founded a second university in Kyoto; and established a large iron foundry. The entire army and naval expansion and military-related infrastructure was to be funded over a ten-year period ending in 1906, for an anticipated cost of £51,500,000.[145]

---

[143] Не дипломат (Not a Diplomat), "Осложнения на Дальнем Востоке" (Complications in the Far East), *Московские ведомости* (*Moscow Gazette*), no. 110, 23 April 1895 (5 May 1895), p. 3.

[144] Giichi Ono, 120; Iguchi, 106–8.

[145] Hackett, 169; "Extracts from 'The Awakening of the East' by Pierre Leroy-Beaulieu, 1900," Du Boulay, 1–4; Leroy-Beaulieu, 164–5, 145–6; Evans and Peattie, p. 53; Giichi Ono, 89; Lone, 182; Oh, "Background," 294. The figures vary on troop numbers, but the general magnitude of the expansion is accurate. For instance, according to Lone, peacetime forces were to be doubled to 164,500 and wartime forces increased from 216,000 to 545,000 (Ibid.).

On the Russian side, between 1895 and 1899, the tsar authorized the construction of 12 destroyers, 19 cruisers, and up to 42 torpedo destroyers to be completed by 1904. The 1894 Russian fleet of 225,000 tons was to be increased to 680,000 tons by 1907. Appropriations for the army, which for 1890 to 1894 had averaged 261 million rubles, would increase to an average of 302 million for the 1895 to 1897 period. Similarly, naval expenditures for these two periods increased from 47 million to 71 million rubles, respectively. These figures excluded the extraordinary appropriations of 90 million rubles in 1898. Thus, the increase in naval appropriations for the years 1891 to 1895 versus the 1896 to 1900 period grew by 52 percent.[146] In 1900, Nicholas II authorized the construction of a Russian fleet in the Pacific 30 percent stronger than that of Japan.[147] A Far Eastern arms race was on. Russian attempts to shore up its Far Eastern defenses with the Trans-Siberian Railroad had inspired Japanese countermeasures leading to an all-out arms race in the Far East.[148] This would culminate in the Russo-Japanese War.[149]

The Sino-Japanese War also wrought important domestic changes in Japan. The war had fueled the development of nationalism. This would become the cement holding together the political enterprise.[150] The war also strengthened Shintoism. Shintoism fused with nationalism and militarism to become Japan's martial ideology.[151] The political balance of power within Japan had shifted. Victory in the field had greatly increased the prestige of the armed forces at the expense of the diplomats. The military victory also had greatly enhanced the prestige of the emperor as commander-in-chief of the armed forces.[152] A clearer definition for the role of emperor emerged. He became a military figurehead lending legitimacy to the military.[153] While this nationalism had helped ease one fissure in the Japanese body politic – that between the cabinet and the Diet – it had created a new one in its stead – between military and civil authority.

On December 29, 1895, the Emperor Meiji (明治天皇) delivered an address at the opening ceremony of the Diet. He emphasized that he had ordered his ministers to focus on "the advancement of the country in the fields of industry, communications,

---

[146] Gatrell, 21–4.

[147] Ford, 232.

[148] "Великая Сибирская дорога" (The Great Siberian Railway), *Московские ведомости* (*Moscow Gazette*), no. 104, 17 April 1895 (29 April 1895), p. 1.

[149] Gatrell, 21.

[150] Hackett, 167; Huffman, 210, 220–2.

[151] Lone, 109–10.

[152] Beasley, *Rise of Modern Japan*, 128.

[153] Lone, 81–5.

and education...As to the defences of the country, it has ever been Our intention to complete them by degrees. Desirous of repairing the industries occasioned during the recent hostilities, and of making necessary provisions for self-protection, We have charged Our Advisers with the task of elaborating the measures to be adopted...Our Empire has already made large progress in civilization. But the nation has a long and arduous journey yet to perform."[154] Japan had become a recognized power, but it remained one of the weaker powers. Regional instability still plagued the Far East. Thus, the Meiji reforms, for all their achievements, had yet to complete their full agenda.

Members of the lower house of the Diet responded to the emperor's address by introducing a draft address to the throne, lambasting Japan's diplomats for retroceding the Liaodong Peninsula. According to the draft address, Japan's possession of the disputed territory had lasted not "twenty days" before converting "into a dead letter...Such conduct cannot fail to seriously injure the prestige of the Imperial House and compromise the dignity of the country." The authors of the address went on to accuse the diplomats of "incapacity" because they had not prevented the development and then success of a coalition. "They had not even the courage to rely upon the justice of their country's cause and reject the demand of the Allies. In a moment of confusion and consternation, they knew only how to bow their heads to the interfering Powers, thereby subjecting the country to unprecedented humiliation and disgrace." They accused the diplomats of bungling post-war Korean policies as well as referring indirectly to the murder of Queen Min.[155] As events in Korea continued to unravel and as the opposition in the Diet kept highlighting this fact, the government responded by dissolving the Diet in February 1896.[156] The suspension directly preceded Marshal (and now also Marquis) Yamagata's departure for Russia to attend the coronation ceremony of Nicholas II and engage in delicate negotiations with Russia. Itō Hirobumi had been scheduled to go but, with continuing opposition to his tenure in office and escalating problems in Korea, his arch-rival Yamagata was substituted.[157] The prestige of the diplomats was eclipsed by the military.

During the war, a new split had emerged, not between public and government, but within the government. By war's end there was a general feeling that the

[154] "The Opening of the Diet," *The Japan Weekly Mail* (Yokohama), 4 January 1896, p. 4.

[155] "The Address to the Throne on the Subject of Foreign Policy," *The Japan Weekly Mail* (Yokohama), 4 January 1896, p. 4.

[156] "The Suspension of the Diet," *The Japan Weekly Mail* (Yokohama), 22 February 1896, p. 215.

[157] "Marshal Marquis Yamagata's Appointment as Special Ambassador to Russia," *The Japan Weekly Mail* (Yokohama), 29 February 1896, p. 237.

military had won the war but the diplomats had lost the peace. Lieutenant-General Miura's complicity in the assassination of Queen Min was one sign of this. An early indication of a developing split had occurred on the eve of the war. In June of 1894, Vice-Chief of the General Staff Lieutenant General Kawakami Sōroku (川上 操六) had withheld information from Premier Itō about a favorable turn taken by the negotiations in Seoul. Regardless of the available diplomatic possibilities, General Kawakami was determined to send a large body of troops to Korea to counter the Chinese forces. Kawakami was one of the key advocates of war. He was born into a lower samurai family in Satsuma and had devoted his career to the army. He had traveled to the West on two occasions to study Western military organization. In 1893, after observing the Chinese army, he concluded that "it is absolutely certain that in a fight we would win."[158] He misled Foreign Minister Mutsu Munemitsu into approving the dispatch of one brigade. Mutsu thought this would entail 2,000 troops, but Kawakami sent a mixed brigade, which meant 7,000–8,000 troops.[159] Victory in war tipped the civil–military balance in favor of the military. As the prestige of the military grew this split widened and the scales fell ever more heavily on the military side. Victory over Russia in 1905 – the first example in modern times of an Asian country defeating a European country – immeasurably enhanced the standing of the armed forces.

Like the Sino-Japanese War, the Russo-Japanese War also greatly enhanced the prestige of the Japanese military at the expense of the Japanese diplomats. During the Sino-Japanese War, Japanese papers drew unfavorable comparisons between the exploits of the military and the backpedaling of the diplomats. According to Foreign Minister Mutsu, "Soon the air was filled with charges that the fruits of victory gained on the battlefield had now been lost at the negotiating table."[160] Three months after the Triple Intervention, the furor still had not died down in the Japanese press.[161] Political parties agitated to bring down the Itō cabinet. Meanwhile, the emperor had expressed his appreciation for Itō's achievements by promoting him to marquis at the end of the war. The political parties, however, blamed Itō personally for the retrocession of the Liaodong Peninsula. This agitation did not cease until the Itō cabinet fell on September 18, 1896.[162] Foreign Minister Mutsu

---

[158] Cited in Young, "Study of Groups," 253.

[159] Hackett, 160–1; Lensen, vol. 1, 130; Oh, "Background," 303; Conroy, 242; Young, "Study of Groups," 250–6.

[160] Mutsu, 249. This was why Mutsu wrote his book.

[161] "Spirit of the Vernacular Press during the Week," *The Japan Weekly Mail* (Yokohama), 27 July 1895, p. 82.

[162] "Spirit of the Vernacular Press during the Week," *The Japan Weekly Mail* (Yokohama), 21

considered the widespread criticism of Japanese diplomats to be unfair and he wrote his memoirs to exonerate himself and his colleagues. He believed that much had been accomplished: "[O]ur freedom to advance so far without any interference from the powers owed more to farsighted diplomacy than to sheer luck."[163] The achievements of his generation were recognized and extolled in the West but, like Li Hongzhang in China, the diplomats were savaged by their own countrymen unversed in the world outside their borders. One of the subsequent hallmarks of the Japanese military appeared in this period: brilliance in the field but incognizance of the full international ramifications of its actions and contempt for the diplomats who did better understand them. This was the first visible sign of the split between the generals and diplomats in Japan that would become so blatant in the 1930s when the military finally pushed the foreign ministry aside.

In contrast to the successes of the military, civil authority tread a rocky road. The trip was mostly downhill after the signal achievement of the 1902 Anglo-Japanese alliance. The diplomatic conundrums of the twentieth century were not easily solved. In 1910, Japan formally made Korea a colony, but the Koreans remained no more cooperative than before.[164] China remained chronically unstable. The Bolshevik Revolution in Russia in 1917 greatly complicated matters. In the 1920s, the Soviet Union made Outer Mongolia the first member of the communist bloc, and in the 1930s the Soviet government began cultivating the ruling Xinjiang warlord. In intramural China, it helped organize and fund the Chinese Communist Party while simultaneously funding the Nationalist Party. These developments were the antithesis of what Japan desired. In the 1920s, the Japanese government tried to enlist Western support to help contain communism in Asia, but Western concerns lay elsewhere. Europe was preoccupied with economic recovery from World War I while the United States turned inward to the hedonism of the Roaring Twenties and isolationism after the stock market crash in 1929. The Japanese economy suffered a downturn upon the end of World War I, and its domestic political life was marked by assassinations and instability. In 1930, with the onset of the Great Depression, the United States passed the Hawley-Smoot Tariff. This raised American tariffs to historic heights. The other powers erected similar tariff walls. Stymied in China, frustrated at home, and excluded from trade, Japanese diplomats rapidly lost any remaining credibility. The military took a very common route to cut through a political Gordian knot: It staged a coup. In

December 1895, p. 670; "The New Cabinet," *The Japan Weekly Mail* (Yokohama), 26 September 1896, p. 333.
[163] Mutsu, 251.
[164] Eckert et al., 259.

1931, the military took over Manchuria without civil approval. The fait accompli had the same effect as a coup in Tokyo. The diplomats were in eclipse and the military was on the rise. With the coup, Japan abandoned its policy of cooperation with the West dating from the Meiji Restoration. Japan veered toward economic autarchy and imperial expansion. The civil–military split that had made its first appearance in the Sino-Japanese War of 1894–5 developed fully in the Sino-Japanese War of 1937 to 1945, with tragic results for Japan and the rest of Asia.

Japan's Greater East Asian Co-prosperity Sphere of the 1930s and 1940s also had its roots in the first Sino-Japanese conflict. The Japanese empire was born in 1895 with the acquisition of Taiwan and the Pescadores. In 1896, General Katsura Tarō (桂太郎), a disciple of Yamagata intimately involved with creating a modern army in Japan, had made clear that "the development of Taiwan should not be confined to the island, but should be planned in terms of an advance into a wider area."[165] The booty from the Russo-Japanese War brought Japan southern Manchuria and half of Sakhalin Island, followed rapidly by the acquisition of Korea in 1910. These constituted the core area of the Japanese Empire.[166] By 1910, Japan had taken everything it had occupied in 1895 and more.

The consequences of the Sino-Japanese War were global with enormous future repercussions. Changed perceptions had a cascade effect on the domestic politics of China and Japan, and on the foreign policies of all powers engaged in the Far East. To this day, China remains determined to reverse the judgment of the war and restore its former preeminence.

---

[165] Schencking: 779; Jansen, *Making of Modern Japan*, 360, 397.

[166] Lone, 123; Paine, 244.

9

The Cultural Dimensions of the Sino-Japanese War

It is the law, as in the arts so in politics, that improvements ever prevail; and though fixed usages may be best for undisturbed communities, constant necessities of action must be accompanied by the constant improvement of methods.[1]

Thucydides (471–400 B.C.)

Do not look at what is contrary to ritual, do not speak what is contrary to ritual, and make no movement which is contrary to ritual.[2]

Confucius (551–479 B.C.)

From a Western point of view, the question immediately arises: Why did the Chinese choose such self-destructive policies during the Sino-Japanese War? By population, geographic extent, resources, traditional primacy, and shorter logistical lines, the Chinese should have won hands down. Yet they were pasted by a small island nation possessing none of these advantages. To answer this question, it is necessary to try to see the world as the Chinese and the nationals of the powers did in the late nineteenth century.

Today, in an era of innumerable dictionaries, how-to books, and crash courses, it is hard to imagine the information void in which Westerners, Chinese, and Japanese interacted in the late nineteenth century. The Industrial Revolution was at its height in the West, but the modern era of global politics was only dawning, and the communications revolution was a long way off. Each country had its own experts on the others, but these people were few and far between. While many educated Japanese were familiar with China, the reverse was absolutely not the

---

[1] Robert B. Strassler, ed., *The Landmark Thucydides: A Comprehensive Guide to the Peloponnesian War* (New York: Free Press, 1996), 40.

[2] Confucius, *The Analects*, book 12, 1.

case. In China travel abroad was stigmatized, so that a foreign assignment, considered indispensable training in Japan, was recognized to be career-threatening in China. Most Europeans and Chinese knew little about each other or Japan.[3] Very few nationals of any of the three had ever traveled to either of the other two.

The interaction of East and West has been particularly tendentious because of a host of unrecognized cultural differences. China and Japan, like Western nations, perceived the world through their own distinct cultural lenses. Sorting out these differences is a difficult task that has confounded generations of diplomats, journalists, and Orientalists, while unawareness of them has led to perceived but unintended snubs, hard feelings, misdirected financial investments, and diplomatic imbroglios. Western Europeans, on the one hand, and Chinese and Japanese, on the other, believed that when they communicated with each other they were using more or less mutually comprehensible terms. In fact, the cultural chasm was so wide, the cultural preoccupations so different, and the underlying assumptions ordering human interactions so divergent that both sides are still sorting out the differences.

In order for someone in a Western cultural orbit to understand Chinese and Japanese actions in the late nineteenth century, it is essential to take into consideration the basic points of cultural departure between the East and West. Particularly before the twentieth century, there were fundamental differences in how each people defined its place in the world, described the nature of history, understood the natural world, applied ethics, and ordered social interactions. Not all of these differences have disappeared. Each of these topics will be discussed in the following pages. From these basic points of departure an overarching commonality is evident within the Far East and within Western Europe and its cultural off-shoot, the United States. Conversely, a stark contrast emerges between the East and West.

The 1890s found China and Japan in the unenviable position of being objects of the virulent strain of imperialism infecting the West. While they both clearly sensed the increasing dangers, they inhabited mental worlds foreign to the West. Frequently they perceived matters differently and, from a Western point of view, often highly illogically. The reverse was also the case – Chinese officials often referred to foreign behavior as "unfathomable" or 叵測.[4]

Educated Chinese found the Western preoccupation with commercial matters to be distasteful at best. In China, merchants held a low social status; high status derived from educational achievements, not from money. While wealth was a possible consequence of high status, it was not the origin. The Chinese elite

---

[3] Howland, 20–42; Chu, "China's Attitudes," 74–84.

[4] Paine, 11, 21–2n.37.

concerned itself, not with crass financial matters but with ethical issues such as the proper ordering of social relations. As a result, they had no high opinion of the merchants who descended upon China *en masse* in the nineteenth century. As an American observer noted in 1895: "It is customary for Mandarins...to regard all foreigners of being greedy only of gain."[5]

Other Chinese ridiculed Western religious beliefs. One highly educated Chinese explained his views on Christianity. While he praised the philosophical teachings of Christ, he criticized the dogmas of the various Christian churches, saying, "We view them as superstitions at least as wild and foolish as those in any Eastern faith; and we take it as an insult to our intelligence to be asked to believe in such ideas as transubstantiation or the virgin birth."[6] For the Chinese, what could be more barbaric than the idea that priests literally transformed the Eucharistic wine into the blood of Christ and the wafer into His flesh, and then their congregations ingested the concoction? In a society that revered its ancestors, the notion of ingesting the most revered ancestor of all was heretical not to mention disgusting. In their minds, equally preposterous and even more ignorant was the idea that a virgin could conceive and bear a child. They knew perfectly well how babies were conceived and were not interested in what they considered to be foolish old wives' tales. Li Hongzhang (李鴻章) was even more blunt: "Men ought always to admire success. I cannot understand why clever men, like some of you Europeans, should actually worship Jesus Christ. Why, that man's life was a failure, and he was actually crucified at the end of it. Now, crucifixion is a very painful death, besides being a degrading form of punishment. How can you call yourselves followers of such a man as that?"[7]

The Chinese made the a priori assumption that Chinese civilization was eternal, supreme, and predestined to triumph. They understood that Chinese dynasties had often been separated by decades of civil war, but they insisted that Chinese history was an unbroken cloth. They presented themselves as guardians of a 5,000-year-old heritage of cultural continuity in contrast to the insipid attempts at civilization by the cultural parvenus inhabiting the rest of the globe. Throughout Chinese history regional loyalties had prevailed over national sentiments, yet they presented the Chinese people as a monolithic group made up overwhelmingly of Han Chinese. The term for the country and the people was the same, lending semantic credence to the Chinese view. Unlike the Europeans, they minimized the linguistic differences

---

[5] Douglas, 70.

[6] Tyler, 213. Tyler made his career in China and served as a naval adviser to China during the Sino-Japanese War.

[7] Little, 184.

within China. Although they recognized that many mutually unintelligible languages were spoken in different Chinese provinces, they called them dialects – variations on a theme – instead of distinct languages.

Whereas the Chinese defined themselves as "the universe" (天下) or "the Middle Kingdom" (中國), the Western Europeans defined the center of the world not as a land mass but as an ocean, the Mediterranean or "middle of the lands." Their center was the sea lanes connecting and integrating the European world. These sea lanes and adjoining river systems linked the Western European world economically, culturally, and militarily. Distance from the sea determined cultural remoteness in Europe, whereas the reverse was the case in China. The cultural center was inland China. As the Chinese looked landward for their cultural center, the Western Europeans looked outward. Scripture urged Christians to "Be fruitful, and multiply, and replenish the earth."[8] Exploration of the world came naturally to the Western European mindset.[9]

The Europeans were aware of the existence of other civilizations, particularly in the Near East. With the spread of Christianity there was a tendency to dismiss these as pagan, but there could be no denial of their existence. In contrast, only in the late nineteenth century did the Chinese learn that civilization had a plural. Until then they had believed that theirs was the only civilization under heaven. It was surrounded by concentric rings of peoples of increasing barbarity. The least barbarous and most tolerable were the sinicized peoples on its northeastern and southern peripheries. These were its traditional tributaries of Korea, Japan, Mongolia, and Annam (Vietnam). A more dangerous group lived on its Central Asian frontiers. These peoples invaded periodically. The Chinese tried to keep them divided and either bought them off with trading privileges or exterminated them.[10]

The Chinese believed that their country was so large that it could not be digested by any other cultural group and thus was destined to outlast the competition. Although foreign groups had occupied China from time to time, the Chinese believed that they had always managed to transform these political conquerors into their own cultural conquests.[11] This view is so fundamental in China that there are

---

[8] *Genesis*, 1:28.

[9] William Theodore de Bary, *East Asian Civilizations: A Dialogue in Five Stages* (Cambridge, MA: Harvard University Press, 1988), 70.

[10] Owen Lattimore, *Inner Asian Frontiers of China*, American Geographical Society, Research Series no. 21 (New York: American Geographical Society, 1940), 238–48, 511–12; Thomas J. Barfield, *The Perilous Frontier: Nomadic Empires and China, 221 BC to AD 1757* (Cambridge, MA: Blackwell, 1989), 275–94; Jerome Chen, *China and the West: Society and Culture 1815–1937* (Taipei: Southern Materials Center, 1985), 26.

[11] Jerome Chen, 25–6.

a variety of terms for it. The modern terms are "to make Chinese" (使中國化) or "to make Han Chinese" (漢化), while there are two traditional terms meaning "to come and be transformed" (徠化 and 嚮化).[12] Similarly, there are two English words for it: sinicization and sinification. The problem with this view is that foreign rule in China accounts for nearly 400 years of the last 1,000 – the Mongols during the Yuan Dynasty (1279–1368) and the Manchus during the Qing Dynasty (1644–1911). Official Chinese histories minimize the cultural impact of these peoples, but recent scholarship suggests otherwise.[13] One author bluntly describes Qing rule in China as the "Manchu occupation."[14] The Chinese, nevertheless, still believe to this day that they have always managed to sinicize the outsider and, prior to the twentieth century, had never been "barbarized" themselves. They also have not drawn attention to the widely varying geographic extent of China. Yet a quick perusal of a historical atlas shows territory varying enormously by dynasty.

Before the Reformation there also had been an illusion of unity in the West. But the vicious religious wars of the sixteenth and seventeenth centuries had shattered such pretenses. Only the Peace of Westphalia in 1648 had finally ended the period of continentwide religious wars. Westphalia had ushered out the symbol of the unity of Christendom, the Holy Roman Empire, and ushered in a new period of

---

[12] Fairbank, "A Preliminary Framework," 9.

[13] Crossley, *passim*; Gertraude Roth, "The Manchu–Chinese Relationship, 1618–1636," in *From Ming to Ch'ing: Conquest, Region, and Continuity in Seventeenth-Century China,* Jonathan D. Spence and John E. Wills, Jr., eds. (New Haven: Yale University Press, 1979), 4, 18, 25; Edmund S. Wehrle, *Britain, China, and the Antimissionary Riots 1891–1900* (Minneapolis: University of Minnesota Press, 1966), 25–6, 73, 78, 115–8; Mark Elliott, "Bannerman and Townsman: Ethnic Tension in Nineteenth-Century Jiangnan," *Late Imperial China* 11, no. 1 (June 1990): 36–74; Mark C. Elliott, *The Manchu Way. The Eight Banners and Ethnic Identity in Late Imperial China* (Stanford: Stanford University Press, 2001), xiv, xviii, 8, 28, 361.
There is also significant evidence of deep-seated ethnic tensions between the Manchus and the Han Chinese. See Kuo, 5; Elliott, "Resident Aliens," 303–5, 391–8; S. L. Tikhvinsky, "Manzhou Rule in China," in *Manzhou Rule in China,* S. L. Tikhvinsky, ed., and David Skvirsky, trans. (Moscow: Progress Publishers, 1983), 24–7; O. L. Fishman, "Qing Policy in Ideology," in Ibid., 142–5; P. M. Ustin, "Pu Songling: Accuser of the Manzhou Conquerors," in Ibid., 150, 156; B. M. Novikov, "The Rising of 1787–1788 in Taiwan," in Ibid., 167; Y. B. Porshneva, "Popular Religious Sects in Opposition to the Qing Dynasty," in Ibid., 184, 187–8; V. P. Ilyushechkin, "Anti-Manzhou Edge of the Taiping Peasant War," in Ibid., 258; L. N. Borokh, "Anti-Manzhou Ideas of the First Chinese Bourgeois Revolutionaries (Lu Haodong Confession)," in Ibid., 297, 307; Hara: 392, 426–7; Lynn A. Struve, ed. and trans., *Voices from the Ming–Qing Cataclysm: China In Tigers' Jaws* (New Haven: Yale University Press, 1993), 262n.5; Jonathan D. Spence, *God's Chinese Son: The Taiping Heavenly Kingdom of Hong Xiuquan* (New York: W. W. Norton, 1996), 115, 160–3, 181–2; Mi Chu Wiens, "Anti-Manchu Thought during the Early Ch'ing," *Papers on China,* East Asian Research Center, Harvard University, 22A (May 1969): 1–24.

[14] Elliott, "Resident Aliens," 204.

modern European states. As a result of this implosion of Christendom, a whole body of international law developed in Europe to govern relations among juridically equal nation-states. War had forced the many lands of Europe to recognize and ultimately live with their differences whereas the myth of homogeneity endured much longer in China.

In fact the Chinese were no more homogeneous than the Western Europeans. The Roman alphabet and the Latin language unified Western Europe in the same way that the ideographic writing system and Classical Chinese did China. The spoken languages in each province of China and each nation of Western Europe varied equally. In both cases, they were written using the same symbols but according to divergent linguistic encoding procedures. Each civilization possessed an overarching common culture, represented in China by Confucianism, Buddhism, and Taoism and in the West by the Greco-Roman classical heritage and the Judeo-Christian religious heritage. Like Christianity, Confucianism was also subdivided into competing schools of interpretation, which, in contrast to the West, generally did not resolve such differences on the field of battle.

In reality, China was no more ethnically homogeneous than Western Europe, with the latter's overwhelmingly Caucasian population, and Chinese history was no more continuous than Western European history. The nature of this discontinuity and heterogeneity, however, differed. In Western history, Europe has not often been united within one great empire. Particularly in modern times, it has been fractured into numerous nation-states despite a common cultural heritage. In China, dynasties and provinces varied as did nation-states in Western Europe. In reality, dynastic control was very loose compared to the levels of local control attained by central governments in the West.[15] Moreover, provincial loyalties in many ways mirrored the national divisions in the West – each province possessed an enduring subculture and dialect that distinguished it from the others. A key basis for individual loyalties was the village of origin. People from the same province and especially from the same village were assumed to have common bonds of loyalty.

These were all myths underlying the Chinese ideology of empire: In reality, Chinese history is not continuous; China is not an immutable location on the globe; its people are not homogeneous; the languages spoken are no more dialects than are the many languages of Europe; China has not managed to eradicate foreign influences; and the world has other great civilizations. In Western terms, imperial China was not a unified state. Rather, it was a vast empire of heterogeneous and often competing parts, very loosely controlled from the center, and often under

---

[15] Chun-ming Chang, 230–1.

siege from internal rebellion and external invasion.[16] Official ideology in China strove to present it as the homogenous and stable nation that it was not.

Unfortunately, the Chinese succumbed to their own propaganda. These myths led to a soporific complacency in the waning years of the Qing Dynasty. As bad as all of the intrusions of the Western and Russian imperialists were, the Chinese had faith that somehow their culture would inevitably emerge triumphant and uncorrupted. Any setbacks were only temporary. The Chinese lacked the omnipresent sense of vulnerability of the Japanese that motivated the latter to study the West so carefully. While the Chinese would resolutely cling to their myths of empire and dismiss westerners as just another group of distasteful barbarians, the Japanese chose to investigate the matter further.

The Japanese, particularly of the early Meiji era (1868–1912), considered their country to be a vulnerable place. Japan is a land of frequent earthquakes where, in an instant, all visible landmarks can be reduced to rubble. The people live on the coast since the interior is mountainous. Earthquakes at sea bring devastating tidal waves while the prevailing air currents bring typhoons to these exposed shorelines. During the Tokugawa period (1600–1867), the Japanese government had pursued a policy of seclusion or "locked up country" (鎖国). Like the Chinese, they have shared an image of their own cultural superiority. In the Tokugawa period, many Japanese believed that, by the will of the gods, Japan was a country of unique virtue and superiority; and that Western influence must be eliminated lest it threaten this virtue.[17] They believed in the divine origin of Japan, of the Japanese, and of the imperial family, a belief embedded in Shintō doctrine. This made the Japanese people superior to all others, including the Chinese.[18] In the Meiji period, these Shintō beliefs were given even greater emphasis as a way to legitimate the westernizing reforms by making them in the name of an emperor, descended from the sun goddess. This was necessary because traditional Japan took the same dim view of unsinicized foreigners as did China. The Japanese sense of their own vulnerability and awareness of Chinese civilization in distinction to Japanese civilization, however, tempered their sense of superiority. They were aware that there was an outside not connected to the Japanese cultural world, whereas the Chinese had always perceived the barbarian world as eventually melding into their own. This difference of awareness would be one factor helping to account for the very different approach that the Japanese eventually took *vis-à-vis* the West.

[16] Elleman, *passim.*

[17] Totman, 376, 482.

[18] Beasley, *Meiji Restoration,* 75.

In addition to different views concerning the nature of civilization, different understandings of the course of history had emerged in the East and West. Traditionally the Chinese have considered history to be cyclical. In imperial China this meant a succession of dynasties the outlines of whose particular histories were similar. In each dynastic succession, a new and virtuous dynasty overthrew a decadent previous one. The new dynasty would flourish for a time until it succumbed to the same corrupting influences that had undermined its predecessor. Decay would eventually reach the point where yet another dynasty would take over. This is known as "the dynastic cycle." Even today in some quarters the ruling communists in China are considered to be just the latest dynasty in an endless succession.

According to traditional Chinese views, dynasties rose and fell in accordance to the waxing and waning of the virtue of their emperors. The emperor must properly punish evil and reward virtue to maintain the harmony of the cosmos.[19] Traditional Chinese notions of governance particularly stressed his ritual responsibilities. He must correctly perform certain sacrifices and successfully delegate the performance of others. Sacrifices of the first order comprised those to the heavens, the earth, imperial ancestors, and to the spirits of the land and the harvests. Second-class sacrifices comprised those to the sun, the moon, the emperors of preceding dynasties, Confucius, the first cultivator, the first mistress of the silk worms, the heavenly spirits, the earthly spirits, and *guandi* (關帝), the tutelary deity of the Qing. The list of third-class sacrifices is even longer.[20] All of these sacrifices had to be ritually correct lest a lack of propriety offend the spirits, who would express their wrath in natural disasters, popular rebellions, and, in the worst case, in a dynastic overthrow. This is a radically different way of explaining natural phenomena from that of the West, which early on with the Greeks gravitated toward empirical explanations based on math and science. Instead of emphasizing current human behavior in conformity with static rules in order to influence the future, the Western educational system increasingly emphasized the analysis of the past and of on-going experiments in order to understand the natural world.

According to Chinese thinking, eventually there always came a time when imperial virtue weakened, and natural disasters and other misfortunes proliferated until they culminated in dynastic overthrow. In Chinese terminology this was

---

[19] Fung Yu-lan, *A History of Chinese Philosophy*, Derk Bodde, trans., vol. 1 (Princeton: Princeton University Press, 1983), 162–5; Wing-tsit Chan, trans., and comp., *A Source Book in Chinese Philosophy* (Princeton: Princeton University Press, 1973), 245.

[20] Boulais, 354–5; Herbert A. Giles, *A Chinese–English Dictionary*, 2nd ed. (1912; reprint, Taipei: Ch'eng-wen Publishing Co., 1978), 802.

known as the loss of the dynasty's "mandate of heaven" (天命) or authority to rule. A lost mandate became a *carte blanche* for the formation of a rival dynasty to replace the one in decay. The concept has not disappeared in China but still looms in the wings.[21] Frequent natural disasters or overly evident decadence of its rulers threatens their enduring mandate to rule.

In imperial times, the goal of a victorious ascendant dynasty was to attain the highest level of virtue of the preceding dynasties. Surpassing their maximum attainments was impossible, for history was cyclical, not progressive. In contrast, many in the West considered history to be linear in the form of time lines and "the march of progress," a common term expressing the Western understanding of human history. Even such conservative Western thinkers as Edmund Burke assumed that change was both inevitable and desirable. Burke wrote in his *Reflections on the Revolution in France,* "A state without the means of some change is without the means of its conservation. Without such means it might even risk the loss of that part of the constitution which it wished the most religiously to preserve."[22] Whereas the West looked forward into the future with the expectation of progress, the Chinese looked upward (上) to their ancestors for approval. For the Chinese, the future was below, in a deep and unseen abyss. In the West, the attainments of illustrious ancestors did not represent the summit of human achievement but rather way-stations on the road to human progress.[23] This deeply held belief in progress led to an emphasis on reform in the West and a penchant for new approaches to reform. In imperial China, there were certainly periods of reform, but these were often presented as an attempt to restore an idealized past, not as a proud trek into *terra incognita,* an image that has long captured the Western imagination.

This difference also reflected divergent views concerning time. In the West, time was perceived to move forward along a horizontal line; in China, time descended along a vertical path. The Chinese characters for above and below are 上 and 下, respectively. Last year was 上年 while next year is 下年; last month was 上月 while the next month is 下月; this morning is 上午 while this afternoon is 下午. These are just a few examples. Westerners marched forward into the future leaving the past behind them, whereas the Chinese looked up to a past eternally pressing

---

[21] The 1989 Tiananmen massacre has been interpreted by some to indicate a loss of the mandate of heaven by the communists. See Orville Schell, *Mandate of Heaven* (New York: Simon & Schuster, 1994).

[22] Edmund Burke, *Reflections on the Revolution in France,* J. G. A. Pocock, ed. (1790; reprint, Indianapolis: Hackett Publishing, 1987), 19.

[23] Robert K. Merton, *Science, Technology & Society in Seventeenth Century England* (New Jersey: Humanities Press, 1978), 224–38.

down on them from above and fell willy-nilly into the future. The West focused on the future while China dedicated itself to the past. East and West were headed toward different points on the compass.[24]

In addition to these fundamentally different understandings of the course of human history, the East and West had equally divergent views concerning the natural world. Chinese in imperial times explained it in terms of the balance between the forces *yin* (陰) and *yang* (陽). They believed that all things and events could be explained in terms of this balance. *Yin* and *yang* represented opposites: The former was negative, passive, weak, and destructive whereas the latter was positive, active, strong, and constructive. This idea was a basis for the role of the emperor as harmonizer of the universe: He had to strive to balance the opposing forces of *yin* and *yang* to insure cosmic harmony. This led to a focus on the correct observance of rituals and correct balance between punishments and rewards in order to insure the continuing harmony in the natural order.

Deciphering the balance of *yin* and *yang* was very complicated and connected with the traditional Chinese doctrine concerning the Five Elements of metal, wood, water, fire, and earth. Interaction among the various elements and between *yin* and *yang* accounted for both change within the universe and also for its essential continuity.[25] Varying balances led to changes, but the dominant element for each era followed in a prescribed succession, thereby explaining the endlessly repeating cycles in history. Deciphering such balances gave rise to highly elaborated theories of divination. These had their own sets of extremely complicated rules, such as those pertaining to the eight triagrams and the sixty-four hexagrams explained by Taoism and in the *Book of Changes* (易經), the classic of Chinese divination.[26] Suffice it to say that by the time of the Greeks, Chinese approaches to understanding the natural world had headed off in a radically different direction from the general development of Western thinking.

The Greeks would lead the West to an emphasis on rationality, logical consistency, and empiricism. This way of looking at the world and endeavoring to understand it ultimately culminated in the scientific method developed during the Scientific Revolution of the seventeenth century. Christianity used Greek analytical methods as a point of departure and developed it further. Many of the first great modern European scientists were Catholic priest-astronomers. During the

---

[24] I am indebted to Bruce A. Elleman for these observations concerning the differences in perceiving time. Chu Djang, "Chinese Suzerainty: A Study of Diplomatic Relation between China and Her Vassal States (1870–1895)" (Ph.D. diss., Johns Hopkins University, 1935), 5.

[25] Wing-tsit Chan, 244–6.

[26] Fung Yu-lan, *History of Chinese Philosophy*, vol. 1, 379; "Daoism," in Embree, vol. 1, 361.

Enlightenment there would be a parting of the ways between the main concerns of the church and the scientific community, so that priests would no longer dominate the ranks of the great scientists. But in both the Western secular and religious communities there was a trend toward a growing reliance on reason to understand the natural and moral worlds. Logic must be consistent. Beliefs must meet the test of rationality. In China, the unity of thought between the religious and secular worlds endured; there was no great dichotomy between the religious and the secular or between faith and reason, the precise boundaries of which so preoccupied Western thinking.

Whereas the Western mind sought fundamental overarching principles that governed the entire natural order, the Chinese had a layered belief system. The natural order was one of waxing and waning belief systems so that Confucianism, Buddhism, and Taoism could all peacefully cohabit the same mental world. Their cyclical view of history did not require logical consistency or the unity of thought. This greatly frustrated Western missionaries and foreign civil servants in China. To them it defied rationality that intelligent Chinese seemed to have few qualms about simultaneously adhering to incompatible belief systems. James Dyner Ball, who lived in China for thirty years and served in the British civil service in Hong Kong, noted "the utter confusion of thought which characterises the Chinese as a race."[27] The Western psyche demanded syncretism; the Chinese did not.

The sources of knowledge about the cosmic order and correct social relations were to be found in the Chinese classics, many written during the Warring States Period (471/403 B.C.–221 B.C.). Confucius died on the eve of this period, which encompassed the lives of Mencius, Xunzi, and the Legalists and witnessed the development of Taoism.[28] The classics were the finite source of human knowledge whose texts should be memorized and whose style should be imitated as closely as possible. There was a sense that there had been a distant golden age that should be restored. In imperial China knowledge of the classics would become the basis for status. The imperial examination system tested this knowledge to determine eligibility for civil service. The humanities reigned. In contrast, in the West knowledge was segregated by field, and each type reigned only in its own quarter.

Medieval westerners initially focused their quest for knowledge in Scripture; from the Renaissance onward they searched more broadly using textual analysis to determine the origin and accuracy of Scripture. They also engaged in scientific

---

[27] James Dyner Ball, *Things Chinese: Being Notes on Various Subjects Connected with China,* 3rd ed. (London: Sampson Low, Marston, 1900), 138.

[28] "Warring States Period," in Embree, vol. 4, 212–3.

experimentation, applied logical consistency, and collected and analyzed data. Ultimately, the Western educational system stressed inductive and deductive reasoning, synthesis, and analysis as the fundamental approaches to knowledge. Unlike in the East, in the West memorization was a secondary, not a primary activity. Potential knowledge was considered to be vast if not infinite, as is indicated by the numerous and proliferating academic disciplines that organize Western universities. Ultimately creativity would be valued over imitation. The goal was to supersede the past, not, as in the case of China, to recreate it. Whereas knowledge was static and backward-looking in China, it was a broad vista in the West beckoning man to explore.[29] It is this very turn of mind that has given "backward" a pejorative connotation in the West, whereas in traditional China, the past, far from being considered inferior to the present, was thought to include a far superior golden age. "Backward" is pejorative to a westerner because of a presumption that the world should and does move "forward." For this reason, in the West it is common to dismiss the ideas of nineteenth-century observers of China because their observations are assumed to be corrupted by prejudice and inherently inferior to those of people living in the present, a time far removed from both the people and time under consideration.

Whereas the West turned to reason and science to understand the natural world, traditional China focused on ethical human relations to harmonize it. If human relations were in harmony, likewise the cosmos. Instead of toward reason, the East gravitated toward ethics, but ethics in an Asian sense. Ethics concerned proper human decorum in a wide variety of concrete social situations between parties of differing status. Ethics in China and Japan did not, as in the West, focus on abstract universalistic rules good for all situations and for all parties.

Confucius paired human relations into five types, each between a superior and an inferior. They were between sovereign and subject, father and son, elder and younger brother, husband and wife, and between friends. It was essential that behavior conformed to norms for propriety and filial piety. Inferiors had to treat superiors with deference while superiors should treat inferiors with forbearance. In the Chinese and Japanese social systems, there was no place for strictly equal relations; equality was a nonexistent category in both countries. Relationships took place in a Confucian framework of infinite gradations of inequality, determined by age, sex, connections, and social status. People did not simply have brothers, but an eldest brother, followed by a second eldest brother or a first younger

---

[29] Merton, 55–136; Paul Hazard, *European Thought in the Eighteenth Century* (Gloucester, MA: Peter Smith, 1973), *passim*; Margaret C. Jacob, *The Cultural Meaning of the Scientific Revolution* (Philadelphia: Temple University Press, 1988), *passim*.

brother, followed by a second younger brother, and so on. The most senior male in a family bore the responsibility for all the others. They in turn owed him loyalty and obedience.

In China, the primary human duty was loyalty to parents or filial piety, whereas in Japan the primary loyalty was to the feudal lord or emperor.[30] In practical terms, this meant that it would not be difficult for the Meiji government to transform a loyalty to the emperor into a very powerful nationalism ultimately in support of an expansionist foreign policy, whereas family and regional loyalties in China hindered the development of nationalism, let alone national unity to face a foreign foe. This hobbled Chinese foreign policy.

The absence of equality in Chinese social relations had enormous consequences in the fields of domestic and international law. There were no absolute rules of conduct, only rules contingent on a particular relative status combined with a particular situation. The degree of criminality depended on the relative status of those involved. This view permeated the Qing legal system. For instance, parents could kill their children without punishment, whereas the violation of filial piety resulting from an accidental homicide of a parent by a child entailed an automatic death penalty.[31] In China, ethics were relative; right and wrong were not absolute moral categories. The propriety of an action depended on the relative status of the persons involved.

Confucianism stressed the virtues of human-heartedness, righteousness, propriety, wisdom, and good faith.[32] The section of the Qing legal code devoted to rewarding virtue lists the following types of commendable conduct: female chastity, faithful widows, longevity, generational familial concord, charity to the poor, wisdom, state service, loyalty to the sovereign, and civil and conjugal loyalty as well as filial and fraternal love.[33] Completely absent in Western thinking was the Chinese application of ethics to the deceased. In the East, human relations extended beyond death. Ancestor worship was an essential ethical responsibility of the living and its neglect incurred the wrath of heaven.

In contrast to the particularistic world of the Chinese, the Western mind gravitated toward universal principles that applied to all individuals regardless of

---

[30] Inazo Nitobe, *Bushido the Soul of Japan: An Exposition of Japanese Thought,* rev. ed. (1905; reprint, Boston: Tuttle Publishing, 1969), 83–4.

[31] Wing-tsit Chan, 78–9; T'ung-tsu Ch'ü, *Law and Society in Traditional China* (Paris: Mouton, 1961), 21–67, 226, 278.

[32] Fung Yu-lan, *A Short History of Chinese Philosophy,* Derk Bodde, ed. (New York: Free Press, 1966), 197.

[33] Boulais, 304–10.

status. The Western penchant for simple but far-reaching principles and reliance on these universal principles to explain particular phenomena gave rise to a focus, not on the differences separating individuals, as was the case in imperial China, but on the overarching similarities uniting them. Many in the West saw a general equality encompassing all individuals and obscuring their differences. This gave rise to the idea of natural rights or universal rights belonging to all human beings.

The philosophical system of the East had nothing comparable to the highly developed theory of natural rights in the West. Christianity espoused the doctrine that all people had souls and in that sense all were equal before God. From this came the notion of natural rights: All individuals possess certain inherent rights simply by virtue of their humanity. Such rights antedated the state and therefore could not be taken away by the state. Indeed, Christianity endorsed the doctrine that all persons including rulers were subject to God's law. From this sprang the concept of equality before the law. In China and Japan, people were not considered equals but as unequal members belonging to a hierarchy of unequal groups whose interests took precedence over those of any individual. The state antedated the individual; therefore state interests took precedence over individual interests.[34] Westerners soon realized that as individuals they had no legal rights while in China or Japan, and that as foreigners they were at the bottom of this hierarchy of human relations.

In the West, laws protected the rights of individuals, whereas in China and Japan individuals remained in the care of the groups to which they belonged. Unlike in the West, this group identity was more important than any individual identity. According to Confucian norms governing propriety, an individual was subservient first to his emperor, second to his family, and third to other groups with which he identified. In all three cases, he was subservient to his elders, both living and deceased. Totally absent was a concern for liberty or free will, two topics that would dominate Western philosophy. In China, the cyclical view of history was on a general level quite deterministic. The cyclical view, combined with the Confucian hierarchy of social relations demanding carefully choreographed behavior, left little scope for free will. Instead, there is a strong thread of fatalism running through Chinese thinking.[35] Each person was born with an immutable fate (命) that determined the general course of his life. Li Hongzhang, one of the Chinese most familiar with Western thinking in the late nineteenth century,

---

[34] Nitobe, 88–9; Harumi Befu, *Japan: An Anthropological Introduction* (San Francisco: Chandler Publishing, 1971), 96–7.

[35] Wing-tsit Chan, 78–9; Donald A. MacKenzie, *China and Japan: Myths and Legends* (1923; reprint, London: Senate, 1994), 315.

argued, "It is a mistake to suppose that success depends on mental ability. It is all a matter of luck. One man is prosperous and another is poor and downtrodden, not because of any mental qualities that either of them may possess, but just according to their good or bad luck."[36] People could not escape their fate or their social obligations.

The preoccupations of Chinese and Western thinking differed and gave rise to different social orders. Differences in approach reflected differences in perceptions. Whereas westerners concerned themselves with such abstractions as the pursuit of truth and justice, easterners focused on concrete social situations. In the West and particularly in the Anglophone world, the hue and cry would be for (individual) liberty and justice; in China, the focus would be on the maintenance of (group) social harmony. The West would pursue the truth via the expansion of human knowledge with the ultimate goal of justice; the Far East would focus on the study of proper social decorum (their definition of ethics) with the goal of social and cosmic harmony. These were radically different world views.

In China, group affiliations were cemented by personal relations or connections, *guanxi* (關係) in Chinese. Such connections were based on the combined links of lineage, interfamily relationships of previous generations, geographic origin, teacher–student ties, professional ties, schoolmate ties, marriage, and sworn brotherhood. *Guanxi* could either be strengthened or weakened by the degree of *ganqing* (感情) – the shared sentiments required for genuine friendship. An individual's power base depended on his *guanxi* network, meaning the number and strength of these common ties. Social networks in both China and Japan were maintained through reciprocity and astute gift-giving. The latter would be considered bribery in the West, whereas in the East the exchange of gifts was an integral part of the social system.[37] According to the *Book of Rites* (禮記): "In the highest antiquity they prized (simply conferring) good; in the time next to this, giving and repaying...was the thing attended to. And what the rules of propriety...value is that of reciprocity. If I give a gift and nothing comes in return, that is contrary to propriety; if the thing comes to me, and I give nothing in return, that also is

---

[36] Little, 184.

[37] Folsom, 108; Lien-sheng Yang, "The Concept of *Pao* as a Basis for Social Relations in China," in *Chinese Thought and Institutions*, John K. Fairbank, ed. (Chicago: University of Chicago Press, 1957), 291. For extensive modern anthropological examinations of gift-giving in China, see Mayfair Mei-hui Yang, 6, 68, 109, 130, 140, 151–2, 196; Yunxiang Yan, *The Flow of Gifts: Reciprocity and Social Networks in a Chinese Village* (Stanford: Stanford University Press, 1996), 14–5, 21, 44–5, 51–2, 68, 173, 175.

contrary to propriety."[38] In contrast to Western literature, which so often focuses on love between members of the opposite sex, friendship is the theme of the great Chinese popular novels, *The Water Margin* (水滸傳)[39] and *Romance of the Three Kingdoms* (三國演義). Similarly, Chinese paintings often feature two friends admiring the surrounding landscape.[40] Interpersonal relations, not individuality, lay at the heart of Chinese life.

The Japanese had an even more elaborately developed hierarchy of in-groups and out-groups than that represented by *guanxi* networks. To a greater extent than the Chinese, these networks were based on mutual indebtedness. The Japanese stressed the fulfillment of obligations to the emperor as the symbol for Japan, to ancestors for their achievements, to parents for their care, to superiors for their forbearance, and to teachers for their pedagogy.[41] As an island nation, the Japanese defined their own borders – geographic and racial – much more precisely than did the Chinese. The Japanese made the a priori assumption that Japan was a closed world composed of a hierarchy of closed mini-worlds. The Japanese were "the insiders" or *uchi* (內) whereas foreigners were eternally "outsiders" or *soto* (外). The Japanese segregated words of foreign origin with a separate alphabet, *katakana*, distinct from the *hiragana* alphabet for native words. The letters of these two alphabets have a one-to-one correspondence. Their only purpose in modern Japanese is to distinguish foreign from native concepts. Within Japan all groups, whether work colleagues, neighbors, classmates, friends, or family members, were insiders facing a world of far more numerous outsiders.[42] There was no comparable notion in Japan to that of sinicization. "Japanization" does not exist as a standard term because it is impossible for a non-Japanese ever to become Japanese. Theirs was and remains an exclusive and entirely hereditary club. This world view would cause the Japanese enormous problems when they set out to build a colonial empire, since colonies entailed incorporation of new lands whereas the Japanese way of ordering the world assumed an unbreachable exclusivity. Their colonial subjects would resent this insurmountable barrier. Exclusivity under the British Empire paled in comparison. Foreigners could and did become British. What was more, the British kings generally married them. A foreign bride for a Japanese emperor would have been absolutely unthinkable for the Japanese.

[38] Cited in Mayfair Mei-hui Yang, x.

[39] The title is also translated as *All Men Are Brothers*.

[40] Folsom, 17.

[41] Ruth Benedict, *The Chrysanthemum and the Sword: Patterns of Japanese Culture* (1946; reprint, Boston: Houghton Mifflin, 1989), 98–113.

[42] Hoye, 3, 19.

In addition to Confucian norms for social conduct, in the late nineteenth century the Chinese and Japanese also shared an emphasis on external appearances over substantive content. What in Western nations would have been considered to be superficial issues were actually matters of extreme importance in both China and Japan. In both of these countries, the concept of "face" played a critical role in human relations.[43] As one American author took the time to observe in 1900: "The history of China when read in the light of a knowledge of this national characteristic ["face"] will reveal the reason for many acts that before seem without sense or rhyme."[44]

---

[43] Much of this account of "face" is based on my earlier research (Paine, 54–7). While the notion of "face" is well accepted in the field of anthropology, few historians have availed themselves of this research. In 1944, Hu Hsien Chin wrote a path-breaking article for *American Anthropologist*, entitled "The Chinese Concepts of 'Face'" (Ibid., vol. 46 [1944]: 45–64). Other relevant sources from a wide variety of disciplines and specializations include: Emily M. Ahern, "The Power and Pollution of Chinese Women," in *Studies in Chinese Society*, Arthur P. Wolf, ed. (Stanford: Stanford University Press, 1978), 277; Dennis Bloodworth, *The Chinese Looking Glass* (New York: Farrar, Straus and Giroux, 1967), 229–303; David Bonavia, *The Chinese* (London: Butler & Tanner, 1980), 57–8; Jerome Chen, 43–4; Ch'ü, 29–30; Prasenjit Duara, *Culture, Power, and the State: Rural North China, 1900–1942* (Stanford: Stanford University Press, 1988), 182; Lloyd E. Eastman, *Family Fields, and Ancestors: Constancy and Change in China's Social and Economic History, 1550–1949* (New York: Oxford University Press, 1988), 37; Wolfram Eberhard, *Guilt and Sin in Traditional China* (Berkeley: University of California Press, 1967); Chang-tu Hu, *China: Its People, Its Society, Its Culture* (New Haven: HRAF Press, 1960), 493; William L. Parish, *Village and Family in Contemporary China* (Chicago: University of Chicago Press, 1978), 260; Jon L. Saari, "Breaking the Hold of Tradition: The Self-Group Interface in Traditional China," in *Social Interaction in Chinese Society*, Sidney L. Greenblatt, Richard W. Wilson, and Amy Auerbacher Wilson, eds. (USA: Praeger Publishers, 1982), 28–66; Richard J. Smith, *China's Cultural Heritage: The Ch'ing Dynasty 1644–1912* (Boulder, CO: Westview Press, 1983), 212–3; Sybille van der Sprenkel, *Legal Institutions in Manchu China: A Sociological Analysis*, London School of Economics Monographs on Social Anthropology, no. 24 (London: Athlone Press, 1962); Richard W. Wilson and Anne Wang Pusey, "Achievement Motivation and Small-Business Relationship Patterns in Chinese Society," in *Social Interaction in Chinese Society*, Greenblatt, Wilson, and Wilson, eds., 196, 198–9, 206; Yan, 133, 167.

Relevant older sources include: Emile Bard, *Chinese Life in Town and Country*, H. Twitchell, trans. and ed. (New York: G. P. Putnam's Sons, 1905), 55; William Gascoyne Cecil and Florence Cecil, *Changing China* (New York: D. Appleton, 1912), 166; Daniel Harrison Kulp, *Country Life in South China: The Sociology of Familialism*, vol. 1 (New York: Teachers College, Columbia University, 1925), 200; Olga Lang, *Chinese Family and Society*, International Secretariat, Institute of Pacific Relations and the Institute of Social Research (New Haven: Yale University Press, 1946), 37; Kenneth Scott Latourette, *The Chinese: Their History and Culture*, 2nd rev. ed., vol. 2 (New York: Macmillan, 1934), 209–10; Arthur H. Smith, *Chinese Characteristics*, 10th ed. (New York: Fleming H. Revell, 1894), 17; Gerald F. Windfield, *China: The Land and the People* (New York: William Sloan Associates, 1948), 30; Martin C. Yang, *A Chinese Village: Taitou, Shantung Province* (New York: Columbia University Press, 1945), 167–70.

[44] Rounsevelle Wildman, *China's Open Door: A Sketch of Chinese Life and History* (Boston: Lothrop Publishing Co., 1900), 7; see also viii–ix, 4–7.

The term "face" comes from Chinese usage. There are numerous idioms in Chinese concerning face.[45] The Japanese have a concept of personal reputation that performs much the same function as "face" does in China. In China, at the most basic level, "face" meant "public reputation," whereby an individual's sense of self-worth was not defined by himself or on any objective standard of achievement but by how others perceived him or the extent to which he had "face." "Face" could be had, given, and lost. It could be had or maintained by ostentatious displays of magnanimity, generosity, or power, which generally far exceeded any direct gains from the display but which served to preserve the imagery of face. The need to keep "face" helps to explain the banquets that the Chinese traditionally lavished on their guests. "Face" could be given by according someone the public tokens of respect which that person might not actually have deserved. In such a case, "giving face" meant to create a fiction or facade to mask a less perfect reality. "Giving face" flattered the receiver and added to his public reputation. Form took precedence over content. In disputes, the winner was expected to make some token gesture "to give face" to the vanquished. If he did not, it indicated a perception that the relations between the two no longer had any future. "Face" could be lost by acts of impropriety, stupidity, and especially by public humiliation. The key was not objective reality but public imagery. Private or concealed impropriety, stupidity, or humiliation did not entail a "loss of face." In these cases, it was important simply to cover one's tracks.

"Losing face" was a horrendous ordeal. In addition to the psychological pain to the victim, it lessened the value of his friendship to others. If lost in a spectacular fashion, it could threaten that Chinese person's *guanxi* network or a Japanese person's in-group connections. If someone had a penchant for "losing face," his acquaintances might conclude that he simply had a bad fate – better to stay away to avoid any chance of contagion. Therefore, Chinese and Japanese strove at all cost to avoid losing "face."

In Japan, there was an imperative to maintain a good reputation. The overarching value was honor. Each person must defend to the death his emperor's, his family's, and his own honor, for a life without respect was not worth living. This meant that the Japanese were extraordinarily sensitive to perceived insults. Allegations of misconduct however slight had to be refuted. Correct behavior had to be maintained: An individual must not live above his station in life. He must maintain self-control at all times. There was negligible latitude for mistakes. Observance of rules provided a way to navigate the perilous waters of social

---

[45] Mayfair Mei-hui Yang, 196.

interaction. Hence the Japanese focus on politeness and proper etiquette: The meticulous adherence to elaborate rules of etiquette minimized the need to clear one's name, a very trying and potentially life-threatening process. Often the only way to clear one's name in Japan was suicide. Only in death could one prove one's sincerity.[46] For all of these reasons, public reputation was essential in both China and Japan.

In the West, an individual's sense of self-worth stemmed from his achievements or his own evaluation of himself, not primarily from the valuations of others. Such notions as "individual conscience," "the immortal soul," and "human dignity" derived from the belief, of religious origin, in the inherent value of the individual regardless of his station in life or relationship to others. In the West, an individual's guilt was primarily before God, before his own conscience, or before the law, irrespective of what his acquaintances concluded, whereas in China and Japan individuals were shamed before their acquaintances. Whereas the West built its political system on a foundation of law and institutions, China rested its on a root-system of interlocking groups with interlocking mutual obligations all cemented by the personal *guanxi* networks and *uchi* affiliations, managed by the senior members of each of these groups. The sources of power were public knowledge in the former but a matter only of speculation in the latter. Thus, China and Japan before the Meiji Restoration retained a particularistic power base while the West from the time of the Romans was evolving in the direction of universalistic legal definitions of political office and political authority.

The Japanese imported China's Confucian ethical system, the classics, and classical Chinese during the sixth and seventh centuries with two critical modifications. They did not adopt the notion of "the mandate of heaven." Their dynasty never lost its authority to rule and remains the longest reigning monarchy in the world. According to Shintō beliefs, a descendant of the Sun Goddess founded the current dynasty in 660 B.C. The Japanese created an institution of the shogunate to serve as the buffer between the political legitimacy vested in the emperor and the actual political power exercised by the shoguns. Like dynasties in China, shogun families rose and fell.[47] The royal family in Japan has endured because, since the twelfth century, it has reigned but not ruled, has had authority but not power. The vicissitudes of governmental policy have not tainted the royal house. The emperor has remained above the infighting and on the throne because

---

[46] Benedict, 116, 134, 141, 147–76.

[47] Beasley, *Meiji Restoration*, 38; John M. Maki, "Emperor," in *Kodansha Encyclopedia of Japan,* vol. 2 (Tokyo: Kodansha, 1983), 203; "Amaterasu Ōmikami," in Ibid., vol. 1, 51.

he has remained the symbol of legitimacy, not the actual locus of power.[48] By the end of World War II, the United States clearly understood the legitimizing function and so permitted Emperor Hirohito (昭和天皇) to remain on the throne.

The Japanese also did not accept the Chinese prejudice against military service. On the contrary, military values suffused traditional Japanese culture. *Shōgun* (将軍) means "general" in Japanese. The shogunate was a military institution. *Bushidō* (武士道) or "the way of the samurai" provided the foundation for Japanese notions of right and wrong. These views emphasized loyalty, honor, and valor.[49] In China, the royal house both reigned and ruled. It oversaw a centralized government staffed by a civilian gentry-scholar elite who disdained military service. Confucianism, not the throne per se, legitimized the system. Therefore, imperial families came and went, but Confucianism endured. Confucianism, through its idealized social hierarchy, legitimized the status of the lettered elite as a group and, through the civil examination system, legitimized their government appointments as individuals. In traditional Japan the warrior class or samurai (侍) ruled, not for reasons of Confucian propriety, but because of the balance of power among the competing feudal lords. Whereas Confucianism was fundamental to the social order in China, it was supplemental in Japan, since a civilian lettered elite was not at the helm and the survival of the imperial family could provide continuity without Confucianism.[50] This meant that it was easier for the Japanese than the Chinese to discard elements of Confucianism in the nineteenth century in order to adopt westernized institutions.

In the nineteenth century, the West barged into China and Japan, assuming the juridical equality of nation-states and of their sovereigns, whereas the Chinese took for granted the inherently hierarchical relations among nations and men, and their own position at the summit of that hierarchy. The Japanese soon understood the potential of the Western system of international relations to undermine Chinese pretensions of primacy over Japan. In contrast, China had nothing to gain from the new system. Both China and the West assumed the indisputable superiority of their own way of understanding and ordering the world. East and West could not even agree on the most basic preliminaries to facilitate their interaction. They had fundamentally incompatible systems.

Guanxi and *uchi* affiliations greatly complicated diplomacy for westerners in the Far East. In the West, foreign relations were conducted among duly appointed

---

[48] Hoye, xiv; Beasley, "Meiji Political Institutions," 666.

[49] Nitobe, xi–xii; Yamamoto, 17–23, 30, 55, 72–3, 115.

[50] Beasley, *Meiji Restoration*, 38, 123.

ministers and representatives with known spheres of authority, whereas in China *guanxi* networks and in Japan *uchi* affiliations were, by their nature, secret – to reveal one's sources of power would vastly reduce their effectiveness. No one showed his hand in the high-stakes poker game of political intrigue. Natives and foreigners alike did not know the extent of an individual's *guanxi* or *uchi* base. In late nineteenth-century China, since the Empress Dowager was in and out of power for the last four decades of the Qing Dynasty, it was often not even clear who ruled. When the Empress Dowager did rule, it was unclear how she secured her authority in defiance of the Manchu laws for succession that gave her, a former emperor's inferior concubine, no quarter. Foreigners found diplomacy with China extremely frustrating at best.

Meanwhile, proliferating private commercial relations expanded the scope of potential disputes. In China, many situations which required a universalistic legal solution in the West were handled through the personalistic intervention of *guanxi*. From the Western point of view, like cases often produced inconsistent results in China. This was because of variations in the unseen *guanxi* networks involved.[51] If a Chinese were arrested, his friends or associates would descend on the magistrate's offices to offer persuasive words or bribes to secure his release. This network extended to the friends of friends so that indirect friendships could be called into play. Chinese formed secret societies, provincial clubs, and guilds as a means of self-protection; thus in times of need, there was a group to call on for help.[52] Foreigners had no such network of connections and therefore were particularly vulnerable while in China and Japan. Without the right of *habeas corpus*, they could be arbitrarily arrested and held indefinitely in the most squalid conditions.

Westerners found diplomacy in China particularly frustrating. In the East, "face" was an integral part of diplomacy: it set up the basic structure for diplomatic intercourse. Westerners, however, did not adhere to the give and take underlying "face." They were generally oblivious to such considerations or the rancor caused by this oversight. They saw negotiations as a utilitarian affair where both sides got down to business as soon as possible so that they could return home with something important accomplished. Westerners tended to be direct and to get to the point fast. Not so in China or Japan. There diplomacy was a carefully choreographed display whose significance lay not simply in the outcome of the negotiations but in the staging of that process. This difference is perhaps more understandable in the television age, when cameramen, by drawing attention to

---

[51] Paine, 81.
[52] Folsom, 18–29.

minor details, can transform the trivial into the sensational. In a sense, the Chinese operated in a psychological video age where the visuals were as important as the fine print.

In 1895, a Chinese-speaking American diplomat, long attached to the legation in Peking, explained as follows: "Nothing so confuses and disconcerts the Chinese as the blunt and outspoken way in which Western people, especially Americans and the English, express their opinions, or seek to accomplish any desired object. They cover up their designs as closely and as modestly as we do our bodies. We expose ours naked." He noted, "Much of the falsehood to which the Chinese as a nation are said to be addicted is a result of the demands of etiquette. A plain, frank 'no' is the height of discourtesy. Refusal or denial of any sort must be softened and toned down into an expression of regretted inability." He continued, "A Chinese very seldom will make an intentionally disagreeable or offensive remark." Instead, he expresses his dissatisfaction indirectly, leaving it up to the listener to draw the appropriate conclusions. "The extent to which the Chinese will go in order to cover up disagreeable truths, and the efforts they will make to disguise their real feelings and motives, are simply astonishing. This is equally true of all grades and classes."[53] This observer did not make the connection with "face," but that was what he was describing.

Japan was even harder than China for the Western mind to fathom. This was because it was a closed world. Westerners might come to Japan, but they were psychologically sealed off behind the smiling facade that the Japanese erected to keep nongroup members out of their interior world. The Chinese explicitly expressed the barrier between their civilization and foreign barbarity with arrogance. This immediately raised hackles in the West. The Japanese tended to be very gracious but totally uncommunicative. Westerners had no idea what the Japanese were really thinking. Whereas the Chinese had the outlook of the inhabitants of a great power long-accustomed to dominion over a vast empire populated by many peoples, the Japanese inhabited an island nation. They kept others out less by force of arms than by a very polite but utterly impenetrable reserve. Since foreigners could not be "Japanized," there was no point wasting the effort in instructing them as the Chinese regularly did in their communications with Western nations. Many Chinese assumed that the West would have to succumb to the force of Chinese civilization and become sinicized. But these very attempts at sinicization infuriated the westerners, who were equally convinced of the superiority of Western civilization and of Christianity.

[53] Chester Holcombe, *The Real Chinaman* (New York: Dodd Mead, 1895), 278, 274, 276, 276–7.

The Japanese shared the basic Chinese system of "face" and *guanxi* but with many subtle twists.[54] Like the Chinese, they emphasized external appearances over substantive content, but they took this emphasis to an extreme unimaginable in China let alone in the West. Japan took China's Confucian framework of superiors and inferiors and elaborated on it to create a far more finely calibrated scale of differentiation. In addition, they ritualized this scale so that each social status required its own prescribed form of behavior. Like China, in Japan, the status distinction between superiors or *meue* (目上) and subordinates or *meshita* (目下) depended on age, generation, social class, rank, education, sex, family ties, employment, birthplace, and so on.[55] There was no absolute status but only status relative to another particular person. Each social interaction required the recalculation of status relative to that of the other person. Before one sentence could be safely uttered this had to be done. Japanese cannot be spoken without choosing a level of politeness that expresses itself grammatically throughout the language in verb forms, prefixes, suffixes, sentence structures, and specific word choices. Such a system of social interaction required years of education to master.[56]

In addition to complicated assessments of status, there were set dialogs for interacting with others. These included standard greetings and farewells; the proper way to walk, sit, bow, and eat; and the proper level of politeness for addressing someone. Each set of rules was dependent on the occasion and on the relative status of the other party. For every social situation, there was one right form of conduct and innumerable wrong ones. Errors even in small details, such as the way to sit in a chair, to enter a room, or to offer a piece of paper to give to another, were considered to be deliberate insults and therefore highly offensive. These rules choreographed daily life in Japan in the manner of their highly ritualized Noh plays.[57] Those not brought up in this system could not possibly decode the constant barrage of sign language surrounding them. Indeed, westerners were generally not even aware that a silent dialog was in progress. The complexity of the system made it extraordinarily easy to "lose face" or make others do so. Errors in conduct automatically translated into a "loss of face" for oneself or for the other person. Either one had committed a blunder or an offense.[58]

---

[54] Boye Lafayette De Mente, *NTC's Dictionary of Japan's Cultural Words* (Lincolnwood, IL: NTC Publishing Group, 1997), 11–3, 21–2.

[55] De Mente, 1–2; Benedict, 51–4.

[56] Agnes M. Niyekawa, *Minimum Essential Politeness: A Guide to the Japanese Honorific Language* (Tokyo: Kodansha International, 1991).

[57] De Mente, 4; Benedict, 48–9, 70.

[58] De Mente, 11–3.

Westerners could not interpret breaches in conduct. If a Japanese broke with the rules of propriety, it meant something specific and something important, requiring the other party, if he knew what was good for him, to understand, process, and respond. Westerners generally expressed themselves directly: In their words, they "got to the point" or "got down to business." This was the last thing that a Japanese would ever contemplate doing. Only untutored children and obnoxious foreigners were direct. The Japanese language was structured to facilitate expressing oneself as vaguely as possible. Only a complete idiot required explicit explanations. Normal people were expected to process the hints and respond appropriately.

Proper responses included deferential behavior to superiors. For westerners this was well-nigh impossible, since their estimation of status did not jibe with the carefully weighted Japanese scale. Moreover, in the Western mind, persons were often treated as equals, whereas this was a logical impossibility in Japan or China. Since no two individuals were exactly alike – even identical twins had a birth order – there was no occasion to treat anyone as a precise equal. The Japanese never expected foreigners to behave like Japanese, since it was believed that this was a genetic impossibility. In Japan, foreigners were off the charts of accepted social behavior.

Westerners also had trouble reading the Japanese because of *tatemae* (建て前) or the facade that masked the underlying *honne* (本音) or reality.[59] In the West individual integrity entailed an aspiration for consistency between private thoughts and public actions.[60] In China and Japan it was taken for granted that these two worlds were distinct and inconsistent. To maintain social harmony, how could it be otherwise? Westerners, who by comparison tended to take things, in their words, "at face value," often accepted the facade as the reality. These were the ones who interpreted the gracious hospitality generally accorded to foreign guests as an accurate indicator of underlying sympathies instead of the rigid decorum for hosting foreign guests, a mere ritual, not a reality.

In contrast, foreigners remarked on the Japanese and Chinese mastery of Western etiquette. "The people of the Far East are not much inclined to come out of their shell. They live an official life, keep to themselves, give receptions extremely well arranged, and correct dinners, where the guests are very well chosen; they never commit a blunder in etiquette; they are themselves scrupulously punctilious in their social duties, irreproachable in their dress and bearing at State functions."[61]

---

[59] De Mente, 6–7.

[60] I owe this observation to Catherine Diamond.

[61] "The War in the East," *The Times* (London), 22 September 1894, p. 5.

Because the Japanese social system demanded a mastery of the rules of decorum, they paid special attention to Western decorum when dealing with westerners. It was a reflexive action, reflecting their culture's emphasis on correct social relations as the overarching moral imperative.

The combination of "face" with *guanxi* or *uchi* affiliations became brittle during interaction with groups that did not adhere to the rules of "face." On the surface, there appeared to be strength in numbers: In times of need no individual could become isolated, but could always enlist the combined powers of his *guanxi* or *uchi* network. But improprieties committed by any individual group member made the entire group "lose face." The situation was worse for families, where the "loss of face" extended beyond the living to the dead and blighted the sacred honor of the ancestors. In the case of the Chinese imperial house, "having face" was the prerequisite to rule. Confucian norms of propriety put the individual at the mercy of the group, since he was subordinate to it, while "face" put the group at the mercy of the individual, since he could damage its sacred honor. As long as everyone played by the rules, the system worked. Enter the West.

* * *

In the nineteenth century, educated Chinese focused on defending a civilization, not a nation. Therefore, they found it hard to adapt that civilization and its underlying belief system in order to fend off the industrializing powers.[62] The whole notion of reform grated against the Chinese ideal of continuity with an idealized past and their unitary conception of civilization. The Chinese educational system had stressed understanding the present in terms of the past. Because the arrival of industrialized and therefore technologically superior westerners was unprecedented, the Chinese were ill-equipped to remake themselves in order to fend off the West. The Western challenge required an iconoclasm that Chinese tradition abhorred. This problem was reinforced by the very success of Chinese civilization over the millennia. In this sense, the Chinese became victims of their own past cultural success. After 5,000 years of imperial triumph, why should China change in the face of a few cultural upstarts? They were but a momentary aberration on the eternity that was China.

The original overarching policy objective for the Chinese was to keep China unchanged, whereas the Japanese goal was the maintenance of national autonomy. Until the Sino-Japanese War most Chinese fundamentally did not believe that the West had anything significant to offer them beyond a few curios. There is a very famous remark made by the Emperor Qianlong (乾隆皇帝) (1711–99), when he

---

[62] Beasley, *Meiji Restoration*, 413.

declined trade overtures made by George III of England. The Qianlong Emperor, who ruled the Qing Empire at the height of its glory, treated the British delegation as a tribute mission. He sent an edict to King George concluding: "We possess all things. I set no value on objects strange or ingenious, and have no use for your country's manufactures."[63] The Qianlong Emperor wrote a poem commemorating the occasion: "England is paying homage" because "My Ancestors' merit and virtue must have reached their distant shores." But "[c]urios and the boasted ingenuity of their devices I prize not."

A century later, Chinese attitudes broadened only to the extent of expressing an interest in Western armaments. At best Western culture was thought to be an inferior barbarian concoction, and at worst a vile contagion. Its impact on China should be minimized, hence all the violence against Christian missionaries, who were considered to be the professional bearers of this cultural contagion. Many Chinese believed that missionary activities constituted a frontal assault on the Chinese way of life. Many of the missionaries would have agreed: They were indeed intent upon changing the Chinese. The Western belief system that they brought with them was highly corrosive to traditional Chinese beliefs, and both China and Japan accurately gauged the seriousness of, if not the optimal response to, this threat.

For the Manchus, reform was a particularly awkward concept. Like all rulers of China, the Manchus were responsible for the well-being of their subjects. This came under increasing threat as the nineteenth century progressed. Overpopulation, natural disasters, and rebellion from within and predation from without threatened the "mandate of heaven" of the Qing Dynasty.[64] Reform would have been particularly difficult for the Manchus since they were not Han Chinese but foreign. The Manchus retained their legitimacy as long as they successfully adhered to the Han Chinese traditions.[65] Openly breaking with these traditions would have undermined their mandate to rule. They did not have the option open to the Meiji reformers in Japan of hijacking the authority of a boy emperor to legitimize a sweeping reform program. Nor did they have the option, also capitalized on by Japan, of fanning the flames of nationalism in support of government policies.[66] Nationalism in China would have been Han nationalism, anti-Manchu by its very nature.[67] The

[63] Hsü, *Rise of Modern China*, 155–63; Alain Peyrefitte, *The Immobile Empire*, Jon Rothschild, trans. (New York: Alfred A. Knopf, 1992), 291.

[64] Paine, 54–5.

[65] Wiens, 2–15; de Bary, 95.

[66] Beasley, *Meiji Restoration*, 412–3.

[67] de Bary, 83–4.

Manchus were not conservative by choice but by necessity. The Empress Dowager Cixi (慈禧太后) did appropriate the authority of two boy emperors, but this simply allowed her to rule, not to reform. The Manchus were hemmed in by their ethnicity. This very real political constraint helps explain what foreigners perceived as China's ostrich-like behavior.

In the mid-nineteenth century, westerners were flush with the fruits of the Industrial Revolution. Their interest in trade with China had only grown since the eighteenth century. The Industrial Revolution put them in a position to force the issue, and force they did, with the Opium Wars (1839–42, 1856–60). The Western solution was to impose their legal system on the areas where they came into contact with the Chinese and Japanese. Westerners regarded extraterritoriality as essential since they considered the Chinese and Japanese criminal codes to be unduly harsh, the judicial systems biased against foreigners, and the commercial laws inadequate to conduct modern business transactions.[68] There was truth in all of these charges. One Western diplomat assigned to the Far East in the late nineteenth century argued that "not even criminals" should be subjected to "the laws of Asiatic countries." He explained: "European travellers in eastern Asia in the early Middle Ages did not find that difficulty for a very simple reason: there was practically no difference between their laws and ours, including all the barbarous forms of torture we, as well as they, practised. The difficulty was that Asia still kept these practices which we gradually discarded as we rediscovered Roman jurisprudence and developed our own."[69] In China, decapitations, torture, and bribery were all common enough features of the judicial process.[70] "In thousand of Yamêns [local government offices] throughout China men are tortured every day, hung up by their thumbs, forced to kneel upon chains, beaten with heavy bamboos, their ankles cracked, their limbs broken. Every week men are publicly crucified and hacked to death by the 'thousand cuts.'"[71] Since conviction required a confession by the accused, often torture was employed to secure the confession.[72] Contract disputes were generally settled within craft and merchant guilds from which foreign

---

[68] Mutsu, 113–5; John King Fairbank, *China: A New History* (Cambridge, MA: Harvard University Press, 1992), 185.

[69] Sands, 73.

[70] For a list of routine tortures and punishments, see Boulais, 2–6.

[71] Henry Norman, *Contemporary Review*, republished as "The Question of Korea," *The Japan Weekly Mail* (Yokohama), 20 October 1894, pp. 461–4. See also, "Europe and Asia," *The North-China Herald* (Shanghai), 14 December 1894, p. 958.

[72] "The Spirit of the Vernacular Press during the Week," *The Japan Weekly Mail* (Yokohama), 25 May 1895, p. 579.

companies were excluded.[73] Meanwhile, Japanese law before the Meiji reforms was an amalgamation of Chinese legal codes, regulating administrative practices, and customary laws. The latter varied by feudal domain. With the exception of tax matters and public order, most disputes between individuals fell outside the scope of Japanese law.[74] This was problematic for westerners whose interests were primarily commercial and whose legal concerns thus focused on contractual disputes and the like. In Japan and China, foreign commerce operated in a legal limbo. Therefore, foreigners were determined to change the way these Chinese and Japanese conducted business. The Chinese and Japanese considered such demands to be a direct and extraordinarily dangerous threat to their national security.

The Chinese responded by trying to hold true to their traditions while the Japanese decided to learn the new rules of the game in order to win against China and the West. Had either the Chinese *literati* or their Manchu overlords experienced a complete change of heart and actively desired reform, they still would have found its implementation to be extremely difficult. This was because China, unlike Japan, lacked a strong central government. During the period of great internal rebellions, provincial governments were becoming increasingly independent of central control as the dynasty gradually lost its mandate to rule. The lack of a unified military in China during the Sino-Japanese War reflected these fracture lines and, in the case of the banner forces, the division between Han and Manchu loyalties. During the capitulation negotiations at Weihaiwei, the Chinese negotiator wrote Admiral Itō Yūko (伊東祐亨) requesting that the lone surviving ship of the Guangdong (廣東) Squadron[75] be allowed to return to its home base in the south: "Excellency – I have the honour to point out that the *Kwangping* [*Guangbing*,廣丙] belongs to the Kwangtung Squadron...Kwangtung had nothing to do with the present war...I promise that she shall not again take part in the war."[76] Clearly, in this negotiator's eyes, China was not at war with Japan, rather the Beiyang Squadron was. This view reflected the long-standing regional division between north and south China. It was reflected administratively by the Beiyang (北洋海軍) and Nanyang (南洋海軍) squadrons or the squadrons of the northern and southern seas. The Viceroy of Zhili had jurisdiction over the Minister of the Northern Seas while the Viceroy of Jiangsu and Zhejiang had jurisdiction over the

---

[73] Fairbank, *China*, 185–6; Folsom, 182.

[74] Beasley, *Modern History of Japan*, 91–2; Lawrence W. Beer, "Legal System," in *Kodansha Encyclopedia of Japan*, vol. 4 (Tokyo: Kodansha, 1983), 375–8.

[75] Other renditions of Canton include Guangzhou.

[76] "War News," *The Japan Weekly Mail* (Yokohama), 9 March 1895, p. 283; "The Surrender at Weihaiwei," *The Japan Weekly Mail* (Yokohama), 16 March 1895, p. 314.

Minister of the Southern Seas.[77] Since most of the fighting during the war was done by Zhili and Manchurian troops, to many Chinese the war had the air of a provincial rebellion and not a conflict involving their personal interests.[78]

Because China was not a unified nation, such provincial rebellions shared the lack of immediacy of external affairs. In the minds of many, these rebellions affected the relevant provincial governor-general and the Manchus but no one else.[79] "More than one Chinaman has been found ready to aid Japan, if there was money in it. The mass of the Chinese have looked on the war as of no import to them, but only an affair of the Emperor or of Li Hung-chang: 'He's got into trouble: let's see how he gets out of it.' Each Viceroy or Governor looks after his own province; why help Viceroy Li? Some soldiers have been killed in battle; why should any one else go? The navy consists of foreign gunboats, drilled by foreigners; it they fail, why should any one else help them out? Let each one mind his own business, and leave the Emperor to his."[80] Provincial cleavages fractured China. Admiral Ding Ruchang (丁汝昌) had poor relations with his officers, in part because he came from further north. Similarly, he had been unable to help defend Port Arthur, in part because of his inability to secure the cooperation of the local authorities.[81] Because of these regional loyalties and prejudices, the authorities in Peking could not concentrate their forces against the enemy. Japan had been free to divide and conquer.

The North-China Herald commented, "One of the great defects of the Chinese system is the lack of unity...The Manchus and Chinese do not draw together – the former are progressive – the latter conservative. The country is one vast jelly-fish without backbone and without nerves – the injury to one part is not felt at the other extremity of the vast mass. Each official has his own particularly selfish aims and that of his family to advance, he cares nothing for his country or its interests. His sole ambition is to acquire wealth and retire from office and leave the responsibility of his deeds, misgovernment and corruption upon his successor."[82]

Provincial leaders had little incentive to come to the aid of other parts of China and many disincentives. Providing military or financial aid to other provinces would diminish their local resources. Should the aid prove successful, they would derive little gain but would feel the loss of the spent resources. Should the

---

[77] Japan, Imperial General Staff, 26.

[78] Powell, 47.

[79] Kuo, 90.

[80] "Japan and China Compared," *The North-China Herald* (Shanghai), 23 November 1894, p. 861.

[81] Rawlinson, 173, 187.

[82] "A Divided House," *The North-China Herald* (Shanghai), 29 March 1895, p. 472.

attempted aid fail, like all those who drew attention by taking the initiative, they would be personally blamed, if not decapitated.[83] Former-minister of the United States to China, George F. Seward, described the predicament of such reformers as Li Hongzhang: "If there was a legislative body he could go before it, state the direction of the desired reform, and, if successful, a legislative enactment would defend the agent sent out to effect the reformation. As one man in an enormous mass of population, with no legislative body to appeal to, he can take only tentative steps. For any failure he is held to the most rigid accountability, and he is subject always to the intrigues of personal or political enemies. Can one wonder that the initiative for reforms in China is almost unknown?"[84] Provincial leaders in China were not fools. Rather, they were operating in the world as they understood it. They knew that, should they fall from power, their *guanxi* networks, so assiduously and meticulously woven over a lifetime, could instantaneously be torn asunder, with a free fall potentially engulfing their entire clan. "Face," filial piety, and responsibilities to ancestors then greatly magnified the trauma of downfall. Under these circumstances, how many Chinese could afford the luxury of nationalism?

It is a small wonder that true nationalism took generations to develop in China. The provincialism of the nineteenth century degenerated into the warlordism of the 1920s and 1930s. This accelerating turmoil on the mainland would reap another war with Japan. During the prolonged Japanese occupation of China in the 1930s and 1940s, Nationalist forces under Jiang Jieshi (Chiang Kai-shek, 蔣介石) and communist forces under Mao Zedong (毛泽东) both cultivated nationalism as the only force capable of uniting their countrymen to expel the Japanese. This was possible since the Manchu–Han cleavage had been resolved with the overthrow of the Qing Dynasty in 1911. When the communists defeated the Nationalists in 1949, they purged the old provincial *guanxi* networks. In doing so, the old China described in this book was finally smothered in its deathbed. But *guanxi* itself survived and flourished.

In the absence of reform, common soldiers had little incentive to fight. In 1895, the United States Secretary of the Navy, Hilary A. Herbert, wrote: "It is really pathetic to contemplate the condition of the Chinese soldiers who had imposed upon them the duty of meeting the well equipped and thoroughly disciplined armies of Japan. Against troops supplied with all the terrible appliances of modern war China men were forced to take the field armed with guns of every conceivable

---

[83] "The Position of a Viceroy in China," *The North-China Herald* (Shanghai), 31 August 1894, p. 346.

[84] Seward, 585.

pattern, some out of date one hundred years back, some with pikes and pitchforks, and some with crossbows."[85] Privates were often paid less than half their entitled pay or were paid only in rations while the cost of their uniforms was sometimes illegally deducted from what little they did receive.[86]

A reporter for *The Pall Mall Gazette* observed that the Chinese soldiers "had no great ideal before them for which to live and die. Ill-paid, ill-armed, and starving, they fought without fire."[87] In a later issue, another column resumed its discussion: "The Chinese soldier is a byword among his own people...Rapacious, cruel, and cowardly, he is the derision of his foes and the terror of his own people. Undrilled, without pay, miserably armed, ill-fed and ill-clad, having absolutely no officers trained to modern warfare, if wounded left to perish on the field, despised by all, callous of everything except his own miserable life – what has he to fight for? Nothing. What has he to lose? Nothing. Then why should he fight? The defence of China has hitherto been entrusted to such men as these, and Japan is making short work of them... fight they would...if only average men were picked, and they were treated, drilled, and led as soldiers should be."[88]

The Deputy Prefect of Fengtian, Li Peiyuan (李培元), ascribed China's defeat to "our utter lack of training. The strangest thing is that upon the advance of the enemy our troops either flee under the subterfuge that they are going to attack the enemy, or, spreading the news that the enemy is approaching (in order to create chaos), resort to rape, plunder, and robbery. Therefore the people do not designate the war as a calamity inflicted on us by the enemy but instead as a catastrophe resulting from our own armies. Above all others this destroys the morale." He continued: "[T]here are instances in which people flee to avoid our own troops while they return when they learn that the enemy are there." He described how the distinguished veteran generals of the Huai Army had retired before the war while their replacements were inexperienced relatives who had gotten their appointments through bribery and then had used their positions to pilfer from the payroll to the great anger of their men. "In the previous campaigns against the Taipings and Nien they [the officers] were fond of war because there were women, silk and property for booty, while in the present campaign against the Japanese there is no such booty to speak of. Consequently they find it unprofitable to engage in the

---

[85] Herbert, 688.

[86] Kuo, 94; Powell, 17; "A Crisis Averted," *The North-China Herald* (Shanghai), 28 December 1894, p. 1055.

[87] "The Lessons of the Naval War in the East," *The Pall Mall Gazette* (London), 2 February 1895, 4th ed., p. 2.

[88] "'Those Despicable Chinese,'" *The Pall Mall Gazette* (London), 13 February 1895, 4th ed., p. 2.

killing of the enemy but they try to derive some profit in the harassing of their fellow countrymen. Those who are most cowardly toward the enemy are exactly those who harass the people the most."[89]

In sum, before the Sino-Japanese War the Manchus could not have reformed China, even if they had wanted to, and their Han subjects had no desire for them to do so. Therefore, they did not. Similarly, provincial leaders outside the war zone had no incentive to provide assistance, and soldiers inside the war zone had little incentive to fight well. Therefore, neither did. This spelled defeat in the field.

Given this calamitous situation, Chinese pride astounded westerners. They keenly felt the Chinese disdain for foreign cultures and self-satisfaction with their own. They considered it to be the grossest and most ill-placed form of conceit. One of the more thoughtful missionary writers, R. H. Graves, noted the "intense self-conceit" of the Chinese, writing: "They have fixed it in their minds as an axiom that the ancient Chinese sages are the Heaven-sent teachers to teach mankind virtue and morals and the principles of political economy. So they deem other literature as beneath their notice."[90] Another foreigner criticized the Chinese educational system for its exclusive concentration on the classics: "Who for instance but raving maniacs...would think of compelling all their mandarins and scholars to devote all their energies to the study of small ancient principalities whose population might be compared to that of the Hawaiian Islands, or the country of Montenegro, but which are all dead thousands of years ago, while living nations which to-day singly possess more power than all those ancient ones put together are not worth a thought in their studies?"[91] Colonel Charles Denby, the American Minister at Peking (1885–98), wrote: "The foundation of the misfortunes of China lies in the overweening conceit fostered by seclusion and ignorance among its governing classes. Proud, haughty, bound up in ceremonial, absolutely ignorant of foreign affairs, the rulers of China are the least intelligent of her respectable people."[92] In contrast, the British Minister to China, Sir Rutherford Alcock, noted in 1863 that the Japanese "have little of the stupid conceit of the

---

[89] Quoted by Kuo, 82–3. Chu also translates excerpts (Chu, *China's Attitudes*, 91–3).

[90] Graves, 39. For similar views see T. Richard, "China's Appalling Need of Reform," *The Chinese Recorder* 25, no. 11 (Nov. 1894): 515; Curzon, 3rd ed., 367.

According to Captain Lang, who trained the Beiyang Squadron for nine years, "[T]he colossal conceit of the Mandarins is only surpassed by their ignorance" ("The Chinese Navy," *The Japan Weekly Mail* [Yokohama], 17 November 1894, p. 572). For similar views, see MacGowan, 598; Michie, vol. 2, 389–90; Ball, 135, 138.

[91] "The Disease of China," *The North-China Herald* (Shanghai), 10 August 1894, p. 219.

[92] Payson J. Treat, *Diplomatic Relations between the United States and Japan, 1853–1895*, vol. 2 (Stanford: Stanford University Press, 1932), 499.

Chinese, which leads them to ignore or deny the superiority of foreign things. On the contrary, they are both eager and quick to discover in what it lies, and how they can make the excellence their own."[93]

During the Sino-Japanese War, Sir Thomas Francis Wade gave an interview. Wade was famous for helping to develop the Wade-Giles Romanization system of Mandarin Chinese and more famous still for his diplomatic work in China from the Opium Wars onward. By the time he had retired to England, he had served as British minister to Peking from 1871 to 1882 and had resided in China for over forty years.[94] He explained the Chinese outlook as follows: "The sentiment of China was very well represented by a Chinese statesman who said to me, 'We intend to adopt Western machinery, but we shall keep our old customs and our old morality.' The more astute Japanese, on the other hand, clearly perceives that you cannot have one without the other: and that the machinery of Western life is merely the fruit, so to speak, of the ideas that underlie it. The consequence with China is that her attempts to adopt Western ideas have been continually defeated by her adherence to ancient and invincible custom."[95] On the eve of the war, the British-owned *North-China Herald* summed up the situation: "Whatever her faults, Japan unquestionably stands for advancement and progress, China – on the other hand – for old-world and ancestral ways, with only such admixture of Occidental ideas as is absolutely unavoidable."[96] Westerners, for their part, were equally arrogant about the achievements of their civilization; the balance of power, however, was on their side.

When all is said and done, the real challenge presented by the West was not in terms of the military hardware that the Chinese self-strengtheners latched onto, but the intellectual challenge in terms of perceiving and understanding the world. The a priori assumptions in the West did not concern the correct performance of ritual, the proper ordering of social relations, the eternal superiority of Western civilization, or its predestined triumph. Certainly some westerners stressed some of these things, but these were not the elemental beliefs underlying Western thought. Rather, there was an assumption that man is rational; that truth is observable and

---

[93] Sir Rutherford Alcock, *The Capital of the Tycoon*, vol. 2 (London: Longman, Green, Longman, Roberts & Green, 1863), 260, cited in part in Beasley, *Meiji Restoration*, 415. For similar views, see Hart to Campbell, 19 August 1894, in *I. G. in Peking*, Fairbank et al., eds., vol. 2, 983. Hart was writing to James Duncan Campbell, nonresident secretary at the London Office of Chinese Customs (Ibid., vol. 1, 8–9).

[94] O'Neill, 347.

[95] "Some English Views on the War," *The Japan Weekly Mail* (Yokohama), 29 December 1894, p. 732.

[96] "Japan," *The North-China Herald* (Shanghai), 20 July 1894, p. 94.

understandable; that nature follows definite knowable principles; that understanding these principles is liberating and constitutes *an* essential, if not *the* essential purpose of life; and that the most basic principles discovered in this manner apply equally to all peoples. Through "the pursuit of knowledge" (a standard turn of phrase encapsulating the Western mind set), man could become the master of his own destiny, not a hostage to an immutable fate that so preoccupied Chinese thinking. Western thought had long gravitated toward universalistic explanations encompassing the entire cosmos. This approach to knowledge had enormous ramifications, which were extraordinarily disruptive and, indeed, highly corrosive, to the cultures of pre-industrial societies and remain so today.

Epilogue:
Perceptions, Power, and War

It is certain that the situation in Asia will grow steadily worse in
the future...and we must make preparations for another war within the
next ten years.[1]

> Marshal Yamagata Aritomo, April 12, 1895,
> Russo-Japanese War (1904-5)

Li Hung-chang contemplated with a woeful mien the row of Japanese
officers who had accompanied the chargé d'affaires and told them in
the presence of European diplomats: "In the next war we shall be
beaten by you again in the same way as last time."[2]

> German Minister to China, Edmund von Heyking,
> Chinese New Year's audience, February 1897

It may be that this competition in Korea will bring about the next
conflict in the Pacific, and even menace the peace of the world.[3]

> Former-United States Secretary of State, John W. Foster, 1903
> Pacific War (1931-45), Korean War (1950-3)

As this work has endeavored to show, in international relations perceptions are
extremely important. Had China not been trounced in war, thus providing the
powers with a spectacle of incompetence, the "scramble for concessions" might
never have ensued. Not just perceptions *by* others, but also perceptions *concerning*
others, matter. The Chinese misconstrued the balance of power both in the world
at large and in their own backyard in Asia. They believed that, because they had
always been dominant, so they would remain. They did not measure their own

---

[1] Hackett, 163–4.

[2] Cited in Lensen, vol. 2, 513.

[3] Foster, *American Diplomacy*, 343.

power relative to that of the Western powers and relative to Japan but assumed their own eternal superiority. They got it wrong in both cases and paid an enormous price for the mistake. Conversely, the Japanese got the essential balance of power right. They perceived Western ascendancy and therefore emulated Western institutions. They perceived Russian ambitions, Korean incapacity, and Chinese weakness and ejected China from Korea. They were unable, however, to reach a settlement with Russia. This would require another war and then some.

Why were Chinese perceptions so off the mark? What so bewildered the Chinese was the problem of rising powers. Under the traditional system in Asia, China was the dominant power, so dominant that it did not recognize the autonomous existence of any other important power. The status quo was to Chinese liking, so the Chinese had no desire to change it. In the nineteenth century, first Britain and France, and then later Germany, Japan, and the United States were all rising powers. Each at the time of its rise had an interest in overturning the international status quo and inserting itself on a higher rung in the international pecking order. In the late eighteenth and early nineteenth centuries, industrialization enabled Britain and France to overturn the traditional balance of power and force their will upon the unindustrialized world. In the second half of the nineteenth century, as Germany, Japan, and the United States joined this new industrial order, each tried to insert itself higher into the ranks of the powers.

Bismarckian Germany and Meiji Japan did so in a remarkably similar fashion: Both countries fought a series of wars, each one for a limited, but incremental, objective.[4] For Japan these were the Sino-Japanese and Russo-Japanese Wars combined with the formal annexation of Korea. The objective was to make Japan a recognized power by demonstrating Japanese military prowess in the field and using it to contain Russian expansion in the Far East and establish a Japanese colonial base on the Asian mainland. The Prussian wars were the Danish War of 1864, the Austro-Prussian War of 1866, and the Franco-Prussian War of 1870–1. The objective was the creation of a unified German state under Prussian hegemony. The Prussian and Japanese militaries both favored more unlimited objectives, such as the toppling of neighboring governments and more extensive territorial gains, but in both cases civil authorities checked these military ambitions to the attainable. The rationale of the diplomats was to moderate their demands in order to forestall a third-power intervention, a lesson the Japanese learned so painfully with the Triple Intervention. The Japanese did not repeat the mistake in the Russo-Japanese

---

[4] The ideas in this chapter concerning wars of limited objectives, the need for a policy–strategy match, Bismarckian Germany, cooperative adversaries, and a sea-denial strategy are all based on the core course taught by the Strategy and Policy Department at the U.S. Naval War College.

War, and Bismarck skillfully avoided the problem altogether. Although successful, these achievements in Japan and Germany came at a cost of heightened civil–military tensions. This growing fissure had ominous portents for the twentieth century, when weakening civil control over military strategy cost both dearly.

The Japanese ultimately derived the wrong lesson from their turn-of-the-century wars with China and Russia. They concluded that they had won. Actually, their adversaries had lost. There is a big difference between these two statements. Chinese disunity, complacency, and incompetence cost China the war. The Japanese had won not so much because they were so very clever – which they were – but rather because the Chinese had done so very poorly. The Chinese unwittingly did much to assist in their own defeat. Had the Chinese been a less cooperative adversary, the Japanese might have found themselves dangerously overextended in Manchuria. The many supplies that the Chinese left behind as they retreated helped the Japanese compensate for their own strained logistical lines. The Japanese experienced grave problems with supply, sanitation, disease, interservice coordination, and inadequate sea transport or "lift."[5] After the war, neither the Japanese leaders nor the public appreciated the great extent to which their victory had depended on Chinese incapacity.

A decade later, in the war against Russia, Nicholas II sent emissaries to the peace table not because the Japanese had destroyed the Imperial Russian Army but because a domestic revolution, the Revolution of 1905, threatened to unseat his dynasty, so that Nicholas could no longer afford a war at that time. Domestic unrest forced Russia to settle, not the Japanese army, which was on the verge of exhaustion.[6] The Japanese then applied their misconstrued lesson from these wars to the United States in 1941. They paid an enormous price for assuming that the United States would prove to be another cooperative adversary and either settle early or assist in its own defeat. Wrong on both counts. The United States, unlike China and Russia and despite the Great Depression, was not beset by internal problems that would cripple its military. On the contrary, the war lifted the United States out of the depression and both the government and citizenry fought to win.

This work also endeavors to show that strategy matters. Undoubtedly this seems to be a painfully obvious observation. In the Sino-Japanese War, however, although the Chinese and Japanese governments both set concrete policy objectives, only the Japanese government matched a strategy to achieve its objective. The

---

[5] Kuwada, 232–62; Iguchi, 88, 90.

[6] Denis Warner and Peggy Warner, *The Tide at Sunrise: A History of the Russo-Japanese War, 1904–1905* (London: Angus and Robertson, 1974), 453–65, 479, 522, 533.

Chinese did not perceive the disconnect between their ambitious policy objective and their inability to achieve it. They needed to downgrade their objective to something less ambitious and inflexible than the status quo eternal and unalterable. They needed to weigh carefully those resources they could effectively bring to bear and, based on this assessment, choose an objective attainable with the means at hand. When they still had a navy, they needed to focus on a sea-denial strategy to impede the Japanese deployment of troops on the Asian mainland. Instead of focusing on convoy duty, as they did, or on the Japanese fleet, as Mahan recommended, the Chinese navy should have targeted the highly vulnerable but absolutely critical Japanese merchant marine and troop transports. If the Japanese could not deliver men or supplies to the Asian mainland, they could not wage war. Under these circumstances China's attrition strategy might have delivered victory. Japan was a country of limited resources. It could not afford to lose many troop transports. The army was Japan's strength and China's weakness. The Chinese had more hope of drowning the Japanese army at sea than of defeating it on land. The result would have been no means certain, but a sea-denial strategy offered China the best chance for success. To make another obvious statement: Foreign policy matters. A country that cannot effectively match a foreign policy strategy to national objectives puts itself at grave risk.

Finally, this work also endeavors to make yet another obvious point that in recent years has not received due attention from the historical profession, namely, that wars matter. They affect everyone regardless of social class, gender, or ethnicity. Defeat in war had disastrous long-term consequences for China that were felt throughout the country, down to the poorest peasant. The consequences of the reversal of the Far Eastern balance of power are still felt in China today. Many once-great civilizations have never recovered from defeat on the battlefield. The borders that define the world as we know it have largely been determined by warfare or lesser power plays. Wars that overturn the balance of power can have catastrophic domestic consequences for the defeated. Dominant powers like the United States today tend to be status quo powers. Dominant powers have no incentive to upset an international status quo that is to their benefit. The opposite is true for rising powers. These days the rising power is China, and the Chinese government is determined to reverse the consequences of the war discussed in this work. If the paths of other rising powers are anything to judge by, the roller coaster ride may just be beginning.

Bibliographic Essay

Although it is a truism in Chinese history that the Sino-Japanese War was a pivotal event, most books devote a paragraph to making this observation before turning to other subjects.[1] To quote one of the most distinguished historians of Japan, Marius B. Jansen, "One of the attractions East Asian history offers its students is the large number of important topics to have escaped investigation in Western scholarship. The war between China and Japan in 1894–5 is unusual even in an underdeveloped field. It was immediately recognized by contemporaries as a turning point in the modern history of East Asia...It is a historical cliché that the Sino-Japanese War of 1894–5 drastically altered not only the international balance of power in East Asia, but also the fate of all three countries involved...Despite the international impact of the war, historical studies of the topic are surprisingly scarce."[2] There is nothing in English aimed at a general audience about this seminal war. This book is an attempt to help redress this balance and give the war the attention that it deserves. Because no prior knowledge of Chinese, Japanese, Korean, or Russian history is assumed, Chapters 2, 3, and 8 provide information well known to specialists but essential for understanding the war and its implications.

Jeffery M. Dorwart, a scholar of American history, concludes his book, *The Pigtail War: American Involvement in the Sino-Japanese War of 1894–1895*, writing, "The war was after all a minor incident in the late nineteenth-century

---

[1] Chung-fu Chang, 33–4; Leroy-Beaulieu, 242–3; Chien, 3; Foster, *American Diplomacy*, 342; Philip Joseph, *Foreign Diplomacy in China 1894–1900: A Study in Political and Economic Relations with China* (London: George Allen & Unwin, 1928), 27, 144; F. G. Notehelfer, *Kōtoku Shūsui: Portrait of a Japanese Radical* (Cambridge: Cambridge University Press, 1971), 35, 40; Aleksandr L'vovich Gal'perin, Англо-японский союз 1902-1921 годы (Anglo-Japanese Alliance 1902–1921) (Moscow: Государственное издательство политической литературы, 1947), 33; Kenneth B. Pyle, "Meiji Conservatism," *The Cambridge History of Japan*, vol. 5, Marius B. Jansen, ed. (Cambridge: Cambridge University Press, 1989), 708; Pierson, 236; Jansen, *Japan and China*, 25; Hugh Borton, *Japan's Modern Century* (New York: Ronald Press Co., 1955), 211; Nish, 3, 37; Bays, 11, 19; Langer, 167, 175, 385.

[2] Jansen et al., 191, 214; Chu, "Sino-Japanese War," 351–2.

diplomacy and politics."[3] In making this statement, Dorwart focused on the direct short-term impact of the war on the United States. In doing so he overlooked its implications for China, Japan, Korea, Russia, and Great Britain. Wars by definition are international events. Their complexity demands research beyond the confines of any one area of specialization or academic discipline. The current work attempts to reduce this problem by considering the Sino-Japanese War from the perspectives of many countries and by relying on scholarship from a variety of disciplines. In particular, Russia has been emphasized because it is all-too-often neglected in histories of the Far East, yet the modern histories of Japan and China cannot be understood without due attention to Russian activities in the Far East. In addition to works from the disciplines of history, government, and economics, I have also branched further afield to use works on philosophy, anthropology, and law in order to explore the cultural dimensions of international relations.

Like so many wars, much of the history of the Sino-Japanese War has been written by the victors. Du Boulay, Eastlake, and Volpicelli, the main nineteenth-century historians of the conflict, all based their works on information released by the Japanese armed forces. Similarly, most of the reporting from the battlefield came from journalists accompanying Japanese forces, since the Chinese forces did not allow the presence of reporters. All of Li Hongzhang's memorials for the war years are unavailable at the Palace Museum Archives in Taipei, Taiwan. Nor have they been included in the voluminous published collections of his works. It is unclear whether these documents were destroyed long ago or whether they remain classified. Although Li's personal secretary for many years, W. N. Pethick, was writing his memoirs at the time of his death, he survived his master by less than a year and his manuscript "disappeared" from his personal effects.[4] At the time of the war, there was no interest on the Chinese side in telling what happened. Finally, within a decade the Russo-Japanese War overshadowed the Sino-Japanese War, since this time the Japanese stunned Western audiences by defeating a great European power.[5] For all of these reasons the Sino-Japanese War has been a neglected war.

The current work does not attempt to provide the definitive statement on the very complicated diplomatic history of the period. For this there are three outstanding dissertations that deserve to be published as books: Bonnie Bongwan Oh, "The Background of Chinese Policy Formation in the Sino-Japanese War of 1894–1895";

---

[3] Dorwart, 135.

[4] Bland, 31.

[5] Lone, 2.

Sung-ping Kuo, "Chinese Reaction to Foreign Encroachment with Special Reference to the First Sino-Japanese War and Its Immediate Aftermath"; and Andrew Changwoo Nahm, "Kim Ok-Kyun and the Korean Progressive Movement, 1882–1884." Oh's dissertation is actually much broader than the title indicates. She follows events from 1864 through 1895 and relies on an exhaustive reading of Korean, Chinese, and Japanese sources. Kuo provides a careful reading of Chinese sources and continues the story through the scramble for concessions. He provides an informative discussion of the domestic factions within China. Nahm provides invaluable guidance through the murky waters of Korean politics, explaining the complex rivalries among the powerful clans.

The one recent book on the war in English by Stewart Lone, *Japan's First Modern War: Army and Society in the Conflict with China, 1894–95*, is a social history focusing on domestic events in Japan. To satisfy historiographers, I will set forth my differences with Lone. According to him, "Based on what the [Japanese] leadership hoped to achieve internationally, the war is clearly a political failure." He argues that it did not achieve Japanese objectives in Korea, it drove China into the arms of Russia, and it conjured images of the "yellow peril" in the West. "The image was thus fixed in 1895 that Japan was not to be trusted and, to a considerable degree, it has remained even to the present day."[6] He concludes: "Japan remained a minor, regional power."[7] These observations, as shown in the present work, are incorrect. Japan had an unfinished agenda in Korea. War or no war, the Russian threat was growing because of the construction of the Trans-Siberian Railway. Moreover, even before the war there had been talk in Russia of running the line through China.[8] Russia had Far Eastern ambitions regardless of Japanese actions. Japan's main objective, which was not emphasized by Lone, was to become a respected power. The "yellow peril" syndrome was but one rather twisted manifestation of this growing respect. All of the great powers regarded each other as one kind of peril or another. Japan had just joined the club. It achieved this key objective as demonstrated by Britain's endorsement of its success with the 1902 Anglo-Japanese alliance. Contrary to Lone's assessment, Japan was a major regional power, as Russia was soon to learn in the Russo-Japanese War of 1904–5. With the exception of the United States, Japan remained the only non-European power to become a recognized power for the next century. To be fair to Lone, his work does not focus on international issues but on domestic politics.

[6] Lone, 179–80.

[7] Lone, 181.

[8] Valliant, 95.

Other works also shed light on the war. For information about Japanese–Korean relations, see Young Ick Lew, "The Kabo Reform Movement: Korean and Japanese Reform Efforts in Korea, 1894"; Kwang Hai Ro, "Power Politics in Korea and Its Impact on Korean Foreign and Domestic Affairs, 1882–1907"; Martina Deuchler, *Confucian Gentlemen and Barbarian Envoys: The Opening of Korea, 1875–1885.* For information about Russian activities in the Far East, see George Alexander Lensen's encyclopedic *Balance of Intrigue: International Rivalry in Korea & Manchuria, 1884–1899.* For further information on Russo–Korean relations, see Yur-bok Lee's *West Goes East: Paul George von Möllendorff and Great Power Imperialism in Late Yi Korea.* Lensen and Lee also provide extensive discussions of Korea's relations with other European powers and the United States. For works focusing on Korea, see Ching Young Choe, *The Rule of the Taewôngun, 1864–1873: Restoration in Yi Korea* and C. I. Eugene Kim and Kan-kyo Kim, *Korea and the Politics of Imperialism 1876–1910.*

The present work does provide a detailed examination of the negotiations for the Treaty of Shimonoseki. For some reason the Chinese and Japanese negotiating records have not been used by the above scholars, although they are in English and have long been available. Lensen relied on a Russian translation of the minutes and on related Japanese records. The Japanese records were microfilmed by the United States government after World War II and exist in microfilm at the Library of Congress under call number MT 2211. See Cecil H. Uyehara, comp., *Checklist of Archives in the Japanese Ministry of Foreign Affairs, Tokyo, Japan, 1868–1945.* For this work, I have used my own microfilm copy made at the Japanese Foreign Ministry Archives in Tokyo. The Chinese minutes were reprinted at the time in what has since become a very rare newspaper, *The Peking and Tientsin Times.* This newspaper was only started in early 1894 and survives on microfilm for the period July 14, 1894 through December 28, 1895. It is contained in a microfilmed newspaper collection entitled, *China Coast Newspapers,* Group III (November 1886–March 1901), and held at Princeton University's Firestone Library. This microfilm was produced by the China Coast Newspaper Project, Center for Research Libraries, Center for East Asian Studies, University of Kansas.

Two English versions of the minutes to the negotiations have survived. They have the same general content but differ in their translations. One was written by Foreign Minister Mutsu Munemitsu's son, Mutsu Hirokichi (陸奥広吉), for the Japanese Foreign Ministry while the other was leaked to *The Peking and Tientsin Times.* All of the many other documents concerning the negotiations and reproduced by *The Peking and Tientsin Times* are the same as those maintained by the Japanese Foreign Ministry Archives. They differ only in paragraph breaks and occasional italicizations. It seems likely that the minutes published by *The Peking and Tientsin Times* were those kept by the Chinese. In comparing the Japanese and Chinese versions of the minutes, discrepancies arise in certain omissions in the Chinese version relating to (1) Li's desire to create an anti-Western alliance with Japan and (2) Li's disparaging attitudes toward his contemporaries in China, including the Guangxu Emperor. Since the Chinese version, unlike the Japanese version, was meant for publication, details that would have aroused the powers or Li opponents in China seem to have been omitted. But these instances are few in number. I have specifically pointed out these discrepancies when they are relevant to the present work.

For the complete cycle of minutes and documents, see: "The Documentary History of the Peace Negotiations between China and Japan," *The Peking and Tientsin Times,* 18 May 1895, supplement, pp. 1–5; "Report of the Verbal Discussions During Peace Negotiations," *The Peking and Tientsin Times,* 8 June 1895, p. 263; "Translated from the Original Chinese Records," *The Peking and Tientsin Times,* 15 June 1895, pp. 267–8; "Translated from the Original Chinese Records," *The Peking and Tientsin Times,* 22 June 1895, pp. 271–2; "Report of the Verbal Discussions during Peace Negotiations," *The Peking and Tientsin Times,* 29 June 1895, pp. 275–6; "Report of the Verbal Discussions During Peace Negotiations," *The Peking and Tientsin Times,* 6 July 1895, pp. 279–80; "Report of the Verbal Discussions during Peace Negotiations," *The Peking and Tientsin Times,* 13 July 1895, p. 283. *The North-China Herald* only reprinted the various treaty drafts and correspondence originally published in *The Peking and Tientsin Times*; it did not publish the daily negotiating record, but summarized it instead. The documents and negotiating record summaries appear from the May 31 through the July 12, 1895, issues. *The Japan Weekly Mail* did not publish the complete run of documents either, but it did reproduce the negotiating record and major treaty drafts. Start with the June 1, 1895, issue.

The documents reprinted in these newspapers conform to the official English-language version of the negotiations kept at the archives of the Japanese Foreign Ministry, 外務省外交資料館 (Ministry of Foreign Affairs, Diplomatic Record Office), 2.2.1-1-6, 会見条約 (Negotiations and Treaty), "The Proceeding of the Peace Conferences Held at Hiroshima and Shimonoseki in 1895." Many of the documents have been published by the Japanese Foreign Ministry in 外務省 (Japan, Foreign Ministry), 日本外交文書 (Diplomatic Records of Japan), vol. 28, part 2, 380–436. For the Chinese-language minutes see Ma Jianzhong (馬建忠) et al., 中國近代內亂外禍歷史故事叢書 (Collection of Historical Accounts of China's Modern Domestic Strife and Foreign Calamities), vol. 17. For the Russian translation, see Captain Marchenko, "Словесные переговоры о заключении мира, веденные в Симоносеки уполномоченными Китая и Японии в марте 1895 года" (Minutes for the Peace Negotiations between the Plenipotentiaries of China and Japan Held in March, 1895, in Shimonoseki).

Many of these documents have also been reprinted in Murinosuke Kajima, *The Diplomacy of Japan 1894–1922,* vol. 1, 195–291. Important missing documents include: the Imperial Rescript from the Emperor of Japan of March 26 apologizing for the assassination attempt on Li Hongzhang; Japan's first draft of a peace treaty of April 1; China's counterdraft treaty of April 9; and Japan's reply of April 10. Kajima provides only summaries for the latter three. Apparently the minutes were also published separately as the *History of the Peace Negotiations, Documentary and Verbal, between China and Japan, March–April 1895* (Tianjin: 1895), cited in Marilyn Blatt Young, *The Rhetoric of Empire: American China Policy 1895–1901* (Cambridge, MA: Harvard University Press, 1968), 242*n.*68.

For those seeking to engage in primary research, there are two excellent Chinese compendia of archival and other documents pertaining to the war. The second collection is meant to be a direct continuation of the first. They are 邵循正 (Shao Xunzheng) et al., eds., 中日戰爭 (Sino-Japanese War), 中國史學會 (Chinese History Learned Society), 7 vols.; 戚其章 (Qi Qizhang), ed., 中日战争 (Sino-Japanese War), 11 vols. Both contain extensive materials from archives, memoirs, and contemporary accounts. While both focus on Chinese materials, they include important translations of Japanese and Western sources as well. For the Japanese side, see Japan, Foreign Ministry (外務省), 日本外交文書 (Diplomatic Records of Japan), vol. 28.

For a guide to locate foreign-language newspapers published in China see King and Clarke, eds., *A Research Guide to China-Coast Newspapers, 1822–1911.* I do not know of any comparable work concerning foreign-language papers published in Japan. *The Japan Weekly Mail* has a section entitled "Vernacular Press," which abstracts important articles from a wide variety of Japanese newspapers, while a section entitled "Imperial Diet" covers domestic politics. Other sections, entitled "Shanghai News" and "Hong Kong News," summarize important events in China. Other world events are summarized under "Summary of News," "Latest Telegrams," "British News," and "American News." *The Japan Weekly News* is available on microfilm.

The North-China Herald and Supreme Court & Consular Gazette (Shanghai) is the weekly version of *The North-China Daily Herald,* which is unavailable for July 1893 through December 1903. The weekly version is available on microfilm. The section entitled, "Abstract of the Peking Gazette," contains summaries or translations of memorials published in the official Chinese government paper, 京報. It also has separate sections for each region of China, so that local matters receive coverage.

After the war broke out, there was a certain amount of rivalry between *The North-China Herald* and *The Japan Weekly Mail,* with the latter excoriating the former for its adherence to Chinese war propaganda. *The Peking and Tientsin Times* generally stayed out of this vendetta, although it was not totally immune. In general such British papers as *The Pall Mall Gazette* and *The Times* of London provided more detailed coverage of the war than such French papers as *Le Temps, Le Siècle,* or *Le Journal des débats politiques et littéraires;* or such German papers as *National Zeitung, Neue Preussische Zeitung,* or *Königlich privilegirte Berlinische Zeitung;* or than the Russian press in general. After the British press, American coverage of Asia was the most detailed. The French papers initially relied heavily on *The North-China Herald* and *The Japan Weekly Mail* as well as on the London press for their information while the Russian press relied on the European press. Meanwhile, throughout the war, the German press relied on a combination of the London press and the British press in Asia. The German press mainly focused on the initial outbreak of the war and then the end game with relatively little coverage of the hostilities themselves. Their attentions remained turned to Africa and the Balkans, the prime concerns of Germany. Of the French press, *Le Journal des débats* provided much more detailed coverage of the war than either *Le Siècle* or *Le Temps.* Within a week of the outbreak of hostilities, *Le Journal des débats* had a correspondent in Tokyo.[9] Only very late in the war did *Le Temps* hire a Far Eastern correspondent. The German and the Russian papers apparently never did.

In Japan, the war led to an explosion in readership of the local press. In fact, some would argue that the Japanese press came of age during the Sino-Japanese War. The Japanese press sent numerous correspondents to the war theater and the coverage was very detailed. Headline followed headline during the hostilities. Censorship laws, however, restricted the coverage. The effects became particularly evident during the peace negotiations, when the Japanese government shut down numerous papers for their frank criticisms of the war settlement. The Chinese press really developed only after the war. During the hostilities, there were vernacular Chinese newspapers but most had been founded and were owned by Western businessmen or missionaries. Therefore, they were more a conduit of information

---

[9] "La Guerre entre la Chine et le Japon" (War between China and Japan), *Le Journal des débats politiques et littéraires* (*Journal of Political and Literary Debates*) (Paris), 5 August 1894, evening edition, p. 4.

from the West to China rather than an accurate reflection of Chinese thinking during the war.[10]

Technical Note

Foreign-language citations in Russian, Chinese, and Japanese that have no author and begin with the title are listed alphabetically by the English translation of that title. Russians used the Julian calendar before the Russian Revolution of 1917. In the nineteenth century, it lagged twelve days behind the Gregorian calendar generally used today. Some Russian newspapers provide both the Julian and Gregorian dates in their masthead. In these cases, I cite the Gregorian date in the notes. For those papers that provide only Julian dates, I cite the Julian date in the notes followed by the Gregorian date in parentheses. Neither *Le Temps* nor *Le Siècle* provided page numbers. Therefore, in my notes, I have only indicated p. 1 for any front-page articles. Otherwise, no page numbers have been indicated.

---

[10] Huffman, 220–3; Joan Judge, *Print and Politics: 'Shibao' and the Culture of Reform in Late Qing China* (Stanford: Stanford University Press, 1996), 19, 21–2.

Bibliography

NEWSPAPERS

萬國公報 (*International Gazette*) (Shanghai)
The Japan Weekly Mail (Yokohama)
日本人 (*The Japanese*) (Tokyo)
Journal de St-Pétersbourg (*St. Petersburg Journal*)
Le Journal des débats politiques et littéraires (*Journal of Political and Literary Debates*) (Paris)
Königlich privilegirte Berlinische Zeitung (*Royal Berlin Newspaper*)
Московские ведомости (*Moscow Gazette, Moskovskie vodomosti*)
National Zeitung (*National Newspaper*) (Berlin)
Neue Preussische Zeitung (*New Prussian Newspaper*) (Berlin)
Новое время (*New Times, Novoe vremia*) (St. Petersburg)
The New York Times
The North-China Herald and Supreme Court & Consular Gazette (Shanghai)
The Pall Mall Gazette (London)
The Peking and Tientsin Times (Tianjin)
國民新聞 (*People's Newspaper*) (Tokyo)
朝日新聞 (*Rising Sun Newspaper*) (Tokyo)
Русские ведомости (*Russian Gazette, Russkie vedomosti*) (Moscow)
申報 (*Shanghai Report*)
Le Siècle (*The Century*) (Paris)
Le Temps (*The Times*) (Paris)
The Times (London)
Владивосток (*Vladivostok*)
The World (New York)

OTHER SOURCES

Ahern, Emily M. "The Power and Pollution of Chinese Women." In *Studies in Chinese Society,* edited by Arthur P. Wolf, 269–90. Stanford: Stanford University Press, 1978.

Akagi, Roy Hidemachi (赤木英道). *Japan's Foreign Relations, 1542–1936, A Short History.* Tokyo: Hokuseido Press, 1936.

Alcock, Sir Rutherford. *The Capital of the Tycoon.* 2 vols. London: Longman, Green, Longman, Roberts & Green, 1863.

Alef, Gustave. "The Adoption of the Muscovite Two-Headed Eagle: A Discordant View." *Speculum: A Journal of Mediaeval Studies* 41, no. 1 (Jan. 1966): 1–21.

Allan, James. *Under the Dragon Flag: My Experiences in the Chino-Japanese War.* London: William Heinemann, 1898.

Allison, Gary D. *Japan's Postwar History.* Ithaca, NY: Cornell University Press, 1997.

Ariga, Nagao. *La Guerre Sino-Japonaise au Point de Vue du Droit International (Sino-Japanese War from the Perspective of International Law).* Paris: A. Pedone, 1896.

Arnold, Edwin. *Seas and Lands.* Rev. ed. London: Longmans, Green, and Co., 1892.

Ball, James Dyner. *Things Chinese: Being Notes on Various Subjects Connected with China.* 3rd ed. London: Sampson, Low, Marston, 1900.

Ballard, G. A. *The Influence of the Sea on the Political History of Japan.* New York: E. P. Dutton, 1921.

Banno, Masataka. *China and the West, 1858–1861: The Origins of the Tsungli Yamen.* Cambridge, MA: Harvard University Press, 1964.

Bard, Emile. *Chinese Life in Town and Country.* Translated and edited by H. Twitchell. New York: G. P. Putnam's Sons, 1905.

Barfield, Thomas J. *The Perilous Frontier: Nomadic Empires and China, 221 BC to AD 1757.* Cambridge, MA: Blackwell, 1989.

Barneby, W. Henry. *The New Far West and the Old Far East, Being Notes of a Tour in North America, Japan, China, Ceylon, Etc.* London: Edward Stanford, 1889.

Barsukov, Ivan Platonovich. Граф Николай Николаевич Муравьёв-Амурский (*Count Nikolai Nikolaevich Murav'ev-Amurskii*). 2 vols. Moscow: Синодальная Типография, 1891.

Bartlett, John. *Famous Quotations.* 14th ed. Boston: Little, Brown, 1968.

Bays, Daniel H. *China Enters the Twentieth Century: Chang Chih-tung and the Issues of a New Age, 1895–1909.* Ann Arbor: University of Michigan Press, 1978.

Beasley, W. G. *Japan Encounters the Barbarian: Japanese Travellers in America and Europe.* New Haven: Yale University Press, 1995.

——. "Meiji Political Institutions." In *The Cambridge History of Japan,* vol. 5, edited by Marius B. Jansen, 618–73. Cambridge: University of Cambridge Press, 1989.

——. *The Meiji Restoration.* Stanford: Stanford University Press, 1972.

——. *The Modern History of Japan.* 2nd ed. New York: Praeger, 1974.

——. *The Rise of Modern Japan.* New York: St. Martin's Press, 1990.

——. *The Rise of Modern Japan.* 2nd ed. New York: St. Martin's Press, 1995.

Bee, Minge C. (皮名舉). "Origins of German Far Eastern Policy." *The Chinese Social and Political Science Review* 21 (1937–38): 65–97.

Befu, Harumi. *Japan: An Anthropological Introduction.* San Francisco: Chandler Publishing, 1971.

Benedict, Ruth. *The Chrysanthemum and the Sword: Patterns of Japanese Culture.* 1946. Reprint, Boston: Houghton Mifflin, 1989.

Beresford, Baron Charles William De la Poer. *The Break-up of China.* New York: Harper & Row, 1900.

Black, John R. *Young Japan. Yokohama and Yedo.* London: Trubner & Co., 1880.

Blackwell, William L. *The Beginnings of Russian Industrialization 1800–1860* Princeton: Princeton University Press, 1969.

Blake, John. *How Sailors Fight: An Account of the Organisation of the British Fleet in Peace and War.* London: Grant Richards, 1901.

Bland, John O. P. *Li Hung-chang.* 1917. Reprint, Freeport, NY: Books for Libraries Press, 1971.

Bloodworth, Dennis. *The Chinese Looking Glass.* New York: Farrar, Straus and Giroux, 1967.

Bonavia, David. *The Chinese.* London: Butler & Tanner, 1980.

Borokh, L. N. "Anti-Manzhou Ideas of the First Chinese Bourgeois Revolutionaries (Lu Haodong Confession)." In *Manzhou Rule in China*, edited by S. L. Tikhvinsky, translated by David Skvirsky, 297–311. Moscow: Progress Publishers, 1983.

Borton, Hugh. *Japan's Modern Century.* New York: The Ronald Press, 1955.

Boulais, Guy. *Manuel du Code Chinois* (大清律例便覽)(*Chinese Legal Code Manual*). Chang-hai: Imprimerie de la Mission Catholique, 1924.

Boulger, Demetrius Charles. *The History of China.* Rev. ed., 2 vols. London: W. Thacker & Co., 1898.

Bounds, Marcella. "The Sino-Russian Treaty of 1896." *Papers on China.* Harvard University. 43 (July 1970): 109–25.

Bourne, Kenneth and D. Cameron Watts, eds. *British Documents on Foreign Affairs: Reports and Papers from the Foreign Office Confidential Print. Part I, From the Mid-nineteenth Century to the First World War, Series A: Russia: 1859–1914.* Vol. 1. University Publications of America, 1983.

Browne, G. Waldo. *The New American and the Far East.* 2 vols. Boston: Marshall Jone, 1910.

Burke, Edmund. *Reflections on the Revolution in France.* Edited by J. G. A. Pocock. 1790. Reprint, Indianapolis: Hackett Publishing, 1987.

Burroughs, Peter. "Defence and Imperial Disunity." In *The Oxford History of the British Empire: The Nineteenth Century*, vol. 3, edited by Andrew Porter, 320–45. Oxford: Oxford University Press, 1999.

Calman, Donald. *The Nature and Origins of Japanese Imperialism: A Reinterpretation of the Great Crisis of 1893.* London: Routledge, 1992.

Cameron, Nigel. *Barbarians and Mandarins: Thirteen Centuries of Western Travellers in China.* New York: Walker/Weatherhill, 1970.

Cecil, William Gascoyne and Florence Cecil. *Changing China.* New York: D. Appleton, 1912.

Chan, Wing-tsit, trans., comp. *A Source Book in Chinese Philosophy.* Princeton: Princeton University Press, 1973.

Chang, Chi-yun (張其昀). 中國歷史地圖 (*Historical Atlas of China*). 2 vols. Taipei: 中國文化大學出版部印行, 1984.

Chang, Chun-ming (張純明). "The Chinese Standards of Good Government: Being a Study of the 'Biographies of Model Officials' in Dynastic Histories." *Nankai Social & Economic Quarterly* 8, no. 2 (July 1935): 219–49.

Chang, Chung-fu *The Anglo-Japanese Alliance.* Baltimore: Johns Hopkins Press, 1931.

Ch'en, Jerome. *China and the West: Society and Culture 1815–1937.* Taipei: Southern Materials Center, 1985.

Chen, Edward I-te. "Japan's Decision to Annex Taiwan: A Study of Itō–Mutsu Diplomacy, 1894–95." *Journal of Asian Studies* 37, no. 1 (Nov. 1977): 61–72.

Chien, Frederick Foo. *The Opening of Korea: A Study of Chinese Diplomacy, 1876–1885.* Hamden, CT: Shoe String Press, 1967.

"China's Extremity." *Blackwood's Edinburgh Magazine* 157, no. 954 (April 1895): 501–16.

Chirol, Valentine. *The Far Eastern Question.* London: Macmillan, 1896.

Cho, Jae-gon. "The Connection of the Sino-Japanese War and the Peasant War of 1894." *Korea Journal* 34, no. 4 (Winter 1994): 45–58.

Choe, Ching Young. *The Rule of the Taewôn'gun, 1864–1873: Restoration in Yi Korea.* Cambridge, MA: Harvard University Press, 1972.

Chow, Jen Hwa. *China and Japan: The History of Chinese Diplomatic Missions in Japan 1877–1911.* Singapore: Chopmen Enterprises, 1975.

Christensen, Thomas J. "Posing Problems without Catching up." *International Security* (Spring 2001): 5–40.

Chu, Samuel C. "China's Attitudes toward Japan at the Time of the Sino-Japanese War." In *The Chinese and Japanese: Essays in Cultural and Political Interactions*, edited by Akira Iriye, 74–95. Princeton: Princeton University Press, 1980.

——. "The Sino-Japanese War of 1894: A Preliminary Assessment from U.S.A." 近代史研究所集刊 (*Proceedings of the Institute for Modern History*) 14 (June 1985): 349–70.

Ch'ü, T'ung-tsu. *Law and Society in Traditional China.* Paris: Mouton, 1961.

Chung, Henry, ed. *Korean Treaties.* New York: H. S. Nichols, Inc., 1919.

Chuzo, Ichiko. "Political and Institutional Reform, 1901–1911." In *The Cambridge History of China*, vol. 11, edited by John King Fairbank and Kwang-ching Liu, 375–415. Cambridge: Cambridge University Press, 1978.

Clausewitz, Carl von. *On War*. Edited and translated by Michael Howard and Peter Paret. Princeton: Princeton University Press, 1976.

Clement, Ernest Wilson. *A Handbook of Modern Japan.* 7th ed. Chicago: A. C. McClurg & Co., 1907.

Cohen, Warren I. *America's Response to China: A History of Sino-American Relations.* 3rd ed. New York: Columbia University Press, 1990.

Coltman, Jr., Robert. *The Chinese, Their Present and Future: Medical, Political, and Social.* Philadelphia: F. A. Davis, Publisher, 1891.

Compilation Committee for the Big Chinese History Dictionary （中国历史大辞典编纂委员会）. Compiled by 中国历史大辞典 (*Big Chinese History Dictionary*). 2 vols. Shanghai: 上海辞书出版社, 2000.

Confucius. *The Analects.* Translated by Raymond Dawson. Oxford: Oxford University Press, 1993.

Conroy, Hilary. *The Japanese Seizure of Korea: 1868–1910: A Study of Realism and Idealism in International Relations.* Philadelphia: University of Pennsylvania Press, 1960.

Cook, Harold F. *Korea's 1884 Incident: Its Background and Kim Ok-kyun's Elusive Dream.* Royal Asiatic Society, Korea Branch. Seoul: Taewon Publishing, 1972.

Coolidge, Archibald C. "The Position of China in World Politics." In *China and the Far East: Clark University Lectures,* edited by George Hubbard Blakeslee, 1–20. New York: Thomas Y. Crowell, 1910.

Cooling, Benjamin Franklin. *Gray Steel and Blue Water Navy: The Formative Years of America's Military-Industrial Complex 1881–1917.* Hamden, CT: Archon Books, 1979.

Cordier, Henri. *Histoire des relations de la China avec les puissances occidentales 1860–1902* (*History of the Relations of China and the Occidental Powers 1860–1902*). 3 vols. Paris: Ancienne Librarie Germer Baillère, 1902.

Crisp, Olga. "Labour and Industrialisation in Russia." In *The Cambridge Economic History of Europe,* vol. 7, part 2, edited by Peter Mathias and M. M. Postan, 308–415. Cambridge: Cambridge University Press, 1978.

——. *Studies in the Russian Economy before 1914.* School of Slavonic and East European Studies, University of London. London: Macmillan Press, 1967.

Crossley, Pamela Kyle. *The Manchus.* Cambridge, MA: Blackwell Publishers, 1997.

Cumings, Bruce. *Korea's Place in the Sun: A Modern History.* New York: W. W. Norton, 1997.

Cunningham, Alfred. *The Chinese Soldier and Other Sketches.* London: Sampson, Low, Marston, 1899?

Curtis, William Eleroy. *The Yankees of the East: Sketches of Modern Japan.* 2 vols. New York: Stone & Kimball, 1906.

Curzon, George Nathaniel. *Problems of the Far East.* 3rd ed. London: Longmans, Green, 1894.

——. *Problems of the Far East.* 4th ed. New York: Longmans, Green, 1896.

D'Autremer, Joseph. *The Japanese Empire and Its Economic Conditions.* London: T. Fisher Unwin, 1910.

Day, Alan J., ed. *Border and Territorial Disputes.* Detroit: Gale Research, 1982.

de Bary, William Theodore. *East Asian Civilizations: A Dialogue in Five Stages.* Cambridge, MA: Harvard University Press, 1988.

De Mente, Boye Lafayette. *NTC's Dictionary of Japan's Cultural Words.* Lincolnwood, IL: NTC Publishing Group, 1997.

Desmond, Kevin. *The Harwin Chronology of Inventions, Innovations, Discoveries from Pre-History to the Present Day.* London: Constable, 1986.

Deuchler, Martina. *Confucian Gentlemen and Barbarian Envoys: The Opening of Korea, 1875–1885.* Seattle: University of Washington Press, 1977.

Dilard, Philip H. *Sir Arthur Sullivan: A Resource Book.* Lanham, MD: The Scarecrow Press, 1996.

Ding, Richu."Dowager Empress Cixi and Toshimichi: A Comparative Study of Modernization in China and Japan." In *China's Quest for Modernization: A Historical Perspective,* edited by Frederic Wakeman Jr. and Wang Xi, 175–90. Berkeley: University of California Press, 1997.

Diósy, Arthur. *The New Far East.* New York: G. P. Putnam's Sons, 1899.

——. "The New Japan." In *Japan as Seen and Described by Famous Writers,* edited and translated by Esther Singleton, 356–63. New York: Dodd Mead and Co., 1904.

Djang, Chu. "Chinese Suzerainty: A Study of Diplomatic Relation between China and Her Vassal States 1870–1895." Ph.D. diss., Johns Hopkins University, 1935.

Dorwart, Jeffery M. *The Pigtail War: American Involvement in the Sino-Japanese War of 1894–1895.* Amherst: University of Massachusetts Press, 1975.

Douglas, Robert K. *Li Hungchang.* New York: Frederick Warne, 1895?

Du Boulay, N. W. H. "Chino-Japanese War, 1894–95." London: typescript, ca. 1903.

du Halde, Jean Baptiste. *Description géofraphique, historique, chronologique, politique, et physique de l'empire de la Chine et de la Tartarie Chinoise (Geographical, Historical, Chronological, Political and Physical Description of the Chinese Empire and Chinese Tartary).* La Haye: H. Scheurleer, 1736.

———. *The General History of China.* London: J. Watts, 1741.

Duara, Prasenjit. *Culture, Power, and the State: Rural North China, 1900–1942.* Stanford: Stanford University Press, 1988.

Dudden, Arthur Power. *The American Pacific: From the Old China Trade to the Present.* New York: Oxford University Press, 1992.

Dumolard, Henry. *Le Japon politique, économique et social (Japan: Politics, Economics and Society).* Paris: Librairie Armand Colin, 1903.

Dupuy, R. Ernest and Trevor N. Dupuy. *The Harper's Encyclopedia of Military History from 3500 B.C. to the Present.* 4th ed. New York: Harper Collins, 1993.

Duus, Peter. *The Abacus and the Sword: The Japanese Penetration of Korea, 1895–1910.* Berkeley: University of California Press, 1995.

Dyer, Thomas G. *Theodore Roosevelt and the Idea of Race.* Baton Rouge: Louisiana State University Press, 1980.

Eastlake, Warrington and Yamada Yoshi-aki. *Heroic Japan: A History of the War between China & Japan.* 1897. Reprint, Washington: University Publications of America, 1979.

Eastman, Lloyd E. *Family Fields, and Ancestors: Constancy and Change in China's Social and Economic History, 1550–1949.* New York: Oxford University Press, 1988.

———. *Throne and Mandarins: China's Search for a Policy during the Sino-French Controversy 1880–1885.* Cambridge, MA: Harvard University Press, 1967.

Eberhard, Wolfram. *Guilt and Sin in Traditional China.* Berkeley: University of California Press, 1967.

Eckert, Carter J., et al. *Korea Old and New: A History.* Cambridge, MA: Harvard University Press, 1990.

Elleman, Bruce A. *Diplomacy and Deception: The Secret History of Sino-Soviet Diplomatic Relations, 1917–1927.* Armonk, NY: M. E. Sharpe, 1997.

———. *Modern Chinese Warfare, 1795–1989.* London: Routledge, 2001.

———. *Wilson and China: A Revised History of the Shandong Question.* Armonk, NY: M. E. Sharpe, 2002.

Elliott, Mark Christopher. "Bannerman and Townsman: Ethnic Tension in Nineteenth-Century Jiangnan." *Late Imperial China* 11, no. 1 (June 1990): 36–74.

———. *The Manchu Way: The Eight Banners and Ethnic Identity in Late Imperial China.* Stanford: Stanford University Press, 2001.

——. "Resident Aliens: The Manchu Experience in China, 1644–1760." Ph.D. diss., University of California, Berkeley, 1993.

Embree, Ainslie T., ed. *Encyclopedia of Asian History*. 5 vols. New York: Charles Scribner's Sons, 1988.

"Emperor Kōmei" (「孝明天皇」). In 「日本大百科全書」 (*Encyclopedia Nipponica 2001*), vol. 9, 42. Tokyo: 小学館, 1986.

Evans, David C. and Mark R. Peattie. *Kaigun: Strategy, Tactics, and Technology in the Imperial Japanese Navy, 1887–1941*. Annapolis: Naval Institute Press, 1997.

Fairbank, John King, ed. *The Cambridge History of China*, vol. 10. Cambridge: Cambridge University Press, 1978.

——. *The Chinese World Order: Traditional China's Foreign Relations*. Cambridge, MA: Harvard University Press, 1968.

——. "A Preliminary Framework." In *The Chinese World Order: Traditional China's Foreign Relations*, edited by John K. Fairbank, 1–19. Cambridge, MA: Harvard University Press, 1968.

——. *China: A New History*. Cambridge, MA: Harvard University Press, 1992.

——. *Trade and Diplomacy on the China Coast: The Opening of the Treaty Ports, 1843–1854*. Stanford: Stanford University Press, 1969.

——, Katherine Frost Bruner, and Elizabeth MacLeod Matheson, eds. *The I. G. in Peking: Letters of Robert Hart Chinese Maritime Customs 1868–1907*. 2 vols. Cambridge, MA: Harvard University Press, 1975.

—— and Kwang-ching Liu, eds. *The Cambridge History of China*, vol. 11. Cambridge: Cambridge University Press, 1978.

——, Edwin O. Reischauer, and Albert M. Craig. *Far East: Tradition and Transformation*. Rev. ed. Cambridge, MA: Harvard University Press, 1989.

"Первые шаги русского империализма на Дальнем Востоке (1888-1903 гг.)" The First Steps of Russian Imperialism in the Far East [1888–1903]). *Красный архив* (*Red Archive*) 52 (1932): 34–124.

Fishman, O. L. "Qing Policy in Ideology." In *Manzhou Rule in China*, edited by S. L. Tikhvinsky, translated by David Skvirsky, 134–49. Moscow: Progress Publishers, 1983.

Fletcher, Joseph. "Ch'ing Inner Asia *c.* 1800." In *Cambridge History of China*, vol. 10, edited by John King Fairbank, 35–106. Cambridge: Cambridge University Press, 1978.

——. "Sino-Russian Relations, 1800–62." In *Cambridge History of China*, vol. 10, edited by John King Fairbank, 318–50. Cambridge: Cambridge University Press, 1978.

Folsom, Kenneth E. *Friends, Guests, and Colleagues: The Mu-fu System in the Late Ch'ing Period*. Berkeley: University of California Press, 1968.

Ford, Harold Perry. "Russian Far Eastern Diplomacy, Count Witte, and the Penetration of China, 1895–1904." Ph.D. diss., University of Chicago, 1950.

Foster, John Watson. *American Diplomacy in the Orient*. Boston: Houghton, Mifflin, 1903.

——. *Diplomatic Memoirs*. 2 vols. Boston: Houghton Mifflin Co., 1909.

Frodsham, J. D. *The First Chinese Embassy to the West: The Journals of Kuo Sung-t'ao,*

Liu Hsi-hung and Chang Te-yi. Oxford: Clarendon Press, 1974.

Fuller, Jr., William C. *Strategy and Power in Russia 1600–1914.* New York: Free Press, 1992.

Fung, Allen. "Testing Self-Strengthening: The Chinese Army in the Sino-Japanese War of 1894–1895." *Modern Asian Studies* 40, no. 4 (1966): 1007–31.

Fung, Yu-lan. *A History of Chinese Philosophy.* 2 vols. Translated by Derk Bodde. Princeton: Princeton University Press, 1983.

——. *A Short History of Chinese Philosophy.* Edited by Derk Bodde. New York: Free Press, 1966.

Gal'perin, Aleksandr L'vovich. *Англо-японский союз 1902–1921 годы* (*Anglo-Japanese Alliance 1902–1921*). Moscow: Государственное издательство политической литературы, 1947.

Garver, John W. *Sino-Soviet Relations 1937–1945: The Diplomacy of Chinese Nationalism.* New York: Oxford University Press, 1988.

Gatrell, Peter. *Government, Industry and Rearmament in Russia, 1900–1914: The Last Argument of Tsarism.* Cambridge: Cambridge University Press, 1994.

Gérard, Auguste. *Ma Mission en Chine (1893–1897)* (*My Assignment in China [1893–1897]*). Paris: Librarie Plon, 1918.

Gerschenkron, Alexander. *Economic Backwardness in Historical Perspective: A Book of Essays.* Cambridge, MA: Belknap Press, 1962.

Geyer, Dietrich. *Russian Imperialism: The Interaction of Domestic and Foreign Policy, 1860–1914.* Translated by Bruce Little. New Haven: Yale University Press, 1987.

Giffard, Sidney. *Japan Among the Powers.* New Haven: Yale University Press, 1994.

Gilbert, W. S. *The H.M.S. Pinafore* 1878. Reprint, Milwaukee: G. Schirmer, n.d.

——. *The Mikado or the Town of Titipu.* 1885. Reprint, New York: Macmillan, 1979.

Giles, Herbert A. *A Chinese-English Dictionary.* 2nd ed. 1912. Reprint, Taipei: Ch'eng-wen Publishing, 1978.

Glinka, G. V., ed. *Азиатская Россия* (*Asiatic Russia*). 2 vols. 1914. Reprint, Cambridge, MA: Oriental Research Partners, 1974.

Graham, Gerald S. *The China Station: War and Diplomacy 1830–1860.* Oxford: Clarendon Press, 1978.

Graves, R. H. *Forty Years in China or China in Transition.* 1895. Reprint, Wilmington, DE: Scholarly Resources, 1972.

Greenblatt, Sidney L., Richard W. Wilson, and Amy Auerbacher Wilson, eds. *Social Interaction in Chinese Society.* USA: Praeger Publishers, 1982.

Gregory, Paul R. *Russian National Income 1885–1913.* Cambridge: Cambridge University Press, 1982.

Griffis, William Elliot. *Corea: The Hermit Nation.* New York: Charles Scribner's Sons, 1911.

——. *Japan in History, Folk Lore and Art.* Boston: Houghton, Mifflin, 1892.

——. *The Mikado: Institution and Person.* Princeton: Princeton University Press, 1915.

——. *The Mikado's Empire.* New York: Harper & Brothers, 1876.

Grimm, E. D. *Сборник договоров и других документов по истории международных отношений на Дальнем Востоке (1842–1925)* (*Collection of Treaties and Other Documents on the History of International Relations in the Far East [1842–1925]*).

Moscow: Издание Института Востоковедения Москва им. Н. Н. Нариманова, 1927.

Gulick, Sidney L. *Evolution of the Japanese: Social and Psychic.* New York: Fleming H. Revell, 1903.

Hackett, Roger F. *Yamagata Aritomo in the Rise of Modern Japan, 1838–1922.* Cambridge, MA: Harvard University Press, 1971.

Hamada, Kengi. *Prince Ito.* Tokyo: Sanseido, 1936.

Hauner, Milan. *What Is Asia to Us? Russia's Asian Heartland Yesterday and Today.* Boston: Unwin Hyman, 1990.

Hayashi, Tadasu. *The Secret Memoirs of Count Tadasu Hayashi.* Edited by A. M. Pooley. New York: G. P. Putnam's Sons, 1915.

Hazard, Paul. *European Thought in the Eighteenth Century.* Gloucester, MA: Peter Smith, 1973.

Hearn, Lafcadio. *Japan: An Attempt at Interpretation.* New York: Macmillan Co., 1913.

"Герб Российской Империи" (Heraldry of the Russian Empire). In *Советская историческая энциклопедия* (*Soviet Historical Encyclopedia*). Edited by E. M. Zhukov, vol. 4, 255. Moscow: Государственное научное издательство «Советская энциклопедия», 1963.

Herbert, Hilary A. "Military Lessons of the Chino-Japanese War." *The North American Review* 160, no. 463 (June 1895): 685–98.

Hirakawa, Sukehiro. "Japan's Turn to the West." Translated by Bob Tadashi Wakabayashi. In *The Cambridge History of Japan*, vol. 5, edited by Marius B. Jansen, 432–98. Cambridge: University of Cambridge Press, 1989.

"His Majesty, the King of Korea." *Korean Repository* 3 (Nov. 1896): 422–30.

Holcombe, Chester. *The Real Chinaman.* New York: Dodd Mead, 1895.

Hou, Chi-ming. *Foreign Investment and Economic Development in China 1840–1937.* Cambridge, MA: Harvard University Press, 1965.

Howland, D. R. *Borders of Chinese Civilization: Geography and History at Empire's End.* Durham, NC: Duke University Press, 1996.

Hoye, Timothy. *Japanese Politics: Fixed and Floating Worlds.* Upper Saddle River, NJ: Prentice Hall, 1999.

Hsü, Immanuel C. Y. *China's Entrance into the Family of Nations: The Diplomatic Phase, 1858–1880.* Cambridge, MA: Harvard University Press, 1968.

——. "The Great Policy Debate in China, 1874: Maritime Defense vs. Frontier Defense." In *Readings in Modern Chinese History,* edited by Immanuel C. Y. Hsü, 258–70. New York: Oxford University Press, 1971.

——. "Late Ch'ing Foreign Relations, 1866–1905." In *The Cambridge History of China,* vol. 11, edited by John K. Fairbank and Kwang-ching Liu, 70–141. Cambridge: Cambridge University Press, 1978.

——. *The Rise of Modern China.* 4th ed. Oxford: Oxford University Press, 1990.

Hu, Chang-tu. *China: Its People, Its Society, Its Culture.* New Haven: HRAF Press, 1960.

Hu, Hsien Chin. "The Chinese Concepts of 'Face.'" *American Anthropologist* 46 (1944): 45–64.

Hu, Sheng (胡绳). *Imperialism and Chinese Politics.* Translation from Chinese. Beijing: Foreign Languages Press, 1981.

Hucker, Charles O. *A Dictionary of Official Titles in Imperial China.* Taiwan ed. Taipei: Southern Materials Center, 1988.

Huet, Auguste. *Quelques réflexions sur la Guerre Navale sino-japonaise (Some Reflections on the Sino-Japanese Naval War).* Paris: Bergen-Levrault, 1896.

Huffman, James L. *Creating a Public: People and Press in Meiji Japan.* Honolulu: University of Hawai'i Press, 1997.

Hummel, Arthur W. *Eminent Chinese of the Ch'ing Period (1644–1912).* 1943. Reprint, Taipei: Ch'eng Wen Publishing Co., 1970.

Hwang, In K. *The Korean Reform Movement of the 1880s: A Study of Transition in Intra-Asian Relations.* Cambridge, MA: Schenkman Publishing, 1978.

Iguchi, Kazuki (井口和起). "日清。日露戦争論" (Discussion of the Sino-Japanese and Russo-Japanese Wars). 日本歴史 *(Japanese History)* 8, no. 2 (June 1985): 85–120.

Iklé, Frank W. "The Triple Intervention: Japan's Lesson in the Diplomacy of Imperialism." *Monumenta Nipponica* 22, no. 1–2 (1967): 122–30.

Illica, Luigi and Giuseppe Giacosa. *Madam Butterfly.* Translated by Rosie Helen Elkin. New York: G. Ricordi & Co., 19??

Ilyushechkin, V. P. "Anti-Manzhou Edge of the Taiping Peasant War." In *Manzhou Rule in China,* edited by S. L. Tikhvinsky, translated by David Skvirsky, 257–73. Moscow: Progress Publishers, 1983.

Inoue, Haruki (井上春樹). 旅順虐殺事件 *(Lüshun Massacre).* Tokyo: 筑摩書房, 1995.

Inouye, Jukichi. *The Japan-China War: On the Regent's Sword: Kinchow, Port Arthur, and Talienwan.* Yokohama: Kelly & Walsh, 1895.

——. *The Japan-China War: The Naval Battle of Haiyang.* Yokohama: Kelly & Walsh, 1895.

Iriye, Akira, ed. *The Chinese and the Japanese: Essays in Cultural and Political Interactions.* Princeton: Princeton University Press, 1980.

——. *Japan & the Wider World.* London: Longman, 1997.

——. "Japan's Drive to Great Power Status." In *The Cambridge History of Japan,* vol. 5, edited by Marius B. Jansen, 721–82. Cambridge: University of Cambridge Press, 1989.

——. "Minds Across the Pacific: Japan in American Writing (1853–1883)." *Papers on China.* Harvard University. 1 (June, 1961): 1–41.

Ishii, Kikujiro. *Diplomatic Commentaries.* Translated and edited by William R. Langdon. Baltimore: Johns Hopkins Press, 1936.

Jacob, Margaret C. *The Cultural Meaning of the Scientific Revolution.* Philadelphia: Temple University Press, 1988.

Jansen, Marius B., ed. *The Cambridge History of Japan.* Vol. 5. Cambridge: University of Cambridge Press, 1989.

——. "Introduction." In *The Cambridge History of Japan,* vol. 5, edited by Marius B. Jansen, 1–49. Cambridge: University of Cambridge Press, 1989.

——. *Japan and China from War to Peace 1894–1972.* Chicago: Rand McNally College Publishing Co., 1975.

——. *The Making of Modern Japan.* Cambridge, MA: Harvard University Press, 2000.

——. "The Meiji Restoration." In *The Cambridge History of Japan,* vol. 5, edited by Marius B. Jansen, 308–66. Cambridge: University of Cambridge Press, 1989.

——. "Mutsu Munemitsu." In *Personality in Japanese History,* edited by Albert M. Craig and Donald H. Shively, 309–34. Berkeley: University of California Press, 1970.

——, Samuel C. Chu, Shumpei Okamoto, and Bonnie B. Oh. "The Historiography of the Sino-Japanese War." *International History Review* 1, no. 2 (April 1979): 191–227.

Japan, Foreign Ministry (外務省). 日本外交文書 *(Diplomatic Records of Japan).* Vol 28. Tokyo: 東京国際連合協会発行, 1953.

Japan, Imperial General Staff. *History of the War between Japan and China,* vol. 1. Translated by Major Jikemura and Arthur Lloyd. Tokyo: Kinkodo Publishing Co., 1904.

Japanese Foreign Ministry. 外務省外交資料館 (Ministry of Foreign Affairs, Diplomatic Record Office), 2.2.1-1-6. 会見条約 (Negotiations and Treaty). "The Proceeding of the Peace Conferences Held at Hiroshima and Shimonoseki in 1895."

"The Japanese Embroglio." *Blackwood's Edinburgh Magazine* 158 (Sept. 1895): 309–32.

Jones, Susan Mann and Philip A. Kuhn. "Dynastic Decline and the Roots of Rebellion." In *The Cambridge History of China,* vol. 10, edited by John King Fairbank, 107–62. Cambridge: Cambridge University Press, 1978.

Joseph, Philip. *Foreign Diplomacy in China 1894–1900: A Study in Political and Economic Relations with China.* London: George Allen & Unwin, 1928.

Judge, Joan. *Print and Politics: 'Shibao' and the Culture of Reform in Late Qing China.* Stanford: Stanford University Press, 1996.

Kajima, Morinosuke. *The Diplomacy of Japan 1894–1922.* 3 vols. Tokyo: Kajima Institute of International Peace, 1976.

——. *The Emergence of Japan as a World Power 1895–1925.* Rutland, VT: Charles E. Tuttle, 1968.

Kamachi, Noriko. *Reform in China: Huang Tsun-hsien and the Japanese Model.* Cambridge, MA: Harvard University Press, 1981.

Kao, Ting Tsz. *The Chinese Frontiers.* Aurora, IL: Chinese Scholarly Publishing, 1980.

Kaser, M. C. "Russian Entrepreneurship." In *The Cambridge Economic History of Europe,* vol. 7, part 2, edited by Peter Mathias and M. M. Postan, 416–93. Cambridge: Cambridge University Press, 1978.

Kazemzadeh, Firuz. *Russia and Britain in Persia 1864–1914: A Study in Imperialism.* New Haven: Yale University Press, 1968.

Keene, Donald. "The Sino-Japanese War of 1894–95 and Its Cultural Effects in Japan." In *Tradition and Modernization in Japanese Culture,* edited by Donald H. Shively, 121–80. Princeton: Princeton University Press, 1971.

Keep, John L. H. *Soldiers of the Tsar: Army and Society in Russia 1462–1874.* Oxford: Clarendon Press, 1985.

Kim, C. I. Eugene and Kan-kyo Kim. *Korea and the Politics of Imperialism 1876–1910.* Berkeley: University of California Press, 1967.

Kim, Key-hiuk. *The Last Phase of the East Asian World Order: Korea, Japan, and the Chinese Empire, 1860–1882.* Berkeley: University of California Press, 1980.

King, Frank H. H. *Money and Monetary Policy in China 1845–1895.* Cambridge, MA: Harvard University Press, 1965.

—— and Prescott Clarke, eds. *A Research Guide to China-Coast Newspapers, 1822–1911*. Cambridge, MA: Harvard University Press, 1965.

Kipling, Rudyard. *From Sea to Sea Letters of Travel*. New York: Doubleday, Page, 1909.

——. "The White Man's Burden." In *Complete Verse*. 1940. Reprint, New York: Doubleday, 1989.

Kissinger, Henry. *Diplomacy*. New York: Simon & Schuster, 1994.

Knapp, Arthur May. *Feudal and Modern Japan*, 2nd ed., 2 vols. Boston: L. C. Page, 1897.

Ko, Seok-kyu. "Activities of the Peasant Army During the Chipkangso Period." *Korea Journal* 34, no. 4 (Winter 1994): 31–44.

Kodansha Encyclopedia of Japan. Tokyo: Kodansha, 1983.

Krausse, Alexis. *China in Decay: The Story of a Disappearing Empire*. 3rd ed. London: Chapman & Hill, 1900.

Kuhn, Philip A. *Rebellion and Its Enemies in Late Imperial China: Militarization and Social Structure, 1796–1864*. Cambridge, MA: Harvard University Press, 1980.

——. "The Taiping Rebellion." In *The Cambridge History of China*, vol. 10, edited by John King Fairbank, 264–317. Cambridge: Cambridge University Press, 1978.

Kulp, Daniel Harrison. *Country Life in South China: The Sociology of Familialism*. 2 vols. New York: Teachers College, Columbia University, 1925.

Kuo, Sung-ping. "Chinese Reaction to Foreign Encroachment with Special Reference to the First Sino-Japanese War and Its Immediate Aftermath." Ph.D. diss., Columbia University, 1953.

Kuropatkin, Aleksei Nikolai. *The Russian Army and the Japanese War*. Translated by A. B. Lindsay, edited by W. D. Swinton. 2 vols. New York: E. P. Dutton, 1909.

Kuwada, Etsu (桑田悦). 近代日本戦争史 (*History of Modern Japanese Wars*). Vol. 1. 日清。日露戦争 (*Sino-Japanese and Russo-Japanese Wars*). Tokyo: 同台経済懇話会, 1995.

Kwei, Chungshu. *Plain Speaking on Japan: A Collection of Articles on the Sino-Japanese Conflict, Originally Published in the Shanghai Evening Post and Mercury under the Column, "As a Chinese Sees It."* Shanghai: China Institute of International Relations, 1932.

Kwong, Luke S. K. *A Mosaic of the Hundred Days: Personalities, Politics, and Ideas of 1898*. Cambridge, MA: Harvard University Press, 1984.

Ladd, George Trumbull. *Rare Days in Japan*. New York: Dodd, Mead, 1910.

LaFeber, Walter. *The American Age: United States Foreign Policy at Home and Abroad*. 2nd ed. New York: W. W. Norton, 1994.

Lamb, Alastair. *Asian Frontiers: Studies in a Continuing Problem*. New York: Frederick A. Praeger, 1968.

Lang, Olga. *Chinese Family and Society*. International Secretariat, Institute of Pacific Relations and the Institute of Social Research. New Haven: Yale University Press, 1946.

Langer, William L. *The Diplomacy of Imperialism 1890–1902*. 2nd ed. New York: Alfred A. Knopf, 1956.

Latourette, Kenneth Scott. *The Chinese: Their History and Culture.* 2nd rev. ed. 2 vols. New York: Macmillan, 1934.

Lattimore, Owen. *Inner Asian Frontiers of China.* American Geographical Society, Research Series no. 21. New York: American Geographical Society, 1940.

LeDonne, John P. *The Russian Empire and the World, 1700–1917: The Geopolitics of Expansion and Containment.* New York: Oxford University Press, 1997.

Lee, Robert H. G. *The Manchurian Frontier in Ch'ing History.* Cambridge, MA: Harvard University Press, 1970.

Lee, Yur-bok. *West Goes East: Paul George von Möllendorff and Great Power Imperialism in Late Yi Korea.* Honolulu: University of Hawai'i Press, 1988.

Lehmann, Jean-Pierre. *The Image of Japan: From Feudal Isolation to World Power, 1850–1905.* London: George Allen & Unwin, 1978.

Lensen, George Alexander. *Balance of Intrigue: International Rivalry in Korea & Manchuria, 1884–1899.* 2 vols. Tallahassee: University Presses of Florida, 1982.

Leroy-Beaulieu, Pierre. *The Awakening of the East: Siberia—Japan—China.* Translated by Richard Davey. London: William Heinemann, 1900.

Lew, Young Ick (Yu Yông'ik). "The Kabo Reform Movement: Korean and Japanese Reform Efforts in Korea, 1894." Ph.D. diss., Harvard University, 1972.

——. "The Reform Efforts and Ideas of Pak Yông-hyo, 1894–1895." *Korean Studies* 1 (1977): 21–55.

Li, Ting-i. *A History of Modern China.* Hong Kong: Oriental Society, 1970.

Lieven, Dominic C. B. *Nicholas II: Emperor of All the Russias.* London: John Murray, 1993.

——. *Russia and the Origins of the First World War.* New York: St. Martin's Press, 1983.

——. *Russia's Rulers under the Old Regime.* New Haven: Yale University Press, 1989.

Lincoln, W. Bruce. *The Conquest of a Continent: Siberia and the Russians.* New York: Random House, 1994.

——. *The Great Reforms: Autocracy, Bureaucracy, and the Politics of Change in Imperial Russia.* Dekalb: Northern Illinois University Press, 1990.

Little, Alicia Bewicke (Mrs. Archibald Little). *Li Hung-chang His Life and Times.* London: Cassell, 1903.

Littlewood, Ian. *The Idea of Japan: Western Images, Western Myths.* London: Secker & Warburg, 1996.

Liu, Kwang-ching. "The Ch'ing Restoration." In *Cambridge History of China,* vol. 10, edited by John King Fairbank, 409–90. Cambridge: Cambridge University Press, 1978.

—— and Richard J. Smith. "The Military Challenge: the North-West and the Coast." In *The Cambridge History of China,* vol. 11, edited by John K. Fairbank and Kwang-ching Liu, 202–73. Cambridge: Cambridge University Press, 1978.

Lone, Stewart. *Japan's First Modern War: Army and Society in the Conflict with China, 1894–95.* London: St. Martin's Press, 1994.

Loomis, H. "Progress in Japan." *Chinese Recorder and Missionary Journal* 25, no. 5 (May 1894): 221–3.

——. "The Status of Japan among the Nations, and her Position in regard to Korea."

Chinese Recorder and Missionary Journal 25, no. 12 (Dec. 1894): 566–70.

Loti, Pierre. *Madame Chrysanthème.* Translated by Laura Ensor. Paris: Edouard Guillaume, 1889.

Lu, David J. *Japan A Documentary History: The Late Tokugawa Period to the Present.* Armonk, NY: M. E. Sharpe, 1997.

Ma, Jianzhong (馬建忠) et al. 中國近代內亂外禍歷史故事叢書(*Collection of Historical Accounts of China's Modern Domestic Strife and Foreign Calamities*), vol. 17, 227–60. Taipei: 廣文書局, 1964.

MacGowan, John. *A History of China, From the Earliest Days Down to the Present.* Shanghai: Presbyterian Mission Press, 1897.

MacKenzie, Donald A. *China and Japan: Myths and Legends.* 1923. Reprint, London: Senate, 1994.

MacMurray, John V. A., comp. *Treaties and Agreements with and Concerning China 1894–1919.* 2 vols. New York: Oxford University Press, 1921.

McGiffin, Lee. *Yankee of the Yalu: Philo Norton McGiffin, American Captain in the Chinese Navy (1885–1895).* New York: E. P. Dutton, 1968.

McKay, John P., Bennet D. Hill, and John Buckler. *History of Western Society,* vol. 2.

McKenzie, F. A. *The Tragedy of Korea.* 1908. Reprint, Seoul: Yonsei University Press, 1969.

McReynolds, Louise. *The News under Russia's Old Regime: The Development of a Mass-Circulation Press.* Princeton: Princeton University Press, 1991.

Mahan, Alfred Thayer. *The Influence of Sea Power upon History, 1660–1783.* 1890. Reprint, Boston: Little, Brown, 1935.

Malozemoff, Andrew. *Russian Far Eastern Policy 1881–1904 with Special Emphasis on the Causes of the Russo-Japanese War.* Berkeley: University of California Press, 1958.

Mancall, Mark. *China at the Center: 300 Years of Foreign Policy.* New York: Free Press, 1984.

——. "The Ch'ing Tribute System: An Interpretive Essay." In *The Chinese World Order: Traditional China's Foreign Relations,* edited by John K. Fairbank, 63–89. Cambridge, MA: Harvard University Press, 1968.

——. *Russia and China, Their Diplomatic Relations to 1728.* Cambridge, MA: Harvard University Press, 1971.

Captain Marchenko. "Словесные переговоры о заключении мира, веденные в Симоносеки уполномоченными Китая и Японии в марте 1895 года." (Minutes for the Peace Negotiations between the Plenipotentiaries of China and Japan Held in March, 1895, in Shimonoseki). *Сборник географических, топографических и статистических материалов по Азии* (*Collection of Geographical, Topographical and Statistical Materials on Asia*). Vol. 71. St. Petersburg: Военная Типография, 1897.

Marble, Frank. "The Battle of the Yalu." *Proceedings of the United States Naval Institute* 21, no. 3 (1895): 479–98.

Martin, W. A. P. *A Cycle of Cathay or China, South and North with Personal Reminiscences.* 3rd ed. New York: Fleming H. Revell, 1900.

Masuda, Koh, ed. *Kenkyusha's New Japanese-English Dictionary.* 4th ed. Tokyo: Kenkyusha, 1983.

Masuda, Wataru. *Japan and China: Mutual Representations in the Modern Era*. Translated by Joshua A. Fogel. New York: St. Martin's Press, 2000.

Mathias, Peter and M. M. Postan, eds. *The Cambridge Economic History of Europe*. vol. 7, part 2. Cambridge: Cambridge University Press, 1978.

Mayers, William Frederick. *Treaties between the Empire of China and Foreign Powers*. 1877. Reprint, Taipei: Ch'eng-wen Publishing, 1966.

Mayo, Marlene J. "The Korean Crisis of 1873 and Early Meiji Foreign Policy." *Journal of Asian Studies* 31, no. 4 (Aug. 1972): 793–819.

Mehnert, Klaus. *Peking and Moscow*. Translated by Leila Vennewitz. New York: G. P. Putnam's Sons, 1963.

Meng, S. M. *The Tsung-li Yamen: Its Organization and Functions*. Cambridge, MA: Harvard University Press, 1962.

Merson, John. *The Genius that Was China: East and West in the Making of the Modern World*. Woodstock, New York: Overlook Press, 1990.

Merton, Robert K. *Science, Technology & Society in Seventeenth Century England*. New Jersey: Humanities Press, 1978.

Michie, Alexander. *The Englishman in China during the Victorian Era*. 2 vols. Edinburgh: William Blackwood and Sons, 1900.

Milward, James A. *Beyond the Pass: Economy, Ethnicity, and Empire in Qing Central Asia, 1759–1864*. Stanford: Stanford University Press, 1998.

Miwa, Kimitada. "Fukuzawa Yukichi's 'Departure from Asia': A Prelude to the Sino-Japanese War." In *Japan's Modern Century: A Special Issue of "Monumenta Nipponica" Prepared in Celebration of the Centennial of the Meiji Restoration*. Edited by Edmund Skrzypczak, 1–26. Tokyo: Sophia University, 1968.

Morris, John. *Advance Japan: A Nation Thoroughly in Earnest*. London: W. H. Allen, 1895.

——. *Advance Japan: A Nation thoroughly in Earnest*. 2nd ed. London: W. H. Allen, 1896.

Morse, Hosea Ballou. *The International Relations of the Chinese Empire*. 3 vols. Shanghai: Kelly and Walsh, 1910–18.

Mosse, W. E. *Alexander II and the Modernization of Russia*. London: I. B. Tauris, 1992.

Moule, Arthur E. *New China and Old: Personal Recollections and Observations of Thirty Years*. London: Seeley, 1891.

Moulton, Harold Glenn and Junichi Ko. *Japan an Economic and Financial Appraisal*. Washington, DC: Brookings Institution, 1931.

Mungello, D. E. *The Great Encounter of China and the West, 1500–1800*. New York: Rowan & Littlefield, 1999.

Murdoch, James. *A History of Japan*, vol. 3. Revised and edited by Joseph H. Longford. 1926. Reprint, Hertford: Stephen Austin & Sons, 1996.

Murray, David. *Japan*. 6th ed. London: T. Fisher Unwin, 1906.

Mutsu,Munemitsu.*Kenkenryoku: A Diplomatic Record of the Sino-Japanese War, 1894–95*. Translated by Gordon Mark Berger. Princeton: Princeton University Press, 1982.

Nahm, Andrew Changwoo. "Kim Ok-Kyun and the Korean Progressive Movement, 1882–1884." Ph.D. diss., Stanford University, 1961.

——. *Korea Tradition & Transformation: A History of the Korean People.* Elizabeth, NJ: Holly International, 1988.

Nakamura, Kaju. *Prince Ito: The Man and Statesman: A Brief History of His Life.* New York: Japanese-American Commercial Weekly, 1910.

Naquin, Susan. *Millenarian Rebellion in China: The Eight Triagrams Uprising of 1813.* New Haven: Yale University Press, 1976.

Nelson, Andrew N. and John H. Haig. *The New Nelson Japanese-English Character Dictionary.* Rev. ed. Rutland, VT: Charles E. Tuttle, 1997.

Nelson, M. Frederick. *Korea and the Old Orders in Eastern Asia.* Baton Rouge: Louisiana State University Press, 1945.

Nevius, John L. *China and the Chinese.* Philadelphia: Presbyterian Board of Publication, 1882.

Nish, Ian, ed. *British Documents on Foreign Affairs: Reports and Papers from the Foreign Office Confidential Print.* Part 1, series E, vol. 5. University Publications of America, 1989.

——. *Japanese Foreign Policy, 1869–1942.* London: Routledge & Kegan Paul, 1977.

Nitobe, Inazo. *Bushido the Soul of Japan: An Exposition of Japanese Thought.* Rev. ed. 1905. Reprint, Boston: Tuttle Publishing, 1969.

Niyekawa, Agnes M. *Minimum Essential Politeness: A Guide to the Japanese Honorific Language.* Tokyo: Kodansha International, 1991.

Norman, Henry. *The Peoples and Politics of the Far East.* London: T. Fisher Unwin, 1901.

Notehelfer, F. G. *Kōtoku Shūsui: Portrait of a Japanese Radical.* Cambridge: Cambridge University Press, 1971.

Novikov, B. M. "The Rising of 1787–1788 in Taiwan." In *Manzhou Rule in China,* edited by S. L. Tikhvinsky, translated by David Skvirsky, 162–82. Moscow: Progress Publishers, 1983.

Oh, Bonnie Bongwan. "The Background of Chinese Policy Formation in the Sino-Japanese War of 1894–1895." Ph.D. diss., University of Chicago, 1974.

——. "Sino-Japanese Rivalry in Korea, 1876–1885." In *Chinese and the Japanese.* In *The Chinese and the Japanese: Essays in Cultural and Political Interactions,* edited by Akira Iriye, 37–57. Princeton: Princeton University Press, 1980.

Ohkawa, Kazushi and Henry Rosovsky. "Capital Formation in Japan." In *The Cambridge Economic History of Europe,* vol. 7, part 2, edited by Peter Mathias and M. M. Postan, 134–65. Cambridge: Cambridge University Press, 1978.

Oka, Yoshitake. *Five Political Leaders of Modern Japan: Itō Hirobumi, Ōkuma Shigenobu, Hara Takashi, Inukai Tsuyoshi, and Saionjji Kimmochi.* Translated by Andrew Fraser and Patricia Murray. Tokyo: University of Tokyo Press, 1979.

Okamoto, Shumpei. "A Phase of Meiji Japan's Attitude toward China: The Case of Komura Juntarō." *Modern Asian Studies* 13, no. 4 (Oct. 1979): 431–58.

O'Neill, Hugh B. *Companion to Chinese History.* New York: Facts on File Publications, 1987.

Ono, Giichi. *Expenditures of the Sino-Japanese War.* New York: Oxford University Press, 1922.

Ono, Setsuko. *A Western Image of Japan: What did the West See through the Eyes of*

Loti and Hearn? Geneva: Imprimerie du Courrier, 1972.

Owen, Thomas C. *The Corporation under Russian Law, 1800–1917: A Study in Tsarist Economic Policy.* Cambridge: Cambridge University Press, 1991.

Paine, S. C. M. *Imperial Rivals: China, Russia, and Their Disputed Frontier.* Armonk, NY: M. E. Sharpe, 1996.

Palais, James B. *Politics and Policy in Traditional Korea.* Cambridge, MA: Harvard University Press, 1975.

Parish, William L. *Village and Family in Contemporary China.* Chicago: University of Chicago Press, 1978.

Parker, Geoffrey. *The Geopolitics of Domination.* London: Routledge, 1988.

Parkinson, Claire L. *Breakthroughs: A Chronology of Great Achievement in Science and Mathematics 1200–1930.* Boston: G. K. Hall, 1985.

Peattie, Mark R. "The Japanese Colonial Empire, 1895–1945." In *The Cambridge History of Japan,* edited by John W. Hall, Marius B. Jansen, Madoka Kanai, and Denis Twitchett, vol. 6, 217–70. Cambridge: Cambridge University Press, 1988.

Peery, R. B. *The Gist of Japan: The Islands, Their People and Missions.* 1908. Reprint, Austin: Book Lab, 1995.

Peyrefitte, Alain. *The Immobile Empire.* Translated by Jon Rothschild. New York: Alfred A. Knopf, 1992.

Pierce, Richard A. *Russian Central Asia 1867–1917: A Study in Colonial Rule.* Berkeley: University of California Press, 1960.

Pierson, John D. *Tokutomi Sohō 1863–1947: A Journalist for Modern Japan.* Princeton: Princeton University Press, 1980.

Polachek, James M. *The Inner Opium War.* Cambridge, MA: Harvard University Press, 1992.

Pollack, David. *The Fracture of Meaning: Japan's Synthesis of China from the Eighth through the Eighteenth Centuries.* Princeton: Princeton University Press, 1986.

Porshneva, Y. B. "Popular Religious Sects in Opposition to the Qing Dynasty." In *Manzhou Rule in China,* edited by S. L. Tikhvinsky, translated by David Skvirsky, 183–93. Moscow: Progress Publishers, 1983.

Porter, Robert P. *Japan the New World Power Being a Detailed Account of the Progress and Rise of the Japanese Empire.* London: Oxford University Press, 1915.

——. *Japan: The Rise of a Modern Power.* Oxford: Clarendon Press, 1918.

Powell, Ralph L. *The Rise of Chinese Military Power 1895–1912.* Princeton: Princeton University Press, 1955.

Power, Jr., Thomas. *Jules Ferry and the Renaissance of French Imperialism.* 1944. Reprint, New York: Octagon Books, 1977.

Pratt, Keith and Richard Rutt, eds. *Korea: A Historical and Cultural Dictionary.* Surrey: Curzon, 1999.

Princeton University, Firestone Library, Rare books. John Watson Foster collection. "Diary written by John W. Foster, Shimonoseki, 1895."

Pyle, Kenneth B. *The Making of Modern Japan.* 2nd ed. Lexington, MA: D.C. Heath, 1996.

——. "Meiji Conservatism" In *The Cambridge History of Japan,* vol. 5, edited by Marius B. Jansen, 674–720. Cambridge: University of Cambridge Press, 1989.

——. *The New Generation in Meiji Japan: Problems of Cultural Identity, 1885–1895.* Stanford: Stanford University Press, 1969.

Qi, Qizhang (戚其章), comp. 甲午战争 (*Sino-Japanese War*). Peking: 人民出版社, 1990.

——, ed., 中日战争 (*Sino-Japanese War*). 11 Vols. Peking: 中华书局, 1989–1996.

Quested, Rosemary K. I. *The Expansion of Russia in Asia, 1857–1860.* Kuala Lumpur: University of Malaya Press, 1968.

——. *"Matey" Imperialists? The Tsarist Russians in Manchuria 1895–1917.* Hong Kong: University of Hong Kong Press, 1982.

Ransome, Stafford. *Japan in Transition: A Comparative Study of the Progress, Policy, and Methods of the Japanese since their War with China.* New York: Harper & Brothers, 1899.

Rawlinson, John L. *China's Struggle for Naval Development 1839–1895.* Cambridge, MA: Harvard University Press, 1967.

Reed, Edward J. *Japan: Its History, Traditions, and Religions with the Narrative of a Visit in 1879.* Vol. 1. London: John Murray, 1880.

Remmey, Paul Baker. "British Diplomacy in the Far East, 1892–1898." Ph.D. diss., Harvard University, 1964.

Reynolds, Douglas R. *China, 1898–1912: The Xinzheng Revolution and Japan.* Cambridge, MA: Harvard University Press, 1993.

Rhee, Syngman. *The Spirit of Independence: A Primer of Korean Modernization and Reform.* Translated by Han-kyo Kim. Honolulu: University of Hawai'i Press, 2001.

Riasanovsky, Nicholas V. *A History of Russia.* 5th ed. New York: Oxford University Press, 1993.

——. *A Parting of Ways: Government and the Educated Public in Russia 1801–1855.* Oxford: Clarendon Press, 1976.

Richard, T. "China's Appalling Need of Reform." *The Chinese Recorder* 25, no. 11 (Nov. 1894): 515–21.

Rieber, Alfred J. "Persistent Factors in Russian Foreign Policy: An Interpretive Essay." In *Imperial Russian Foreign Policy,* edited by Hugh Ragsdale, 315–359. Cambridge: Cambridge University Press, 1993.

Rittner, George H. *Impressions of Japan.* New York: James Pott, 1904.

Ro, Kwang Hai. "Power Politics in Korea and Its Impact on Korean Foreign and Domestic Affairs, 1882–1907." Ph.D. diss., University of Oklahoma, 1966.

Roberts, J. A. G. *China through Western Eyes: The Nineteenth Century.* Bath: Alan Sutton, 1991.

Robertson-Scott, J. W. *The People of China: Their Country, History, Life, Ideas, and Relations with the Foreigner.* London: Methuen, 1900.

Rosen (Rozen), Roman Romanovich. *Forty Years of Diplomacy.* 2 vols. London: George Allen & Unwin, 1922.

Ross, John. *The Manchus, or The Reigning Dynasty of China: Their Rise and Progress.* 1891. Reprint, New York: AMS Press, 1973.

Rossabi, Morris. *China and Inner Asia: From 1360 to the Present.* New York: Praeger Press, 1975.

Roth, Gertraude. "The Manchu-Chinese Relationship, 1618–1636." In *From Ming to Ch'ing: Conquest, Region, and Continuity in Seventeenth-Century China,* edited by

Jonathan D. Spence and John E. Wills, Jr., 1–38. New Haven: Yale University Press, 1979.

Russell, John Robert. "The Development of a 'Modern' Army in Nineteenth Century Japan." Masters' thesis, Columbia University, 1957.

Saari, Jon L. "Breaking the Hold of Tradition: The Self-Group Interface in Traditional China." In *Social Interaction in Chinese Society*, edited by Sidney L. Greenblatt, Richard W. Wilson, and Amy Auerbacher Wilson, 28–66. USA: Praeger Publishers, 1982.

Sadie, Stanley, ed. *The New Grove Dictionary of Opera*. 4 vols. London: Macmillan, 1992.

Sands, William Franklin. *At the Court of Korea: Undiplomatic Memories*. 1930. Reprint, London: Century, 1987.

Sansom, G. B. *The Western World and Japan: A Study in the Interaction of European and Asiatic Cultures*. New York: Alfred A. Knopf, 1951.

Sauvage, Maxime Joseph Marie. *La guerre sino-japonaise 1894–1895 (Sino-Japanese War 1894–95)*. Paris: L. Baudoin, 1897.

Schell, Orville. *Mandate of Heaven*. New York: Simon & Schuster, 1994.

Schencking, J. Charles. "The Imperial Japanese Navy and the Constructed Consciousness of a South Seas Destiny, 1872–1921." *Modern Asian Studies* 33, no. 4 (Oct. 1999): 769–96.

Scherer, James A. *Japan To-day*. Philadelphia: J. B. Lippincott, 1904.

Schulman, Irwin Jay. "China's Response to Imperialism, 1895–1900." Ph.D. diss., Columbia University, 1967.

Schwartz, Benjamin. *In Search of Wealth and Power: Yen Fu and the West*. Cambridge, MA: Harvard University Press, 1964.

Schwartz, William Leonard. *The Imaginative Interpretation of the Far East in modern French Literature, 1800–1925*. Paris: Librairie Ancienne Honoré Champion, 1927.

Scidmore, Eliza Ruhamah. *China: The Long-Lived Empire*. New York: Century, 1900.

———. *Jinrikisha Days in Japan*. New York: Harper & Brothers, 1891.

Seton-Watson, Hugh. *The Russian Empire 1801–1917*. Oxford: Oxford University Press, 1967.

Seward, George F. "Li Hung-chang." *Chinese Recorder and Missionary Journal* 25, no. 12 (Dec. 1894): 584–7.

Shao Xunzheng (邵循正), et al., eds. 中日戰爭 (*Sino-Japanese War*). 中國史學會 (Chinese History Learned Society). 7 vols. Shanghai: 新知識出版社, 1956.

"Sichuan-Hubei White Lotus Rebellion" ("川楚白莲教起义"). In 中国大百科全书 (*Chinese Encyclopedia*), 中国历史 (*Chinese History*), vol. 1, 113–14. Peking: 中国大百科全书出版社, 1992.

Sims, R. L. *A Political History of Modern Japan 1868–1952*. New Delhi: Vikas Publishing House, 1991.

Sladen, Douglas. *Queer Things about Japan*. London: Anthony Treherne & Co., 1903.

Smith, Arthur H. *Chinese Characteristics*. 10th ed. New York: Fleming H. Revell, 1894.

Smith, Richard J. *China's Cultural Heritage: The Ch'ing Dynasty 1644–1912.* Boulder, CO: Westview Press, 1983.

Spector, Stanley. *Li Hong-chang and the Huai Army: A Study in Nineteenth-Century Chinese Regionalism.* Seattle: University of Washington Press, 1964.

Spence, Jonathan D. *The Chan's Great Continent: China in Western Minds.* New York: W. W. Norton, 1998.

——. *God's Chinese Son: The Taiping Heavenly Kingdom of Hong Xiuquan.* New York: W. W. Norton, 1996.

——. *The Search for Modern China.* New York: W. W. Norton & Co., 1990.

Stoddard, John L. *Japan.* Chicago: Belford, Middlebrook & Co., 1907.

Storry, Richard. *Japan and the Decline of the West in Asia 1894–1943.* New York: St. Martin's Press, 1979.

Strassler, Robert B., ed. *The Landmark Thucydides: A Comprehensive Guide to the Peloponnesian War.* New York: Free Press, 1996.

Struve, Lynn A., ed. and trans. *Voices from the Ming–Qing Cataclysm: China In the Tigers' Jaws.* New Haven: Yale University Press, 1993.

Suh, Young-hee. "Tracing the Course of the Peasant War of 1894." *Korea Journal* 34, no. 4 (Winter 1994): 17–30.

Sun, Kefu (孙克复) and Guan Jie (关捷), eds. 中日甲午陆战史 (*History of the Land Engagements of the Sino-Japanese War*). Harbin: 黑龙江人民出版社, 1984.

Sun Tzu. *The Art of War.* Translated by Samuel B. Griffith. London: Oxford University Press, 1963.

Suzuki, S. *The Surgical and Medical History of the Naval War between Japan & China, 1894–95.* Translated by Y. Saneyoshi. Tokyo: Z. P. Maruya, 1901.

Swartout, Jr., Robert R. *Mandarins, Gunboats, and Power Politics: Owen Nickerson Denny and the International Rivalries in Korea.* Asian Studies at Hawaii, no. 25. Honolulu: University of Hawai'i Press, 1980.

Switzerland, Politisches Departement. *Documents relatifs à la révision de la Convention de Genève du 22 Août 1864 (Documents Concerning the Revision of the Geneva Convention of 22 August 1864).* Berne: Imprimerie Stæmpfli, 1906.

Synn, Seung Kwon. *The Russo-Japanese Rivalry over Korea, 1876–1904.* Seoul: Yuk Phub SA, 1981.

Szamuely, Tibor. *The Russian Tradition.* New York: McGraw-Hill, 1974.

Tabohashi, Kiyoshi (田保橋潔), 日清戦役外交史の研究 (*A Diplomatic History of the Sino-Japanese War [1894–1895]*). Tokyo: 刀江院刊, 1951.

Taira, Shigesuke. *The Code of the Samurai.* Translated by Thomas Cleary. Boston: Tuttle Publishing, 1999.

Takahashi, Hidenao (高橋秀直). 日清戦争の道 (*Road to the Sino-Japanese War*). Tokyo: 東京創元社, 1995.

Takahashi, Sakuyé. *Cases on International Law during the Sino-Japanese War.* Cambridge: Cambridge University Press, 1899.

Takemichi, Hara. "Korea, China, and Western Barbarians: Diplomacy in Early Nineteenth-Century Korea." *Modern Asian Studies* 32 (2 July 1998): 389–430.

Takeuchi, Tatsuji. *War and Diplomacy in the Japanese Empire.* Garden City, NY: Doubleday, Doran & Co., 1935.

Tan, Qixiang (谭其骧), ed. 中国历史地图集 (*Historical Atlas of China*). 8 vols. Shanghai: 地图出版社, 1980.

Taylor, Bayard. *Japan in Our Day*. New York: Charles Scribner's Sons, 1881.

Terry, T. Philip. *Terry's Japanese Empire Including Korea and Formosa*. Boston: Houghton Mifflin, 1914.

Thomas, J. E. *Modern Japan: A Social History since 1868*. London: Longman, 1996.

Tikhvinsky, S. L. "Manzhou Rule in China." In *Manzhou Rule in China*, edited by S. L. Tikhvinsky, translated by David Skvirsky, 5–66. Moscow: Progress Publishers, 1983.

——, ed. *Manzhou Rule in China*. Translated by David Skvirsky. Moscow: Progress Publishers, 1983.

Tindall, George Brown and David E. Shi. *America: A Narrative History*. 4th ed. 2 vols. New York: W. W. Norton, 1996.

Toby, Ronald P. *State and Diplomacy in Early Modern Japan: Asia in the Development of the Tokugawa Bakufu*. Stanford: Stanford University Press, 1991.

"Tokugawa Iemochi" ("德川家茂"). In 「日本大百科全書」 (*Encyclopedia Nipponica 2001*), vol. 16, 873. Tokyo: 小学館, 1986.

Totman, Conrad. *Early Modern Japan*. Berkeley: University of California Press, 1993.

"Travel Literature." In *New Catholic Encyclopedia*, vol. 14, 266–7. New York: McGraw-Hill, 1967.

Treat, Payson J. "China and Korea, 1885–1894." *Political Science Quarterly* 49, no. 4 (Dec. 1934): 506–43.

——. *Diplomatic Relations between the United States and Japan, 1853–1895*. 2 vols. Stanford: Stanford University Press, 1932.

Tsiang, T. F. "Sino-Japanese Diplomatic Relations, 1870–1894." *The Chinese Social and Political Science Review* 17, no. 1 (April 1933): 1–106.

Tuchman, Barbara W. *Stilwell and the American Experience in China, 1911–1945*. New York: Macmillan, 1970.

Tung, William L. *China and the Foreign Powers: The Impact of and Reaction to Unequal Treaties*. Dobbs Ferry, NY: Oceana Publications, 1970.

Twitchett, Denis and John K. Fairbank, eds. *The Cambridge History of China*. Vols. 10–11. Cambridge: Cambridge University Press, 1978.

Tyler, William Ferdinand. *Pulling Strings in China*. London: Constable, 1929.

Tzou, Byron N. *China and International Law: The Boundary Disputes*. New York: Praeger, 1990.

Ulam, Adam B. "Nationalism, Panslavism, Communism." In *Russian Foreign Policy: Essays in Historical Perspective*, edited by Ivo J. Lederer. New Haven: Yale University Press, 1962.

U. S. Adjutant-General's Office, Military Information Division. *Notes on the War between China and Japan*. Washington, DC: Government Printing Office, 1896.

Ustin, P. M. "Pu Songling: Accuser of the Manzhou Conquerors." In *Manzhou Rule in China*, edited by S. L. Tikhvinsky, translated by David Skvirsky, 150–61. Moscow: Progress Publishers, 1983.

Uyehara, Cecil H. comp., *Checklist of Archives in the Japanese Ministry of Foreign*

Affairs, Tokyo, Japan, 1868–1945. Washington: Photoduplication Services, Library of Congress, 1954.

Valliant, Robert Britton. "Japan and the Trans-Siberian Railroad, 1885–1905." Ph.D. diss., University of Hawaii, 1974.

van Creveld, Martin. "Through a Glass Darkly: Some Reflections on the Future of War" *Naval War College Review* (Autumn 2000): 25–44.

van der Sprenkel, Sybille. *Legal Institutions in Manchu China: A Sociological Analysis.* London School of Economics Monographs on Social Anthropology, no. 24. London: Athlone Press, 1962.

Vladimir [Zenone Volpicelli]. *The China-Japan War Compiled from Japanese, Chinese, and Foreign Sources.* Kansas City, MO: Franklin Hudson Publishing, 1905.

Vogel, Ezra F. *The Four Little Dragons: The Spread of Industrialization in East Asia.* Cambridge, MA: Harvard University Press, 1991.

Wakeman, Jr., Frederic. *Strangers at the Gate: Social Disorder in South China 1838–1861.* Berkeley: University of California Press, 1966.

Walton, Joseph. *China and the Present Crisis with Notes on a Visit to Japan and Korea.* London: Sampson, Low, Marston, 1900.

Wang, Y. C. *Chinese Intellectuals and the West 1872–1949.* Chapel Hill: University of North Carolina Press, 1966.

Warner, Denis and Peggy Warner. *The Tide at Sunrise: A History of the Russo-Japanese War, 1904–1905.* London: Angus and Robertson, 1974.

Wawro, Geoffrey. *The Austro-Prussian War: Austria's War with Prussia and Italy in 1866.* Cambridge: Cambridge University Press, 1996.

Wehrle, Edmund S. *Britain, China, and the Antimissionary Riots 1891–1900.* Minneapolis: University of Minnesota Press, 1966.

Wesson, Robert. *The Russian Dilemma.* Rev. ed. New York: Praeger, 1986.

Weston, Walter. *Mountaineering and Exploration in the Japanese Alps.* London: John Murray, 1896.

Widmer, Eric. *The Russian Ecclesiastical Mission in Peking during the 18th Century.* Cambridge, MA: Harvard University Press, 1976.

Wiens, Mi Chu. "Anti-Manchu Thought during the Early Ch'ing." *Papers on China.* Harvard University. 22A (May 1969): 1–24.

Wildman, Rounsevelle. *China's Open Door: A Sketch of Chinese Life and History.* Boston: Lothrop Publishing Co., 1900.

Williamson, Alexander. *Journeys in North China, Manchuria, and Eastern Mongolia; with Some Account of Corea.* London: Smither, Elder, 1870.

Wilson, H. W. *Ironclads in Action: A Sketch of Naval Warfare from 1855 to 1895.* Boston: Little, Brown, 1896.

Wilson, James Harrison. *China: Travels and Investigations in the 'Middle Kingdom'–A Study of Its Civilization and Possibilities together with an Account of the Boxer War.* 3rd ed. New York: D. Appleton, 1901.

——. *China: Travels and Investigations in the "Middle Kingdom:" A Study of Its Civilization and Possibilities with a Glance at Japan.* New York: D. Appleton, 1887.

Wilson, Richard W. and Anne Wang Pusey. "Achievement Motivation and Small-

Business Relationship Patterns in Chinese Society." In *Social Interaction in Chinese Society*, edited by Sidney L. Greenblatt, Richard W. Wilson, and Amy Auerbacher Wilson, 195–208. USA: Praeger Publishers, 1982.

Windfield, Gerald F. *China; The Land and the People.* New York: William Sloan Associates, 1948.

Witte, Sergei Iul'evich. *The Memoirs of Count Witte.* Translated and edited by Sidney Harcave. Armonk, NY: M. E. Sharpe, 1990.

Wright, Mary C. "The Adaptability of Ch'ing Diplomacy: The Case of Korea." *The Journal of Asian Studies* 17, no. 3 (May 1958): 363–82.

——. *The Last Stand of Chinese Conservatism: The T'ung-Chih Restoration, 1862–1874.* 1957. Reprint, Stanford: Stanford University Press, 1962.

Yamamoto, Tsunetomo. *Hagakure: The Book of the Samurai.* Translated by William Scott Wilson. Tokyo: Kodansha International, 1979.

Yan, Yunxiang. *The Flow of Gifts: Reciprocity and Social Networks in a Chinese Village.* Stanford: Stanford University Press, 1996.

Yang, Lien-sheng. "The Concept of *Pao* as a Basis for Social Relations in China." In *Chinese Thought and Institutions,* edited by John K. Fairbank, 291–309. Chicago: University of Chicago Press, 1957.

Yang, Martin C. *A Chinese Village: Taitou, Shantung Province.* New York: Columbia University Press, 1945.

Yang, Mayfair Mei-hui. *Gifts, Favors & Banquets: The Art of Social Relationships in China.* Ithaca: Cornell University Press, 1994.

Yokoyama, Toshio. *Japan in the Victorian Mind: A Study of Stereotyped Images of a Nation 1850–80.* Houndmills, Basingstoke, Hampshire: Macmillan, 1987.

Young, Ernest P. "A Study of Groups and Personalities in Japan Influencing the Events Leading to the Sino-Japanese War (1894–1895)." *Papers on China.* Harvard University. 2 (Aug. 1963): 229–75.

Yuan, Tao-feng (袁道豐). "Li Hung-chang and the Sino-Japanese War." *T'ien Hsia Monthly* 3, no. 1: 9–17.

Yim, Dong Jae. "The Abduction of the Taewôngun: 1882." *Papers on China.* Harvard University. 21 (Feb. 1969): 99–130.

Zakaria, Fareed. *From Wealth to Power: The Unusual Origins of America's World Role.* Princeton: Princeton University Press, 1998.

Index

Printed in Great Britain
by Amazon